The Routledge Handbook of Translation and Activism

The Routledge Handbook of Translation and Activism provides an accessible, diverse and ground-breaking overview of literary, cultural, and political translation across a range of activist contexts.

As the first extended collection to offer perspectives on translation and activism from a global perspective, this handbook includes case studies and histories of oppressed and marginalised people from over twenty different languages. The contributions will make visible the role of translation in promoting and enabling social change, in promoting equality, in fighting discrimination, in supporting human rights, and in challenging autocracy and injustice across the Middle East, Africa, Latin America, East Asia, the US, and Europe.

With a substantial introduction, thirty-one chapters, and an extensive bibliography, this Handbook is an indispensable resource for all activists, translators, students, and researchers of translation and activism within translation and interpreting studies.

Rebecca Ruth Gould is the author of *Writers and Rebels: The Literatures of Insurgency in the Caucasus* (2016). Her translations include *After Tomorrow the Days Disappear* (2016) and *The Prose of the Mountains* (2015). She is Professor, Islamic World and Comparative Literature at the University of Birmingham.

Kayvan Tahmasebian is a Marie-Curie Fellow at the University of Birmingham. He is a poet, critic, and the author of *Isfahan's Mold* (2016), *Lecture on Fear and Other Poems* (2019), and co-translator of *High Tide of the Eyes: Poems by Bijan Elahi* (2019).

Routledge Handbooks in Translation and Interpreting Studies

Routledge Handbooks in Translation and Interpreting Studies provide comprehensive overviews of the key topics in translation and interpreting studies. All entries for the handbooks are specially commissioned and written by leading scholars in the field. Clear, accessible and carefully edited, *Routledge Handbooks in Translation and Interpreting Studies* are the ideal resource for both advanced undergraduates and postgraduate students.

The Routledge Handbook of Translation and Politics
Edited by Fruela Fernández and Jonathan Evans

The Routledge Handbook of Translation and Culture
Edited by Sue-Ann Harding and Ovidi Carbonell Cortés

The Routledge Handbook of Translation Studies and Linguistics
Edited by Kirsten Malmkjaer

The Routledge Handbook of Translation and Pragmatics
Edited by Rebecca Tipton and Louisa Desilla

The Routledge Handbook of Translation and Technology
Edited by Minako O'Hagan

The Routledge Handbook of Translation and Education
Edited by Sara Laviosa and Maria González-Davies

The Routledge Handbook of Translation and Activism
Edited by Rebecca Ruth Gould and Kayvan Tahmasebian

The Routledge Handbook of Translation, Feminism and Gender
Edited by Luise von Flotow and Hala Kamal

The Routledge Handbook of Translation and Cognition
Edited by Fabio Alves and Arnt Lykke Jakobsen

For a full list of titles in this series, please visit www.routledge.com/Routledge-Handbooks-in-Translation-and-Interpreting-Studies/book-series/RHTI.

The Routledge Handbook of Translation and Activism

Edited by Rebecca Ruth Gould and
Kayvan Tahmasebian

LONDON AND NEW YORK

First published 2020
by Routledge
4 Park Square, Milton Park, Abingdon, Oxon OX14 4RN
605 Third Avenue, New York, NY 10017

First issued in paperback 2023

Routledge is an imprint of the Taylor & Francis Group, an informa business

British Library Cataloguing-in-Publication Data
A catalogue record for this book is available from the British Library

Library of Congress Cataloging-in-Publication Data
A catalog record has been requested for this book

ISBN 13: 978-1-03-257017-4 (pbk)
ISBN 13: 978-1-138-55568-6 (hbk)

DOI: 10.4324/9781315149660

Typeset in Times New Roman
by Swales & Willis, Exeter, Devon, UK

Publisher's Note
The publisher has gone to great lengths to ensure the quality of this reprint but points out that
some imperfections in the original copies may be apparent.

For Mona Baker, a translator-activist
without whom translation studies,
like this book, is unthinkable

Contents

Contents

Contents

Acknowledgements

First and foremost, we would like to thank the contributors who made this work possible through their dedication to our collective project. We would like to extend our particular thanks to Omid Mehrgan for his detailed critique of the introduction. Thanks are also due to our Routledge editors, Eleni Steck, Louisa Semlyen, Hannah Rowe, and Adam Bell.

Rebecca would like to thank Ruth Bush, Luis Perez-Gonzalez, and Emanuelle Santos for their helpful discussions about this project, and, above all, Mona Baker for making it possible. The European Research Council provided support for research on global literary theory related to this project through the European Union' s Horizon 2020 Research and Innovation Programme under ERC-2017-STG grant agreement no. 759346. Her abiding debt to her family—Brenda, Beth, and Kate Gould—persists across her every book and every creation.

Kayvan is grateful to the European Commission for supporting his research project *Transmodern* (Marie Sklodowska-Curie Individual Fellowship H2020-MSCA-IF-2018 grant agreement number 842125). His work on *Transmodern* provided an opportunity to rethink the ever-expanding relations of translations and activism.

Contributors

Eylaf Bader Eddin is a PhD candidate in Arabic and Comparative Literature at the universities of Aix-Marseille, France, and Marburg, Germany. His research focuses on translation and the language of protests, especially in Syria, as well as on revolutionary archives and performance. His latest publication (in Arabic) is *When They Cried 'Forever': The Language of the Syrian Revolution* on the occasion of the Sadiq Jalal al-Azim Cultural Award in 2018.

Michela Baldo is an honorary fellow in Translation Studies at the University of Hull and holds a PhD in Translation Studies from the University of Manchester. Her research revolves around two strands. One is the written and audio-visual translation into Italian of Italian-Canadian works. On the topic she has published various articles and book chapters and authored a book, *Italian-Canadian Narratives of Return: Analysing Cultural Translation in Diasporic Writing* (2019). Her second strand of research revolves around the role of translation in Italian queer transfeminist activism, with its links to the Ispanophone and Francophone contexts. On this topic she has published various articles and co-edited a book, *Il re Nudo. Per un archivio drag king in Italia* (2014). She has also co-translated into English with Elena Basile the book *Queer Theories* (Routledge, forthcoming) by Italian scholar Lorenzo Bernini. At present she is co-editing a special issue of the translation journal *TIS* (Translation and Interpreting Studies) on translation and LGBT/Queer activism.

Paul Bandia is Professor of French and Translation Studies in the Department of French at Concordia University, Montreal, Canada. He is an Associate Fellow of the W.E.B. Du Bois Institute at the Hutchins Center for African and African American Research at Harvard University. He is currently the President of the Association for Translation Studies in Africa (ATSA) and a member of the Executive Council of the International Association for Translation and Intercultural Studies (IATIS). Professor Bandia is the author of *Translation as Reparation: Writing and Translation in Postcolonial Africa* (2008), editor of *Orality and Translation*, special issue, *Translation Studies*, vol. 8, no. 2 (2015), *Writing and Translating Francophone Discourses: Africa, the Caribbean, Diaspora*. Studies in Comparative Literature 78 (2014); co-editor of *Charting the Future of Translation History* (2006), *Agents of Translation* (2009), and *Rencontres Est-Ouest/East-West Encounters*, *TTR* (Traduction, Terminologie, Rédaction: Études sur le texte et ses transformations), vol. 1 (2010).

Partha Bhattacharjee is an Assistant Professor of English, Amity Institute of English Studies & Research, Amity University Patna. He obtained his PhD (English) from the Department of Humanities and Social Sciences, Indian Institute of Technology Patna in

2019. He completed his MA (2012), BEd (2013), and MPhil (2016) from the University of Burdwan. For his PhD, he worked on Trauma Studies, Memory and Postmemory Studies in Comics and Graphic Narratives under the supervision of Dr Priyanka Tripathi, Assistant Professor of English, Department of Humanities and Social Sciences, Indian Institute of Technology Patna. His research interests include South Asian literature, gender studies, and comics studies. Apart from a chapter in an edited volume with Routledge, he has published in reputed journals like *PSA Newsletter*, *GNOSIS*, *IUP Journal of English Studies, Language in India*, and *Journal of English Language and Literature*. His proposals have been accepted in reputed International Conferences (Comics Studies Society 2019; IGNCC 2019; ImageTech, UF 2018; South Central Modern Language Association 2018; Jadavpur University Comics Festival 2017).

Veruska Cantelli is Assistant Professor of Interdisciplinary Studies at Champlain College, Vermont, US. Before joining the Core Division at Champlain College, she taught in the Center for Global Communication Strategies at the University of Tokyo. She is the co-editor of *Mediterranean*, an anthology of migrant journeys.

Pin-ling Chang is Associate Professor at the Department of Applied Linguistics and Language Studies, Chung Yuan Christian University, Taiwan. She earned her PhD degree in Translation Studies from Newcastle University, UK. Her research interests focus on identity and ideology in translation and interpreting history and practice in the Chinese-language world. Her publications, published by Palgrave (2014) and *LANS–TTS* (2016), demonstrated the ideological factors and significance of interpreting in seventeenth-century colonial Taiwan, while her latest journal paper in the 2017 special issue of *The Translator* uncovered the ideological nature and implications of China English in translation.

Ayşe Düzkan is an activist, writer, editor, journalist, and translator. Her books include *Çalar Saat* (1994), *Erkekliğin Kitabında Yazmaz Bu* (2006), *Behiç Aşçı Kitabı* (2006), and *05 17* (2018). Her translations include *SCUM Manifesto* (Valerie Solanas), *Leila Khaled: Icon of Palestinian Liberation* (Sarah Irving), and *Freedom is a Constant Struggle* (Angela Davis). She currently has columns in *Yeni Yaşam* and www.artigercek.com.

Brahim El Guabli is Assistant Professor of Arabic Studies at Williams College, Massachusetts, US. His work probes questions of archives, memory, and strategies of rewriting history in contexts of mass violence in the Maghreb and the Middle East. His book manuscript, which investigates the significance of the concomitant emergence of cultural production about Moroccan Jews and political disappearance in post-1999 Morocco, is entitled *Other-Archives: Rewriting the Nation in Post-1956 Morocco*.

Aria Fani is an Assistant Professor in the Department of Near Eastern Languages and Civilization at the University of Washington. He worked as a volunteer and social advocate at the East Bay Sanctuary Covenant (EBSC) between January 2017 and August 2019. He is currently serving EBSC as an academic adviser on a project called Amplifying Sanctuary Voices, which aims to educate the San Francisco Bay Area public on the reasons why asylum seekers flee their homes. His writes about and teaches courses on different aspects of translation studies.

Morad Farhadpour is a leading Iranian leftist philosopher. He was born in 1958 in Tehran. A widely read essayist and translator, and member of the new Iranian left, he has translated Walter Benjamin, Theodor W. Adorno, and many other critical theorists into Persian. He is the author of three essay collections: *Depressed Reason: Reflections on Modern Thought* (1999), *Western Winds* (2003), and *Fragments of Thought* (2008-2009).

Sahar Fathi is a long-time government employee. She has served as adjunct faculty at Seattle University and the University of Washington School of Law, and her academic work has been published in a variety of law journals. Her research focuses on local government responses to institutional and structural racism, hate crimes and immigrant and refugee integration, and the evolution of racism in the law.

Elena Fiddian-Qasmiyeh is Professor of Migration and Refugee Studies at University College London where she is Co-Director of UCL's Migration Research Unit and Director of the Refuge in a Moving World interdisciplinary network. Her recent books include *The Ideal Refugees, South-South Educational Migration, Humanitarianism and Development, The Oxford Handbook of Refugee and Forced Migration Studies*, and *The Routledge Handbook of South-South Relations*.

Min Gao is a PhD candidate in the Translation Research and Instruction Program (TRIP) at State University of New York at Binghamton. Her current research interest focuses on literary translation and subtitle translation.

Rebecca Ruth Gould is the author of *Writers and Rebels: The Literatures of Insurgency in the Caucasus* (2016), and was awarded the University of Southern California Book Prize in Literary and Cultural Studies and the best book award by the Association for Women in Slavic Studies. Her translations include *The Death of Bagrat Zakharych and other Stories by Vazha-Pshavela* (2019), *After Tomorrow the Days Disappear: Ghazals and Other Poems of Hasan Sijzi of Delhi* (2016), and *The Prose of the Mountains: Tales of the Caucasus* (2015), and, as co-translator with Kayvan Tahmasebian, *High Tide of the Eyes: Poems by Bijan Elahi* (2019). Her activism focuses on Palestine and Chechnya. She is director of the European Research Council-funded project "Global Literary Theory" and Professor, Islamic World and Comparative Literature at the University of Birmingham.

Tania P. Hernández-Hernández is a Lecturer in Translation Studies at the Centre for Literary and Linguistic Studies of El Colegio de México. She holds a PhD in Translation and Intercultural Studies from the University of Manchester, UK, with a thesis on the role of translation in the internationalisation of the press. Her research interests lie in the fields of sociology of translation, translation and the production and circulation of knowledge, and translation and mass media.

Noelle Higgins is Associate Professor in Law at Maynooth University, Ireland. She has a PhD in International Law and an MA in Irish. She researches in the area of public international law, particularly in the field of human rights law.

Amanda Hopkinson is an academic, writer, and literary translator. A former director of the British Centre for Literary Translation at the University of East Anglia and Visiting Professor at City, University of London, she is currently a director of the Warwick

Translates Summer School. Author of over twenty non-fiction works on Latin American and European popular culture, literature, and photography, and translator of over fifty translations from the Spanish, French, and Portuguese, her most recent translations are *The Hole* by Mexican writer and activist, José Revueltas (2018) and the selected anthology of Portuguese short stories, *Lisbon Tales* (2019).

Sarah Irving is a Postdoctoral Fellow at the Centre for Concurrences in Colonial and Postcolonial Studies, Linneaus University, Sweden. Her current research focuses on historiography, gender, and indigenous knowledge production in Late Ottoman and Mandate-era Palestine.

Moses Kilolo manages the Mabati-Cornell Kiswahili Prize for African Literature and is the project lead for the Jalada Africa language and translation project. The inaugural *Jalada* translation issue, which he conceptualised and for which he continues to provide editorial coordination, features the single most translated short story in the history of African writing. Moses served as the Managing Editor for *Jalada* Africa between 2014 and 2018. His writing has been published in *Saraba*, *Veem House of Performance*, and *Radio Africa Magazine*, among others. He writes in Kikamba, Kiswahili, and English.

Amanda Laugesen is Associate Professor and Director of the Australian National Dictionary Centre at the Australian National University. She is the author of a number of books, articles, and dictionaries. She is the author of *Taking Books to the World: American Publishers and the Cultural Cold War* (2017) and *Globalizing the Library: Librarians and Development Work 1945–1970* (2019).

Kuan-yen Liu is currently a Lecturer in the School of Humanities and Social Science at the Chinese University of Hong Kong, Shenzhen. He received his PhD in Comparative Literature at the University of California, Santa Barbara. His current research focuses on the interactions of Pre-Qin philosophy, Song-Ming Confucianism and Qing thought with Western science, philosophy, and socio-political theory in late-Qing Chinese (1840–1911) thought and translation.

Kobus Marais is Professor of Translation Studies in the Department of Linguistics and Language practice of University of the Free State, Bloemfontein, South Africa. He has published two monographs, namely *Translation Theory and Development Studies: A Complexity Theory Approach* (2014) and *A (Bio)semiotic Theory of Translation: The Emergence of Social-cultural Reality* (2018). He also published two edited volumes, one with Ilse Feinauer, *Translation Studies beyond the Postcolony* (2017), and one with Reine Meylaerts, *Complexity Thinking in Translation Studies: Methodological Considerations* (2018). His research interests are translation theory, complexity thinking, semiotics/biosemiotics, and development studies.

Hazel Marsh is Senior Lecturer in Latin American Studies at the University of East Anglia. Her research interests include popular music and social activism, politics and popular culture, collective memory and identity, music and social movements, and the use of popular music in the construction of political discourses. She has published on George Borrow's construction of Gypsy identity, popular music and the Mexican student movement of 1968, and Venezuelan cultural policy in the Chávez period. She is the author of the monograph *Hugo Chávez, Alí Primera and Venezuela: The Politics of Music in Latin America* (2016).

Miriam Bak McKenna is a Postdoctoral Research Fellow in the School of Law at Lund University, Sweden. Before this, Miriam was a Doctoral Candidate at the University of Copenhagen, and a visiting researcher at Toronto University and the University of Cambridge. She holds degrees in law and art history from the University of Western Australia, as well as an LLM in Legal Theory from the University of Copenhagen. Her research interests encompass the history and theory of international law, with a particular focus on the history of self-determination and decolonisation, law and aesthetics, and materialist and feminist approaches to international law.

Omid Mehrgan received his PhD in 2018 from the Department of Comparative Thought and Literature (formerly The Humanities Center) at Johns Hopkins University, Maryland, US, where he currently is a part-time research assistant and lecturer. He wrote his thesis on Adorno's *Aesthetic Theory* analysed through Kleist, Hegel, and Marx. Before joining Hopkins, he worked in his hometown Tehran, Iran, as a critic, translator, and co-translator of theoretical works from German and English, particularly in the Critical Theory tradition, into Persian. Mehrgan wrote a monograph called *Ilāhıyāt-i tarjuma: Walter Benjamin va risālat-i mutarjim* (*Theology of translation: Walter Benjamin and the task of the translator*) (2008).

Khushmi Mehta is a PhD student in Art History at the Graduate Center, City University of New York, with a focus on Modern and Contemporary South Asian art. She received a BA with Distinction in Visual and Critical Studies from the School of the Art Institute of Chicago in 2018. Her research practice concerns the visibility of cultural pluralism in postcolonial Indian art. Her recent writing on *Vrishchik* (1969–1973), an artists' periodical from Baroda, explores the periodical's role as a platform to voice socio-political concerns and dissent against a totalising perception of a single visual culture for the nation. Interested in curatorial practices and archival collections, she has previously worked at art institutions such as Christie's, the Art Institute of Chicago, the Museum of Contemporary Art Chicago, and the Hans Ulrich Obrist Archive.

Hafida Mourad is Assistant Professor at the Faculty of Letters and Human Sciences, Agadir, Morocco. She holds a PhD in Literature and Translation Studies. She is also a freelance translator (Arabic–English–French). She obtained her MA in Translation Studies from King Fahd School of Translation in Tangier, Morocco, and her BA in postcolonial studies and travel narratives from the University Mohamed V-Rabat. Her areas of interests are postcolonial translation, postcolonial studies, and translation studies.

Mukoma wa Ngũgĩ is an Associate Professor of English at Cornell University, New York, US and the author of *The Rise of the African Novel: Politics of Language, Identity and Ownership*, the novels *Mrs. Shaw, Black Star Nairobi, Nairobi Heat*, and two books of poetry, *Logotherapy* and *Hurling Words at Consciousness*. He is the co-founder of the Mabati-Cornell Kiswahili Prize for African Literature.

Bidisha Pal is a Research Scholar at the Department of Humanities and Social Sciences (English), Indian Institute of Technology (Indian School of Mines) Dhanbad, Jharkhand,

India. Her areas of interest include translation studies, Dalit literature, Indian writing in English, subaltern studies, and modern and postmodern literature. She is presently working on her dissertation, entitled *Role of Translation in Mainstreaming Dalit Literature: A Study of Bengali Dalit Writings*. She has presented papers at national and international conferences on literature and language and published in international journals and book chapters.

Yousif M. Qasmiyeh is a poet, translator, and doctoral researcher at the University of Oxford's English Faculty. In addition to teaching Arabic at the University of Oxford, Yousif is Writer-in-Residence for the Arts and Humanities Research Council–Economic and Social Research Council-funded Refugee Hosts research project, the Arabic language researcher on the Prismatic Translation project, and the Creative Encounters Editor for the *Migration and Society* journal.

Mehrdad Rahimi-Moghaddam has an MA in Translation Studies from the University of Tehran, Iran. He received his BA in Translation Studies from the University of Isfahan. His current research focuses on literary translation, literary criticism, and comparative and world literature.

Bhakti Shringarpure is Associate Professor of English at the University of Connecticut (Storrs) and editor-in-chief of *Warscapes* magazine. She is the author of *Cold War Assemblages: Decolonization to Digital* (2019) and editor of *Literary Sudans: An Anthology of Literature from Sudan and South Sudan* (2016).

Malaka Shwaikh gained a PhD in Middle Eastern politics from the Institute of Arab and Islamic Studies of the University of Exeter. She is Associate Lecturer in Peace and Conflict Studies at the University of St Andrews. Her research interests cover prison dynamics, hunger strikes, the Israeli–Palestinian conflict, and oral history projects in occupied Palestine.

Kayvan Tahmasebian is a Marie-Curie Fellow at the University of Birmingham, and Principal Investigator of *Transmodern*, a Horizon 2020-funded project on the position of translated literature within modern Iranian literary theory. He is a poet, critic, and the author of *Isfahan's Mold* (2016), *Lecture on Fear and Other Poems* (2019), and co-translator (with Rebecca Ruth Gould) of *High Tide of the Eyes: Poems by Bijan Elahi* (2019). His work has appeared in or is forthcoming in *Wasafiri, Modernism/Modernity, Twentieth Century Literature,* and *The Kenyon Review*.

Marta Natalia Wróblewska holds a PhD in Applied Linguistics from the University of Warwick. She has worked as a translator of scientific and literary texts. Currently she works at the National Centre for Research and Development in Warsaw, Poland.

Manuel Yang is an Associate Professor in the Department of Studies on Contemporary Society at Japan Women's University. He studies transatlantic and transpacific history from below, with particular emphasis on the peoples, cultures, and movements that create various commons that seek to replace capitalism and empire. He is currently working on the Japanese translation of Mike Davis, C.L.R. James, and Peter Linebaugh.

1

Introduction

Translation and activism in the time of the now

Rebecca Ruth Gould and Kayvan Tahmasebian

When we were mid-way through editing this volume, we received a message from one of the contributors. She was headed to prison in less than two weeks and asked us to hurry with our edits, since she did not know whether she would have access to electronic communication from within her prison cell, or whether she would be released before the book was published. She therefore asked us to make any requests as soon as possible. Her situation represented in acute form the pressures under which many of us—translators, activists, and academics concerned with the politics of language—labour.

The author, Ayşe Düzkan, is just one of the thousands of intellectuals, authors, academics, and translators, currently being persecuted by the Turkish state as political prisoners. While their 'criminal' acts of bravery deserve our commendation, their persecution by the Turkish government reminds us of high stakes of intellectual solidarity. Similar stories are told in this volume in relation to Palestinians in Gaza, Guatemalan, El Salvadoran, Syrian, and Sahrawi refugees, student protestors in Mexico and Taiwan, revolutionaries in Venezuela, Iran, Poland, and Italy, and prisoners in Morocco. Düzkan's chapter, entitled 'Written on the Heart, in Broken English,' is a timely account of the capacity of translational activism to expand the horizons of our political commitments, in her case to transnational feminism and anti-imperial politics (Chapter 13). Düzkan's message to us was a sobering reminder of just how much the theme of this book—the intersection of translation and activism—affects our daily lives. As an activist who has helped to change discourse in Turkey around feminism and Palestine, and who inspired a translator collective through her work on *Ben Bir Feministim* (I am a Feminist), Düzkan knows whereof she speaks. Like many contributors to this volume, from across Africa, the Middle East, South and East Asia, and the Americas, her example reveals what can happen when translators conceive their agency in collective terms and when they conceptualise their activism in relation to their work as translators.

Our contributors work at the intersections of translation and activism in different ways. For some of the contributors to this volume, translational activism is a scholarly enterprise. For others, translational activism is a practice that can land—and which already has landed—them in prison. For others, translational activism lies at the heart of their anticolonial agenda (Bandia's afterword provides an overview of this dimension).

For yet others, translational activism refers to simple acts of translating with love, fidelity, and care. For all of us, readers, translators, and activists alike, the meaning and function of this intersection, along with the possibilities it opens, are unstable and subject to constant revision. This introduction reviews the chapters in this volume from the point of view of their interpretations of the concept of translational activism, after which we turn to questions of agency, temporality, and the precarious condition in which translational activism finds itself today. Activism, as we understand it, can take many forms. Although it necessarily has a public dimension, the public status of activism may not be visible to everyone. As Bandia decribes in his afterword, activism is 'a form of opposition or resistance to power' (515) that is premised on the agency of the subject. Given the central role played by agency in constituting what Walter Benjamin called the 'task of the translator,' in regards to language, the link between translation and activism is both intrinsic and necessary.

Four paradigms of translational activism

Across the many chapters that constitute this volume, four paradigms of the translator-activist can be identified: that of witness-bearer, of voice-giver, as vernacular mediator, and as revolutionary. The translator as witness-bearer is taken up in the chapters by El Guabli, and Hopkinson and Marsh, as well as in more personal terms, by Düzkan and Qasmiyeh. When the translator acts as witness-bearer, the boundary between author and translator is often rendered invisible. The particular kind of agency of the translator as witness-bearer often merges with that of the poet, including the poet who translates his own poems, as in Qasmiyeh's chapter. It is no coincidence that Qasmiyeh, who in this volume reveals the impossibility of locating an origin for himself as a poet and as a refugee, is also a translator of his own verse from Arabic into English. Qasmiyeh's chapter is distinguished by his inclusion of his own poems, meaning that his activism is manifested with respect to his own self. In contrast to this poetic approach, El Guabli documents how Moroccan writers became witness-bearers of their imprisonment during the Years of Lead under the Moroccan king Hassan II.

The second paradigm, of the translator-activist as a voice-giver, is explored in several of the chapters, particularly those by Fathi and Fani, who consider the crucial role of interpreters who help refugees from Central America navigate the asylum process within the United States. The translator-activist as a voice-giver puts into words the perspectives and experiences of oppressed and silenced peoples. Refugees and migrants feature frequently among those whose voices have been suppressed and whom the activist translator helps to make audible. In Fathi and Fani as throughout this volume, translators act in a capacity that exceeds the role typically assigned to them; they are transposers of words from one language to another. In order to be effective, an interpreter must acutely grasp the political context for the asylum seeker's claim and be able to translate that context into the terms of the target culture. Interpreters must be familiar with the legal system through which refugees pursue their claim. Generalised knowledge of the refugee's language is often not enough; the interpreter must be equipped with a nuanced understanding of the refugee's specific dialect, in other words, their vernacular.

However, it is not only in the formal capacity of interpreter that translators give voice to those whose voices are marginalised within mainstream discourse. Writing about Palestinian and Sahrawi refugees in south-west Algeria respectively, Shwaikh and Qasmiyeh and Fiddian-Qasmiyeh show us what happens when the translator's role as voice-giver is undervalued or ignored: Orientalisms of various kinds interfere, and stereotypes proliferate. The translator-interpreter's role in this context is to dispel the myths and prejudices that accumulate through lack of first-hand contact with the represented subjects, particularly in contexts of war and other circumstances marked by grossly disproportionate distributions and abuses of power.

This brings us to the third paradigm into which the translational activisms represented in this volume are embedded: of the translator as renderer of so-called minor tongues, and of literary and non-literary vernaculars, into metropolitan languages, or in some cases as renderers of metropolitan languages into vernaculars. Irving, Higgins, Mehta, and Pal and Bhattacharjee each give us ample material for reflection on the translator's contribution to the vernacularising process in Palestine, Ireland, Gujarat, and Bengal, respectively. Irving shows how translators act as mediators, making vernacular forms of Arabic accessible to the world. While Higgins showcases the role of vernacularisation—here understood as the right of people to speak and be spoken to in their native languages in court—in the context of oral interactions, Mehta and Pal and Bhattacharjee focus on the translator's contribution to expanding the viability and accessibility of 'minor' languages. In these instances, as with the translator as witness-bearer, the translator-activist acts in the capacity of an artist, inventing new forms and generating new meanings from felicitous if unexpected linguistic juxtapositions.

The fourth paradigm of translational activism that emerges in this volume is that of the translator as a revolutionary. This role includes translators who are physically stationed on the barricades or their virtual equivalent (as with Chang), who pioneer new class alliances (as with Gao) or in more mediated senses, intellectuals who come to terms with the aftermath of revolution (as with Mehrgan), and who shape the climate of debate preceding it (as with Liu). Focusing on Syria amid the ongoing war, Bader Eddin (like Chang) takes us beyond the figure of the individual translator and introduces us to a case study involving translation as a collective act. Focusing on the translation of anonymous sprayed writing (which he distinguishes from 'graffiti') on the walls of wartime Aleppo, the modality of translation that is Bader Eddin's subject helps us understand how translational activism works outside liberal conceptions of individual agency. In the case of both Chang and Bader Eddin, activist translation is a collective act that transpires on socal media.

The figure of the Syrian translator who works in a collective capacity, bearing witness to wartime atrocity, calls to mind Düzkan's insistence in her chapter that 'working collectively takes more time and is harder than working alone or in a hierarchy but the result is more powerful' (219). It is not incidental that five of the chapters included in this volume are co-authored, in some cases by authors from different countries and geographies, who bring their varying knowledge and experience into conversation with each other. Such collaborations are political even when not intended as such. Having outlined the scope of what the contributors to this volume mean by 'translation' and 'activism,' let's consider our own interpretation, as editors, of what makes a translation activist, and thereby reveal what we have learned about translation while collaborating on this work.

What makes a translation activist?

At the end of his chapter in this volume, Marais distinguishes between 'agency' and 'activism.' 'While … translators can also be activists,' he writes, and 'particular contexts may call for activism by translators,' it does not follow 'that activism is the only form that agency can take. Translators are agents through their semiotic work even if they do not have a particular activist agenda' (107). This distinction between agency and activism highlights the infinite capacity of the translator-interpreter to intervene in the political realm. At the same time, it leads us to reflect on the extent to which activist translation must be deliberate. As mediators between rulers and the public, *akyeame* (linguists) influenced Akan society, even when their role was primarily defined in relation to their service to the king. Analogously, in Mandate Palestine, informants, dragomans, and fixers disrupted conventional understandings of power in their society even when they served the colonial system (Chapter 7). Similarly, translators of Dalit memoirs in Bengali contribute to a political project by giving voice to oppressed minorities even when this plan is not explicitly articulated (Chapter 23). The importance of the agency/activism distinction lies in its positing the infinite potentiality of translator's agency, that in turn extends our conception of activism beyond liberal notions of agency.

The fact that a translation is normally considered activist only when it consciously pursues a plan for social, political, or educational change suggests the limits of existing conceptions of activist translation. In contrast to existing models, we hold that translational activism should be evaluated and appreciated in terms different from accuracy or fidelity to the original. We consider a translation to be activist whenever and however it stirs readers and audiences to action. The goal of provoking the reader may stand in tension with—and even contradict—a literal rendering of words on the page. Equally, an activist agenda may motivate a translator to intervene with the meanings and tones of the original. Such interventions do not mean relinquishing the translational mandate; rather they represent translation's reconfiguration. If there is a fidelity inhering in activist translation, it is to the 'situation' identified by Farhadpour in his essay 'Thought/translation' (which appears in English for the first time in this volume), which is intrinsically and irrevocably political. This situation is comprised of the socio-political contexts into which the translated text seeks to intervene.

Activist translators reconfigure the text alongside the context in which they write. This points to another important characteristic of activist translation: its timeliness. Translations can only be activist at certain times and within certain social circumstances. For example, Ali Shari'ati's translation of Franz Fanon's *The Wretched of the Earth* (1961) into Persian in 1963 played a role in propagating anticolonial ideas in Iran with the purpose of toppling a colonialist-dependent political regime, leading to the 1979 revolution. Assessed in terms not merely of message but also, and more importantly, of impact, Shari'ati's work could not sustain the ideological requirements generated by the reformist demands that emerged from Iranian society during the early 2000s, as documented in Mehrgan's chapter in this volume.

Activist translation takes place in what Walter Benjamin calls *Jetztzeit* (the time of the now) in his 'On the concept of history.' In Benjamin, the moment of 'now' contains the possibility of revolution in contrast to the ruling class's 'homogeneous empty time' (Benjamin 2003 [1968]: 396). Through their translations, activist translators intervene to redeem time in its revolutionary discontinuity, hence contributing to a history of the oppressed, a history that must be written in the future tense. Benjamin identifies a secret agreement between past and present generations. The past exists not only to give us lessons, but also to make it possible for activists to bring to fruition in the present what past generations failed to achieve in the past. Continuities across time make such fulfilment possible.[1]

Mona Baker reveals the primary mechanism of counter-narratives in the time of the now when she describes how the translator participates in social change by 'framing narratives' (Baker 2006). On this view, the revolutionary potential of a text from times past is released and actualised in a translation that, in the process of rendering a temporal framework, recontextualises the original. Activist translation shows how translation relates to the original as to an *'ibrat* (teaching or lesson in Arabic and Persian), changing the shape of its time and its place. Along with showcasing the empty structure of homogenous time, which can be endowed with any revolutionary or reactionary content, the concept of *'ibrat* suggests that the very rendering-into of different temporal frameworks, whatever they may be, has a disruptive and liberating effect, which defines the work of translation.

Each chapter in this volume elaborates a lesson of resistance, dissidence, protest, reform, or overthrow instigated or sustained by translators who give voice to marginalised minority groups. They narrate stories of political change brought about through the agency of translators. The diverse backgrounds of the narrators of these stories, which include scholars and activists, speak to the practical orientation of activist translation, which *act*s rather than merely copying out words, sentences, and paragraphs into the target language. Having outlined our understanding of activist translation alongside the four paradigms through which it is activated, we will now briefly introduce each of the chapters to this volume, before inviting the reader to enter the multilingual and politically divergent universes they evoke. Having distinguished the chapters from each other according to their participation in the four paradigms of translational activism, the final section of this introduction focuses on empirical overlaps, on the view that such contexts are relevant for assessing the role of activism, and in order to emphasise contrasts as well as similarities.

Chapter overviews

Hopkinson and Marsh (Chapter 16) treat *testimonio*, in the form of commission reports, interviews with human rights activists, memoirs, and songs, as a genre of activism that resists the oblivion induced by genocides and related forms of oppression in Argentina, Guatemala, Mexico, and Venezuela. They explore the ties of activism to memory, and document the challenges of translating the activist voice inherent to testimonial literature between the individual and the collective. Hopkinson and Marsh also reveal the translational core of testimonial songs as a translation of lived experiences across modalities—from experiences to words, from symbols to song. This chapter's engagement with the disappeared in Argentina's Dirty War (1976–1983), those murdered in the Mayan genocide, and suppressed during the Mexican Student Movement brings to light the ways in which activist artists and writers move between idea and praxis, translating the individual and the collective to and from each other.

When the original is an activist text, then its translation into another language, in another place and another time, has a birthright as an activist text as well. This situation describes Yang's study of the translation of Marx for the Japanese New Left movement of the mid-twentieth century (Chapter 5). Analogously examining the late-Qing Chinese translation of Social Darwinism as a prelude to Cultural Revolution, Liu (Chapter 27) examines the politicisation of the theory of evolution in its passage from Europe to Asia. While his sources—particularly British social Darwinists such as Huxley—are not explicitly activist, their Chinese translations become activist by recontextualising the original for a late-Qing audience. Liu thereby illuminates the ways in which activist translations not only translate texts but also translate temporal and regional contexts.

Both Fathi (Chapter 18) and Higgins (Chapter 17) explore the relationship between activist translation and legal and civil rights, albeit from diametrically opposed points of view and in radically different contexts. While Fathi defends the right to have an interpreter in immigration courts, Higgins demonstrates that low-quality interpretation can infringe on due process rights, including a fair trial. Whereas both authors seek legal support for minority languages, instead of defending the right to have an interpreter in courts, the right not to have an interpreter is defended in Higgins' work. Both chapters consider multilingualism from a human rights perspective and demonstrate how the erosion of legal and constitutional norms restricts marginalised groups' access to justice.

McKenna (Chapter 19) examines human rights vernacularisation through a case study of women's human rights activists in the Muslim world. Her chapter focuses on attempts by human rights activists, marginalised groups, policy makers, and legal professionals to translate human rights 'on the ground' in order to counter the reproduction of gender inequality and to open up the emancipatory potential of critical rights discourse. Such positioning situates women human rights activists on the vanguard of two different struggles: against the (false) universalism of human rights on the one hand, and against local gender and cultural stereotypes that deny agency to individual women on the other.

Fani (Chapter 24) examines the interpreter's work as an advocate for El Salvadoran and Guatemalan asylum seekers in the US. Based on his experience as an immigration rights advocate, Fani clarifies how a successful appeal in an immigration court depends on tailoring the immigrant's personal trauma to accommodate an abstract 'set of criteria enshrined in our legal institutions.' While accurately translating the asylum seekers' stories, the activist interpreter must make visible the victims' stories within recognised institutional categories in the target legal system. Fani shows how the interpreter is committed to eliciting the story the victim often withholds due to shame at its revelation or because asylum seekers think that the stories of their suffering lack significance and are unworthy of being told.

Qasmiyeh and Fiddian-Qasmiyeh's work with refugees from the Western Saharan war (Chapter 25) reveals the citational and re-citational mechanisms involved in the misrepresentation of refugees for political ends. The authors elaborate on how analysts, observers, and interpreters systematically and uncritically 're-cite'——that is, merely repeat or perpetuate—longstanding misrepresentations of Sahrawi refugees. Thus, the activist translator-interpreter's task consists of unveiling the ideological distortions that inhibit refugees' attempts at self-determination and independence. Instead of outlining how interpreters attempt to fit refugees' appeal into recognised institutional categories, as Fani does in his chapter, Qasmiyeh and Fiddian-Qasmiyeh document how interpreters can redeem refugees from corrupted political categories and falsified media representations.

Activist translation in Moroccan testimonial literature from the Years of Lead (1956–1999) is characterised by El Guabli (Chapter 15) as a form of co-writing. El Guabli argues that the co-writing and prefatory and paratextual practices he describes in his chapter are translations in their own right. Co-writing as translation involves processes of comprehension, narration, formulation, and articulation of both the events narrated and their emotional charge. Moreover, prefaces translate prisoners' voices into a language or register that makes them accessible to wider readership. This process is also observed in the standardisation of refugees' stories within the institutionally recognised categories documented by Fani.

Translational activism for Rahimi-Moghaddam and Laugesen (Chapter 11) is defined as resistance against integration into colonialist cultural programmes through the propagation of counter-narratives. Rahimi-Moghaddam and Laugesen demonstrate how in Iran during the 1960s, in the context of the influential state-sponsored Franklin Book Programme, individual Iranian translators functioned as 'organic intellectuals,' to use the term coined by Italian Marxist Antonio Gramsci (see Wróblewska and Yang's chapters in this volume); they translated leftist literary works that challenged the hegemonic cultural programmes of the ruling regime. Wróblewska (Chapter 2) reflects on different understandings of the term 'translation' scattered across Gramsci's prison notebooks in order to show how translation intervenes into existing power relations and affects the composition of what Gramsci refers to as the 'historical bloc,' with reference to the social order that produces and re-produces the hegemony of the dominant class through a nexus of institutions, social relations, and ideas. Wróblewska's chapter investigates how different translations of Gramsci's prison notebooks into English and Polish, alongside editions of these notebooks in Italian, challenge or reinforce the existing power relations in their cultural milieu.

Drawing on understudied African contexts, Marais (Chapter 6) puts forward the distinction between agency and activism that, as noted above, can help to broaden the concept of translational activism. His chapter focuses on the West African figure of the linguist (*okyeame*) and the linguist's staff (*okyeame poma*) as a mediator between the ruler and the public, who has the ability to influence society without consciously embarking on an activist project. Unusually for scholarship on translational activism, which tends to focus on modern and contemporary contexts, Marais focuses on precolonial translation practices in developing his semiotic theory of translation.

In her contribution to this volume, Düzkan (Chapter 13) offers an account of her first-hand experience in Turkey of translating in solidarity with the international feminist movement. Düzkan recounts how translating for feminist collectives led to resistance against linguistic hegemonies, most notably of global English. In this context, the translator's goals are achieved through the creation of networks of solidarity among activists who write in non-metropolitan languages yet who are compelled for various reasons from time to time to communicate in their own versions of 'broken English.'

In the context of discussing the role of dragomans, fixers, and interpreters in Mandate Palestine, Irving (Chapter 7) suggests a revision to the way these roles are often defined at the service of colonial powers. This chapter makes an effective case for distinguishing the interpreters' work from work that facilitates colonial projects by documenting how the translations by individuals such as Elias Nasrallah Haddad, Judy (Judeh) Farah Docmac (and Khalil Baydas) challenged conventional understandings of political power. Irving shows how this loosely defined group of Palestinian-Arab translators defended colloquial and vernacular forms of Arabic while insisting on visions of society that defied both the colonialist Zionist projects and the Arab nationalism that was hegemonic during their eras.

As a leader of leftist political thought in contemporary Iran, Farhadpour (Chapter 4) defends a controversial thesis according to which the only true form of thought for modern Iranian intellectuals has been translation. He explains the politicisation of European critical theory through translation projects during the fervent reformist movements of Iran during the late 1990s and demonstrates how even the indirect involvement of theoretical discourse with the everyday in the marginal translation projects pursued in Iranian newspapers during this period advanced a radical political agenda.

In the wake of Farhadpour's theorisation of translation as a political practice, Mehrgan (Chapter 29) reflects on his experience as an activist translator in the days of political reform in Iran. Mehrgan shows how translation was transformed into political activism in response to what he identifies as the 'dichronism' that afflicted Iranian intellectual life after the 1979 revolution. The politicised undecidability between tradition and modernity in the Iranian cultural scene, according to Mehrgan, reveals itself in different modalities of translation and in different translational strategies adopted by translators in post-revolutionary Iran.

Cantelli and Shringarpure (Chapter 26) address the intersection of translation and activism by introducing the idea of migrant feminist food translation studies. Exploring the intersections of gender, culture, memory, and activism, they investigate translations of recipes by women from the Gaza Strip, Sahrawi, Syrian, Somalian, and Eritrean refugee camps and detention centres. Over the course of such explorations, translation becomes an act of resistance against narrow dehumanising classifications of migrants and refugees.

For Mehta (Chapter 22) as for Pal and Bhattacharjee (Chapter 23), translational activism entails translating marginalised ethnic groups. Whereas Pal and Bhattacharjee investigate Bengali Dalit memoirs and autobiographies translated into English with the aim of securing a wider readership, Mehta views 'cultural and linguistic multiplicities as a form of resistance to a totalising national culture in the precarious state of a newly post-independence nation.' In both contexts, the translator's activism consists of affirming multiplicity against a backdrop of homogenising representations of the nation and the role of art.

Like Yang's exploration of Yoshimoto Taka'aki's translation of Marx, Gao's examination of Lu Xun's translational activism and his theory of 'hard translation' (Chapter 28), and Baldo's discussion of the Italian translation of Judith Butler's *Notes Toward a Performative Theory of Assembly* (2015) for Italian queer transfeminist groups (Chapter 3) exemplify how activist translation can inspire political movements with dreams of emancipation while providing a template for their realisation.

In the context of African translation, Kilolo (Chapter 21) calls for translation into and among African languages. He introduces a practical means of facilitating a multilingual conversation across nearly two thousand African languages without collapsing into dependency on a single unifying language. Transposing Kilolo's concern with African literary multilingualism to the conceptual domain, Ngũgĩ (Chapter 20) takes up the idea of alternative indigenous knowledge production across a multiplicity of African languages, defying calls for a single African theory of translation, and instead revealing the infinite capacity for generating theory that is immanent to and relevant for African literatures.

In a North African context, Mourad (Chapter 10) develops the metaphor of the activist translator as *maroon*, and of translation as *marronage* (escape from slavery), with reference to American writer Paul Bowles' efforts to preserve and translate Moroccan oral folk narratives. Mourad argues that Bowles' translations can be considered activist inasmuch as they challenge concept of national identity and blur the boundaries between what is regarded as 'American' and 'Moroccan' literature. In an even more direct sense, Shwaikh gives voice to indigenous perspectives against totalising colonialist representations (Chapter 8). Her chapter informs readers about the sensitivities of translation in war-zones with particular reference to the ongoing siege of Gaza. According to Shwaikh, translation should be able to generate an 'alternative approach to knowledge production by indigenous people,' in order to challenge the hegemonic misrepresentations of oppressed peoples that dominate the media (also see Qasmiyeh and Fiddian-Qasmiyeh in this volume).

Chang (Chapter 30) expounds a model of digital translation activism by recognising the significant role played by volunteer translators during the Taiwanese Sunflower Student Movement of 2014. During this movement, live reports were translated and posted online in the hope of amplifying the protest into the broader world. While Chang is concerned with the role of amateur translators in changing social spaces, Hernández-Hernández (Chapter 12) seeks activism in the context of professional journalism by engaging with the left-leaning newspaper *Le Monde diplomatique en español* (the Spanish edition of the well-known French periodical) in Mexico and Argentina in 1970s–2000s.

Bader Eddin (Chapter 9) discusses the translation of sprayed writing linked to the Syrian war on social media. With reference to a widely circulated image from Aleppo dating to 2016, he warns against the oversimplification of the disastrous wartime conditions in Syria by the images that circulate, via social media, around the world. Through his theoretically astute analysis, Bader Eddin outlines an activist role for the translator as the corrector of the false representations of war who constantly—and often anonymously—retranslates the messages inscribed on the walls.

Finally, in his afterword, Paul Bandia brings together the divergent threads of our global narratives under the rubric of postcolonial and anticolonial contexts. He thereby identifies what is arguably the single most recurrent feature of translational activisms: their resistance to coercive political regimes, and to colonial regimes in particular.

Across the unprecedented range of geographies, cultures, languages, and temporalities assembled here, translators, activists, translation theorists, and writers from many different backgrounds teach us to think in new ways about the intersections of translation and activism, as well as the meanings of translation and activism as such. While the individual chapters move in many different and often unanticipated directions, we like to think of this volume as an activist endeavour in its own right, and as one that is greater than the sum of its parts. Our collaborative work—with our contributors and with each other—has been an education in the art of thinking beyond the self. May the wide-ranging theoretical, scholarly, and empirical insights offered in these chapters inspire readers in the ways that they have affected editors: to incorporate their lessons into their own professional and personal lives.

Note

1 We express our gratitude to Omid Mehrgan, whose comments on Benjamin are paraphrased here.

References

Baker, Mona (2006) *Translation and Conflict: A Narrative Account*. London and New York: Routledge.
Benjamin, Walter (2003 [1968]) 'On the Concept of History,' in *Selected Writings, Vol. 4: 1938–1940*. Eds. Howard Eiland and Michael W. Jennings. Cambridge: Harvard University Press. 389–400.

Part I
Theorising translation and activism

2

Theory, practice, activism
Gramsci as a translation theorist

Marta Natalia Wróblewska

Introduction: Gramsci and the question of language

Antonio Gramsci (1891–1937) was one of the twentieth century's most influential figures in political theory and political activism. Founder of the Italian Communist Party, he influenced an entire generation of scholars, union activists, and politicians. When in 1926 Mussolini's Fascist government introduced a wave of emergency laws which saw the opposition parties delegalised, Gramsci, alongside several leaders of the communist movement, was arrested on charges of conspiracy and attempting to incite a civil war. The prosecutor who sentenced Gramsci to prison, despite the fact that he was protected by parliamentary immunity, allegedly declared: 'we must stop this brain from functioning for 20 years' (Togliatti 1937). Ironically, the *Prison Notebooks*——a collection of reflections and essays on a range of topics, from politics, through philosophy to literature, written during Gramsci's confinement between 1929 and 1935——testify to how Gramsci's brain continued to function during the entire period of his imprisonment, and long after his death continued to have an impact on readers and activists. Gramsci's concepts, including 'cultural hegemony,' 'organic intellectuals,' and 'subalternity' (Gramsci 2000; Hoare and Sperber 2015) have penetrated not only into academic discourse but also into journalistic and political genres.

Alongside his engagement in politics, Gramsci was a keen linguist and a polyglot. His interest in languages can be traced back to his childhood experience of multilingualism. He was born into a family of Arbëreshë (Italo-Albanian) descent (Carlucci 2013: 124) and spent his formative years in a small town in central Sardinia where dialects of Sardinian were spoken alongside Italian (or indeed dominated the linguistic landscape) (Carlucci 2013: 31). Gramsci's personal experience of bi- and multilingualism may have pushed him to study and practise translation. He studied linguistics for four years at the University of Turin before he renounced his studies in favour of journalism and political activism in the Italian Communist Party and left the university without graduating. Gramsci's involvement with languages continued in his later life: his Russian wife, Julia, was an aspiring translator and Gramsci himself translated from German and Russian, treating this activity as an intellectual exercise during the years he spent in prison. Translation exercises were part of his studies (this is the case for his translations of Marx's texts) and a pastime (in the case of translations of fairy tales of the brothers Grimm, which Gramsci sent as a gift to his children).

In approaching Gramsci's theory of translation, it is necessary to take note of the fragmented and sometimes eclectic nature of his writings. The notebooks are composed of separate notes sometimes just a few sentences long, sometimes spanning several pages, where the same concepts return in various constellations and contexts. This form of Gramsci's writings was no doubt shaped by the material conditions in which they were produced: writing in solitary confinement, Gramsci was only permitted a limited number of notepads and books at any one time. He often returned to previous reflections in subsequent notes, and rewrote extensive parts of the notebooks in separate notepads.

The web-like, elliptical quality of the notebooks constitutes a significant challenge for translators of his work. It can also be problematic for a student seeking to use a particular concept from Gramsci's intellectual repertoire. While Gramsci's writing can be challenging, the form of the *Prison Notebooks* reveals his creativity in maintaining his intellectual activity under harsh conditions of material scarcity, psychological strain, and deteriorating health. Gramsci's heroic intellectual work, undertaken in defiance of fascism, is a form of political activism, in accordance with his principles of engaged scholarship. Indeed, Gramsci was convinced that it is the responsibility of intellectuals to contribute to the dissemination of political thought and the education of the public. Combining as they do qualities of the philosophical essay and the intellectual diary, rich in references both to previous fragments by the author and various external texts (classics of literature, popular novels, and current press alike), Gramsci's notebooks call to mind in contemporary terms a personal blog.

Gramsci reflected on questions related to language in several notes, most of which are collected in Notebook 11 under the title 'On the translatability of scientific and philosophical languages' (interestingly, out of the original thirty-three notebooks, four were entirely dedicated to translation exercises). Gramsci's reflections on language fall under the academic fields of language policy (the role of dialects and the standard language in shaping national identity), sociolinguistics (the historically shaped variants used by groups from different class backgrounds), and philosophy of language (the question of untranslatability between different linguistic systems). The reflections on translation and translatability presented in the *Prison Notebooks* flow logically from Gramsci's understanding of language as such. While Gramsci was an eclectic thinker and did not present a systematic analysis of any of these problems, his observations on the way cultural and political realities shape language, and how in turn language interlinks with ideology, were pioneering.

The originality of Gramsci's approach to language and translation has attracted scholars' attention only relatively recently (ground-breaking publications include Lo Piparo 1979; Boothman 2004; Ives 2004a; publications in the area of linguistics and translation studies which recognise Gramsci's role include: Wagner 2011; Carlucci 2013). Gramsci's thought has influenced contemporary reflections on the culturally conditioned nature of translation (an approach sometimes dubbed 'cultural translation,' i.e. a type of translation which recognises and accounts for the culturally conditioned nature of language on the level of words and entire texts—Trivedi 2007). It has been convincingly argued that Gramsci influenced Ludwig Wittgenstein's thinking about the nature of language which found its expression in his ground-breaking *Philosophical*

Investigations (1953). This influence was due to the mediation of the Italian economist, Piero Sraffa, who knew both Gramsci and Wittgenstein (Sen 2003). The *Investigations*, which emphasised the role of rules and conventions in meaning and sense making, were critical in inspiring a strand of pragmatically oriented studies on language use in context (Bach 2004; Hoenisch 2006).

Through the mediated impact of Gramsci's thought on linguists as well as on the general understanding of the link between culture and power in the areas of philosophy, political sciences, cultural studies, and literature, Gramsci has stimulated the many 'linguistic turns' in twentieth-century social sciences and humanities (Ives 2004b: 12–32, 126–165). Certain themes from his notebooks have been also picked up by scholars working in the field of (critical) discourse analysis, and incorporated into theories of social representations in media, literature, and culture generally. In this sense, Gramsci is a forerunner of modern approaches to translation which stress the agency of the translator in rendering text in a different language and in mediating between cultures (Bassnett 1998; Lefevere 2016).

Concepts of translation (and activism) in Gramsci

A number of differing accounts of translation and translatability in Gramsci have been put forward in recent years (Frosini 2003; Boothman 2010; Gaboardi 2015). Here I propose a typology of three meanings that can be ascribed to 'translation' in Gramsci's work (see also Wróblewska 2020; Briziarelli n.d. for an analogic three-fold model): (1) translation between languages; (2) translation between paradigms; and (3) translation between theory and action. This categorisation links translation to political action.

Translation between languages

In its most literal sense, 'translation' means transferring meaning from one national language to another. For Gramsci, translation never consists in simply rendering words or sentences in a different language, but always requires mediating between entire cultures (Gramsci 1994: 207). When writing of translation between languages Gramsci often puts the name of the language in quotation marks, indicating that the word (for instance 'French' or 'Italian') stands for a broader reality which has been shaped in the course of historical processes and which represents cultures that often differ materially and economically (Gramsci 1995/1999: 450–451).

Translation between paradigms

The second understanding of 'translation' in Gramsci's thought is connected to transmission from one paradigm into another. Such translation can take a variety of forms: 'translation' may signify rendering theories created within one national culture in the language of another culture, each of which will be shaped by its own unique historical and economic development (linking back to the first understanding of translation). For example, Gramsci criticised the inability of the philosopher Giuseppe Ferrari to translate from 'French' social theory to the 'Italian' (Gramsci 1992: 140), as the latter existed in the context of a society which was economically and politically less advanced. In order to be effective, a translator must exploit parallels between the source and the target culture, taking into account their different points of development.

Translating between paradigms may also refer to scholarly paradigms. In a famous remark, Gramsci noted ironically that some philosophers and scholars tend to use 'their own Esperanto' and believe that 'everything that is not expressed in their language is a delirium, a prejudice, a superstition' (Gramsci 1995/1999: 447). 'Language' stands here for a professional jargon, rooted in the professions' theories and values. An analogy can be drawn with contemporary academia, in which context different schools of thought and disciplines have developed their own parlance to a degree which sometimes makes them hermetic and in need of 'translation' in order to be understood. Gramsci praised some scholars contemporary to him for their ability to translate between the methodologies of different disciplines. For instance, in his view philosopher and mathematician Giovanni Vailati was able to translate between geometry and algebra, between hedonism and Kantian morals, and between normative and applied economics, while political economist Achille Loria could express an economic argument using the 'language' of Adam Smith, Ricardo, or Marx (Gramsci 1995/1999: 452).

Translation between paradigms may refer to translation between different scholarly methods. Gramsci argues that on a basic theoretical level 'translation' must be possible within the triad philosophy–politics–economy (Gramsci 1971/1999: 745). He asks for instance whether 'Machiavelli's essentially political language can be translated into economic terms, and if so, in which economic system it could be reduced' (Gramsci 1971/1999: 346). This understanding of translation may seem distant from the literal meaning of the term, but actually it only takes one step further the recognition, present already in the previously mentioned examples, that linguistic practices reflect the cultural, social, and political conditions of a given era, and therefore that one can identify homologies between them (Briziarelli, n.d.: 3).

Translation between theory and action

In keeping with his Marxist convictions, Gramsci was not interested in pure theory. He strived to apply theory to political reality. His 'philosophy of praxis' aimed to unite theoretical thought and practical applications. Hence, the third meaning of 'translation' in Gramsci relates to translation between theory and practice, that is translating speculative philosophy into a philosophy of praxis. Gramsci equated philosophy and politics, thought and action, when he wrote: 'everything is political, even philosophy or philosophies … and the only "philosophy" is history in action, that is, life itself' (Gramsci 1971/1999: 676). The relationship between thought (theory) and practice (particularly political strategies and techniques) can be conceptualised as the third category in Gramsci's theory of translation.

This understanding is of course closely connected to the previous category—translating between paradigms or structurally analogous socio-political contexts. Thus, a theory must first be expressed in a 'language' adequate to the reality of a given historical moment (characterised by particular material conditions of production, or, in terms of classical Marxism, by the material base), before it can become a point of reference for political action and struggle. Gramsci reflects on the relationship between practice and theoretical ideas when he writes that all philosophies are born not from former philosophies but from real social developments. He concludes that:

every truth, even if it is universal and even if it can be expressed by an abstract formula of a mathematical kind (for the sake of theoreticians) owes its effectiveness to its being expressed in the language appropriate to the specific concrete circumstances. If it cannot be expressed in specific terms, it is a Byzantine and scholastic abstraction, good only for phrase mongers to toy with.

(Gramsci 1971/1999: 437–438)

If the evolution of speculative philosophy into a philosophy of praxis can be considered the ultimate scope of Gramsci's project of social emancipation, we see that this level of translation must necessarily be based on two previous steps. In reverse conceptual order these are: (1) the translation of notions and ideas from a specific source reality into a specific target reality, often requiring (2) the translation of a particular text between two languages.

The concept of historical bloc and activism

An influential Gramscian concept which is helpful in theorising the relation between translation and activism is 'historical bloc,' which refers to Gramsci's unique take on the previously mentioned Marxist dyad of base and superstructure. Rejecting mechanistic and static accounts of the relationship between underlying economic realities and the social attitudes and cultural phenomena which they shape, Gramsci argued for an understanding of the two spheres as mutually dependent.

Gramsci wrote: 'Structures and superstructures form a "historical bloc." That is to say the complex, contradictory and discordant ensemble of the superstructures is the reflection of the ensemble of the social relations of production.' He continued to argue that there exists a 'necessary reciprocity between structure and superstructures, a reciprocity which is nothing other than the real dialectical process' (Gramsci 1971/1999: 366). As an example of the practical implications of this mutual link between the base and superstructure, Gramsci stated that traditional politics usually lags behind economic processes —precisely because it belongs to the sphere of superstructure which is, in traditional Marxist theory, dependent on the hard economic base. However, he argued for the possibility of a different kind of politics, which can consciously address economic realities, giving rise to a 'new, homogenous politico-economic historical bloc' (Gramsci 1971/ 1999: 167–168). The realisation of the mutual, dialectical relationship between base and superstructure is linked to a recognition of the unity of theory and practice, of the broad social masses and those responsible for the production of politics, of ideas—the intellectuals. On the level of theoretical reflection, the consequence of admitting the concept of historical bloc is that individual notions, constellations of ideas or facts cannot be understood on their own, in isolation—on the contrary, they must be perceived as historically conditioned, set in a broader social context and always dynamically evolving as part of a 'totality' (Jay 1984; Boothman 2017).

The concept of historical bloc has been used by Gramsci scholars in a narrower sense, to denote a particular social constellation of powers, marked by 'a historical congruence between material forces, institutions and ideologies, or broadly, an alliance of different class forces' (Gill and Law 1993: 93–94). The concept of 'historical bloc' suggests that, for social change to take place, it is not enough for the material, economic conditions (the 'base' in Marxist terms) to change, but that a shift must also occur on the level of ideas and concepts. This development would normally be initiated by the 'organic intellectuals'—that is, an intellectual elite which emerges as a sub-group of any social group which is striving towards dominance, giving this group a 'homogeneity and awareness of its own function' (Gramsci 1971/1999: 5, 10). These ideas and concepts would later be taken up and put into practice by other classes, leading to a new structure of power, a new hegemony.

Against this background, translation performed on the first two of the above-described levels (between languages and paradigms) intervenes into the existing power relations and alters the composition of the historical bloc. Hence it may constitute a case of theory as praxis, or translation in the third of the discussed meanings of the term. While in his writings Gramsci does not explicitly cast translation as a form of activism, one can see how this connection emerges from the core notions of his thinking.

A neat example of translation understood in Gramsci's terms can be found in his own translations. In translating the Grimm tales from German into Italian, Gramsci eliminated references to Christian faith and transferred the stories into the context of his native Sardinian countryside. Such was Gramsci's attempt to tell the same tales while transplanting them into a different cultural context (Borghese 2010: 148–155). In this instance, a rendering of a text in a different language mediates between two different national contexts (the first level of 'translation'). At the same time, a rendering of a story rooted in Catholic morality in the context of a more universal ethics is also a translation between paradigms (the second level of 'translation'). Such a translation provides a consciously lay instruction to the younger generation.

The idea of education was fundamentally linked to that of hegemony, as according to Gramsci every hegemonic relationship is necessarily 'an educational relationship and occurs … in the international and worldwide field, between complexes of national and continental civilisations' (Gramsci 1971/1999: 666). Hence, Gramsci's *liberated* translations of the Grimm fairy tales belong also to the third category of translation: theory translated into practice.

Translating Gramsci—a comparative view

In an attempt to connect translation and activism, and to exemplify how the three levels of Gramscian translation can illuminate contemporary contexts, I will turn, once again, to the example of his own work—namely the shape in which Gramsci's notebooks have reached readers in three different linguistic contexts. I will show how these texts can either challenge the existing hegemonic structure of power, or on the contrary, how they contribute to reinforcing it. Whichever it may be, the notebooks constitute an intervention into the historical bloc. I will focus here on examples from three quite different publishing markets: the Italian, the Anglo-Saxon, and the Polish one.

A student browsing through the existing editions of the *Prison Notebooks* in Italian, English, and Polish would reach the conclusion that Gramsci 'speaks' very differently—and to different audiences—in each of these languages. This is due to the contexts that have shaped the politics of translation, editing, commentary, and critique over the course of the past decades. The reshaping of Gramsci's texts by editors and translators was made possible by the very form of the core of Gramsci's theoretical writings, particularly their division into a web-like structure of loose yet interconnected notes of different length. Below, I discuss the shape which the notebooks took in three different countries, linking their linguistic features to characteristics of the relevant political contexts.

Italian: Gramsci liberated

The division of the notebooks into separate interconnected notes was problematic already for the editors of their first Italian edition. Work on it commenced shortly after World War II and was personally supervised by Palmiro Togliatti, Gramsci's comrade and leader of the Italian Communist Party (who however is not listed among the editors; see Daniele 2005). The first Italian edition of the notebooks, edited by Felice Platone (Gramsci 1948–51), reordered Gramsci's notes, grouping them into thematic sections, rendering the text more accessible for a non-specialised reader. Furthermore, fragments of the original notebooks were censored or manipulated to fit the party agenda: for instance, positive remarks on Trotsky (a leader of the Soviet Communist Party, later exiled for opposing Stalinist rule) were removed, as were negative comments about Engels and internal Soviet politics. These choices were all linked to the Communist Party's ambition to construct an image of Gramsci as its symbolic leader, a monumental hero: dedicated husband and father (as evident from his equally hastily published, and also partly manipulated, *Letters from Prison* (*Lettere dal carcere*) (1947)), and brilliant intellectual, whose arguments were to provide a firm foundation of current party line. That the volume was published by the prestigious Italian publisher, Einaudi, and not one belonging to the party, gave a clear signal that Gramsci was not only a left-wing intellectual; he was also a modern Italian intellectual *par excellence*.

The first edition of Gramsci's writings, although accessible to the general public due to the convenient re-ordering of the notes under thematic headings, was criticised by scholars for violating the original 'organic' form of the philosopher's writings and for containing several 'ideologisations' and 'mummifications' (Bermani 1991). In 1964, Togliatti himself admitted that his methodology while working on Gramsci's manuscript was exceedingly cautious, due to the 'Stalinist times' (Bermani 1991). A request for a critical, unabridged, and unbiased edition of Gramsci's writings which would 'liberate' his thought paved the way for a new edition, a project carried out by the same publisher under the editorship of Valentino Garratana (Gramsci 1975). This edition was based on a careful re-reading and transcription of the original hand-written notebooks. Words which were previously altered as they were considered a code used by Gramsci (for instance 'philosophy of praxis' would stand simply for 'Marxism') were rendered in their original form, censored fragments were reinstated, and original orthography was used, even where this meant using antique forms. The notes were reproduced as in the original notebooks and assigned numbers (e.g. Q1§1 stands for notebook 1, note 1) to facilitate cross-referencing and consultation of the original. In the footnotes, the editors meticulously indicate crossed-out or illegible words, or Gramsci's notes to himself such as *vedere* (check), *cercare il punto* (find the exact place), *cfr* (confront). Additionally, abundant footnotes provide editors' expert comments and explanations. This ambitious editorial project testifies to a completely new vision of Gramsci's legacy. No longer is he figured as an exponent of one strand of thought (communism) and a near-contemporary of the editors and readers. Instead, he is one of the great minds of Italian philosophy, whose words deserve to be reproduced and studied with painstaking care. In later years, the advent of digital technologies has made possible the publication of the notebooks in accessible formats: first as a CD-ROM in 2007 (Gramsci 2007b), followed by the excellent online gramsciproject.org, established in 2012, which enables any reader to easily cross-check different notes (Filippini 2016). In the future, another website may reproduce the original, digitalised *Notebooks* (currently accessible only at Gramsci's family home in Ghilarza or as a travelling exhibition). The scrupulous approach of the editors of the second Italian edition and the attention conferred by Gramsci scholars around the world to every detail of his writings have cast the *Prison Notebooks* almost as a sacred text.

The history of the successive Italian editions shows how Gramsci's work was initially manipulated in the service of a political agenda to later become liberated, testifying to the multivalent legacies of the original work. At the same time, the scholarly apparatus of the second edition makes the text less accessible to a non-specialised reader, thus rendering Gramsci's work somewhat remote for many activists.

English: Gramsci's plural voice

The shape and character of two Italian editions have obviously influenced the English translations of the *Prison Notebooks*. There are no less than five edited selections from the notebooks in English.

The first two appeared the same year, 1957, in the British and American market respectively. Both were based on the first Italian edition. Besides reproducing the biases contained in the Italian original, the translators also partly re-shaped the texts according to their own political agendas. The first American selection from the *Notebooks* carries the title *The Open Marxism of Antonio Gramsci* (Gramsci 1957b) and was translated by Carl Marzani, an interesting figure who had worked as an American intelligence officer, a left-wing activist, and the head of a left-wing publishing house, Marzani & Munsell. The publication is rather odd in its shape: Gramsci's original text was translated only in fragments (sentences or even entire paragraphs are omitted). The notes are rearranged rather freely and information on source paragraphs is not provided. Words or phrases which the translator deemed 'esoteric' for the American reader were removed or 'decoded' to be replaced with what the translator considered to be synonyms (Marzani 1957). Finally, Gramsci's text is interwoven with editor's notes, which often link the content of the notes to current political affairs and debates within contemporary American politics. This curious approach gives the text the feeling of a political pamphlet, which uses Gramsci's authority to reinforce the translator's personal opinions. This translational methodology caused the text to age quickly, since many of its allusions are no longer current.

The year in which Marzani published *Open Marxism* in the US, a similar compilation of Gramsci's writings, including a selection of notes from the *Prison Notebooks*, appeared in Great Britain—*The Modern Prince and other Writings*, translated by Louis Marks (Gramsci 1957a). The section containing a selection from the *Prison Notebooks* is preceded by a biographical introduction and includes explanatory footnotes by the translator. Although *The Modern Prince* is a more rigorous edition than *Open Marxism* (for instance it follows the original division into notes), like Marzani, Marks modified some of the expressions originally used by Gramsci, for instance decoding 'philosophy of action' as 'Marxism.' While the volume was instrumental in drawing attention to the figure of Gramsci in Great Britain, it cannot but seem to be an approximate translation, which glosses over or distorts certain notions which were to become foundational to Gramscian scholarship, such as the concept of *praxis*.

The late 1960s and 1970s witnessed a wave of interest in the figure and thought of Gramsci. In the UK, this can be partly attributed to the popularity of a theatrical play produced in 1971 by the Royal Shakespeare Company, which included Gramsci among its protagonists (Boothman 2004–2005). This point is interesting for our argument, as it demonstrates how a rendering of a body of work into a completely different language (drama, instead of philosophical argument) can contribute to the dissemination of an idea, and, in consequence, also affect practice. In this case, a newly found curiosity for Gramsci's work amongst the Anglophone public paved the way for the publication of the third Anglophone edition of Gramsci's work: the *Selections from the Prison Notebooks* (Gramsci 1971/1999) which constituted for many years the main point of reference for those wanting to study Gramsci, as well as the *Letters from Prison* (an American edition published in 1973, a new British one in 1974 (1988), followed by a 'definitive' edition in 1994). Each of these successive editions greatly contributed to the awareness of Gramsci's dramatic life and his personality.

Since the *Selections from the Prison Notebooks*, translated by Quintin Hoare and Geoffrey Nowell-Smith, was published four years before the publication of the critical Italian edition, the organisation of the text followed the earlier one, with the notes grouped into thematic sections. The *Selections* were a carefully prepared edition, with abundant explanations provided by the translators—both scholars of Gramsci's work and Italian culture. In response to comments submitted by readers and commentators, certain inaccuracies and omissions present in the first edition were gradually addressed in the several ensuing ones. The *Selections* focused mainly on Gramsci's writings on social and political issues. To address an interest in Gramsci's work on culture and language which continued to grow over the following decade, the Lawrence & Wishart publishing house decided to publish a selection of notes under the title *Selections from Cultural Writings* (Gramsci 1985), selected, edited, and translated by a highly qualified team of specialists in the areas of Gramsci's work and of translation: William Boelhower, David Forgacs, and Geoffrey Nowell-Smith.

1995 brought the publication of *Further Selections from the Prison Notebooks*, prepared by Derek Boothman, a scholar who has studied extensively the topic of translation in Gramsci's work as well as the various translations of his works. This edition complements the *Selections* (1971), as it includes previously omitted notes on religion, education, and economics. Importantly for the present chapter, it includes the notes devoted to the translatability of scientific and philosophical languages. Unlike the previous *Selections* (1971) and *Cultural Writings* (1985), published with Lawrence & Wishart, *Further Selections* (1995) used the system of numeration of notes, allowing the reader to cross-reference the original with ease.

By the mid-1990s, most of the *Prison Notebooks* had been translated into English by different translators and according to different thematic constellations. The lack of clear numeration of notes in most of the published translations considerably hindered cross-referencing of the translations, reconstructing the position of particular notes in the entirety of the notebooks or consultation with the original. The work of creating a 'definite' translation, which would reproduce the order of the second, critical Italian edition of 1975, and which would take stock of decades of debates on Gramsci's thought and lexicon, was undertaken by Joseph A. Buttigieg. The result was a three-volume edition of the *Notebooks*, complete with an introduction and extensive notes (Gramsci 1992, 1996, 2007a; also re-published as a three-volume set: Gramsci 2011).

An overview of the English translations of the *Notebooks* produced in the span of half a century reveals much about changing attitudes to translation as well as the evolving interpretation of Gramsci's oeuvre in relation to the history of philosophy and political thought. While the first editions make a somewhat instrumental use of Gramsci's work, casting it as a convenient commentary to current political debates, subsequent ones emphasise the global significance of the *Prison Notebooks*; the final edition is reminiscent of editions of religious texts, in its meticulous and reverent attitude to the source. The many superseding editions and translations, together with reviews and commentaries by Gramsci scholars, testify to the vibrancy of the debate on Gramsci's thought amongst the public on both sides of the Atlantic and to the huge effort of the translators, all of whom were also keen readers of Gramsci.

In conclusion, we may say that an Anglophone reader can access a wide variety of translations of the *Prison Notebooks*. This situation facilitates an awareness of Gramsci's many voices. The proliferation of Gramsciana generates a variety of paths through which the *Prison Notebooks* can be read: from accessible publications for those wishing to be acquainted with Gramsci for the first time (Gramsci 2000) to the monumental critical edition for specialists.

Polish: Gramsci, the dead classic

There are two Polish translations of Gramsci's *Notebooks*, neither of which carries the title *Prison Notebooks*. The first edition, entitled *Pisma wybrane* (*Selected Writings*) was published in 1961 in two volumes. It is a compilation of Gramsci's writings based on the first Italian edition, combined with selected letters and an essay on the Southern Question (1949). In the Polish edition, the paragraph and notebook numbers are not listed (not even in the table of contents, as had been done in the corresponding Italian edition). This confers on the text an illusion of uniformity, even though the original character of the *Notebooks* is explained in the introduction. Otherwise, the edition follows quite closely the choices of the Italian editors, for example with the inclusion of a glossary of Gramsci's 'codes.'

When the first Polish translation of the *Notebooks* appeared, Poland was a communist state with an official ideologically driven policy of publishing: translations of works by Marxist authors were commissioned with prominent specialists and published with great care by national publishing houses. This enabled a very early (1950) publication of Gramsci's *Letters from Prison* (*Listy z więzienia*) prepared by prestigious leftist literary publisher Czytelnik. The Polish edition of the *Notebooks* (1961) was among the first in the world; selections from the text appeared in print earlier only in Serbo-Croat (1951), Spanish (1958), and Russian (1959). The *Notebooks* were published by Książka i Wiedza, a publishing house with leftist traditions dating back to the pre-World War II period. It was the fifth book to appear in the prestigious series Biblioteka myśli socjalistycznej (Library of Socialist Thought). The notes to be included were selected by Ludovico Tulli, translator of Polish literature into Italian, in consultation with specialists from the Gramsci Institute in Rome. The translation was entrusted to the distinguished literary translator Barbara Sieroszewska and the support of several leading Polish intellectuals is acknowledged in the foreword.

The second Polish edition, published in 1991, and based on Garratana's critical edition, is entitled *Zeszyty filozoficzne* (*Philosophical Notebooks*). It was published as part of another prestigious series: Biblioteka Klasyków Filozofii PWN (Library of the Classics of Philosophy of the Polish National Scientific Publishers). A major change between the two editions is the organisation of the text. In the second edition, the organisation finally follows the structure originally given to it by Gramsci, i.e. it is divided into separate (numerated) paragraphs and not merged into one seemingly uniform text.

The editor of the second Polish edition, Sław Krzemień-Ojak (the author of one of the two monographs on Gramsci in Polish), deemed that the first translation was accurate enough to be reprinted after thirty years from its first publication. The paragraphs translated earlier by Sieroszewska were included in the new edition with only small amendments and were complemented with fragments published for the first time, translated by Joanna Szymanowska.

In effect, though there are two Polish editions of the *Notebooks*, one published thirty years after the other, we can effectively speak of a single translation executed by one translator and later seamlessly complemented by another. The only differences between the two editions are minor editorial ones and even these can be usually attributed to alterations in the source text, and not to changes in the style or policy of translation or shifts in the interpretation of particular Gramscian notions. Furthermore, the editors did not seize the opportunity to correct mistranslations or linguistic slips present in the first version (for examples, see Wróblewska 2020).

While being well-known experts in the field of Italian literature, Sieroszewska and Szymanowska, the Polish translators of the *Prison Notebooks*, are not specialists in the field of Marxism, or radical theory in general, in contrast to the English-language translators, who are all avid readers and recognised commentators on Gramsci. The English editions of the *Notebooks*, as we have seen, all include introductions and notes from the translators, which is not the case with the Polish editions, in which the translators remain largely invisible. In the Polish editions, it is the editors who play the role of the readers' guides to Gramsci's thought.

In the contemporary Polish intellectual panorama, Gramsci remains a rather distant intellectual figure, 'a classic' rather than a relevant voice in current philosophical and political discussions. The existing translations of the *Prison Notebooks* seem to reinforce such an approach. The first edition casts him as a classic of Marxist thought, the second as a classic philosopher *tout court*. This framing of Gramsci's work seems to be a conscious choice on the part of the editors. In the introduction to the second Polish edition we read that, although Gramsci's work has been a topic of intellectual reflection worldwide for decades, currently interest in his work has diminished:

> everything has been published, every detail of his biography has been studied, all historical material exhausted, all possible variants of interpretation tried out … and while for decades [Gramsci] has been part of the living tradition, he has now been shifted to the area of respected legacy … This is how we present him in the current edition.
>
> *(Krzemień-Ojak 1991)*

After the Polish economic transformation of 1989, all theory associated with the socialist regime became suspect and was scrapped from university education programmes. Thinkers associated with the left quickly became intellectually unfashionable. In consequence, academic traditions of Marxist reflection were abandoned, and scholars often hastily concealed traces of engagement with leftist theory from their resumes. These historical circumstances cast light on the above-cited words from the introduction to the second Polish edition of Gramsci's *Notebooks*. It is quite likely that the project of a new edition of Gramsci's writings had been initiated before the Polish economic transformation of 1989, but the volume appeared on the market when it was clear that the communist regime has been dismantled and that any presentation of Gramsci as a classic must come with a proviso.

In conclusion, while we can say that Garratana's critical edition of 1975 enables Gramsci to speak in his own voice, and the many existing English translations allow readers to hear the author's multiple voices, mixed sometimes with those of the translators, in Polish Gramsci's words are distant, muted, and at times distorted. The very shape of the two editions of the *Notebooks* (hard-cover elegant volumes) and the venue of their publication (in 'classics' series) cast the author as a historical thinker rather than a theorist whose ideas can invigorate contemporary politics.

Progressive activism in Poland—why we are losing and can Gramsci help?

In contemporary Poland, a large majority of the young generation supports right-wing political parties and movements, which often capitalise on a strong and crude anti-communist component—in the parliamentary election of 2015, over 60% of voters aged under 30 cast their votes for right-wing parties (Winiewski et al. 2015: 2). According to one common hypothesis (Kozłowski 2015), this tendency can be attributed to the fact that the young generation doesn't have any other 'language' in which to voice their dissatisfaction and develop a critique of current social and political conditions, including their experienced relative deprivation (Winiewski et al. 2015: 9–10) apart from the dominant right-wing nationalist and xenophobic one. At the same time, leftist movements find themselves without a common symbolic framework: postmodern currents, popular in academia, are perceived by the wider public as overly complex and abstract, while classical Marxist theory is strongly associated with the previous system and its flaws.

During the last decade, the nationalist agenda has gained many endorsers in intellectual circles. There emerged an entire intellectual environment composed of journalists, writers, and academics who enthusiastically support nationalist tendencies within society by developing its theoretical base. The historical-political reflection these authors put forward often bears traces of conspiracy theory, including linking all progressive political movements (feminism, LGBT+ rights, ecology) to communism, which in post-communist Poland is an accusation not to be taken lightly. With the boom in 'patriotic' publishing (popular and academic books, weekly magazines) and intellectual events (debates, exhibitions), far-right nationalism gained a certain intellectual legitimacy. At the same time, audio-visual production, such as patriotic films, music, and the rise of a merchandise industry (nationalist-themed t-shirts, gadgets) ensured the proliferation of symbols of the nationalist agenda in popular culture. From a theoretical perspective, this alliance between academics, intellectuals, and the broader public has taken the form of what Gramsci referred to as 'historical bloc.'

Can Gramsci's 'open Marxism' become a reference point in political debates and struggles over hegemony in contemporary Poland? Could a new edition of Gramsci's works constitute an intervention into the historical bloc? A lack of contemporary publications on Gramsci's thought certainly hinders the enterprise of re-introducing his voice into intellectual debate. A strategy of bringing back Gramsci's thought to Poland, not just for the purposes of historical scholarship, but as a valuable voice on urgent contemporary issues, can build on the Gramscian classification of levels of translation presented in the first part of this chapter.

On the level of translation between languages, a new, accurate, and well-researched edition of Gramsci's essential writings would be necessary for reviving Gramsci's legacy. On the level of translating paradigms, a critical introduction or commentary would help clarify Gramsci's concepts, express them in a language relevant for the stage of societal development in which Poland currently finds itself, and relate such reflections to current political problems, such as the rise of the hegemonic nationalist discourse. Such a postulated new translation may encompass more than just a publication, and the book itself wouldn't necessarily have to be a typical scholarly hard-back edition. The publication could draw on the possibilities offered by technology (following the example of several international online projects dedicated to Gramsci) and new editing trends. A multimodal publication, a comic book, a Twitter account, and an open-access e-book with an online forum for debates are all options.

Finally, on the third level, that of translating theory into practice, a Gramscian reflection on the current hegemony of nationalist thought and imagery in Polish politics and the role of the unity of the 'historical bloc' (intellectuals and broader society united around a set of symbols representing values) could inspire those supporting progressive movements to strive towards a united front, one which would also build on an appropriate set of symbols, including elements of popular culture. For Gramsci's voice on contemporary issues to be heard in contemporary language, his thought would have to be translated on all three of the above-described levels. While it may be excessively optimistic to expect that 'translating' Gramsci in any of the above-discussed levels would significantly affect the current state of affairs, such an undertaking could disrupt the composition of the currently dominant historical bloc.

From translation theory to activist practice: personal reflection and conclusions

In this concluding section, I wish to briefly reflect on my own work as translator, intellectual, and activist, in the light of Gramsci's theory of translation, introduced above. The last decade has been for me the time of intellectual and political coming of age, which happened to take place in a period characterised by growing hostility towards the values and theories I cherish the most. A pressing need developed for me to understand the social processes at work: the consolidation of nationalist attitudes amongst my peers and the disavowal of women's and minorities' rights which had previously seemed to have been well secured. I reflected extensively on these topics in my academic and partly academic publications.

I also translated into Polish authors whom, I believed, could offer important insights into the current state of affairs. These included the feminist Shulamith Firestone, whose observations on the impact of biology on the position of women in society seemed oddly timely four decades after the publication of her *The Dialectic of Sex*. All this frantic reading, thinking, commenting, writing, and translating did not bear the expected fruit. Despite some modest scholarly recognition, few readers reacted outside my own intellectual circle. I discovered, to my dismay, that my translation of Firestone was being used as a reference in papers written from ultra-conservative positions, to illustrate the so-called madness of feminist theory. Disappointed, for a while I abandoned this engaged strand of my work, returning to critical theory.

After a while however, passively observing the spreading of nationalistic, xenophobic, misogynistic symbols and slogans in the media, in popular culture, and in public spaces (posters, graffiti, sticker art) became impossible. Compelled to react in a way which would have tangible effects, I turned this time to a different repertoire to express myself. Blog posts constituted one channel: I wrote in Polish about the concept of 'mansplaining,' suggesting a suitable Polish translation for the term and denouncing the practice of organising 'manels' [all-male panels], which are usually considered a non-issue in Poland. Satirising the surge of popular 'identity' clothing, featuring 'patriotic' (often anti-communist, anti-EU) symbols, I produced a t-shirt with the logo of one of the largest workers' cooperatives from the time of People's Poland. To mark the Polish Day of Independence (11.11), which is often an occasion for demonstrations verging on xenophobia and always a celebration of uniquely male heroes and role-models, I produced, together with a collective of female friends, two forms of simple artwork. We created a zine featuring the female and feminist heroes of Polish history as well as a set of stickers with progressive slogans, intended to be used oppositionally in public spaces to cover up hateful messages against minorities and migrants (for further details on these interventions see Christensen et al. 2018: 871–874).

These improvised micro-interventions stimulated an animated response. My blogs and tweets on 'mansplaining' and 'manels' provoked comments and gave rise to online discussions, my 'People's Poland' t-shirt stirred up conversations also amongst strangers, and I have handed out many sets of 'progressive' stickers and even received requests for the sticker templates from activist groups in other cities which had requested them in order to print their sets. It was interesting to see that these little bits of writing, produced impromptu and in a playful spirit (quite different from the continuous strain and stress of academic work) were actually more effective in drawing attention to the issues I found pressing than my scholarly publications. It was almost as if the further away from academic writing my intervention was, the more powerful; the less verbose, the more widely it was read. That said, these activist moments could not have taken place, were it not for the theoretical moments which preceded them: my awareness and understanding of the current state of political affairs, and my urge to intervene were fuelled by my theoretical, academic background.

How can these small acts of web or urban activism be reframed in terms of Gramsci's theory of translation? Referring to the first level of translation—translation as mediating between languages and cultures—I would see my engagement in translating feminist theory (Firestone), but also concepts such as 'mansplaining' and 'manel' as an effort to situate international progressive thought within the conditions of Polish culture. In doing so, I used a language which was not overly rooted in arcane feminist theories and did not assume the readers' progressive views. In short, I translated in a way that would be adequate to the particular stage of social development that we currently find ourselves in. Referring to the second level of translation in Gramsci's theory, my efforts to communicate my ideas in more popular formats, which would not alienate those who are not familiar with academic genres or who find fashionable scholarly jargon too abstract or off-putting, can be considered as an attempt to translate some of the feminist, progressive concepts I have been working with into a different, more accessible paradigm. Finally, given the activist and collaborative spirit in which these interventions were produced, they may be seen as an attempt to translate theory into practice, situating themselves on the third level of translation.

Being a translator under the conditions of contemporary capitalism, where we are constantly battling against deadlines as well as against challenges brought by technology and globalisation, often leaves little space for us to reflect on our social responsibilities. Translators are rarely recognised as scholars, activists, and intellectuals and even more rarely are they rewarded for their contributions to the critique of culture. And yet, Gramsci's example—his inspired work, as well as his heroic life—testifies to the necessity of conceiving of our work within its broadest possible social and political contexts, particularly in adverse times. If we do not think of our work as an intervention, however small, into the historical bloc our work will remain, in Gramsci's words, 'a Byzantine and scholastic abstraction, good only for phrase mongers to toy with.'

Related topics

Activist Translation, Alliances and Performativity; Translators as Organic Intellectuals; Thought/Translation.

Further reading

Carlucci, Alessandro (2013) *Gramsci and Languages. Unification, Diversity, Hegemony*. Chicago: Haymarket Books.

A recent and thorough discussion of the importance of language in Gramsci's bibliography and his work.

Gramsci, Antonio (1975) *Quaderni del carcere*. Ed. Valentino Garratana. Torino: Einaudi.

Critical edition of the Prison Notebooks in Italian, scroupolously prepared by a team of expert editors from the Istituto Gramsci in Turin. Includes ample annotations, which however avoid giving a single interpretation of the notes.

Gramsci, Antonio (2011) *Prison Notebooks, Vol. 1–3*. Trans. Joseph Buttigieg. New York: Columbia University Press.

Critical edition of the Prison Notebooks in English, widely considered the 'ultimate' English translation, complete with insightful introduction and extensively annotated.

Lo Piparo, Franco (1979) *Lingua, intellettuali, egemonia in Gramsci*. Bari: Laterza.

First publication drawing attention to the importance of language in Gramsci's thought.

References

Bach, Kent (2004) 'Pragmatics and the Philosophy of Language,' in *The Handbook of Pragmatics*. Eds. Laurence R. Horn and Gregory L. Ward. Oxford: Blackwell. 463–487.

Bassnett, Susan (1998) 'The Translation Turn in Cultural Studies,' in *Constructing Cultures: Essays on Literary Translation*. Eds. Susan Bassnett and André Lefevere. Bristol: Multilingual Matters. 123–140.

Bermani, Cesare (1991) 'Il Gramsci di Togliatti e il Gramsci liberato,' in *L'impegno* 9 (2) [online]. Available at: www.storia900bivc.it/pagine/editoria/bermani291.html [accessed 27 July 2019].

Boothman, Derek (2004) *Traducibilità e processi traduttivi. Un caso: A. Gramsci linguista*. Perugia: Guerra.

Boothman, Derek (2004–2005) 'Le traduzioni di Gramsci in inglese e la loro ricezione nel mondo anglofono,' in *inTRAlinea* 7 [online]. Available at: www.intralinea.org/archive/article/Le_traduzioni_di_Gramsci_in_inglese [accessed 27 July 2019].

Boothman, Derek (2010) 'Translation and Translatability: Renewal of the Marxist Paradigm,' in *Gramsci, Language and Translation*. Eds. Peter Ives and Rocco Lacorte. Lanham: Lexington Books. 107–133.

Boothman, Derek (2017) 'Gramsci's Historical Bloc: Structure, Hegemony and Dialectical Interactions,' *Movimento-revista de educação* 6: 131–150.

Borghese, Lucia (2010) 'Aunt Alene on Her Bicycle: Antonio Gramsci as Translator from German and as Translation Theorist,' in *Gramsci, Language and Translation*. Eds. Peter Ives and Rocco Lacorte. Lanham: Lexington Books. 135–169.

Briziarelli, Marco (n.d.) 'The Translation of Politics and Politics of Translation: Gramsci and the Philosophy of Communicative Praxis.' Working Paper [online]. Available at: www.academia.edu/ 29298902/The_translation_of_politics_and_politics_of_translation_Gramsci_and_the_Philoso phy_of_Communicative_Praxis [accessed 27 July 2019].

Carlucci, Alessandro (2013) *Gramsci and Languages. Unification, Diversity, Hegemony*. Chicago: Haymarket Books.

Christensen, Jannick Friis, Sarah Anne Dunne, Melissa Suzanne Fisher, Alexander Fleischmann, Mary Mcgill, Florence Villesèche, and Marta Natalia Wróblewska (2018) 'Powerful Writing as Writing "with",' *Ephemera—Theory and Politics in Organization* 18: 865–879.

Daniele, Chiara (2005) *Togliatti editore di Gramsci*. Rome: Carocci Editore.

Filippini, Michele (2016) 'Gramsciproject.org: una «digital library» semantica per nuovi percorsi di ricerca,' *Studi culturali* 2: 259–272.

Firestone, Shulamith (2011) 'Dialektyka Płci. Rozdział 1,' in *Res Publica* [online]. Available at: www. academia.edu/12692375/Shulamith_Firestone_Dialektyka_płci_rozdz.1 [accessed 27 June 2019].

Frosini, Fabio (2003) 'Sulla «traducibilità» nei Quaderni di Gramsci,' *Critica Marxista* 6: 1–10.

Gaboardi, Natalia (2015) 'Il concetto di 'traducibilità' in Gramsci,' *Gramsciana* 1: 91–108.

Gill, Stephen, and David Law (1993) 'Global Hegemony and the Structural Power of Capital,' in *Gramsci, Historical Materialism and International Relations*. Ed. Stephen Gill. Cambridge: Cambridge University Press. 93–125.

Gramsci, Antonio (1947) *Lettere dal carcere*. Eds. Palmiro Togliatti and Felice Platone. Torino: Einaudi.

Gramsci, Antonio (1948–51) *Quaderni del carcere*. Ed. Felice Platone. Torino: Einaudi.

Gramsci, Antonio (1949) *La questione meridionale*. Torino: Tipografia Popolare.

Gramsci, Antonio (1957a) *The Modern Prince and Other Writings*. Trans. Louis Marks. London: Lawrence and Wishart.

Gramsci, Antonio (1957b) *The Open Marxism of Antonio Gramsci*. Trans. Carl Marzani. New York: Cameron Associates.

Gramsci, Antonio (1961) *Pisma wybrane*. Trans. Barbara Sieroszewska. Warszawa: Książka i Wiedza.

Gramsci, Antonio (1971/1999) *Selections from the Prison Notebooks*. Trans. Quintin Hoare, Geoffrey Nowell-Smith. London: Lawrence & Wishart.

Gramsci, Antonio (1973) *Letters from Prison*. Trans. Lynne Lawner. New York: Harper and Row.

Gramsci, Antonio (1975) *Quaderni del carcere*. Ed. Valentino Garratana. Torino: Einaudi.

Gramsci, Antonio (1985) *Selections from Cultural Writings*. Trans. William Boelhower, David Forgacs, and Geoffrey Nowell-Smith. Cambridge: Harvard University Press.

Gramsci, Antonio (1988) *Gramsci's Prison Letters—Lettere dal Carcere*. Trans. Hamish Henderson. London: Zwan Publications.

Gramsci, Antonio (1991) *Zeszyty filozoficzne*. Ed. Sław Krzemień-Ojak. Trans. Barbara Sieroszewska and Joanna Szymanowska. Warszawa: Wydawnictwo Naukowe PWN.

Gramsci, Antonio (1992) *Prison Notebooks, Vol. 1*. Trans. Joseph Buttigieg. New York: Columbia University Press.

Gramsci, Antonio (1994) *Letters from Prison. Vol. 1*. Ed. Frank Rosengarten. Trans. Raymond Rosenthal. New York: Columbia University Press.

Gramsci, Antonio (1995/1999) *Further Selections from the Prison Notebooks*. Trans. Derek Boothman. London: Lawrence & Wishart/The Electric Book Company.

Gramsci, Antonio (1996) *Prison Notebooks, Vol. 2*. Trans. Joseph Buttigieg. New York: Columbia University Press.

Gramsci, Antonio (2000) *The Gramsci Reader, Selected Writings 1916–1935*. Eds. David Forgacs and Eric Hobsbawm. New York: New York University Press.

Gramsci, Antonio (2007a) *Prison Notebooks, Vol. 3*. Trans. Joseph Buttigieg. New York: Columbia University Press.

Gramsci, Antonio (2007b) *Quaderni del carcere* [Versione digitale in Cd-Rom]. Ed. Dario Ragazzini. Torino: Einaudi.

Hoare, George, and Nathan Sperber (2015) *An Introduction to Antonio Gramsci: His Life, Thought and Legacy.* London: Bloomsbury Publishing.

Hoenisch, Steve (2006) 'A Wittgensteinian Approach to Discourse Analysis,' in *Critisicm.com* [online]. Available at: www.criticism.com/da/lw_da.html [accessed 21 July 2019].

Ives, Peter (2004a) *Gramsci's Politics of Language: Engaging the Bakhtin Circle and the Frankfurt School.* Toronto: University of Toronto Press.

Ives, Peter (2004b) *Language and Hegemony in Gramsci.* London: Pluto Press.

Jay, Martin (1984) *Marxism and Totality: The Adventures of a Concept from Lukács to Habermas.* Berkeley: University of California Press.

Kozłowski, Michał (2015) 'Youngsters and Refugees, or How Exile Changes Eastern Europe,' in *Open Democracy* [online]. Available at: www.opendemocracy.net/can-europe-make-it/michal-kozlowski/youngsters-and-refugees-or-how-exile-changes-eastern-europe [accessed 27 June 2019].

Krzemień-Ojak, Sław (1991) 'Wprowadzenie,' in Antonio Gramsci, *Zeszyty filozoficzne.* Ed. Sław Krzemień-Ojak. Trans. Barbara Sieroszewska and Joanna Szymanowska. Warszawa: Wydawnictwo Naukowe PWN. vii–xxxvii.

Lefevere, André (2016) *Translation, Rewriting, and the Manipulation of Literary Fame.* London: Routledge.

Lo Piparo, Franco (1979) *Lingua, intellettuali, egemonia in Gramsci.* Bari: Laterza.

Marzani, Carl (1957) 'Translator's Note,' in Antonio Gramsci, *The Open Marxism of Antonio Gramsci.* Trans. Carl Marzani. New York: Cameron Associates. 15.

Sen, Amartya (2003) 'Sraffa, Wittgenstein, and Gramsci,' *Journal of Economic Literature* 41: 1240–1255.

Togliatti, Palmiro (1937) 'Antonio Gramsci capo della classe operaia italiana,' in *Lo Stato operaio* 5–6 [online] May–June 1937. Available at: https://quadernidelcarcere.wordpress.com/su-gramsci/antonio-gramsci-il-capo-della-classe-operaia-italiana/ [accessed 27 June 2019].

Trivedi, Harish (2007) 'Translating Culture vs. Cultural Translation,' in *Translation—Reflections, Refractions, Transformations.* Eds. Paul St-Pierre and Prafulla C. Kar. Amsterdam: John Benjamins Publishing Company. 277–287.

Wagner, Birgit (2011) 'Cultural Translation: A Value or a Tool? Let's Start with Gramsci!,' in *Goethezeitportal* [online]. Available at: http://publikationen.ub.uni-frankfurt.de/frontdoor/index/index/docId/23347 [accessed 27 June 2019].

Winiewski, Mikołaj, Łukasz Jurczyszyn, Michał Bilewicz, and Marta Beneda (2015) 'Podłoże prawicowych preferencji wyborczych młodych Polaków,' Report of Centre for Research on Prejudice, Warsaw [online]. Available at: http://cbu.psychologia.pl/uploads/images/foto/Pod%C5%82o%C5%BCe%20prawicowych%20preferencji%20wyborczych%20m%C5%82odych%20Polak%C3%B3w2.pdf [accessed 28 June 2019].

Wittgenstein, Ludwig (1953) *Philosophical Investigations.* New York: MacMillan Publishing Company.

Wróblewska, Marta Natalia (2020) 'Translations of the 'Prison Notebooks' into Polish—A Gramscian Analysis,' in *Revisiting Gramsci's Notebooks.* Eds. Francesca Antonini, Aaron Bernstein, Lorenzo Fusaro, and Robert Jackson. Leiden: Brill. 101–121.

3

Activist translation, alliances, and performativity

Translating Judith Butler's *Notes Toward a Performative Theory of Assembly* into Italian

Michela Baldo

Introduction

This chapter theorises a concept of activist translation, understood as a political and, often, oppositional act, capable of producing social transformation (Tymoczko 2007, 2010; Wolf 2012; Baker 2013). It takes inspiration from the recent translation into Italian, by Federico Zappino, of Judith Butler's *Notes Toward a Performative Theory of Assembly* (Butler 2015), which has been translated as *L'alleanza dei corpi* (*The Alliance of Bodies*) (Butler 2017). Butler's book deals with a specific form of activism, one centred on public demonstrations and protests.

In this chapter, I first give some background information on the translation of Butler's book, and its reception in Italy; subsequently, I discuss what it means to engender collective protest through activist translation. Firstly, by drawing on the idea of the performativity of bodies gathered in public demonstrations, I analyse the performative aspect of this translation; in particular, I look at how the public presentations of the book's translation mobilised Italian queer transfeminist[1] groups that are committed to fight against precarity, much like the groups discussed by Butler, and what kind of impact the debates raised around the translation have had on them. Secondly, I examine the extent to which we can theorise translation in activist scenarios as an 'alliance,' a term borrowed from the title of the translation of Butler's book, and which is widely used in Italian queer transfeminist circles. Understanding translation as an alliance bears similarities with Mona Baker's (2016b) and other translation studies scholars' (Tymoczko 2007; Wolf 2012; Castro and Ergun 2017b) theorisation of activist translation as the creation of networks of solidarity across languages and cultures. Concepts like 'alliance' and 'solidarity,' as they are used by Butler, have occasionally been criticised both by the translator of *L'alleanza dei corpi* (Butler 2017) and by the Italian transfeminist groups and individuals who attended the presentations of the book's translation. This chapter will thus move from the criticism generated by Butler's translation in relation to these terms to an exploration of the uses of such criticism for current understandings of activist translation.

The translation into Italian of Butler's *Notes Toward a Performative Theory of Assembly*

In 2017, Federico Zappino translated Judith Butler's *Notes Toward a Performative Theory of Assembly* (2015) as *L'alleanza dei corpi* (*The Alliance of Bodies*). Zappino had previously translated other works by Judith Butler into Italian, including *La vita psichica del potere. Teorie del soggetto* (2013), the translation of *The Psychic Life of Power: Theories in Subjection* (1997), and *Fare e disfare il genere* (2014), a retranslation of *La disfatta del genere* (2006), which is the translation of *Undoing Gender* (2004). *L'alleanza dei corpi* was published by the Milanese independent publisher Nottetempo,[2] and the book was presented in various locations in Italy, including Rome, Bologna, and Milan. Zappino has also translated into Italian a book by the queer theorist Eve Kososky Sedgwick, *Epistemology of the Closet* (Sedgwick 2011), and a book by lesbian radical feminist Monique Wittig, *The Straight Mind* (Wittig 2019).

In *L'alleanza dei corpi*, Butler uses the theory of gender performativity, which she had developed in her previous works, as the point of departure for a discussion of precarity and public protests. She analyses what public assemblies signify under current economic and political conditions, critically discussing movements of dissent such as those of Tahrir Square, Occupy Wall Street, Black Lives Matter, and others. Butler understands demonstrations as public forms of performative action, as 'embodied forms of expression, ways of making political demands even when speech is absent' (Berbec 2017). Performativity thus refers to the expressive dimension of physical bodies when gathering together, a dimension that does not rely on speech. This gathering also generates a new understanding of the public sphere of appearance essential to political life. Moreover, the public mobilisation of bodies makes visible the ontological precariousness and material precarity of people who gather publicly. While precariousness refers to the condition by which 'one's life is always in some sense in the hands of the other' (Butler 2009b: 14), and to the fact that all lives 'can be expunged at will or by accident' (Butler 2009b: 25), precarity designates the material aspect of such precariousness. Butler defines precarity as a 'politically induced condition of maximised vulnerability and exposure for populations exposed to arbitrary state violence, to street or domestic violence' (Butler 2015: 33). Indeed, the aim of public demonstrations is to protest against the political and economic forces that are implicated in the creation of such material precarity. The latter also implies that people are interdependent, resistant, and grievable, that is that their life matters. Butler thus conceives the assembly of bodies as a performative enactment of precarity, which in turn becomes a site for the assembly and, eventually, for an alliance of bodies.

As Federico Zappino stated in two interviews (Baldo and Zappino 2018; Zappino 2017c), the decision to translate the word 'assembly' with 'alleanza [alliance],' rather than with its literal translation into Italian, namely 'assembramento,' is justified by the importance the translator himself, and current queer transfeminist groups in Italy, place on the notion of alliance, a term which seems to be used more and more among these groups. The term alliance, which I will discuss further in this chapter, is understood as a way to strengthen queer feminist struggles by bringing together other groups involved in similar struggles. Alliance was indeed used by Butler in the second chapter of the book, which is based on a paper presented in Venice in 2011, in the aftermath of the protests related to the Occupy Wall Street movement. Assembly, instead, for Butler (2015) refers to the public gatherings of people who get together in public spaces to protest. Following from this, Zappino (Baldo and Zappino 2018) argues that the assembly has to be understood as a moment preceding the alliance, as a moment when bodies, which are not yet political subjectivities, assemble. Translating 'assembly' with the term 'alleanza' [alliance] can thus be perceived as an indication of the intention to focus on the potential outcome of the assembly of bodies, that is, the potential formation of alliances among different subjectivities.

The importance of the term 'alliance' also becomes evident from the many reviews of the translation, which have appeared between 2017 and 2018, given also the popularity of Judith Butler and the fact that Zappino was already well known for his previous translations and public discussions of Butler's work. One of these reviews (Presentazione Alleanza dei corpi 2017) aimed at promoting the presentation of the translation in Bologna, in April 2017, in an activist space called Mediateca Gateway,[3] by representatives of the transfeminist collective Smaschieramenti and of the collective Connessioni precarie,[4] which both work on the notion of precarity. The insightful interventions by a series of activists, other than that of Zappino, at this presentation stressed the possibilities offered by Butler's work to think about alliances against neoliberal governance; with its hierarchies and exclusions, and the competitive ethos that maximises the precarity of our lives and separates our bodies, neoliberalism silences our senses and our desires to reach out to other bodies. Such desires can constitute the premise for an alliance that can oppose this neoliberal, forced isolation and fragmentation, and produce social transformation. This view was particularly expressed by activist Renato Busarello from Smaschieramenti, who stated that Butler's L'alleanza dei corpi does what queer movements are currently trying to do in Italy, that is, trying to form alliances between LGBTQ+ groups and other groups based on the notion of a shared precarity. Busarello stressed the fact that, in a current political situation where LGBTQ+ rights are weaponised against other rights (see, for example, the pinkwashing rhetoric used by Israel against Palestinians),[5] it is impossible to engage in activism without thinking of expanding one's alliances.

The notion of precarity in its relation to the questions of capitalism, neoliberalism, and austerity politics is indeed a central topic of discussion within Italian queer transfeminist collectives. Transfeminist collectives such as Laboratorio Smaschieramenti (2008), mentioned above, Cagne sciolte (2013),[6] a transfemininst collective from Rome working mainly on violence against women and LGBTQ+ subjects, Consultoria Transfemminista Queer Bologna (2013),[7] working on notions of health, and especially SomMovimento NazioAnale (2012),[8] a national network of transfeminist movements (around which I gravitate), which include Laboratorio Smaschieramenti and many other collectives and individuals, have made clear that the exclusion of transgender subjects from feminism is now over, and seek ways to combat precarity through the creations of networks of mutual support.

Other reviews of L'alleanza dei corpi placed emphasis on the new idea of 'the people' that the book foregrounds; this idea consists of an alliance among different groups against a political system that ignores the needs of the population,[9] and which can oppose the fragmentation and inequalities produced by the neoliberal system. Some of these reviews (Barberis 2017) also emphasised the fact that the term 'queer' in Italy,[10] which is borrowed from English and is now used by various Italian queer collectives, refers not to an identity but to an alliance, as stated by Butler, and that the alliance is not only among different groups, but also among parts of ourselves; as Dominijanni (2017) observed, everybody, every identity, is an assembly of various elements.

Still other reviews (such as Terranova 2017) highlight, instead, the question of the occupation of public space as a form of resistance against neoliberalism, by way of making visible—through this embodied performance—the precarity of the people gathering in public assembly[11]; at the same time, they show that precarity and vulnerability can be transformed into activist tools (I corpi alleati 2017). Some of these reviews are also interested in the question of livability—that is, how to find ways to live a better life by connecting to others—or they focus on the dialogue between Butler's text and feminism. They show, for example, that feminism is the catalyst for a vast array of alliances (Guacci 2017) or that Butler's text resonates strongly with the Italian women's movement. Arts events and projects taking inspiration from the book have also been organised. These include 'L'alleanza dei corpi,'[12] an art installation that borrowed the title of the translation of Butler's book; it was hosted by the M-Gallery (a collaboration between Sardegna Teatro and EXMA Exhibiting and Moving Arts), in 2017, and contained performances, videos, talks, and a library space reflecting on how the creation of joint actions, and of alliances of bodies, can promote resistance against neoliberal capitalism.

The reviews of Zappino's translation, the presentations and the artistic projects and events based on it, all insisted on the importance and relevance of the concept of alliance. However, in some interviews (Zappino 2017b, 2017c; Baldo and Zappino 2018)[13] as well as during the presentations of the translation,[14] as one review indicates,[15] Zappino stated that Butler's text is prone to criticism because it does not give readers sufficient tools to conceptualise the feasibility of such an alliance. For Zappino, the problematic aspect of Butler's thesis is the fact that Butler—although laying the basis for a performative theory of democracy or, rather, a theory of the crisis of democracy—does not consider the price that an alliance among diverse groups might entail, and what conditions would support the building of such an alliance. This was also an issue raised by both the public and the discussants who attended presentations of Zappino's translation,[16] and who contended that Butler outlines a method without proposing solutions.

Zappino (2017b) states that an effective alliance among different groups affected by precarity is objectively difficult to achieve; for example, groups fighting against economic precarity caused by unemployment might not think that their battle shares a common ground with those fighting against the precarity caused by their racialisation, disability, or discrimination based on their sexuality and/or gender identities. Thus, despite the fact that often a wider alliance among different groups opposing precarity is possible, this might be halted because power differentials establish hierarchies among different types of oppression, for example in terms of which oppression is more worth fighting than others. For Zappino (Zappino 2017b; Baldo and Zappino 2018), these power differentials are represented by the concepts of masculinity, whiteness, class, and ableism, which should be the first targets of our contention. Zappino (2017b) thus defines Butler's book as a populist one since it aims at glorifying the concept of 'the people' in the name of a radical democracy based on radical equality. However, since this radical equality still does not exist, the term 'populist' in this sense acquires the meaning of demagogic: Butler focuses on the notion of creating popular consensus among different groups, rather than on the inequalities that challenge this unitary idea of people. Such an idea of consensus and democracy, Zappino continues, might be problematic if we do not oppose the hierarchies mentioned above, and, more specifically, if we do not engage in a fight against heteronormativity. Zappino (2017a) affirms that, before embarking on the task of recomposing differences and making alliances, we need to break the power differentials that compose such differences, and thus paradoxically to embark on a sort of queer separatism. He articulates this idea more in depth in his recent book, *Comunismo queer* (*Queer Communism*) (Zappino 2019). In the book he identifies heterosexuality, understood as the heteropatriarchal system in which we live, at the heart of the oppression of women, gay, lesbians, and trans and intersex people and sees this as a way of production of *our* (as LGBTQ+ people, including myself as a lesbian woman) inequalities. Heterosexuality as a 'mode of production,' for Zappino (2019: 50), precedes capitalism and thus alliances among LGBTQ+ groups and anticapitalist groups which do not aim at overturning heterosexuality risk maintaining the same oppression and precarity they claim to fight against.

Given these premises, it is clear that Zappino's translation has contributed to the circulation of discourses, which—while praising Butler's theories in general—are more concerned with the potentialities of establishing alliances based on the assembly of bodies in the public space than with the analysis of the assemblies of bodies themselves. These discourses thus move the focus slightly away from the utopian side of Butler's text and towards the more practical potentialities, but also to the potential problematic aspects of her theorisations. We can therefore say that the Italian translation of Butler's text moves the text forward as it is interested in exploring what could happen after bodies assemble, and how these assemblages might give rise to more established alliances. This view, which was especially voiced at the presentations of *L'alleanza dei corpi*, tells us also something about the importance of these presentations for the reception of LGBTQ+ work in Italy. In a country where LGBTQ+ studies are generally not taught at university, LGBTQ+ or other leftist activist spaces become the venues where, through such, usually numerous, presentations, queer theory is produced by activists, for activists, and for the wider public. Thus the presentations of the translations are important moments for activism.

As we have seen above, the discussion of Butler's *L'alleanza dei corpi* at a presentation in Bologna (and this is valid for other presentations in the same city or other cities) has tapped into the questions that have preoccupied the queer feminist collective Smaschieramenti for a while, that is, the notion of alliances, and how to make them. The presentations of translations are thus performative, as they are productive moments for activism, as the next sections will illustrate better. Moreover, like other activist gatherings, they are highly charged affective moments. In relation to this, if the presentations of the previous translation of Butler's *Undoing Gender* by Zappino (Butler 2014) had catalysed a widespread optimism, the presentation of *L'alleanza dei corpi* has instead reflected more the anxieties related to the feasibility of such an alliance, as anticipated above (Zappino 2019, personal communication, 14 August).

Activist translation and performativity

The presentations of Butler's translation touched on two important concepts: performativity and precarity. I believe that these concepts can be employed to discuss the meaning and importance of activist translation, and queer feminist translation specifically. If we look at the scenario presented above, in her *Notes Toward a Performative Theory of Assembly*, Butler links the notion of performativity with that of precarity. In her view (Butler 2009a), gender performativity refers to the fact that gender is a certain type of enactment, or action, as it is prompted by obligatory norms that dictate what gender should or should not be; it involves the reproduction through repetition of gender norms, a repetition that always risks undoing such norms in unexpected ways. Precarity, on the other hand, refers to the condition in which certain populations suffer because of the lack of social and economic support, and consequently 'become differentially exposed to injury, violence, and death' (Butler 2009a: ii). Precarity is linked to gender norms because those who do not abide by such norms are at risk of harassment and violence, and therefore in a precarious condition. Gender norms have to do with visibility, with recognition and thus with those who can be read, or understood, as a living being worth of living. Not abiding by gender norms, indeed, impacts on such recognition.

How can we, then, theorise activist translation with reference to Butler's notions of precarity and performativity? As I have argued elsewhere (Baldo 2017a; Baldo and Inghilleri 2018), translation in queer feminist spaces can be better understood when analysed through the lens of performativity.

The word 'performativity' has become increasingly visible in recent debates within the fields of theatre translation, and translation and performance studies, leading scholars to refer to a 'performative turn' in translation studies (Bigliazzi, Kofler and Ambrosi 2013). As a concept, performativity has been used by Keith Harvey in relation to gender performativity in a gay context (2000) and, more specifically, to camp talk, and its translation between English and French. However, performativity has a much broader spectrum that exceeds the field of theatre and performance studies. Douglas Robinson (2003), a translation scholar who has discussed the notion of performativity at length, considers translation to be performative, because it does something to its audience; it produces an effect on the receivers of the translation. His theory of translation performativity derives from Austin's (1962) speech act theory, which suggests that performative utterances, as opposed to constative ones, perform actions rather than simply conveying information. Speech act theory also informs Butler's theory of gender performativity, which Sandra Bermann draws on in her discussion of the potential links between Butler's theory and the notion of translation. By referring to Derrida's (1977, 1985) theory of iterability, according to which translation entails repetition leading to meaningful transformations, Bermann (2014) suggests that it is this citational aspect of translation—similarly to the citational aspect of gender—that allows translations to produce change by exaggerating, displacing, and queering normative expectations across gender, culture, and language.

Hence, we can affirm that translation is performative because it involves a series of transformative acts. Michaela Wolf (2017), drawing on anthropologist Victor Turner, links the performative turn to the social turn in translation studies, and stresses the fact that the political and social dimension of translation becomes apparent through performative practices. By drawing on the meanings of the verb 'perform' (which stands for 'to do,' 'to finish,' 'to build,' 'to make'), she conceives of performativity as a process. Translation, for Wolf (2017), is performative because it constitutes meaning by exploring differences during the process itself, thus following in the footsteps of Turner's conceptualisation of the processual and conflictual way in which culture is produced. The progression of performative actions is therefore subject to institutional and social conditions, and is a process characterised by a transformative force. This performativity of translation is also explored by Butler (2009a: x) herself, who affirms that the practice of translation is 'a way of producing—performatively—another kind of we,' so as 'to negotiate the right to speak,' to expose and resist the violence of power, and 'to find the language to which to lay claim to rights to which one is not yet entitled.'

To summarise, performativity has to do with the productivity of translation. This productivity means that translation can produce political transformation. If we refer to the activist translation scenario illustrated in the previous section, we could say that the Italian translation of Butler's *Notes Toward a Performative Theory of Assembly* is performative because it plays a role within Italian queer feminist activism, by contributing to the elaboration and creation of new discourses about what it means to protest and to create alliances. As argued by Tymoczko (2010: 231), mobilised translators, using a series of textual and paratextual strategies, 'often become founders of discursivity,' that is, they are not merely importing new discourses in a target culture but initiating new discourses. Translation involves the transformation of the source text, which often takes unexpected paths and, consequently, becomes a very different cultural product in the target culture. Beyond that, it has to do with the transformation of the target activist community as well. The presentations of Butler's translated books in transfeminist spaces—as in the case of other translations by Butler, and translations of other queer feminist theorists or activists (Baldo 2017a; Baldo and Inghilleri 2018)—play an important role within the activist landscape, since translations are presented, read, discussed, and contested in groups; they thus become a source of inspiration for art work, as I explained in the previous section of this chapter, when I mentioned the art installation based on *L'alleanza dei corpi* and hosted by the M-gallery, and for activism, for example through the use of slogans at demonstrations or as conceptual inspiration. The term *alleanza dei corpi*, or simply *alleanza*, for instance, was used to define a series of initiatives by SomMovimento NazioAnale and Smaschieramenti in the years 2017 and 2018, which will be discussed more in depth further in this chapter. The term stressed the importance of forming alliances among transfeminist and other groups. A previous translation by Zappino, of Butler's *Undoing Gender* (Butler 2014), has become a source of inspiration for an edited book on the notion of gender and neoliberalism, which Zappino edited and published in 2016 (Zappino 2016), and which includes essays by many of the activists who took part in the book presentation. And again *L'alleanza dei corpi*, according to Zappino (2019, personal communication, 14 August), became a source of inspiration for his book *Comunismo Queer* (Zappino 2019). Moreover, these translation presentations bring together people who are interested in the same themes and gravitate around the same activist spaces, contributing to initiate at times new book projects. This is discussed in this volume, for example, by Düzkan, who puts emphasis on the powerful aspect of working together on translation projects within feminist collectives. Performativity therefore has to do with this traffic of bodies, discourses, and translations. Since performativity, as affirmed by Butler (2015), refers to the concept of 'expressivity,' we can think of these bodies gathered together as a way in which translation speaks not only through words, but also through non-verbal means. Since, as Butler affirms, the gathering of bodies in public places is performative because it makes visible the precarity of those bodies, the gathering of people produced through, and in the aftermath of, the presentation of these translations likewise makes visible the precarity of translation.

Queer feminist activist translation is a precarious and vulnerable activity and for various reasons: it is most often performed voluntarily, and thus it is unpaid work; it is published at times by small publishing houses[17] or often just online in activist blogs and websites, as it is considered too niche or too radical; finally it is often not granted the same recognition that other translations enjoy, especially because it is mostly collective work, and therefore does not bear the signature of an author. Although this is not the case for the translation of Butler's work analysed here, where the author is named, and for other translations of her work, because of the cultural capital Butler enjoys, it is certainly the case for many other translations. The reason behind all this is that translation, in most contexts, is a 'taken for granted' and 'un-problematised activity,' considered as a 'feminine' activity and given less importance than authorship (Chamberlain 1988). This is even more the case for queer feminist translation; thinking of queer feminist activist translation in performative terms, in the footsteps of Butler, may then help recognise and value its existence, consider it as an event worth of attention and discussion, and reveal the potential of this activity to queer assumptions and transform (hetero)normative, consolidated perceptions.

Similarly to the bodies gathered in public demonstrations, which become a tool to demand rights in order to fight precarity, shedding a light on activist translation, on the gathering of bodies at the presentations and discussions of translated books, may hold the potential to subvert the status quo, the precarity experienced by translation in general and activist translation more specifically. How? Activist translation performed in transfeminist spaces is most often guided by the urgency to speak, to make visible the precarity caused by not abiding by gender and sexuality heteronorms. This urgency of gathering together offers the possibility to create and/or consolidate networks of affective support that, through translation, participate in the making of a different space, one which has the potential to counteract that same precarity that brought the bodies together in the first instance. In this sense, activist translation is performative and transformative. Moreover, it can be considered performative as the translation and discussion of *L'alleanza dei corpi* have certainly boosted the interest in the concept of alliance and have possibly stressed even more among transfeminist circles the importance of forming new networks and alliances among groups whose precarity stems from the same heteropatriarchal roots, as the next section discusses in greater depth.

Activist translation, solidarity, and alliances

Along with the concept of performativity, the translation of Butler's work into Italian under the title *L'alleanza dei corpi*, as stated earlier on, puts emphasis on the concept of alliance. In this last section I discuss activist translation through the lens of this concept, and theorise activist translation—and queer feminist translation more specifically—as a kind of alliance. The concept of alliance can be discussed in conjunction with another concept, to which it is often linked in studies on activist translation: solidarity. A good starting point is the work of translation scholar Mona Baker, who, in her latest edited volume (2016a), analysed translation within the political economy of protest movements, using the Egyptian revolution as a case study. Baker focuses on themes (such as protests and demonstrations) and scenarios (including Tahrir Square in Egypt) similar to those analysed by Butler (2015). According to Baker (2016b: 1), translation must be conceptualised as 'an integral element of the revolutionary project' and as a force participating in the creation and consolidation of networks of solidarity. Translation is what enables protest movements to connect and share experiences across the globe, thus allowing the activists to position themselves within a broader struggle. The values that inform contemporary movements, as Baker (2016b) states with reference to some of the authors of her edited collection as well as other scholars, such as Maeckelbergh (2011), differ from those that oriented traditional politics. These include a commitment to 'horizontal, non-hierarchical forms of interaction,' the 'rejection of representational practices,' 'an embrace of diversity and pluralism' (Baker 2016b: 10), and the promotion of solidarity between activists all over the world, as well as between activists who do not translate and activists who do.

Baker's idea of activist translation therefore emphasises the notion of solidarity. She uses the concept not only in this latest publication (2016a), but also in previous work (Baker 2013), when commenting on various activist networks of translators such as *Babel*, *Ecos*, and *Tlaxcala*, and the importance placed by these on issues such as altruistic action and collective authorship. Baker's work inserts itself within the so-called 'sociological turn' in translation studies (Angelelli 2014), and more specifically within the 'activist turn,' to borrow a term introduced by Michaela Wolf (2012). Angelelli (2014: 1) defines the 'sociological turn' as the increasing interest paid by the discipline 'to the agency of translators and interpreters, as well as social factors permeating the communicative and social act of translation and interpreting.' The 'activist turn,' by contrast, is explained by Wolf (2012) as the increased focus, in recent studies of translation, on the political factors that have contributed to mold the 'habitus' (a term taken from Bourdieu) of translators in contexts of activism. Talking about the activist agenda of translation means for Wolf (2012: 140) emphasising 'specific situations where the translator's intervention is shaped by a specific pattern of beliefs or convictions which follow a certain specific program mostly connected with solidarity and social claim.' The concept of solidarity is also used by scholar Tymoczko (2007), in relation to her discussion of the concept of engagement. The term 'engagement' comes from the old French and refers to concepts such as commitment, involvement, participation, the assumption of obligations, entering into conflict, and so on. Tymoczko (2007, 2010) favours the term 'engagement' to that of 'resistance,' which—along with 'engagement'—has been widely used in the conceptualisation of activism, and which was popularised by translation scholar Lawrence Venuti (1995, 1998, 2010). According to Tymoczko (2007, 2010), Venuti borrowed the term from the activist movements opposing occupying forces and fascist governments during World War II, and used it in his theorisation of the concepts of foreignisation; he stated that foreignisation is the disruption of the linguistic expectations of the target language, including the expectation of fluency, which mark translation as foreign. Foreignisation is thus a translation strategy that aims at resisting the aggression and violence of monolingual Anglo-American culture, with its ethnocentric tendency to reduce and domesticate the foreign text to Anglo-American, imperialist target language values.

Tymoczko criticises the concept of *resistance* as theorised by Venuti. She argues that it implies that an antagonist and opponent are known and well defined, whereas various descriptive studies of translation seem to show, instead, that there is no agreement among translation scholars on what should be resisted in translation. In addition, resistance, in Venuti's terms, refers to the opposition against the 'cultural enclosure and cultural dominance of readers in the United States' (Tymoczko 2007: 211), and might not be an argument suited for subaltern cultures already flooded with foreign linguistic impositions. Moreover, since resistance implies being reactive rather than proactive, as it refers to an act of opposition to a force or power, it 'is restrictive with respect to initiative, limiting the translations to a more passive role' (2007: 210). The notion of 'engagement' does not exclude that activist translation might be engaged in resistance against a specific power but allows the term to include much more, especially because it is not possible to oppose everything about a specific source culture and translators have to negotiate their way around by making choices on what to prioritise (Tymoczko 2010). The term 'engagement,' instead, suggests that activist translations have a proactive dimension, because they initiate ethical, political, and ideological actions based on a commitment to specific principles as well as actions involving solidarity. Indeed, engagement means 'acting together with,' and engaged translators usually join with others in collective action (Tymoczko 2007), thus forming alliances. In addition to including the concept of solidarity and alliance, the term 'engagement' also brings forward the performative aspect of activist translation and, more specifically, the illocutionary and perlocutionary aspect of translation. Activist translation is 'translation that rouses, inspires, witnesses, mobilizes, incites to rebellion,' and that aims at participating in social movements and at 'achieving demonstrable social and political change' (Tymoczko 2000: 26).

Similarly to Tymoczko (2007, 2010), Baker (2007) criticises Venuti's notion of resistance, arguing that the dichotomy between foreignising and domesticating is not suitable for an explanation of the wide variety of choices and negotiations that activist translators make, in relation to the texts and authors they translate, and the communities in which they act. Commenting on the paper of an author included in her edited volume on the Egyptian revolution, Baker (2016b: 4–5) stresses that the aim of the struggle against neoliberal policies is not only 'to counter hegemonic narratives promoted by powerful institutions, but also to allow activists to build networks of solidarity across linguistic and national boundaries.' Solidarity, in its links to the notion of engagement and alliance, is thus an important concept for both Tymoczko (2007) and Baker (2016b), whereas it does not belong to Venuti's theorisations (1995, 1998).

The 'Solidarity as translation' project of the University of Vienna[18] takes into account three forms of solidarity, namely national, Christian, and socialist. Solidarity for the purposes of this chapter has to be understood as a socialist solidarity. It is a solidarity derived from the social class struggle and understood as a common fight against capitalism. This socialist solidarity differs from solidarity understood in a Catholic sense, which refers instead to the idea of assistance for those in need (although certain characteristics, such as mutual obligation and love, might be present in the activist solidarity I am discussing here).

Although Tymoczko and Baker give emphasis to the notion of solidarity, and hardly mention the term alliance, preferring to that the term 'network of solidarity' for example (Baker 2016), alliance appears quite often instead, in relation to the concept of solidarity, in the work of feminist translation scholars. Both alliance and solidarity are mentioned extensively in Castro and Ergun's (2017b) edited book on transnational feminism and translation, another highly relevant work for the present discussion, which deals with translation in queer transfeminist contexts in Italy. In the introduction to their edited collection, Castro and Ergun (2017a: 1) foreground the important role that translation plays 'in the making of feminism transnational'; they envision transnational feminism as a polyphonic space and as 'a model for cross-border dialogue, resistance, solidarity and activism.' Translation thus enters the project of creating transnational solidarity and alliances, although translation, the authors specify, can also disable 'crosscultural encounters, dialogues and alliances among feminists' (Castro and Ergun 2017a: 8), as also confirmed by some of the papers featuring in their edited collection.

In the same edited collection, the contribution by Santaemilia (2017) focuses on the idea of building interdisciplinary alliances among feminist translation scholars, while that of Tissot (2017) refers to the idea of translation as an activity involved in the reconceptualisation of a universality that should not reproduce its ethnocentrism, and should instead pay attention to otherness. Tissot (2017) understands transnational solidarity as a call for imagining and building new alliances not rooted in the colonial claim of an essentialist 'woman' identity, or in a global sisterhood grounded in the illusion that women are the victims of the same patriarchal oppression around the world; rather, this solidarity should be based on the recognition of hierarchies and differences among women. These transnational solidarities should therefore incorporate a multiplicity of perspectives, voices, and narratives. Reimóndez (2017), another author included in the volume, on the other hand, stresses that the possibility of building transnational solidarity and alliances among feminists rests on the awareness, by feminist translators, that transnational feminist conversations are often held in hegemonic languages such as English (see Düzkan, in this volume), with the consequence that conversations in other languages are not granted such visibility or access. Similarly, Pas and Zaborowska (2017) discuss the difficulties of applying feminist concepts that are taken for granted in English to other non-hegemonic languages. In sum, for most of the feminist translation scholars contained in this book it is impossible to imagine the formation of alliances, understood as short- or long-term relationships, without an ongoing praxis of translation, and they seem to invoke solidarity as a premise for, or a characteristic of, such alliances.

Given these premises, solidarity and alliances—two terms used in translation studies scholarship, with reference to activist translation and feminist translation—need to be problematised, as the specific case of the translation into Italian of Butler's work on performativity and precarity teaches us. If the act of translating might be considered an activist act, aimed at forming international alliances among activist groups and collectives that share the same political agenda, such an act cannot be considered smooth as it is often imbued with issues of power imbalance between languages and cultures; these may at times silence the privileges and the hierarchies existing between such languages and cultures, as studies of postcolonial translation, feminist translation, translation in the context of migration, and activist translation have shown over the course of the past three decades.

If we transpose this discourse to the specific case study analysed here, in the context of the reception of *L'alleanza dei corpi*, we can see that alliances are not only a dominant theme of discussion in transfeminist groups in Italy, but also a common activist praxis. The network of transfeminist queer groups called SomMovimento NazioAnale, mentioned in a previous section of this chapter in connection with the presentation of *L'allenza dei corpi*, and around which Federico Zappino gravitates (although he is not an active member of it) has put forward the urgency of constructing alliances with groups of African and other migrants based in Italy, such as the group Coordinamento Migranti Bologna,[19] which includes migrants mainly coming from African countries. Indeed, SomMovimento NazioAnale supported the demonstration organised by migrants in Macerata and Florence, in the spring of 2018, and in Modena in July 2018,[20] against racism and fascism in Italian politics.[21] On 14 July 2018, they also organised the international day of solidarity in the city of Ventimiglia (situated at the border between Italy and France), which supported the cause to grant migrants a European residency permit. Moreover, SomMovimento NazioAnale has created alliances with the sex workers movement called Ombre Rosse,[22] in preparation for the national demonstration to denounce violence against women, held on 25 November 2017 in Rome, and also in preparation for the National Women's Strike of 8 March 2018. It thus supported Ombre Rosse in its fight for the decriminalisation of sex work, and for the recognition of sex work as work.

The word used by SomMovimento NazioAnale to define these invoked alliances with other collectives and groups was 'solidarity.' This choice of wording was based on the premises that a transfeminist politics is intersectional and focused on the struggle against precarity, sexism, racism, and fascism. The latter all have the same heteropatriarchal roots, based on the belief of the supremacy of the white, heterosexual, and cisgender male over all other non-male (i.e. female, transgender, or gender queer), non-heterosexual, and non-white and/or migrant subjectivities.

These alliances, invoked on the basis of a shared heteropatriarchal oppression, which is also linked to the notion of precarity as discussed by Butler, are encouraged not only by SomMovimento NazioAnale, but also by the now well-known feminist movement against male violence, Non Una di Meno,[23] which has taken inspiration from the Argentinian movement Ni Una Menos. Non Una di Meno was created in Italy in 2017, and is currently one of the largest feminist movements in Italy. Since its inception, it has organised various protests and gender strikes (for example on 8 March), it has written a national plan against violence on women, and it has formed links with the global movement as it developed in various other countries (Spain, other Latin America countries, Germany, Turkey, the UK). At present, Non Una di Meno is working to address the demands raised by women, migrants, and precarious workers against current Italian reactionary politics, which are patriarchal, neoliberalist, and racist.

Alliances, according to the above-mentioned Italian collective Connessioni precarie,[24] intensify and multiply struggles; they make movements stronger and better equipped to face the dominance of far-right nationalist groups in Italy and elsewhere, as heteropatriarchal oppression can no longer be addressed solely on a national scale, given the globalised world we live in and the globalised nature of exploitation and violence against women. If we link this to what we previously stated in relation to activist/feminist translation, translation can become a form of solidarity that might circumvent censorship in a specific national state, help increase the pressure on violent regimes, and confer longevity to the struggles (Baker 2016c), as it contributes to the building of international activist networks fighting the same struggle.

However, while this is certainly a positive goal, solidarity, as the criticism related to the translation of Butler's work (2015, 2017) has demonstrated, should be problematised if we want to give a more precise account of the complexities and hierarchies existing within activist groups themselves. In fact, these groups are not immune to the persistence of some of the forms of oppression that they are invested in fighting against, a fact the above-mentioned feminist movements are very much aware of. Zappino (2017b, 2018, 2019), the translator of *L'alleanza dei corpi*, for example, warns us about the fact that the oppression of LGBTQ+ minorities—even when perceived as sharing certain characteristics with other groups that fight against economic precarity, for instance—might still constitute a condition for the privilege of these other groups. Consequently, not recognising this and the hierarchies existing between groups might hinder the formation of effective alliances. Examples are represented by two, relatively recent, episodes amply discussed among queer feminist groups (see also Zappino and Ardilli 2017) and known as 'the rape of Parma' and the 'incidents at the Bari Pride.'[25] The former refers to the rape, in 2010, of a female activist by fellow male activists as part of the antifascist centre in Parma called RAF, and the efforts at covering up this case by the rapists and their activist friends by slut shaming the victim. The case shows the contradictions lying in a self-definition of antifascism that does not take into account sexism. The second case refers to an episode that happened during the LGBTQ+ pride in Bari in 2017. During the parade and during a party organised after it, a group of male antifascists, who had collaborated as allies in the organisation of the Pride, exercised homotransphobic and sexist violence by shoving, and verbally insulting and threatening women and LGBTQ+ subjectivities. These two episodes show how sexism and homotranshobia might be often still present within activist groups that are LGBTQ+ allies, and define themselves as anticapitalist, antifascist, and antisexist.

Moreover, the presence of sexism in activist movements, including LGBTQ+ groups, is a topic which has been amply discussed by the aforementioned feminist movement *Non Una di Meno*, which organised two workshops on the theme.[26] Moreover, Zappino, at one presentation of his translation of *L'alleanza dei corpi*,[27] and in his *Comunismo Queer* (Zappino 2019), stated that since LGBTQ+ minorities are often not united among themselves, they should invest energies in becoming better allies of each other. He also states that a populist invocation of an alliance with other movements, in order to seek consensus, might risk replicating the normalisation of these power relationships based on gender, race, class, and so on; this is often an operation favoured by capitalism (Zappino 2017b, 2019). However, Zappino (2019) continues, these power relations exploited by capitalism for its advantage are not caused by capitalism itself but by the heteropatriarchal regime preexisting it, as mentioned above. Thus, an alliance that overlooks this, and fights only to overturn capitalism and precarity, might be very ineffective.

Similarly to what was discussed above, Mortada (2016: 130) comments on the fact that the revolution of Tahrir Square brought to the fore the sexism existing within activist groups fighting against the regime of Mubarak, arguing that not only mainstream discourses but also some activist discourses 'tend to impose a passive role on Arab and Muslim women, projecting them either as victims or submissive subjects.'

With this knowledge in mind, and with the awareness that conflicts continuously cross feminist movements themselves, we could say that creating effective networks of solidarity through translation is a complex matter; in addition to the fact that translation further exploits and misinterprets discourses in the passage from one language and culture to another, it risks obscuring the power hierarchies present within movements. This misinterpretation is, for example, at the centre of Scholz's (2014) critique of transnational feminist solidarity, again with reference to the protests of Tahrir Square. She says that transnational feminist solidarity must find strategic and responsible ways to obtain more complete information about specific foreign feminist movements, in order to avoid focusing only on a few selected aspects of these, thus missing a chance to form a more accurate and nuanced vision of the facts.

As Selim (2016: 85) argues, in order to avoid 'misconstruction and misunderstanding of complex histories and political economies of domination and struggle,' we should aim for what she calls 'deep translation,' which she opposes to 'crisis translation.' Whereas 'crisis translation'—a translation done in emergency mode, for example in situations of protest—might translate into a sort of touristic and superficial voyeurism, which forecloses the possibility for real solidarity, 'deep translation moves beyond image and spectacle' (Selim 2016: 84) in order to build more sustained, international solidarity networks. Using the terminology employed in relation to the Italian translation of Butler, we could compare 'crisis translation' to the assembly of bodies, and 'deep translation' to the notion of alliances. In order to build more sustainable alliances we need to engage in deep translation, which presupposes that we are situated in a specific location, committed to the place of struggle and that we engage in a long series of actions and negotiations that take time and effort.

In conclusion, if the discussion of the assembly of bodies by Butler points toward the urgency, the enthusiasm, and the thrilling energy that protest movements performatively generate, translating the 'assembly' into a wider and effective alliance is a far more complex operation: one that requires a more sustained effort and a constant awareness of the hierarchies of power in place.

Conclusion

In this chapter I have analysed the notions of performativity, solidarity, and alliances, taking inspiration from the translation into Italian of Butler's *Notes Toward a Performative Theory of Assembly* (2015). Using the notions of performativity in connection to that of precarity, as theorised in Butler's book, and drawing from the reception of the book's translation within queer transfeminist groups in Italy, I have examined the implication and fruitfulness for activist translation of Butler's concepts. I have linked the concept of performativity to activist translation, and for two reasons. Firstly, because translation participates in the act of producing and making new discourses visible; secondly, because it creates new activist networks and alliances among activists. I have also discussed the act of forming new alliances in relation to the notion of solidarity. Solidarity is a recurrent term in studies on activist translation, and this chapter has attempted to problematise this concept in view of the criticism raised by the translation of Butler's book into Italian. If solidarity is certainly a productive term for studies on translation and activism, we also need to take into account the ways in which activist translation—understood as an act of solidarity—can obscure the complexities and power hierarchies existing in certain activist contexts, and between different translational contexts.

Related topics

Written on the Heart, in Broken English; Feminism in Translation; Resistant Recipes.

Notes

1 Transfeminist groups are feminist groups whose feminism is informed by transgender politics and queer theory and politics. Further explanation of the term is given in the next section of this chapter.

2 Nottetempo self-defines as an independent publisher, and is especially interested in making accessible to the wider public works of philosophy and politics, and in publishing new emerging Italian narrative authors.

3 Mediateca Gatway is a media library in Bologna which contains an archive of social activist movements since the 1960s, and that often hosts presentations of books related to LGBTQ+ activism. The video of the presentation of *l'alleanza dei corpi* on 24 April 2017 is available at: www.facebook.com/mediateca.gateway/videos/809971542512787/

4 Smaschieramenti is a queer feminist collective from Bologna created in 2008 initially as a space of reflection on masculinity. In recent years Smaschieramenti has concentrated its work on questions of gender and sexuality in their intersection with the concept of precarity. Connessioni Precarie is a collective formed of Italians and migrants that centres its activism on the notion of economic precarity as a global characteristic of contemporary work. See https://smaschieramenti.noblogs.org and www.connessioniprecarie.org [accessed 20 March 2010].

5 Pinkwashing refers to a variety of marketing and political strategies aimed at promoting products, countries, people, and so on through an appeal to gay-friendliness, in order to be perceived as progressive, modern, and tolerant.

6 Cagne sciolte is a transfeminist group from Rome. It was formed in 2013 and has worked mainly on fighting against slut-shaming and violence against women and LGBTQ+ subjects. See https://cagnesciolte.noblogs.org [accessed 20 March 2010].

7 See https://consultoriaqueerbologna.noblogs.org [accessed 20 March 2010].

8 SomMovimento NazioAnale was formed in 2012 with the idea of uniting various transfemininst groups and individuals in Italy in order to strengthen the struggle against heteropatriarchy and neoliberalism at national but also transnational level. See https://sommovimentonazioanale.noblogs.org [accessed 20 March 2010].

9 www.reset.it/libri/alleanza-dei-corpi-butler [accessed 8 October 2019]; see also https://queerographies.com/2017/02/13/lalleanza-dei-corpi/ [accessed 8 October 2019] and *Cultweek*.

10 On the various uses of the meaning of queer in Italian, see Baldo (2017b). Queer in Italy can be used as an umbrella term to refer to LGBT people, or in a de-politicised way as a fashionable foreign term used in commercial contexts, or as a highly political term when used by some queer feminist groups, which claims the derogatory aspect of the term used by US and UK activists.

11 In the website of *Cooltura* the phrase used is 'manifestare per manifestarsi,' a word play that means 'to demonstrate to make oneself visible.' www.lacooltura.com/2017/05/judith-butler-corpo-focolaio-resistenza/ [accessed 21 March 2019].

12 See www.sardegnateatro.it/content/lalleanza-dei-corpi [accessed 22 March 2019].

13 Along with the interview released for RSI (Swiss radio television) in February 2017 (Zappino 2017c) and the Skype interview with the author of this chapter (Baldo and Zappino 2018), Zappino was interviewed by the magazine *Che fare* in May 2017 (Zappino 2017b).

14 See the presentation of the translation by Nottetempo edizioni in January 2017 in Milan, and at the LGBT space Cassero in Bologna on 21 April 2017.

15 See the review of Zappino's translation within the magazine *I diavoli*. www.idiavoli.com/recensioni/corpi-alleati-judith-butler-politica/ [accessed 22 March 2019].

16 This question was raised by lecturer Marzia Vaccari at the presentation of the translation at LGBT centre Cassero on 21 April 2017, by Cristina Morini at the presentation of Zappino's translation in Milan in January 2017, and by Angela Balzano and Paola Rudan at the presentation of Zappino's translation on 24 April 2017 at Mediateca Gateway in Bologna.

17 Although the publisher of *L'Alleanza dei Corpi*, Nottetempo, is a prestigious (and not small) publisher, LGBTQ+ works in Italy are also published by small publishing houses interested in LGBTQ+ themes. The situation is indeed very complex as publishers like Meltemi, which is a well known publisher, have published the translation of most of the work by Butler and other postcolonial, feminist and radical thinkers (Spivak, Hall, Gilroy), while other radical feminist work in Italian translation has been published by small publishers such as Golena (for what concerns Spanish transfeminism, see Baldo and Inghilleri 2018), or Ombre Corte for what concerns Monique Wittig for example (see Wittig 2019).

18 See www.oeaw.ac.at/en/ikt/research/translation/solidarity-as-translation/ [accessed 17 March 2019]

19 See https://it-it.facebook.com/coordinamentomigranti.bologna.7 [accessed 12 August 2019].

20 See www.radiondadurto.org/2018/07/04/modena-sabato-7-luglio-manifestazione-delle-e-dei-migranti-per-una-liberta-senza-paure/ [accessed 8 October 2019].

21 For an account of the intersection between racism, fascism and sexism in the current Italian politics, dominated by a coalition of right and conservative parties, see Giuliani (2018).
22 Ombre Rosse is a collective of sex workers born in Rome in 1992. See www.facebook.com/collettivoOmbreRosse/ [accessed 14 August 2019].
23 See the website of the movement at https://nonunadimeno.wordpress.com [accessed 20 March 2019].
24 See www.connessioniprecarie.org/2019/03/18/the-connecting-breach-the-transnational-power-of-the-feminist-strike/ [accessed 20 March 2019].
25 In relation to the rape of Parma see also www.ilfattoquotidiano.it/2016/12/17/stupro-in-centro-antifascista-di-parma-il-sessismo-resiste-anche-tra-i-movimenti-di-sinistra/3266048/. In relation to the incidents of at the Bari Pride see www.facebook.com/notes/transfemministe-queer-bari/scritti-cozzali-di-frocie-indecorose/1376453625805978/ [accessed 15 Augusts 2019].
26 See the report of these workshop at the following page https://nonunadimeno.wordpress.com/2017/02/08/tavolo-sessismo-nei-movimenti/ [accessed 8 October 2019].
27 See the podcast of the presentation by Federico Zappino of *L'alleanza dei corpi* at Cassero on 21 April 2017. www.cassero.it/alleanza-dei-corpi-judith-butler-podcast/ [accessed 20 March 2019].

Further reading

Baker, Mona (ed.) (2016) *Translating Dissent: Voices from and with the Egyptian Revolution.* New York and London: Routledge.

This edited collection focuses on the topic of activist translation in situations of protests, specifically with reference to the Egyptian revolution, which is also one of the scenarios mentioned in Butler's *Notes Toward a Performative Theory of Assembly.*

Baer, Brian, and Klaus Kaindl (eds.) (2017) *Queering Translation, Translating the Queer. Theory, Practice, Activism.* New York and London: Routledge.

This edited book includes several chapters (Addison-Smith 2017; Baldo 2017a; Démont 2017; Nossem 2017), on the meaning of queer translation and on the notion of translation and activism in queer scenarios which provide a deeper understanding of the notion of queer translation discussed in this handbook chapter.

Wolf, Michaela (2012) 'The Sociology of Translation and Its 'Activist Turn',' *Translation and Interpreting Studies* 7 (2): 129–143.

This article specifically focuses on the activist turn in translation studies and thus covers some of the basic concepts underpinning this chapter.

Robinson, Douglas (2003) *Performative Linguistics: Speaking and Translating as Doing Things with Words.* London and New York: Routledge.

The book draws on the notion of performative linguistics by Austin, Searle, Derrida, and others and argues that translation is strictly linked to that notion, as it is an effective tool for reproducing words as doing something to their audience.

Butler, Judith (2009) 'Performativity, Precarity and Sexual Politics,' *AIBR. Revista de Antropología Iberoamericana* 4 (3): i–xiii.

This article by Butler well summarises the interconnections between the notion of gender performativity and precarity in relation to LGBTQ minorities.

References

Addison-Smith, Mark (2017) 'Years Yet Yesterday: Translating Art, Activism, and AIDS across the Visual and the Verbal,' in *Queering Translation, Translating the Queer.* Eds. Brian Baer and Klaus Kaindl. New York: Routledge. 206–224.

Angelelli, Claudia (ed.) (2014) *The Sociological Turn in Translation and Interpreting Studies*. Amsterdam and Philadelphia, PA: John Benjamins.

Austin, John (1962) *How to Do Things with Words*. Oxford: Clarendon Press.

Baker, Mona (2007) 'Reframing Conflict in Translation,' *Social Semiotics* 17(2):151–169.

Baker, Mona (2013) 'Translation as an Alternative Space for Political Action,' *Social Movement Studies* 12 (1): 23–47.

Baker, Mona (ed.) (2016a) *Translating Dissent: Voices from and with the Egyptian Revolution*. New York and London: Routledge.

Baker, Mona (2016b) 'Beyond the Spectacle. Translation and Solidarity in Contemporary Protest Movements,' in *Translating Dissent: Voices from and with the Egyptian Revolution*. Ed. Mona Baker. New York and London: Routledge. 1–18.

Baker, Mona (2016c) 'Interview with Philiph Rizk,' in *Translating Dissent: Voices from and with the Egyptian Revolution*. Ed. Mona Baker. New York and London: Routledge. 225–238.

Baldo, Michela (2017a) 'Queer Translation as Performative and Affective Undoing. Translating Butler's Undoing Gender into Italian,' in *Queering Translation, Translating the Queer*. Eds. Brian Baer and Klaus Kaindl. New York: Routledge. 188–205.

Baldo, Michela (2017b) 'Frocie, femminelle, terrone, polentone e favolosità varie. Quando il queer è di casa,' in *Queer Italia Network* [online] 13 May. Available at: https://queeritalia.com/2017/05/13/frocie-femminelle/ [accessed 14 August 2019].

Baldo, Michela, and Moira Inghilleri (2018) 'Cultural Resistance, Female Voices. Translating Subversive and Contested Sexualities,' in *The Routledge Handbook of Translation and Culture*. Eds. Sue-Ann Harding and Ovidi Carbonell Cortés. New York: Routledge. 296–313.

Barberis, Sarah (2017) 'Judith Butler e il corpo delle minoranze,' review of *L'alleanza dei corpi*, in *Cultweek* [online] 6 March. Available at: www.cultweek.com/judith-butler/ [accessed 21 March 2019].

Berbec, Stephanie (2017) 'An interview with Judith Butler,' in *Verso Books* [online] 30 June. Avaliable at: www.versobooks.com/blogs/3304-an-interview-with-judith-butler [accessed 6 March 2019].

Bermann, Sandra (2014) 'Performing Translation,' in *A Companion to Translation Studies*. Eds. Sandra Bermann and Catherine Porter. Hoboken, NJ: Wiley-Blackwell. 285–297.

Bigliazzi, Silvia, Peter Kofler, and Paola Ambrosi (2013) 'Introduction,' in *Theatre Translation in Performance*. Eds. Silvia Bigliazzi, Peter Kofler, and Paola Ambrosi. London and New York: Routledge. 1–26.

Butler, Judith (1997) *The Psychic Life of Power: Theories in Subjection*. Stanford, CA: Stanford University Press.

Butler, Judith (2004) *Undoing Gender*. New York and London: Routledge.

Butler, Judith (2006) *La Disfatta del genere*. Trans. Olivia Guaraldo. Roma: Meltemi.

Butler, Judith (2009a) 'Performativity, Precarity and Sexual politics,' *AIBR. Revista de Antropología Iberoamericana* 4(3): i–xiii.

Butler, Judith (2009b) *Frames of War: When is Life Grievable?* New York: Verso.

Butler, Judith (2011) 'Bodies in Alliance and the Politics of the Street,' lecture held by Judith Butler in Venice in September 2011 [online]. Availabale at: http://eipcp.net/transversal/1011/butler/en [accessed 14 January 2019].

Butler, Judith (2013) *La vita psichica del potere: Teorie del soggetto*. Trans. Federico Zappino. Torino: Mimesis.

Butler, Judith (2014) *Fare e disfare il genere*. Trans. Federico Zappino. Milano: Mimesis.

Butler, Judith (2015) *Notes Toward a Performative Theory of Assembly*. Cambridge, London: Harvard University Press.

Butler, Judith (2017) *L'alleanza dei corpi*. Trans. Federico Zappino. Milano: Nottetempo.

Castro, Olga, and Emek Ergun (2017a) 'Introduction: Re-Envisioning Feminist Translation Studies: Feminisms in Translation, Translations in Feminism,' in *Feminist Translation Studies. Local and Transnational Perspectives*. Eds. Olga Castro and Emek Ergun. New York and London: Routledge. 1–12.

Castro, Olga, and Emek Ergun (eds.) (2017b) *Feminist Translation Studies. Local and Transnational Perspectives*. New York and London: Routledge.

Chamberlain, Lori (1988) 'Gender and the Metaphorics of Translation,' *Signs* 13(3): 454–472.

Démont, Marc (2017) 'On Three Modes of Translating Queer Literary Texts,' in *Queering Translation, Translating the Queer*. Eds. Brian Baer and Klaus Kaindl. New York: Routledge. 157–171.

Derrida, Jacques (1977) *Limited Inc.* Evanston, IL: Northwestern University Press.

Derrida, Jacques (1985) 'Des Tours de Babel,' in *Difference in Translation*. Ed. Joseph Graham. New York: Cornell University Press. 165–207.

Dominijanni, Ida (2017) 'La Scommessa del Popolo,' review of *L'alleanza dei corpi*, in *Alfabeta2* [online] 8 April. Available at: www.alfabeta2.it/2017/04/08/speciale-judith-butler-lalleanza-dei-corpi/ [accessed 22 March 2019].

Düzkan, Ayşe (2020) 'Written on the Heart, in Broken English,' in *The Routledge Handbook of Translation and Activism*. Eds. Rebecca Ruth Gould and Kayvan Tahmasebian. New York and London: Routledge. 217–221.

Giuliani, Gaia (2018) *Race, Nation and Gender in Modern Italy: Intersectional Representations in Visual Culture*. London: Palgrave MacMillan.

Guacci, Rosaria (2017) 'L'alleanza dei corpi,' review of *L'alleanza dei corpi*, in Website of the Libreria delle Donne di Milano [online]. Avalaible at: www.libreriadelledonne.it/puntodivista/lalleanza-dei-corpi/ [accessed 10 August 2019].

Harvey, Keith (2000) 'Translating Camp Talk. Gay Identities and Cultural Transfer,' in *The Translation Studies Reader*. Ed. Lawrence Venuti. London and New York: Routledge. 402–422.

'I corpi alleati di Butler e la politica della strada,' (2017), review of *L'Alleanza dei Corpi*, in *I diavoli* [online] 8 March. Available at: www.idiavoli.com/recensioni/corpi-alleati-judith-butler-politica/ [accessed 22 March 2019].

Maeckelbergh, Marianne (2011) 'Doing Is Believing: Prefiguration as Strategic Practice in the Alterglobalization Movement,' *Social Movement Studies* 10 (1): 1–20.

Mortada, Leil-Zahra (2016) 'Translation and Solidarity in Words of Women from the Egyptian Revolution,' in *Translating Dissent: Voices from and with the Egyptian Revolution*. Ed. Mona Baker. New York and London: Routledge. 125–136.

Nossem, Eva (2017) 'Queering Lexicography: Balancing Power Relations in Dictonaries,' in *Queering Translation, Translating the Queer*. Eds. Brian Baer and Klaus Kaindl. New York: Routledge. 172–187.

Pas, Justine, and Magdalena Zaborowska (2017) 'The Other Women's Lives: Translation Strategies in the Global Feminisms Project,' in *Feminist Translation Studies. Local and Transnational Perspectives*. Eds. Olga Castro and Emek Ergun. New York: Routledge. 139–150.

'Presentazione de l'*Alleanza dei Corpi* di Judith Butler,' (2017) review of Butler's *L'alleanza di corpi* (2017) [online]. Available at: www.facebook.com/events/presentazione-di-lalleanza-dei-corpi-di-judith-butler/1694806563869596/ [accessed 15 August 2019].

Reimóndez, María (2017) 'We Need to Talk … to Each Other: On Polyphony, Postcolonial Feminism and Translation,' in *Feminist Translation Studies. Local and Transnational Perspectives*. Eds. Olga Castro and Emek Ergun. New York and London: Routledge. 42–45.

Robinson, Douglas (2003) *Performative Linguistics: Speaking and Translating as Doing Things with Words*. London and New York: Routledge.

Santaemilia, José (2017) 'A Corpus-Based Analysis of Terminology in Gender and Translation Research: The Case of Feminist Translation,' in *Feminist Translation Studies. Local and Transnational Perspectives*. Eds. Olga Castro and Emek Ergun. New York and London: Routledge. 15–28.

Scholz, Sally (2014) 'Transnational Feminist Solidarity and Lessons from the 2011 Protests in Tahrir Square,' *Global Discourse* 4 (2–3): 205–219.

Sedgwick, Eve Kosofsky (2011) *Stanze Private*. Trans. Federico Zappino. Rome: Carocci editore.

Selim, Samah (2016) 'Translating in a State of Emergency,' in *Translating Dissent: Voices from and with the Egyptian Revolution*. Ed. Mona Baker. New York and London: Routledge. 77–87.

Terranova, Annalisa (2017) 'Butler, l'alleanza dei corpi' che salva la democrazia agonizzante,' review of *L'alleanza dei corpi*, in *Lettera 43* [online] 23 April. Available at: www.lettera43.it/it/

articoli/cultura-e-spettacolo/2017/04/23/butler-lalleanza-dei-corpi-che-salva-la-democrazia-ago
nizzante/210125/ [accessed 24 March 2019].

Tissot, Damien (2017) 'Transnational Feminist Solidarities and the Ethics of Translation,' in *Feminist Translation Studies. Local and Transnational Perspectives*. Eds. Olga Castro and Emek Ergun. New York and London: Routledge. 29–41.

Tymoczko, Maria (2000) 'Translation and Political Engagement,' *The Translator* 6 (1): 23–47.

Tymoczko, Maria (2007) *Enlarging Translation, Empowering Translators*. New York and London: Routledge.

Tymoczko, Maria (2010) 'The Space and Time of Activist Translation,' in *Translation, Resistance, Activism*. Ed. Maria Tymoczko. Amherst and Boston, MA: University of Massachusetts Press. 227–254.

Venuti, Lawrence (1995) *The Translator's Invisibility: A History of Translation*. London and New York: Routledge.

Venuti, Lawrence (1998) *The Scandals of Translation*. London and New York: Routledge.

Venuti, Lawrence (2010) 'Translation as Cultural Politics: Régimes of Domestication in English,' in *Critical Readings in Translation Studies*. Ed. Mona Baker. London and New York: Routledge. 65–79.

Wittig, Monique (2019) *Il pensiero eterosessuale*. Trans. Federico Zappino. Verona: Ombre Corte.

Wolf, Michaela (2012) 'The Sociology of Translation and its 'Activist Turn',' *Translation and Interpreting Studies* 7 (2): 129–143.

Wolf, Michaela (2017) 'A 'Performative Turn' in Translation Studies? Reflections from a Sociological Perspective,' *TransCultural* 9 (1): 27–44.

Zappino, Federico (ed.) (2016) *Il genere tra neoliberismo e neofondamentalismo*. Verona: Ombre corte.

Zappino, Federico (2017a) 'Spirito di scissione in Gramsci. Dalla prospettiva del separatism queer,' in *Opera Viva magazine* [online] 17 September. Available at: https://operavivamagazine.org/ideo logia-e-spirito-di-scissione-in-gramsci/ [accessed 19 March 2019].

Zappino, Federico (2017b) 'Zappino: L'alleanza dei corpi di Judith Butler,' written interview with Federico Zappini on *L'alleanza dei corpi*, in *Che Fare* [online] 24 May. Available at: www.che-fare.com/federico-zappino-lalleanza-dei-corpi-di-judith-butler/ [Accessed 24 March 2019].

Zappino, Federico (2017c) 'Judith Butler *L'alleanza dei corpi*,' radio interview, in RSI [online]. Available at: www.rsi.ch/rete-due/programmi/cultura/attualita-culturale/Judith-Butler-L'alleanza-dei-corpi-8588104.html?fbclid=IwAR0j1M1ThIwDoxrYSx7eRbSpw3NGw7sF_s Ra3DKsJ4FR0JGPNSIGdk3iylQ [accessed 24 March 2019].

Zappino, Federico (2019) *Comunismo queer*. Milano: Meltemi.

Zappino, Federico, and Deborah Ardilli (2017) 'La volontà di negare. III. I nostri amici e noi,' in *Lavoro Culturale* [online] 27 July. Available at: www.lavoroculturale.org/volonta-di-negare-nostri-amici/?utm_source=feedburner&utm_medium=feed&utm_campaign=Feed%3A±lavorocul turale%2FupUZ±%28il±lavoro±culturale%29 [accessed 14 August 2019].

Interviews cited

Baldo, Michela, and Federico Zappino (2018) 'Skype Interview with Federico Zappino on *L'alleanza dei corpi*.' 26 September 2018.

4

Thought/translation

Morad Farhadpour

Farhadpour, prismatically translated: philosophical prose and the activist agenda

by Kayvan Tahmasebian and Rebecca Ruth Gould

When we first began to conceptualise the shape and structure of *The Routledge Handbook of Translation and Activism*, Morad Farhadpour was among the first theorists of translation to occur to us. This is in part because of the respect he commands among leftist Iranian activists, and also, just as importantly, the author's conceptual originality, and his ability to think translation far beyond the borders into which it is traditionally circumscribed. We chose a text that directly addressed the intersection between thought and translation and which merges these processes into a single cognitive act. Our engagement with Farhadpour's text proved enlightening, as much as for the meanings we were able to convey in English as for those which did not cross the translational divide. The translation of dense philosophical prose presents challenges that have not received the same attention as has poetry and other genres.

The text included below is a translation in the broadest sense of the term, which includes adaptation (*eqtebās*), abridgement (*ekhtesār*), summary (*talkhis*), and rewriting (*bāznevisi*). The version presented here can be compared to the more literal version presented on our companion website.[1] Both versions have been approved by Farhadpour; both serve radically different ends. The version included in this volume is intended for the non-specialist reader who may be encountering not only Farhadpour, but Iranian intellectual thought, for the first time, alongside an array of other voices from across the world. The rendering in the online supplement aspires to a more precise rendering of the original. In adopting this dualistic approach, we reproduce the translational method of the poet-translator Bijan Elahi, who chose to render the German Romantic poet Hölderlin through a precise literalism and the Sufi mystic al-Hallaj according to a broader understanding of translation.[2] Elahi chose this approach because he recognised that, just as no original text can be entirely reproduced in any other context, so too, no translation will serve all times, places, and functions.

The translation offered here abridges the Persian text, reducing passages that in English might come across as repetitive and rebarbative, erasing certain irresolvable contradictions which appear like distractions in the English text, and removing characteristic Persian rhetorical features. In general, we seek to meet the aesthetic ideals of English in terms of concision and precision, while removing aesthetic features, such as ornate and abstract language, that only have traction in Persian. Were Farhadpour's text intended to be read alongside the philosophers he draws from, such as Gadamer and Hegel, it goes without saying that our translation would have been different as well. We are presenting Farhadpour's work as a standalone text, that must be accepted (or rejected) alongside other works of different genres and outlooks. Our aims in including this text are more rudimentary than those that animate the dense hermeneutical tradition to which Farhadpour is so clearly indebted.

Although he writes as a theorist rather than as an activist, the relevance of Farhadpour's understanding of translation to activist praxis is clear. In making translation cognate with thought, Farhadpour suggests that every thinker is potentially a translator, and every act of communication and adaptation is an act of translation. When Farhadpour broadens the meaning of translation beyond its conventional boundaries, he thereby opens it to activist agendas. At the same time, he also narrows the concept of translation so that readers unfamiliar with the Iranian context will better be able to understand its transformative political capacity. Farhadpour parts ways with the intellectuals who paved the way for the Iranian revolution such as Jalal Al-e Ahmad and Ali Shari'ati in advocating for the necessary mediation of Iran's past and of Islamic learning by European philosophy. While Farhadpour embraces the European legacy without reservation, he also recognises that exclusive absorption in European traditions can inhibit Iranians' access to their own past. Within this framework, Farhadpour rethinks translation as a means of reconciling contemporary Iranians with their pasts.

We can distinguish two conceptions of translation in Farhadpour's essay: hermeneutic and Lacanian. Farhadpour reports how he shifted from a hermeneutic approach to translation to a Lacanian one. He also explains how these two conceptions arise from his own 'situatedness' within two different socio-political conditions. Farhadpour's use of the concept of 'situation [*vaz'iyat*],' resonates with the notion of philosophical situation adopted by the French philosopher Alain Badiou, whom Farhadpour has translated into Persian.

The hermeneutic conception of translation—entailing translating one's own tradition—does not distinguish between the original (*ta'lif*) and translation (*tarjoma*). In Persian, '*ta'lif*' and '*tarjoma*' are used as opposites, the first meaning 'authorial work' and second meaning 'translation.' *Ta'lif-e tarjomayi*—a noun phrase that recurs at key points in Farhadpour's text —which literally translates as 'translational authorial work'—is a hybrid genre combining authorial work and translation. These works are presented as original creations in Persian when in actuality they contain a considerable amount of unacknowledged and acknowledged translations. The phrase *tailīf-e tarjomayi* establishes Farhadpour's insight that all modern Iranian creations are also translations.

The hermeneutic approach to translation distinguishes between felicitous and infelicitous translations in terms that parallel the distinction between deliberative (*āgāahāna*) and non-deliberative (*nā-āgāahāna*) translations. Deliberation is a function of the extent to which a text makes itself available to translation. Non-deliberative translations conceal the text's translatability. In the hermeneutic translational method, the self is mediated through the understanding of the other, which is best achieved through deliberative translation.

Farhadpour shifts to a Lacanian model of translation that challenges this homogeneity. In the Lacanian model, any understanding is structured by misunderstanding. The choice to privilege deliberative over non-deliberative translations appears meaningless when considered in light of the fact that even a deliberative translation is based on misunderstanding. In the Lacanian conception, translation does not conceal the internal gaps of its situation; rather, translation reveals the gaps and voids internal to language itself. In other words, in this second approach to translation, deliberative translations can be as deceptive as non-deliberative ones. For Farhadpour, the shift in his approach to translation from a hermeneutic to a Lacanian method is a response to the political changes in Iran, including the shift from radical reformist to depoliticised post-reformist conditions.

Alongside the contextualising approach that has guided our approach to translating Farahadpour, we have drawn on Matthew Reynolds' concept of 'prismatic translation' to make sense of the many variant versions that productively interact with each other.[3] Reynolds recognises that 'different translations can also be made by the same person; indeed, the potential for multiplication is latent in any act of translation in the moment of its happening.'[4] Prismatic translation suits our multifaceted approach to Farhadpour, as well as Farhadpour's approach to translation, for it captures the multiplicity of renderings that inevitably arise in the process of adapting a text as rich as this one for different audiences. Reynolds registers an acute absence within contemporary translation studies when he observes that 'the idea that translation is fundamentally multiplicatory—that its essence is not reproduction but proliferation—has been difficult to hold consistently in focus and to theorise.'[5] Farhadpour's reflections on the consubstantiality of thought and translation—indeed on their shared identity—shed light on the relation between translation and activism, and indeed translation and action of any kind: they help us to see how multiplicity in language generates possibility in political life.

This selection below is abridged, with the permission of the author, from Morad Farhadpour, Fragments of Thought: Philosophy & Politics *(Tehran: Tarh-e Now, 2009), 231–264. Except where noted, all notes are in the original Persian, including the two passages below in bold type.*

Morad Farhadpour: a biographical sketch

Morad Farhadpour was born in 1958 in Tehran, during the reign of Mohammed Reza Shah Pahlavi (1941–1979). He is a widely read essayist and translator, and member of the new Iranian left. His father was a journalist and member of Iranian Parliament under the Pahlavis. During a short stay in London, where he was studying English in the years leading up to the Iranian revolution of 1979, Farhadpour became affiliated with Marxist student opposition groups that campaigned across Europe for the overthrow of Mohammed Reza Shah. Farhadpour returned to Iran in 1979, and has lived in Tehran ever since.

From 1979 to 1981, Farhadpour was the youngest member of a theoretically minded division of Trotskyists who developed their own theory of what the revolution meant. Farhadpour wrote and translated for a few short-lived Marxist periodicals (such as the theoretical quarterly called *Jadal*), as did many other members of the intelligentsia. For the next two years he worked as a member of an intellectual Marxist circle that published *Kavosh* (a theoretical quarterly) and *Basijeh: The Voice of Critical Communism*, first in Germany and then in Iran. After the collapse of the political and revolutionary spirit of those years, Farhadpour turned to literature, poetry, and theology until the path was paved socially and politically for more direct political and theoretical interventions during the mid-1990s.

Farhadpour was a prominent figure of the Iranian reformist movement of the late 1990s. The reformist era opened up a space for intellectuals like him to write and translate. It was on the pages of journals like *Arghanun, Rāh-e-now,* and *Kiān* that Farhadpour contributed to reformist intellectual debates by translating modern European philosophy, literary and cultural theory. Farhadpour translated Theodor W. Adorno and Walter Benjamin among others for *Arghanun* and played a central role in popularising the Frankfurt School among Iranian reformist intellectuals. He achieved much of this influence as a translator. In 1999, Farhadpour translated the philosopher David Couzens Hoy. This was followed in 2000 by Farhadpour's translation of Marshall Berman's seminal study of modernist aesthetics, *All That is Solid Melts into Air* (1982).

While first and foremost a critical theorist and a translator of critical theory into Persian, Farhadpour has also made a distinctive contribution to Iranian intellectual thought by introducing modern Christian theology to Iran. He translated two books by Adorno's dissertation supervisor, the Christian socialist Paul Tillich. He also translated an introduction to the thought of the German protestant theologian Wolfhart Pannenberg. In addition to his work as a translator, Farhadpour's introductions to these translations are important and memorable.

From 1998 to 2004, Farhadpour was associated with *Arghanun*, a state-sponsored journal named after the *organon*, the standard collection of Aristotle's six works on logic, and published by the Ministry of Culture. When this journal closed in 2004, Farhadpour led a group of young leftist journalists and translators belonging to a circle that called itself *rokhdād*, meaning 'event.' 'In search for a philosophical system to support a kind of radical emancipative thought and praxis,'[6] Farhadpour was drawn to translating contemporary critical thinkers such as Slavoj Žižek, Giorgio Agamben, and Alain Badiou. The outputs of the circle were published in a website which ceased to operate after the 2009 Green Movement. All in all, Farhadpour has translated and co-translated over twenty-five works of European critical theory. With Omid Mehrgan (another contributor to this volume, currently based in the US), Farhadpour translated Max Horkheimer and Theodor W. Adorno's *Dialectic of Enlightenment* and Walter Benjamin's selected essays.

Farhadpour's leftism has been contrasted with other dominant intellectual currents within post-revolutionary Iran, including Ahmad Fardid's Islamic Heideggerianism, Abdolkarim Sorush's Islamic reformism, Tudeh leftism, and other Marxist trends in Iran, and Sayyed Javad Tabatabai's theory of decline in Islamic social sciences and Iranian political thought.[7] In an essay on Heidegger, Farhadpour describes the German philosopher as a 'reactionary revolutionary'[8] who nonetheless cannot be denounced and discarded as 'just another German Fascist.'

Farhadpour's essays have been collected in three collections: first, *Depressed Reason: Reflections on Modern Thought* (1999), *Western Winds* (2003), and *Fragments of Thought* (2008–2009). These essays cover a wide range of subjects: German intellectual movements, Serbian violence during the Balkan Wars, postmodernist relativism (a literary trend within Iranian reformism), Iranian idealism, and translation theory. While his thinking is not systematic, it is everywhere pervaded by a conception of translation that reaches beyond conventional understandings of this practice as the mere conveyance of a message from one language into another.

Alongside his theoretical writings, Farhadpour is a prolific literary critic. He has introduced and translated J. R. R. Tolkien and edited and translated a collection of Latin American short stories. Farhadpour's translations (with the Iranian sociologist Yousef Abazari) of European modernist poetry, called *Ketāb-e shāʿerān*, make a significant contribution to Iranian literary criticism.

Distinguished as an essay writer, translator, and teacher of the younger generation of Iranian writers, poets, translators, and activists, for more than two decades, Farhadpour has played a central role in shaping leftist intellectual debates in Iran. A younger generation of Iranian leftist journalists and translators, including Omid Mehrgan and

Saleh Najafi, has been directly influenced by Farhadpour's ideas and positions with respect to Iranian and international politics, philosophy, and art.

Farhadpour currently lectures in private institutes, such as Porsesh Institute in Tehran, in order to develop his ideas and to inspire the young generation. In a recent interview with the Iranian daily newspaper *E'temad,* Farhadpour warns that international leftist thought is suffering a legitimacy crisis in relation to the masses. He expresses his hope of bringing about an emancipative event, in a world wherein all protest movements tend to be suppressed by state power and corrupted by capitalist interventions.

Select bibliography

Original works by Farhadpour

Morad Farhadpour, *Depressed Reason: Reflections on Modern Thought ('Aql-e afsorda)* (Tehran: Tarh-e now, 1999).
Morad Farhadpour, *Western Winds (Bād-hā-ye gharbi)* (Tehran: Hermes, 2003).
Morad Farhadpour, *Fragments of Thought (Pāra-hā-ye fekr)* (Tehran: Tarh-e now), vol.1 (On Art and Literature), 2008; vol.2 (On Philosophy and Politics), 2009.

Translations by Farhadpour

Alan badiu: falsafa, honar, siyāsat, 'eshq (Alain Badiou: philosophy, art, politics, love) (Tehran: Gam-e now, 2010).
Alain Badiou, *Bonyād-e kolli-gerāyi: pol-e qeddis va manteq-e haqiqat* (Tehran: Mahi, 2008), co-translated with Saleh Najafi. A translation of *Saint Paul: The Foundation of Universalism.*
Alain Badiou, *Farziya-ye komunism* (Tehran: Nashr-i markaz, 2017), co-translated with Saleh Najafi, a translation of *The Communist Hypothesis.*
Walter Benjamin, *Arusak va kutuleh* (The puppet and the dwarf) (Tehran: Gam-e now Publishing House, 2006), co-translated with Omid Mehrgan. A translation of Benjamin's selected essays.
Marshall Berman, *Tajroba-ye moderniteh* (Tehran: Tarh-e now, 2000). A translation of *All That is Solid Melts into the Air.*
Farhadpour's translations of Žižek, Badiou and Agamben are found in three volumes of *Ketāb-e rokhdād* (Book of Event):
Allan Douglas Galloway, *Pannenberg: elāhiyāt-e tārikihi* (Tehran: Serat, 1973). A translation of *Wolfhart Pannenberg.*
Max Horkheimer and Theodor W. Adorno, *Diyālektik-e rowshangari* (Tehran: Gam-i now Publishing House, 2005), co-translated with Omid Mehrgan. A translation of *Dialectic of Enlightenment* (1944).
David Couzens Hoy, *Halqa-ye enteqādi: adabiyāt, tārikh va hermenutik-e falsafi* (Tehran: Roshan-garan va motale'at-e zanan Publishers, 1999). A translation of *The Critical Circle: Literature, History, and Philosophical Hermeneutics* (1982).
Islavoy jijek: gozida-ye maqālāt: nazariya, siyāsat, din (Slavoj Žižek: selected essays on theory, politics and religion) (Tehran: Gam-e now, 2005).
Qānun va khoshunat: gozida-ye maqālāt-e Jorjo Agāmben, Kārl Eshmit, Vālter Benyāmin, ... (Law and violence: selected essays of Giorgio Agamben, Carl Schmitt, Walter Benjamin, ...) (Tehran: Gam-e now, 2010).
Sevvomin karāna-ye rud, dāstān-hā-ye kutāh az nevisandegān-e āmrikā-ye lātin (The river's third bank: twelve Latin American Stories) (Tehran: Roshangaran, 1992).
Paul Tillich, *Shojā'at-e budan* (Tehran: Entesharat-e 'elmi va farhangi, 1987). A translation of *The Courage to Be* (1952).
Paul Tillich, *Elāhiyāt-e farhang* (Tehran: Tarh-e now, 1997), co-translated with Fazlollah Pakzad, a translation of *Theology of Culture* (1959).
J. R. R. Tolkien, *Derakht va barg (si dāstān-e takhayoli)* (The tree and the leaf: three fantastic stories) (Tehran: Tarh-e now, 2008).

Thought/translation

Morad Farhadpour Rendered by Kayvan Tahmasebian and
Rebecca Ruth Gould

I

In 1999, in the preface to *Depressed Reason* (*'aql-e afsorda*), I related translation to thought in this way:

> In the past years, I have frequently emphasised that in the contemporary era, begin-
> ning roughly with the Constitutional Revolution and ending perhaps in a future not
> so near, translation, in its broadest sense, is our only true form of thought. My per-
> sonal experience as a translator and an author as well as the achievements of others
> in these two realms are evidence of this.

So, the main idea is that for us the only true form of thought is translation. This idea matters because it is related to the concept of situation (*vaz'iyat*).

We all must begin our arguments from within a particular situation. Therefore, we are not concerned with 'should' and 'should not'; our question addresses neither the abstract nor the ideal. It does not aim at what thought 'should be' but is instead concerned with actual reality or the actuality of thought.

The emphasis on the situatedness of thought is one of the main achievements of philosophical hermeneutics, which is rooted in a Hegelian tradition. Prioritising translation and introducing it as the true form of thought resulted directly from my choice of hermeneutics as my philosophical stance at that time. In the first part of this discussion, I demonstrate this hermeneutic aspect of the problem through the concept of translation. In the second part, I will try to show how a necessary passage from this hermeneutical space to a so-called Lacanian space takes place, and how in this process the concept of translation is transformed from within.

As far as the modern situation is concerned, it is necessary to introduce thought as something other than the action of an abstract un-situated subject. The concept of situation is meaningful only when we recognise that the very question concerning it is, as such, the outcome and a feature of belonging to a particular situation. Our dilemma does not consist in facing a choice between two abstract universals (*koll-e entezā'i*), tradition and modernity. The scrutiny that is already attached to tradition and modernity attests to our location within modernity. If we were not already modern, the contrast would pose no dilemma for us. However, when thought admits that it is situated, it loses its abstract and ideological quality. Extracting the categories of tradition and modernity from within a situation, here modernity, leaves them neither pure nor ideal. Rather, such categories are meaningful only within the context of particular historical conditions.

One of my purposes in translating Marshall Berman's *All That is Solid Melts into Air* was to introduce modernity as a concrete experience (*tajroba-ye enzemāmi*). Also, in several articles on the subject of tradition, especially 'Ideological Traditionalism,'[9] I tried to demonstrate that the abstract category of tradition used by ideological traditionalism is an outcome of the modern situation. In this context, it has a nihilistic meaning that eradicates all living tradition. Thought that takes its own situatedness seriously cannot see itself facing a choice between the two abstract universals, tradition and modernity. It experiences both as evolving processes and traditions, concrete and specific traditions. The most important part of our critical argument is that thought becomes ambiguous and abstract when we regard a problem without a situation.

Regarding our historical situation, this hermeneutical choice of being situated is manifested in other intellectual paradigms as well. For example, in the debates around a certain kind of Islamic Heideggerianism, mainly proposed by Ahmad Fardid, I am interested in the point at which this theoretical problematic (*mo'zal*) becomes dialectical, i.e. where the problem of *Weststruckness* (*gharb-zadegi*) comes to be formulated as 'even West is West-struck,' thereby transferring the gap between East and West to within West itself. In this way a gap or tension is introduced into the European self-conception. At the same time, it becomes impossible to define the East as an independent, solid and original (*asil*) totality or identity against this West-struck West. Like it or not, the gap is drawn inside us. To know the West critically, or to negate the West, is impossible without negating the East. Any attempt to do so transforms an ahistorical and abstract negation into a definite negation and amounts to the Hegelian 'negation of negation [*nafy dar nafy*].'

The negating subject is not faced with a spiritual or religious choice between two universals, West and East, or tradition and modernity. Rather, it experiences the tension between the two concretely, within itself. To experience this tension means to restore it to a situation. We recognise that the choice as such emerges from within a modern situation, that is, from the fissure of the self in relation to the other. The historical fact that we are undertaking this very choice shows that we live and think in a particular situation, that is, in the modern world. Within modernity, nothing and no one owns a pre-defined fixed identity. Everyone must construct their own identity, or essence, through historical discourses, narratives and images. As a result, only reflection on the situation can reveal the historical and concrete essence of thought.

This dialectical movement can also be discerned in certain aspects of Iranian leftist thought. Failing to reflect on itself or to define itself as situated, leftist thought conceptualised the passage into capitalism in a dogmatic, abstract, and as a result, arbitrary way. Different theories, including dependency theory, were proposed to explain Iran's transition from pre-capitalist or feudalist conditions into capitalism without recognising how these theoretical paradigms may deprive leftist thought of its political purpose.

Leftist thought would have traction only once society passed structurally into the capitalist mode. In the absence of such a development, leftism would become merely a benevolent sermon or a call for an imaginary socialism. As in the paradigm of tradition and modernity that reveals itself as an abstract choice between two totalities, both of which lack self-reflection, any form of thought that is unaware of its status within a specific historical situation, leftist or otherwise, reproduces itself in the form of an arbitrary general choice.

Most recently, this process (*farāyand*) has become evident in debates around religious intellectualism (*rowshanfekri-ye dini;*). Such debates characterise the attempts of a tradition or a theoretical discourse to confront its inner tensions, to overcome its abstraction and to discover its historical role. Given that the most important quality of thought is reflexivity, any attempt to overcome abstraction and to attain self-consciousness can take an abstract form and become indistinguishable from self-delusion.

A striking example of this reflexive turn can be seen in stagnate epistemological frameworks that repeat the primal event of this tradition: Abdolkarim Soroush's epistemological arguments, which are informed by the philosophy of Karl Popper. Similarly, Sayyed Javad Tabatabai's theory of the 'impossibility of thought [*emtenā'-e tafakkor*]' casts doubt on the possibility of thinking within all of our intellectual traditions. Despite its historical trappings, Tabatabai's theory lacks any concrete historical content. In Tabatabai's thought, the attempt to overcome abstraction and to understand the causes of the weakness and impotence of [Iranian] thought ironically resulted in pure abstract generalisations, therefore reproducing the same impotence on a wider scope.

Meanwhile, this 'impossibility' or poverty of thought dialectically reappears in Tabatabai's work itself in the guise of a philosophy that answers to all academic norms: voluminous books, each an ocean of historical facts and philosophical insights demonstrating the singular truth that explains and deciphers our intellectual history *tout court*. Condensing the entire history of our thought into a few books, Tabatabai argues that all Iranian intellectuals, except the author himself, are ignorant and incapable of thinking. His effort to overcome abstraction and dogmatism turns dialectically into its antithesis and produces an idealistic yet hollow discourse, which is rooted in the historical situation of our modernity. This modernity is characterised by, among other things, the proliferation of [a hybrid genre combining] authorial work and translation (*ta'lifāt-e tarjomayi*) and the production of voluminous books covering the history of ideas from Aristotle to modern times. These works, ranging from encyclopaedias to handbooks, devalue European philosophy through their misrepresentation of European thought.

This conceptual structure, which is at the same time an historical process, is one that I call 'concretised-historicised thought.' It drew me to hermeneutics: the most interesting philosophical tradition at that time, because hermeneutic philosophy is concerned with the situatedness of thought. For this reason, when my friends and I decided to start a translation project, we chose books that spanned the hermeneutic tradition, from Schleiermacher and Dilthey to Heidegger and Gadamer. My translation of David Couzens Hoy's *The Critical Circle* was the result of such a choice.

The unification of thought and translation is accomplished through the return to situation. As we saw, this particular situation, called modernity, creates a necessary encounter whereby the self is shaped through its confrontation with the other. As a result, the question can never be posed in terms of a pre-existing, pre-historical subject faced with a choice between tradition and modernity. Rather, the subject and the choice are outcomes of modernity and, *eo ipso*, of the confrontation between self and other. What matters is the dialectics of self and other.

In a Hegelian-Lacanian sense, the main point is the internal gap and negation that the other creates. Encompassing this gap, I become a subject with self-consciousness. Extending this further, we actually confront the concept of translation in its different layers and aspects, from the broad meaning of cultural transfer to translation in its specific sense, translation as the dialectical motif which Gadamerian hermeneutics derives from the relation of thought to situation.

If understanding and thought are situated, then all understanding of the other requires a transfer from one situation to another. In other words, understanding is primarily related to interpretation and translation. Transfer (*enteqāl*) is a spatial, temporal and at the same time verbal metaphor: transfer from one place to another, from one time to another and ultimately from one language to another. The concept of translation can reflect this historical and cultural dialectics. In this dialectics, recognition of oneself *through* an other often means recognition of oneself *as* an other. Recognising oneself *through* an other involves an understanding of translation as negativity: it interiorises the alterity (*ghayriyat*) that is concretely located in the source culture, especially in its traditional texts.

Tradition is a space in the continuity of which one can regard, from a new position, oneself and one's own history as an other, as something alien that is still connected to oneself. This opens the way to a critique of tradition and invigorates it. The opposite is also true: when I, as an Easterner, confront a European or Western civilisation as such, when I want to know it and internalize it, *I have to confront the other as not-I or as the negative side of my interiority.* Perhaps an example can elucidate the dialectical interweaving of self and other that is tied to different layers of the concept of translation, and to our knowledge (*shenākht*) of modernity and the West (as other) as well as our knowledge of our own past. When I foreground the concept of translation, putting it forward as the main form of thought, I mean that not only our relation to European modernity but also and more importantly our relation to ourselves is established through translation.

If any kind of thought can be considered a kind of translation, then we need to translate, not only in order to know Kant and Hegel, but also to know our own past. We need to translate Mulla Sadra and Ibn Sina, and, more importantly, Saʿdi, Hafez and Ferdowsi for ourselves. When we develop this conception of translation along with the dialectics of the particular and the universal entailed in this concept, the central role of the metaphor of translation becomes apparent. In simplest terms, we all know that, as modern subjects, we are inside modernity, thereby confronting the history of modernity and its philosophical attempts at self-understanding. In fact, modernity's self-reflection, in any form, is inevitably part of our self-reflection. This truth obliges us to translate and publish Hegel and Kant into Persian.

It is only in this way that we recognise our 'identity [*hoviyyat*]' or 'lack of identity [*bi-hoviyyati*],' as well as our premodern, so-called 'authentic self [*hoviyyat-e asil*],' or 'the self of the self [*khishtan-e khish*].' This recognition is the product of modern historical situation. As a result, in order to properly and consciously import our own past into modernity and history—a past that has always had a foothold in history through Ibn Sina and other Islamic philosophers—we should 'translate' the works of Islamic philosophy in both the restricted and broad senses of the term. Distinguished figures such as Ibn Sina, Abu Rayhan Biruni, Mulla Sadra should cease being cultural heritage—mere inheritances from the dead past—and become a living tradition.

This type of translation necessarily has various aspects and layers. We should be able to provide comprehensible Persian texts of the works of Farabi, Ibn Sina, Mulla Sadra, and so on. More importantly, we should be able to interpret these works in the context of our current situation. This is translation in the broadest sense. We should draw Ibn Sina and Mulla Sadra, among others, into our tensions, decisions, and concrete experiences of our situated subjectivity.

Now we begin to see how different branches and layers of the hermeneutic act of translation are intertwined: in order to be able to draw Ibn Sina and Mulla Sadra into our situation, we need to incorporate Kant and Hegel. When understood (even if through translation), Kant and Hegel enable us to incorporate Ibn Sina and Mulla Sadra into modern Persian thought. This is true also for texts that do not require translation in the narrow sense, such as the poetry of Hafez, Sa'di, and Ferdowsi.

To make Hafez, Sa'di and Ferdowsi meaningful for ourselves, we must translate them into the current situation. They should be criticised and rethought from the point of view of modernity. To be meaningful in the modern situation requires our coming to terms with the utter meaninglessness of this 'sacred literary treasure.' This can be accomplished in different forms and through different literary and critical theories. We need to be familiar with Barthes, Derrida, new criticism, structuralism and other theoretical traditions and literary-critical tools to give us different understanding of our own tradition.

Despite what is usually thought, neither the philosophical category of translation nor the metaphor of translation posits a passive state or a shameful native subject because its apparent role is limited to praising the West. To the extent that translating Hegel and Kant is necessary for making Ibn Sina and Hafez accessible to us Iranians, European philosophical texts stand in need of interpretation that reaches well beyond merely verbal translation. However, this interpretation is derived from our own convoluted situation. Part of it consists of traditions that belong only to us, such as the works of Ibn Sina, Hafez, and others that distinguish our historical situation from the Argentinian or Icelandic ones.

Close reading, criticising and engagement with these works, among many other factors, enable me (the Iranian reader) to understand Hegel differently. But if my dialectical relation to Hegel goes beyond reading Hegel's books in Persian then this dialectics surely extends to all my intellectual history, including all my past. Apart from this dialectical excess such books will gather dust on the shelves, or worse, turn into tools for the fabrication of university degrees. In all these cases, we are concerned with the actuality of thought; therefore, the question is not whether I can decide to use Hegel to comprehend my own past or not. This comprehension either takes place, in which case I will be forced to use parts of European philosophy, whether I like or acknowledge it or not, or it does not.

The same logic is followed when considering the opposite side of the relation. I either comprehend Hegel according to my own situation or I don't comprehend him at all. Nothing remains to be said if I do not comprehend Hegel and keep the translation of his *The Phenomenology of Spirit* into Persian 'on the shelf' in both the literal and figurative sense of the term, either not reading it at all or only consulting it for 'valuable philosophical knowledge' that is separated from and irrelevant to my situation.

When I understand Hegel, my situation with all its diversities, paradoxes, traditions, complexities and gaps partakes in this comprehension. This involvement is not arbitrary or a matter of choice. A subject who lacks any situation can only choose between abstract ideas and ideals. This is not thought but the dead remains of a mystical and 'spiritual' culture that is incapable of self-reflection. It is built on misunderstanding and falsity, like the ideological traditionalism prevalent in Iran, which is in fact the worst form of nihilism.

Situatedness is indeed what determines the fate of thought and its relation to truth (*haqiqat*) or falsehood (*kezb*). Rimbaud's famous phrase, 'one must be absolutely modern,' affirms this.[10] However, the word 'must' here, as we will see, is not a universal and moral 'must.' Rimbaud's phrase is not only different from but also contradicts Taqizadeh, who said 'one must be modern from head to toe.'

As I argued, the claim that translation is the only true form of thought implies that there is no thought that is not translation in some way. To translate or not to translate is not an option. In the contemporary era, whatever we do is essentially translation. This is just another way of emphasising our participating in today's situation: the modern world we all live in. To clarify this aspect of the question, we need to refer to another key concept of Gadamerian hermeneutics. In explaining the problem of understanding, Gadamer distinguishes between *subtilitas explicandi* and *subtilitas intelligendi*, a distinction that has been common to all versions of hermeneutics since antiquity.[11]

Throughout the history of theological and literary hermeneutics, that is, in all attempts to interpret and understand sacred texts and ancient literary works, one encounters these two notions. *Subtilitas explicandi* refers to what Schleiermacher describes as a technical interpretation. This hermeneutic method or subtlety is mainly limited to philology; it makes a text meaningful through the application of philological techniques, editing texts and removing the technical problems that burden all philological endeavours. *Subtilitas intelligendi*, on the other hand, serves to clarify the author's intention and discover the true meaning veiled by the text, especially in cases that involve textual ambiguity and where misunderstanding is likely.

Schleiermacher's hermeneutics consists of becoming familiar with all that seems strange or foreign. This is why Schleiermacher believes that the text must be understood as the author intended, and sometimes even better than the author understands. One has to grasp the hidden meaning in the text, intended by the author, through empathy (*ham-deli*), that is by putting oneself in the author's situation and reconstructing their intellectual horizon. Therefore, we first use a set of philological techniques to make the text technically comprehensible (*subtilitas explicandi*), then, through empathy with the reconstructed world of the author, we attain an understanding of the original text (*subtilitas intelligendi*). Obviously the second aspect has a psychological rather than a philological nature since it involves a form of *pathos*, that is, empathy.

Gadamer adds to this classical typology a third aspect, called *subtilitas applicandi*.[12] In his view, this aspect expresses the hermeneutical truth: every understanding is situated in a certain historical horizon. This performative dimension shows exactly that understanding and interpreting a foreign text or a foreign culture, even understanding the past, require that the horizon of the text or of the past fuse with the horizon that surrounds the interpreter in their historical situation. For Gadamer, the foreign text must be understood according to the requirements and exigencies of the existing situation, which are intrinsic to understanding.

Highlighting *applicatio*, Gadamer emphasises that hermeneutic understanding is not a pure theoretical knowledge (*episteme*). Rather, it consists of that kind of knowledge that Aristotle called practical (*hekmat-e 'amali*): *phronesis*. Understanding is necessarily practical; its significance is only realised when it is put into practice or performed (like a play or a game). In contrast to the applied sciences, such as engineering, understanding never applies a pre-existing theory. From the very beginning, it is a performative act. Performativity or being applicable to a certain situation is inherent to understanding. At the same time, performance and application are not optional and arbitrary.

Textual understanding, like historical understanding, does not happen through universal theoretical principles that can be used to discover the meaning of a text or an event. Examples can be drawn from literary and legal hermeneutics. In literary hermeneutics, a director's understanding of a play is simply the director's production (*ijrā'*) of that play. No director can claim that there is a distance between her understanding of the play and its performance. In fact, from the moment a director interprets a play, it is being interpreted according to the requirements and exigencies of its performance. The performative or practical dimension is present in their understanding from the start. In addition, the director's understanding will ultimately be judged in light of the performance. No director can claim after the production that the play they had in mind is not identical with the play that has been performed, unless the performance has failed due to contingent and external causes such as poor acting or the failure of stage design.

Legal hermeneutics functions in a similar way. Judges reveal their understanding of how general laws apply in any particular case by the decision (*hokm*) they make. Here too, judges' understanding and interpretation of law is expressed in their decisions. In fact, it is through applying the law in a particular case that judges reinterpret and clarify their understanding of it. A judge comprehends the general law in terms of a particular situation, a particular case. This is accomplished through applying it in that particular situation. This example illustrates the relation among the three dimensions of hermeneutics: understanding, interpretation, and application. It shows that understanding always involves a non-arbitrary practical dimension.

Combining the above results with our discussion about translation leads us to this conclusion: *For us Iranians, more than for any other culture, translation is the performative dimension of understanding.* This axiom (*hokm*) logically follows from and supplements the previous one, that today translation is the true form of thought for us. Our understanding, whether of Europe or of modernity or of our own past and present, always entails a performative dimension which usually manifests itself as translation. In other words, all of us, in so far as we think and understand, are active translators. This return to translation is an essential part of our self-reflection. It is a part of the historical self-understanding of the thinking subject in its concrete situation. Here the distinction between an authorial work (*ta'lif*) and a translation fades and the priority of one over the other ceases to matter.

One can say that in this sense everything is translation and the only meaningful distinction is between felicitous and infelicitous translations. This distinction is manifested in the different types of translated authorial works (*ta'lifāt-e tarjomayi*). Works that do not reflect on their relation to translation and pretend not to be translations can be described as infelicitous translations, in contrast to the second type or felicitous translations. This first type of works claims to be pure and absolutely original 'authored works,' while in fact they are nothing but secondary literature: fragments badly translated and haphazardly stitched together. Recently, alongside these translated authorial works, we witness a second type: authorial translations (*tarjoma-hā-ye ta'lifi*) in which an inaccurate verbatim translation of a philosophical text is later published as an original work. In these instances, ignoring the performative dimension of translation turns these works into bad and barren translations. By contrast, wherever thought becomes sensitive to its performative dimension, and therefore to translation, it becomes felicitous. More precisely, it becomes a form of understanding, understanding oneself, understanding modernity and understanding the other. From this vantage point, true thought is simply the distinction between deliberative and non-deliberative translation (discussed below).

The issue of translation cannot be reduced merely to translating the books deemed worthy of translation. What matters is how thought becomes concretised with reference to an historical situation, which provides the criteria for choosing the texts that should be translated. Whenever the act of translation turns into a medium for situating thought, the situation itself—with its tensions, paradoxes and inner processes—provides the criteria for deciding what to choose for translation and to what extent translation should be in an intralingual form and in what contexts it should acquire its broader meaning. In this way, translation manifests itself as a tension between European philosophy and modernity as it is experienced by us Iranians. So far, we have dealt with the hermeneutic aspect of translation. In the next section, the relation of history to modernity will be presented through another interpretation of the meaning of translation.

II

As argued above, the self is recognised through recognition of the other. Our past serves as an other to ourselves. Can we define the self as a self-contained, solid, and authentic (*asil*) identity? Or should we ascribe authenticity to translation that plays a decisive role in shaping thought and self-consciousness? If the answer is yes, our selves can be completely restored, via an other, and through a process called 'deliberative translation.' Deliberative translation facilitates transparent and complete self-awareness with recourse to 'the only possible form of thought in our situation.'

So, it seems that after many ups and downs, paradoxes and tensions, and after overcoming the intellectual poverty of abstraction, our dialectical odyssey can reach a happy ending, thanks to the magic of 'deliberative translation.' This happy ending would generate a harmonious self capable of critical reflection yet still connected to its authentic past. This identity would be constituted by a combination of tradition and modernity, as it picks up the best parts of the past and the present in the 'supermarket of history.'

Deliberative translation's conception of the historical identity of the thinking subject and its insistence on the relation of history to thought is the concern of philosophical hermeneutics. This conception confers an ontological significance on situatedness. This is the main function of concepts of temporality in Heidegger and historicity in Gadamer. These categories facilitate the transformation of the dialectics of situatedness into an abstract ontological discourse. But as Walter Benjamin says, Heidegger's historicity is an attempt to save historical thought, and the very concept of history for phenomenology— an attempt that ends in failure.[13] Engaging with historicity as a part of hermeneutics but without referring to the history of hermeneutics itself, Gadamer too ends up with the same solid 'I' that attains a complete understanding of itself through the other.

However, the difference between history and historicity is present in hermeneutic philosophy itself. Historicity—the axiom that all understanding is essentially bound to an historical situation—is a contingent and therefore changeable axiom. Gadamer himself refers to a possible future in which people no longer think historically. Moreover, empirical history also confirms the existence of many ahistorical cultures, civilisations and societies in the past. One can go further and claim that even right now all people in all cultures *do not* think historically. The credibility of historicity as an existential or ontological situation is therefore open to challenge. Despite this proclivity for 'ontologisation,' Gadamer's genuine, deep and detailed description of the understanding of history is a major achievement in European intellectual history. However, his philosophical hermeneutics is radically fissured as a general theory of understanding: it argues for situatedness but extends it, ontologically, to all times and places, while leaving these questions unanswered: Why was such a hermeneutic view developed only in Europe? Is Gadamer's hermeneutics itself an historical phenomenon? Are there any historical limits in the self-understanding of hermeneutics? What, if any, are its blind spots?

The emergence of hermeneutics from within a particular historical experience drives us towards an essential, and yet concrete and non-idealistic, concept of history. In the course of the evolution of European hermeneutics, external challenges compounded by internal crises in these humanist and historicist traditions paved the way for the passage from hermeneutics to structuralism and, later, poststructuralism. New theories emerged about subject, meaning, and truth, mainly inspired by Freudian and Lacanian psychoanalysis. Void and gap become the main elements in the definition of the subject (*nafs*). The hermeneutic interpretation of the relation between self and other was questioned, especially its assumption that one can reach a homogeneous and perfect recognition of oneself or a recognition of a perfect and homogeneous self through confrontation with the other.

We have previously encountered this perfect authentic subject or self in Iran under the rubric of return to 'the self of the self [*khishtan-e khish*],' pseudo-religious, mystic and spiritual readings of Heidegger and theories of *Weststruckness (gharb-zadegi)*.[14] As indicated earlier, the fundamental point about these theories is the thesis of the *Weststruckness* of the West itself. From this point of view, both West and East are homogeneous, self-sufficient, and mutually exclusive totalities.

In this way a kind of negativity or a gap is internalised by the West and consequently by us, who are, according to that theory, part of the historicity (*havālat-e tārikhi*) of Europe. As a result, the universal homogeneous sphere of modernity emerges no longer as a closed totality against our previous Eastern life but as a gap within this life, as a line that divides any worldview or value system and, in this way, connects to the universal: universal morals, universal values, scientific facts, and so on. The universal, or universality, is always and everywhere realised as a void or crack at the heart of the full and empirical content of any particular substance (*jowhar*), any particular form of life or social system, but never as an abstract and encompassing sphere beyond all particular spheres.

This gap is produced by the negative, abyss-like, nihilistic dimension of modernity. It is also this very dimension that forms the basic ground of modern globalisation. If modernity is globalised, it is because, although generated by a particular lifestyle dominant in Europe, it relates to that life through creating gaps and holes in it, whether in politics, economy, ideology, culture or in Europeans' individual psyches. This hole, this gap, is transferrable to the furthest ends of the world exactly as the negative, as a wind-like nothingness with no positive grounding.

The globalisation of modernity is an effect of this negative aspect or void, of the fact that modernity is not related to a particular content. Notions such as 'religion and democracy,' 'tradition and modernity' and 'the impossibility of thought' (as set forth in the pseudo-historical writings of Javad Tabatabai) gain currency as a result of efforts to fill this void. Such notions characterise a thought that has no particular referent. In particular, they demonstrate that thought flees any determined situation, such as modernity, or when forced to face it simply presents it as a full and complete whole for instance, in the figure of 'autonomous reason,' or ultimately in the form of a tool (technology) that Europeans have and which we lack. Such a thought denies its situatedness in modernity because it never dares to admit that the 'essential' characteristics of modernity are crisis, change, disruption and negativity. In other words, the very thing that Europe possesses and we do not is the lack itself.

In order to realise the idea or spirit of modernity, we need subtraction (internalising the lack and paradox), not addition (filling the void). Modernity is produced by rupture. Even in Europe, autonomous reason was questioned during the evolution of philosophy, as a metaphysical surrogate for categories such as 'being,' 'substance' or 'God.' Modernity cannot be characterised by a pure rationality reliant on super-historical, scientific and epistemological bases (*mabāni*).

Modernity knows no basis but *the critical* (in both senses of the word, as criticism and as crisis). What makes up the modern is the internal gap and void of modernity itself. It is this critical aspect of modernity that joins us to the universal by separating us from any particular life, opinion, religion, and historical content. The reference of thought to the contemporary situation entails a continual return to critique, crisis, and rupture, and not to an autonomous subject or a fundamental rational project, even one presented within the framework of a consistent formal, normative system as in Kant and later Habermas.

As in Fichte's subjectivist idealism, the conditions of rationality and the bases of reason are simply the inquiry into the conditions of this rationality itself. Although this Kantian conception of reason has no particular content or metaphysical substance, it follows a formal, *a priori,* and transcendental consistency, which subjects it to the existing situation and system. For this reason, subjectivist idealism always leads to reformism. The existing system and capitalism itself act more radically than does formal Kantian-Habermasian thought in its movement toward universality. In its movement toward universality, such a formalist philosophy is always left behind by the existing system.

Well ahead of this kind of critique, capitalism itself generates more crisis, tension, rupture, conflict and negativity in the body of society and in the individual's mind and body. That is why capitalism easily incorporates any radical challenge or desire into itself. Thinking that is unable to understand universality in terms of a gap—a short circuit between the singular event and the true universal—but which tries to explain it in terms of a formal, *a priori* consistency, is more attached to all sorts of particular contents than capitalism, a system that easily transcends any given content.

This is why capitalism flourishes even in places like Saudi Arabia where there is not a single trace of Habermas's rational liberal democracy. It is able to dissolve and transform the particular content of any form of life or life-world. By contrast, Habermas's formal thought confronts, in its first encounter, the ambiguities of this particular Arabian way of life, challenging its formal principles and turning it into a merely reformist discourse: an impotent form of educated nagging that gradually moves toward an unrealisable ideal.

III

If, in line with Hegelian thought and Adorno's negative dialectics, we replace the hermeneutic paradigm with a paradigm derived from Lacanian psychoanalysis, structuralism, and poststructuralism, then any return to the historical situation of thought comes to signify a return to a gap or a void, rather than to a solid and complete identity. If we extend this insight to thought itself, which has translation as its primary metaphor, we will recognise that any thought that has its own situation as its point of departure is a thought that is chosen more than it chooses. It chooses what it already is as its identity, like a person or a subject whose freedom is defined as a forced choice based on a retroactive structure. This structure describes the shaping of the subject according to the mechanism of interpellation in its Althusserian sense.

However, in the context of this structure, our metaphor of translation is also raptured. As a result of all these points it becomes obvious that any concept or metaphor for translation must incorporate that gap and crisis into itself. We cannot simply put authentic thought, or what we have defined as deliberative translation, on top of a so-called non-deliberative translation that merely disseminates self-deception. If this internal gap exists, then any form of translation and any form of thought generates a fissured subject. This means that, according to Lacan, thought is always intermixed with misunderstanding in one way or another. *There is a lack of understanding at the heart of any understanding.* We fill this void or lack with fantasies or imagined stories. According to Lacan, truth is always structured like a fiction. Gadamer's hermeneutics ignores this gap at the heart of understanding, or in Freudian terms disavows it. He identifies truth with perfection and richness of meaning or with the accumulation of supplementary interpretations.

In this way, the metaphor of translation, as a centre that gathers everything into a consistent whole, falls apart. The vision of deliberative translation as the only mode of 'genuine thought' ceases to persuade. What was formerly excluded, namely non-deliberative translation, is made manifest again and then internalised. One reason for this is the process of repoliticisation that is the inevitable result of a risky dive into a situated thought.

In Badiou's philosophy, the concrete situation of thought is understood not as an epistemological system but in terms of a truth-procedure. This procedure begins with naming an event and remaining faithful to it. The subject is an effect and an aspect of this truth-procedure, not a thought that chooses 'freely.' The subject is chosen according to a structure similar to the experience of blessing; it is called by a voice or a vocation such as love, revolution, artistic creation, or scientific discovery. The subject is an effect of this choice and of this acceptance. The subject and its freedom are produced by an act through which we choose an identity we always had. We choose to be Iranians, Blacks, workers, activists, and leftist. We become, retroactively, subjects who enjoy these particular identities. Choosing reveals the potential of the subject. But in order to choose we must already be subjects.

There is no thinking subject without identity and situation. The act of choosing, of becoming a subject, is only possible in the context of a retrospective structure. However, this 'forced choice' in face of the vocation of history, this choosing to be what we have already been, testifies to the truth of freedom: the subject's identity is not natural, existential, substantial or innate. Rather, existence as such and its maintenance depend on a thought beyond language and the recognition of its 'objective conditions.'

As Mallarmé notes, any thought is a throw of dice. Therefore, the radical subject can maintain its thought as a 'logical revolt' by submitting to the risk. At this juncture, a person's being, or her 'passion and reason [*shur va sho'ur*],' becomes politicised. In the course of subjectification, we do not confront the transfer of knowledge through an education system. Rather, we confront a risk that already involves the danger of misunderstanding. Only by submitting to this constructive misunderstanding internal to itself can the subject move toward a comprehensive and correct understanding of the situation, in other words, toward truth. This conception of the structure of the subject, thought and truth places in a new perspective what we already criticised under the rubric of non-deliberative translation. Bearing this in mind, we should critically examine books such as Babak Ahmadi's *Structure and Interpretation of the Text* (*Sākhtār va ta'vil-e matn*), but this time without foregrounding the category of 'non-deliberative translation' in our critique.[15] The aim of this return is to remove the ambiguity and one-sidedness latent in this category. It does not aim to moderate or dilute the radical nature of our previous criticism. The positive role of such books in education and knowledge expansion among a particular class of readers necessitates a new interpretation of their historical function.

Now with regard to the new sense of translation as a thought containing a void and inner gap, and according to the dialectical relation between understanding and misunderstanding in a particular situation, it can be argued that thinking based on non-deliberative translation has been more effective than what we imagined. Unlike the hermeneutic judgement that prioritised felicitous and deliberative translations, non-deliberative translation has opened up new spaces and introduced new forms for thought. However, we aim to go beyond recognising the productivity of misunderstanding or than insisting on irrelevant notions of fidelity to the original. In the hermeneutic framework, the dialectic of understanding and misunderstanding becomes an ontological structure, which plays the role of a Hegelian synthesis in this transformation. This synthesis automatically imposes unity, homogeneity, and peace on the historical situation.

Despite affirming misunderstanding in the context of the historical evolution of understanding, Gadamer ultimately subjects this evolution to an ahistorical universality. What is lost here is the concrete and historical quality of thought, the situatedness that goes beyond the subject in complexity and breadth. Risk-taking and fidelity to an unrealised and unfinished truth disappear. In other words, everything that highlights the political nature of thought as a risky act, everything that is perceived as an uncanny, new and incomprehensible rupture, is hereby erased.

From this point of view, the main problem of non-deliberative translation is not their misunderstanding and hastiness compared to deliberative, perfect and clear translation. Rather, it is the veiling of this political aspect of thought. Concrete thought resembles a performative sentence or a promise more closely than an affirmative sentence, the truth or falsity of which can be determined at any moment through empirical verification. The attempt to prove *truth as an enunciation* (*qowl*) exposes thought to all the gaps, misunderstandings, complexities, paradoxes and voids implied in the historical situation as well as to the possible emergence of an event on the margins of this void. The principal meaning of being concretely situated is precisely this.

This new conception of the relation between thought and translation, and the dialectic of understanding and misunderstanding, is a product of altered social circumstances and the new emphasis on the political dimension of speculative thought. Throughout the 1990s and the early 2000s, as the reformist movement and its fervid political stances transformed our historical situation, even a radical theoretical discourse could be efficacious as a manifestation of open-mindedness on the margins of the reformist movement. Back then, it was not necessary for a theoretical discourse to directly address the political situation, for the density and attraction of political change, struggles for power, and different types of political passions were adequate to facilitate the rapid transformation of any theoretical discourse into journalism.

In this period, theory could play a more critical role by distancing itself from the political scene, rather than directly addressing political problems. Marginal translation projects, or so-called 'cultural work [kar-e farhangi],' could nurture radical critique, or at least prepare the ground for it. Translation projects introduced new texts and concepts into Iranian culture. This kind of thought could as well be a preliminary but effective form of radical politics thanks to the dynamism of the reformist movement.

However, after the collapse of the reformist movement, Iranian society became more and more de-politicised. We witnessed a convergence between theory and politics: politics, especially radical politics, increasingly took refuge in theory. Meanwhile, following the principle already discussed, theory—that is, theory as a form of situated thought related to translation, that does not consider translation as a return to a perfect, homogeneous, riskless thought—became more and more political, in form as well as in content.

To what extent is this new situation different from earlier periods? For previous periods, we distinguished between deliberative and non-deliberative translations. How to distinguish one theoretical project from another when we believe even a deliberative translation contains a gap of misunderstanding or unconsciousness? So long as theory links itself to truth, it presents itself epistemologically as a kind of tension or rupture rather than as a positive force or a visible measure of progress. Truth lies beyond representation within the present situation. We must change the existing epistemological paradigm in order to make the representation of this truth possible.

This reveals the indeterminacy and inconsistency at the heart of the project of radical thought, and of this new conception of thought/translation. A rupture in the existing epistemological system can be minute, like a small change in point of view that displaces everything. What was irrelevant suddenly becomes an important problem. Thus, what is chosen is based on a judgement or decision that cannot be proven within the framework of an existing epistemological paradigm. Any justification for this decision must remain faithful to the thought it evokes and maintain the rational consistency of this thought and the universality of truths that are raised by it. This justification has a retrospective structure.

As far as the distinctions between all theories are concerned, everything depends on how these discourses—whether as translated originals (tarjoma-ye ta'lifi) or simply as translations (tarjoma)—function: whether they try to cover up and fill in this inner void with mythological and ideological narratives, or not. The ideological nature of these discourses derives from their conformity to prevailing conditions. Radical thought is indeterminate; it separates itself, fundamentally, from the big Other, or the symbolic realm, which is always contaminated with risk and ambiguity.

Ideological thought or thought/translation does not reveal its inner misunderstanding or gap. It does not preserve this gap as a productive tension at the heart of theory or theoretical act. Rather, it covers up this gap with an ideological narrative that is both delusional and demagogic. The main difference between all theoretical discourses lies in what they conceal. This is not a celebration of the infinite set of postmodern differences that can justify the existence of anything and everything. In fact, the affirmation of ambiguity and difference in the form of postmodernist infinite multiplicity can be an ideological strategy for getting along with the chaotic and fluid space of modern capitalism.

As Badiou suggests, philosophy should distance itself from the fluid circulation of perceptions, imaginations, information, opinions, and beliefs that constitute modern capitalist discourse. Can this discourse highlight its unresolved tension or gap? In psychoanalysis, what is defined as law, what Lacan calls the name of the father, always has an ideological role. There is no hidden repressed desire somewhere 'inside' us. To the contrary, the desire we experience in the disguise of a denied fantasy is a veil that resolves tension and covers up the gap; it hides the hole produced by the trauma of encountering the other and the mystery of the other's desire. In Lacanian psychoanalysis this scar or gap that tears apart our 'natural and innate' order is called 'symbolic castration.' This castration makes desire possible and makes us capable of desire. The perverse and digressive nature of desire (*meyl*) is affirmed in language through its links to passion and perversion (*māyel*). The inscription or the trace of the unconscious is a gap and rupture on the surface, not a hidden treasure inside. The unconscious is the discourse of the other. In order to discover it, one must look at the other.

The Lacanian structure of the subject resembles Kant's description of the transcendental subject. In Kantian philosophy what makes objective experience possible and consistent is what can never be experienced. What makes us ethical subjects in search of infinite good and evil is breaking with our natural desires. Kant's transcendental subject, like Lacan's notion of fantasy, is a veil that turns our sense data into a consistent image of reality at the same time as it covers our inner void or lack of essence, namely, our lack of access to our own noumenal reality.

The above points can be summarized as follows. By proposing translation as the only true form of thought in our age, we aim to make thought return to its historical and concrete situation. We also move away from abstract negation to determinate negation, a movement that conditions the attainment of truth and radical critical theory. This movement involves two stages. In the first stage, which I described with the help of Gadamerian hermeneutics, the abstract narcissism of thought is disrupted by the idea of translation. This stage can be described by the formula thought/translation. But this formula leaves dichotomies and polarities intact and reproduces them in a new framework. We must bear in mind that 'situation,' 'concretisation,' and even 'thought' and 'translation' are themselves mere abstractions.

Overcoming the abstraction of thought depends on a constant action at the heart of thought itself, the act of driving every concept towards its ultimate and dialectical limits, where it will overcome its abstract stagnation through the mediation of its opposite. However, the risk of falling into abstraction is always there. This risk can never be overcome in an absolute and *a priori* way. Situatedness also means partaking of the ambiguity of the situation. Removing this ambiguity depends on the evolution of the situation itself and also preserving thought's openness and sensitivity to a changing situation.

The formula thought/translation entails both overcoming the abstraction and recognising the danger of falling into it again. In the first stage, the dialectical concept of translation—understood as the negative, the tension, or the inner gap within modern thought—was mistakenly defined as something substantial. This only reproduced the abstract nature of thought in the form of the opposition between deliberative and non-deliberative translation. This opposition, itself an effect of the hermeneutic interpretation of the metaphor of translation that prevailed during the reformist movement, once again distorted our historical understanding of the situation and the situatedness of thought. Transforming the metaphor of translation, indicated by the turn to Lacanian theory, was a reaction to this problem. This transformation can be most clearly and succinctly formulated as follows:

Thought/translation → deliberative translation/non-deliberative translation → ~~thought-translation~~

In our new post-reformist period, the convergence of politics and theory amid the general depoliticisation and intensification of theory leaves no doubt that reflection on how to internalise the so-called objective and external paradoxes of translation as thought—or how to move from thought/translation to ~~thought/translation~~—is essential to any form of critical theory that pursues radical politics under present conditions.

Related topics

Translators as Organic Intellectuals; The Political Modes of Translation in Iran; Theory, Practice, Activism.

Notes

1 For a literal rendering of Farhadpour's text, see https://transactivism.hcommons.org/supplementary-material/.
2 Gould, Rebecca Ruth and Kayvan Tahmasebian (forthcoming) 'Translation as Alienation: Sufi Hermeneutics and Literary Modernism in Bijan Elahi's Translations,' *Modernism/Modernity* (currently available at: http://dx.doi.org/10.17613/y35x-ah23).
3 The idea of prismatic translation is first introduced in Reynolds, Matthew (2016) *Translation: A Very Short Introduction* (Oxford: Oxford University Press), 87.
4 Reynolds, Matthew (2019) 'Introduction,' in *Prismatic Translation,* ed. Matthew Reynolds (London: Legenda), 1.
5 Reynolds, 'Introduction,' 2.
6 'Ruzgar bar vefq-e morād,' *E'temad*, no.3771 [online] 16 March 2017. Available at: www.etemadnewspaper.ir/1395/12/26/Main/PDF/13951226-3771-7-6.pdf (This is an anonymous report of a meeting with Farhadpour).
7 See, respectively, Mirsepassi, Ali (2017) *Transnationalism in Iranian Political Thought: The Life and Times of Ahmad Fardid* (New York: Cambridge University Press); Soroush, Abdulkarim (2009) *The Expansion of Prophetic Experience: Essays on Historicity, Contingency and Plurality in Religion* (Leiden: Brill); and Tabataba'i, Sayyid Muhammad Husayn (2012) *Kernel of the Kernel: Concerning the Wayfaring and Spiritual Journey of the People of Intellect (Risāla-yi lubb al-lubāb dar sayr wa sulūk-i ulu'l albāb): A Shi'i Approach to Sufism* (Albany: SUNY Press).
8 Farhadpour, Morad (2009) 'Hāydeger: enqelābi-ye mortaje' (Heidegger: A Reactionary Revolutionary),' in *Para-hā-ye fekr (falsafa va siyāsat)* (Fragments of Thought: Philosophy and Politics) (Tehran: Tarh-i now), 97–125.
9 See Farhadpour, Morad (2003) *Bādhā-ye gharbi* (Western Winds) (Tehran: Hermes Publishing House).
10 Farhadpour refers to Rimbaud's phrase '*il faut être absolument moderne,*' in *A Season in Hell and Illuminations*, trans. and ed. Bertrand Mathieu (Rochester: BOA Editions, 1991), 53 (bilingual edition) [translators' note].
11 For further on this distinction, see Babich, Babette (2017) *Hermeneutic Philosophies of Social Science* (Berlin and Boston: Walter de Gruyter), 227 [translators' note].
12 Gadamer, Hans Georg (1975) *Truth and Method* (New York: New York Seabury Press), 278.

13 The author refers here to Benjamin, Walter (2002) *Arcades Project* (Cambridge: The Belknap Press). N3.1, 463 [translators' note].
14 The author refers her to the theories of Jalal Al-e Ahmad and Ali Shariʿati, discussed in the biographical sketch above. For a relevant discussion, see Davari, Arash (2014) 'A Return to Which Self?: ʿAli Shariʿati and Frantz Fanon on the Political Ethics of Insurrectionary Violence,' *Comparative Studies of South Asia, Africa, and the Middle East* 34 (1): 86–105 [translators' note].
15 Ahmadi, Babak (1991) *Structure and Interpretation of the Text* (*Sākhtār va taʾvil-e matn*) (Tehran: Markaz). It is one of the first books to introduce Iranian readers to modern European theories of reading, including hermeneutics, structuralism, and poststructuralism.

Further reading

Soroush, Abdolkarim (2009) *The Expansion of Prophetic Experience: Essays on Historicity, Contingency and Plurality in Religion*. Tr. Nilou Mobasser and Forough Jahanbakhsh. Leiden: Brill.

A much-debated contribution to Iranian religious intellectualism containing Soroush's programme for reforming Islamic traditionalism. Soroush argues in this work for a number of compromises between Islam and modernity.

Berman, Marshall (1982) *All That Is Solid Melts into Air: The Experience of Modernity*. New York: Simon and Schuster.

A seminal study of modernist aesthetics. Translated into Persian by Farhadpour and foundational to his efforts to theorise modernity in an Iranian context.

Horkheimer, Max, and Theodor W. Adorno (1969 [1944]) *Dialectic of Enlightenment*. Tr. John Cumming. New York: Herder and Herder.

A key text of the Frankfurt School and the most complete statement of Horkeimer and Adorno's critique of industrial modernity. Horkeimer and Adorno trace the rise of fascism in the middle of the twentieth century to shifts in relations of production.

Benjamin, Walter (1999 [1982]) *The Arcades Project*. Tr. Howard Eiland and Kevin McLaughlin. Cambridge: Harvard University Press.

Benjamin's posthumously published manuscript, compiled between 1927 and 1940, documenting the texture of modern urban life in the form of collage. This palimpsestial work has served as an allegory for translation for many theorists.

5

Translating Marx in Japan

Yoshimoto Taka'aki and Japanese Marxism

Manuel Yang

In 2008, as a central component of my PhD dissertation at the University of Toledo, I translated *Karl Marx*, a historically important intervention in Japanese Marxism by the radical thinker Yoshimoto Taka'aki (or Ryūmei, as he was known during the 1960s). Yoshimoto was a major poet, critic, theorist of language, culture, and state, who was at the centre of Japanese intellectual debates during the second half of the twentieth century. I discovered his work accidentally on the shelf of Perry Casteñeda Library at the University of Texas, as an undergraduate student, when I was studying Marx with Harry Cleaver, the autonomist Marxist economist who co-translated Antonio Negri's *Marx Beyond Marx* (1984) and undertook solidarity work for the 1994 Zapatista uprising (much of it involving translating political materials from multiple languages into English for the listserv Chiapas95). Cleaver introduced me to Peter Linebaugh's *The London Hanged* (1991), a sweeping history of capitalism, capital punishment, and class struggle of the condemned. Reading it propelled me to pursue my graduate studies with its author and move to the 'Interior,' or the American Midwest, in 1998.

Cleaver was an American New Left student activist who took part in the civil rights and anti-Vietnam-War movements. So was Linebaugh, who participated in the 1968 general strike at Columbia University, whose local Students for a Democratic Society (SDS) invited E.P. Thompson, a leading voice of the British New Left and social historian, who pioneered 'history from below,' to speak at their gathering. Thompson lectured on William Blake on that occasion and, years later, recalled the encounter thus:

> In 1968 I gave an early lecture on Blake at Columbia University (in New York City), at a time of excitement when some sort of campus revolution against the Moral Law was going on, and I startled the audience by acclaiming William Blake as 'the founder of the obscure sect to which I myself belong, the Muggletonian Marxists'. Instantly I found that many fellow-sectaries were in the room.
>
> *(Thompson 1993b: xx–xxi)*

This meeting prompted Linebaugh, an SDS member, to sail across the Atlantic to work with Thompson at Warwick University, write his PhD dissertation on the struggle of the criminalised working class, and, after returning to the United States in the mid-1970s, engage in activism with prison inmates in the wake of rebellion at Attica Corrections Facility, a crucial experience that he needed to revise his dissertation into the manuscript of *The London Hanged*. From Linebaugh and Thompson, I learned not only that, in Thompson's words, '[r]adical history ... must be as good as history can be' (Thompson 1993a: 364) but also, as with Cleaver's example, that activism and scholarship can be organically and passionately connected, sharpening each other's focus and drawing a different kind of collective, intellectual energy from each other.

Hence there was a certain political and historical sense in taking up Yoshimoto as the subject of my graduate research. He was born in the same year as Edward Thompson, in 1934, deeply influenced by Marx, and, also like Thompson, had a huge hand in the making of the New Left, albeit in Japan. Both were poets who criticized an economically determinist, state-centred version of Marxism and reread Marx through their experiences of war, working-class life, popular consciousness. Thompson affirmed the agency of workers and commoners in his historical work, drawing from the revolutionary Romantic poetics of Blake and Wordsworth. Yoshimoto's poetry, which combined existential and intellectual insights out of his proletarian experience into a distinctively contemporary form, became a leading work of the so-called modernist 'Wasteland' [*Arechi-ha*] poets, whose major motif was the renewal of human agency in the face of destruction. Can we speak of a 'global New Left' that crisscrossed the Atlantic and the Pacific, linking America, Europe, and Asia through the power of poetic imagination and activist social energy (see Chapter 4)? If so, what are its historical characteristics and what would be its common vocabulary, literally and ideologically? These questions rose to my mind at the time, no doubt, because, in the immediate aftermath of the 1999 World Trade Organization protest in Seattle, as I was witnessing the rise of anti-globalisation or global justice movement, I was also perusing the manuscript of *The Many-Headed Hydra* (2000) (which Linebaugh co-authored with Marcus Rediker, historian of pirates and slave ships), a history recovering the hidden and lost connections among global, trans-Atlantic revolutionary forces from the seventeenth to the eighteenth centuries. I started to wonder how we might start piecing together a global history of social struggles in our own times in a similar vein, retrieving hidden, lost connections among participants who may not have been even aware of each other's existence (which appears to be the case with Yoshimoto and Thompson).

A passage in the Introduction to *The Many Headed-Hydra* mentions the activist role of translators in forging history from below:

> The power of numbers was expanded by movement, as the hydra journeyed and voyaged or was banished or dispersed in diaspora, carried by the winds and the waves beyond the boundaries of the nation-state. Sailors, pilots, felons, lovers, translators, musicians, mobile workers of all kinds made new and unexpected connections, which variously appeared to be accidental, contingent, transient, even miraculous.
>
> *(Linebaugh and Rediker 2000: 6)*

Although Linebaugh and Rediker are here talking about the multitude of insurrectionary and revolutionary activities that circulated from the mutiny of the sailors of the shipwrecked *Sea-Venture*, which inspired Shakespeare's *The Tempest* (1611), to the 1640s English Revolution to the Irish, American, and Caribbean rebellions of the late eighteenth century, their statement may just as well apply to the later period of capitalist modernisation in the nineteenth and twentieth centuries, when the subalterns of Africa, Asia, and the Middle East experienced imperialism first-hand and organised massive anti-colonial movements against their European rulers, fuelled by the efforts of activists who were 'banished or dispersed in diaspora, carried by the winds and the waves beyond the boundaries of the nation-state' (Linebaugh and Rediker 2000: 6). Translation became a vector of intense social antagonism in this historical context, both as a means of domination, to propagate the virtues of Western imperialism and its modernising effects, and as a means of liberation, to share dissent and mobilise popular forces against imperialist and economic exploitation.

Origins of modern Japan and translating Karl Marx

When Japan embarked on a full-fledged process of capitalist state development after 1871, as the modern Meiji government displaced the feudal Tokugawa regime, translation functioned as a critical node of this capitalist modernisation, virtually in all spheres of scientific knowledge and cultural expression. In this period of intra-imperialist rivalry, Japan sought to escape the assault of Western imperialist domination, as it befell South and Southeast Asia as well as China, by becoming an imperialist power itself. The intellectual rationales for its domestic modernisation and foreign colonisation of Korea, Taiwan, Manchuria, and other parts of East Asia were partly supplied by Eurocentric theories of racialism, social Darwinism, and historical stages, drawn from translation and extrapolation of Herbert Spencer, John Stuart Mills, Jean-Jacques Rousseau, and Adam Smith. The first translations of Karl Marx's writings also appeared during this halcyon period of Japanese capitalism.

Tymoczko has noted 'Western imperialism' to be a 'dominant ideological perspective' that renders 'most [Western] statements about translation that date before the demise of positivism … relatively useless for current theorizing about translation' and argued for the need to develop a non-Eurocentric translation theory, doing away with Eurocentric presuppositions 'based on Greco-Roman textual traditions, Christian values, nationalistic views about the relationship between language and cultural identity, and an upper-class emphasis on technical expertise and literacy' (Tymoczko 2006: 14–15). While her call for exploring plurilingual/pluricultural life, oral cultures, diverse textual categories, translation processes in other cultures, non-professional translators, non-Western meanings of translation, and relationships between text and translation, as ways of combating such Eurocentric assumptions are suggestive, in understanding the historical function of translation in modern Japan it is crucial to study what it has historically absorbed from West European and American forms of capitalism, namely, industrial labour-discipline, mechanisation, and computerisation of the publishing industry, commodified mechanisms of global market exchange and consumerism, and international copyright laws. This is because the very process of modernisation, which is none other than what Marxists conventionally theorised as the problem of 'transition from feudalism to capitalism,' invariably involves 'Westernisation' to some degree, homogenising production and culture— including that of translation and publication—to a high degree. Hence contemporary Japanese and British translators have more in common with each other in terms of translation cultures and practices than they do with their preindustrial predecessors, and any serious comparative theory of contemporary translation will have to take into account the existing global capitalist system and its overwhelming impact on the transformation of translation in order to carefully parse its regional and cultural differences.

Japanese translation of Marx was as much a product of such globalising effect of capitalist development as it was a response to it. We can divide the history of Japanese Marxist translation into four phases: early socialism (1871–1923); interwar Marxist social science (1924–1938); post-war Japanese Communist Party (JCP) hegemony (1945–1955); and heterodox and New Left dispensation (1956–1975). The period of early Japanese socialism is characterised by its inchoate, robust radical social energy, located as it was during the incipient moments of primary accumulation, when peasant landholding was expropriated through the privatising *chiso kaisei* (land tax reform) policy and common sacred spaces were enclosed and integrated by the state into a vehicle of emperor-centred state Shinto. Various kinds of unique ideological hybridisation and rapid political conversion took place in a short span of time. For example, Abe Isō (1865–1949), Ikuta Chōkō (1882–1936), Takabatake Motoyuki (1886–1928), Kawakami Hajime (1879–1946)—major figures of early Japanese socialism who produced uneven translations of Marx's *Capital* (1867)—all underwent a concatenation of intellectual and political conversions that ran the gamut of Christianity, liberalism, Marxism, and anarchism. In the case of Takabatake, who translated Karl Kautsky's *The Economic Doctrines of Karl Marx* (1887) in 1919 and completed the first Japanese version of *Das Kapital*, volumes 1–3, in 1919–1925, the final political terminus was the rightwing stance of patriotic national socialism. Sakai Toshihiko (1871–1933) and Kōtoku Shūsui (1871–1911) are representative figures of this period as well, both founding editors of *The Commoners' Newspaper* (*Heimin shinbun*), a radical left periodical whose wide influence far exceeded its short run from 1903 to 1905. *The Commoners' Newspaper* printed Katayama and Kōtoku's first Japanese abridged translation of *The Communist Manifesto* (1848) from Samuel Aveling Moore's English version, using down-to-earth, if not entirely accurate, language to recast Marx and Engels' political program on the eve of the 1848 European revolution to accentuate its relevance for an East Asian agrarian island society going through the throes of enclosure of the commons and industrial exploitation of labour. What the early Japanese socialists may have lacked in linguistic and theoretical sophistication, they more than made up for in their practical revolutionary activism that was as spontaneously creative and hybrid as it was short-lived, destroyed by state violence: Kōtoku was executed on the trumped-up conspiracy charge of an attempted assassination of the emperor ('The Great Treason Case'), alongside eleven fellow militants, in 1911. Katayama escaped a similar fate only because, at the time, he was still serving a two-year sentence for his part in the 1908 'Red Flag Incident' in which radicals attending a welcoming party for the journalist Yamaguchi Koken (who had been imprisoned for fourteen months for writing an article entitled 'Kick Your Mother and Father' criticising the feudal family structure and had just been released) took to the streets and waved red banners that said 'Anarcho-Communism,' 'Socialism,' and 'Socialist Revolution,' shouting 'Long live the anarcho-communist revolution!' These activists laid the foundation of Japanese radical politics and disseminated anarchist, socialist, and Marxist ideas as an organic part of their revolutionary practice.

Although the shift from early Japanese socialism to interwar Marxist social science, which reached its apogee during the 1930s in the celebrated 'debate on the Japanese capitalism [*Nihon shihon-shugi ronsō*],' is not entirely discrete, it emerged in the vacuum left behind by the state repression of leftwing political activities, including The Great Treason Case and the June 1923 arrest of activists who were in contact with the Communist International (Comintern), preparing the grounds for the organisation of the JCP. Those Marxist activists, economists, and writers associated with the non-Communist magazine *Rōnō*

(*Workers and Peasants*), who viewed Japan as having already achieved a bourgeois revolution in the Meiji period, calling for the formation of a mass anti-bourgeois political party and for a single-stage socialist revolution that was not beholden to Russian Leninist or German social democratic model but based on uniquely Japanese socioeconomic conditions, came to be called Rōnō-ha; they formed the political antecedents to the leftwing current of the post-war Japan Socialist Party (JSP). Opposed to the Rōnō-ha and closely following the Comintern's directives were the Kōza-ha ('Lecture Faction') Marxists, so named because of their multi-authored seven-volume *Lectures on the History of Japanese Capitalist Development* published in 1932–1933 by Iwanami Shoten Publishers, which would become an important promoter of post-war Japanese democracy after World War II. Kōza-ha deemed Japan's simultaneously semi-feudal and semi-capitalist society as necessitating a two-stage revolution, a bourgeois-democratic one that would sweep away its feudal remnants, most especially entrenched in the absolutist emperor system, before it could undergo a socialist transformation. In order to empirically prove these two seemingly marginal doctrinal differences in Marxist theory of historical stages, a considerable amount of social and economic data was collected, sifted, and marshaled in theoretically pathbreaking arguments, and some of the most important foundations of Japanese social science were laid. As Andrew Barshay put it summarily:

> Ultimately, Marxism's claim to synonymity with social science derived from its analysis of Japanese society itself, one that reflected—but in important ways transcended—all the tensions and problems just described. Its chief contribution took the form of the 'debate on Japanese capitalism' that ran from the late 1920s to the late 1930s. Occasioned by political disagreements over revolutionary goals and strategy, its task was the historical characterization of the developmental process of Japanese capitalism and the modern state.
>
> *(Barshay 2004: 55)*

In retrospect, the so-called 'debate on Japanese capitalism' is not without its obvious faults: crudely stadialist conception of capitalist development, failure to grasp the historical significance and variety of the Japanese commons, reliance on a singularly developmentalist logic, analytical absence of popular social agency, and culturally refined concept of class. However, despite these shortcomings, the echoes of the debate would resonate throughout post-war Japan, given their earnest collective effort to liberate historical and social research from the realm of nationalist myth-making and bring to it, with all its ideological and stadialist limitations, a rational, empirical analysis grounded in revolutionary commitment.

Significant impetus for the debate stemmed from the collective translation of Marx's writings, the publication of which became embroiled in a bidding war divided along Kōza-ha and Rōnō-ha lines. The translation associated with the Kōza-ha, with the official approval of the JCP, was planned by the combined force of Iwanami and four other publishers, with the cooperation of the Ōhara Institute of Social Research, Japan's oldest social science research organisation founded in 1919 by Ōhara Magosaburō, the CEO of the textile company Kurano Industries, Chūgoku Hydroelectric Company, and Chūgoku Association Bank. However, through negotiations with David Riazanov, the founder of the USSR's Marx-Engels Institute and editor of Marx and Engel's original writings, the scholars affiliated with Rōnō-ha managed to secure the translation rights and published their effort in twenty-nine volumes by Kaizō-sha in 1928–1933 and 1935. This was the edition Yoshimoto

Taka'aki read in the aftermath of World War II, the primary source for his 1963 *Karl Marx*. With the mass arrest of Kōza-ha scholars who wrote *Lectures on the History of Japanese Capitalist Development* in the 1936 'Com-Academy Case' and of non-Communist Marxist and socialist scholars of Rōnō-ha in the 1937/1938 'Popular Front Case,' the largely academic debate of Marxist social science was cut short.

Post-war Japanese Marxism, Yoshimoto Taka'aki's reading of Marx, and the New Left

With Japan's defeat in World War II, some of the Kōza-ha and Rōnō-ha Marxists restructured their positions under the respective aegis of the JCP and the JSP, putting together a series of research projects and publications which established the framework of post-war Japanese social science and contributed considerably to the formulation of public policy. While its lines of investigation diversified and public influence widened, what Marxist scholarship gained in number and institutional presence, it lost in its susceptibility to shifting ideological dictates and tended to prioritise political expediency within party politics over actually existing class struggles. These limitations were, of course, implicit from the outset in the original debate, as it was a discourse for and by intellectuals, anchored in an idealised image of the Soviet state, assuming capitalist economic development as an invariable and necessary stage in the transition to socialism—limitations which turned into stultifying constrictions, once the earlier historical context of nascent industrial capitalism and emperor-centred authoritarian state had transformed into one of fully developed industrial-consumerist capitalism and parliamentary democratic state under US military hegemony. In other words, what had originally been a critical method of analyzing the origin and contradictions of Japanese capitalism had become an instrument of enforcing and stabilising its dominant rule, not least of all the dictates of authoritarian power structure. Yoshimoto Taka'aki considered both of these major currents of the Old Left as ideologically limited, the Rōnō-ha/JSP line representing a nationalist agrarianism that set the limit of Japanese liberalism and the Kōza-ha/JCP line a quasi-internationalism that slavishly followed the authority of the Third International, neither able to respond meaningfully to the subsequent post-industrial, financialised development of Japanese capitalism (Yoshimoto 2002: 120–122).

Nowhere is this institutional co-optation clearer than in the two veterans of Rōnō-ha Marxism and major ideologues of the left wing of the JSP, Ōuchi Hyōe (1888–1980) and Sakisaka Itsurō (1897–1985). Their translation of *The Communist Manifesto*, still in print since 1951, is the most widely read Japanese version of Marx and Engels's most famous political tract. Sakisaka, professor at Kyushū University, had a leading role in editing and translating the Kaizō edition of Marx and Engels's works and was the primary editor of the fourteen-volume *Collected Works of Marx/Engels* (*Marukusu/Engerusu senshū*), published by Shinchō-sha in 1956–1962. Ōuchi taught economics at Tokyo University, served as a president of Hōsei University, and, given his paramount role in advising the Bank of Japan, was repeatedly asked by post-war administrations of Hatoyama Ichirō and Yoshida Shigeru to assume the position of minister of finance, which he refused. His pupil Arisawa Hiromi worked in the Yoshida cabinet to implement the 'priority production system,' enhancing post-war industrial development through emphasis on steel and coal production, and later led the way in building nuclear power, as the chairman of the Japan Atomic Industrial Forum. The premise of Ōuchi and Sakisaka's Marxist economics was industrial capitalist development, which they helped facilitate at the level of both theory and policy.

Sakisaka, with whom Ōuchi headed the Socialist Association, a theoretical research group that heavily influenced the JSP's political orientation, took an active role in teaching Marx's *Capital* to the JSP labour activists involved in the historic 1960 Miike coal miners' strike. He also drafted the 'Socialist Association Thesis' in the late 1960s, which was adopted as the Association's mission statement expressing support for the Socialist bloc, class struggle against Japanese monopoly capital, 'dictatorship of the proletariat' by peaceful means. For both Sakisaka and Ōuchi, 'socialism' meant a variant of Marxist-Leninist state socialism and they took the side of the Soviet state in the repression of the 1956 Hungarian Revolution and 1968 Prague Spring. Moreover, Sakisaka was not above uttering homophobic statements, as when, during a dialogue with the gay activist Tōgō Ken, he informed him that his 'sickness' of being homosexual would be cured under Soviet socialism and warned the publisher Shōgakkan that he would never agree to an interview if they ever brought 'such a perverted man' into his presence again (Tōgō 2002: 164–165).

Preceding Sakisaka's 1956–1962 Shinchō-sha translation of Marx and Engels, the most ambitious post-war translation project was undertaken by the JCP's Marxist-Leninism Research Institute, which presided over the twenty-three-volume *Collected Works of Marx-Engels* (*Marukusu-Engerusu senshū*). Ōtsuki-shoten published them in 1949–1952 and, seven years later in October 1959, commenced publishing the most authoritative and referenced translation of the fifty-three-volume *Marx-Engels Werke*, popularly known as *Maru-En zenshū* (an abbreviation for *The Complete Works of Marx-Engels*), and continued to do so for the next thirty-two years. Given its significant, if ideologically circumscribed, contributions to Marxist scholarship and extensive political influence over social movements, the JCP had a hegemonic role in determining post-war intellectual discourse and fared no better than the JSP in terms of its general authoritarian conformism and developmentalist ideology; in fact, its party discipline was arguably even more restrictive, dominant, and divisive in setting the parameters of left politics, given its close and unstable relationship with other members of the Comintern, particularly the USSR and People's Republic of China (PRC). The establishment of the PRC in 1949 became the basis of the historic factionalism that tore the party apart in the early 1950s. Seeing the revolutionary success of the PRC in the geographic proximity of East Asia prompted some JCP activists to try their hand at organising Maoist-style guerrilla warfare in the rural areas. They constituted a, more or less, nationalist-oriented current called Shokan-ha (Impression Faction); they were opposed by a current called Kokusai-ha (International Faction) that affiliated themselves with the USSR and advocated a parliamentary path to socialism.

The factionalist division within the JCP demoralised a generation of activists and demonstrated the ill effects of its authoritarian party structure, which distorted genuine popular revolutionary aspirations through the prism of idealised ideologies imported from abroad. As the prewar 'debate on Japanese capitalism,' the very theoretical framework of which was laid down by the Comintern's 1927 and 1932 theses on Japan, was departing the realm of debate and entering into the contradictory terrain of real capitalism and working-class life, JCP's pretension as the party of popular democratic revolution became increasingly unsustainable. It was this glaring failure to ground intellectual activity in popular consciousness, to instead forcibly impose on the latter foreign translations of Marxism under the guise of revolutionary indoctrination, which offended Yoshimoto Taka'aki, who had no experience of prewar left politics (which had been all but suppressed by the time he came of age during the war), and instigated him to reason against the Pharisees of the Old Left.

Yoshimoto was a true believer in the Japanese war effort, for which he was prepared to die, as did so many other working-class youths like him, ultimately for the sake of the emperor. When this rationale fell apart at the end of World War II, Yoshimoto had to confront why he had found it so personally convincing in the first place. When he heard the emperor's radio announcement declaring the Japanese surrender, why did a profound sadness come over him, choking him up when he went for a swim afterwards (Yoshimoto 1994: 123)? Why could he not shake off a sense of embarrassment at the sight of returning soldiers who had sworn they would fight to the bitter end but instead were scrounging for their next meal for themselves and their families?

No less bewildering was the discrepancy between the wartime propaganda of *kichiku beiei* (American and British demonic beasts) and the actual conduct of the American soldiers stationed in Japan during the occupation. Prior to the commencement of the occupation, Yoshimoto and many others fled Tokyo for the countryside, fearing the invading Americans would massacre the men and rape the women, as they had been led to believe by wartime propaganda. When this did not happen and Yoshimoto returned to the city, he was surprised to find ill-disciplined GIs carousing with women in the streets and Supreme Commander for the Allied Powers (SCAP) making regular public announcements regarding its policies. He keenly felt that the Japanese had been defeated not so much by the Americans' overwhelming technological power but by the Americans' unruly democratic culture and individualism.

This post-war experience of defeat, along with the subsequent one of failed labour union activism and that of the 1960 anti-Anpo (US–Japan Mutual Security Agreement) struggle, marked the formation of Yoshimoto's political thought and underwrote his radically distinctive way of reading Marx. What Yoshimoto witnessed in the brief interlude between the Japanese defeat in the war and the establishment of US occupation was a society without a state, a society out of which emerged spontaneous forms of mutual aid and associations, along with free individual expressions of nihilism, decadence, survival— something that was utterly inconceivable under the rule of the wartime state, which dictated the strictest discipline over everyday life, including language, cultural expression, and personal behaviour, according to the absolutist ideology of the emperor. This was the crucial moment when he realised, contra the Hegelian view, that 'society is far larger and the state is smaller in comparison' (Yoshimoto Taka'aki Kenkyūkai 2001: 68).

However, for such an existential insight to take full-fledged theoretical form a decade later in *Communal Illusion* (1968), backed by creative close reading of mythological texts and customary social practices, it was necessary for Yoshimoto to cross the 'river of fire,' to borrow William Morris's famous phrase in describing his political conversion, in the factory and in the streets. After the war, Yoshimoto joined the rank-and-file working class in Tokyo, hopping from one precarious, low-paid job to another and doing his best to make use of the knowledge of chemistry he had picked up in college. An important turning point was his experience at the Seito ink plant, where he headed a labour union to demand basic improvements in working conditions according to the newly legislated labour law. The sudden ostracism Yoshimoto faced at his workplace in the wake of his failed labour activism drove him to eventually leave his job and, more importantly, explore the merciless 'ethic of rebellion' (the subtitle of 'An Essay on Book of Mathieu [*Machiu-sho shiron*]' (1954)—Yoshimoto's choice of the French phonetic spelling was meant to distinguish it as a non-religious intervention) through a secular, political reading of the Gospel According to Matthew. In the aftermath of the war, he had briefly attended a Christian church, where he learned much but also felt an enormous discrepancy between the religiously formalised, sanctimonious services and the ruthlessly uncompromising, combative ethical worldview expressed in the New Testament, especially the Gospel of Matthew. Yoshimoto explored the latter as a way to confront the existential, philosophical meaning of the labour struggle he had just undergone in 'An Essay on Book of Mathieu,' declaring:

> Human beings can believe in revolutionary thought while walking cunningly through the system and can also despise revolutionary thought as they are forced to defend poverty and irrational laws. This is because free will makes choices. But only the absolute nature of relations determines the human condition. Only when we try to rupture this contradiction do we gouge out the base of our conception. At that moment our loneliness exists. Loneliness asks itself: What is revolution? As long as we cannot rupture the contradiction in human survival.
>
> *(Yoshimoto 2014c: 250)*

Here social consciousness is posited not as a product of social being but as an autonomous activity that is irreducible to a particular class position or social function, an existential awareness of the intractably alienated relationship in which it finds itself and yet tries, even in hopeless isolation, to struggle against this social contradiction. This passage has been interpreted variously, but there is no doubt that it reflects Yoshimoto's experience of defeat as a working-class activist and poet. Yoshimoto did not join the JCP and, in fact, kept a critical distance from it, distrusting its self-serving, falsifying propaganda about wartime responsibility and the Russian Red Army. Thus, the battle he waged in the factory was not ideologically motivated but emerged out of proletarian necessity. At the same time, this necessity was not deemed an inevitability, an economically determined set of perceptions and choices; rather, it had to be perceived as such and acted upon, forged and determined in consciousness, the consequence of which also had to be faced in solitude.

Yoshimoto started to methodically compose poetry after his work shifts. He would sit alone and put himself in a trance-like state, weaving together words that came to him from the depth of his silent, solitary contemplation. The enormous corpus of verse produced during this period, compiled under the title *Sundial Verses* (*Hidokei-hen*), was a living proof that this poetic realm of expression was autonomous. Poetic language was produced by a sort of permanently free and independent zone of consciousness that could not be colonised by the imperative of the labour process, state power, or political ideology. The dominant trend of leftwing Japanese literary criticism at the time was to make political content and utility the measure of aesthetic value. Moreover, JCP-affiliated intellectuals publicised a list of writers they deemed collaborators during the war, even though many of the critics themselves had supported the war effort and concealed their own record of collaboration. Yoshimoto took this hypocrisy to task and vigorously defended the autonomy of literature in a series of highly influential polemical essays.

It was during a brief period in 1949 when the physically and mentally exhausted Yoshimoto left the factory life for graduate school at the Tokyo Institute of Technology that he found the time to seriously study Marx's work and classical economics. As a formative working-class poet, under the mentorship of a neighborhood tutor Imauji Otoji, during the war he had acquired verbal facility in sensitively exploring his emotional sensibility. Although his contemporaries showed him the way to express his interior life more fully, their silence on social and political matters and collusion with militarist state propaganda left a serious gap in his understanding of the world.

Marx gave Yoshimoto a critical and rational means of analyzing capitalist socioeconomic relations, wage and money, labour process, and production. Although Marx was not the only source of his post-war social, economic, and political education, he stood head above shoulders among the giants of radical social thought:

> Compared to *Das Kapital*, *German Ideology* is no more than a book of genius. Lenin's *Imperialism* is no more than a book of political philosophy written by a genius practitioner. And Rudolf Hilferding, the author of *Finance Capital*, is no more than a world-class Marxist economist.
>
> *(Yoshimoto 2014a: 257)*

His initial impressions of reading Marx is recorded in a short comparative essay on Marx and Rimbaud ('Notes on Rimbaud and Karl Marx's Methods' (1949): Yoshimoto 2016), in which Marx's scientific method is described as an inverted image of Rimbaud's poetics. Years later Yoshimoto used a New Testament trope for conversion in describing his experience of reading Marx as that of 'scales falling from his eyes' (Yoshimoto and Tajika 1999: 54).

In 1963, in his seminal book on Marx, Yoshimoto would call Marx a 'master [*kyoshō*]' who conceivably appeared once every millennium. This statement would sound like messianic hero worship, were it not for the qualification he immediately added:

> The person I am dealing with here is probably a master who would appear only once every thousand years, but the difficulty of reproducing his life is no different from that of a commoner who lives and dies anonymously. The value of innumerable commoners who were repeatedly born, grew up, raised a family, subsisted, got old and died in anonymity is exactly the same as that of a person who only appears once every thousand years.
>
> *(Yoshimoto 2015a: 65)*

This can be superficially understood as a variation of a banal view that holds the equal worth of all human lives, but drawing the equivalence between a millenarian genius and an anonymous commoner in such a way highlights an essential feature of Yoshimoto's conception of intellectuals. Yoshimoto saw that leftwing intellectuals during the war abdicated their autonomy and, sooner or later, conformed to the doctrine of the emperor state, many of them actively aiding in the spread of war fever. The few Communist leaders who refused to recant their political faith and remained in jail did so in reverence to the Soviet state, still fetishising state power and, no less egregiously, divorced from popular consciousness. Hence Yoshimoto opposed the vanguardist notion of revolutionary intellectuals and political parties which appointed themselves the primary agents in charge of shaping working-class consciousness and disciplining their cadres. He also took exception to the liberal variant of this view, which considered the public in need of education in democratic citizenship. Instead Yoshimoto proposed the need for intellectuals to incorporate what he called the 'image of the multitude [*taishū no genzō*]' into his thought-process in order to avoid the siren song of state and institutional power.

The 'multitude' posited in the 'image of the multitude' is none other than the figure of the anonymous commoner whom Yoshimoto contrasted to the genius of Marx. As a student of chemistry and natural sciences, he considered the ever-increasing sophistication, knowledge, and abstraction of intellectual process to be an ineluctable, natural extension of human reason and curiosity; the 'multitude' are conceived as the people who are alienated entirely from this process, those who are consumed completely in the activity of physical survival and subsistence. Such a purely non-intellectual 'multitude,' of course, does not exist in reality, and Yoshimoto does not intend the concept to function as a stand-in for sociological reality. Rather he conceives of it as part of a self-critical existential method that turns the intellectual process upside down once it reaches the pinnacle of knowledge and abstraction, sloughing off its privileges to absorb the realm of non-intellectual subsistent life on its own terms.

Such an existential conception of the intellectual, in which the emphasis is not on enlightening or influencing the masses but on how intellectuals engage their thought-process and expression, is radically different from the position of the Marxist-Leninist vanguard and the liberal public intellectual as well as from that of the Gramscian organic intellectual (see Chapter 11). Antonio Gramsci's work first entered the lexicon of the Japanese left by way of a reformist current in the JCP and JSP, which went under the rubric of 'structural reformists [kōzō-kaikaku-ha].' The emergence of this group coincides with the appearance of the Japanese translation of a six-volume collection of Gramsci's writings, published in 1960–1964 by Gōdō-shuppan, a leftwing publisher also known for the translations of Palmiro Togliatti, Louis Althusser, and Étienne Balibar's *Reading Capital* (1965), and books critical of nuclear energy. Although the structural reformists were originally inspired by Eurocommunism and shared a gradualist approach to socialism through parliamentary election and popular movements, their political ramifications took a different course within the JCP and JSP. Given that the main currents of the JCP had already been distancing themselves from the USSR as an unblemished authority, it was the structural reformists who adopted a pro-Soviet stance and, eventually splitting away from the JCP, formed their own small political parties and organisations; on the other hand, in the JSP, structural reformism became an ideology of its rightwing faction, expressing an opposition to doctrinaire Marxist-Leninism and an adamant defence of parliamentary politics, with very little to distinguish it from social democracy. Structural reformism was consequently attacked by the JSP's leftwing current under Ōuchi Hyōe and Sakisaka Itsurō's leadership, who deemed it a species of 'opportunism' and 'reformism,' accommodating itself shamelessly to capitalism. In a twist of historical irony, the term 'structural reform' will be revived in the 1990s as a slogan for neoliberal dismantling of state intervention and welfare, destroying not only its nominal notion of socialism but also its association with social democracy.

Of course, the Italian Communist Party's institutionalised interpretation—alongside that of its Japanese subset, with its own specific, complex local inflections—of Gramsci hardly exhausts the polysemic layers, nuances, and themes found in the Sardinian Marxist's writings, and there are significant overlaps, as well as differences, between Yoshimoto and Gramsci's respective notion of the intellectual. Like Gramsci, Yoshimoto had a sustained interest in traditional popular culture, folklore, and ethnology in order to grasp the structure of popular *mentalité*. Unlike Gramsci, Yoshimoto's purpose was to clarify the mechanism of communal illusion cohering in the state. Ultimately, Gramsci was interested in crafting a revolutionary strategy to seize and keep popular power, with his creative reading of Machiavelli's *Prince* as a strategic manual for the revolutionary party, his vocabulary of war of position and manoeuvre in capturing proletarian hegemony, his nuanced analysis of culture all reflecting a political will to power to mobilise the disparate sectors of the popular class and construct a historic bloc toward the formation of a revolutionary class-for-itself, mediated in the last instance through a properly functioning vanguard party.[1]

When Yoshimoto was faced with the necessity of political action during the 1960 mass protest against the renewal of the US–Japan Mutual Security Agreement, the so-called anti-Anpo movement, as New Left student leaders approached him, Sinologist Takeuchi Yoshimi, and other older independent leftwing intellectuals who were critical of the JCP's authoritarianism to 'sympathetically observe' their part in the struggle (Yoshimoto 2007: 108), he was impressed by the young activists' independence of spirit and refusal to seek directives, their attempt to forge a path of radical autonomy free from the influence of orthodox Marxism and Japanese nationalism. His response was not to establish a more authentic and organic revolutionary vanguard party, as some of the sectarian groupuscules of the New Left did and about which he was highly critical, but to act spontaneously in relation to the contingency of the changing situation. The June Action Committee, a collective of radical intellectuals which Yoshimoto helped organise to work with the main current of the Zengakuren (short for *Zen Nihon Gakusei Jichikai Sō Rengō*, it stands for 'All-Japan League of Student Self-Government') students to undertake direct action in June 1960 against the undemocratic passage of the Anpo treaty, did not seek to acquire hegemony over the movement, had no long-term strategy, and made its decisions on the fly. As far as Yoshimoto was concerned, the Anpo crisis was hardly a revolutionary situation. After the movement expanded and intensified in the wake of Prime Minister Kishi Nobusuke's forcible passage of the Anpo treaty on May 20 in the House of Representatives, made possible by the physical removal of Socialist Party members with the use of rightwing thugs and police force, Yoshimoto believed that the most that the movement could aim to accomplish was pushing the Kishi administration out of power—which eventually happened as Kishi resigned under popular pressure.

In Yoshimoto's sober estimation, what was fought out on the streets as tens of thousands of people encircled the National Diet and demanded the dissolution of Anpo, the institutional foundation of Japan's subordinate alliance with the US in the East Asian Cold War, was not the defence of constitutional democracy or the making of a socialist revolution in solidarity with the Second or Third World. Rather, it was intellectual and political autonomy from state power, political parties, and institutional structures, signaling the formation of a new radical sensibility he witnessed among the young militants of Zengakuren, which brought together a polymorphous conclave of student activists who were opposed to the repressive state apparatus of post-war Japanese democracy as well as to the repressive democratic centralism of the JCP. In contrast to the JCP's heavy-handed approach in regulating demonstrations and suppressing dissident political expressions, with their appeal to Japanese national independence to mobilise its supporters against Anpo, the Zengakuren militants invented new forms of direct action, as they took over the streets and, inheriting a confrontational style of demonstration from the post-war labour movement, moved in snake-like formation to rout the capture of the riot police, crashing their way through the gates of the Diet building. JCP denounced their unruly anti-authoritarian militance as an act of 'an anticommunist, counterrevolutionary group of Trotskyist provocateurs' (Kōan-chōsa-chō 1960: 11) while other student radicals across the world saw in it powerfully disciplined self-organisation.

This was also recognised contemporaneously by the sociologist C. Wright Mills when he penned his 'Letter to the New Left' in 1960 on the pages of the *New Left Review*. After surveying the concurrent insurrections in Turkey, South Korea, Cuba, Taiwan, and Great Britain, he paused on Okinawa, at the time still under US occupation, and Japan:

On Okinawa—a US military base—the people get their first chance since World War II ended to demonstrate against US seizure of their island and some students take that chance, snake-dancing and chanting angrily to the visiting President: 'Go home, go home—take away your missiles' (Don't worry, 12,000 US troops easily handled the generally grateful crowds; also the President was 'spirited out the rear end of the United States compound'—and so by helicopter to the airport) ... In Japan, weeks of student rioting succeeded in rejecting the President's visit, jeopardise a new treaty with the U.S.A., displace the big-business, pro-American Prime Minister, Kishi.

(Summers 2008: 264, 265)

Here Mills clearly sees the Japanese students playing an integral part in the making of the nascent global New Left and, at the conclusion of his rousing trans-Atlantic proclamation, makes them the mouthpiece of this inchoate new radical movement against the dismissive voice of political realism: '"But it's utopian, after all, isn't it?" No—not in the sense you mean. Whatever else it may be, it's not that; tell it to the students of Japan.' Mills, to my knowledge, was not acquainted personally with anyone in the Japanese New Left, least of all Yoshimoto, but his two major sociological texts (*White Collar: The American Middle Classes* (1951) and *The Power Elite* (1956)) and two important political tracts (*The Causes of World War Three* (1958) and *Listen, Yankee!: The Revolution in Cuba* (1960)) were translated into Japanese within a few years of their original publication. In 1960, E.P. Thompson, Mills's confrère in the Anglophone New Left edited and published *Out of Apathy*, a collection of essays which set the political tone of the first British New Left, with contributions from Raphael Samuel, Stuart Hall, Peter Worsley, Alasdair MacIntyre, and Kenneth Alexander.

In many ways, *Out of Apathy* is comparable to the Japanese collection *The Myth of Democracy: Intellectual Summation of the Anpo Struggle* (*Minshu-shugi no shinwa: anpo-tōsō no shisōteki-sōkatsu*), also published in 1960, showcasing the leading voices of the new radical dissent in Japan, including Yoshimoto, Kyushū's charismatic Maoist poet and organiser Tanigawa Gan, novelist Haniwa Yutaka, Trotskyist theoretician Kuroda Kan'ichi, French studies scholar Morimoto Kazuo, and Marxist philosopher Umeda Katsumi. *Out of Apathy* affirmed the necessity of radical political commitment against the ideology of apathy bred and generalised by the Cold War, and Thompson raised the banner of 'socialist humanism' in opposing the Stalinist cult of personality and authoritarian party discipline, which he had renounced in 1956 after the Soviet repression of the Hungarian Revolution. On the other hand, *The Myth of Democracy*, as its title suggests, saw the historical significance of the Anpo movement to lie in exposing the hollowness of post-war Japanese democracy, which failed to follow even the rudimentary protocol of representative democracy in legislating a treaty that affected the lives of all its constituency. For Yoshimoto, the new political agency that rent asunder the veil of democratic illusion was the 'independent left [*dokuritsu sayoku*],' which the Zengakuren students embodied and which, unlike the JCP and JSP that abided by the Stalinist notion of 'socialism in one country,' understood revolution as an international process requiring the dissolution of the state (Yoshimoto and Tajika 1999: 229–230).

Out of Apathy (1960) was translated into Japanese, published three years later in 1963, the same year Yoshimoto published *Karl Marx*. The book had no traction in the debate among their Japanese counterparts, due in no small part to the politics of translation: the publisher of the Japanese version was Iwanami, a venerable bearer of post-war democratic values responsible for printing respectable voices of liberalism and the Old Left, and its translators (Fukuda Kan'ichi, political science professor of Tokyo University's Law Faculty and president of Meiji Gakuin University specialising in modern democratic theory, co-editor and translator of Isaiah Berlin's work; Kawai Hidekazu, Gakushūin University's political scientist in the field of English politics and prolific translator of Isaiah Berlin, Bertrand Russell, Eric Hobsbawm, and Bernard Crick; and Maeda Yasuhiro, Chiba University professor of political science and translator of Crick's *In Defense of Politics* (1962)) were all close associates of Japan's most influential liberal political scientist Maruyama Masao, whom Yoshimoto especially targeted for a lengthy critique also in 1963.

According to Yoshimoto, Maruyama fetishises Western liberal values as an idealised standard to measure the development of post-war Japanese democracy, to say nothing of its premodern political history, on the basis of his 'hatred, or mechanism of escape, against the life history of really existing human beings' (Yoshimoto 2014b: 52). In 1968, as if living out Yoshimoto's critique in real life, Maruyama, a renowned professor in the most prestigious Faculty of Law (with its close association with the upper echelons of the state bureaucracy) at Tokyo University, the most elite institution of higher education, made his notorious denunciation against a new generation of student militants who rushed into his department's research library and accidentally destroyed a few of its primary documents. 'Not even the Nazis had committed this kind of atrocity!' he remarked in reaction to the students' action. Such a hyperbolic statement of victimhood on the part of the great liberal professor and leading exponent of democratic governance exposed the respected position of elite privilege he enjoyed and the vitriol he would reflexively pour on anybody who would transgress it even slightly. Yoshimoto's inspired polemic on this incident, published in the small independent magazine *Shikō* which he had co-founded in 1960 and continued to edit for the subsequent three decades, circulated widely among student radicals. This work defined an argumentative style of non-sectarian radical criticism, which was personal, plebeian, and uncompromisingly principled, sharing many qualities found in Edward Thompson's arguments within and outside English Marxism, such as his debate with Perry Anderson in 'The Peculiarities of the English' (1965), 'An Open Letter to Leszek Kolakowski' (1973), and an extensive screed against Louis Althusser in *The Poverty of Theory* (1978).

Although Yoshimoto and Thompson never encountered each other, translating Yoshimoto's *Karl Marx* for my doctoral dissertation was motivated by a desire to stage such an imaginary encounter against the backdrop of the making of the New Left and renewal of independent Marxism, comparative moments of working-class composition, and the contemporary history of global capitalism and US-centred imperialism. In the intervening ten years, I never did manage to return to this work but I have come to realise the meaning of 'translation' to be much broader than the one I grasped as a graduate student, namely the linguistic transfer of meaning from one language to another. The expanded sense of translation involves what Yoshimoto and Thompson were each doing, according to their respective historical experiences, in reading Marx against the grain to create new radically grounded ways of rethinking class, politics, ideology, history, and poetics from below. It also involves what Thompson's pupil and my mentor Peter Linebaugh elaborated in his 1981 piece 'What If C.L.R. James Had Met E.P. Thompson in 1792?,' bringing the Trinidadian Marxist's anticolonial Afro-Caribbean experience face to face with the English Marxist historian's narrative of antinomian artisans and commoners through the prism of the revolutionary 1790s, concerning which both had written extensively in their classic books, respectively, *The Black Jacobins* and *The Making of the English Working Class*. In this chapter, I wanted to renew a similar but more modest aspiration: to start asking anew 'What if Yoshimoto Taka'aki had met E.P. Thompson in 1960?' I know that such a work of translation cannot be solely a scholarly pursuit but—and this is what I have learned above all from Yoshimoto's struggle to be not so much a Marxist as to do what Marx did for his own times—a secular 'pilgrim's progress' that digs deeply to discover, in Gauguin's famous triad of questions, where we came from, who we are, and where we are going in relation to our particular experience of class struggle and social antagonism.

Related topics

Thought/Translation; Theory, Practice, Activism; The Political Modes of Translation in Iran.

Notes

1 According to Rocco Lacorte, Gramsci saw 'translation' in the amplified sense of facilitating the relationship between theory and practice as a central characteristic of Marxism: 'it represents a theory of praxis, namely, of how (revolutionary) political and historical action works. Second, translatability is the theory of the necessity that theory becomes practice (and vice versa). Finally, theory *as such* is (a form of) praxis—*when* and *to the extent that* it becomes praxis, that which constitutes the ground to justify its autonomy on the theoretical level' (Lacorte 2018: 20). Broadly speaking in the history of Marxism, Gramsci represents a significant antidote against the economic determinism and bureaucratic party politics of the Second International, a 'cultural turn' towards the appreciation of popular consciousness, customs, and language, which had been marginalised in the passive conception of superstructure in the more dogmatic versions of Marxist base-superstructure theory. Yoshimoto's theory of communal illusion, a term he borrowed from *The German Ideology*, and linguistic theory of literary expression, whose paired key concepts of self-expression and indicative expression are inspired respectively by 'use-value' and 'exchange-value' in Marx's labour theory of value, also belong in this genealogy of rereading or 'translating' Marx according to the particularities of human consciousness and agency, as do Edward Thompson, Jean-Paul Sartre, Herbert Marcuse, among other defining figures of the New Left. Needless to say, beyond this fundamental commonality, many significant differences exist and their 'translatability' with each other cannot be properly understood without situating each of these figures in their specific historical contexts, in the long arc of regionally varying forms and exigencies of capitalist development, class struggles, and Marxism with which they were interacting and to which they were responding.

Further reading

Hobo Nikkan Itoi Shinbun (2015) *Yoshimoto Taka'aki no 183 kōen* [online]. Available at: www.1101.com/yoshimoto_voice/ [accessed 6 October 2019].

Itoi Shigesato, renowned copywriter and impresario of Japanese media culture, was an avid supporter of Yoshimoto in his later years and his office has digitised this free archive of Yoshimoto's 183 lectures, dating from 1964 to 2008, in both podcast and transcript format. Covering everything from literature, philosophy, and religion to politics, agriculture, and language—including a debate with Jean Baudrillard in 1995 (A169)—these recordings showcase Yoshimoto's range and power as one of the greatest contemporary Japanese intellectuals. The original recording of 'Contemporary Times and Marx' can be heard here as well (A004).

Maruyama, Masao, and Shūichi Katō (1998) *Honyaku to nihon no kindai*. Tokyo: Iwanami-shoten.

Maruyama Masao and Katō Shūichi, two leading liberal intellectuals of Japanese post-war democracy, engage in an informed, wide-ranging discussion of the role of translation in the development of Japanese modernity.

Okazaki, Jiro (1983) *Marukusu ni motarete — jichōshōgaiki*. Tokyo: Seido-sha.

A memoir by a Rōnō-ha Marxist economist who was a central figure in the contemporary Japanese translation of Marx, including *Das Kapital*, *Theories of Surplus Value*, and Marx–Engels correspondence. His memoir reveals the unstinting collaborative work required by such a massive translation project, as well as the Socialist Party bigwig Sakisaka Itsurō's manipulative power politics in hijacking the project and monopolising the majority of royalties and in claiming credit for himself. A year after the publication of this book, in 1984, Okazaki and his wife organised and disposed of all of their possessions, leaving on a journey from which they never returned.

Yoshimoto, Taka'aki (2014–2015) *Yoshimoto Taka'aki mishūroku-kōenshū*. Tokyo: Chikuma-shobō.

A twelve-volume selection of Yoshimoto's uncollected lectures on Japan, agriculture, city, literary expression, writers, biological life, and religion further shows the capacious range of his voracious intellectual practice, which relied as much on the spoken as the written word.

Yoshimoto, Taka'aki (2015) *Yoshimoto Taka'aki zenshū: dai 9-kan 1964–1968*. Tokyo: Shōbunsha.

The ninth volume in *The Complete Works of Yoshimoto Taka'aki*, which commenced publishing in March 2014 and is still ongoing, covers a crucial period in Yoshimoto's life when his influence on the Japanese New Left was at its zenith and includes the original text of *Karl Marx* as well as essays that theorised intellectual 'autonomy' from existing left ideologies.

References

Barshay, Andrew E. (2004) *The Social Sciences in Modern Japan: The Marxian and Modernist Traditions*. Berkeley: University of California Press.

Kōan-chōsa-chō (1960) *Anpo-tōsō no gaiyō: tōsō no keika to bunseki*. Tokyo: Kōan-chōsa-chō.

Lacorte, Rocco (2018) 'Translation and Marxism,' in *The Routledge Handbook of Translation and Politics*. Eds. Jonathan Evans and Fruela Fernandez. London: Routledge. 17–28.

Linebaugh, Peter, and Marcus Rediker (2000) *The Many-headed Hydra: Sailors, Slaves, Commoners, and the Hidden History of the Revolutionary Atlantic*. Boston: Beacon Press.

Summers, John (ed.) (2008) *The Politics of Truth: Selected Writings of C. Wright Mills*. Oxford: Oxford University Press.

Thompson, Edward (1993a) *Persons & Polemics: Historical Essays*. London: The Merlin Press.

Thompson, Edward (1993b) *Witness against the Beast: William Blake and the Moral Law*. New York: The New Press.

Tōgō, Ken (2002) *Jōshiki o koete — okamano michi 70-nenn*. Tokyo: Potto-shuppan.

Tymoczko, Maria (2006) 'Reconceptualizing Translation Theory: Integrating Non-Western Thought about Translation,' in *Translating Others*, vol. 1. Ed. Theo Hermans. Manchester: St. Jerome. 13–32.

Yoshimoto Ryūmei/Taka'aki (1965) *What is Beauty in Language?* Tokyo: Keiso-shobo.

Yoshimoto Taka'aki Kenkyūkai (ed.) (2001) *Yoshimoto Taka'aki ga kataru sengo-55-nen*, vol. 5. Tokyo: Sankōsha.

Yoshimoto, Taka'aki (1994) *Haikei no kioku*. Tokyo: Takarajimasha.

Yoshimoto, Taka'aki (2002) *Chō-'sensō'-ron*, vol. 2. Tokyo: Askii Communications.

Yoshimoto, Taka'aki (2007) *Jicho o kataru*. Tokyo: Rocking On.

Yoshimoto, Taka'aki (2014a) *Yoshimoto Taka'aki zenshū: dai 6-kan 1959–1961*. Tokyo: Shōbunsha.

Yoshimoto, Taka'aki (2014b) *Yoshimoto Taka'aki zenshū: dai 7-kan 1962–1964*. Tokyo: Shōbunsha.

Yoshimoto, Taka'aki (2014c) *Yoshimoto Taka'aki zenshū: dai 4-kan 1952–1957*. Tokyo: Shōbunsha.

Yoshimoto, Taka'aki (2015a) *Yoshimoto Taka'aki zenshū: dai 9-kan 1964–1968*. Tokyo: Shōbunsha.

Yoshimoto, Taka'aki (2015b) *Yoshimoto Taka'aki zenshū: dai 11-kan 1969–1971*. Tokyo: Shōbunsha.

Yoshimoto, Taka'aki (2016) *Yoshimoto Taka'aki zenshū: dai 2-kan 1948–1950*. Tokyo: Shōbunsha.

Yoshimoto, Taka'aki and Nobukazu Tajika (1999) *Watashi no sensōron*. Tokyo: Bunkasha.

Contemporary times and Marx

Yoshimoto Taka'aki (October 12, 1967 at Chuō University)
Translated by Manuel Yang

Editors' note: The abridged version of Manuel Yang's translation of Yoshimoto Taka'a-ki's 'Contemporary Times and Marx' introduces the reader to the broad sense of translation in Yoshimoto's work. 'Translation' in this context looks beyond the rendering of texts in new languages to encompass the adaptation of ideas and contexts. In this lecture, the New Left Japanese intellectual Yoshimoto Taka'aki, whose work and legacy are described in detail in Yang's chapter in this volume, explains the exigency of adapting Marx's ideas to the post-war Japanese socio-political circumstances. Yoshimito's contemporary, the writer, translator, and member of the Iranian New Left, Morad Farhadpour, has similarly drawn on the European critical tradition to develop his concept of activist translation in conjunction with what he calls 'situatedness' (see Chapter 4).

Thanks for the introduction, I am Yoshimoto. This year coincides with the hundredth anniversary of the publication of *Capital*, but it would be my twentieth anniversary because I first read and got acquainted with *Capital* twenty years ago. I recall this was about two, three years after the end of the war.

I will first talk about what shaped Marx's intellectual views, what he was thinking. Germany during Marx's time was a 'holy state,' so to speak, integrating Christian divine rights and state power, virtually in a state of slumber. In European countries, apart from Germany, what today we would call anti-establishment movements and labour movements were developing, albeit sporadically. But such real movements were few and far between in Germany. Nevertheless, in this seemingly slumbering Germany, German philosophy or the system of German idealism had at the time reached its ultimate peak as an almost completely idealist dialectic, with Hegel at the top. Here everything from the general problem of consciousness to the problems of family, state, and law were investigated thoroughly. This was in contrast to other European countries where real movements were developing but ideas or philosophy that propelled them as theoretical principles were weak.

So the following was assumed: in order to develop in a real sense a movement that internationally connected the whole of Europe, ideas or philosophy must rework German idealism in a distinctive form and this real movement must emulate the real movements occurring in relatively modernised parts of Europe outside Germany. In other words, the intellect will have to rework German idealism and the real movement will have to apply what it learns from the ongoing workers' movement and other movements of the intelligentsia, integrating those two things with each other. This is how Marx's intellectual work started.

By the way, twenty years ago, right after the end of the war, when we think about what Japan was like at the time, or what Japanese philosophy under the so-called emperor state was like, it was completely different from Marx's situation and what was around us was only reactionary philosophy, conservative philosophy. If Japanese conservative, reactionary philosophers had managed to accomplish great things during the war, we might have been able to rework that and develop, to some extent, intellectual problems in the context of the real workers' movements. I don't know why, but no great reactionary philosophy or great conservative philosophy emerged under the Japanese emperor state that lasted throughout the war, a state that was reactionary or theocratic to the core, saturated with residues of ancient institutions.

For example, during the war, those contemporary ideologues of the citizens' movement went through the war merely in the dual sense: psychologically disliking the war but still picking up the gun and carrying on with the war. Liberal or conservative philosophies were not perfected in any high degree. For example, during the war, the philosophers who rationalised the war were those of the Kyoto School, who weren't any good at all. And the more reactionary, rightwing ideologies developed only in prehistorical forms, such as those espousing the theory of the social organic body, advocating that a state socialist or agrarian-centred revolution was to be realised under the emperor's charismatic being. Thus, we greeted the post-war era in a condition where Marxists had obviously attached themselves to either or both of these tendencies, or did not do any meaningful intellectual work at all.

Hence, from my own experience, I was convinced that something philosophical, a philosophical point of origin that needed to develop after the war did not even exist in the first place. Philosophical problems existed as something I had no choice but to explore on my own. So I started thinking differently, and I thought about the problems of Christianity and also thought through such subject matters as Japanese classics, literature, philosophy, and went on to be concerned with Marx as well, and, as I was doing this, I had no intention of seeking to learn from Japanese Marxists, those Marxists who, during the war, either remained silent or took part in reactionary philosophical rationalisation of the war. Thus, my experience was one of going directly to Marx.

As I was thinking out of this experience, the biggest shock I received from Marx involved the philosophy of the state. Which means I got a great shock from how Marx conceived the state as a communal illusion. This is because, according to our experience of the war, our point of departure was how we ought to place more emphasis on the state rather than the individual, that is, the individual within civil society or the family, and I remember the jolt I got in coming across Marx's idea that this state, which we thought we had to emphasise more, was nothing more than an illusion masked under a sense of communality (*taishū*).

And, as we keep examining Marx's writings, from his early period to the later years, that is, until *Capital*, we can see that his study of the state was more or less perfected and ended with his treatise critiquing Hegel's philosophy of law. Henceforward, Marx would stick his neck into the problems of economics or economic categories. The completion of *Capital* is therefore considered to be his final destination, but, speaking strictly from how I was understanding the problem, what became an important question was how to develop Marx's philosophy of state, which had reached its peak as a critique of Hegel's philosophy of law.

This way of stating the problem may seem at first glance inappropriate for celebrating the one hundredth anniversary of *Capital*, but when we think about how Marx conceives economic categories in *Capital*, we see that in his study, in his theoretical, scientific elucidation of economic categories, in which economic categories are developed within their inner structure, they are conceived in such a phase that the problems of communality (that is to say, those of state, religion, law, art) can be abstracted. As we understand it, Marx never considered economic categories as entirely determining the historical tendency of humanity. So, if we were to deem economic categories as important, as the primary factor in the movement of human history and explicate them accordingly, the economic categories are conceived in the phase of abstraction in which communal categories can be placed at a distance and abstracted.

So-called materialist dialectics and historical materialism were developed in Russia after the 1920s, but I consider them invalid because they were developed more or less with the assumption that economic categories constitute all categories. At least I wanted to state at the beginning that this point is what distinguishes me entirely from the so-called Marxists (or, to use my term, 'Russian Marxists').

About twenty years ago, when I started engaging myself with Marx, what you know generally as the *Economic and Philosophical Manuscripts* had not yet been translated in Japan. So that means I was only able to read it about six, seven years ago. I believe this is a crucial piece of writing in making sense of Marx's system as a whole. Because, without the theory of self-alienation or the theory of alienation at the foundation, the study of such problems as those of communality, state, law, religion, and art becomes quite difficult to undertake. In short, without such a theory, the problem of communality is only raised at the level of producing, at best, a countereffect of relative autonomy, as the superstructure is moved and changed by the base. Today I would like to start my argument a little bit from this standpoint.

Alienation, or self-alienation, is of course not a concept that Marx was the first to use, as it was already used by Hegel, but, when we think about the significance of this concept of self-alienation for Marx, the first significance is essentially as follows. A human being cannot exist without an objectified act in relation to another human being (or this could be in relation to nature as well). When human beings undertake the objectified act of survival, that is, to fulfill the necessary conditions for existence, their very self becomes correspondingly alienated from the original self. In other words, the self too receives a countering effect and influence. Or the objectified act is not possible without receiving a countering effect—this is the philosophy of nature which lies at the foundation of Marx's theory of alienation.

If we were to make an easily understandable outline, we can say that when such a philosophy of nature is represented in a civil society whose basic structure is made up of economic categories, and it is transplanted on to civil society, what is established is the relationship of self-alienation as economic categories. This means the relationship of self-alienation and alienation is established between the worker and the product that is the result of his/her labour, as well as vis-à-vis the capitalist who possesses and develops profit from that product following a fixed law and vis-à-vis the organised worker.

Accordingly, transplanting, which also means representing, this category of natural philosophy as economic category, the basis of civil society, is what we call alienation or self-alienation. The concept of self-alienation means alienation or self-alienation not only within the relations in the category of natural philosophy but also in transplanting the category of natural philosophy into the economic category of civil society. Of course, such relations are established within the inner structure of civil society.

Human relationships that make up these economic categories as their base are what produce the world of ideas or the world of communality, and, if this is so, transplanting the various relations of life in this civil society or various economic categories into the category of communal illusion is also alienation. This is so-called idealist alienation or idealist self-alienation. The concept of alienation is simultaneously a spatial concept and a chronological concept. To put it differently, transforming something into the phase possessed by all human categories, such a concept is also called alienation. This is the basic structure of Marx's theory of alienation.

The current trend in examining Marx takes many forms. For example, it is possible to find faults in the materialist dialectic and historical materialism that is the basis of Russian Marxism, which was developed in Russia after the 1920s, and compensate for and correct them with some kind of philosophy. That is, for instance, what Sartre and his Japanese adherents have done. As I just stated, this is the position of the so-called Marxists in Japan, to compensate for or correct the development of Russian Marxist philosophy. Yet another position for Marxists is to argue that the materialist dialectics in the real sense cannot be developed without taking into account the theory of alienation or the self-alienation theory of ideas, which deals with the problem of communality, in other words, the problem of the state, as well as the problems of law and art. These positions of examining Marx symbolise their respective perspective. This is the reason why these various positions can only appear in the form of ultimately forcing their way of looking on to the very thing they are examining.

By the way, a systematic theory of alienation is important because, as I stated earlier, without having such a theory, we cannot approach the world of illusoriness, which is to say, the problems of state, law, and art. In other words, otherwise we don't have a theory of power. Hence the theory of alienation—and it doesn't matter what we call it —is carried all the way to *Capital* as an important problem and dominates the philosophy of nature in *Capital*. The logic is established as a crossing point between the philosophy of nature as a theory of alienation and historiography of nature which sees the history of the humanity as the process of natural history.

My own concern is obviously related to the field of literature, in which I've worked hard, and to the problem of communality, which Marx temporarily stopped concerning himself with his critique of Hegel's philosophy of law, and these are the issues that preoccupy me now. This is largely where my thinking has developed.

[…][1]

There are places where the consciousness of the consanguineous group retains power, depending on which race you're talking about. I think one of those places is Japan. There are those races and places where the state was formed in the form where such elements have been entirely extinguished. Speaking in this sense, the states are as different regionally as, to exaggerate a little, they are in their essential structure. Thus, to think you can grasp all this in a unified, theoretical fashion is no good, it's a big mistake, and, if you want to grasp it in a unified, theoretical way, we know that state theory in a universal sense cannot be formed unless we study how economic categories always alienate communal categories and we start thinking about the philosophy of the state, state theory, at that level of abstraction.

This is where our position completely differs from that of the self-avowed Marxists. What the Russian Marxists do most honestly is dealing with the influence that the state as communal illusion receives from various economic categories. This is the concept of *Macht* (power). *Macht* is an illusory function that for the time being became independent from the regional people (*taishū*), and this *Macht* is manifested in so-called law. Law is a right, a duty. That is, where *Macht* is, there is law; and where law is, there are those who impart it as right and the people who use it as a duty. That is the concept of *Macht*. And when we go from *Macht* to the concept of *Gewalt* (force), this is the state of power that imparts duty as duty even if right is not extracted independently. In short, in this instance, such things as force and violence become acceptable.

So, speaking of law, if legal duty is always executed in a certain sense, the demand for rights from the side of the people will offset it properly. That means, for instance, law as a neutral concept, that is, concept of power. When this turns into *Gewalt*, it is the form where only duty is imposed and rights are completely ignored; in other words, a form of condition where *Macht* alienates itself absolutely.

Such a concept can also be found in Engels, and, generally, the Japanese Russian Marxists' understanding of the problem is to argue for the need to carefully distinguish this concept. But, as we stated just now, we are fundamentally critiquing Engel's *Origins of the State*. If we fail to do this, we can't resolve the problem no matter what.

In its totality illusoriness is restricted by various economic relations of civil society, by economic categories, but, once we want to treat the problem of illusoriness as an inner structure, we can think about it by setting aside economic categories in a fixed position. Or, to put this inversely, we must think about it by setting them aside. Speaking in terms of the problem of the origin of the state, there are primitive societies that are communist and there are races that practice despotism and there is no unitary feature among them. Engels studied them as if they had a logically unitary, theoretical stage, or a real stage. But in actuality there is no such thing. So, when we are explicating the problem of illusoriness in its inner structure, surely we will become aware of the problem in such a way that we can set aside economic categories in a particular place, where economic categories relate as a structural element. If so, this means the problem of illusoriness or the problem of communal illusion can be treated in terms of its inner structure. This doesn't mean that we necessarily have to make rationalisations by always roping in economic categories. These are the problems we're dealing with.

The reason the Japanese state was called the familial state in the wartime period was because the residual institution of the clan system remained intact for the most part. As to why it remained intact, it is probably due to the fact that Japan is a separate island. And when we consider the separate island that is Japan, it is better to think of *honshū* (main island), *hondo* (mainland, or Japan proper) as a relatively new entity. This means that regions in the south and north are old. We can thus trace this problem back to the period preceding agricultural society. For example, in Okinawa today such problems as reverting to *hondo* are proposed in diverse ways, and, when we think about them, I think we should not forget that people living in Okinawa, Amami, and other regions in the south view themselves as older strata of Japanese. That is, they are probably thinking, old Japan is actually where we are and we are the ones who are older while you are of mixed blood, having intermingled with all kinds of people like the Koreans and the southern race and becoming a race that we can't make head or tail of. That is the same perspective shared in the north.

Let's now consider whether today an antiestablishment can constitute communality on its own against state power as communal illusion. In reality this cannot be constituted. In reality what can be inverted in relation to communal illusion is only individual illusion. So antiestablishment communality cannot be constituted intrinsically. But it can be constituted with an additional condition. As to what this condition is, the people (*taishū*) who support the state as communal illusion on the most idealist basis (or this could be a realistic basis), on the basis of illusoriness—when we think of people not as people who have some kind of philosophy or ideology but as we abstract them considerably as people who have none of this, that is, people who are abstracted to such a degree that they have no particular sense of being dominated by the state even if they are, and, if we can keep incorporating into our consciousness the understanding of the problem or the nature of the problem posed by such people as philosophy or ideology, then perhaps we can constitute an antiestablishment communality. If you do not incorporate this into your consciousness and start thinking about political organisation or political communality, antiestablishment communality, with only the ideologically educated people as its referent, it will always become closed up inside. If this closes up, it will always invert itself in relation to the people. This is what bureaucracy is.

For example, the reason for the degeneration of the Leninist establishment in Russia stems from this problem. Although Lenin wanted to think about the primary principle of the party by positing a communality that keeps incorporating the problems of perfectly ordinary people, the actual problem was that it only got closed up inside. If this keeps getting distorted, of course, this will turn into a bureaucracy and, if it acquires power, it will itself exert force or violence as state power, that is, try to do more than exercise *Macht*; in short, it ends up in the form that also self-alienates *Macht*. Such problems can exist as well.

As I stated earlier, the communality of relational illusion has a layer in which the stage of the clan system never goes to the origin of the state. In the language of legal scholars, unless the form based on territorial communality is not established in relation to consanguinity, there is no transition to the communality of the state itself. That is, we can say that the wall directly facing consanguineous groups stops generally in the clan system. The extent to which the residual institution of this clan system is powerful or not could constitute a factor determining the mechanism of power in the respective tribal states. In other words, the absolute structure of each respective state power would be different for each currently existing state. There is no way this problem could be resolved, no matter how detailed we do it in the form where everything comes out of economic categories. Economic categories cannot extract laws except at a particular level of abstraction. This degree of abstraction will lead to absurdly wrong conclusions unless we investigate, within the totality of reality and the totality of illusoriness, the phase of the degree of abstraction possessed by economic categories.

That is what distinguishes Marx from Engels. Marx does not say anything in the least dubious because he understands. He has said nothing more than, essentially, that the state is a communal illusion. If you were to say more than that, as Engels does, and try to integrate it with economic categories, you end up doing something that appears rational but is quite absurd. The states are so different from each other that we can almost say, with each so-called race, it is going to be different. That is where Marx truly excels. That is, he understands. In case you are dealing with economic categories, he understands what position these categories assume in the totality of categories. He never presumes to do anything dubious, such as trying to make up a law on issues where, beyond a certain point, there is no doubt that empirical proof or counterproof could conceivably be raised. If a stadial law is to be produced, he posits a particular degree of abstraction from the beginning and considers the law only at that point. This is the case with the structure of *Capital*. In my view, there is basically no mistake in *Capital*. The reason is, if you remove the abstraction or the phase of economic categories, what it says would in fact be quite wrong. For instance, he says one hour of person A's labour and one hour of person B's labour are the same; here the problem is one of time. But, actually, this is not true. For instance, if A is someone who is hardworking and likes to work and B is indolent and lazy, the quantity as well as the quality of the product made in the same one hour of labour are, of course, going to be different. That is, in real categories, what he says is wrong. But the reason we can consider them to be equivalent is because he posits a particular degree of abstraction there. It is because he grasps well the phase of economic categories in the totality of categories. So, in the case of one hour of person A's labour, it is one hour of labour made up entirely of natural time. There is no other nuance besides this. But if we think realistically, if we take individual illusion into consideration, for a particular person under particular conditions, there are cases when you think the work lasted only for thirty minutes even after working for one hour or there are times, for example, when just an hour of work feels like 'I've worked for about ten hours.' If the time of consciousness is taken into account, what Marx says becomes completely wrong. But this can be abstracted. It can be abstracted when you are thinking in economic categories, when you are dealing with it in terms of a particular law, in terms of inner structure. He does not make a mistake because he grasps well the degree of abstraction and the phase of such economic categories. That is why he can also extract a particular law. If these categories are taken away, then it would be true that such stupid things cannot be said. In that case, A and B are completely different, their abilities are also different, everything is different. In this sense, Engels was not great. Engels himself said and thought that, after Marx's death, he assumed Marx's mantle, developing what Marx could not do. But that's not so. You have to understand how it would be dubious if you say more than what is possible, that is, understand the categories that cannot be stated in terms of laws. And when we are thinking about philosophy or fundamental principles, we could occasionally make mistakes unless we clearly grasp the phase in the world produced by such abstraction, by the ideas of all human beings. Engels committed those kinds of mistakes. Marx made sure he did not speak about such dubious matters. In short, that is one of the crossroads confronted by philosophy and thinkers.

Contemporary researches on Marx are ongoing and Marxism is developing in diverse ways, but these are completely different from the phase in which we find ourselves. We do not consider Russian Marxism or Chinese Marxism as significant issues; our phase is located at the place where we bring up problems and can develop them further. I believe the future will properly decide which one of these intellectual trends is going to win out. That is one of the lessons Marx has taught us, although he has not stated this explicitly. When we think about the question of what will smash the existing state philosophically and fundamentally, we will realise that the first thing that must be smashed is mythology. Without smashing mythology, nothing else can be smashed. I think that is one of the greatest lessons that Marx's greatness teaches us, namely, in Marx's words, 'there was never a case in which ignorance prospered.'

Notes

1 In the removed passage, Yoshimoto critiques Engels's *The Origin of the Family, Private Property, and the State* (1884), a foundational text of Marxist state theory, on the basis of customary practices on Okinawa's Kudaka Island, whose matriarchal ritual demonstrates the structure of dual power in which the women hold religious authority while their brothers assume political authority. According to Yoshimoto, this dual power is the basis of the emperor system, defining the peculiarities of the Japanese state, which Engels's stadialist theory and Russian orthodox Marxism fail to explain but which can be accurately analysed on the basis of adumbrating Marx's theory of alienation as a point of departure. For Yoshimoto, to theoretically demystify the origins of state power, which was equally fetishised by Japanese wartime ultranationalism, Marxist-Leninism, and post-war democracy, meant to intellectually free oneself of its ideological force field.

Part II
The interpreter as activist

6

Okyeame poma[1]

Exploring the multimodality of translation in precolonial African contexts

Kobus Marais

Introduction

In translation studies, African contexts have not only been underrepresented (Chibamba 2018: 2), but they have also largely been limited to postcolonial theoretical constructs (e.g. Bandia 2008; Inggs and Meintjes 2009; Naudé et al. 2017—in Bible translation). Recent developments in translation studies have focused more attention on Africa. This includes the formation of the Association for Translation Studies in Africa (2018) with its first conference in 2018 (ATSA Conference 2018). In the process, translation on the continent has been studied from different conceptual angles such as development studies (Delgado Luchner 2015; Footitt 2017a, 2017b; Marais 2014; Tesseur 2020) or medical interpreting (Batchelor 2018) and refugee interpreting (Delgado Luchner and Kherbiche 2018, 2019). Recent studies have also started to question the relevance of postcolonial constructs in thinking about translation in Africa (Bandia 2012, 2013; Marais and Feinauer 2017).

Studies about precolonial translation practices in (sub-Saharan) Africa are even more limited. Although my knowledge of work in this field might itself be limited, I am aware of a handful of monographs only, namely excellent work by Ricard (2011)[2] and Mazrui (2016) and the recent PhD theses by Ajayi (2018), Awung (2018), Chibamba (2018) and Talento (2018). One of the obvious reasons for this lack of information is the oralate[3] nature of precolonial African societies, namely that there are no written translations to be studied. This is, however, only a problem if translation is conceptualised as interlingual (between languages) only (Jakobson 2004 [1959]). If translation is conceptualised more broadly to include all semiotic activity (Marais 2019), precolonial Africa renders significant information about translation practices through its artefacts and practices.

Against this background, read together with Tymoczko's (2007) arguments about the internationalisation of translation studies, there seems to be a need for studying precolonial translation practices, in particular as they relate to the emergence of social-cultural reality. I present a case of such precolonial practice and link it to multimodal[4] semiotic theory in order to argue that translation as an interlingual practice is a European theoretical construct that can be deconstructed by data from precolonial practices and that this (non-European) data call for expanding the conceptualisation of translation itself.

In this chapter, I present data from the West African context, focusing on the notions of *okyeame* and *okyeame poma*, to make an argument regarding precolonial translation practice, multimodality and the agency of the translators in this context. I link this data to Peirce's notion of indexical signs as a method for understanding the emergence of social-cultural reality (Parmentier 2016) and social-cultural agency.

Methodologically, I have to clarify that I am an outsider to the Akan culture. Furthermore, I have no primary data but rely in total on secondary data, which I reference copiously. In particular, I make ample use of Yankah's (1995) specialist work on the *akyeama* and *akyeama poma*, which was the most authoritative source I found on this topic. My interpretation of this secondary data might thus be skewed towards my interests and remains open for debate.

Okyeame

In translation studies, precolonial translation practices in Africa have traditionally been linked to orality (Finnegan 2007; Jousse 2000; Ong 1967, 1995), based on the links between translation studies and literary studies. Bandia (2008, 2015) has established himself as the foremost translation studies scholar in this line of thinking, arguing that even written literary texts by African authors could be regarded as translations of an oral narrative into a written narrative. This line of argument holds true, in my opinion, but it limits the scope of translation studies to intralingual (rewording within a language) or interlingual translation. As Chibamba (2018) shows, and as is known about the rest of the world, not even in postcolonial Africa is translation interlingual only. Ajayi (2018) equally argues that one theoretically needs more than interlingual translation to understand translation practices in precolonial Africa, referring to precolonial Nigeria. I thus decided to explore the evidence on the 'linguist's staff' to see whether the theoretical and methodological conceptualisation above would allow insight into translation practices in precolonial African society and culture.

References to the 'linguist's staff' appear in various writings on West African politics, economics and society (Bennett n.d.: 434; Brokensha 1964: 19; Dickson 1966: 429; Lechtman 1988: 133; Owusu 1979: 94). In a particularly interesting case, an Asante chief, Akrofi, was deposed as chief by the English administration because he appointed himself as king (Brokensha 1964). One of the charges against him was that he appointed a 'linguist,' which was the prerogative of kings only. So, who was 'the linguist' and what was the 'linguist's staff,' which is still found in postcolonial politics (Owusu 1979: 94)?

The context in which I am talking about the 'linguist' and the 'linguist's staff' is the Akan-speaking people in the central, southern and southwestern part of modern Ghana (Ross 2002: 21). This language, which is a Niger-Congo language, has about 9.1 million speakers (Eberhard et al. 2019) with a number of dialects. It is a language of wider communication and the de facto national working language (Eberhard et al. 2019). The

Asante is the biggest group in this area (Ross 2002: 19), and Asante is listed as a dialect of Akan with about 2.8 million speakers (Eberhard et al. 2019). The linguist and linguist's staff probably originated with the Asante[5] people, although it also occurs among other groups (Yankah 1995: 19). While archaeological evidence from the area dates back to about the tenth century CE, the Asante political history is said to have its origin in 1701 CE in a precolonial empire that lasted until 1901 (Muller 2013: 15), although this empire started emerging as early as the seventeenth century (Blackpast 2019). This was followed by a colonial era under British rule from 1901 to 1957 CE and a postcolonial era from 1957 CE to the present (Muller 2013: 15). Since 1978, the language has been written in Latin script (Eberhard et al. 2019).

Of particular interest in this chapter is the 'linguists,' known as *akyeama* (singular *okyeame*) and their ceremonial staffs (*akyeama poma*) (see Figure 6.1 for an example). My interest was originally raised by one of my colleagues, a theoretical linguist specialising in African languages,[6] and I pondered its implications for multimodal translation for a while. I also had in the back of my head a study that one of the MA students in our department did a few years back (Tshovhewaho 2013) in which he studied ways in which royal language in Tshivenda[7] was translated for the general public, i.e. intralingual translation. At that point, I did not see the link with multimodal translation as the student just focused on intralingual translation between Royal Tshivenda and ordinary Tshivenda, and I am not sure if the task of interlingual translation in the South African context is as institutionalised as it is in West Africa. While I have not done an extensive, original study on the topic, I think that the evidence that I managed to obtain is sufficient to draw initial conclusions on which further research can be based.

Chiefs usually have more than one *okyeame*, sometimes as many as twelve (Yankah 1995: 89). Interestingly, the female rulers had their own spokespeople who were mostly female but did not carry a staff (Yankah 1995: 100). The reason for this difference was that male chiefs were concerned with the public domain, and the staffs carried messages to their hosts/enemies while the female rulers were concerned with female issues in the kingdom (Yankah 1995: 100).

The word *okyeame* in general has the meaning of 'rhetorical excellence' (Yankah 1995: 5), i.e. being skilled in a variety of rhetorical abilities, and is embedded in the role that rhetorical acuity plays in many African societies and politics. Yankah (1995: 15) also lists similar occurrences in the Americas, Indonesia and the Philippines. As he (1995: 6) points out, based on the reference to 'rhetorical excellence,' the translation of *okyeame* with 'linguist' is wrong, and he argues that one should maintain the term *okyeame* rather than try to translate it—a suggestion which I take up in the rest of this text. Yankah suggests that, in terms of modern linguistic (pragmatic) theories, the *okyeame*'s work could be conceptualised as reported speech, surrogation,[8] spoken language or face-to-face communication. He makes clear (1995: 16) that the practices on the ground are much richer than the theoretical conceptualisation allows.

The tasks of the *okyeame* are wide-ranging in nature and require a high level of skill. Some scholars suggest that the *okyeame* is an advisor, judicial advocate, military attaché, foreign minister, prime minister and political trouble-shooter (Ross 2002: 89). Others suggest mediating speech, envoy, counsellor, consultant and ritual officiant in libation prayers (Yankah 1995: 34). Important for my argument is to note that *akyeame* did not only use verbal language but also visual icons (Yankah 1995: 34), making use of what Yankah calls an 'intercultural semiotic' (1995: 35). While

Figure 6.1 'Linguist staff finial representing a seated man pointing at his eye,' wood and gold leaf. Gift of Alfred C. Glassell, Jr., The Museum of Fine Arts, Houston.

men made use of staffs, female *akyeama* used garments (Yankah 1995: 3) with symbolic messages, again engaging in translating meaning from one material form to another. He is adamant about the fact that it is virtually impossible to separate the verbal and the visual in the case of the *okyeame*. He (1995: 114) argues that the king's speech can be animated in two ways by the *okyeame*, namely supplementative and substitutive. The former means that the *okyeame* speak after the king and complete his speech so that the two speeches could be juxtaposed. In the second case, the *okyeame* speaks on behalf of the king, who may or may not be present. The *okyeame*'s role included protecting the king should he make verbal mistakes in communication (Yankah 1995: 90). The *okyeame* is also confidant and counsellor, and he should have

[a]n uncommon familiarity with traditional lore, custom, and history, as well as wisdom, experience, and skills in the forensic arts, oratory, logic, diplomacy, and public relations. ... the quintessence of moral virtues: sincerity, loyalty, probity, and selfless devotion.

(Yankah 1995: 88)

In another description, Yankah puts it as follows:

Indeed, formal discourse within the royal domain scarcely qualifies as communication without an intermediary who smooths out the rough edges of talk. These roughnesses need not involve malicious words; they may be stylistic, structural, lexical, or thematic; for the *okyeame* is in many cases both a master of occult science and lord of diplomacy. In the *okyeame*'s care, royal words, whether whispered or spoken, may be paraphrased, elaborated, punctuated with history, ornamented with metaphor, enlivened with proverbs and allegories, or even dramatized outright. Through the art of the surrogate orator, royal words are refined, poeticized, and made palatable for public consumption.

(1995: 22)

The *okyeame* was thus an official at the Akan court. He was the highest official in the court and was 'not only the spokesman for the chief but also an advisor, an intermediary with his subjects, a store of knowledge, a legal expert, an ambassador, and occasionally, a ritual officiator' (Asare 2011: 18). Another source (Quarcoopome 1996: 104) describes the *okyeame* as 'the spokesperson of the chief but also an advisor, an intermediary with his subject, a store of knowledge, a legal expert, an ambassador, and occasionally, a ritual officiator.' An *okyeame* must come up with the words, proverb, saying, or metaphor that will most accurately express what the chief is saying or what is being said to the chief. This means that an *okyeame* must not only be a good speaker but must also know as much or more about the social and political system as the chief he serves (Quarcoopome 1996: 18) and

articulate, eloquent, and concise in interpreting the ruler's thoughts and traditional lore in a clear and assertive manner. In particular, he must be adept at proverbial language because, in a traditional chief's court, there is hardly any serious conversation that does not use proverbs and sayings.

(Quarcoopome 1996: 104)

Akyeame lead representatives for any delegation sent to make enquiries from deities. They also lead delegations to deliver messages from one chief to another. Delegations to inform another chief of the death of a chief would always have an *okyeame* to perform acts of representation, mediation, judicial advocacy, political troubleshooting and the preservation and interpretation of royal history (Quarcoopome 1996: 18–19). The *okyeame*'s most visible public role is as principal intermediary between the ruler and those who seek his counsel, leading to the popular characterisation of his profession as being that of a linguist. Drawing upon vast knowledge and considerable oratorical and diplomatic skills, the *okyeame* eloquently engages in verbal discourse on behalf of the chief and his visitors. He relays the words of visitors to the king and transmits the king's response, often with poetic or metaphorical embellishment (Clarke n.d.: 2). It was his primary duty to recast the chief's pronouncements as proverbs, to convey the meaning of the chief's words in a witty, appealing way to instruct, inform, educate and entertain the people. However, the *okyeame* was much more than a wordsmith or the reciter of little moral snippets. His vast knowledge and wisdom—especially of the wisdom contained in the proverbs—made him an invaluable adviser to the chief, often requiring him to act as diplomat, counsellor, legal advisor, historian, ambassador and even a military attaché (Imagawa and Joffe 2017: 2).

The *okyeame* is thus an official in the royal court of the Akan, entrusted with a wide variety of communicative tasks that relate to the royal house, the politics of the state and its communication with its citizens and other states.

Apart from determining the tasks, it is also important to understand the motivation for the position of *akyeame* and the broader role they played in society (see Yankah 1995: 31ff. for a history). The social background to the *okyeame* is the avoidance of face-to-face communication because of the sacredness of the royal office (Yankah 1995: 88), what Yankah calls 'the politics of avoidance.' These practices, including avoiding direct gaze, is aimed at protecting the ego of the royal person (Yankah 1995: 88), which is aimed at protecting the sanctity of the royal person. The kingdom was legitimised by means of religious ritual and by hiding the messages of the elite from the general populace in the rituals (Yankah 1995: 90). Muller (2013: 90) argues that ritual allows for socially embodied knowledge in a 'symbolically constituted' environment. Ritualisation, as it were, mutes the communication process because it says what it wants to say without saying it, appealing to embodied knowledge, not 'systematic thinking' (Muller 2013: 90). This ritualisation or embodiment of practice should interest translation studies scholars. It entails a double translation process. It entails translating ideas into practices. It also entails translating those practices into ritual practices, ensconcing them in ritual contexts so that they appear ordained and unquestionable. The translation practice was also twofold in another sense. The royals communicated with the spirits, communicating this message to their *akyeame* while the *akyeame* then communicated this message to the general populace, using proverbs and myths (Muller 2013: 90; see also Ajayi 2018).

Physical and communicative avoidance additionally works at mystifying the position of the chief (Yankah 1995: 101). Linguistic avoidance, e.g. euphemisms, is also used to ensure the sanctity of royalty (Yankah 1995: 106). The avoidance is used specifically when the king is implicated (Yankah 1995: 107), such as in cases where the king was understood to have promised something but he did not intend it as such. Muller (2013: 15) points out that Asante royals are viewed as mediators between the spiritual and the social world. She ascribes the rise and longevity of the Asante kingdom to the rulers' mediating role between their subjects and the spiritual world (Muller 2013: 82). Yankah

(1995: 19) confers that the motivation for the use of *akyeame* would be the need to separate royalty from ordinary life for safety reasons but primarily for the link between religious legitimisation and the state. The dangers that originated with the populace that could threaten the king were also mediated in this way (Yankah 1995: 22), and the *okyeame* also protected the populace from the spiritual power in the wrath of the king by softening his words.

The aim of the practices of the *okyeame* is consensus (Yankah 1995: 23), a key component for the stability of the precolonial political system. The *okyeame* aimed at consensus not only in royal settings but also in cases of storytelling (Yankah 1995: 23) as well as other contexts. Commenting on what has been said allows the audience to voice their agreement. Some of this work includes meta-communication with the aim of creating synergy between speaker and audience to 'diffuse the hazards of performance' (Yankah 1995: 26). Oral performance, as modern interpreters know, is fraught with dangers because of its immediacy. The same holds for royalty in oralate cultures.

Because of their relationship with the spirits, kings were seen as more powerful than normal human beings and their words were believed to have force that could be deadly. This is why they communicated through the *akyeame* who aimed at managing these forces (Yankah 1995: 101). Because they believed that words have 'magic potency' (Yankah 1995: 101), the *okyeame* could break this power or soften it by paraphrasing, not using the exact same words. The *akyeama* thus did more than merely intralingually 'translate' words. They had a wide-ranging communicative function with implications in many areas of society such as politics, diplomacy and religion. They also partook in rituals, translating meaning into ritual practices (Yankah 1995: 101). In oralate societies, ritual keeps alive historical knowledge (Yankah 1995: 101), but perhaps one should study modern political and social systems from this perspective, i.e. the translation of meanings into ritualised meanings, which I think is among the things that Baker (2006) had in mind with her link between narrative and translation. Knowledge of the divine was seen as intuitive and thus not to be spoken about overly much. Silence thus played an important role in this context (Yankah 1995: 103).

It is important to take note of Schildkrout's (1987: 184) argument that Asante culture made ample use of cultural borrowing, though Yankah (1995: 35) points out that this point is debatable. What and how much has been borrowed is not directly relevant to my argument. Rather the point is that the importation of social-cultural artefacts or practices always entail a translation process, as conceptualised above, because the meaning of the artefact/practice changes with the change of context and time. In Schildkrout's (1987: 184) words, 'cultures have a pre-existing system of classification and evaluation, a pervasive cosmology which influences the utility and attractiveness of the new items.' This links strongly to Olivier de Sardan's (2005: 23) view that development is a meaning-making process of adapting to new information, artefacts of practices.

It is important to distinguish between *akyeame* and bilingual interpreters (Yankah 1995: 29). One should think of the *akyeame* in broader categories such as diplomacy (Yankah 1995: 30). As early as the ninth century CE, this position was known (Yankah 1995: 30). These diplomats were not mere parrots but had to exercise judgement and use their rhetoric and cultural skills (Yankah 1995: 31). In all of these respects, the social, political, judicial and so forth are linked to the aesthetic (Yankah 1995: 111). Aesthetics is not relegated to literary art only but made manifest in everyday situations.

Like the modern translator, the *okyeame* is vulnerable because of her or his intermediary position (Yankah 1995: 108). Both the royal house and the public/other states, as the two sides between which the *okyeame* mediates, could find problems with their renditions.

In the position of the *okyeame*, we have an example of a communications expert with wide-ranging skills and influence playing a central role in politics, religion, the judiciary and diplomacy (Yankah 1995: 37–39) by translating messages in a variety of contexts and in a variety of material forms.

Okyeame poma

As indicated above, the *akyeame* did not translate only words. They also used their staff (*poma*) in the communication process, adding a multimodal dimension to the communication. For this chapter, I did not delve into the ritualisation of the *okyeame's* practices, which in itself would constitute a fascinating translation process.

The *okyeame poma* is a symbol in West African politics that 'show clan identity in terms of lineage or ancestry, ethnography, beliefs, values, philosophies among others' (Asare et al. 2016: 226). While the office of *okyeame* dates from precolonial times (as early as the seventeenth century (Quarcoopome 1996: 104) or even earlier (Yankah 1995: 29–30)), the *okyeame poma* seems to be based on official staffs representing British colonial powers and thus of later origin (Clarke n.d.). It should be noted that Schildkrout (1987: 306) argues that the history of the use of the *poma* is more complex than that because there is evidence of the Baule to the west carving *poma* earlier in history. In particular, *poma* given as gifts to chiefs (Schildkrout 1987: 188) or just artefacts in society at large (Schildkrout 1987: 306) were widespread among the Asante in the nineteenth century. Apart from being a symbol of the power of the *akyeame*, the *poma* itself carries meaning (Yankah 1995: 36), resulting in a 'double-layered mediation strategy.' The sculpting work on the finial of the *poma* is an indication of a particular value, carrying semiotic import. 'As eponymous totems, as personified voices of the gods and ancestors, the animals have a semeiotic significance and are spokesmen of a way of life' (Hellbusch 1978: xix). The more *poma* he had available, the more powerful a king was regarded to be. The *okyeame* would sit next to the king, holding the *poma* in his right hand (Yankah 1995: 36).

The carvings on the *poma*, while iconic signs of particular animals or other referents, were indexical of the power of the *okyeame* as well as of certain proverbs and thus, simultaneously, symbolic of particular cultural values and meanings (Asare 2011; Beckwith and Fisher 1999: 373–375; Obeng and Obeng 2006: 127–128; Quarcoopome 1996: 104). This shows the link between different types of sign and the reason why an interlingual theory of translation only does not suffice to explain translational phenomena. The *okyeame poma* entails this translation process in quite some detail. As a case in point, let us consider one such staff, the picture of which I had taken from the work of Asare et al. (2016: 229). While Asare et al. deal with the use of these motifs in textile design, he explains the proverb and the meaning captured in the motif.[9]

Iconically, the artwork on the *poma* depicts a lion and a child with the child touching the lion. Indexically, the *poma* points to the authority of the *okyeame*, but also to a proverb from the Asante culture. It is this second indexical meaning that is translated by Asare et al. (2016: 229) into the words 'a child does not know the lion.' Depending on the context in which it is interpreted, the sign could also have other indexical meanings, such as being an index of a foreign culture, of African art or of a particular development in African politics. The meaning of a child touching a lion thus has to be translated, i.e. the meaning has to be processed, because it is not self-evident. It is not 'in' the iconicity. Even the indexicality is not given. It needs to be determined. This semiotic work needs to be done to engender meaning. In the context of the Asante, Asare et al. (2016: 229) argue that the artwork on the *poma* points to the proverb 'A child does not know a lion,' which is, in Peircean terms, a symbolic sign that can be engendered to mean that ignorance can be dangerous. The further implications would be that one should be knowledgeable rather than ignorant. Part of the function of the *okyeame* would be to select the appropriate *poma* for the appropriate occasion, thus performing semiotic work by interpreting the situation and constraining the audience's interpretation thereof.

The *okyeame* has to choose an *okyeame poma* and a metaphorical proverb that wisely illustrates a solution to the state of affairs he had to address. The *okyeame poma* functions as semantics, which is the relationship between phrases or symbols and what they represent or their meaning (Baule Prestige Staff n.d.). In this way, the words and images together create the meaning that the *okyeame* wants to convey.

Multimodal translation

The question now remains: where is the translation? If one argues that the term 'translation' refers to interlingual translation only, there is no translation involved in the process described above. If, however, one argues that translation is a technical term that refers to semiotic work done to constrain the semiotic process, the process described above is rich in translation actions. So, what semiotic work was done in the example above? Firstly, the creator(s) of the *poma* performed semiotic work, choosing a particular one from the possible proverbs (symbolic meanings) and translating that symbolic meaning into iconic meaning, i.e. the sign of the lion and the child. The *akyeame* then had to do semiotic work by interpreting the situation that they had to mediate and then choose an appropriate *poma*, the meaning of which they would explain to the audience and work into their interaction with the audience.

An interesting point about the semiotic work described above is that it oscillates between idea and matter. The material *poma* is a translation of the ideational proverb while the materiality of the chosen *poma* is translated into a speech, a set of ideas, by the *okyeame*. The idea expressed by the proverb is, obviously, already a translation from previous processes. Somewhere in the past, human beings had had experiences that they translated into the proverb. No translation process is thus limited to a particular source system and a particular target system, which is why I coined the terms 'incipient' and 'subsequent' systems. The proverb is an incipient sign system (one of many possible ones) for this particular *poma*, but it is a subsequent system to other translation processes. Equally, the *poma* is one (of many possible) subsequent sign system to the proverb, but an incipient sign system for the *okyeame*.

Furthermore, the semiotic work seems to entail an oscillation between icons, indexes and symbols, as Peirce theorised it. Assumed theories of meaning in translation studies tend to either absolutise the materiality of the sign or dematerialise it to the point of having virtually no materiality. The analysis above shows that all representamens[10] need to be instantiated in material form to be observable. Even private thoughts in the brain, the so-called *res rationis*, or what Deacon (2013) calls 'ententionality,' need the brain as a material substance for its existence. In my view, however, these ententional features are not reducible to the brain and the materiality in which they become intersubjective. The ententional emerges from the material, co-exists with it and is irreducibly interwoven with it.

In my view, these are the kind of practices that translation studies scholars need to study to get a better understanding of the forms that 'translation,' generally conceptualised below as negentropic semiotic work, takes in various contexts. While all of these forms are of the basic category of translation, i.e. working on semiotic material for a particular purpose, they also all differ in that specific contexts require specific forms.

In the remainder of the chapter, I work out some of the aspects of such a semiotic theory of translation.

A semiotic theory of translation

Contra the Toury (1995) school of thinking, I conceptualise 'translation' as a technical term. In this technical conceptualisation, translation is negentropic semiotic work performed with the aim of constraining 'semiotic material' (Marais 2019: 137–142) in order to guide interpretation (Aguiar et al. 2015). Seeing that the whole of reality is subject to a tendency towards equilibrium (entropy) and that entropy can only be countered by work (in the physicist sense of the word) or negative entropy (negentropy), I argue that semiosis is also subject to entropy and that the creation of meaning entails work (negentropy) to counter this entropy. Translation is work because it is aimed against the entropic tendency to which meaning making is also subject. In particular, translation works against both the equilibrium and chaotic tendencies in meaning making, namely that something can mean only one thing (equilibrium) or that something can mean anything (chaos). If a semiotic process is in equilibrium, it is no longer a difference that makes a difference. In contrast, maximum entropy, i.e. if there is no structure in meaning making, would cause maximum chaos, which might work in certain aesthetic contexts but not in general communication. Translation is thus semiotic work done with the aim of keeping semiosis in a state at the edge of chaos.

Translation is thus always a process in time (and sometimes in space[11]) that pertains to meaning making and meaning taking, i.e. semiosis. As explained above, it is negentropic because it imposes constraints on semiotic processes. It is called 'work' because it imposes constraints on the semiotic process in order to make it possible to understand meaning (Aguiar et al. 2015: 12). In other words, if some organism wants to understand something or wants to communicate with another organism so that the other organism can understand, the communicating organism has to constrain the semiotic process in which they both take part. It has to limit the semiotic process of which it is part to a particular aspect thereof, or it has to limit all the possible meanings it could communicate to another organism to a particular set of meanings. This is done by choosing specific semiotic material, e.g. sounds, images, smells, tastes, touches, and structuring them in a particular way to exclude as many meanings as possible and to guide the other organism as closely as possible (Sperber and Wilson 1986) to the set of meanings that the sender intends. As hermeneutics and communication studies have shown over the years, this is never an exact process, but rather one of creating possible meanings by constraining all meaning.

In general communication, the aim is to perform semiotic work in order to structure the semiotic material to obtain the maximum clarity. Note here that the aim at maximum clarity does not entail absolute clarity or certainty but refers to the economy of using semiotic material as explicated in relevance theory and other versions of pragmatics. All users of semiotic material seem to be aware of the need to limit the potentially unlimited number of interpretants to which a representamen can give rise. This aim is never achieved absolutely, but hopefully sometimes, in the pragmatic sense of the word. In other words, if the representamen can be structured in such a way that it guides the receiver of the sign towards the most plausible interpretant, the semiotic work has been successful.

The point of my argument is that semiosis, like metabolism, is a constant process of meaning making, and like metabolism, it requires work to constrain it, e.g. through genres or text types, to be meaningful. Semiotic material is thus constantly being worked, i.e. being translated. The information an organism gets through its senses is worked by relating it to meaningful concepts that the organism already knows. These concepts are worked into, in the case of human beings, words that are uttered. These words are worked into concepts by the hearer, who then works them into a response. So, between transduction (the physical-chemical changes in signals received by the senses) and translation (the physical-chemical brain processes that change the form of meaning and the meaning of form), meaning is constantly being worked over.

For translation studies, the major implication of the above is that translation is not limited to interlingual translation, as some translation studies scholars still prefer it. Rather, translation refers to processes that are always semiotic, utilising the full range of semiotic material. Even interlingual translation is intersemiotic translation. For this reason, I suggested (Marais 2019: 144–145) to do away with Jakobson's categories of intralingual, interlingual and intersemiotic translation because, from my perspective, all translation is intersemiotic, i.e. between semiotic systems. It would thus rather make sense to take a systems perspective on the matter and talk about intra-, inter- and extra-systemic translation. Then one is free to choose the level of observation, determining a particular system, to which intra-, inter- and extra-systemic translation is relative. This thinking allows for multimodal translation in principle because it does not stipulate what the material form of the semiosis in the translation process is. Meaning through photos and meaning through words are thus equally translation processes, though constrained by the different affordances and constraints of their materiality. The point is that meaning is not only created through spoken or written language. Meaning is created through customs, through practices, through artefacts, through social conventions, through technological advances, and so on. The whole of society/culture is a web of meaning, work done by living organisms in response to an environment, meaning-making work to make sense of or to respond sensibly to an environment. This web of meaning has been/is being created through translation, which means that all of society/culture has a translational aspect to it. This is the domain of study in translation studies, and this is how translation studies can study precolonial translation practices.

This conceptualisation opens the possibility of studying translation practices in precolonial contexts without having to presuppose the existence of written records. Written records would be only one kind of data to work with, among others like cultural practice, artefacts, customs, and so forth. All of the latter would entail a translation process, i.e. constraining semiotic material in order to make meaning. Before dealing with the data, however, I would like to delve more deeply into the concepts that Peircean semiotics offers in this regard, namely indexicality.

Indexicality

The next step would thus be to present a specific method for studying multimodal translation processes, i.e. processes in which neither the incipient nor the subsequent semiotic systems (Marais 2019: 123–125) entail language. If one defines translation as a process that includes all possible forms of semiosis, the problem is to find a method with which to study translation processes that did not take place in language (spoken or written) or about which one cannot ask people by using language. Regarding the first category, how does one study the translation of a painting into dance? Alternatively, how does one study the translation of music into photography? These kinds of questions are usually asked within intermediality or multimodality studies, and they present interesting analyses. However, scholars of intermediality have not yet come up with a way of describing the translation process in detail as one can do with interlingual translation. In other words, they do not yet have a way of mapping different mediums onto one another, as one would be able to map different languages on one another.

There is, however, an even more difficult problem. If my definition of translation holds, it means that what we call society or culture is the effect of translation, i.e. negentropic semiotic work. Social relations and culture emerge from this semiotic work, but the question is then: how can one study this work? In human beings, social relations and cultural practices quite often, if not mostly, take place at the level of tacit knowledge. Some of it is even purposefully shifted to that domain, as Muller (2013: 90) argues about the use of ritual in the maintenance of national coherence in the Asante kingdom. The embodied nature of knowledge and meaning means that one cannot ask people to explain their society or culture because they would not necessarily know why they do things in certain ways. Anthropology has also had to deal with this problem, to which they responded with the methodology of observation and immersion.

In my case, I am not primarily interested in the social relations or cultural practices as such but in the semiotic work that went into creating them. I am interested in the translational aspect of the emergence of these relations and practices. Based on the work by Parmentier (2016), I thus propose that we study society and culture as the effects of the semiotic work that created them. Parmentier, thinking in Peircean terms, suggests that anthropology should be interested in the meaning of social and cultural practices and artefacts. Using the Peircean notion of indexicality, one would thus be able to study society and culture as indexes of the processes that created them just like a footprint in the sand would be an index of the process that created it. Peirce conceptualised a sign as the relationship between a sign-vehicle, which he called the representamen, an object to which the representamen refers and an interpretant, which mediates between the representamen and object to give what is commonly called the meaning. Zooming in on the relationship between representamens and object, Peirce suggested three categories of relationships, namely iconic, indexical and symbolic. Broadly speaking, iconic representamens bear a resemblance to their objects and symbolic representamens have a law-like or generalised relationship with their objects. In the first case, a photo of granddad stands in an iconic relationship to granddad while the word granddad stands in a symbolic relationship to granddad. Peirce calls the third type of sign an index, that is, a representamen that stands in a real (causal or spatial) relationship to the object. Thus, the photo of granddad is an index of the camera that took the photo or the track of a lion is an index of the lion that walked in this particular spot.

Similarly, the notion of index allows one to study the traces of semiotic work as indicative of the semiotic work that went into their creation. One could thus consider a building from a number of angles. In physical terms, one could study the forces that influence it, drawing conclusions as to the strength of the materials needed. One could also study the building from the point of view of the people using it, considering the sizes of the rooms needed (such as offices for a bank and construction space for the building of an engineering company). One could also study the building from the perspective of the semiotic work that went into constructing it. For instance, large windows on the northern side of a building (in the southern hemisphere) could be an index of green values that have influenced the design.

With such a method, one could present arguments about the meaning-making processes that lie behind cultural artefacts or processes. Understanding the meaning of cultural processes and artefacts would be helpful in a number of ways. It could help with critical analyses, but especially in the case of the link between translation and development, it could help development practitioners understand the meanings of existing practices in communities in which they suggest changes. This method could also allow an understanding of meaning making in cases where it is not advisable to ask people about their practices or in cases where the practices are embodied to the point where people would not be able to express their understandings in words.

These arguments will, however, need to be made specifically for each case because signs do not mean in general, they mean in a context. Peirce made this clear when he conceptualised a sign as something standing for something else to someone 'in some respect.' The aim of this method would thus be to view cultural artefacts or practices as interpretants, i.e. the result of a meaning-making process. From the interpretant, one would then investigate and present arguments about possible semiotic processes of which the artefacts are indexes (or traces). There will, obviously, also be counter-arguments that need to be considered because the fact that the representamen stands in an indexical (real) relationship with the object does not mean that this relationship is self-evident. Because it is a semiotic relationship, it needs to be argued.

With this broadened conceptualisation of translation and a methodology for studying it, translation studies scholars can try to understand precolonial translation practices by means of arguing indexically about the artefacts and other forms of social and cultural evidence that are available.

Conclusion

The conceptualisation and data presented above seem to indicate that all translators have agency because they perform semiotic work from which emerges social-cultural practices, structures and artefacts. While it is true that translators can also be activists (Tymoczko 2007, 2010) and that particular contexts may call for activism by translators (Colon Rodriquez 2019), it does not mean that activism is the only form that agency can take. Translators are agents through their semiotic work even if they do not have a particular activist agenda. Complex social and cultural systems could emerge with and without particular intentions of all the agents in the system.

In the case I presented, the *akyeame* clearly had agency, shaping and influencing various spheres of Akan society and culture. I doubt, however, if one can call them activists in the modern sense of the word. Rather, it seems to me that activism is but one subcategory of agency and that agency can take various forms in various contexts. What needs further study, however, is the relation between intention, agency and the emergence of social-cultural systems.

Related topics

The Single Most Translated Short Story in the History of African Writing; Against a Single African Literary Translation Theory; Translator, Native Informant, Fixer.

Notes

1 This is the Akan term that has been commonly translated as 'the linguist's staff.' Later in the article, I discuss the problems with this translation, which is why I used the original term and not the translation here. The term is pronounced *akyeamepoma* [àtɕìàmípómá], with thanks to Dr Reggie Akuoko Duah.
2 Because I do not read French, I did not have access to this book though I met Ricard once and had some discussions with him about his impressive work.
3 'Oralate' is a term used in orality studies to indicate cultures that are pristinely oral. Orality is common in many cultures that also have a written culture, i.e. oral and written modes of communication coexist. Oralate refers to cultures where there are no concomitant written cultures.
4 Multimodality refers to communication in which different modes of representation are combined, e.g. written text with photos and diagrams.
5 Also spelled 'Ashante' (Yankah 1995: 1).
6 I thank Dr Kristina Riedel for making me aware of this notion.
7 A language in the Southern Bantu group and one of the eleven official languages of South Africa, spoken mostly in the northern Limpopo Province.
8 Speaking on behalf of someone, i.e. spokesperson.
9 Interested readers can consult sources in the reference list referring to the Akan culture to see more of these motifs.
10 The technical term in Peircean semiotics to denote the 'sign' or 'sign vehicle.'
11 For example, information generated in a car factory in Germany needs to be localised in South Africa, changing the space in which the information operates. Alternatively, consider performing a Christmas pantomime conceptualised in Germany (where Christmas means snow) in South Africa (where Christmas usually means sweltering heat), i.e. the translation needs to account for the change in space.

Further reading

Milton, John, and Paul Bandia (2009) *Agents of Translation*. Amsterdam: Benjamins.

This collection of essays explores the role of translators as agents in various contexts of development.

Sturge, Kate (2007) *Representing Others: Translation, Ethnography and the Museum*. Manchester: St Jerome.

This book explores the links between translation and the kind of ethnographic work that can shed light on pre-colonial translation practices.

'Translation and Development' (2018) Special edition of *The Translator* 24 (4).

This collection of articles explores a variety of aspects concerning the relationship between translation and development in a number of different contexts. It provides an initial basis for comparing the role that translation practices play in the development of society.

References

Aguiar, Daniella, Pedro Ata, and Joao Queiroz (2015) 'Intersemiotic Translation and Transformational Creativity,' *Punctum* 1 (2): 11–21.
Ajayi, O. Francis (2018) 'Translational and National Consciousness in Nigeria: A Socio-historical Study,' PhD thesis, Concordia University, Montreal, Quebec, Canada.

Asare, Daniel K. (2011) 'The Use of Asante Linguist Staff Symbols in Textile Design, Master of Fine Art (Textile Design) thesis, Kwame Nkrumah University of Science and Technology.

Asare, Daniel K., Ebenezer K. Howard, and Abdul F. Ibrahim (2016) 'The Aesthetic and Philosophical Values of Asante Linguist Staff Symbols in Textile Design,' *International Journal of Innovative Research and Development* 5 (8): 225–237.

Association for Translation Studies in Africa (2018) [Online]. Available at: https://atranslationstudie safrica.wordpress.com/ [accessed 15 October 2019].

ATSA Conference (2018) [Online] Available at: https://atranslationstudiesafrica.wordpress.com/atsa-conference/ [accessed 15 October 2019].

Awung, Felix (2018) 'Representing Africa through Translation: Ferdinand Oyono's *Une Vie de Boy* and *Le Vieux Nègre et la Médaille* in English,' PhD Thesis, University of the Free State, Bloemfontein.

Baker, Mona (2006) *Translation and Conflict. A Narrative Account.* New York: Routledge.

Bandia, Paul (2008) *Translation as Reparation: Writing and Translation in Postcolonial Africa.* Manchester: St Jerome.

Bandia, Paul (2012) 'Postcolonial Literary Heteroglossia: A Challenge for Homogenizing Translation,' *Perspectives: Studies in Translatology* 2 (4): 419–431.

Bandia, Paul (2013) 'Translation and Current Trends in African Metropolitan Literature,' in *Intimate Enemies: Translation in Francophone Contexts.* Eds. Kathryn Batchelor and Claire Bisdorff. Liverpool: Liverpool University Press. 235–251.

Bandia, Paul (2015) 'Introduction: Orality and Translation,' *Translation Studies* 8 (2): 125–127.

Batchelor, Kathryn (2018) 'Interlingual Translation and Healthcare Communication in West Africa,' Paper read at the First Conference of the Association for Translation Studies in Africa, Stellenbosch, 25–26 May 2018.

Baule Prestige Staff (n.d.) [Online]. Available at: www.randafricanart.com/Asante_staff.html [accessed 15 October 2019].

Beckwith, Carol, and Angela Fisher (1999) *African Ceremonies.* New York: Harry N. Abrams Inc.

Bennett, George (n.d.) 'The Gold Coast General Election of 1954,' *Parliamentary Affairs* 7 (4): 430–439.

Blackpast (2019) [Online]. Available at: www.blackpast.org/global-african-history/ashanti-empire-asante-kingdom-18th-late-19th-century/ [accessed 15 October 2019].

Boakye, Emmanuel O. (n.d.) 'Symbols on Asante Linguist Staffs,' [Online]. Available at: www.google.co.za/search?source=hp&ei=4OnjW7rhIou5kwWI1LawAg&q=linguist±staff±articles&oq=linguist±s&gs_l=psy-ab.1.1.35i39k1l2j0l8.579.7574.0.10762.23.17.2.0.0.0.436.2003.2-2j3j1.6.0....0...1c.1.64.psy-ab..17.6.1432.0..0i131k1j0i10k1j0i30k1j0i10i30 [accessed 15 October 2019].

Brokensha, David (1964) 'Chief Akrofi of Larteh, 1885–1900,' *Transactions of the Historical Society of Ghana* 7: 12–23.

Chibamba, Mwamba (2018) 'Translation Practices in a Developmental Context: An Exploration of Public Health Communication in Zambia,' PhD dissertation, University of Ottawa, Ottawa.

Clarke, Christa (n.d.) 'Linguist Staff (Okyeamepoma) (Asante Peoples),' [Online]. Available at: www.khanacademy.org/humanities/art-africa/west-africa/ghana/a/linguist-staff-okyeamepoma-asante-peoples [accessed 15 October 2019].

Colon Rodriquez, Raul E. (2019) 'A Complex and Transdisciplinary Approach to Slow Collaborative Activist Translation,' in *Complexity Thinking in Translation Studies: Methodological Considerations.* Eds. Kobus Marais and Reine Meylaerts. New York: Routledge. 152–179.

Deacon, Terrence W. (2013) *Incomplete Nature: How Mind Emerged from Matter.* New York: WW Norton & Company.

Delgado Luchner, Carmen (2015) 'Setting up a Master's in Conference Interpreting at the University of Nairobi: An interdisciplinary Case Study of a Development Project Involving Universities and International Organisations,' PhD Thesis, University of Genève, Genève.

Delgado Luchner, Carmen, and Leila Kherbiche (2018) 'Without Fear or Favour?: The Positionality of ICRC and UNHCR Interpreters in the Humanitarian Field,' *Target* 30 (3): 408–429.

Delgado Luchner, Carmen, and Leila Kherbiche (2019) 'Ethics Training for Humanitarian Interpreters,' *Journal of War and Culture Studies* 12(3): 251–267 (Special Issue).

Dickson, K. B. (1966) 'Trade Patterns in Ghana at the Beginning of the Eighteenth Century,' *Geograhical Review* 56 (3): 417–431.

Eberhard, David M., Gary F. Simons, and Charles D. Fennig (eds.) (2019) *Ethnologue: Languages of the World*, 22nd ed. Dallas, TX: SIL International. Online version: http://www.ethnologue.com [accessed 10 February 2020].

Finnegan, Ruth (2007) *The Oral and beyond: Doing Things with Words in Africa*. Oxford: James Currey.

Footitt, Hilary (2017a) 'International Aid and Development: Hearing Multilingualism, Learning from Intercultural Encounters in the History of OxfamGB,' *Language and Intercultural Communication* 17 (4): 518–533.

Footitt, Hilary (2017b) *Translating Development*. [Online]. Available at: https://modernlanguagesresearch.blogs.sas.ac.uk/2017/10/30/translating-development/ [accessed 20 November 2017].

Hellbusch, Judy A. (1978) 'Animal Symbolism in Akan Art: Literature in Wood and Brass,' Master of Arts thesis, California State University, Northridge.

Imagawa, Misaki (2015) 'You Get the Message?: Ashanti Linguist's Staffs,' [Online]. Available at: www.beprimitive.com/blog/you-get-the-message-ashanti-linguists-staffs [accessed 15 October 2019].

Imagawa, Misaki, and Glen Joffe (2017) 'The Power of Proverbs: Ashanti Linguist's Staffs,' [online]. Available at: www.beprimitive.com/blog/two-way-communication-ashanti-linguists-staffs [accessed 15 October 2019].

Inggs, Judith, and Libby Meintjes (2009) *Translation Studies in Africa*. London: Continuum.

Jakobson, Roman (2004 [1959]) 'On Linguistic Aspects of Translation,' in *The Translation Studies Reader* (2nd ed). Ed. Lawrence Venuti. London: Routledge. 138–143.

Jousse, Marcelle (2000) *The Anthroplogy of Geste and Rhythm*. Durban: Mantis Publishing.

Lechtman, Heather (1988) 'Reviewed Work: Red Gold of Africa: Copper in Precolonial History and Culture by Eugenia W. Herbert (Book Review),' *Technology and Culture* 29 (1): 130–133.

Marais, Kobus (2014) *Translation Theory and Development Studies: A Complexity Approach*. London: Routledge.

Marais, Kobus (2019) *A (Bio)semiotic Theory of Translation: The Emergence of Social-cultural Reality*. New York: Routledge.

Marais, Kobus, and Ilse Feinauer (eds.) (2017) *Translation beyond the Postcolony*. Newcastle: Cambridge Scholars Press.

Mazrui, Alamin M. (2016) *Cultural Politics of Translation: East Africa in a Global Context*. New York: Routledge.

Muller, Louise (2013) *Religion and Chieftancy in Ghana: An Explanation of the Persistence of a Traditional Political Institution in West Africa*. Zurich: Lit Verlag.

Naudé, Jacobus A., Cynthia L. Miller-Naudé, and Johannes T. Makutoane (2017) 'Bible Translation in Postcolony Africa: Reclaiming Humanness through Bible Translation Performance,' in *Translation Studies beyond the Postcolony*. Eds. Kobus Marais and Ilse Feinauer. Newcastle upon Tyne: Cambridge Scholars Press. 154–209.

Obeng, Samuel G., and Cecilia S. Obeng (2006) *From Linguistics to Cultural Anthropology: Aspects of Language, Culture and Family Issues in Ghana (West Africa)*. Muenchen: Lincom Europa.

Olivier de Sardan, Jean-Pierre (2005) *Anthropology and Development. Understanding Contemporary Social Change*. London: Zed Books.

Ong, Walter J. (1967) *The Presence of the Word: Some Prolegomena for Cultural and Religious History*. Minneapolis: University of Minnesota Press.

Ong, Walter J. (1995) *Orality and Literacy*. New York: Routledge.

Owusu, Maxwell (1979) 'Politics without Parties: Reflections on the Union Government Proposals in Ghana,' *African Studies Review* 22 (1): 89–108.

Parmentier, Richard J. (2016) *Signs and Society: Further Studies in Semiotic Anthropology*. Bloomington: Indiana University Press.

Quarcoopome, Nii O. (ed.) (1996) *African Form and Imagery: Detroit Collections*. Detroit: Detroit Institute of Arts.

Ricard, Alain (2011) *Traduction et apartheid: Esquisse d'une anthropologie de la textualite*. Paris: CNRS Editions.

Ross, Doran H (2002) *Gold of the Akan from the Glassell Collection*. Houston: Museum of Fine Arts.

Schildkrout, Enid (1987) *The Golden Stool: Studies of the Asante Center and Periphery (Anthropological Papers of the American Museum of Natural History)*. New York: American Museum of Natural History.

Sperber, Dan, and Dianne Wilson (1986) *Relevance: Communication and Cognition*. London: Basil Blackwell.

Talento, Serena (2018) 'Framing Texts/Framing Social Spaces: The Conceptualisation of Literary Translation and Its Discourses in Three Centuries of Swahili Literature,' PhD Thesis, University of Bayreuth, Bayreuth.

Tesseur, Wine (2020) 'Listening, Languages and the Nature of Knowledge and Evidence: What We Can Learning from Investigating 'Listening' in NGOs,' in *Learning and Using Languages in Ethnographic Research*. Eds. Robert Gibb, Annabel Tremlett, and Julien Danero Iglesias. Bristol: Multilingual Matters. 193–206.

Toury, Gideon (1995) *Descriptive Translation Studie—And Beyond*. Amsterdam: John Benjamins.

Tshovhewaho, O. Israel (2013) 'Intralingual Translation of the Venda Royal Language,' MA mini-dissertation, UFS, Bloemfontein.

Tymoczko, Maria (2007) *Enlarging Translation, Empowering Translators*. Manchester: St Jerome.

Tymoczko, Maria (ed.) (2010) *Translation, Resistance, Activism*. Amherst: University of Massachusetts Press.

Yankah, Kwesi (1995) *Speaking for the Chief: Okyeame and the Politics of Akan Royal Oratory*. Bloomington: Indiana University Press.

7

Translator, native informant, fixer

Activism and translation in Mandate Palestine

Sarah Irving

Introduction

In colonial environments, figures such as the interpreter, dragoman, fixer and native informant are rarely viewed as radical or even as possessed of serious agency. On the contrary, they are more likely to be viewed with suspicion, as collaborators with or at least unwitting facilitators of the colonial project. They might be suspected of passing on information that is useful to the coloniser, of giving them skills with which to infiltrate and manipulate indigenous society, or working for colonial institutions in ways which undermine the colonised society and/or anti-imperial struggles. Certainly, these figures tend not to fit into central understandings of activist translation, rarely fitting into translation movements with articulated political aims (Tymoczko 2000) or performing translations that support the actions of radical political groups (e.g. Baker 2016). But, drawing on feminist critiques of the content of activism and Freirean notions of pedagogy as activism (Courington 1999; Freire 1970), this chapter argues that the colonial encounter is one in which definitions of what constitutes activism should incorporate actions which lie outside the realms of formal politics, but which are still intended to affect knowledge and discourse.

This argument is advanced via three case studies of a loose group of Palestinian Arab translators—Elias Haddad, Stephan Hanna Stephan, Jalil Irany and Judeh Docmac—and their interventions into debates around Palestinian selfhood, culture and nationality during the 1920s, 1930s and 1940s. The first study looks at the ways in which several of these men approached transcription and transliteration of colloquial Arabic by foreign ethnographers; the second examines Elias Haddad's translation of Gotthold Lessing's story of Jewish–Christian–Muslim tolerance, *Nathan the Wise* (*Nathan der Weise* 1779/2004); finally, I consider how Haddad and Stephan articulated ideas of Palestinian society through the language manuals they authored. These cases all take place in Mandate Palestine (1917–1948), when Britain, having occupied this part of the Ottoman Empire during World War I, ruled the territory under a League of Nations Mandate under which it was tasked with building structures of self-government for a future independent state. They employ ideas of activism that pay attention to everyday behaviours as well as high-profile acts of political or armed resistance, thus recognising the potential for radicalism in more understated contexts. Palestinian politics in this period is often viewed solely in terms of a small number of factions, headed by elite families and with (often tense and conflictual) links to the British authorities. Looking for other forms of activism, alongside the dominant nationalist groupings, thus permits more nuanced views of opposition to British colonialism and to Zionism, and understanding of the diversity of opinions amongst Palestinians under Mandate rule. The examples of Haddad, Stephan, Irany and Docmac rest on ideas of translation which, as elaborated by David Katan and Kate Sturge, involve not just the interpreting of language but more broadly of culture, explaining and elucidating behaviours, values and ideas between people seen as occupying different cultural spaces and therefore in need of explication in order to understand the meanings underlying their encounters (Katan 2009; Sturge 2007). It is in this interpretative space, where the translator has the power to shape understandings, affect the terms of contact between coloniser and colonised and imbue different peoples with certain characteristics, that their potential for activism is situated.

This broad understanding of activism has a number of methodological implications. It permits the inclusion of a wider range of figures—including those such as dragomans and translators—as actors in political debates and discourses, in this case in the conversations happening in the Arab community of Mandate Palestine. Subsequent historiographies of liberation and resistance movements often obscure the diversity of ideas and visions of a future desirable society held amongst colonised peoples (Coakley 2004; Trouillot 1995: 22, 28–9, 31–69); as studies of social movements highlight, a national liberation movement comprises not just organisations such as political parties, but survives only with broad networks of informal supporters (see Willems and Jegers 2012 for a useful summary). But such an understanding of activism also makes certain demands, many of which parallel those broadenings of definitions of translation which Tymoczko argues are necessary in order to understand its activist potential (2014 [2007]: 189–92 et passim). Amongst these are the widening of source materials beyond canonical works and high culture to less literary texts and archival objects such as notebooks and diaries. Another is the use of ways of reading which historicise and contextualise, drawing on the lessons of relational history to see writings in response and tension with other thinkers of the time and place (Bernard 2013; Lockman 1996). Finally, biographical, long-term views of the subject permit particular statements and ideas to be highlighted as existing dynamically, as argument, push-back, reaction and stance, the products of activism in the context of the moment.

Linked to this is the necessity of considering the judgements and decisions of Arab Palestinians against the events and standards of their own moment, evading the teleological tendencies of much scholarship on the period, which reads the actions of Palestinians under British rule as if they should have foreseen the 1948 Nakba (catastrophe), as the foundation of the State of Israel is termed in Arabic. As Bhambra points out, 'contrasting "indigenous" developments with those initiated from "outside" perpetuates the reified categories of "Europe"' (2007: 142). In this case, to define 'activism' in the Palestinian context solely in terms of the British–Zionist–Arab triangle that seems so clear to many post-1948 writers obscures the ways in which Palestinian Arabs living under the Mandate tried to think through the possibilities for their country in the unstable and hostile environment of British Mandatory occupation. Activism in the

1930s, for instance, was also about considering an independent Palestinian future and the nature of society within it; as such, differences between Palestinian thinkers were not just those arising from the coloniser–colonised relationship, but from political and social conversations happening in the Arabic-speaking world as well.

The translator's many roles

Before considering translation as a form of activism in pre-Nakba Palestine, a sense of who actually performed it is necessary, and highlights the varied social roles to which forms of translation are key. Translating and interpreting included formal roles linked to the ruling power—be it the Ottoman Empire or the British Mandatory authorities—and myriad less institutional practitioners; as Hermans points out, the many challenges of translation studies include the narrow selection of terms available to discuss a huge range of social phenomena, and the fact that these phenomena themselves differ in nature and meaning in different societies (2003: 380, 384). In the English-language writings of those using translators, the first of many words used to denote some form of translation role in the setting of late Ottoman and Mandate Palestine is dragoman, derived from the Arabic word *tarjumān*, meaning a translator, via Greek and Italian. A conventional definition is: 'An interpreter; strictly applied to a man who acts as guide and interpreter in countries where Arabic, Turkish, or Persian is spoken' (OED Online 2019). In the Ottoman period during which Elias Haddad, Stephan Stephan and the other subjects of this chapter grew up, translators with official status were embedded within branches of the state, with the head dragomans of the Ottoman ministries effectively acting as deputy ministers; the dragomans of the foreign consulates, meanwhile, combined language functions with the tasks of a cultural go-between and practical manager (Bosworth 2012).

In Anglophone travel literatures the word 'dragoman' was mainly used for less official figures. These included self-employed fixer-interpreters (or, from the late nineteenth century onwards, those working for tourism agencies) who helped tourists, pilgrims and other visitors in the course of their travels (e.g. Lonni 2011). They were licensed by the Ottoman and later the British authorities and in modern environments would coincide with the professional interpreter/fixer who provides both linguistic help and local knowledge—cultural and logistical—to journalists, aid workers and other foreigners. However, the services they provided overlapped with a looser category, that of educated, bi- or multilingual persons who helped European and American scholars with translation to and from Arabic and with the interpretation of cultural norms and references. These, as we shall see, were often teachers or government employees (like the men who appear in this chapter), and might carry out their work for pay, as part of their own intellectual projects, or a combination of the two. Finally, one might identify the classic creator of literary texts, the usual image of the translator, who in this setting ranges from elite men such as Ruhi al-Khalidi, with the ability to put substantial time aside to write and translate (Gribetz 2016: 41–52), to middle-class professionals who incorporated translation into the fringes of their working lives, such as Elias Haddad. Often one person might fit into several of these classifications. Indeed, sometimes it is only when we look at activities across the different fields that we can identify patterns that suggest an activist intentionality, a point that highlights the usefulness of long-term and biographical approaches when considering how we analyse the social and political roles of translators.

Despite the absence of a coherent literature on the subject of dragomans, interpreters and native informants in the Palestinian context, a survey of publications yields scattered examples and insights. Mairs and Muratov have done important work on the idea generally, and particularly on the case of Solomon Negima, a dragoman who ushered a wide range of European and American clients around southern Syria in the Late Ottoman period. Negima's case, especially, highlights the potential for the local informant to shape the perceptions and ideas of those for whom they interpret and plan trips, via the choices and framing of sites visited (Mairs 2016: 10–15 et passim; Mairs and Muratov 2015: 4, 29–30). Those dragomans attached to consulates had official status under the Ottoman political system and often represented their employers at events and in local negotiations; they thus possessed a certain discretionary power and influence, while shaping the perceptions of their employers regarding local events and social dynamics (De Ballobar 2011; Lonni 2011). And, as I have argued elsewhere, local men whose formal role mainly comprised logistics and daily interpreting for Western archaeologists should also be understood as influencing cultural and historical understandings (Irving 2017).

The footnotes of many Euro-American biographical and ethnographic writings on Palestine, however, reveal that the kinds of tasks entrusted to dragomans and interpreters were not only taken up by those for whom this was their main form of employment. Indeed, one of the main groups that engaged in 'amateur' interpreting and translation (both linguistic and cultural) was schoolteachers, presumably because they were educated men likely to be able to speak one or more European languages. An unstudied example is Dschirius Jusif (also known as Jirius Abu Yusif), who taught at the Lutheran school at the Muristan, in the centre of the Old City of Jerusalem, but who was also a contributor to a collection of traditional stories collected in his native village of Bir Zeit (near Ramallah) and published by the German folklorists Paul Kahle and Hans Schmidt (Patai 1998; Schmidt et al. 1930). Several of the figures whose works appear in this chapter follow a similar pattern of formal teaching—to local students and to foreign adult learners of Arabic—alongside informal help to visiting scholars in Palestine.

This latter group includes Elias Haddad (1878–1959), whose presence is interwoven into all three case studies described below and who thus warrants a brief biographical treatment. Born in southern Lebanon to a Christian family, his father died when he was about ten. The young Elias was sent to the Syrian Orphanage, a German Lutheran institution in Jerusalem. He remained at the Orphanage for almost his entire professional life, becoming a teacher of Arabic and, during the Mandate period, head of subject and finally of the whole school. As discussed below, he published a number of manuals and textbooks in German and English for learners of colloquial Arabic, taught officials of the Mandate administration (including a number of High Commissioners) and translated two books from German to Arabic. Alongside this, he authored and co-authored numerous articles on folk literature and social practices in Palestine and Transjordan, at times working with the German-American orientalist Hans Henry Spoer (Irving 2018b: 93–108, Tamari 2009: 97–110), and provided help for the ethnographic projects of researchers such as Hilma Granqvist. Elias Haddad thus in many ways exemplifies the informal version of the dragoman role, fulfilling all its functions but in a casual or voluntary capacity and thus able to some extent to dictate the terms of his contribution (and to withdraw his labour should he so choose).

The ethnographer as translator

In the literature on ethnography in Palestine before 1948, Finnish anthropologist Hilma Granqvist's studies of women, motherhood and childbirth in the village of Artas are often singled out for their sympathetic treatment of their subjects, focus on subaltern groups in Palestinian society and most of all absence of the nigh-obsessive search for Biblical parallels often seen in British and US scholarship (Furani and Rabinowitz 2011: 477–9, Weir 1975: 6–9). A small village of mainly Muslim families, south of Bethlehem, the inhabitants had traditionally been responsible for protecting pools which, connected by an aqueduct, were one of Jerusalem's main water supplies. Foreign missionaries had also been attracted to the well-watered and picturesque site since the mid nineteenth century. Although Granqvist (1890–1972) undoubtedly produced sensitive and perceptive studies of the families of Artas, whilst struggling against an academic system biased against her as a woman (Suolinna 2000: 323; Weir 1975: 8–9), she was substantially dependent on a series of intermediaries and translators in her quest to understand the peasants of whom she wrote. The most notable of these was Louise Baldensperger (1862–1938), known in the village as 'Sitt Luisa,' the daughter of missionaries who had moved to the area in the nineteenth century.

Granqvist's notes, held in her archives in London, highlight the importance of discussions of translation when considering the role of the anthropologist in a colonial setting. Ethnography has long been described as a kind of translation of cultures. The notion that a professional anthropologist can act as a simple bridge, explaining the culture they have studied to their academic audience has, though, been increasingly problematised. Issues such as the close ties between anthropology and colonialism (Sturge 2007: 35–55), the fundamental questioning of the idea of bounded cultures between which understanding can be clearly translated for the target readership (Bachmann-Medick 2006: 34, 36; Sturge 2007: 5–13) and the ability of a writer, especially one from a colonising system, to represent the dynamic complexes of meaning and behaviour they observe (Bachmann-Medick 2006: 36; Sturge 2007: 56, 68, 90) are only some of these questions. As Sturge discusses (2007: 31–2, 40–59), one of the frequent lacunae from anthropological works, whether of classic colonial-era ethnographers or later scholars influenced by ideas of representation and voice, is recognition of the role of local interpreters, sometimes dubbed 'native informants,' an '"in-between" as a special source of anthropological knowledge' (Bachmann-Medick 2006: 39) who were often key in both linguistic and cultural translation for the newcomer and thus of profound significance in shaping ethnographic accounts. It is this role which, from the detailed annotations and letters of Granqvist's archives, can to some extent be reconstructed and analysed. Furthermore, specific translation strategies adopted by different anthropologists should be identified and their political implications recognised, in the light of the impacts this has on how subjects and their agency are portrayed (Sturge 1997: 23–6).

From amongst her Palestinian Arab networks Granqvist drew significantly on the advice of at least three such people: Elias Haddad (1878–1959), Stephan Stephan (-1894–1949) and Judeh Docmac (1904–after 1987). This help took various forms, such as annotations and translations of some of her field notes, informal letters and conversations, and language lessons with Elias Haddad, whose 1909 manual for self-teaching Arabic (discussed below) she used, according to the *ex libris* label of the copy in her archive. This case study thus argues that the Arab Palestinian who demands accuracy and precision of a European anthropologist in their transliterations of village women's talk, and corrects their notes time and again, can be understood as defending the rural dialect from Eurocentric assumptions of superiority.

Elias Haddad's life story has been sketched above, and it overlaps with that of Stephan Hanna Stephan. The latter was, like Haddad, educated at the Syrische Waisenhaus, although as a member of the Syrian Orthodox community from Beit Jala (near Bethlehem) he did not maintain Haddad's life-long association with the orphanage. Instead, for the entire period of British rule in Palestine he worked for the Mandate authorities, initially at the Treasury but for the most part as a library assistant, translator and researcher at the Department of Antiquities (Irving 2018a: 45–51). He published numerous papers on Palestinian material and rural culture in the *Journal of the Palestine Oriental Society* and annotated translations of Arabic and Ottoman Turkish inscriptions and texts—most notably a six-part translation into English of the Palestine sections of Evliya Celebi's seventeenth-century travelogue, the *Seyāḥat-nāme*—in the *Quarterly of the Department of Antiquities of Palestine* (Irving 2018a: 48–51; Tamari 2009: 100–3). Stephan also made a brief foray into writing Arabic phrasebooks and manuals for speakers of English and German, and authored several travel guides for British soldiers during World War II (Irving 2018a: 52–4). In many respects Stephan might be viewed as a cultural intermediary *par excellence*, interpreting not just the historical languages of Palestine to Anglophone audiences, but delivering his research back to the Arabic-speaking population in the shape of broadcasts on history and folklore on the Arabic service of the British-run radio station, which reinforced the notion that the rural culture of Palestine was worth recording and passing on (Irving 2018a: 51–2).

Judy (Judeh) Farah Docmac is the least studied of Granqvist's helpers. Judeh, the spelling used in his Mandate employment file (Kalisman 2015a: 600), is the more conventional transliteration of his name; the spelling Judy, used in most sources, is probably an Anglicised spelling reflecting the Palestinian pronunciation of the Arabic letter *tā' marbūṭa*. A more usual transliteration of his surname today would be Duqmaq. Born in 1904, by the age of nineteen he was, like Haddad, employed as a teacher in Safad and received consistently excellent reports from the British Mandate authorities' inspectorate of education. Keen and ambitious, he took extra classes and, after a tussle in which the Mandate Director of Education refused his resignation, he left in 1927 to work for the German Lutheran school in Bethlehem (Kalisman 2015b: 73–4), finally ending his career as pastor of the Christmas Church in Bethlehem. Despite the irritation of the Mandate's education department at his departure for what one official referred to as 'the Germans' (Kalisman 2015b: 74), Docmac seems to have remained an active member of the Anglophone Protestant community in Jerusalem throughout the period of British rule (Bishop 1961: 272). He was also an active member of a number of Freemasons' lodges in Jerusalem, which probably strengthened his relationships with Anglophone elite communities, joining the King Solomon's Temple Lodge in 1944 and later translating masonic rituals into Arabic. He was still active in Freemasonry as late as 1987 (Lodge of King Solomon's Temple No. 4611 2019).

During 1961 and 1962, while still the headmaster of the Lutheran school in Bethlehem, Docmac aided investigations into how the Dead Sea Scrolls had been found, translating between members of the Ta'amreh Bedouin family who had made the original discovery and American researchers attempting to piece together the details of events over ten years earlier (Kiraz 2005: xxvi–xxvii). Emphasising the entangled nature of intellectual and socialised relations in this milieu, Stephan Stephan had been among the first scholars to whom the scrolls had been shown in the late 1940s. As this chapter discusses, Docmac also carried out substantial work on Granqvist's notes, re-transcribing large bodies of handwritten text in the late 1950s and early 1960s. Docmac and Granqvist maintained an epistolary friendship for many years after she returned to Finland from Palestine (by then the Jordanian-controlled West Bank), founded on shared time and conversation with Arab intellectual circles at the home of Docmac and his wife (Sirignano 2013: 167–72).

In these biographical sketches, we witness three different men raised in Mandate Palestine, and with lifelong involvements in teaching Arabic, engaging with Granqvist's Artas notes at different points in her research. In these notes, she transcribed the *'āmmiyya*, or colloquial Arabic she heard in the village, in notebooks. My own readings of the contents of Granqvist's archives at the Palestine Exploration Fund confirms Sirignano's findings that Elias Haddad re-transcribed Hilma Granqvist and possibly Louise Baldensperger's field notes, endeavouring to replicate as closely as possible, using the conventional Arabic alphabet, the pronunciation of the rural dialect, and commenting on meaning and tone (Sirignano 2014, 2017; Palestine Exploration Fund (PEF) Granqvist archives, 'Opus'). The mixture of handwritings and notes on the documents indicates that Haddad did this in the early 1930s, whilst Granqvist was still in Palestine, perhaps even working together with her on the manuscripts. Letters exchanged between them show that Stephan Stephan, slightly later in the same decade, helped Granqvist after she had returned to Finland, correcting the versions of the transcriptions and translations she was incorporating into her printed articles and books (PEF Granqvist archive 364–79). Judeh Docmac, meanwhile, only became involved several decades later, when Granqvist managed to obtain funding to return to Palestine and follow up on her earlier research, but continued to draw on the notes she and Haddad had produced twenty years earlier.

According to Sirignano's sociolinguistic analyses of Haddad and Docmac's work on Granqvist's notes, their approach to her material was very different (Sirignano 2013: 167–72, Sirignano unpublished PhD research 2017). Haddad's transcriptions from the 1930s, as Sirignano demonstrates, endeavoured to replicate the sounds and texture of the dialect spoken by the peasant community of Artas; examples include attempts to use the ordinary Arabic alphabet to convey the rural pronunciation of the latter *kāf* as a *ch* instead of a hard *k,* instead of adopting Perso-Arabic or *'ajami* scripts adapted to create letters not used in conventional Arabic. Haddad's methods convey, it seems, an interest in preserving as closely as possible the exact words and phrases as they were spoken in the Palestinian countryside. He may have considered this colloquial speech to be fated to decline in the face of better education of native speakers of Arabic (Haddad and Albright 1927: i), but he also appears to have deemed it worth recording as part of the nativist anthropological project of which he and Stephan, along with figures such as Tawfiq Canaan and 'Omar Salih al-Barghuthi were a part (Tamari 2009: 109–10). As far as can be seen from their correspondence, Stephan followed a similar linguistic practice.

Docmac, on the other hand, 'tends to standardise the Arabic dialect of the Artas peasantry' (Sirignano 2013: 168), creating a version which contains the formal meaning of Granqvist's fieldnotes but which, unlike Haddad's, conveys less of the manner in which the originals were spoken. There is a sense of dialogue not only between Haddad, Stephan or Docmac and Granqvist, but also between Haddad (and perhaps

Stephan) and Docmac over their views on how colloquial Arabic should be dealt with in scholarly contexts. Although all three men might be categorised as members of an educated colonised elite, whose careers and expertise were embedded in the educational networks systems of European empires, they demonstrate divergent approaches to their native language and particularly to its rural dialects. These are differences which emerged not from the coloniser–colonised relationship, but from debates within the Arabic-speaking world which took place in the context of the *nahda* (or 'Arabic renaissance') from the late nineteenth century onwards, and of pan-Arab nationalist visions of a unified, linguistically uniform and politically powerful Arab world (Haeri 2003: 10–12, 63–4; Versteegh 1997: 72–82). Intersecting with nativist ethnographic ideas about Palestinian culture, Haddad, Stephan and Docmac's different interventions into Granqvist's notes become a conversation about how the region might be decolonised, and about what that meant for the language(s) spoken within it in the future.

The relationships between Granqvist on the one hand and Haddad, Stephan and Docmac on the other also shed light on the complexities of intellectual interactions in this colonial environment. All three men were essentially tasked with checking and correcting Granqvist's grasp of their native language, conferring upon them some form of authority. However, she was a white European, at least nominally backed by the institutional weight of the European university system and of the social norms of the Mandate regime in Palestine, and she was paying them to deliver a service. Stephan's letters to her are often confident and authoritative, but at times he also displays a colonised subservience. In one letter, Stephan sends Granqvist his best wishes for her 'important work on Palestine,' highlighting his concern for Palestine as an issue, and suggesting that he saw ethnographic work such as Granqvist's as significant for Palestine itself. The tone also asserts Stephan's right and ability to judge Granqvist's work (Letter from St. H. Stephan to Hilma Granqvist, 17 March 1932, PEF 367). In one letter Stephan writes that: 'We never had this idea and have to learn a lot from the West. We just have to prove that we Orientals are students who are quick and eager to learn' (Stephan Stephan to Hilma Granqvist, 15 April 1932, PEF Granqvist archive, unnumbered).

At the same time, Granqvist, perhaps influenced by previous encounters with male anthropologists, was wary of Stephan and of Tawfiq Canaan, his and Haddad's best-known Palestinian colleague in the anthropological field, as male published scholars. Her field notebooks mention her fears that they might appropriate her work, given that—at the time, in 1931—she felt that they carried more weight in ethnographic circles than she (Granqvist daybook, 17 February 1931). Granqvist may have failed to perceive the power inherent in her own position, but her sense of vulnerability and her articulation of it as a function of their established scholarly status complicate usual narratives about the European anthropologist and their informants. Perhaps in contrast with more confident scholars, this opened up a space for the native speakers of Arabic who interpreted for Granqvist, corrected her notes and edited her manuscripts to articulate their own linguistic ideas and priorities, and to defend a space for a colloquial form of the language rejected in almost all European institutions of the time, where Arabic was still conveyed as a 'dead' language, existing only on the literary or religious page (Mcloughlin 2002: 74, 96, 130), and against strands within Arabic scholarship and elite culture which predicted the imminent demise of colloquial forms (Chejne 1969: 151–68; Haeri 2003: 10–12, 63–4, 76).

The literary translator as activist

In the first half of 1932, Elias Haddad published the first Arabic translation of Gotthold Ephraim Lessing's German Enlightenment play, *Nathan der Weise* (1799/2004), under the title *Nāthān al- ḥakīm*. This was less than two years after violence had erupted in Palestine in the shape of the Western Wall or Buraq riots of 1929 when at least 133 Jews were killed by Arab rioters and around 116 Arabs killed in turn, mainly by British forces; in Europe, meanwhile, fascism was on the rise. The plot of the play, which is set in Jerusalem under the reign of Salah ad-Din (1138–1193; the English Saladin), blends Jewish, Christian and Muslim characters and a series of blurred and mistaken identities into a parable intended to illustrate the inseparability and equality of the three Abrahamic faiths. Throughout the nineteenth and twentieth centuries it was largely viewed as a key narrative of tolerance and amity (Meyer 2005: 286–91, Robertson 1998: 105). Some voices have questioned the extent to which the central character, an elderly Jewish merchant called Nathan, is actually permitted to 'be Jewish,' as opposed to an assimilated enlightenment figure (Robertson 1998: 115–16).

Haddad's published text of *Nāthān*, printed at the Syrian Orphanage, is accompanied by substantial paratextual materials written by him: an introduction to the play's themes (Lessing 1932: 3–4); a biography of Lessing (12–13), his research and opinions and an account of the controversial events leading up to his writing of *Nāthān* (4–9); summaries of the main characters (9–11); notes on aspects of the plot (14–20); and footnotes to his translation. These, combined with a consideration of the translated text itself, convey something of Haddad's thinking and intentions in publishing such a translation at such a time, and what he wanted to say by doing so. In terms of understanding *Nāthān al-ḥakīm* in the context of translation theories, we might see it as 'thick translation'; with his copious paratextuals, Haddad seems to be foreshadowing Appiah's exhortation to translate African texts for American academia in order to 'continue the repudiation of racism […], the need to extend the American imagination [… beyond] the narrow scope of the United States; the desire to develop views of the world elsewhere that respect more deeply the autonomy of the Other' (1993: 818). On one level this is true; Haddad's annotations bring the German writer and his well-known ethical aims closer to the Arabic readership. Combined with this, though, is something more like the activist translations described by Tymoczko, in which the translator claims an active right to define the text and to overtly frame its meanings (2014 [2007]: 115, 193–6, 230–8).

Haddad's primary concern in his paratextual writings and his choice of source text is to stress the need for rationality and for tolerance between faiths, and to oppose mystical extremism and divisiveness (Lessing 1932: 3–4, 15–16). These themes animate the original play, and are also reflected in the circumstances of Lessing's authorship of it; Lessing adopted the theatrical form as a means of conveying his ideas about rationality and religion after his exemption from censorship for printed works (granted to approved writers by local rulers in this period) was revoked during a heated public debate over faith and rationality in late eighteenth-century Germany (Nisbet 2013: 601). Haddad makes it clear in his introduction that he is linking the play's ideas to his own environment. He cites recent Middle Eastern history in his arguments (Lessing 1932: 3–4). And although he is using a work from the European Enlightenment to express his views, he clarifies that he does not see Europe as the source of such values, and instead highlights the fact that when a European author wanted to write about wisdom and tolerance, he looked to the Jerusalem of Nathan and Salah ad-Din for his example (Lessing 1932: 19).

It was not uncommon for translators of European literature into Arabic, especially plays, to transpose the action into a Middle Eastern setting, to please audiences as well as to make political and social points: examples include two plays loosely based on *Nathan the Wise* performed in Beirut and Cairo in the late nineteenth century, as well as versions of works by Molière and Shakespeare (Dressel 2006: 351–70; Hanna 2016: 57; Litvin 2011: 79–100; Moreh and Sadgrove 1996: 83–105), but there was no need for Haddad to do so in this case. His choice was a foundational part of his statement.

The location of interfaith tolerance in the Arab, Islamicate East rather than Europe is also highlighted by one of Haddad's few overt interventions as translator. For the most part, his standard Arabic (*fusha*) text follows Lessing's Enlightenment German faithfully in register and meaning, but there is one noticeable change: Recha, adopted daughter of Nathan and actually the offspring of Salah ad-Din's brother and a Christian noblewoman, is in Haddad's version Arabised as Rayhana. The choice of name could simply be a matter of domestication, the translation strategy of making a text more acceptable to the target audience by rendering foreign elements more culturally familiar. But it is also possible that, given his deep professional knowledge of the Arabic language and of aspects of regional culture and history, Haddad was making a deliberate reference to Rayhana bint Zayd, the Jewish wife or concubine of the Prophet Muhammad, who according to some versions of this story converted to Islam after she was acquired by him as part of the spoils of war (Yitzhak 2007: 2–5). In renaming Recha —the only example in the Arabic text of such a change—and by choosing this specific name, Haddad connects an example of interfaith relations from the earliest and most sacred point of Islamic culture, to Ayyubid Jerusalem, and thence to the same city in the 1930s. The impact of the change is further emphasised by the faithfulness of the rest of the text to the German original, following much of it line by line and refusing to, for example, correct geographical oddities which might well have stood out to Haddad's own readership; nearby locations such as the River Jordan and city of Damascus are, for example, named in the original and in Haddad's translation alongside Lessing's orientalising lists of far-off places—India, China, Persia, Babylon, the Tigris (Lessing 1932: 28, 52). If Haddad had sought to fully domesticate his text, destinations like these which were not unusual for twentieth-century Palestinians would have been switched for somewhere more distant, and his failure to do so suggests a pressing reason to change Recha's name for Rayhana.

How should we read Haddad's resort to a European text to make his point? For Tageldin, writing on Egyptian translators of European texts into Arabic in the nineteenth century, such practices are part of the 'seduction' of the East by the West, a means by which orientalist and imperialist ideas managed to infiltrate Egyptian culture and thought (2011: 7–23). On the other hand, Tageldin admits the possibility of the translator's agency, through which such transfers can be seen as strategic (2002: 199). This opens up the possibilities articulated by others who see translated works as a neutral space in which ideas experienced as conflictual or controversial within the translator's own society can be debated at a remove and in less combative ways (Marti-Lopez 2002: 77–9, Zubeida 1999: 20). Given the values implicit or explicit in much of Haddad's other work—be it language manuals, ethnographic articles or helping foreign scholars and officials with their Arabic—a commitment to coexistence is entirely at home in his worldview and values. In recreating *Nathan der Weise* in Arabic and framing it using paratextuals that emphasise Levantine values and ideas over descriptive details, Haddad is not domesticating a foreign idea (Venuti 1995), but re-domesticating domestic values which had been foreignised by the Other.

One of the continuing questions surrounding Haddad's translation of *Nathan* is this: to whom was he directing his plea for tolerance and rational, secular coexistence? The most obvious answer seems to be his fellow inhabitants of Mandate Palestine. If we assume that the text's 1932 publication followed work done in 1930 or 1931, it came in the wake of the Western Wall or Buraq riots of 1929, at the time the worst instance of violence between Arabs and Jews in the country. A tantalising additional point here is the enigmatic mention in a Chicago Jewish community newspaper in 1931 of funds from the estate of Harold Wiener, a British Jewish lawyer killed in Palestine in the riots of 1929, earmarked specifically for the translation of *Nathan* into Arabic:

> Lessing's famous philo-Semitic play, 'Nathan the Wise,' is to be translated into Arabic, presumably for the purpose of stimulating good will between Jew and Arab in Palestine. The decision was made by the Board of the London Spanish-Portuguese Community, in which Sir Francis Montefiore is the head, in disposing of the estate left by the late Harold Wiener, famous scholar and friend of the Arabs, who was killed by Arabs during the August, 1929, riots in Palestine. Before his death Wiener had indicated that he would like to see the classic drama translated.
>
> *(Chicago Sentinel 1931)*

The London Spanish and Portuguese Jews' Congregation (now known as the S&P Sephardi Community), which administered Wiener's legacy, no longer has records of how his estate was disbursed (S&P Sephardi Community, Email exchange to Sarah Irving, 'Accessing Congregation archive records,' June/July 2016), but the dates and the circumstances fit, and it is likely that Haddad's social and professional circles overlapped with those of Wiener, who had been a visiting scholar at the American School of Oriental Research and had good relations with British and German scholars (Albright 1929: 22; Petrie 1928: 1). If Haddad's translation was inspired by acquaintance with, or even funded by, Wiener, this makes it even more fully expressive of relations between Muslims, Christians and Jews in the increasingly tense atmosphere of 1930s Palestine.

A second possibility also exists: that Elias Haddad, embedded within the German community of Palestine, was seeking to counter the rise of open antisemitism within Europe. Although Adolf Hitler's Nazi Party did not come to power until early 1933, a year after the publication of *Nāthān al- ḥakīm*, a few German Palestinians—mainly from the Templer community, but including Lutherans with whom Haddad lived and worked—had already shown enthusiasm for Nazi policies (Nicosia 1979: 243; Wawrzyn 2013: 4, 12, 74). Such a clear-cut aim on Haddad's part seems remote as early as summer 1932. But it cannot be completely discounted as part of the general background against which he chose to assemble his call for rationalism and tolerance, and to overtly locate it within the cultures and religions not of Enlightenment Europe, but of the Islamicate East. This overall stance meshes with his approach to Granqvist's notes and Haddad's own ethnographic output, in which he respects and co-operates with the work of European scholars and writers, but also asserts the value and interest of Levantine Arab culture and language in a way which, in the context of Mandate Palestine, had clear political implications.

Teacher as translator/teaching as translation

The notion that communicating with those who speak another language will necessarily lead to mutual understanding is often hackneyed and inaccurate: in situations of unequal power, occupation or colonialism, an enemy who speaks the language of the colonised is one who can rule and oppress all the more effectively. How then, should we understand the role of Palestinian Arabs who taught British officials in the Mandate administration the local tongue—not just the literary written Arabic of ancient texts, but the colloquial ('āmmiyya) used by ordinary people about their daily business? What role might a conception of activism play in understanding the political function of such language pedagogy? Whilst language teaching may appear distant from conventional understandings of translation, if (following ideas made implicit or explicit by Sturge (2007) or Tymoczko (2014 [2007])) we consider it as part of the repertoire or 'cluster' (Tymoczko 2014 [2007]) of cultural and linguistic interpretation carried out by figures such as Haddad and Stephan, its potential to further elucidate these liminal activist practices becomes clear.

His first venture into writing language manuals for foreign learners of Arabic highlights Elias Haddad's conviction that such books could be a medium for conveying information about the nature of Palestinian society, and not just grammar and vocabulary. The *Manual of Palestinean* [sic] *Arabic for Self-Instruction* (1909) contains a range of sample phrases for learners to memorise. Beyond standard content such as hotel bookings and travel arrangements, examples include political statements such as 'How conditions would change if the Pasha would go from here!' and 'The liberty which the Sultan gave to the people is a blessing' (Spoer and Haddad 1909: 80, 104). Other sentences challenge the orientalist stereotypes of some European-authored Arabic textbooks, suggesting that bribery was no longer tolerated under the new rule of the Young Turks (101) and that railways, cars, inventors and photography were everyday features of Levantine life (92, 105, 129–43, 166). Combined with these assertions of modernity and political change, though, is the insistence on the use of a colloquial form of Jerusalemite Palestinian Arabic, a prioritising of 'āmmiyya which prefigures Haddad's work with Granqvist. Although manuals for Egyptian and Syrian-Lebanese had been published, this was the first specifically for Palestinian, as well as being an early example by a native speaker. The introduction asserts the need for a textbook not focused on 'Egyptian or Libanese' or containing too much 'modern, literary Arabic … not belonging to the vernacular and not understood by the populace' (Spoer and Haddad 1909: iii–iv). Colloquial usages typical of the region are given, such as *hŏom* or *hŏon* (human plurals in standard Arabic) for non-human plural nouns and an assimilated letter *jīm* (ج) in the definite article is given in the transliterated phrases–such as *j-jmâl* for camels and *j-jabr* for algebra (5, 77, 95, 143).

That Haddad's commitment to defending Palestinian 'āmmiyya remained a lifelong stance is clear from the foreword of Haddad and Jalil Irany's 1955 *Standard Colloquial Arabic,* which celebrates both men's roles as 'pioneers in the promotion of the teaching of colloquial' (n.p.). Written by Eric Bishop, then a lecturer in Arabic at the University of Glasgow, Haddad and Irany's 'friendship' and teaching, which 'render-[ed] service both to God and men' was said to have been of value to 'many British officials under the Mandate' (Haddad and Irany 1955: n.p.). This rosy image of Haddad and Irany is perhaps borne out by the fact that both men taught British administration staff for twenty years or more, from the early 1920s onwards. Neither needed to undertake this role; both had secure jobs, Haddad at the Syrian Orphanage and Irany as a teacher and later headmaster in reform schools run by the Mandate administration's Department of Social Welfare. In Haddad's case, his range of textbooks and manuals for Anglo- and Germanophone learners of Arabic, published over a span of five decades, suggests a genuine zeal for conveying the local, spoken form of the language to foreigners, alongside the culture and values with which he associated it. His approach is captured in a review of the 1955 book, his last publication, which called it: 'a useful unpretentious piece of work, founded on long teaching experience' (Serjeant 1956: 401).

However, despite their co-operation on the 1955 volume, their respective careers suggest that Haddad and Irany had rather different relationships with and attitudes to British Mandate rule. Irany was a long-term employee of the Department of Social Welfare, working at several of its boys' reform schools until he became head of the main Reformatory School at Bethlehem. He received an MBE in the 1946 King's Birthday Honours list (*Palestine Gazette* 1946: 573), an appellation that he continued to use after the British exit from Palestine and his own retirement. Haddad, by contrast, socialised and co-operated with many Europeans, and 'taught those of the High Commissioners who found time for Arabic' (Bishop 1961: 272), but was never formally employed by the British government in Palestine. Rather, he worked for the German-run Syrian Orphanage.

The one exception to this is telling: Haddad spent a brief period in the 1940s at the Middle East Centre for Arab Studies (MECAS), established by the British government to train diplomats, military officers and spies. Initially based in the requisitioned Austrian Hospice in Jerusalem in 1944, it was transferred to Shemlan, in southern Lebanon, in 1947 (Craig 1998: 12–24). Elias Haddad worked at MECAS for a short period in Jerusalem and Shemlan. It is unclear whether his service there was entirely voluntary: Eric Bishop describes him as having been 'requisitioned' (1961: 272) and he certainly seems to have made as speedy an exit as possible from the institution once it moved across the Lebanese border (Craig 1998: 18, 168). This may have simply been a matter of loyalty: he was occupied with re-establishing the Syrian Orphanage in the village of Khirbet Qanafar, also in southern Lebanon, but by the mid-1940s Haddad's loyalty to and patience with the British may well have been sorely tried. The Orphanage's facilities had been used as a British military camp during World War II and a number of its staff, both German and Arab, interned as enemy aliens or as sympathisers; Haddad, as one of the few not confined, appears to have spent considerable time and effort during the war finding safe places for the many children dependent on the German institution for their home and education (Schneller 2009: 112–13; Schneller School 2010: 7). Not a fierce Palestinian nationalist but one whose writings had for several decades asserted the value of Levantine Arab language and civilisation, he may also have found the deputy director of MECAS, the passionate Zionist and later Israeli politician Aubrey (Abba) Eban an abrasive boss. Certainly, the latter was described by another colleague as a 'dedicated Zionist' who openly campaigned whilst at the Centre and who wrote fiery articles for the Jewish press (Craig 1998: 17).

Certainly, Haddad does not seem to have left his mark on an Arabic curriculum, which was described by one veteran as having a 'heavy concentration on grammar and little systematic attempt to teach colloquial,' although he is said to have 'tried his hand' at introducing it on Eban's departure (22). In contrast, then, to his early attempts to introduce cultural and political knowledge into language manuals and his acceptance of the role of teaching Arabic to higher officials in the British Mandate administration, Haddad's contribution at Shemlan seems to have been limited both by the institution itself and his own inclinations as the ideological environment around him changed. Both as an intentional form of activism which puts forward arguments, thoughts and values, and as the more mute defiance of withdrawal and absence, Arabic teaching and guidance as carried out by Haddad, Irany, Stephan and other Arab instructors were shot through with political considerations, in the content and the type of Arabic conveyed, and in the relationship with learners and fellow teachers.

Conclusion

The interventions of Stephan Hanna Stephan, Jalil Zand Irany, Elias Nasrallah Haddad and Judy Farah Docmac, through translation and interpretation, in the linguistic and literary fields of Mandate Palestine tell a story of diversity and divergence, as well as of cultural tactics that—implicitly or explicitly—argued or supported particular visions of Palestinian values and identities. Through literary translation, Haddad laid claim to 'civilised' values not as Western gifts to Eastern peoples, but as indigenous ways of being embedded in historical examples such as Saladin and Nathan. Indeed, his re-domesticated tale of Ayyubid Jerusalem suggests, it was to the East that Gotthold Lessing had to look in order to find the story through which he could urge these virtues on the eighteenth-century German public. In their editing of Granqvist's field notes and their teaching of colloquial Arabic to Europeans in Jerusalem and Shemlan, Haddad, Stephan and Irany insisted on the validity of a local Palestinian language. In doing so, they both intervene in regional debates concerning the place of colloquial versus formal languages, and they take a position vis-à-vis those who saw formal or classical Arabic as the only version worth promoting and teaching in foreign universities.

Particularly when viewed alongside Haddad and Stephan's ethnographic writings, their advocacy of 'āmmiyya must be seen not only as a position in support of the everyday language, but also of the Palestinian culture which both men recorded in articles for academic journals and which Stephan also delivered in Arabic on Palestinian radio. At times these views placed them in tension with mainstream political currents, especially with pan-Arab tendencies that regarded colloquial Arabic as threatening the collective tongue with linguistic and thus national fragmentation, at times in collusion with European colonial intent (Haeri 2003: xi, 9–12, 63–4). But the quiet, patient but insistent activity—activism?—of these unostentatious scholars conveyed images of Palestine and its people which must be considered alongside those of more mainstream and vocal political voices. As such, their legacies remind us that the various types of activisms possible under the headings of translation and interpretation are not just those of identifiable schools of literary translation or of groups of interpreters with defined political identities and purposes. For those whose professional circumstances or personal styles of communication ruled out overt activisms, the margins and interstices of texts and archives can reveal other forms of stance-taking and attempts at education and persuasion that also deserve to be seen as forms of active engagement in struggles for justice and independence.

Related topics

Translation in the War-Zone: Writing as Hospitality; Resistant Recipes.

Further reading

Halperin, Liora R. (2014) *Babel in Zion: Jews, Nationalism, and Language Diversity in Palestine, 1920–1948*. New Haven: Yale University Press.

An important study of the complex and fractious role of languages in Mandate Palestine, and the political processes by which Hebrew was imposed in the Yishuv.

Kilito, Abdelfattah (2008) *Thou Shalt Not Speak My Language*. Trans. Waïl S. Hassan; (2001) *The Author and His Doubles: Essays on Classical Arabic Culture*. Trans. Michael Cooperson. Syracuse: Syracuse University Press.

Writing in both Arabic and French, but widely available in translation, Abdelfattah Kilito's works offer a range of challenging, complex, poetic contemplations of the relationships between language, identity, authenticity and imperialism.

Scoville, Spencer (2015) 'Reconsidering Nahdawi Translation: Bringing Pushkin to Palestine,' *The Translator* 21 (2): 223–236.

Scoville's sensitive and historically informed study is some of the rare work on translation in Late Ottoman and Mandate Palestine, and especially valuable in that it addresses the under-studied relationship of Palestinians with Russian language, literature and culture.

References

Albright, William Foxwell (1929) 'Mr Harold Wiener,' *Bulletin of the American Schools of Oriental Research* 35: 22–23.

Appiah, Kwame Anthony (1993) 'Thick Translation,' *Callaloo* 16 (4): 808–819.

Bachmann-Medick, Doris (2006) 'Meanings of Translation in Cultural Anthropology,' in *Translating Others*, Vol. 1. Ed. Theo Hermans. Manchester: St Jerome. 33–42.

Baker, Mona (2016) 'The Prefigurative Politics of Translation in Place-based Movements of Protest: Subtitling in the Egyptian Revolution,' *The Translator* 22 (1): 1–21.

Bernard, Anna (2013) *Rhetorics of Belonging: Nation, Narration and Israel/Palestine*. Liverpool: Liverpool University Press.

Bhambra, Gurminder (2007) *Rethinking Modernity: Postcolonialism and the Sociological Imagination*. Basingstoke: Palgrave Macmillan.

Bishop, Eric (1961) 'Jerusalem Byways of Memory,' *The Muslim World* 51 (4): 265–273.

Bosworth, Clifford (2012) 'Tardjumān,' in *Encyclopaedia of Islam* (2nd ed). Eds. Peri Bearman, Thierry Bianquis, Clifford E. Bosworth, Emeri van Donzel, and Wolfhart P. Heinrichs [online]. Available at: http://dx.doi.org/10.1163/1573-3912_islam_COM_1179 [accessed 20 March 2019].

Chejne, Anwar (1969) *The Arabic Language: Its Role in History*. Minneapolis: University of Minnesota Press.

Coakley, John (2004) 'Mobilizing the Past: Nationalist Images of History,' *Nationalism and Ethnic Politics* 10 (4): 531–560.

Courington, Chella (1999) '(Re)Defining Activism: Lessons from Women's Literature,' *Women's Studies Quarterly* 27 (3): 77–86.

Craig, James (1998) *Shemlan: A History of the Middle East Centre for Arab Studies*. Basingstoke: Macmillan.

De Ballobar, Conde (2011) *Jerusalem in WWI: The Palestine Diary of a European Diplomat*. Eds. Eduardo Manzano Moreno and Roberto Mazza. London: IB Tauris.

Dressel, Diana (2006) 'Intisar al-Fadila aw Haditha al-ibna al-Isra'iliyya as an Adaptation of *Nathan der Weise*,' *Journal of Semitic Studies* 11 (2): 349–371.

Freire, Paolo (1970) *Pedagogy of the Oppressed*. New York: Continuum.

Furani, Khaled, and Dan Rabinowitz (2011) 'The Ethnographic Arriving of Palestine,' *Annual Review of Anthropology* 40: 475–491.

Granqvist, Hilma (1931) *Dagbok XII (February)* [online]. Avaialable at: http://granqvist.sls.fi/#/publication/29/cover/ [accessed 15 October 2019].

Gribetz, Jonathan (2016) *Defining Neighbours: Religion, Race, and the Early Zionist-Arab Encounter*. Princeton: Princeton University Press.

Haddad, Elias, and William Foxwell Albright (1927) *The Spoken Arabic of Palestine for Use in Beginners' Classes*. Jerusalem: Palestine Educational Company.

Haddad, Elias, and Jalil Irany (1955) *Standard Colloquial Arabic*. Al-Quds: Dar al-Aytam al-Islamiyya.

Haeri, Niloofer (2003) *Sacred Language, Ordinary People: Dilemmas of Culture and Politics in Egypt*. New York: Palgrave Macmillan.

Hanna, Sameh (2016) *Bourdieu in Translation Studies: The Socio-Cultural Dynamics of Shakespeare Translation in Egypt*. Abingdon: Routledge.

Hermans, Theo (2003) 'Cross-cultural Translation Studies as Thick Translation,' *Bulletin of the School of Oriental and African Studies* 66 (3): 380–389.

Irving, Sarah (2017) 'A Tale of Two Yusifs: Recovering Arab Agency in Palestine Exploration Fund Excavations 1890–1924,' *Palestine Exploration Quarterly* 149 (3): 223–236.

Irving, Sarah (2018a) '"A Young Man of Promise": Finding a Place for Stephan Hanna Stephan in the History of Mandate Palestine,' *Jerusalem Quarterly* 73: 42–62.

Irving, Sarah (2018b) 'Intellectual Networks, Language and Knowledge under Colonialism: The Work of Stephan Stephan, Elias Haddad and Tawfiq Canaan in Palestine, 1909–1948,' Unpublished PhD thesis, University of Edinburgh, Edinburgh.

Kalisman, Hilary (2015a) 'Bursary Scholars at the American University of Beirut: Living and Practising Arab Unity,' *British Journal of Middle Eastern Studies* 42 (4): 599–617.

Kalisman, Hilary (2015b) 'Schooling the State: Educators in Iraq, Palestine and Transjordan: c. 1890-c. 1960,' PhD thesis, University of California, Berkeley.

Katan, David (2009) 'Translation as Intercultural Communication,' in *The Routledge Companion to Translation Studies*. Ed. Jeremy Munday. Abingdon: Routledge. 74–92.

Kiraz, George (2005) *Anton Kiraz's Dead Sea Scroll Archive*. Piscataway: Gorgias Press.

Lessing, Gotthold (1932) *Nathan al-Hakim*. Tr. Elias Nasrallah Haddad. Jerusalem: Syrian Orphanage/Dar al-Aytam al-Suri.

Lessing, Gotthold (1779/2004) *Nathan the Wise*, adapted and translated by Edward Kemp. London: Nick Hern Books.

Litvin, Margaret (2011) *Hamlet's Arab Journey: Shakespeare's Prince and Nasser's Ghost*. Princeton: Princeton University Press.

Lockman, Zachary (1996) *Comrades and Enemies: Arab and Jewish Workers in Palestine, 1906–1948*. Berkeley: University of California Press.

Lodge of King Solomon's Temple No. 4611 Website [online]. Available at: http://kingsolomonstemple.homestead.com [accessed 15 October 2019].

Lonni, Ada (2011) 'Translating Between Civilisations: The Dragoman in Clarel's Nineteenth-Century Jerusalem,' *Leviathan* 13 (3): 41–48.

Mairs, Rachel (2016) *From Khartoum to Jerusalem: The Dragoman Solomon Negima and His Clients (1885–1933)*. London: Bloomsbury.

Mairs, Rachel, and Maya Muratov (2015) *Archaeologists, Tourists, Interpreters: Exploring Egypt and the Near East in the Late 19th-Early 20th Centuries*. London: Bloomsbury.

Marti-Lopez, Elisa (2002) *Borrowed Words: Translation, Imitation and the Making of the Nineteenth-Century Novel in Spain*. London: Associated University Presses.

Mcloughlin, Leslie (2002) *In a Sea of Knowledge: British Arabists in the Twentieth Century*. Reading: Ithaca Press.

Meyer, Reinhart (2005) 'Lessing on the German-speaking Stage in the Federal Republic of Germany, Austria and Switzerland, 1945–1990,' in *A Companion to the Works of Gotthold Ephraim Lessing*. Eds. Barbara Fischer and Thomas Fox. Rochester: Camden House. 283–300.

Moreh, Shmuel, and Philip Sadgrove (1996) *Jewish Contributions to Nineteenth-Century Arabic Theatre*. Oxford: Oxford University Press.

'News Brevities' (1931) *Chicago Sentinel*, 13 February: 27.

Nicosia, Francis (1979) 'National Socialism and the Demise of the German-Christian Communities in Palestine during the Nineteen Thirties,' *Canadian Journal of History/Annales Canadiennes d'Histoire* 2: 235–255.

Nisbet, Hugh (2013) *Gotthold Ephraim Lessing: His Life, Works, and Thought*. Oxford: Oxford University Press.

OED Online (2019) Oxford: Oxford University Press [online]. Available at: www.oed.com/view/Entry/57428?redirectedFrom=dragoman#eid [accessed 20 June 2019].

Palestine Gazette 1499, 13 June 1946, 573–574.

Patai, Raphael (1998) *Arab Folktales from Palestine and Israel*. Detroit: Wayne State University Press.

Petrie, Flinders (1928) *Gerar*. London: British School of Archaeology in Egypt.

Robertson, Ritchie (1998) '"Dies hohe Lied der Duldung"? The Ambiguities of Toleration in Lessing's *Die Juden* and *Nathan der Weise*,' *Modern Language Review* 93 (1): 105–120.

Schmidt, Hans, Paul Kahle, and Dschirius Jusif (1930) *Volkserzählungen aus Palästina: gesammelt bei den Bauern von Bir-Zet und in Verbindung mit Dschirius Jusif in Jerusalem*. Göttingen: Vandenhoeck und Ruprecht.

Schneller, Ludwig (2009) *The Life and Work of Father Johann Ludwig Schneller, Founding Father of the Syrian Orphanage*. Trans. Ramsey Bisharah. London: Melisende.

Schneller School (2010) *Strategic Plan* [online]. Available at: www.schneller-school.org/Files/jlss_strategic_plan.pdf [accessed 15 October 2019].

Serjeant, Robert (1956) 'Standard Colloquial Arabic (Review),' *Bulletin of the School of Oriental and African Studies* 18 (2): 401.

Sirignano, Rosanna (2013) 'Mother and Child in Palestine: The Artas Material in Hilma Granqvist Nachlass at the Palestine Exploration Fund,' *Studi Interculturali* 3: 159–181.

Sirignano, Rosanna (2014) 'Popular Wisdom and Marriage Customs in a Palestinian Village: Proverbs and Sayings in Hilma Granqvist's Work,' *Studi Interculturali* 4: 189–208.

Sirignano, Rosanna (2017) 'Female Anthropologists in the Arab World: European Orientalism and Palestinian Culture in the Field Notes of Hilma Granqvist (1890–1972),' Unpublished PhD thesis, University of Heidelberg, Heidelberg.

Spoer, Hans, and Elias Haddad (1909) *Manual of Palestinean [sic] Arabic for Self-Instruction*. Jerusalem: Syrian Orphanage.

Sturge, Kate (1997) 'Translation Strategies in Ethnography,' *The Translator* 3 (1): 21–38.

Sturge, Kate (2007) *Representing Others: Translation, Ethnography and Museum*. Manchester: St Jerome.

Suolinna, Kirsti (2000) 'Hilma Granqvist: A Scholar of the Westermarck School in Its Decline,' *Acta Sociologica* 43 (4): 317–323.

Tageldin, Shaden (2002) 'The Sword and the Pen: Egyptian Musings on European Penetration, Persuasion and Power,' *Kroeber Anthropological Society Papers* 87: 196–218.

Tageldin, Shaden (2011) *Disarming Words: Empire and the Seductions of Translation in Egypt*. Berkeley: University of California Press.

Tamari, Salim (2009) *Mountain Against the Sea: Essays on Palestinian Society & Culture*. Berkeley: University of California Press.

Trouillot, Michel-Rolph (1995) *Silencing the Past: Power and the Production of History*. Boston: Beacon Press.

Tymoczko, Maria (2000) 'Translation and Political Engagement: Activism, Social Change and the Role of Translation in Geopolitical Shifts,' *The Translator* 6 (1): 23–47.

Tymoczko, Maria (2014 [2007]) *Enlarging Translation, Empowering Translators*. Abingdon: Routledge.

Venuti, Lawrence (1995) *The Translator's Invisibility: A History of Translation*. London: Routledge.

Versteegh, Kees (1997) *The Arabic Language*. Edinburgh: Edinburgh University Press.

Wawrzyn, Heidi (2013) *Nazis in the Holy Land, 1933–1948*. Berlin: Walter de Gruyter.

Weir, Shelagh (1975) 'Hilma Granqvist and Her Contribution to Palestine Studies,' *British Society for Middle Eastern Studies Bulletin* 2 (1): 6–13.

Willems, Jurgen, and Marc Jegers (2012) 'Social Movement Structures in Relation to Goals and Forms of Action: An Exploratory Model,' *Canadian Journal of Nonprofit and Social Economy Research* 3 (2): 67–81.

Yitzhak, Ronen (2007) 'Muhammad's Jewish Wives: Rayhana bint Zayd and Safiya bint Huyayy in the Classic Islamic Tradition,' *Journal of Religion and Society* 9: 1–14.

Zubeida, Sami (1999) 'Cosmopolitanism and the Middle East,' in *Cosmopolitanism, Identity and Authenticity in the Middle East*. Ed. Roel Meijer. Richmond: Curzon Press. 15–34.

8

Translation in the war-zone

The Gaza Strip as case study

Malaka Shwaikh

In November 2018, I received a phone call from a producer of a major media outlet, based in the United Kingdom. They were planning a visit to Gaza[1] to produce a special broadcast about everyday life, including the weekly protests organised by Palestinians who hope to highlight their deteriorating living conditions to the outside world. 'We never have done something as in depth in Gaza before,' the producer told me. She then asked if I could link them to English-speaking Palestinian youth in the Strip. I offered my help, on the condition that they would centralise those voices and give them a chance to express themselves. Media can transform people's lives, for better or worse. It has worked miracles on issues, most recently the case of Jamal Khashoggi (d. 2018), the Saudi journalist who was killed in his country's embassy in Istanbul. Media can make a difference in the case of Gaza too.

I was excited to see what would come next. Yet, to my dismay, the four-hour BBC Radio 4 Today Programme allotted less than twenty minutes' airtime to the Palestinian youths.[2] Whenever a Palestinian spoke, it was immediately followed by rebuttals beginning with the phrase 'Israel says …' and 'Israel defends itself ….' No such right of reply was given to Palestinians following Israeli claims about them. This is a familiar feature of European and American media reporting on the Gaza Strip and on the entirety of Palestine. The rest of the programme focused on 'ordinary' Israelis. It was chilling to hear the dehumanisation of Palestinians across the board. One Israeli settler was asked about the plight of kids facing starvation a few miles away. She responded by complaining she could not walk her dog. Her BBC interviewer did not note the incongruity. The Israeli youth interviewed for the programme were never interrupted as they spoke and were given more time and space to speak about their daily life than were the Palestinian interviewees. Most importantly, this popular programme provided no historical context for the longest conflict in the Middle East. Without such context, the mainstream narrative that dehumanises the Palestinians and their struggle remains unchallenged. As Mona Baker argues (2006: 472), experience cannot be changed without simultaneously changing the narratives that underpin them. Such narratives circulate around the world, largely in and through translation.

When the interviewer asked Israeli youths about 'families who in 1948 ended up in Gaza,' she did not provide the reasons behind 'ending up' there, in terrible conditions, with their homes and villages to which they are forbidden access often within eyesight. At the same time, in order to provide what she called 'balance,' the interviewer gave airtime to a British-Israeli girl who had lived in Israel for just five years because, as the interviewee said, '[her] dad is a Zionist.'[3]

Informed by these interviews, this chapter examines knowledge production specifically in the Gaza Strip, since other parts of Palestine are more widely accessed by scholars. I interview Palestinian journalists, translators, and activists from Gaza who worked with European and American scholars to understand how language is used in their communication, how helpful it is to speak a different language in a war-zone country, and whether indigenous points of view are engaged by orientalist discourse. I also examine how the ongoing Israeli siege on the Gaza Strip contributes to the process of knowledge production by allowing a certain category of people to enter and leave the Strip. The chapter finally provides recommendations to deal with the sensitive situation in Gaza.

The account noted above is relevant to this chapter on activism and translation in the Gaza Strip on two grounds. First, Euro-American media bias towards Palestinians overwhelmingly shapes global media narratives of the conflict (Said 1981). Indigenous Palestinian voices are almost entirely absent from this media. Second, and as a result of this bias, Palestinians have stopped trusting European and American knowledge and content producers, whether it is media platforms, activists, or translators.[4] By way of moving beyond this stalemate, this chapter adopts an indigenous ethnographic approach to the use of language in translation in war-zone areas. Inspired by Grande (2004: ix), who opened her book by stating 'I am a Quechua woman [and this is] not only who I am but also, in these "postcolonial" times, an identity, I feel [...] obligated to claim,' I am also an indigenous woman, a Palestinian from the Gaza Strip. This is not only who I am but also an identity I am increasingly obliged to assert in these times, when media practices, translation, and epistemologies informing coverage and reportage of Palestine are rooted in the imperialist mentalities that are seemingly inherent in orientalist journalism and activism (Said 1981). These practices proliferate within and outside the university. They are advanced through a web of power relations that are part of colonialism's power/knowledge construct with an ongoing, long history of 'research through imperial eyes' (Smith 2012: 58; Al-Hardan 2014: 64).

This power/knowledge nexus continues to structure the 'contemporary coloniality' (Al-Hardan 2014: 61) of literature on Palestine. Imperial and colonial power relations fundamentally structure arguments relating to Palestine. While the continuous impact of colonialism takes different shapes and forms, it consistently undermines colonised peoples, through different means, including language, as documented in this chapter.

The ongoing struggle of indigenous Palestinians against Israeli colonisation seeks to exercise the fundamental right to represent ourselves with our own voices, language, and words, in contexts wherein Palestinians are often spoken of or about by opposing or biased observers (Abu-Saad 2008: 1902). This is clearly the case even when Palestinians lack full mobility and opportunities to resistance, as in Israeli prisons.[5] They embark on hunger strikes (Shwaikh 2018; Shwaikh and Gould 2020) to stress their right to represent themselves on their own terms: to stress, for example, like the Irish hunger strikers of 1981 (Beresford 1987), that they are 'political prisoners,' not 'criminals.' But how does language even matter in the context of imprisonment? For prisoners, it is central to their anticolonial resistance to a settler colonial project that subjects the entire Palestinian population to unjust policies of extrajudicial assassination, expulsion, loss of land, destruction of homes, and exile. As Walid Dakka, a Palestinian held in Israeli jails since 1986, elaborated on the significance of using 'political prisoners' to identify Palestinians held in Israeli prisons:

> What are we dealing with here? With a definition? Can this or that definition do anything to add or detract from the prisoners' conditions of confinement, or to release those we seek to release? The answer is: Yes! The definition we are demanding is a political definition and not a legal one, and not only a theoretical position of principle derives from it, but also a politically practical one.
>
> *(cited in Baker 2010: 65)*

Dakka's statement clarifies the significance of having clear linguistic criteria to characterise Palestinians in Israeli jails. Similarly,[6] this chapter aims to develop an alternative approach of knowledge production by indigenous people, just as Palestinian oral history projects seek to develop such alternative narratives from within Palestine and by the Palestinian people.

Historical overview

In 1948, war between the new, well-equipped Israeli state and poorly organised Palestinian forces and armies from the neighbouring Arab states erupted. The war ended catastrophically for the Palestinian people who lost their lands and became refugees or were internally displaced peoples. Between December 1947 and 1949, 800,000 Palestinians were forced to leave their lands during the *Nakba* (Arabic for 'catastrophe'). Five hundred and thirty villages and towns were destroyed. Some 160,000 managed to stay in the 78 percent of the land that was turned into a Jewish state in 1949, though their wealth, land, and society were destroyed (Pappé 2006; Qumsiyeh 2011: 98–99; Lentin 2013: 8–9).

Already by 1949, Palestinian society had been devastated, fragmented between refugees and displaced persons, isolated and dispersed around the world. The newly established Israeli state was trying to rid itself of most non-Jewish natives through ethnic cleansing. It could not, however, stop Palestinians from trying to return: between 2,700 and 5,000 Palestinians were killed from 1949 to 1956, mostly unarmed. The majority were peasants trying to return to their lands in order to harvest crops (Morris 1993: 28–68; Masalha 1996: 55). Some of the Palestinians who managed to reach their lands have stayed there to this day (Qumsiyeh 2011).

From that point onward, Palestinians began to emphasise the importance of education as a method of resistance, particularly as their traditional way of making a living (agriculture) was taken away by force. Students formed their own students' leagues to represent themselves and reclaim their agency. The first union was set up in Cairo in 1954 (Qumsiyeh 2011: 104–105). Tension between indigenous Palestinian Arabs and the Jewish settlers continued. Eventually, another war, called the *Naksa* (Arabic for 'defeat'), erupted in 1967 between Israel on the one hand and Egypt, Jordan, and Syria on the other, for control of the areas occupied in 1948. Consequently, another 250,000 Palestinians were made refugees, some for the second time. The rest of historic Palestine was occupied, including all of the Gaza Strip. In 1967, Israel started building settlements to gradually move Palestinians from the areas they occupied.

The contemporary moment (2000s) is a critical period for the Palestinians. Other than their emphasis on education as a way of resistance, Palestinians continue to fight settler colonial language framework in order to represent themselves with their own voices. A case in point where such resistance took place is the imposition of the word *yasidi* (Arabic for 'lord' or 'sir') on Palestinians in Israeli prisons (1969–1973). Prisoners were required by the Israeli authorities to use it at least three times a day. The Israeli Prison Services (IPS) staff recorded prisoners' names. If they did not use *yasidi* in their responses, through forgetfulness or in dissent, they were punished, cursed at, and isolated (Abu Atwan 2007).

Although *yasidi* may seem a mere linguistic choice, its usage cannot be understood apart from the settler colonial contexts in which prisoners are located. The Israeli authorities use every means at their disposal to oppress the colonised, and language is just one means of achieving this goal. The specific language usage of *yasidi* has two aspects. It reveals and shapes the psychology of the colonial jailers. On a more subtle and insidious level, such terminology controls how people think, forcing a single perspective on a socially complex situation that inevitably reflects the viewpoint of the group in power. If one compares this to South African usage of the word *baas* ('boss' in Afrikaans), which was imposed on black people in that country during the apartheid period (1948–1994), the same type of subjugation is revealed. White settlers insisted on being addressed that way, and it became common usage. By the simple, united refusal to use *yasidi* and the support of collective hunger strikes between 1968 and 1973, as well as the spread of such protests to other prisons, the prisoners prevailed. The obliteration in 1973 of the word *yasidi* from the prison's dictionary, meant metaphorically, was probably one of the first and most lasting achievements of prison hunger strikes (Al-Qaimari 1981: 69). This example reveals the importance of dignity in the prison context. This theme continues to be the number one priority in hunger strikes to this day, as seen most recently in the collective strikes of 2012, 2014, and 2017, and their achievements go beyond basic needs to winning dignity (Shwaikh 2018: 81). It is also a theme that continues to shape much resistance, as the subsequent sections show.

Writing about the Strip

Having established the importance for Palestinians of resisting settler colonial language within and outside prison, I now turn to examining how translation facilitates repression rather than representation in the Palestinian case. To do so, I interviewed five professionals based in the Gaza Strip. They are: Maram Humaid, a freelance journalist who has worked in the field of Arabic–English translation for eight years; Hind al-Khoudary, a freelance journalist who works regularly with international media outlets; Abeer Ayoub, a journalist from Gaza currently based in Amman, who used to work with European and American journalists before 2007; H. Saleh, a journalist who regularly works with American and European economists and journalists, and, finally, M. Badawi, who works within the Gaza's Ministry of Interior, that facilitates the work of foreign journalists before and after they arrive to the Strip.

Each of my interviewees has dealt with journalists from Europe or North America, mostly as part of their work in translation and journalism. These interviews took place over Skype, from my location within the UK between November 2018 and May 2019. The interviewees were all located in Gaza. All interviews were conducted in Arabic. With the help of these interviews, I examine knowledge production specifically in the Gaza Strip, examining how the siege on Gaza contributes to the process of knowledge production by allowing a certain category of people to enter and leave the Strip. Before venturing out into this critical terrain, I first briefly review the situation in Gaza since the Israeli siege was imposed in 2007.

But what is the Gaza Strip? The Gaza Strip is a 365-square-kilometre Palestinian territory to the east of the Mediterranean Sea and in the southwest of Palestine (Jabba 1997: 20–21; Abu Saif 2016; Jebril 2018: 177). The majority of those living in the Gaza Strip today are refugees. The area is of high density, and its population is mostly children and youth. In 2020, it is set to reach 2.2 million, up from 2.13 million projected in 2012 (UN Report 2017: 3). Israeli forces first occupied it back in 1967, following the *Naksa*. Under the administration of the Egyptian authorities, the Gaza Strip has been struggling to survive and flourish. It remains neglected in scholarship despite its political centrality (Roy 2007).

Several attempts, initially sponsored by international mediators, including the United States, to put to an end the conflict in Palestine have failed. The most famous among these was the drawn-out Oslo peace process between the Israeli government and the Palestinian Liberation Organization (PLO), which produced the Palestinian Authority (PA). The PA arrived in the Gaza Strip in 1993 to start the self-governing process, at a time when the Strip was still under Israeli occupation (Kelman 2007: 292). The peace process, however, did not bring peace. Arguably, the situation has become worse in all respects for the people of Gaza since it was signed in Oslo. In 2000, Palestinians initiated a five-year *intifada* (Arabic for uprising), to protest against the continuing Israeli occupation of their lands and resources (Pressman 2003: 114–132). In 2005, when the uprising ended, the Israeli government, headed by then prime minister Ariel Sharon, announced and later implemented a plan to withdraw from the Gaza Strip. A year later, Hamas won the Palestinian parliamentary election. In 2007, the Israeli siege on Gaza began, and the living conditions started deteriorating.

'It impacts on all aspects of our life […]. We, in Gaza, do not have control over what gets in or out. It is either the Egyptian or the Israeli authorities who do,' al-Khoudary said. Unemployment, poverty, lack of freedom of speech and movement, and several Israeli attacks followed. No one is safe. Since 2008, Gaza has witnessed three major wars: in 2008, 2012, and 2014. During these difficult years, Gaza saw the loss of thousands of people and great damage to its limited resources. Since then, the Israel-imposed siege has continued to intensify, limiting imports and exports, the movement of people, and the activities of fishermen as well as farmers in their daily work (Alfar et al. 2017: 1–9; UN report 2017).

Beyond its impact on Palestinians' ability to travel, this siege has impacted economic conditions as well as Palestinians' intellectual activities. In the first war on Gaza in 2008, which lasted twenty days, there were severe cuts in the electricity supply. There was little internet access. No exposure to the outside world. No clean water. People who started coming from the outside were typically foreigners with a lot of money who live comfortable lives (Humaid and Shwaikh 2018). Palestinians who managed to leave the Strip were still attached to this life that once traumatised them.

The constant political instability in the Strip impacted on knowledge production immensely. During the siege period, libraries have suffered a lack of visitors. Clubs where books are read and exchanged and where intellectually inclined youth gather are a rare sight today. Before the siege started, libraries had regular visitors and reading clubs were flourishing. Now, printed newspapers are less widespread than before. People check social media more often than before (Badawi and Shwaikh 2018). '2018 was a hard year for reading in Gaza,' Maram Humaid commented. She added that the culture of reading is in danger. People who read do so mostly to escape the harsh reality of Gaza. Those who used to read do not feel any relief from doing so any more. The few remaining libraries have tried to engage the people of Gaza. Books are on sale most times, but with more than 70 percent discounted, hardly anyone buys. More important than reading, Humaid added, is access to electricity, clean water, and food. Additional stress is produced by internal political rivalries between supporters of Hamas and Fatah, headed by Mahmoud Abbas, who is also the head of the PA and the PLO.

The process of knowledge production has also been worsened by limitations on freedom of movement to and from the Strip. In the Palestinian territories, there is no functioning airport. The only airport, Yasser Arafat International Airport in Rafah city, southern Gaza Strip, opened in 1998 and closed in 2001 as it was severely damaged by Israeli airstrikes (Mong 2005). There are two border crossings in Gaza, to the north (Erez) and to the south (Rafah). They are controlled by external as well as internal parties: mostly Israel, the PA, and Hamas, which has controlled Gaza ever since it received the majority of votes in the legislative election in 2006 (Roy 2011). This was followed by violent clashes between Hamas and Fatah supporters in the Strip. Importantly, being ruled by a party does not necessarily mean supporting it, especially if one 'has never been part of the election process in the Strip before,' said twenty-eight-year-old interviewee H. Saleh. Meanwhile, European and North American sources continue to portray all people of Gaza as if they subscribed to the same ideology, dehumanising them in an orientalist way that ignores their political and non-political differences and ignoring their right to resist a brutal occupation.

Attempts to write about what Palestinians in Gaza go through tend to become polemically enmeshed in the study of results, not causes, with emphasis on the responses combined with obliviousness to the context in which such responses occur: the focus falls on clichés such as 'Hamas and terrorism,' and Palestinian militant groups' use of rockets, without comparable criticism of the Israeli forces' use of indiscriminate violence. This is often followed by a discussion of the sequence of events and who starts shooting or rocket firing. The narrative often provides very little context (Baker 2006: 462–484). It is not the aim of this chapter to provide answers to any of these questions, but it is important to note that, while these debates continue to overdetermine Euro-American media representations, on the ground, life is getting more wretched. As with the example of the BBC with which I opened, Palestinians' accounts are not made the central focus of journalists' interest, which often simply perpetuates the colonial orientations of the governments where it is produced.

Who is allowed into the Strip?

For Euro-American journalists and translators, Israeli-controlled checkpoints are the most convenient way to enter the Strip. The Egyptian-controlled checkpoint, on the other hand, is more dangerous since it is close to the Sinai Peninsula, a haven for the ISIS militant group (McKernan 2017; Human Rights Watch Report 2019). Israeli journalists find it much harder to enter the Strip from either checkpoint. Abeer Ayoub noted that *Haaretz* columnist Amira Hass, whose views are popular among many Palestinians, used to live in Gaza until around 2005 when Israel withdrew from the Strip (Ayoub and Shwaikh 2018). She was very close to several non-governmental organisations working in Gaza but was then warned as an Israeli citizen that her presence in the Strip was a danger to her life. As Israel withdrew from the Gaza Strip, a new Israeli law prevented those with blue IDs (denoting Israeli citizenship) from entering Gaza. Jewish journalists who reside in Israel and have another nationality are eligible to receive an Israeli passport automatically, but those who work in the Strip often ask the Israeli government not to issue them a passport.

> One day, I was working with a Jewish journalist in Gaza who got a message asking him to collect his new Israeli passport. He left the Strip immediately to ask the government to withdraw his passport. He did not need it. It causes more harm than good,

Ayoub commented.[7]

Other than Israeli journalists, only a limited category of journalists are allowed into the Strip. Their political affiliations, academic orientations, and history of activism are thoroughly reviewed by Israeli and Hamas authorities to determine their 'eligibility' to enter.[8] Prior to their visit, they need to apply for two special permits, one from the Israeli authorities and the other from the Hamas authorities. Sponsorship from an individual or a group in Gaza is also required by the Hamas authorities to let them in. The sponsor is responsible for facilitating their visit. This may include translating for and co-working with them. Sponsors are briefly interrogated by Hamas authorities, and their passports are temporarily confiscated. Journalists' passports are taken too. As soon as journalists enter the Strip, they may be asked to show their permit and identity cards several times. This demonstrates the extent to which Palestinians are wary of the outside world.

Travel procedures have become more complicated over time. Permits have become harder to obtain. Sponsorships from an individual or a group are not easy to obtain either. If things go wrong, the sponsor will be mostly in trouble with the authorities in Gaza. Those who manage to enter the Strip are dealt with vigilantly by people who are often thirsty to get their narratives across, and who hope that their voices will be centralised. Professionals interviewed for this chapter explained how their accounts are repeatedly manipulated by the media organisations or individuals they work for or with, making it harder every time they deal with Euro-American knowledge producers.

> The stories we tell are not only manipulated to serve specific agendas. They are also fabricated. We do not speak spontaneously any more with Euro-American journalists. They are often very nice when speaking to us but they write about us in a completely different way.

said Maram Humaid.

'I am always suspicious, I have a "security obsession,"' interlocutor M. Badawi, who works within the Gaza Ministry that facilitates journalists' work and issue their permits, noted, agreeing with Humaid on the need for a security obsession.

In the Strip, people are often vigilant when dealing with Euro-American journalists. This is especially the case amid events of major geopolitical significance, to which Euro-American countries are significant contributors. In 2018, the Trump decision to recognise Jerusalem as the capital of Israel and to move the American embassy to Jerusalem significantly impacted American–Palestinian relations, not only on the official level but also domestically, within Palestine (Khalidi 2018: 93–102). In May 2018, around the time Trump's decision was made, Maram Humaid was facilitating an eighteen-day trip for an American photojournalist in the Strip, to document everyday life. Residents were not happy to receive the photojournalist or deal with her. She was not allowed into several houses or to take pictures of their properties. 'All this was because she is from America. It is a sensitive issue. 2018 was a catastrophic year because of the Trump administration's position on Jerusalem. It was a bloody year in Gaza too,' Humaid commented. However, it was not only because of Trump that the Jerusalem's move was allowed to happen but also because of the 'media bias that stayed neutral most of the times, abandoning Palestinian scars,' Humaid added.

This emergent anti-Americanism within Gaza was less evident before the siege started on the Strip. Abeer Ayoub recounted, 'there have never been attempts before to prevent journalists from entering one's houses.' The change in attitudes may refer to the sense of betrayal the Palestinians of Gaza have felt since the siege started, not only from Americans, as people and as a leadership, but also the international community as a whole. Even when Maram tried to tell people that the photojournalist is Australian, they received a response that this is not any different, showing that it is not only about Trump but overall a sense of betrayal from the west and sensitivity towards all foreigners.

'The language we spoke, not the one we understood'

In everyday life, language is vital, not just to communicate. 'It is the most important thing,' according to al-Khoudary. In Gaza, using the local language may help to establish warm relations with the indigenous population too, as this section shows. History teaches us that learning other languages in the war-zone can challenge existing power/knowledge dynamics. Anti-apartheid leader Nelson Mandela once said, 'If you talk to a man in a language he understands, that goes to his head. If you talk to him in his own language, that goes to his heart' (cited in O'Toole 1996: VI). Mandela so strongly believed this that he learnt the language of his oppressor, Afrikaans, while imprisoned on Robben Island. He also devoted himself to learning everything about Afrikaans culture, from literature to history, to music. His linguistic approach helped him to speak the language with the white warders, and he unintentionally benefited from the effect of his ability with foreign languages. This is because Mandela capitalised on the benefits of using someone else's language. When a person makes the effort to speak someone else's language, even if only basic phrases, they communicate to them that they are understood, their cultures are respected and that their identity is recognised. They see them as a human being, in the words of another South African, Trevor Noah (2016).

Echoing Mandela's and Noah's statements, Humaid commented, 'I am very happy when I see journalists coming to the Strip with some Arabic. It becomes easier to communicate.'[9] They win 'more trust' among the people, she added, emphasising that she would appreciate it if all journalists try to speak to us in 'the language we speak, not the language we understand.' Translators and journalists in Gaza prefer those who speak Arabic. It makes conversation and communication easier. 'It is not only I who need to study to understand you. You need to study to understand me too. It is more of a psychological barrier,' Humaid explained. But there is a group of people who know Arabic but chose to not uncover their ability to understand it. Humaid commented that it becomes clear a few hours later that journalists or academics do understand it from how they react to things and their way of speaking. 'With all honesty, this made translation and journalism much harder. I became scared of the journalist,' Humaid said. Hamas security guards in Erez know about this issue and often advise Palestinians fixers and translators to exercise caution when dealing with journalists and academics from outside the Strip. For example, no information deemed 'sensitive' should be disclosed in front of them, even if in Arabic, because they may know the language but not have disclosed this.

Interlocutors interviewed for this research emphasise the importance of being accepted as they are and in their native languages. Both Humaid and Ayoub said they appreciate the efforts made by journalists to learn Arabic in order to better understand their conditions and to be understood. Ayoub dealt with journalists who tried hard to learn Arabic, paying high fees for private lessons not only to help themselves understand normal conversations with their interviewees but also to make the work of Ayoub easier. 'When there was an update in a story he wrote, he would write messages to people responsible in Arabic. It was clear it was not a perfect message but I appreciate that he tried,' Ayoub recounted in a story about a European journalist she worked with. 'This made a lot of difference,' she added. It is important to learn the mother tongue, though it can be problematic: 'If they tried to speak in a Hebrew or Israeli-Arabic accent, for example, the people in Gaza will think they are Israelis and stop coordinating with them,' Humaid added.

Culture and politics matter too

Interlocutors also relate to how culture and language are not often respected by Euro-American knowledge producers in the Strip. 'Journalists are often insensitive,' said M. Badawi. He added that they do not understand the political sensitivity of many issues in the Gaza Strip, as the examples below indicate. An inconsiderate word or an unauthorised picture can easily destroy one's family in Gaza. Humaid, for example, worked with journalists who took pictures and videos without taking into consideration the political and cultural sensitivity of the moment. Some took pictures without having permission or after they were clearly instructed not to. Humaid narrated:

> One day, an uncle of a martyr was about to break the camera of a journalist who without permission was taking pictures of women who just lost their loved ones, screaming and without a headcover. In a conservative society like Gaza, this is not allowed. But even though this message was clearly channelled to the journalist, she tried to take pictures still.

This not only violates the trust between the oppressed population and the Euro-American visitors but may also impact their mutual relations for years to come.

In the Gaza Strip, protests were planned by youths from 30 March 2018 (Land Day)[10] to 15 May (*Nakba* Day)[11] to highlight the Palestinian right of return to the homes from which they were expelled in 1948. These protests were named Great March of Return. These were initially planned to last for a few weeks but have continued as of this writing (July 2019) on a weekly basis. Israel used live fire to respond to non-violent protesters, causing several amputations.[12] A report published by United Nations Office for the Coordination of Humanitarian Affairs (OCHA) dated 27 March 2019 states that 120 amputations were carried out 'as the result of injuries sustained during demonstrations, including 21 children, with 22 people paralysed due to spinal cord injuries and nine people suffering permanent sight loss' (OCHA 2019). Maram accompanied journalists while they were reporting on some sixty cases, all male protestors between twenty-six and twenty-seven years old. Journalists were not interested in the context or the background for their stories, why they protested, or what their life was like before joining such a protest. 'All they wanted was to document the operation through which their legs were amputated and to create an album of this for their audience,' Humaid said. It appears that many Euro-American journalists and news agencies care more about receiving likes and shares on social media than respecting the families of Palestinians affected by Israeli violence.

Another tragic incident took place in 2011 when the child Amal Jaroucheh was killed by an Israeli missile in Gaza. As her body was covered on the way to burial, and people in the mosque were praying over it, the sunlight shone over it. Of course, this sunlight would naturally create a striking image for photographers, but for photographers to 'come one after another and move the body left and right to take a [perfect] picture was beyond imagination.' 'The girl turned into a doll, moving according to the photographers' lens,' an interlocutor in a recent work of Arabic journalism by Marah al-Wadia said (2017).

Arabic-language journalism can sometimes be problematic too and fail to centralise the voices of those interviewed. Al-Wadia herself questioned the practice of publishing pictures of martyrs in the first place, for example (2017):

> From the Palestinian viewpoint, we do not exaggerate when we say that 'media' has become the most contentious space. The focus should not be to display blood-soaked stories, but rather to talk about them and Palestinian heroism. Many questions arise here. Are journalists seeking to get as many shares as possible via sensationalism? Is the aim of publishing images to reveal the horrors of the occupation? What about it being an occupation, primarily? Is not that enough? We should know better.[13]

> في فلسطين، لا نبالغ حين نقول إن "الاعلام" صار المساحة الأقسى ليس بعرض القصص المخضبة بالدماء، وإنما باستهواء الحديث عنها وعن البطولات الفلسطينية، ثمة أسئلة كثيرة تطرح نفسها. هل الصحفيون باتوا يسعون إلى الحصول على أعلى عدد ممكن من المشاركات؟ هل الهدف من نشر الصور أن نعرف، نحن الفلسطينيون خصوصا والعرب عموما، بشاعة الاحتلال؟ وماذا عن كونه احتلالا؟ ألا يكفي هذا؟ يُفترض أننا نعلم.

> [*fi filistin, la nubaligh hin naqul in 'al-ilam' sar al-masaha al-aqsa lais be'rq al'qisas al-mokhadba be-adimaa, w inama bi istihwaa al-hadith anha w an al-butulat al-falastiniya, thamat as'ila kathira tatrah nafsaha. Hal al-sahafiyun batu yas'awn ila al-husool 'ala a'la 'adad mumkim min al-mosharakat? Hal al-hadaf min nushr al-suwar an na'rif, nahn al-falastiniyun khususan w al-'rab 'umuman, basha'at al-ihtilal? W matha 'an kawnihi ihtilalan? Ala yakfi hatha? Yuftarad annana na'lam.*]

In another account, a Euro-American journalist wanted to talk to Humaid about the lost corpses of martyrs in Gaza. 'Most corpses are of militants,' she explained. 'It is not safe or secure to tell [the journalist] names.' The journalist did not only push Humaid to the limit to disclose names of those militants but also identified her in the piece in a 'problematic way.' Humaid, who is a freelance journalist, was portrayed as a supporter of Hamas. 'I was shocked that she identified me this way,' Humaid commented. The journalist was contacted afterwards but refused to change the piece, which left Humaid shocked and upset. This journalist's behaviour confirms Mona Baker's work (2010), which explains how the turmoil that interpreters like Humaid experience partially results from how they are narrated by others, the Euro-American journalist in this case. Baker also examines what she refers to as the 'chasm' which gradually 'opens up between their own sense of identity, their own personal narrative, and the identity and narrative imposed on them by other parties who both need and fear them' (2010: 204). Humaid was needed by the journalist throughout her work in Gaza. She was feared by the same journalist, who provided her with sponsorship to stay in Gaza in that period. Without Humaid's facilitation, the journalist would not have been able to work freely in the Stip. But as soon as she left, this need was gone. The translators interviewed for this chapter were perceived as journalists' friends, villains, victims, or foes,[14] depending on the journalist's inclinations, often without regard to actuality. Sometimes, they were perceived to possess all of these characteristics together, depending on where the journalists were located at the time and how much they needed the Gaza-based interpreters and translators.

The interviews conducted for this research show that Palestinians' hopes are constantly shattered by the irresponsible coverage of their experience by American and European journalists. The journalists interviewed for this chapter agree that, even when Gaza is reported on, the types of issues covered by Euro-American media are often irrelevant to everyday reality in Gaza. There is often a lengthy interval of silence in the reporting of news from Gaza, and when media outlets decide to travel there, they cover issues that are not of importance to the residents in the Strip. Humaid recalled that, in 2016, a major British media agency finally travelled to Gaza after a long period of silence. The coverage, however, was on why, during council elections, Hamas chose to display roses instead of pictures of women candidates. 'These are not that important issues when it comes to the miserable situation in Gaza. One cannot leave the Strip for four years [during which time thousands of Palestinians were killed] and come back to focus on this,' Humaid commented.

Alternative media include al-Shabaka as well as Twitter accounts of Palestinians writing and capturing the reality on the ground on a daily basis. A few of the most significant such accounts are @Omar_Gaza, @Hind_Gaza, @shawajason, @MaramGaza, and @sarahsaftawi. Palestinians living abroad, such as myself, follow these accounts and check them daily in order to keep up to date with life in the Strip, where my family lives today.

Who is responsible?

When Euro-American journalists finish their work in Gaza, they head to Israel-controlled Erez checkpoint, passing through Jerusalem towards their final destination. Those who helped them throughout their journey in the Strip cannot accompany them beyond Erez. The siege makes it impossible for the Euro-American journalists to be accompanied by Palestinians from Gaza beyond this checkpoint. The responsibility of Euro-American journalists remains significant. They have more resources to centralise voices and change stereotypes. 'Little by little, Gaza can come out of these stereotypical images,' Ayoub commented. 'It just needs effort by all parties.' Palestinians, journalists, and others, are equally responsible in this regard. They need to 'know their priorities, to diversify their topics, and to present human stories in unique ways. It needs not to be the same story all the time. They need to make sure there are always new approaches,' Ayoub added. Both Humaid and Ayoub noted that the siege is a major barrier to better coverage. If there were no siege, there would be 'more of a chance to get things done in Gaza. Only open the borders. We do not need aid. We just need to be given a chance,' Ayoub noted.

Importantly, all interlocutors recognised that they cannot force journalists to write the way they want. Agencies require that someone from their team write. The challenge is to build strong and genuine relationships with the journalists and change stereotypes. 'Some foreign journalists have more knowledge about Gaza than I do. They have impact,' Ayoub noted. Some foreign journalists, on the other hand, have very little knowledge. For Ayoub, it is important to build 'good relations with them' whatever the amount of knowledge they have. Also, it is important to be part of the process. Some journalists come to the Strip with preconceptions they want to prove. Ayoub explained that one of the preconceptions is 'everyone in Gaza wears a headscarf.' One Euro-American journalist came to the Strip and met with a fixer who has a headscarf. Her dad gave her a lift and stayed with them through the interviews. Later the journalist wrote a story about 'Gaza where everyone wears a headscarf and has a male guardian.' Ayoub advised journalists who work in the Gaza Strip not to have such preconceptions. 'Go and investigate, try to know if this is right or wrong. Do not go to prove it. Look at what they have in common, go deeper into things. Look into the root causes,' Ayoub said. 'If needed, do get into the superficial details. Try the unique and sweet way, the world understands it. Just go and think more deeply and discover it yourself.'

Awareness is important on the fixers' sides. There are questions that put people's life in danger. When Wafa al-Bis, a Palestinian ex-political prisoner in Israeli jails, was freed, Ayoub was asked to facilitate an interview with her. The Euro-American journalist asked, 'Now you are free, would you go back to do another military operation like you did before imprisonment?' This is a question that would put al-Bis's life in danger, especially if answered affirmatively, as had happened in similar cases before (see Al-Wadia 2017). Ayoub told the journalist it was not a reasonable question and asked her to change the question, which emphasises the agency of the journalist. When the question could be edited or restructured, Ayoub did so, but there were times when there was no way for this to be done.

Ayoub's first job as a fixer and translator was with a journalist from *The Independent*.[15] It was to interview Ismail Haniyah, then the Prime Minister and Hamas leader. 'This was not an easy job. All the Hamas leaders were around,' Ayoub recounted. The difference between this journalist and the one above is that the latter knew what he wanted from Haniyah, without being culturally or socially insensitive, and this made their jobs easier. When Haniyah did not answer the question, the journalist asked, 'Ask the question again.' Ayoub had no choice but to ask him to repeat the question.

It is impossible to underestimate the importance of being sensitive and respectful of cultural differences and aware of political contexts in the war-zone. Making an effort to learn the language spoken in Gaza or at least to be acquainted with cultural differences makes a huge difference. Pictures should never be taken without permission from local residents, and all journalistic pieces should be accurate and not written solely to collect likes and shares. Most importantly, journalists who visit Gaza from the outside should always remember that media coverage can transform one's life and it has done so for countless residents of Gaza, for better and for worse. The journalist, activist, and translator all collectively share a moral obligation to harness the media's power to bring about peace and relief from suffering, and to prevent it from causing further harm.

Related topics

Translator, Native Informant, Fixer; Resistance, Activism and Marronage in Paul Bowles's Translations of the Oral Stories of Tangier; Translating Mourning Walls.

Notes

1 Gaza city, Gaza, the Strip, and the Gaza Strip are used interchangeably to refer to the Gaza Strip which includes several cities, including the Gaza city.
2 The programme was aired on 13 June 2019. It is not currently available on the BBC site (www.bbc.co.uk/sounds/play/p06vttg0) but a tweet referencing the programme can be found here: https://twitter.com/BBCr4today/status/1073622384517767169.
3 Zionism refers to the support of creating a Jewish state in Palestine (Mayamey 2010: 2–29).
4 Knowledge producers in this chapter refers to journalists, academics, and translators.
5 Before Israeli withdrew from the Gaza Strip in 2005, Israeli prisons were spread throughout the occupied territories, including the Strip.
6 The Israeli authorities perceive Palestinian prisoners held as 'criminals' and 'terrorists' responsible for causing security threats to the State. Palestinians, on the contrary, as well as Egyptians, Jordanians, Syrians, and Lebanese, from countries that have been involved in the Arab–Israeli war of 1967, see themselves as 'political prisoners ['asra siyasun],' held for national-political reasons as in resisting the occupation. On the national reasons, if a Palestinian and an Israeli throw stones, they are treated differently by the Israeli authorities (for more see Nashif 2008; Dakka 2009).
7 An anonymous source explains this story further to me, '[it looks like] the journalist was on a resident visa first, which is the visa that can 'roll over' into a passport. All other visas you need to submit paperwork when applying for a passport. A resident visa is only open to Jews.' He added that the journalist would need to 'go to the Misrad Hapnim (Ministry of Interior in Israel), and tell them to switch his visa from resident to work because having an Israeli ID number would be unsafe for him.'
8 The Israeli authorities and the Hamas authorities have different criteria in terms of whom they accept. Most of these are related to the political background of the person, how well connected they are, and the work they wish to do in the Strip.
9 The above statement is powerful but one would say that some Israeli soldiers speak Arabic. They do but the interaction they have with the Palestinians in Gaza is very limited to times of wars. Even Israeli journalists are not allowed in the Strip with their passports, as the chapter explores.
10 In 1976, the Israeli government announced a plan to expropriate thousands of dunams of land for state purpose. The Palestinians responded with a general strike and marches in Arab towns from the Galilee to the Negev, in which six unarmed Palestinians were killed and one hundred were wounded. Since then, this day has been commemorated as a tribute to those who have failed in the struggle to hold on to their land and identity, not only of the Palestinian citizens of Israel but of the Palestinians everywhere. It is an important day in the Palestinian collective memory, one that emphasises their right to resistance of Israeli colonisation (Hawari 2018).
11 *Nakba* (Arabic for 'catastrophe') refers to the Israeli systematic ethnic cleansing against the indigenous Palestinians, which saw its peak in May 1948 (Pappé 2006).

12 For more on the Great March of Return, see Abusalim (2018).
13 Translation was slightly amended.
14 For further on these characteristics, see Baker (2010: 204–209).
15 The name of the journalist is not disclosed for unclear reasons.

Further reading

Barkuzar, Dubbati, and Abudayeh Haneen (2018) 'The Translator as an Activist: Reframing Conflict in the Arabic Translation of Sacco's *Footnotes in Gaza*,' *The Translator* 24 (2): 147–165.

This article explores the translator's influence in the Arab translation of Joe Sacco's novel *Footnotes in Gaza*, arguing that the Palestinian translator sees himself as an activist and aims to reframe the Palestinian cause as people struggling for independence.

Roy, Sara (2007) *Failing Peace: Gaza and the Palestinian-Israeli Conflict*. London: Pluto.

Roy used more than two thousand interviews and extensive first-hand experience to examine the political and socio-economic reality in the Strip, providing a unique context to the situation there.

Sacco, Joe (2009) *Footnotes in Gaza: A Graphic Novel*. London: Jonathan Cape.

A graphic novel about Rafah, a city to the south of Gaza. Sacco travelled throughout Gaza and immersed himself in its daily life and wrote the book to capture the essence of its tragedy.

Tymoczko, Maria (2000) 'Translation and Political Engagement,' *The Translator* 6 (1): 23–47.

Examining the translation of Irish literature into English, this article examines the possibility of using translation to achieve a geopolitical agenda.

References

Abu Atwan, Monqiz (2007) 'The Prisons since 1967,' MA thesis, Birzeit University, BirZeit.
Abu-Saad, Ismael (2008) 'Where Inquiry Ends: The Peer Review Process and Indigenous Standpoints,' *American Behavioural Scientists* 51 (2): 1902–1918.
Abu Saif, Atef (2016) *The Drone Eats with Me: A Gaza Diary*. Boston, MA: Beacon Press.
Abusalim, Jehad (2018) 'The Great March of Return: An Organiser's Perspective,' *Journal of Palestine Studies* 47 (4): 90–100.
Alfar, Abd ElRahman, Samir Mdallah, and Eman Alkhoudary (2017) 'The Reflections of Israeli Siege over Economic and Social Indices on Gaza Strip,' *Journal of Global Economics* 5 (3): 3–9.
Al-Hardan, Anaheed (2014) 'Decolonising Research on Palestinians: Towards Critical Epistemologies and Research Practices,' *Qualitative Inquiry* 20 (1): 61–71.
Al-Qaimari, Atta (1981) *The Prison is Not for Us*. Israeli Prison of Nafha: Nafha Prison.
Al-Wadia, Marah (2017) 'Filistin … sahafiyun fi saradiq al-aza [Palestine … Journalists in the Funeral Marquee],' *Al-Jazeera* [online]. Available at: http://journalism.aljazeera.net/ar/ajr/article/2017/10/171008120007723.html [accessed on 15 October 2019].
Baker, Mona (2006) 'Translation and Activism: Emerging Patterns of Narrative Community,' *The Massachusetts Review* 47 (3): 462–484.
Baker, Mona (2010) 'Interpreters and Translators in the War Zone,' *The Translator* 16 (2): 197–222.
Beresford, David (1987) *Ten Men Dead*. New York: HarperCollins.
Dakka, Waleed (2009) 'Moulding of Consciousness,' [online]. Available at: www.safsaf.org/12-2009/asra/walid-dakkah.htm [accessed on 3 July 2019].
Grande, Sandy (2004) *Red Pedagogy: Native American Social and Political Thought*. Maryland: Rowman and Littlefield Publishers.
Hawari, Yara (2018) 'Palestine Land Day: A Day to Resist and Remember,' [online]. Available at: www.aljazeera.com/indepth/opinion/palestine-land-day-day-resist-remember-180330054113738.html [accessed 8 June 2019].
Human Rights Watch Report (2019) 'If You Are Afraid for Your Lives, Leave Sinai,' [online]. Available at: www.hrw.org/report/2019/05/28/if-you-are-afraid-your-lives-leave-sinai/egyptian-security-forces-and-isis [accessed 4 July 2019].

Jabba, Richard (1997) 'Suitability Analysis for Determining New Residential Developments in Gaza Strip, Palestine,' *University of Rhode Island Digital Commons* [online]. Available at: http://cite seerx.ist.psu.edu/viewdoc/download?doi=10.1.1.1011.3877&rep=rep1&type=pdf, 20–21 [accessed 15 October 2019].

Jebril, Mona (2018) 'Academic Life under Occupation: The Impact on Educationalist at Gaza's Universities,' *University of Cambridge* [online]. Available at: https://core.ac.uk/download/pdf/151178568.pdf, 177 [accessed 15 October 2019].

Kelman, Herbert (2007) 'The Israeli-Palestinian Peace Process and Its Vicissitudes: Insights from Attitude Theory,' *American Psychologist Association* 62 (4): 292.

Khalidi, Rashid (2018) 'And Now What? The Trump Administration and the Question of Jerusalem,' *Journal of Palestine Studies* 47 (3): 93–102.

Lentin, Ronit (2013) *Thinking Palestine*. London: Zed Books.

Mandela, Nelson (2007) *Wisdom for the Soul of Black Folk*. Ed. Larry Chang. Washington, DC: Gnosophia Publishers.

Masalha, Nur (1996) 'The 1956–57 Occupation of the Gaza Strip: Israeli Proposals to Resettle the Palestinian Refugees,' *British Journal of Middle Eastern Studies* 23 (1): 55–68.

Mayamey, Babak (2010) 'Zionism: A Critical Account 1897–1948. The Development of Israel and the Exodus of Palestine from a 'New Historian' Perspective,' *POLIS Journal* 4 [online]. Available at: www.polis.leeds.ac.uk/assets/files/students/student-journal/ma-winter10/mayamey-e.pdf [accessed 15 October 2019].

McKernan, Bethan (2017) 'Isis in Egypt; What is Their Presence in Sinai and Have They Previously Claimed Terror Attacks in the Region,' *The Independent* [online]. Available at: www.independ ent.co.uk/news/world/middle-east/isis-egypt-sinai-terror-attack-presence-claim-map-insurgency-explained-who-are-they-a8073866.html [accessed 15 October 2019].

Mong, Adrienne (2005) 'Ground in Gaza, But Hoping to Fly Again,' *NBC NEWS* [online]. Available at: www.nbcnews.com/id/7900217/ns/world_newsmideast_n_africa/t/grounded-gaza-hoping-fly-again/#.XR4e9-v0ldg [accessed 4 July 2019].

Morris, Benny (1993) *Israel's Border Wars, 1949–1956: Arab Infiltration, Israeli Retaliation and the Countdown to the Suez War*. Oxford: Clarendon Press.

Nashif, Esmail (2008) *Palestinian Political Prisoners: Identity and Community*. London: Routledge.

Noah, Trevor (2016) *Born a Crime: Stories from a South African Childhood*. New York: Spiegel and Grau.

O'Toole, Garson (1996) *At Home in the World: The Peace Corps Story*. Washington, DC: United States Government Printing Office.

Pappé, Ilan (2006) *Ethnic Cleansing of Palestine*. London: Oneworld Publications.

Pressman, Jeremy (2003) 'The Second Intifada: Background and Causes of the Israeli-Palestinian Conflict,' *The Journal of Conflict Studies* XXIII (2): 114–132.

Qumsiyeh, Mazin (2011) *Popular Resistance in Palestine*. London: Pluto Press.

Roy, Sara (2011) *Creating Civic Communities: Engaging the Islamist Social Sector*. Princeton, NJ: Princeton University Press.

Said, Edward W. (1981) *Covering Islam: How the Media and the Experts Determine How We See the Rest of the World*. New York: Vintage.

Shwaikh, Malaka (2018) 'The Dynamics of Prison-Based Hunger Strikes,' *Jerusalem Quarterly* 75: 78–90.

Shwaikh, Malaka, and Rebecca Ruth Gould (2020) *Prison Hunger Strikes as Civil Resistance: A Global Perspective on Political Resistance in Prisons, International Centre on Nonviolent Conflict*. Washington, DC: International Center on Nonviolent Conflict Research Monograph Series.

Smith, Linda Tuhiwai (2012) *Decolonising Methodologies*. London: Zed Books.

UN Report (2017) 'Gaza Ten Years Later,' *United Nations Country Team in the Occupied Palestinian Territory* [online]. Available at: https://unsco.unmissions.org/sites/default/files/gaza_10_years_later_-_11_july_2017.pdf, [accessed on 15 October 2019].

United Nations Office for the Coordination of Humanitarian Affairs (OCHA) (2019) 'Approaching the First Anniversary of the 'Great March of Return' Protests in Gaza,' [online]. Available at: www.ochaopt.org/content/approaching-first-anniversary-great-march-return-protests-gaza [accessed 15 October 2019].

Interviews cited

Al-Khoudary, Hind, and Malaka Shwaikh (2018) 'Interview with Hind al-Khoudary,' 31 December 2018.
Ayoub, Abeer, and Malaka Shwaikh (2018) 'Interview with Abeer Ayoub,' 17 December 2018.
Badawi, M., and Malaka Shwaikh (2018) 'Interview with M. Badawi,' 1 December 2018.
Humaid, Maram, and Malaka Shwaikh (2018) 'Interview with Maram Humaid,' 15 November 2018.
Saleh, H., and Malaka Shwaikh (2018) 'Interview with H. Saleh,' 31 December 2018.

Part III

The translator as activist

9

Translating mourning walls

Aleppo's last words

Eylaf Bader Eddin

Introduction

Translation in times of conflict is an especially difficult task, as translators often play the role of activists, exposing their viewpoints in their work, despite their best attempts at neutrality. In December 2016, for example, many online English newspapers and magazines reported on the displacement of civilians from Aleppo. After a bloody fight, which had raged since 2012, the armed Syrian opposition and regime forces signed 'a truce providing for a ceasefire, and the evacuation of both civilians and militants from eastern Aleppo' (Aljazeera 2016). Upon hearing this, civilians went into the streets, and sprayed the city's walls with messages to the effect that they had been condemned to leave the city by force. Syria witnessed like other Arab countries a huge wave of protests in 2011 and then 'in February 2012 the revolution officially took the shape of the armed one' (Bishara 2013: 199). Gradually the situation escalated into regional and international interventions that moulded the uprising as a proxy-war. It is important to highlight here that Assad's regime 'prevented the Arab and international journalists to cover without the presence of the Assad's forces' (Ḥazīn 2012) which forced journalists later to get translated data from activists with the absence of trust of the regime media outlets, as happened with Aleppo 2016. In the absence of more, and better, translations concerning these events, photos and images took the place of words, creating a 'non-translation, mistranslation and/or disputed translation,' as Apter (2006: 14) describes translation into Arabic after 9/11. In such cases, the preference for image over translation gives rise to less text, and more semantic ambiguity. Here, translation serves as a quotation—at best —or, less ideally, as a commentary lacking cultural weight and context. Assuming that readers already understand the spray painters' intentions, online activists seek to convey political messages, rather than promote an understanding of the cultural aspects of a phenomenon like Aleppo's walls. This is obvious from the way in which English media covered the Aleppine displacement. Broadly speaking, the walls of Aleppo were reported on with photos rather than words, a strategy which, one way or another, conveyed a flat, simplistic scene, devoid of cultural and artistic nuance. The representation of Aleppo's walls by activist translators, and political activists, on English websites transformed a cruel disaster involving displaced civilians into a flowery event full of hope and romance. In this chapter, I argue that the use of images as translations omits rich layers of meaning, and confounds attempts 'to bring back a cultural other as the same' (Venuti 1995: 18). Such substitution invariably overlooks the essential meaning and intention of the writing, captions and images themselves, while preventing the original utterance from being seen as a conscious act (Appiah 1993: 809). By combining Appiah's 'thick translation' with Roland Barthes' method of reading images, I aim to recover the complexity of the sprayed writing, in contradistinction to 'graffiti' as a term, while unpacking the cultural content that has been lost in the English translations of both journalists and activists, alike.

The act of spraying

Between the 14 and 16 of December 2016, a number of activists managed to spray messages on Aleppo's city walls, before being forcibly displaced. Almost immediately, tens of photos of their messages went viral on Facebook and Twitter (one of them, containing two lines from a poem by the Syrian poet Nizar Qabbani (1923–1998), will be analysed later in this paper). To fully understand the circumstances surrounding such acts of spraying, one must contact the sprayers themselves. Despite the fact that most English websites described the contents of such photos as 'graffiti,' activists, in semi-structured interviews, characterised them as no more, nor less, than messages to the outside world. Ghith Beram, one of the activists in the spraying campaign, says:

> You might see them as art, as a person studying them, or you can call them graffiti, but I see them as an act of *baḫḫ*, which means 'spraying.' I did not spray the lines for artistic reasons. I sprayed them because I wrote what my heart told me to do, because of the deep sorrow I had, because of us being displaced from our city. I wanted to send messages to the silent world; primary messages of love.
>
> *(Bader Eddin and Beram 2017)*

Salem Abu alNaser, who had the idea of Aleppo's walls, shares Beram's position. He does not consider the act of writing on walls as art, but rather as an attempt to inform the world about the displacement of Aleppo's civilians (Bader Eddin and Abu alNaser 2017).

Uncovering a writer's motivations for placing these symbolic products on Aleppo's walls raises a number of questions. How best to describe such symbolic products? Are they murals, or graffiti? Are they perhaps best characterised by the activists' own terms, *baḫḫ* (spraying), or *ḥīṭān* (walls)? What is the difference between such terms, in the context of both Syria, generally, and Aleppo, in particular?

Murals, graffiti, *baḫḫ*, *ḥīṭān*

Prior to recent events, writing on walls in Syria was used only for the purposes of advertising, or to praise Hafiz Assad, or his son (as the walls of most military barracks and Baath Party buildings attest). Despite the use of walls as a means of resisting Assad, since March 2011, the term 'graffiti' has not been popular in Syria. The phenomenon most resembling graffiti is referred to as *ḥīṭān*, which means 'walls,' not 'graffiti.' The term 'graffiti' was used for the first time in April 2012, during the so-called Freedom

Graffiti Week—an international campaign that passed through most Arab countries, including Syria (Ratta 2012). After this campaign passed, Syrians reverted to calling graffiti *baḥḥ*.

> [With] this singular exception, Syrians knew and know graffiti by other names, like *baḥḥ*, or *ḥīṭān*. Thus, it is difficult to determine the name of the writing on Aleppo's walls. From *baḥḥ*, other terms like 'spray man' (*a-r-rajul al-baḥḥāḥ*) or 'spray woman' (*al-mar'a al-baḥḥāḥ*) have been derived, which emphasises the act of spraying more than the product in Arabic. At the end of 2011, in Damascus especially, activists organised themselves into *baḥḥ* brigades, each of which contained anywhere from five to ten spray men or women. Further complicating the question of nomenclature is the fact that wall writing has deep roots in Arab history.
>
> *(Al-Aṣbahānī 1972)*

Kitāb adab al-ġurabā (Book of Strangers), by Abu Faraj Al-Iṣbahānī (897–967), offers many examples of the use of walls as message holders (as in the case of the hanging poems, or *al-Mu'allaqāt* (Suspended Odes)) as using walls for hanging poetry, which was an Arabic cultural phenomenon for hanging the most outspoken poems on Ka'ba in Mecca in Pre-Islamic Arabia.

What then, to call the writing on Aleppo's walls? A mural is 'a large picture that has been painted on the wall of a room or building,' while graffiti is 'words or drawings, especially humorous, rude, or political, on walls, doors, etc. in public places' (Woodford 2003). Given their linguistic content, the walls of Aleppo resemble graffiti more than they do murals. Nor should we fail to consider the mural's traditional function of 'beautifying [a] specific location' (Gottlieb 2008: 2). While this might have been the case in Saraqib—where activists decorated destroyed walls with murals—it does not apply to Aleppo, where civilians were being displaced, and had no need to decorate the walls before leaving. Thus, Aleppo's walls are not murals. A further distinction relates to the question of permission, or authorisation. Graffiti is usually written as an act of resistance, and is considered 'an act of vandalism' (Walsh 1996: 12). If Aleppo's walls are graffiti, then they should necessarily reflect the sprayers' resistance to a given authority—which they do not, in all cases, except for some moments when the regime's forces have the city. Nor is the question of authorisation, or permission, of any great import in the context of a forced displacement. Thus, Aleppo's walls should not be considered graffiti.

As neither 'graffiti' nor 'mural' describes the sprayings in Aleppo—and as they contain characteristics of both forms—I propose referring to them simply as 'the walls of Aleppo.' The sprayers, for their part, do not consider their works to be graffiti; this term reduces the long history of *baḥḥ* in Syria, which dates back to the 2008 TV series, *Spotlight*, a satire show that criticised the regime on different topics. Adnan Ezraay, the writer of the Al-rajull al-baḥḥāḥ episode, was arrested after his last series, entitled 'Fawq as-saqf' in 2012 (Aljazeera 2012). Many activists call spraying on walls *baḥḥ* to the extent that *Al-Watan Radio*, pro-revolution media, states 'al-rajull al-baḥḥāḥ is active again in Deraa' (2019), which highlights the importance of using *baḥḥ* rather than graffiti in the Syrian context. Furthermore, the term 'walls' is deeply rooted in Syrian cultural history, and reflects a greater variety of cultural and political aspects than the contemporary term, 'graffiti.' In addition, 'graffiti' as a term does not echo the cultural characteristics of the Syrian particularity of Syria and Aleppo and the artists (painters) themselves do not see it as graffiti. Moreover, all of the mentioned influence of the term took its shape and meaning not as a copy of the concept of graffiti, as was shown in the term definition difference, but of *baḥḥ* as a different act of graffiti. This is seen in Al-Iṣbahānī's book in Arabic (not the translation), the painters and the Syrian series *Spotlight*. All of these sources mention writing on walls as *baḥḥ*. 'Wall' also lends a certain particularity to the act of spraying in Aleppo, and in Syria generally. I believe thick translation can be rendered not only on the level of the text itself but also on the level of the technical terms that have some nuances in both cultures (source and target language texts). Despite the fact that graffiti can serve the meaning of 'walls, it deprives the term of cultural nuances. For all of the reasons mentioned 'wall' thickens the act and the product of the sprayed poetic line and it reflects more multiple cultural echoes than graffiti.

The English news

English translations of Aleppo's walls have appeared on the BBC and in *The Huffington Post UK*, *Middle East Eye*, *The Daily Mail*, *Mass Appeal* (a cultural magazine), *The Independent*, *Buzz Feed*, *EA Worldview* and elsewhere. Using Google search results from the period within two months of the civilian displacement (15 December 2016 to 15 February 2017), I found references to the wall I intend to analyse (with translations of its two poetic lines) on the following sites: *The Daily Mail, Mass Appeal, Huffington Post*, BBC and *Middle East Eye*. All of these sites offered a short, single-paragraph description of the situation in Aleppo, before inserting the photos with activists' translations, as found on social media. All of the headlines included quotes from the activists' translations, which were reproduced and not revised, or, at most, reduced to platitudes, such as: '"Goodbye … One day, we will return": Syrians spray-paint moving messages on their homes ahead of their evacuation from Aleppo' (Robinson 2016)—in this case, with no link to the original image.

The *Huffington Post*, meanwhile, regarded the Aleppine walls as messages of hope, taking their cue from a man who spray-painted messages to his fiancée. A photo of the couple—standing in the city's ruins and mournfully contemplating a wall that says, 'We will return'—doesn't stop the editors from titling the piece: '"We will return": Syrian newlyweds fleeing Aleppo leave behind messages of hope' (Abdelaziz and Cook 2016). The BBC also regards the walls as 'Words of hope' (BBC 2016), without adding more than a single sentence, and a few-second-long video. *Mass Appeal* magazine, known especially for its interest in graffiti, presents the photos in four sentences, providing readers with a single activist's translation (Turco 2016). But did the walls represent mere words of hope and love, as the English media would have had it?

Thick translation and its demands

In this chapter, my working definition of translation is that it be 'readable and transparent'; negotiating between domestication, and resisting foreignisation, translation aims to 'bring back the cultural other as the same' (Venuti 1995: 18). In the case of Aleppo's walls, this negotiation is vital; 'the cultural other' cannot simply be reproduced in a translation of the walls' sprayed text and simple iconography. The photos themselves are texts, open to multiple interpretations. Although the walls contain only simple sentences, or single words, activists' English translations managed to universally omit their cultural context. Translation is more than 'an attempt to find ways of saying in one language something that means the same as what has been said in another,' because the relationship between languages is not a parallel one, and rarely offers exact equivalents (Appiah 1993: 808). Depending on the translation's aim and audience, a given translator positions him- or herself either closer to, or further from, the original context. If translation does not involve a certain resistance to the target language, it invariably settles closer to the readers' established knowledge and culture, encouraging them to see it not as a translation, but as a distinct text from their own culture. In the case of the aforementioned headlines, such shifts contribute to a flat understanding of events in Aleppo, and in Syria generally. Such translations were presented carelessly to English audiences, without considering the ways in which activist translators may have imposed their own perspectives on the walls—to say nothing of the sprayers' original intentions.

This chapter does not suggest the best possible translations for the walls of Aleppo; rather, I will offer a number of possible translations for a single wall, while commenting on those already extant. My aim in providing more than one translation for the same text is to illustrate the text's multiplicity of possible readings. Therefore, I will use thick translation to produce more than one translation of a single wall, while providing a semiotic interpretation aimed at revealing the wall's deeper cultural significance. I proceed from the premise that existing translations of the wall in question omit four key cultural aspects. The first of these is the fact that the wall's lines come from Nizar Qabbani's poem 'The Brutal Poem,' which describes a violent love in a violent context. Surprisingly, the sprayer did not reproduce Qabbani's lines exactly. Perhaps he or she considered the message a new work in a new context; or maybe, the sprayer simply relied on intertextuality to lend Qabbani's lines additional meaning (a process which, naturally, complicates attempts at translation). Second, the varied media outlets' attempts to translate the image, as image, ignored the lines' performativity, and prevented them from being recognised as acts. Instead, they prompted readers to interpret and react to them on the basis of pre-existing translations. Third, by failing to appreciate the walls as acts of mourning, all of the outlets overlooked the obvious cultural connection between Aleppo's walls and the ancient Arabic tradition—popularised in pre-Islamic poetry—of 'aṭlāl (standing by the ruins) which is seen in the introductory lines of many poems, like Imru'lQays (501–540 CE) in the Prc-Islamic time or later by al-Nuffari in the tenth century. Finally, the English-language media's emotional presentation of the walls transformed them into superficial words of hope and love; that is, into instruments by which to manipulate the readership's emotions. In the following, thick translation challenges the conventional reading of these websites, by uncovering the walls' suppressed meanings and cultural dimensions, beyond the narrow goals of activists and media agents.

Walls, arts and memory

Language and memory, reinforced by childhood processes of native language acquisition, are constantly shaping our realities by carrying texts we have memorised into new contexts (Becker 1995: 185). To understand Aleppo's walls, therefore, one must first understand the complex interplay between language and cultural and linguistic memory. The walls of Aleppo could not have been created, were it not for

Eylaf Bader Eddin

a combination of cultural and lingual memory. Cultural memory is 'a privatization of history and it happens with an insistent collective rememoration [remembrance] "this happened, this really happened": one can be deeply suspicious of cultural memory, but lingual memory is an acquired access' (Spivak 2008). When creating or writing something on a specific occasion—drawing spontaneously on one's linguistic memory—the act of writing derives from previous acts of memorising culture and language (culture, in terms of collective historical, or individual, memory; language, in terms of textual memory, and its re-contextualisations). To understand the general background of writing on walls, and the specific choice of these lines by Qabbani, one must first consider the cultural and lingual memory of Aleppo's citizens. Culturally, the practice of writing (which symbolises the act of recording memory) resonates with a profusion of elements in both ancient, and modern, Arabic art history. Some likely sources for the cultural practice of wall-writing are those normally taught in Syrian schools, like 'Ukaẓ Souk, where Arabs gathered to perform poetry seasonally' (Al'Alusī n.d.: 267), and the Suspended Odes, or al-Mu'allaqāt, of the Ka'ba, which were treasured for their eloquence. Contemporary history is likewise rich in models, such as the wall-art that accompanied recent social movements in Tunisia, Egypt and Syria, not to mention the Palestinian resistance. Such movements have made extensive use of resistance walls, especially in Syria, where the regime's iron fist rendered a quick spray on the walls of a government building a meaningful and effective act of protest. Such examples highlight the role of memorialisation, and the tradition of wall-art, in Arabic history, confirming the interviewees' assertions that Aleppo's walls are more than mere graffiti.

More than one possibility

Thick translation offers the possibility of translating a single text in multiple ways, in order to reflect the text's richness, as well as the impossibility of translating its linguistic context into another language. It aims to produce a detailed description of the text, which captures dimensions that conventional translation overlooks. The walls of Aleppo simultaneously engage multiple contexts; as I suggest, a single wall has at least two contexts (that is, excluding its strictly visual character, which adds another layer of complexity). For this reason, I will offer several English translations of the same wall. To complement my thick translation, I employ Barthes' method of reading images, which opens new possibilities for analysing layers of meanings in colour, and the semantic of words. Barthes' mechanism combines the linguistic practice with the visual, and with semiotics, by scrutinising the signifiers on an image's surface. My interpretation of the wall in question, therefore, involves three phases: (1) a study of the existing translations; (2) the development of alternative, 'thick,' translations; and (3) a second phase of thick translation, based on Barthes' method of reading images.

Depending on what the translator wants to illustrate, the translations shown in Table 9.1 vary in their negotiation of domestication and foreignisation. Some leave the text in the domain of the author; others seek to bring it closer to the reader. This interplay between the text in the source language, and its translation, ultimately tells us more about the translator than it does about the text itself.

All four translations fail to catch the intertextuality between the sprayed lines and the poem from which they come. With the exception of the *Daily Mail*, three of the four media outlets prefer to quote a ready-made Syrian activist's translation, rather than produce their own.

152

Table 9.1 Different translations from different activist translators for the same wall (Figure 9.1); the first translation is rendered by the *Daily Mail*

Translation[1]	Translator
1 'Love me far from the country of misery and oppression, far from out city that has had enough of death.'	*Daily Mail*
2 'Love me away from the land of oppression and repression, away from our city which has had enough death.'	*Mass Appeal*, quoted from Twitter
3 'Love me away from our city that got enough of oppression, hatred, & death! Graffiti from Aleppo.'	*Huffington Post*, quoting from Twitter user 'Susan Ahmad'
4 'My friend Haleem n #aleppo graffitied a love letter 2 his girlfriend lives n Turkey: love me away from our destroyed home. Last day n siege!'	*Middle East Eye*, quoting Twitter user 'Zeina Erhaim'

The *Daily Mail*'s translator, however, chooses not to make a literal translation, as evinced by his or her decision to translate *kabt* as 'misery.' Though *kabt* can have many meanings in Arabic—including 'suppression'—'misery' is not one of them. Here, a decision has been made to gloss Syrian voices. The word '*bilād* [countries/homelands],' which is plural, is translated in the singular—a change which, though it specifies the place with which the sprayer is concerned, loses the original's sense of an appeal to one's home country. Usually, *yā bilādī* (literally, 'Oh, my countries') refers to the speaker's homeland, emphasising one's sincere relation to one's country.

Consider also the phrase 'has had enough of death'; the Arabic original carries the sense of having eaten to fullness, while the English suggests a certain fatigue with death. Of course, fatigue does not do justice to the Syrian catastrophe, which has resulted in hundreds of thousands of deaths since 2011. 'Has had enough of death' thus prevents readers from appreciating the cultural import of the metaphor of being sated. This metaphor is sarcastic, because it also carries the positive meaning of having more than enough food. Therefore, the poetic line says that the city is sated, having devoured more than enough of its own people.

The remaining three translations were written by Syrian activists, in the hopes of conveying events to an English audience. The first, which appeared on *Mass Appeal*, is an attempt at a literal translation. It can be accepted as that, although translating *bilād* as 'land' makes it seem as though the sprayer wanted to express the fact that all Arab countries suffer from oppression and repression. 'Land' here generalises the meaning of the Arabic (although it's an adequate literal translation). Finally, this translation also lost the original's metaphorical reference to food, by employing the phrase 'enough of death.'

The last two translations are paraphrases that combine the two poetic lines into one, with the effect of glossing over the agony of Aleppo's civilians. Susan Ahmad's version adds hatred to the wall's linguistic realm; it also eliminates the reference to *bilād*, limiting the geographic context to 'our city.' Meanwhile, Zeina Erhaim adds 'our home,' and removes 'city,' which further reveals the subjectivity of the sprayer's experience. She also employs the 'domestic' word, 'girlfriend,' which is rarely used in Syrian culture (which prefers 'fiancée' or 'beloved'). Domestication is also evident in Erhaim's declaration that her friend 'Haleem' took part in painting the graffiti—an assertion that lends authenticity to the message. What makes this final translation the most domesticated of all, however, is Erhaim's self-evident use of social media conventions, like the use of '2' for 'to,' 'n' for 'in,' and so on.

No less revealing than these rough activist translations are the English-language articles that accompanied them. The BBC, for example, devoted just one sentence to the walls of Aleppo: 'As residents are evacuated from eastern Aleppo, one phrase has been chanted and left behind in graffiti again and again' (BBC 2016). Below this sentence, on their website, appeared a short video, in which a noticeably sad and angry sprayer says, 'We are coming back here.'

Despite the obvious gloom associated with documenting the civilian displacement, live, with the world watching, the BBC nonetheless managed, in the post's headline, to interpret the walls as 'words of hope.' Similarly, an article from *The Huffington Post* touchingly describes a 'heartbroken' couple, as they say goodbye to the city in which they were raised. Despite their obvious misery, and words of lamentation, this article also insists on characterising the walls as 'messages of hope' (Abdelaziz and Cook 2016). *Mass Appeal*'s presentation of the walls is no less perfunctory: a four-sentence paragraph accompanied by photos of Aleppo taken by the Syrian activist, Iyad El-Baghdadi, who also provides a translation. *Middle East Eye* likewise introduces the above photo (Figure 9.1) with a very short, three-sentence introduction, without commenting on an additional list of photos of walls from Aleppo, gathered from activists on social media. Like the other outlets, it repeats the well-worn claim that Syrians have been leaving messages of hope before evacuating. All of these articles are characterised by an enormous gap between their content and their headlines. Most of them describe the wall-writings as words of hope and love, or as romantic acts. But do Aleppo's walls really convey hope and love?

Keeping in mind that there is no perfect translation, I propose to supplement the aforementioned translations with four of my own, each of which focuses on a specific characteristic of the source text (Table 9.2).

In the first two translations, I tried to translate Qabbani's poetry literally, by maintaining the word order, and respecting the number of sentences in Arabic. Here, however, as in all the translations previously considered, I could render neither the context of the poem from which the lines originally derive, nor that of Aleppo. In the first translation, I attempted to convey the metaphor of being full of food, with 'our death-sated city.' In the second, I used the adjective 'bloated' to suggest death, and the swelling that attends corpses in a state of decay ('bloated' also has the advantage of expressing death's smell). In translating *kabt* and *qahr*, I followed the pattern established by the media outlets, selecting different equivalents for each translation: I thereby sought to reflect the tremendous weight of oppression and repression that Syrians have faced in their modern history. The third translation attempts to express the fact that, for the painter of these words, writing on walls is a means of leaving the defeated city of Aleppo (in my view, the events surrounding the civilian displacement delivered a blistering defeat to the revolution, and a huge victory to the regime). To render the line's musicality in English, and to give a hint that the original was poetry, I chose the opening address, 'Oh, Love!' which departs from the imperative, and shifts the translation into a more openly lyrical realm. Finally, as the departure of civilians from Aleppo was seen as the revolution's turning point—the moment in which the tide turned in favour of the regime—I added 'defeated' to describe the feelings of those civilians and activists forced to leave.

Figure 9.1 One of the Walls of Aleppo: 'Fall in love with me, far away from the country of persecution and suppression, far away from our death-sated city. Besieged Aleppo, the
last day.' Untitled photograph by Haleem Kawa (2016).

Table 9.2 Possible translations

Fall in love with me, far away from the country of persecution and suppression, far away from our
death-sated city. Besieged Aleppo, the last day.

Love me away from the country of oppression and suppression, away from our bloated city of death.
Besieged Aleppo, the last day.

Oh, Love! Take me away from our defeated country, away from our dead city. Besieged Aleppo, the
last day.

Love me away from our country of subjugation and stifling, away from our sated city full of death.
Besieged Aleppo, the last day.

Thick translation and Barthes

As mentioned above, my intention is not to provide a definitive English version of
this particular wall. No single version could capture every dimension of the original
lines, nor unite the varied emphases of the preceding translations. For this reason,
I have chosen to provide a thick translation, which will reveal not only more cultural

aspects and layers of meaning, but illuminate the multiple contexts of Aleppo's walls. The type of thick translation that I pursue incorporates Barthes' method of reading images. Originally, thick translation was an analytical tool for 'untranslatable' texts (or, texts which translation cannot readily encompass), not a means of reading images in foreign languages like Appiah's proverb (1993). In this sense, thick translation elaborates both local and structural manoeuvre sides that Cheung suggests in treating '*xin*, *da*, and *ya*' (2007: 23). Structuralising and localising a translation help to 'bring depth and breadth to the representation of culture, even if the representation can never be total, never complete' (2007: 32). There are definitely more cultural dimensions that I did not mention but the offered thick translation makes the readers 'travellers not tourists,' which activates their senses of touching the shed lighted points and details (2007: 32). Based on my understanding of Barthes, I divide the interpretive process into three movements: the linguistic message, the symbolic message and the literal message. This combination of translational and visual interpretation improves and systemises the mechanism that thick translation can be extracted from a text that contains visual and textual elements, alike.

Linguistic message

The difficulty in extracting the linguistic message from our image results, as Barthes implies, from the fact that the message resides in the image's 'caption'—which, in this case, is a translation (Barthes 1977: 153). As Barthes explains, 'linguistic message is indeed present in every image: as title, caption, accompanying press article, film dialogue, comic strip balloon' (1977: 155). For the purposes of this article, the 'caption' can be said to be the English translation of the sprayed text, which, as we have seen, differs from translator to translator. Such variability poses a significant obstacle to reading the image; as Barthes argues, the 'caption' should help us to 'identify purely and simply the elements of the scene and the scene itself … [it is] a description that is not complete' (1977: 156).

The original photo of the sprayed poetic lines has no caption; it was added later on social media, or in online magazines, as an act of translation, or as an attempt to orient readers with respect to the image. It is an act of violence that brands the text with a very specific, and singular, meaning. The 'caption' encourages readers to read the photo in a particular way, if only because it 'helps me [as a reader] to choose the correct level of perception, permits me to focus not simply my gaze but also my understanding' (Barthes 1977: 156). The translator's power is enormous, for here, the linguistic message (caption) not only identifies the image; it offers itself as an interpretive guide. Thus, in the case of our photo, we may conclude that the translation as caption is the key element directing the reader's senses toward a specific meaning. And yet, the caption itself is multiple, having been produced by a number of different translators, each of whose editorial choices control the interpretation of the photos themselves. Before moving to consider the photo's denotative (literal) and connotative (symbolic) messages (both of which stem from its linguistic message), we should briefly consider its elementary visual signs.

Visual signs

Analysing, or even identifying, an image's signs requires 'anthropological knowledge' (Barthes 1977: 154), which varies from person to person, depending on an individual's ability and experience. An English speaker confronted by the image of our wall might infer a wholly different set of signs than the one recognised, for example, by the original sprayer of the text. I, personally, see the following: the photo consists of two lines sprayed on a wall. These lines are from Nizar Qabbani. They speak of love, death and place. At the bottom of the image are the spray cans used to write the lines. The text is written in different colours; dominant are red and black. In addition to the writing, there appears a flag with three green stars. The black writing says 'Ḥalab al-muḥāṣarah, aḫir yūm [Besieged Aleppo, the last day of the siege].' The red lines quote the poetry. The lower part of the wall is worn out, and surrounded by rubble, while the upper part has been repainted with a pale colour to make it look new. The street seems to have been destroyed. The date and place of the act of painting are written. The lines are written in a grammatically accurate way; they include the taškīl vocalisation of the important letters, and, rhythmically, end with the correct word from the original poem. Vocalisation is used to confirm that this is the right way to pronounce the lines to keep their musicality and meaning, knowing that sometimes non-vocalised words can lead to different meanings and understandings. For this reason, vocalisation illustrates the painter's cultural and educational background. The last words of each line are kabt and mawt. Such accuracy shows that the sprayer was singing, or chanting, the lines before spraying them. Critical, also, is that the photo is set in Aleppo. As Barthes insists, the visual signs must be mentioned not only to reveal them, but to invent a method for their interpretation. An image's tripartite messages are inseparable: they depend on each other, in the system of signification.

Connotative visual signs

To be sure, the weight of the image's signifying content is textual, not visual. Nonetheless, the signs of ruin are omnipresent: the wall is worn out; its dim, pale colour reflects Aleppo's state of siege. To complement our reading of the wall, we might examine the layers of meaning that accumulate by virtue of the image's colour symbolism. Whether or not such symbolism is intentional, as Barthes argues, colour—in combination with the reader's cultural knowledge—can enrich the act of interpretation. The main colours used here are red and black. In Arabic culture, as in most cultures, colours have specific significations. While these significations may differ from place to place, the colours here play a salient linguistic role in orienting the reader's senses toward the wall. Red, for example, is commonly used as a sign of blood, love or even revolution, as in this line from Aḥmad Shawqī (1868–1932):

وَلِلْحُرِّيَّة الحَمراءِ بابٌ بِكُلِّ يَدٍ مُضَرَّجَةٍ يُدَقّ

(Shawqī 2012: 456)

The red freedom has a door, knocked by a *blood-stained* hand.

(Shawqī 2012: 456)

Here, Shawqī describes freedom as red, suggesting that it cannot be attained without blood sacrifice, or martyrdom. In Arabic, red is also associated with love and romance. In the case of our image, red may have two meanings, both of which suit the situation in Aleppo. The first is, indeed, love and romance—if one reads the lines strictly as a love poem. The second stands for the bloodshed the city witnessed during its years of resistance, blood spent in the name of revolution, and freedom. The small, Syrian revolutionary flag on the left supports this claim.

Black, for its part, has a very negative connotation, relating to death, or people who are deceived. In the Qur'an, for example, God describes those who have done good deeds as having white faces. The faces of those who have not done good deeds are black.

يَوْمَ تَبْيَضُّ وُجُوهٌ وَتَسْوَدُّ وُجُوهٌ فَأَمَّا الَّذِينَ اسْوَدَّتْ وُجُوهُهُمْ أَكَفَرْتُم بَعْدَ إِيمَانِكُمْ فَذُوقُوا الْعَذَابَ بِمَا كُنتُمْ تَكْفُرُونَ.

(Qur'an 3:106)

On the day (i.e. the day of Resurrection) when some faces will become white and some faces will become black; as for those whose faces will become black (to them will be said): Did you reject Faith after accepting it? Then taste the torment (in Hell) for rejecting Faith.

(al-Hilâlî and Khân 2006: 79)

Another signification of black in Arabic culture is the melancholic alienation of being away from the homeland. For example, in describing his longing for home, the Andalusian poet Ibn Zaydun (1003–1071) tells those around him that 'my days with you are black,' because he is out of his homeland.

حالت لفقدكُم أيامنا فغدت سودا وكانت بكم بيضا ليالينا.

(Ibn Zaydun 1994: 299)

Our days away of you have gone longing for you, clad in black prior to that they were white.

(Ibn Zaydun 1994: 299)

Black can also mean danger. In military parlance, 'the black flags' refer to the flags of death and danger, used by troops. In our photo (Figure 9.1), black adds emphasis to the words 'Besieged Aleppo, the last day.' It invokes the state of siege itself, and warns readers of imminent danger. Thus, the sprayer's use of colour adds significant layers of meaning to the wall, while reflecting his experience of life under siege.

As stated, however, colour is but one aspect of the wall's symbolism; the photo's third, or literal, message can only be extracted by interpreting the sprayed text. To do so, I will consider the lines in their two, complementary contexts: that of Qabbani's poem, and that of besieged Aleppo.

The literal message of the poem (Qabbani's original: the 'internal' context)

The sprayed lines are taken from Nizar Qabbani's famous poem, *al-Qaṣīdah al-'Mutawaḥišah*, in English 'The Brutal Poem' (1970), from his collection, 'The Brutal Poems' (1970, as cited in Qabbani n.d.). Notwithstanding their obvious differences, the poem, and the catastrophe in Aleppo, share the same violent context. The poem's title already alludes to the experience of love in a cruel place, opening yet another horizon for interpretation: namely, Qabbani's country, and its brutal characteristics. As the title further implies, the poem's use of language is likewise cruel; as it develops, it employs increasingly violent vocabulary. The poem begins with a reference to autumn, as the death of nature, and proceeds to thunder. Then, Qabbani invokes the cruelty and savagery of the Mongols (a reference to their repeated invasions of Damascus), before invoking an earthquake. The poem accelerates in its rhythm of violence, eventually reaching the lines sprayed on our wall, which conclude with a reference to 'this city, visited neither by love, nor God.'

Table 9.3 Violence expressions gradually increased through Qabbani's poem

Fall in love with me … and blend in with the lines of my palm. Fall in love with me for a week, or days or hours. For it is not I whose obsession is 'eternity.' I am November/Autumn, the month of winds, rains and cold … I am November… So sweep through me like a thunderstorm…	أحبيني .. بلا عقد وضيعي في خطوط يدي أحبيني .. لأسبوع .. لأيام لساعات .. فلست أنا الذي يهتم بالأبد.. أنا تشرين .. شهر الريح، .. والأمطار .. والبرد.. أنا تشرين فانسحقي كصاعقة على جسدي ..
Fall in love with me … with all the savagery of the Mongols, with all the density of jungles, with all the ferocity of heavy rains. Obliterate me altogether … Do not become civilised… For the entirety of urban civilisation has shattered on your lips.	أحبيني .. بكل توحش التتر.. بكل حرارة الأدغال كل شراسة المطر ولا تبقي ولا تذري.. ولا تتحضري أبدا.. فقد سقطت على شفتيك كل حضارة الحضر
Fall in love with me … like an earthquake, like an untimely death … Let your bosom, kneaded with sparks and matches, attack me like a ferocious wolf … exactly as the rains batter island coasts. I am a fateless man … So be my fate … Keep me on your bosom, like a word written in stone.	أحبيني.. كزلزال .. كموت غير منتظر.. وخلي نهدك المعجون.. بالكبريت والشرر.. يهاجمني.. كذنب جائع خطر وينهشني .. ويضربني .. كما الأمطار تضرب ساحل الجزر.. أنا رجل بلا قدر فكوني .. أنت لي قدري وأبقيني .. على نهديك.. مثل النقش في .. الحجر
Fall in love with me … without asking 'How?' Never stutter in coyness, or fall down in fear. Fall in love with me, without complaints. Does the sheath complain on receiving the sword? Be the sea and its harbour. Be the homeland and exile. Be clear weather and the hurricane. Be serenity and unrest/violence.	أحبيني .. ولا تساءلي كيفا.. ولا تتلعثمي خجلا ولا تتساقطي خوفا أحبيني .. بلا شكوى .. أيشكو الغمد .. إذ يستقبل السيف؟ وكوني البحر والميناء.. كوني الأرض والمنفى وكوني الصحو والإعصار كوني اللين والعنفا
Fall in love with me … in myriad ways. Never be monotonous, like summer, for I hate summer. Fall in love with me, and admit it. I refuse to be loved voicelessly. I refuse to hide love in a grave of silence.	أحبيني .. بألف وألف أسلوب ولا تتكرري كالصيف.. إني أكره الصيف.. أحبيني.. وقوليها لأرفض أن تحبيني بلا صوت وأرفض أن أواري الحب في قبر من الصمت
Fall in love with me … far away from the country of persecution and suppression, far away from our death-sated city. Since our city came into existence, it has experienced no love. God has overlooked it … (Qabbani 1970 [as cited in Qabbani n.d.]: 652–656)	أحبيني .. بعيدا عن بلاد القهر والكبت بعيدا عن مدينتنا التي شبعت من الموت.. بعيدا عن تعصبها.. بعيدا عن تخشبها.. أحبيني .. بعيدا عن مدينتنا التي من يوم أن كانت إليها الحب لا يأتي.. إليها الله .. لا يأتي (Qabbani 1970 [as cited in Qabbani n.d.]: 652–656)

Extracting the poem's violent images, and connecting them, gives the following excerpt (Table 9.3).

Gathering the above stanza's violent images reveals Qabbani's attempt to create a dichotomy between life versus death, on the one hand, and woman versus homeland, on the other. It also illuminates the Aleppo context, in which two of the lines were sprayed. Of course, it is difficult to know if the sprayer knew the whole poem, since Qabbani was mentioned neither on the wall itself, nor in the semi-structured interviews that I conducted. Nonetheless, the poem's setting, and description of the 'city,' perfectly illustrate Aleppo in ruins. The poem's original date of publication, 1970, is also highly significant, as that year marks the beginning of the Baath party's reign in Syria (1963 to present time). As in so much contemporary Arabic poetry, Qabbani's romantic entanglement with a woman can here be said to reflect his troubled relationship to his homeland.

Aleppo: the external context

In my view, the Aleppo context in which the lines were sprayed can best be understood in light of Qabbani's poem. Of course, the relevance of the poem, in its entirety, to the situation in Aleppo might not have been the sprayer's main reason for choosing the lines. Considering, however, the importance of linguistic memory in recalling linguistic patterns from an individual's background, to help him or her express the present moment, a brief consideration of the line's intertextuality should prove illuminating.

The Syrian regime promoted Qabbani by marketing only his love poetry, as if his writing lacked political dimensions. And yet, in many of his love poems as in this one, political messages can be read between the lines. This enables a dialogue between the poem's context, and that of 2016 Aleppo, especially because 'any text is constructed as a mosaic of quotations; any text is the absorption and transformation of another' (Kristeva 1986: 37). The sprayer who wrote the lines on the wall is a reader of Qabbani's text, whose spraying gave rise to a new dialogue, woven into the context of the old one. Thus, there is no ignoring the fundamental relationship between Qabbani's poem and the wall in question.

The lines were sprayed at the end of the siege of Aleppo, a city whose history and geographic location imbue it with layers of meaning that enrich the walls' context. In this case, re-contextualising poetry creates a new social reality, undertaken by civilians as their sole, and final, means of resisting the regime's forces. Before the forced evacuation, most of Aleppo's walls had been destroyed, and people were living in ruins. Thus, Qabbani's vocabulary of destruction perfectly suits the reality of Aleppo in 2016. While the poet's lines were cited by an individual who wanted to send a message to his beloved, they express the state of all civilians. People were deceived, and betrayed, by those events; they left Aleppo in accordance with the stanza's final lines—bereft of both God and love.

Another layer of meaning emerges when one considers the relation between the act of spraying, and the ancient, pre-Islamic custom of *al-wuqūf 'ala al-'aṭlāl* (standing by the ruins). Isbahānī's book on the history of wall-poetry among the Arabs, *The Book of Strangers*, offers ample evidence that writing poetry on walls is a deeply rooted cultural tradition. Though the book does not specifically mention the poetry of mourning, it remains a good reference, detailing a number of walls that still exist. In pre-Islamic times, walls were used for cultural purposes, as in the case of the hanging poems (*al-Mu'allaqāt*).

What unites the old custom of wall-writing and the walls of Aleppo is the deep feeling of sorrow expressed in Qabbani's lines. This elegiac sensibility leads us back to the ancient practice of lamenting the ruins, in which poets would begin their poems by remembering the ruins of the city in which their beloveds had lived. Seen in this light, the words sprayed on the walls of Aleppo were hardly words of hope; they mourned Aleppo, lamenting its destruction and its people's displacement. They were written to inform the world about a dire civilian catastrophe, unfolding in the ruins of a once proud city.

Conclusion

Activist translators succeeded in transmitting messages to the Euro-American media, which effectively purged Aleppo's walls of their profound cultural and historical content. This was possible, of course, only to the extent that the translators and sprayers shared a common goal. Susan Ahmad, whose translation was quoted in *The Huffington Post*, describes the mechanism of translation as follows:

> I have been working for many years as a professional translator of Syrian news and events. As translators, we do not always think in the complexities of the terms, or consider the literal meaning of words. What we mainly care about is that the English audience gets the intended message. The translation reflects my understanding of the intended message. This is why I decide not to translate word-for-word, but add or delete words, according to what I think makes a more powerful appeal to human consciousness. I see the photos as words of hope and love, as I understand them. We want to keep the western audience informed about the death of those people in Aleppo in 2016, and everywhere in Syria. We used to have a closed Facebook group in which foreign journalists—who do not speak Arabic—share the information we've translated about Syria.
>
> *(Bader Eddin and Ahmad 2018)*

If the aim of both activist translators, and spray-painting activists on the ground, was to send messages of hope and love to the world, their mission was a success: English websites universally portrayed the walls of Aleppo as words of hope and love. Yet, if those English websites provided a forum for the voices of activists, and activist translators, they also robbed Aleppo's walls of their profound cultural importance. This article has used thick translation to defy the activists' short cuts, and return meaning to the curt paraphrases on Aleppo's walls. Here, thick translation has revealed not only the walls' multiple layers of meaning, but also their multiple contexts. It has restored their suppressed cultural significance, even if only within the framework of my humble interpretation (which, after all, is just one reading of the cultural layers that have accumulated to Qabbani's lines since he wrote them).

Just as the sprayed lines have a direct, intertextual relation to Qabbani's poem, that poem poignantly illustrates the context of Aleppo, both during and after the siege. Qabbani's poetry witnessed 'a shift after the Naksa in 1967, and became nationalist, reflecting the consecutive Arab defeats' (Raḍwān 2004: 17). This shift is evident in poems like 'When Will They Declare the Death of the Arabs?' (Qabbani n.d.: 140). There, Qabbani bemoans the metaphorical imprisonment of all people—especially women, whom he identifies with the homeland. As he writes elsewhere, 'the one who loves a woman, is able to love his homeland' (1981: 33). Thus, in Qabbani's verse, 'love,' 'woman' and 'homeland' are synonymous; they represent a semantic cluster that perfectly reflects the multiple contexts of the sprayed lines we have considered (i.e. their simultaneous nature as an expression of romantic love, addressed to a woman, and a lamentation for the destruction of Aleppo). Such semantic aggregation has close parallels in the ancient Arab custom of 'standing by the ruins,' as *'aṭlāl* is 'longing for a place … where one has been together with a beloved or trusted person' (Müller 1999: 43). Given the linguistic memory at work in reviving such a cultural habit, it seems inappropriate to regard the walls of Aleppo as mere graffiti, or murals. They are, as the sprayers themselves call them walls (*ḥīṭān*), or spray (*baḥḥ*), depending on the cultural and historical load of the term itself in Syria. Nor are they merely words of hope and love. 'Hope and love' is a painfully limited, short-sighted interpretation. Though it might have served the activists' desire to present an affective story about their suffering, this interpretation plasters over the ultimate defeat of the resistance, and the failure of the 2011 Syrian revolution.

Related topics

Civil Resistance through Online Activist Translation in Taiwan's Sunflower Student Movement; Translating for *Le Monde diplomatique en español;* The Dialectics of Dissent in Postcolonial India.

Note

1 All of the non-cited translations from Arabic, except for the ones taken from the media outlets, are my own.

Further reading

Apter, Emily (2006) 'Translation after 9/11,' in *The Translation Zone*. Princeton: Princeton University Press. 12–22.

Apter's book deals with the shifts and changes of the linguistic, cultural and translational dimensions of translation and calls for determining a zone for translation to lessen the ignorance gap of translation and its cultural characteristics. This is shown in her chapter on the importance of translation, after 9/11, in the United States. With respect to the invasion of Iraq, it argues that a dearth of qualified Arabic translators allowed media and politicians to substitute images as translations of events; many such examples are provided.

Barthes, Roland (1977) 'Rhetoric of the Image,' in *Image, Music, Text*. Tr. Stephan Heath. London: Fontana Press. 32–51.

Barthes presents different ways of reading images as texts. By analysing a pasta advertisement, the essay offers a clear approach to interpreting images, which involves dividing the interpretive act into several messages, while combining the visual and the textual.

Venuti, Lawrence (1995) *The Translator's Invisibility: A History of Translation*. London: Routledge.

Venuti's book is a classic reference for translation throughout history. It demonstrates translation's domesticating function, which—by virtue of a translation's fluency and readability—renders translators invisible. In contrast to 'thick translation,' domestication of the source language tends to obscure significant cultural dimensions.

References

Abdelaziz, Rowaida, and Jesselyn Cook (2016) 'We Will Return:' Syrian Newlyweds Fleeing Aleppo Leave behind Messages of Hope,' in *The Huffington Post* [online] 17 December. Available at: https://www.huffpost.com/entry/syrian-newlyweds-aleppo-graffiti_n_5852cc b9e4b0c05ff31ff1af?guccounter=1 [accessed 14 February 2019].

Al'Alusī, Maḥmūd Šukrī (n.d.) *Bulūġ al-irb fī ma'rifat 'ḥwāl al-'arab*, Volume 1. Cairo: al-Maktabah al-'Ahliyah.

Al-Aṣbahānī, Abū Faraǧ (1972) *Adab al-ġurabā'*. Beirut: Dar al-kitāb al-jadīd.

Aljazeera (2012) 'Fannanū Sūryyah 'ala al-Miḥak aṮ-ṯawrah,' in *Aljazeera* [online] 8 May. Available at: https://bit.ly/2GqUMv4 [accessed 14 February 2019].

Aljazeera (2016) 'Itifāq Hudnah Wa 'Iḫlā' Šarq Ḥalab,' in *Aljazeera* [online] 13 December. Available at: https://bit.ly/2EfA5A2 [accessed 14 February 2019].

al-Hilâlî, Muhammad Taqî-ud-Dîn, and Muhammad Muhsin Khân (2006) *Translation of the Meanings of the Noble Qur'ân in the English Language*. Madinah: King Fahd Complex for the Printing of the Holy Qur'ân.

'al-Rajul al-Baḥḥāḫ Yanšaṯṯ Fī Dar'a Wa Yuqliq Qūwāt al-Assad,' (2019) in *Watan Radio* [online] 7 February. Available at: https://watan.fm/news/syria-news/120516 [accessed 14 February 2019].

Appiah, Kwame (1993) 'Thick Translation,' in *Callaloo* 16 (4) [online]. Available at: https://bit.ly/2DF5udn [accessed 14 February 2019].

Apter, Emily (2006) *The Translation Zone*. Princeton: Princeton University Press.

Badawi, El-Said, Michael G. Carter, and Adrian Gully (2004) *Modern Written Arabic: A Comprehensive Grammar*. Oxon: Routledge.

Barthes, Roland (1977) *Image, Music, Text*. Trans. Stephen Heath. London: Fontana Press.

Bassnet, Susan, and Harish Trivedi (1999) *Postcolonial Translation: Theory and Practice*. London: Routledge.

BBC (2016) 'Aleppo Syria battle: evacuees graffiti words of hope,' in *BBC* [online] 16 December. Available at: https://bbc.in/2S1COQV [accessed 14 February 2019].

Becker, Alton L. (1995) *Beyond Translation: Essays toward a Modern Philology*. Ann Arbor: University of Michigan Press.

Bishara, Azmi (2013) *Sūryyah: Darb al-'Alām Naḥww al-Ḥuriyyah Muḥāwalah Fī a-Tarīḫ al-Rāhin*. Doha: Arab Center for Research & Policy Studies.

Cheung, Martha P.Y. (2007) 'On Thick Translation as a Mode of Cultural Representation,' in *Across Boundaries: International Perspectives on Translation Studies*. Eds. Dorothy Kenny and Kyongjoo Ryou. Newcastle: Cambridge Scholars Publishing. 22–36.

Gottlieb, Lisa (2008) *Graffiti Art Styles: A Classification System and Theoretical Analysis*. Jefferson: McFarland.

Ḥazīn, Abdulḥalīm (2012) 'Sūryyah: Aṣ-Ṣaḥafīyūn Yaddfa'un aṯ-Ṯaman,' in *Sky News Arabya* [online] 22 February. Available at: https://bit.ly/2BwNi5j [accessed 14 February 2019].

Ibn Zaydun, Aḥmad (1994) *Dīwān Ibn Zaydun*. Beirut: Dār alKitab al'Arabi.

Kristeva, Julia (1986) *Word, Dialog and Novel: The Kristeva Reader*. Ed. Toril Moi. New York: Columbia University Press.

Mahmoud, Osha (2016) 'Syrians are Leaving Graffiti all over Aleppo with Messages for Assad,' in *Middle East Eye* [online] 15 December. Available at: https://bit.ly/2GMHfgv [accessed 14 February 2019].

Müller, Kathrin (1999) 'Al-ḥanīn ilā l-awṭān in early adab-literature,' in *Myths, Historical Archetypes and Symbolic Figures in Arabic Literature: Towards a New Hermeneutic Approach*. Eds. Angelika Neuwirth, Birgit Embaló, Sebastian Günther, and Maher Jarrar. Beirut: Orient-Institute der DMG. 33–58.

Qabbani, Nizar (1981) *al-Mar'ah fī ši'rī wa ḥayātī*. Beirut: s.n.

Qabbani, Nizar (n.d.) *al''māl al-Kāmila Li Nizār Qabbani*, 1st and 2nd vols. Beirut: Manšurāt Nizar Qabbani.

Qur'an (2008) Medina: King Fahd Qur'an Printing Complex.

Raḍwān, Mammad (2004) *Asrār al-qaṣṣā'id al-Mammnu'ah li ša'ir al-ḥubb wa al-ḥuryyah*. Damascus: Dār al-kitāb al-'arabī.

Ratta, Donatella Della (2012) 'Syria: Art, Creative Resistance and Active Citizenship,' in *Freemuse* [online] October. Available at: https://bit.ly/2IedhEo [accessed 14 February 2019].

Robinson, Julian (2016) 'Goodbye … One Day, We Will Return:' Syrians Spray-paint Moving Messages on their Homes Ahead of Their Evacuation from Aleppo,' in *Daily Mail* [online] 16 December. Available at: https://dailym.ai/2BBlaOO [accessed 14 February 2019].

Shawqī, Ahamd (2012) *Šawqīyyāt*. Cairo: Hindāwī for Publishing.

Spivak, Gayatri Chakravorty (2008) 'More Thoughts on Cultural Translation,' in *European Institute for Progressive Cultural Policies* [online] April. Available at: http://eipcp.net/transversal/0608/spivak/en [accessed 14 February 2019].

Turco, Bucky (2016) 'The Heartbreaking Graffiti of Aleppo,' in *Mass Appeal* [online] 16 December. Available at: http://archive.massappeal.com/the-heartbreaking-graffiti-of-aleppo/ [accessed 14 February 2019].

Venuti, Lawrence (1995) *The Translator's Invisibility: A History of Translation*. London: Routledge.

Walsh, Michael (1996) *Graffito*. Berkeley: North Atlantic Books.

Woodford, Kate (ed.) (2003) *Cambridge Advanced Learner's Dictionary*. Cambridge: Cambridge University Press.

Interviews cited

Bader Eddin, Eylaf, and Salem Abu alNaser (2017) 'Interview with Salem Abu alNaser,' 27 January 2017.

Bader Eddin, Eylaf, and Susan Ahmad (2018) 'Interview with Susan Ahmad,' 17 December 2018.

Bader Eddin, Eylaf, and Ghith Beram (2017) 'Interview with Ghith Beram,' 30 January 2017.

10

Resistance, activism and marronage in Paul Bowles's translations of the oral stories of Tangier

Hafida Mourad

Introduction

Over the course of the last two decades, translation studies has undergone a rapid paradigm shift. Its focus has moved away from linguistic bound towards socio-cultural perspectives of translation. Following the cultural and sociological turns, the 'activist turn' (Wolf 2013) is central to contemporary translation theory as scholars are more concerned with translation as a source of empowerment and resistance. In contrast with the peripheral and marginalised position previously attributed to trans-lation and translators, scholars have come to reveal multiple ways that present trans-lation and translators as 'active' rather than 'passive' agents. Activist translations refer to key translations and translation movements that have contributed in one way or another to social, political or cultural change. As Tymoczko puts it, translations within this framework constitute 'records of cultural contestations and struggles' (2010: 3) with 'ethical, political, ideological rather than mere communicative object-ives' (Tymoczko 2010: 300).

Engaged translators are active agents who play a critical role in social change. They make special selections and use specific translation strategies in order to intro-duce, serve or foster an ideology or agenda 'that explicitly challenge[s] the dominant narratives of the time' (Baker 2010: 23). This chapter situates Paul Bowles's transla-tions of Moroccan oral stories within this framework of translation as activism. Activist translation in this chapter refers to the translator's challenge to dominant representations of culture and literature in relation to both source (post-independence Morocco) and target culture (US post-World War II (WWII)) throughout Bowles's journey of expatriation towards emancipation. In this chapter, I highlight the strat-egies adopted by Bowles as translator to communicate his resistance to mainstream culture in the US post-WWII, and, more importantly, to foster his own perception regarding 'authentic' Moroccan culture.

The chapter also makes use of Jean-Mark Gouanvic's metaphor of translation as marronage, a form of cultural cross-pollination derived from the 'slaves who took to the mountains [...] in order to escape white masters' (Gouanvic 2000: 107). Gouanvic (2000) considers resistance in translation by looking at marginalised groups as translator figures. He develops an interesting analogy between the translator and the 'maroon,' the runaway slave who successfully breaks free from the control of the white man. Gouanvic draws on Pierre Bourdieu's ideas of resistance to domination by cultural producers who find themselves in 'a position of being dominated and that of a position of resistance to the imposition of power which denied the individual the right of "feeling justified in existing as he does"' (Bourdieu 1997: 280, cited in Gouanvic 2000: 105).

Paul Bowles and his translations: an overview

Paul Frederic Bowles was born on December 30, 1910 to middle-class parents in New York, and died in 1999 in Tangier, Morocco. Until 1946, Bowles was successfully pursuing a career of music composition in New York, collaborating with Orson Welles, Tennessee Williams and others on music for stage and orchestral pieces. It was not until his encounter with Morocco that he solidly established a career in fiction writing. Throughout the 1930s, Bowles spent his time travelling all over Europe and North Africa, and composing music. When *Partisan Review* accepted his short story 'Distant Episode' in 1947, Bowles decided that he could seriously go on writing fiction. The same year, the young American traveller and composer came to the conclusion that Tangier, which he previously visited in 1931, was the place where he wanted to be more than anywhere else (Bowles 1972: 247) and it was there 'that Bowles came of age as a writer of fiction. And it was in the flamboyant, mystical cult of *kif* (cannabis) smoking that Bowles found his métier' (Davis 1993: 103).

From 1923 to the late 1950s, Tangier, also referred to as 'Tangiers,' 'Tan-ja' and 'Tingis,' was a melting pot where peoples of various cultures and races co-habited. During this time, the city was unique for two main reasons. Politically, unlike the rest of Morocco, which was under direct French or Spanish rule, Tangier was considered international. Geographically, the city served as the nexus that linked North Africa and Europe, connecting the Mediterranean to the Atlantic Ocean. The city's strategic geographic location has always intrigued the interest and greed of the most powerful and imperialist powers, namely, Great Britain, France and Spain. In 1923, Tangier was declared an international zone (*la zone internationale de Tanger* (French)—*Tan-ja addaw-liya* (Arabic)) under the joint administration of France, Spain and Great Britain with the signing of the Tangier protocol registered in League of Nations Treaty in 1924. Later, other European countries (Portugal, Belgium, the Netherlands, Sweden and, later, the United States) joined the city's administration until its reintegration into independent Morocco in 1956.

In 1947, Bowles settled in the international zone of Tangier and wrote successful works including *The Sheltering Sky* (1949) and *Let it Come Down* (1952), novels of alienation which tackle the themes of cultural encounter between American expats and the natives in the North African desert and International Tangier, respectively. *The Spider's House* (1955) narrates an anti-colonial uprising in Fez that also explores the dilemma of the American tourist in an alien society and the gap of misunderstanding created by the clash of different cultures. Bowles also wrote short stories and essays such as *A Hundred Camels in The Courtyard* (1962) and *Their Heads Are Green and*

Their Hands Are Blue: Scenes from the Non-Christian World (1963). Many of these texts take place in Tangier and invoke the culture, mentality, religion and the mindset of the North African other.

In Tangier, the self-exiled American artist encountered a group of poor and illiterate young boys; namely, Ahmed Yacoubi, Larbi Layachi, Mohammed Mrabet, Abdesslam Boulaich and Mohammed Choukri, known in Morocco as the 'Tangerian' or 'Tanjawi' storytellers, which means the storytellers from the region of Tangier. These young men were not professional storytellers until they met with Bowles, who encouraged them to tell him stories, which he translated and published in the English language. Many of these stories have been directly inspired by Moroccan oral tradition, perpetuated through generations and traditionally recognised in Morocco as tales and legends. In addition, the storytellers whom Bowles translated also relied in their storytelling on their imagination and daily adventures with foreigners in international Tangier.

Bowles's translations of Moroccan oral stories began in the late 1950s. His first collaborations were with Ahmed Yacoubi with the publication of his tales or short stories 'The Man and The Woman' (1956), 'The Man Who Dreamed of Fish Eating Fish' (1956) and 'The Game' (1961). Bowles translated Larbi Layachi's semi-autobiography *Life Full of Holes* in 1964, and Mohammed Mrabet's novel *Love With a Few Hairs* in 1967, followed by several other collaborations. Bowles's collaboration with Mrabet was more significant. They produced thirteen narratives in the form of the short story, the novel and the autobiography. Their literary productions include *The Lemon* (1969), *M'hashish* (1969), 'The Boy Who Set the Fire' (1974), 'Hadidan Aharam' (1975), *Look & Move On* (semi-autobiography in 1976), 'Harmless Poisons, Blameless Sins' (1976), *The Big Mirror* (1977), 'The Beach Café & The Voice' (1980), 'The Chest' (1983) and 'Marriage with Papers' (1986).

Bowles also published collections of his translated tales by various authors under the title *Translations from the Moghrebi* (1986) and *Chocolate Creams and Dollars*, by various authors (1992). The word 'Moghrebi' is the equivalent of Moroccan and, by using this word, Bowles refers to spoken (colloquial) Arabic, also referred to as *da-ri-ja* (dialect), the non-written Arabic version spoken in Morocco. The dialect slightly varies according to every region in Morocco. By using this word, Bowles emphasises the oral nature of the source texts.

Following the oral tradition in Morocco, these texts were narrated orally by the storytellers either directly to Bowles or recorded on tape. Bowles listened, transcribed, translated and did the editing, which involves cutting the text into chapters, paragraphs, sentences, and punctuation, and also keeping the storytellers on good terms with their publishers. After Bowles published these stories in America and London, the texts were re-translated into many other European languages. Some of them were later translated into standard Arabic.

The oral storytellers with whom Bowles collaborated could neither read nor write their proper works. They were considered illiterate according to conventional understandings of literacy. They used Moroccan dialect and Spanish to communicate with their translator, who likewise could neither read nor speak standard Arabic, which he explicitly denounced in his conversation with Elghandour (2012), a Moroccan scholar, as being a language imposed on Moroccans by the Arabs.

Compared to the oral storytellers with whom Bowles collaborated, Mohammed Choukri was different. He learnt to read and write in standard Arabic at the age of twenty-one. When he met with Bowles, he could write his own stories. Choukri was famous for his successful autobiography *For Bread Alone* (1973), which first appeared in Bowles's English translation, then in French as *Le Pain Nu* (1980), translated by the Moroccan Francophone writer Tahar Ben Jelloun, before it was finally permitted to be published in its Standard Arabic version in Morocco in 2000, having been censored since 1983 for 'containing extreme pornographic scenes which do not fit with our [Moroccan] social and religious traditions' (Green and Karolides 2014).

When they first appeared, the stories of Tangier were welcome neither at home nor in the US. It is quite significant that the oral tales translated by Bowles were produced during a critical time in the history of both source (post-independence Morocco) and target culture (post-WWII US), a time of political movements and social revolutions. The texts shed strong light on the dark reality of life in the international zone of Tangier, the life of the marginalised class of society. The storytellers of Tangier used informal and sometimes shocking language as they openly tackled social taboos, and brought up sensitive issues that were not tolerated in the traditional Moroccan society of the time. The translations were heavily criticised by Moroccan intellectuals not just for their content but also for being narrated in Moroccan Arabic by illiterate storytellers, and therefore, not conforming to the standard conventions of Moroccan and Arabic literature. In his article 'Une Technique de viol [A technique of rape]' published in *Le Monde* newspaper in 1972, Tahar Ben Jelloun, a well-established postcolonial Moroccan writer, denounced Bowles and described his translations of the Moroccan storytellers as 'bastard literature' (Mourad 2016b).

The late 1950s and early 1960s, that coincide with the publication of the translations, mark major social and cultural movements and revolutions in the US. The sexual and drug-fuelled revolution (also known as the psychedelic sixties) provoked radical modifications in the values and principles of the modern world. This counter-culture also marked a turning point in American literature, especially with the formation of the beat movement and literature which challenged 'traditional' modernist literature by bringing to light social taboos and sub-cultural themes, notably drugs and sexuality (Diehl 1974).

Bowles's translations of the oral stories of Tangier (like his fiction) challenged the conventions of mainstream culture and literature. The stories clearly defied conformism and traditional values (imposed) at home by shedding strong light on the lavishness and extravagance that the post-war renegades dwelled in in the international zone. All the stories that Bowles translated emphasised unregulated consumption of *kif* and sexual relations between foreigners and native boys in Tangier. The translations represented Tangier as an alternative place for the disillusioned to lose themselves and unleash their non-conformism (the beat generation, for example). The texts carefully depicted the social freedom that characterised life in the international zone and challenged US social norms, especially the traditional notion of family (Mourad 2016b). Most of the texts (for example, *Love with a Few Hairs*, *Look and Move On* by Mohammed Mrabet) focus on sexual relations between foreigners and native boys.

Bowles distanced himself from the counter-culture writers and poets in the US. However, he shared affinities with them. 'I was never part of a group,' Bowles says, 'but I felt sympathy for the beats' (a conversation with McInerney 1983: 191). Despite his reluctance as a counter-culture icon, Bowles's stories and translations of *kif* tales and sexual encounters between the natives and foreigners enhanced the beats' efforts to challenge conformity at home. It is, therefore, not surprising that Bowles's translations as well as his own stories where similar themes are celebrated ('A Hundred Camels in the

Courtyard' is an example) were embraced, and, most importantly, encouraged by the beat writers as well as by the non-conformist publishing houses in the US like Black Sparrow Press, Grove Press and City Lights.

On October 19, 1961, Allen Ginsberg (one of the beat writers) wrote to Bowles to say: 'if you have nothing available,' Lawrence Ferlinghetti 'might be interested in 70–100 pps of Jacoubi's [Yacoubi] stories maybe, with comments or intro or reminiscences by you [Bowles]' (Miller 1994: 332). Lawrence Ferlinghetti is the co-founder of the American City Lights Booksellers & Publishers. Like the other non-conformist publishing houses Black Sparrow Press and Grove Press that published most of Bowles's fiction and translations of the Tangerian oral storytellers, City Lights was a haven for the counter-culture writers and poets in America. It published the works of both Paul Bowles and the storytellers in the US (Mourad 2016b).

In this vein, Bowles's translations as well as his literary productions conform with the definition of activism as a form of solidarity (Tymoczko 2010) and alliance (Baldo 2020). In her conceptualisation of translation as activism, Tymoczko distinguishes between two forms of activism: resistance and engagement. She considers the first one to be reactive and, therefore, 'restrictive and limiting the translator to a more passive role than is required or desirable' (Tymoczko 2010: 210). The metaphoric meaning of activism as engagement, however, implies commitment and suggests action that goes beyond reaction or opposition to external power or force (Tymoczko 2010: 210). It is, therefore, 'proactive' in the sense that suggests actions that might 'involve solidarity with other people' (Tymoczko 2010: 210).

As a rebel, Bowles's early departure from the US and his representation of the exotic and the 'primitive' can be considered a form of resistance, an attempt to undermine progress, development and order that the US appeared to represent. Bowles despised his 'Americanness' to the extent that he shunned everything American by adopting an exotic, unmodern lifestyle. In his words:

> I don't like America. I never go there. I haven't been there in 26 years, and I hope to never go again … It would be better if it didn't exist at all, and a nice atom bomb would finish it off. I would be pleased.
>
> *(Elghandor 1994: 11)*

Like all translations, Bowles's did not happen in a vacuum. His selection of exotic and marginalised forms of culture communicates his dissatisfaction with the modern world in general and life in the US in particular. Bowles's selection of texts which depict marginalised and socially unregulated modes of living in the international zone of Tangier also 'titillated the counter-culture' at home (Edwards 2005: 81), especially the beat writers who followed him to Tangier (William Burroughs, Allen Ginsberg, Jack Kerouac). His representation of Tangier as a place for escape for those who were unsatisfied with their lives at home, embodied in Bowles's fictional characters (Port and Kit in *The Sheltering Sky* and Dyar in *Let it Come Down*), defied America's political objectives after WWII. Edwards explains how American media supported exaggerated and popular representations of Tangier 'as decadent and dissolute that even murder was unexceptional' in order to contain the challenging potential of the city as an exotic escape (2005: 141). For Bowles, however, Tangier was a dream city. In a conversation with Davis (1993), Bowles describes the North African city as a haven where you could live for nothing and get whatever you wanted. Right after the war Tangier was extremely cheap; you never asked the price of anything, you just took what you saw. It was amazing. You got a terrific rate on the dollar, higher than anywhere. People were living in Paris and all over Europe, but they kept their bank in Tangier ... and also it was a beautiful place to live.

(Davis 1993: 108)

Right after the war, Tangier 'drew a wide range of travellers whose motivations for staying on as expatriates may have grown out of the trauma of the war' (Walonen 2011: 2). In the words of one of the beat writers, William Burroughs,

Tangier is one of the few places left in the world where so long as you don't proceed to robbery, violence or some sort of crude, anti-social behavior, you can do exactly what you want. It is a sanctuary of noninterference.

(Burroughs and Grauerholz 1998: 128)

A lifestyle of extravagance, gay sexuality and excessive liberty in the 'sanctuary of noninterference' was strongly depicted in the tales of the Tangerian storytellers, especially their semi-autobiographies: Mohammed Mrabet's *Look and Move On* (1976), Ahmed Yacoubi, *Life Full of Holes* (1964), Mohammed Choukri, *For Bread Alone* (1973) as well as Mrabet's *Love with a Few Hairs* (1967), *The Lemon* (1969), *Mhashish* (1969) and others. Bowles's careful selection of these texts, as I will discuss in the following section, suggests a high level of engagement. The translator's commitment to translating what was regarded as 'low' and 'marginalised' forms of Moroccan culture through his collaboration with the illiterate class of society was one of his main resistant translation strategies.

Bowles's resistant translation strategies

There is no single textual or discursive strategy ... Activist translation strategies are selected, invented and improvised for their tactical values in specific situations, contexts, places and times.

(Tymoczko 2010: 230)

Engaged translators simplify translated texts in order to serve specific engaged purposes. Sometimes activist translation strategies turn on the insertion of the foreign into a culture and at other times they turn on the refusal of the foreign.

(Tymoczko 2010: 230)

In his representation of Moroccan culture, Paul Bowles exclusively concentrated on the primitive and marginalised forms of low culture manifested in popular practices such as witchcraft, the habit of *kif* (cannabis) smoking, popular figures like *Aicha Quandicha* (a female ghost) and *djin* (ghosts) and non-Islamic rituals. The oral tradition of storytelling that Bowles translated strongly depicts these popular beliefs and practices perpetuated mostly among uneducated and marginalised classes of society. By shedding light only on this part of the culture, Bowles deliberately excluded institutional and written Arab culture in Morocco (Mourad 2016a), which he denounces as being non-Moroccan in an interview with the Moroccan scholar A. Elghandor. Bowles states, 'I think I have left out a great deal, oh yes, an enormous amount, but I do that on purpose; it's not a mistake. I had no intention of giving a fair picture' (Elghandor 1994: 27).

As Tymoczko puts it, translation is 'the primary activist achievement' (2010: 229). Engaged translations make decisions, special choices and selections in order to achieve specific engaged purposes. The translator's deliberate choice of a culture or an aspect of it reveals the translator's agency. At other times, the translator's silence or choice not to translate reveals agency (Tymoczko 2010: 230). In Bowles's case, it is his decision to discard a huge amount of the culture and give only a partial or an incomplete representation by translating what he personally perceives as 'authentic' Morocco: pre-Islamic Morocco, the Berber versus Arab, oral versus written culture and uneducated layman versus educated elite. Bowles's selective approach to Moroccan culture and the possibility of reform (modernisation), especially after independence, highlights his active agency as a translator.

During his lifelong residence in Tangier, Bowles avoided the educated Moroccan minority and criticised their attempts to 'cease being themselves and become Westerners' (Bowles 1963: viii). Bowles feared that, after independence, Moroccans would cease to be Moroccans. In 1955, he published *The Spider's House*, a novel set in Fez (a Moroccan city) during the Moroccan nationalist uprising in 1954. In this novel, Bowles transmits his rejection of the modernisation of postcolonial Morocco. In a conversation with the Moroccan scholar Abdelaziz Jadir, Bowles criticises 'the metamorphosis of the country towards the perpetuation of the goals pursued by the French coloniser, that of making Morocco an open market for French goods, business and values, which completely counteracts Moroccan standards' (Jadir 2011: 65, my translation).

Bowles's translations, which were initiated after Morocco's independence, resonate with his statement to Jadir. The translations attempt to textually preserve what he regarded as authentic Morocco as opposed to the fake metamorphosing Morocco. In this context, Bowles's translations of locally underappreciated and uneducated storytellers can be seen as an act of resistance to change and modernisation after Independence.

The selection of a specific text genre, here the oral narratives of Tangier, is a main activist strategy adopted by the translator. Textual selection involves manipulation both in disseminating as well as 'in blocking communication and refusing to transmit cultural information' (Tymoczko 2010: 230). Other forms of activist translation strategies that we can trace in Bowles's translation include manipulation and amplification.

In his introduction to the autobiography of Larbi Layachi (pseudonym DrissCharhadisemi), *Life Full of Holes*, Bowles acknowledges his interference with the original oral text by imposing an episode that the author (Larbi Layachi) wanted to leave out completely. For more clarification, let us quote at some length what Bowles writes in this concern:

> One of these [sequences that the author wanted to add to his text] was the episode in 'The Shepherd', where the narrator insists on spending the night at the tomb of Sidi BouHajja in order to see if the 'bull with horns' will appear. When he [Larbi Layachi] had appended this bit and listened to the playback, he decided that it was not interesting; and was for leaving it out. This was our only occasion for disagreement. I [Bowles] wanted to include it because, although it was incidental to the story, the passage was a clear illustration of the persistence of pre-Islamic belief: the appearance of the ancient god in a spot whose initial sanctity has been affirmed by

the usurping faith. During the rural celebrations, the Bull is still decorated with flowers and ribbons and medals, and led through the streets to be sacrificed. I [Bowles] explained to him [Layachi] why I thought the passage ought to be included, knowing in advance that he would disapprove any suggestion to the effect that his ancestors had been something else before embracing Islam. We let the subject drop, he having agreed, if not wholeheartedly, to allow the episode to be incorporated into the text.

(Layachi 1964: xvi)

The sequence of the 'Bull with Horns' in Layachi's narrative emphasises a pre-Islamic ritual which highlights Bowles's personal attitude regarding Moroccan Arab versus pre-Islamic Berber culture, as previously discussed in this section. Bowles wanted to emphasise the Berber dimension of Moroccan culture because he believed it represents the authentic Moroccan before being, as he describes it, 'ruined by the Arabs' (Elghandor 1994: 12). The sequence that Bowles insists on inserting conveys the translator's personal conviction that the primitive, the intuitive and the irrational represent an authentic aspect of humanity in contrast to the rational, orderly and the religious which Bowles rejected throughout his life.

Engaged translators can also be committed to enhance or challenge certain narratives. For example, 'ontological narratives are personal stories we tell ourselves about our place in the world and about our own personal history' (Baker 2010: 25). In a similar vein, Bowles states: 'when I got here [Morocco] I said to myself "Ah, this is the way people used to be, the way my own ancestors were thousands of years ago. The natural man. Basic humanity ... It all seemed quite natural to me"' (Halpern 1993: 130). Bowles had a personal conviction before coming to Morocco that primitivism is the natural state of being. 'I don't think it was very important when we were going on all fours,' he states, 'but I suppose going on all fours is a natural way for human beings to live. In other words, let's go back to non-existence, that's my [Bowles's] idea, to the past' (Elghandor 1994: 18).

Bowles's convictions go against the beliefs and intentions of Layachi, the author. As a Moroccan Muslim, Layachi refuses to include anything that would (mis)represent his culture as primitive, chaotic, backward or unreligious. This can be justified by his hesitation regarding whether to keep the scene or to discard it all together. Despite the author's disagreement, the translator clearly imposes his voice on a text that is not his own. Bowles imposes his beliefs on to a text that was not meant to serve the purpose that the translator makes it serve. This is a clear case of manipulation. It highlights the power of the translator to intervene with the original text to either transmit a personal message, enhance a doctrine or ideology, as well as reconstruct the target text in order to fit a pre-existing personal and public ideological framework or narrative (Baker 2006).

Bowles's agency as a translator is also manifested in the simplicity of the language of his translations. While it is not possible to compare Bowles's translations with that of the original oral texts, comparing the translations themselves demonstrates that there is a deliberate inclination by the translator towards using over-simplified English. The English that Bowles uses in his translated texts, compared with his own texts, is simple, plain and straightforward. This can be read as an attempt by the translator to carry the fingerprint of the illiterate in order to convey an image of a simple-minded North African man and to emphasise the average, uneducated, primitive Moroccan, whom Bowles wants to represent as authentic versus the educated, modern sophisticated man, whom Bowles regards as the fake Moroccan.

In all his translations, Bowles preserves words in Moroccan Arabic, which emphasises the translator's attempt to accentuate the orality of Moroccan culture in contrast to written Arabic culture. While Bowles has intentionally kept Moroccan Arabic words and expressions in his translations, he did not provide any English equivalents of these words, even though many of them were simple and translatable words.

The following are examples we find in some of Mrabet's tales translated by Bowles and published in a collection titled *The Boy who Set the Fire and Other Stories*:

'I swear you *khay* [brother] we'll never sell it' ('Si Mokhtar')
'*hamdul'lah* [thanks to Allah] you are alive for me' ('Si Mokhtar')
'*Ya rajel* [hey man] she said' ('The Spring')
'*Ouakha* [OK], they said.' ('Ramadan')
'To me he says: Allah y chafih. [May Allah cure or heal him]' ('The Well')

Bowles did not include footnotes or glossaries in these stories, something that he opted for only in some of his own texts such as 'A Hundred Camels in the Courtyard.' In his *Collected Stories and Later Writings* (2002), he provides a glossary for different Moroccan cultural concepts that he has included in his texts. For example, the concept of *baraka* is defined by Bowles as 'Blessedness, those with Baraka are believed to enjoy divine protection' (2002: 1047) In Islam, the Arabic word 'baraka' is a concept which refers to constant flow of blessedness and grace transmitted from Allah to the most devout or chosen ones. Similarly, the Moroccan Arabic words *fasoukh and cirfhalek* were respectively defined by Bowles as 'incense used to ward off evil Spirits' (2002: 1048); 'go away' (2002: 1048).

Like his translations of the oral stories of Tangier, Bowles used the same strategy of incorporating Moroccan Arabic words and expressions into the stories that he wrote himself. For example, in 'He of the Assembly,' Bowles writes 'Mustapha saw that He of The Assembly was *mkiyef maarassou* and was not interested in money' (1962: 244). The Moroccan expression '*mkiyef maarassou*' refers to the state of joy or the good mood that the person, here the assembly, experiences as a result of smoking *kif*. In all his translations, however, Bowles did not explain the Moroccan words and expressions. Therefore, we are left to think that the translator aimed to accentuate the foreignness of the English version of the Moroccan text in order to assert the Moroccan identity of the translations and emphasise their embeddedness within Moroccan oral tradition; thereby giving the texts a foreignised, exotic Moroccan flavour.

Venuti (1995) describes foreignisation as a translation strategy whereby the translator deliberately keeps foreign elements from the original text. Venuti considers foreignisation to be a resistant strategy that enables the disruption of the target language's cultural codes to register the linguistic and cultural differences of the foreign text; thus, exerting an 'ethno-deviant pressure' on the values of the target culture (Venuti 1995: 81–94). This translation strategy produces 'something that cannot be confused with either the source-language text or a text written originally in the target language' (Neubert and Shreve 1992: 6). The result is a new, strange, hybrid and exotic text that is a neither/nor; in this case, neither Moroccan nor American.

Even in his own writings about Morocco, only some and not all of Bowles's writings incorporate glossaries for the words and expressions which he kept in Moroccan Arabic.

Interestingly, Bowles's Moroccan characters used Moroccan dialect in his three major novels—*Let it Come Down*, *The Sheltering Sky* and *The Spider's House*—without giving strict definitions of the foreign words and phrases that Bowles incorporated in his texts. The following are examples from *The Spider's House* and *Let it Come Down*: 'Stenna, Stenna [wait, wait],' 'Chouïa, Chouïa [slowly, slowly]' (Bowles 1955: 214), 'Inaal din—[cursing] he said savagely under his breath' (Bowles 1952: 39).

While Bowles could have used English words to achieve a 'smooth' text accommodated to the American culture/language and that could be easily read and understood by its audience, it seems that Bowles's objective was to achieve a counter-effect: to write a text which does not adhere to but rather 'disrupts target language [here American] cultural codes' (Venuti 1995: 42) and challenges the norms of mainstream literature. The desired result of this strategy is to create something which does not adhere, but defies the cultural and linguistic conventions of both the source/Moroccan and the target American text/culture. This challenge is also clearly manifested in Bowles's mixing of the cultural and linguistic codes as well as the voices of the two texts. Rather than assimilating the source text to the target text, he constructs a hybrid rather than a homogeneous text.

Bowles's writings and translations of Moroccan oral stories can be associated with a literature of resistance that advocates cross-cultural mixtures and hybrid perspectives that result from cross-cultural encounter. In this context, Bowles's hybrid texts and translations can be read as attempts to break down the norms and the conventions of the target culture and American literature by retaining aspects from the foreign culture and language. This idea is also related to the translation of the language and customs of foreign and marginalised cultures into American English. In this regard, D'Amore writes that the adoption of a foreignising approach in translation is a clear form of resistance to and a demonstration of non-conformity (2009: 122). The rejection Bowles faced as a writer of fiction when he has just started his career as a fiction writer supports this argument.

The hybridity in Bowles's texts and translations of the oral stories defies conformity and challenges the concept of the 'national' (both Moroccan and American) mainstream literature. In his translations, the use of Arabic and English in the same text illustrates this hybridity. This appears even at the level of the word unit. For instance, in Mrabet's story 'Ramadan,' Bowles invents the word *salaam-ing* to emphasise the Moroccan form of greeting and salutation. While the root of the word belongs to Arabic language, Bowles uses English grammatical structure by adding the gerund -ing to the Arabic word 'salaam [greeting]' in order to forge a new word, which is neither Moroccan nor American, but like the translations themselves, reflects the cultural intersection between the two cultures, languages and voices.

Translation: marronage, emancipation

It is not until recently that the practice of translation in colonial and postcolonial contexts has been partly liberated from its colonising stigma in order to become also a means of liberation and power for colonised and dominated subjects. In addition to serving colonial power in enhancing cultural and political domination, postcolonial translation theorists have asked 'how translation might contribute to exposing, challenging and decolonising the legacy of colonialism and various forms of neo-colonialism in a postcolonial era' (Hui 2009: 200).

In a metaphor of translators as 'colonised individuals,' Gouanvic, borrowing Bourdieu's remark on K, the protagonist of Kafka in *The Trial*, proposes an interesting analogy between the real colonised nations and translators as dominated nationals, given the fragile and marginalised position that they occupy in their society (2000: 12). Commenting on the character of K, Bourdieu writes: 'Robbed of the power to give sense to his life, to express the meaning and direction of his existence, he [K] is condemned to live in time determined by others, alienated. This is exactly the destiny of the dominated' (1997: 279–80, cited in Gouanvic 2000: 101).

Given the fact that Bourdieu is not addressing a real situation of the colonised, Gouanvic remarks that Bourdieu's comments can also be applied to 'those within a nation,' the 'dominated nationals' (2000: 101). Domination in this context is clearly symbolic, experienced from within or at the level of the individual rather than from without or at the state level (2000: 101). In relation to this idea, we can say that Bowles was a 'dominated national': he was colonised from within by his own American identity and culture. Mostly, Bowles resisted the fact that there was no room for him as an artist in America of the 1930s and 1940s. In this concern Bowles states that

> Thirty or forty years ago, when I was in my formative stage, there didn't seem to be a place for the artist there [US]: he was considered to be an outsider. I resented that more than anything else, I suppose, the general attitude that any artist, particularly a creative artist … was an outcast, a pariah.
>
> *(Evans 1993: 47)*

Bowles shunned European civilisation, modernism, progress, technology, rationalism,and intellect. He criticised the decadence of consumer culture and mass production. At the same time, he believed that human authenticity was best realised in primitive modes of being, which he chased and tried to preserve by translating oral stories of magic and superstition, and recording indigenous music of Morocco. For Bowles, primitiveness meant the natural state of humanity, a state of being that he praised, advocated and tried to embody himself.

Bowles's ideas about world culture and American culture in particular 'distanced him from what is imagined as "normal" in the US' (Edwards 2005: 311), by placing him at the margin of what is regarded as American culture. In this context, Gouanvic writes that, like colonised nations, 'dominated nationals' are social outcasts who live at the fringes of society and undergo a symbolic form of violence by being denied 'the power to live their own lives, by not recognising the legitimacy of their aspirations, thereby denying them the power to direct their own destinies' (2000: 102). Indeed, Bowles never succeeded in justifying his choices to his American peers. Following his definitive departure to North Africa, Edwards explains how the American media could not forgive Bowles his permanent residence in a remote place and how his reviewers were not satisfied with the fact that he dedicated his career to representing life outside the US (Edwards 2005).

Inevitably, colonisation triggers resistance and rejection triggers rejection. 'If you were rejected,' Bowles states, 'you reject back' (Evans 1993: 47). Bowles's resistance to and disdain of American culture was communicated through his early departure from the US; by dedicating his time and career to representing an alternative life outside the US, his thematic choices, both in his fiction as well as his translations, further reflected his renunciation of his native land. From North Africa, Bowles wrote about American hostages who, like himself, departed from home looking for a shelter from the bourgeois ideals of industrial progress and teleological rationality. His own fiction, *The Sheltering Sky* (1949), *Let it Come Down* (1952) and *The Spider's House* (1955), took as subject encounters of Anglo-Americans with remote places and natives who live there. Like Bowles, his protagonists escaped their identity by travelling towards exotic cultures in order to lose themselves in the North African desert (for example, Kit and Port in *The Sheltering Sky*) or in the international zone of Tangier (for example, Dyar in *Let it Come Down*), or another remote place that became their shelter towards freedom. *The Sheltering Sky*, Bowles's first novel, was an explicit rejection of American culture. Set in the Algerian Sahara, it recounts the story of an American couple (Port and Kit) who left America in order to abandon 'the decadence of the West, attempting to escape the incursion of what the novel calls "The mechanistic age"' (Edwards 2005: 315).

Bowles embodies Gouanvic's description of the dominated as a 'maroon' writer and translator. In his attempt to destabilise the image of translation as a site of domination, Gouanvic coined the concept of 'marronage,' through an analogy with literary translation 'as resistance in the context of colonialism.' As noted above, Maroons are originally 'slaves who took to the mountains during the seventeenth and eighteenth centuries in the Caribbean in order to escape white masters' (Gouanvic 2000: 107). In their escape, 'Maroons affirmed the possibility of liberty, of freedom, in their desire for a liberated state' (Gouanvic 2000: 106).

Gouanvic figuratively considers the translators and writers, the so-called *écrivains maudits* (cursed writers) those 'who do not play by the rules of the game, protesters' to be the maroons of the source culture 'as they attempt to remove themselves from the hold of legitimacy' (2000: 106). Developing this metaphor, Gouanvic asserts the possibility of liberty through translation.

The recurrent theme of running away (*marronage*) from American culture into remote spaces like the desert in Bowles's *The Sheltering Sky*, Tangier in his 'Distant Episode' or the Caribbean in 'Pages From Cold Point,' in addition to celebrating homosexual encounters with the natives in his writings and translated stories, can all be read as a form of defiance, an attempt to free the self and as an expression of the European protagonist's dissatisfaction with the post-war condition and his disappointment with the concept of the nation and its values. Paul Bowles, the traveller and fiction writer, is an ideal manifestation of this American character.

When he settled in the international zone of Tangier in 1947, Bowles already decided that he did not want the life that post-WWII America had to offer him. Instead, he chose to leave and observe far from home the major economic and political changes, which he dreaded and criticised eagerly and openly in interviews and through his fiction. This has made of him one of the most prominent literary figures who reacted early to the political, social and economic aftermath of the war in the US and tried to break free from domestic values and mainstream ideals of suburban America by devoting his career to representing alternative realities outside the US.

Bowles's marronage can be considered as one of the translator's main strategies of resistance. 'Marronage' here means Bowles's choice of representing and translating exclusively the marginalised, the poor, the illiterate, the backward, the foreign and the exotic 'other' as resistance and defiance of the confining norms and boundaries of society, both source (Moroccan) and target (American), which brings a symbolic form of liberty to the translator and to the translated subject alike. Gouanvic further notes that translation becomes a site for resistance when maroon translators select the 'least cynical writers, those who are the least directly and exclusively market-oriented' (2000: 107). In line with Gouanvic's metaphor, both the storytellers of Tangier and Bowles were Maroons in the sense that both were marginalised, dominated/colonised and *maudits* (cursed) in their own societies. They were rebels and resisters to different forms of domination. While the storytellers experienced colonisation in its political sense and resisted mostly its social ramifications, Bowles was dominated, symbolically, from within or at the individual level by his American identity which suffocated him to the extent of disdain.

Both Bowles and the Moroccan oral storytellers lived at the periphery of their societies due to their non-conformist lifestyle and literary productions which challenged mainstream social and literary standards. Accordingly, they became outcasts in their communities, for expressing their different realities, 'the meaning of their world' (Gouanvic 2000: 106), in their own terms. In the light of this allegory of marronage, Bowles's translations brought symbolic freedom to himself as a maroon writer and translator as well as to the storytellers of Tangier, whom Bowles translated in order to transmit his rebellious voice and ideas.

Conclusion

The concept of activism in translation challenges the perception of translators as non-active or passive agents and calls for placing translators and translations within their social, cultural and political contexts in order to reveal their agency and understand their activism. In this chapter, I approached the translations of the American self-exiled novelist, composer and translator Paul Bowles from this perspective in the light of Tymoczko's definition of translation as both a form of resistance and engagement. In this respect, this chapter discussed how Bowles's translations of the oral stories of Tangier communicate the American expatriate's resistance to mainstream representations of culture and literature both at home (US) and in exile (Tangier, Morocco). For Bowles, translation, in addition to his fiction, constituted a main tool not only in communicating his dissatisfaction with life at home, but in encouraging alternative (or unrestrained) modes of existence outside the US, also embodied in his fictional characters as well as in his own lifestyle.

As highlighted by many translation theorists (for example, Tymoczko (2010), Baker (2010) and others), engaged translators make use of different translation strategies to serve their agendas that can be of social, cultural, ideological or political nature. In this chapter, I emphasised Bowles's selective approach to Moroccan culture as a main resistant translation strategy. Translators' choices are key in understanding and revealing their (sometimes hidden or latent) activism, especially in the translation of oral texts, as is the case with Bowles's translations. In this respect, Tymockzo writes that the 'translator's choices and decision making was one of the first steps in exploring the agency of the translator' (2010: 211).

In the absence of the source (oral) text, resistant translation strategies can also be traced in paratextual elements such as footnotes, prefaces, glossaries and sometimes in the absence of these. In relation to Bowles's translation strategies, I have demonstrated how his choice of not including glossaries, for example, and incorporating Moroccan Arabic words and expressions in his English text reflect the translator's wish to break down and transcend conventional norms of mainstream Moroccan and American literature.

Related topics

The Dialectics of Dissent in Postcolonial India; Writing as Hospitality.

Further reading

Milton, John, and Paul Bandia (2009) *Agents of Translation*. Amsterdam: Benjamins.

An inspiring collection of essays that investigate cases where agents are responsible for major historical, cultural and literary shifts.

Tymoczko, Maria (2000) 'Translation and Political Engagement,' *The Translator* 6 (1): 23–47.

Through the example of the translation of Irish literature into English, Tymoczko studies how translation movements can lead to the achievement of significant geopolitical results.

Tymoczko, Maria (2015) *Enlarging Translation, Empowering Translators*. London: Routledge.

Tymoczko discusses how an enlarged perception of translation sheds strong light on the agency and empowerment of translators.

References

Alameda, Soledad (1993) 'Paul Bowles: Touched by Magic,' in *Conversations with Paul Bowles*. Ed. Gena Caponi-Tabery. Jackson: University Press of Mississippi. 218–226.

Baker, Mona (2006) *Translation and Conflict: A Narrative Account*. New York: Routledge.

Baker, Mona (2010) 'Translation and Activism: Emerging Patterns of Narrative Community,' *Massachusetts Review* 47 (3): 462–484.

Baldo, Michela (2020) 'Activist Translation, Alliances and Performativity: Translating Judith Butler's *Notes toward a Performative Theory of Assembly* into Italian,' in *The Routledge Handbook of Translation and Activism*. Eds. Rebecca Ruth Gould and Kayvan Tahmasebian. London: Routledge. 30–48.

Ben Jelloun, Tahar (1972) 'Une Technique de Viol,' in *Le Monde* [online] 9 June. Available at: www.lemonde.fr/archives/article/1972/06/09/une-technique-deviol_2392430_1819218.html [accessed 10 October 2019].

Bowles, Paul (1949) *The Sheltering Sky*. New York: New Directions.

Bowles, Paul (1952) *Let It Come Down*. New York: Random House.

Bowles, Paul (1955) *The Spider's House*. New York: Random House.

Bowles, Paul (1962) 'A Hundred Camels in the Courtyard,' in *Bowles Collected Stories & Later Writings*. Ed. Paul Bowles. San Francisco: City Lights. 223–274.

Bowles, Paul (1963) 'Their Heads Are Green and Their Hands are Blue,' in *Bowles Collected Stories & Later Writings*. Ed. Paul Bowles. San Francisco: City Lights. 698–962.

Bowles, Paul (1972) *Without Stopping: An Autobiography*. London: Peter Owen.

Bowles, Paul (2002) *Collected Stories & Later Writings*. New York: Library of America.

Bowles, Paul (2006) *A Distant Episode: The Selected Stories*. New York: Harper Collins.

Breit, Harvey (1993) 'Talk with Paul Bowles,' in *Conversations with Paul Bowles*. Ed. Gena Caponi-Tabery. Jackson: University Press of Mississippi. 3–5.

Burroughs, William S., and James Grauerholz (1998) *Word Virus: The William S. Burroughs Reader*. New York: Grove Press.

D'Amore, Anna Maria (2009) *Translating Contemporary Mexican Texts: Fidelity to Alterity*. New York: Peter Lang.

Davis, Stephen (1993) 'Interview: Paul Bowles,' in *Conversations with Paul Bowles*. Ed. Gena Caponi-Tabery. Jackson: University Press of Mississippi. 102–110.

Diehl, Digby (1974) *Drug Themes in Fiction*. Rockville: National Institute of Drug Abuse.

Edwards, Brian (2005) 'Sheltering Screens: Paul Bowles and Foreign Relations in American Literary History,' in *Morocco Bound: Disorienting America's Maghreb, from Casablanca to the Marrakech Express*. Ed. Brian T. Edwards. Durham: Duke University Press. 307–334.

Elghandor, Abdelhaq (1994) 'Bowles's Views of Atavism and Civilization: An Interview with Paul Bowles,' *A Review of International English Journal* 25 (2): 7–30.

Evans, Oliver (1993) 'An interview with Paul Bowles,' in *Conversations with Paul Bowles*. Ed. Gena Caponi-Tabery. Jackson: University Press of Mississippi. 38–58.

Gouanvic, Jean Mark (2000). 'Legitimacy, Marronnage and the Power of Translation,' in *Changing the Terms: Translating in the Postcolonial Era*. Eds. Sherry Simon and Paul St-Pierre. Ottawa: University of Ottawa. 101–111.

Green, Jonathon, and Nicholas J. Karolides (2014) *The Encyclopedia of Censorship*. New York: Facts on File.

Halpern, Daniel (1993) 'Interview with Paul Bowles,' in *Conversations with Paul Bowles*. Ed. Gena Caponi-Tabery. Jackson: University Press of Mississippi. 86–101.

Hui, Wang (2009) 'Postcolonial Approaches,' in *Routledge Encyclopedia of Translation Studies*. Eds. Mona Baker and Gabriela Saldanha. London: Routledge.

Jadir, Abdelaziz (2011) *al-hi-war al-akhir bulbulz Mo-ha-mmadshuk-ri*. Beirut: Jadawil.

Layachi, Larbi (1964) *A Life Full of Holes*. Trans. Paul Bowles. New York: Grove Press.

McInerney, Jay (1983) 'Paul Bowles in Exile' in *Conversations with Paul Bowles*. Ed. Gena Caponi-Tabery. Jackson: University Press of Mississippi. 180–191.

Meyers, Jeffrey (2011) 'The Oddest Couple: Paul and Jane Bowles,' *Michigan Quarterly Review* 50 (2): 171.

Miller, Jeffrey (1994) *In Touch: The Letters of Paul Bowles*. London: Harper Collins.

Mourad, Hafida (2016a) 'The Orientalist Leanings in Bowles's Translation and Representation of Moroccan Culture,' *International Journal of English Language & Translation Studies* 4 (3): 91–103. Available at: http://www.eltsjournal.org/archive/value4%20issue3/10-4-3-16.pdf [accessed 28 March 2020].

Mourad, Hafida (2016b) 'Paul Bowles's Translations in the Context of the American Counterculture,' *Arab World English Journal* 4: 162–172.

Mrabet, Mohammed (1969) *M'hashish*. Trans. Paul Bowls. San Francisco: City Lights.

Mrabet, Mohammed (1989) *Look and Move on*. Trans. Paul Bowls. London: Owen.

Mrabet, Mohammed (2004) *Love with Few Hairs*. Trans. Paul Bowls. Casablanca: Moroccan Cultural Studies Journal.

Neubert, Albrecht, and Gregory M. Shreve (1992). *Translation as Text*. OH: Kent State University Press.

Simon, Sherry, and Paul St-Pierre (2000) *Changing the Terms: Translating in the Postcolonial Era*. Ottawa: University of Ottawa.

Stewart, Lawrence Delbert (1974) *Paul Bowles: The Illumination of North Africa*. Carbondale: Southern Illinois University Press.

Turner, Victor (2011) *The Ritual Process: Structure and Anti-structure*. NJ: Adline Transaction.

Tymoczko, Maria (2010) *Translation, Resistance, Activism*. Amherst: University of Massachusetts Press.

Venuti, Lawrence (1995) *The Translator's Invisibility: A History of Translation*. London: Routledge.

Walonen, Michael K. (2011) *Writing Tangier in the Postcolonial Transition: Space and Power in Expatriate and North African Literature*. Farnham and Surrey: Ashgate Pub.

Wolf, Michaela (2013) 'The Sociology of Translation and Its "Activist Turn",' *Translation and Interpreting Studies* 7 (2): 129–143.

11

Translators as organic intellectuals

Translational activism in pre-revolutionary Iran

Mehrdad Rahimi-Moghaddam and Amanda Laugesen

Introduction

Many scholars have addressed the role of translation as a transcultural process in bringing about political modernity (Balay 1998; Shafiee Kadkani 2011). However, few of these studies give translators their due recognition in the narratives of the country's modern history. Accounts of Iranian modernity often fail to consider its 'translational origins' in detailed textual terms (Gould and Tahmasebian forthcoming), and the figure of the translator and their motivations, background, and political orientation in shaping the texts that have been central to modern Iranian cultural life. In an attempt to fill this gap, and building on scholarly conversations that have been devoted to the study of the translator in the last decade (Delisle and Woodsworth 2012), especially in line with what Chesterman has called 'Translator Studies' (2009), this chapter focuses on some prominent Iranian translation activities and literary translators, and aims to shed further light on the much-neglected dissident role of the translators. It begins by briefly examining the history of translation in Iran, followed by a closer study of the politics of translation in Pahlavi Iran under the regime of the Reza Shah and his successor Mohammed Reza Shah Pahlavi, until the 1979 revolution. A closer look at a Cold War translation program and the leftist Iranian translator, Behazin, follows. This chapter draws on the scholarly literature on translation in Iran, as well on translators' notes and other written accounts, as well as archival material.

A study of translators in Iran can shed significant light on the politics of translation. In particular, the chapter elucidates how political activism can be undertaken within a regime of censorship through the act and practice of translation. It thus adds to a growing scholarly literature (e.g. Haddadian-Moghaddam 2014; Kinnunen and Koskinen 2010) that argues for considering translators as agents. Through the selection of certain topics and texts for translation, translators could express their political views. But this chapter also argues that translation can be a political tool used by both the state as well as those who seek to resist the state. Tymoczko has drawn our attention to the question of power and translation, importantly noting the limitations ultimately placed on translation as a political act (2000: 31, 41; 2006: 446).

This chapter particularly focuses on the role of translators and translations in post-coup Iran through to the end of the Mohammed Reza Shah Pahlavi's regime in 1979. While championing culture and education, the Shah's regime developed a security state that cracked down on opposition and dissent. This chapter also considers the ways in which translation and translators could be used as a means of reinforcing the regime's goals to influence Iranian political views, primarily through an examination of a US-funded translation and publication operation, Franklin Book Programs (FBP: 1953–1978). FBP was part of an attempt to thwart (or at least counter) the impact of leftist translations (Haddadian-Moghaddam 2014: 109).

While some translators and intellectuals (Parviz Natel-Khanlari, Ehsan Yarshater) worked with the regime through programs such as FBP to buttress its cultural and political agenda, others (such as Behazin, Shamlu, and Shari'ati) used translation as a means of political resistance. In the absence of a coherent political opposition to the Pahlavi regime throughout the 1950s, and due to widespread censorship, translators helped to consolidate and transmit oppositional political discourse. This was being undertaken both in the area of theoretical works, such as Shari'ati's translation of Fanon; and in the literary world that was witnessing a rise in the number of translations of socialist realist novels, notable among them works of Gorky, especially his *Mother* (1906). Gramsci's notion of 'organic intellectuals' will be used in order to shed further light on the critical role of translators and their politically motivated translations in the period of the Shah.

A brief historical survey of different modes of activist translation in pre-1953 Iran

The inception of modern Iranian translation history can be traced to the Russo-Persian wars (1804–1813) in which Iran suffered a crushing defeat that resulted in the signing of the Treaty of Gulistan and the annexation of northern Azerbaijan by the Russian empire. A second Russo-Persian War (1826–1828) led to another humiliating defeat for Iran that lost the rest of the South Caucasus to Russia under the Treaty of Turkmenchay. These defeats had significant impacts both for the ruling Qajar dynasty (1789–1925) and the political elite active in *Dār al-saltana* (the seat of royalty) of Tabriz led by Prince 'Abbas Mirza (1789–1833) and Qa'em Maqam Farahani (1779–1835), then Iran's chancellor (Amanat 1993: 35). It was in the aftermath of these events that the Qajar rulers realised how desperately they needed to embark on a project of modernisation, and they turned to the translation of foreign texts as one means of doing so.

During the wars, Prince Abbas Mirsa urged people in his circle to initiate the translation of military texts so that he could modernise various facets of Iran's military strategy and tactics. Afshar suggests that '[i]t is likely that the first book translated into Persian [from a European language] was an account of Napoleon's wars of 1805–1806 against Austria and Russia' (2003: 279). The Prince took a keen interest in history, as he was hopeful that through a careful study of history he could 'find out about the reason of progress in the west and the failure and decline of his own country' (Adamiyat 1975: 163). Historical texts thus also found their way into translation into Persian.

The next phase of modern Iranian translation history begins around 1851 with the establishment of Dār al-Fonun (Polytechnic) in which Amir Kabir, then royal vizier to Naser al-Din Shah, gathered foreign secretaries of government, Christian Iranians, and instructors who were mostly brought from Austria (Adamiyat 1975: 379; Azarang 2015: 248). Edward Burgess (1810–1855), who was British, and Jules Richard (1816–1891), who was French, were among these translators (Azarang 2015: 248). Dār al-Fonun became a centre for modern Iranian education, and the teaching of foreign languages was central to its curriculum. Many students and translators who studied at or worked with Dār al-Fonun went on to become prominent politicians. Although Amir Kabir played a fundamental role in the formation of these modern institutes, the patronage of Naser al-Din Shah was also critical. The Shah was interested in knowing more about the modern world, and, like Prince Abbas before him, the most reliable sources for such knowledge were considered to be translated works from other countries. Some of the translated works included biographies of Alexander of Macedonia, Peter I, Frederick the Great, Christopher Columbus, and Napoleon Bonaparte (Amanat 1997: 430).

Naser al-Din Shah's fascination with history, geography, travelogues, and daily news led to the opening of the Royal Translation Bureau (*dār al-tarjoma-ye nāseri*), an institution solely dedicated to translation. The main figure of this institution is Eʿtemād-al-Salṭana, a prolific translator of French texts who, as Kia writes, 'denounced modern ideas as dangerous and detrimental to the security and stability of the Qajar state and openly advocated censorship' (Kia 2001: 108). The Shah also became increasingly concerned with the potentially disruptive influence of such texts both on the public and on the circle around him, and how they might encourage criticism of Qajar policies. Perhaps for this reason, translations were decreed to remain 'exclusively for [the Shah's] own personal use and out of the reach of the public' (Amanat 1997: 430).

It is at this juncture that institutional censorship began to take shape in Iran. Eʿtemā-d-al-Salṭana suggested the establishment of formal censorship following the Iranian printing of *Resāla-ye hajv-e solāla* (Pamphlet on satire of dynasties), a satire against the Shah by Sheikh Hashem Shirazi, then located in Bombay (Mumbai). Vejdani (2014: 18) observes that '[t]he imperial court astutely avoided translating histories that were unflattering to the Qajar dynasty.' However, he also argues that, despite the court's best intentions, 'such critical translations did appear in British India, where diasporic Iranians were unfettered by Qajar print censorship.' *The Virgin's Kiss* (1850) by George W. M. Reynolds, and François Fenelon's *Les Aventures de Télémaque* (1699) were among the first translations banned from publication and circulation in Iran (Bakhtiyar and Arabzadeh 2009: 16). Two factors impeded the publication of the translation of *The Virgin's Kiss*: at the time of its completion, upheavals had taken over the country and political pressure on the press and print was at its highest. Furthermore, Mohammad Hossein Forughi, as the head of the translation bureau at the time, was suspected of cooperating with the dissenting magazine *Qanun*. These heightened pressures eventually led to the arrest of the translator of *The Virgin's Kiss*, Seyyed Hossein Khan Shirazi, for being guilty of working with Mirza Malkam Khan (a dissident in exile and publisher of *Qanun*) (Adamiyat 1992: 78–79). The fate of the other translation, *Télémaque*, was much worse: due to its hints of politics, Naser al-Din Shah ordered published versions to be stashed underground until they decayed totally (Yaghmaee 1970: 364).

In the years that followed and outside the imperial court, newspapers and magazines circulated among the masses. Within this media form, many translated items appeared. Scholars have examined the role of these translations in mobilising the masses (Abrahamian 1979: 398). One of the most significant newspapers to carry translated items was *Akhtar* (1875–1896). Published under the editorship of Mirza Mahdi Khan Tabrizi and Mohammad Taher Tabrizi, by an Iranian political diaspora residing in Ottoman Turkey,

Akhtar played a key role in bringing about dramatic changes both in Persian prose and news-writing style. It included translations of items from European newspapers (Lawrence 2018: 249). Due to the low rate of literacy among Iranians at the time, there were some limitations on how effectively these translations could play a role in mobilising the masses or modernising the country (Azadibougar 2010). However, Rastegar (2007: 143) emphasises the significant role of 'public readings,' where newspapers or books such as *Adventures of Hajji Baba, of Ispahan* (1824) were read aloud, suggesting that an older oral public culture was meshing with the emerging modern print culture, and helped to circulate political and cultural ideas.

The most important of all the translations of this period is *The Adventures of Hajji Baba, of Ispahan*, written by James Justinian Morier, and published in London in 1824, and in the same year in a French edition in Paris. It was translated into Persian by Mirza Habib Esfahani (1835–1893), a Persian poet and translator who had fled to Istanbul after being accused of having satirised Iran's prime minister. The story of Hajji Baba revolves around the son of a barber from Isfahan who goes through ups and downs in the course of his life, working in many jobs and travelling to distant lands. Since it lacks a coherent plotline, each chapter can be read on its own as a separate adventure. Kamshad singles out two books that appeared at the beginning of the Constitutional Revolution and which, he argues, 'greatly influenced the coming events, the awakening of the people, and the literary revival' (2011: 17). One is *Siyāhat-nāma-ye Ebrāhim Beg* (Travelogue of Ibrāhim Beg); the other is *The Adventures of Hajji Baba, of Ispahan*.

It has become a cliché to argue for the crucial influence that this translation exerted at the time, both in terms of its stylistic characteristics and its political and oppositional stance. As Haddadian-Moghaddam rightly suggests, 'for Esfahani, the Persian translator, the ethics of political progress were higher than the ethics of fidelity to the foreign text as one way to exercise his agency in exile' (2011: 59). Kamshad goes so far as to claim that, '[s]ocially and politically the book had an immense influence on the awakening of the people and on bringing forth the [Constitutional] Revolution' (2011: 26). *Hajji Baba* had many themes that were of interest to Iranian political exiles, including its criticism of Iranian society and the Iranian state. This led readers to contrast Iran with countries such as Turkey and Britain, often to the detriment of Iran. As mentioned previously, clandestine political meetings of Iranians in exile 'provided the settings for the reading of texts such as *Hajji Baba* within the context of a political reformist discourse' (Rastegar 2007: 143).

Hajji Baba can be considered as a milestone in Iranian translation history because of Esfahani's agency and awareness of the influence that translations exerted on Iran's public discussion and culture, and the way that translation served as a means to criticise institutional power. Esfahani's translation method 'allowed him to amplify the meaning, intensify the corruption of the ruling class, and the rampant poverty and religious demagoguery of the time in Persia' (Haddadian-Moghaddam 2014: 76). Both within the court and within the broader Iranian cultural community, the importance of translations was recognised, and both sides were acutely aware of their power and effect.

Translation was also employed as a tool against tyranny in the years leading up to Iran's Constitutional Revolution. Notable translators of this era include Talibov Tabrizi (translation and exposition of Japan's Meji constitution), Mirza Fath ʿAli Akhundzadeh (self-translator of Maktubat), Mirza Aqa Khan Kermani (incomplete translation of Fenelon's *Télémaque* along with translations of parts from Bernardin de Saint Pierre's *Le café de Surat* in *Haftād-o-do mellat*), and Mirza Malkam Khan (translations of parts of

Mill's *On Liberty*) (Parsinejad 2003). Adamiyat examines Abd al-Husayn Mirza-ye Qajar's translation of Syrian writer and political reformer Abd al-Rahman al-Kawakibi's influential work, *The Nature of Despotism and the Struggle Against Enslavement* (1900). In the preface to this translation, the translator explicitly claims that his aim in translating this important political work was 'awakening the people and inciting them … to progress and civility' (Adamiyat 1985: 317).

From the very beginning of Iranian modernity, translation had a strong presence in the Iranian political scene and played a formative role in shaping political discourse. Odabaei (in Ansari 2016) demonstrates the crucial impact of the vocabularies imported through translations on the formation of new discourses which in turn generated new identities. He notes how terms such as 'liberty [*horiyat*],' 'constitutionalism [*mashruteh*],' and 'fraternity [*okhovat*]' were introduced into the Iranian political vocabulary at a crucial point in the country's history through the process of translating texts from European nations.

Many scholars have discussed the role of intellectuals in contemporary Iran, and have reflected on the formation and origins of these intellectuals. Notable among these are the studies of Mirsepassi (2000) and Gheissari (2010). Both of these scholars acknowledge the crucial role that translations played in the overall development of Iranian intellectuals; for instance, Mirsepassi takes into account the fact that Iranian intellectuals became familiar with the modern world 'particularly through translations of European texts' (2000: 56). But it strikes one as an odd case to see that translations are being discussed without there being any trace of translators. That is to say, in none of these accounts are translators deemed notable enough to be included for extended discussion. These scholars take the fact of translators for granted, but in doing so, they risk effacing a critical professional class who through their translation work paved the way for both formation and articulation of new discourses throughout society. Apart from this outright negligence, some even go as far as criticising the flow of translation from the west as a cause of an 'inferiority complex' among Iranians due to their illogical 'expectations concerning the actual and potential functions of the translated ideas and texts' (Gheissari 1998: 52). According to Gheissari, one of the outcomes of a strong flow of translations from the west was a gradual development of 'a metaphysic of translation among the intelligentsia' in relation to 'the status of the text and all the expectations surrounding it' (1998: 52). In stark contrast to this, we argue that, among Iranian translators, the source text was only one component in the overall apparatus of a final book, and through their prefaces, footnotes, commentary, and manipulations, these translators were used to making the translation utterly fit within the Iranian context. Thus, notions such as fidelity to the source text or loyal translation were not foremost concerns in their practices. Furthermore, to say that the expectations of both the intelligentsia and the people from these translations were unjustified is also, in our opinion, a claim rooted in the political and historical realities of Iranian society. Also, through adopting Gramsci's concept of Organic Intellectuals, and thus considering translators as a sub-class of Iranian intelligentsia, we will emphasise the dissident nature of their practices.

Politics, power, and committed literature in Iran, 1930s–1979

In 1937, following the passage of a law against 'collectivist' organisations that decreed that membership in certain groups could result in prison terms of up to ten years, many of Iran's leftist activists were arrested and tried. Notable among them was the legendary group, called the Fifty-Three (*Panjāh-o se nafar*), which included political activists such as Taqi Arani, Ehsan Tabari, Iraj Iskandari, and the writer Bozorg Alavi. One of the charges laid against them was 'translating such "atheistic tracts" as Marx's *Das Kapital* and the *Communist Manifesto*' (Abrahamian 1982: 155). These translations were undertaken within a group formed around the Iranian Marxist paper *Donya*. Prior to their arrest, a series of Marxist texts such as the *Communist Manifesto* and a May Day pamphlet were published anonymously in 1936 in Tehran. It is believed that Arani was the translator behind those texts (Jalali 2018: 220). Iraj Eskandari, in his 1970 translation of Marx's *Das Kapital*, points to the fact that on many occasions there were discussions between him and Taqi Arani on the necessity of translating Marx's oeuvre (13). In the very same preface, Eskandari asserts that '[t]he dictatorial regime of Reza Shah, through abandoning democracy, dissolving of all progressive political parties and groups along with establishment of police state, hindered the translation and composing of [Marxist] works' (Eskandari 1970: 12). Eskandari writes that he began translation of *Das Kapital* in the summer of 1935; however, in 1937, while a good proportion of the translation was finished, he was arrested and the work remained incomplete (Eskandari 1970: 14). After his release from prison, due to the fact that the previous translation was lost, he embarked on translating the book once again.

The 1941 Anglo-Soviet invasion of Iran saw British and Soviet troops occupying southern and northern Iran respectively. Three weeks after this invasion, Reza Shah (1878–1944), who had become Shah of Iran in 1926, establishing the Pahlavi dynasty to succeed the Qajars (1789–1925), abdicated and was forced into exile in Johannesburg, South Africa. He was succeeded by the crown prince, Mohammad Reza Pahlavi. The abdication of Reza Shah in 1944 and the vacuum of power that followed put a temporary end to two decades of suppression and dictatorship. The nucleus of the Fifty-Three fed into the Tudeh party of Iran, which quickly became active in Iran's political scene. With its rising popularity among the masses as well as the urban middle class, many intellectuals became sympathisers with this political movement. As Abrahamian notes, many members of the Tudeh were 'the country's intellectual luminaries' (Abrahamian 2018: 113).

According to Abrahamian (1982: 165), the fall of Reza Shah marked the beginning of an era of 'the politics of social conflict,' in part caused by the sudden emergence of previously oppressed political organisations. One of these political organisations was Iran's communist party, the Tudeh Party of Iran (1941). The ycars 1941–1953 (1953 was the year of the US-led coup against Iran's Prime Minister Mossadegh) were the apex of activities by communist and Marxist groups in Iran. The Tudeh can be considered as the mainstream communist party of Iran through until the early 1970s. Its presence in labour organisations and trade unions also attracted a large number of sympathisers (Abrahamian 1999: 81). The demise of Tudeh was mainly due to the adoption of alternative strategies by a new and younger generation of dissidents; in the 1970s mainstream opposition groups were guerrilla fighters who had a disdain for concepts such as political struggle and parties. Thus, while some were still insisting on the necessity of political struggle, others embraced armed-struggle tactics as the quickest way to undermine the regime's authority. Despite these internal differences, the Iranian left played a key role in '[providing the] ideas which fuelled the [Iran's 1979] Revolution' (Mirsepassi 2000: 160).

The left in Iran in this period (through to the 1979 revolution) comprised diverse groups and changed across time. In fact, as Gheissari and Nasr note, 'there were all strands of leftist ideas extant in Iran,' including 'Marxist-Leninists, Trotskyites, and Maoists' (2006: 82). Mirsepassi (2000: 161) usefully distinguishes four distinct phases of the history of the left in Iran. The first period from 1906 to 1937 is distinguished by 'a militant, revolutionary communist movement' which came to an end with Reza Shah's ascendancy to power (1926–1941). The second period from 1941 to 1953 was 'the interregnum between the two dictatorships,' in which the Tudeh revived itself, bolstered by its Soviet links. The 1953 CIA-sponsored coup against Prime Minister Mohammad Mossadegh marked the end of this second phase. The third period from 1954 to 1970 was when the Tudeh Party and labour unions were suppressed and banned, as the regime of Mohammad Reza Shah strengthened its grip on power through massive modernisation projects and close ties with the US. The fourth period from 1970 to 1978 is distinguished by the rise of leftist groups such as Organization of Iranian People's Fedaian, who were 'espousing armed struggle against the Pahlavi regime as the regional pillar of U.S. imperialism.'

The years 1941 to 1953, ending with the coup, are thus considered by many as a decade marked by the explosion of translated works. Writers and translators seized the opportunity to publish works in line with their own political commitments and beliefs. Fani describes this period as 'a phenomenal juncture of translation history,' in which literary translations increased public awareness of political issues (in Khojaste Rahimi and Shabani 2010: 49). Consequently, '[m]uch of Iranian literature became a *littérature engagée*' (Mozaffari 2005: 3) Leftist translators began translating politically committed literature (Talattof 2000: 4) on a vast scale. Chief among the literary writers whose works were translated were Maxim Gorky and Bertolt Brecht.

One of the most critical events of modern Iranian literature that took place in this period was the formation of the First Iranian Writers Congress (Nakhostin kongera-ye nevisandegān-e irān) in 1946, initiated by the Iranian Cultural Association and the Soviet Union with the assistance of the literary branch of the association. Seventy-eight Iranian writers, poets, and translators were invited to this event. The guest list included the poet laureate Mohammad-Taqi Bahar, Nima Yushij, Bozorg Alavi, Sadeq Hedayat, Sadeq Choubak, Ali-Akbar Dehkhoda, Ehsan Tabari, Mahmoud E'temadzadeh (Behazin), and Abd al-Hossein Noushin. Each person presented their work to the audience, and critical issues relating to Iran's literature were discussed and disputed. The overriding atmosphere of the program was the espousal of leftist political ideas in the literary world. This can be demonstrated through the themes of the presentations, which revolved around freedom, justice, and the condition of the poor within Iranian society. The event ended with a five-point manifesto. The first point stressed the importance of 'advocating rightness and justice, and opposition to oppression' and 'fighting against the foundations and remnants of fascism' (Nakhostin kongera-ye nevisandegān-e irān 1978 [1947]: 303). As Talattof (2000: 68) posits, this event facilitated 'the dissemination of Marxist literary theory and the upsurge of committed literature.'

Due to the political, cultural, and sociological conditions of the time, literature was frequently employed in service of political aims. As Talattof (1996: 124) argues, literary works were the most important medium through which political groups could reach their audience. According to him, literature 'was the single medium capable of presenting ideas to the dissatisfied public' (1996: 124). Yet, while Talattof demonstrates the crucial role of literature at this time, he neglects to focus on translation and translators. With the growing presence of censorship after the 1953 coup, translations became much more common in the Iranian literary field. They created the channels through which politically sensitive material was circulated. Translators justified such publications by calling them foreign accounts that had nothing to do with the Iranian situation.

In 1951, Mohammad Reza Shah, following the rise of a series of political pressures, appointed Mohammad Mossadegh as prime minister of Iran. Mossadegh sought to increase the power of parliament and Iran's control over its oil resources. Mossadegh passed the nationalisation of oil bill into law immediately after he gained his office. Britain in particular was unhappy with this, and it was eventually decided that the only viable last option was ousting Mossadegh (Gasiorowski 1987). Eventually, Anglo-American cooperation between the CIA and MI6 in an operation codenamed Operation Boot on the British side and TPAJAX on the American side resulted in the 1953 Iranian coup and overthrow of Mossadegh. (Abrahamian 2013).

Print propaganda was crucial to the way US influence was wielded within Iran after the coup. Materials were 'written by CIA propaganda specialists and translated into Persian' (Gasiorowski 2013). Translation and book publishing became part and parcel of the US propaganda war against communists and communism in Iran. The crucial strategic value of Iran, the fierce confrontation of the superpowers in the Middle East, and the dominance of communism among a notable portion of Iranian political activists, all contributed to a war of propaganda. Translation played a key role for both sides and occupied a central place in their projects.

After the 1953 coup, the Shah took centre stage in Iran's political and cultural scene. He was admired by the Americans for the 'resolute attitude Iran [is] taking vis-à-vis communists' (Alvandi 2016: 19). The best illustration of the Shah's determination to suppress communist opposition was the establishment of Iran's notorious secret police, SAVAK (Sāzemān-e Ettelā'āt va Amniyat-e Keshvar), a highly sophisticated secret service formed under the guidance of the CIA and trained by Mossad, Israel's intelligence service. SAVAK became omnipresent in all spheres of Iranian life. Many Iranian authors, artists, and translators at some point in their careers wound up in the Shah's prisons, and some were severely tortured and even beaten to death (Abrahamian 1999).

SAVAK's concern with intellectual life led to its meddling in the literary sector, and thus it eventually became one of the main censorship agencies, the other being the Composition Bureau of the Ministry of Culture and Art (Edāre-ye Koll-e Negāresh-e Vezārat-e Farhang va Honar) (Boroujerdi 1996: 49). The publishing industry in Iran was also politicised, as all books were scrutinised lest they criticised the Shah or commented negatively on the country's political situation. Reza Baraheni (a world-renowned Iranian writer), Mahmoud Dowlatabadi (an Iranian novelist), Gholam-Hossein Saedi (Iranian playwright, 1935–1985), and Mahmoud E'temadzadeh (Behazin, see discussion below) were among the most notable literary activists who were arrested. Torture rose dramatically 'in scope, intensity, variety, and sophistication' (Abrahamian 1999: 105). A harrowing account of the Shah's prisons can be found in *God's Shadow: Prison Poems* (*Zel Allāh: She'r-hā-ye zendān*) (1976) based on renowned Iranian writer Raza Baraheni's 102 days of solitary confinement and torture.

The dominance of SAVAK's censorship apparatus in the publishing field forced writers to use symbolic language so that they could escape the grip of censorship and convey their resentment of the Shah's tyrannical regime. As Sandler notes, writers often 'made use of allegory and symbolism and allusion, even vague writing that could be taken in a hundred different ways, to say what they had to say' (1986: 249). Also, as Boroujerdi observes, the reader 'is struck by the amount of symbolism, allegory, metaphor, and allusions used to avoid the institution of censorship' (1996: 48, 49) in the literature of the 1960s and 1970s. Samad Behrangi's *Māhi Siāh-e Kuchulu* (*The Little Black Fish*) (1968) is a prime example of a text that employed allegory and metaphorical language to address the political issues of the time. In this short story an old fish recounts the story of a small black fish to her 12,000 children, in which the little fish despite all the pressures of her environment embarks on going from the small stream in which she is living towards the sea on her own. Throughout this journey, the little fish encounters several characters such as a lizard and a pelican. The lizard gives a knife to the little black fish and instructs her on how to escape from the pelican. Overall, the allegorical aspects of the story can be interpreted as a defence of armed struggle in the face of tyranny.

It was within this context that Iranian literature reached the apex of an ideological phase (extending from the 1940s to 1979) that has been referred to as 'committed litera-ture [*adabiyāt-e mota'ahed*]' (Talattof 1996: 3). According to Shamisa, a prominent Iran-ian literary critic, the term *ta'ahod* has its roots in Jean-Paul Sartre's concept of engagement (Shamisa 2006: 406). However, as Alavi notes, 'the idea that literature, and especially poetry, should serve "the people" in their struggle against oppression was articulated in Iran before the publication of Sartre's essays' (2013: vii, viii).

In the second part of this chapter, we considered how nineteenth- and twentieth-century translators in Iran paid special attention to the political ramifications of their translations and attempted to choose works in line with their political ideology. We could argue that this was the inception of a 'committed literature,' and that it was through translations that the concept of literature in the service of the people could be realised. Early-twentieth-century translations in Iran played a key role in sowing the seeds of an idea that was to blossom much later. There is no doubt that the theoretical underpinnings of committed literature were nourished later by Marxist aesthetics but this should not lead one to exclude earlier attempts by Iranian intellectuals to fuse political and literary themes in their output.

Translators as organic intellectuals

As the preceding account of the early development of translations in Iranian society has demonstrated, many translations became political by disrupting the dominant discourses of the time. Along with showing that translators in Iran have been in the vanguard of change in shaping the dominant discourses of society, we argue here that they have also been organic intellectuals.

To elucidate the role of translators who generated an alternative political vision through their translations, we draw on the concept of organic intellectuals put for-ward by Gramsci in his *Prison Notebooks* (also see Wróblewska (Chapter 2), in this volume). In 'The Formation of the Intellectuals,' Gramsci asks a pivotal ques-tion: 'Are intellectuals an autonomous and independent social group, or does every social group have its own particular specialised category of intellectuals?' He fur-ther asserts,

> every social group, coming into existence on the original terrain of an essential function in the world of production, creates together with itself, organically, one or more strata of intellectuals which give it homogeneity and an awareness of its own function not only in the economic but also in the social and political fields.
>
> *(Gramsci 1971: 5)*

Gramsci's concept of the organic intellectual helps us see how translators in Iran were attempting to articulate certain worldviews that aimed at forming and consolidating the political hegemony of their own class.

Within the difficult political context of the Shah's regime, many translators began to translate texts with explicit and implicit leftist themes. The core group of writers, dedicated to committed literature, were mostly leftist sympathisers. This was in part because the very foundations of their committed approach to literary activity had its roots in Marxist aesthetics. The leftist literati naturally had a keen interest in committed international writers. Writers such as Mikhail Sholokhov, Maxim Gorky, Romain Rolland, Bertolt Brecht, and Pablo Neruda became some of the acclaimed and commonly translated authors of this generation.

Perhaps the strongest demonstration of the committed approach to literature was the formation of the Writers' Association of Iran (*kānun-e nevisandegān-e irān*) in 1968. This came about in response to a government initiative that aimed at convening major Iranian writers, poets, and translators through a 'Congress of Iranian Writers and Poets.' Many of the Iranian literati refused to take part in the program (Karimi-Hakkak 1985: 193). As a result, the idea was abandoned. Following this victory, writers who had protested convened independently and conducted the first meeting of the Writers' Association of Iran. The members of the first executive board were Simin Daneshvar, Mahmoud E'temedzadeh (Behazin), Nader Naderpur, Siyavash Kasra'i, and Daryoush Ashouri (Karimi-Hakkak 1985: 195). This was the first time that a coherent bloc of writers had convened to discuss the important issues affecting intellectuals. They also issued a statement protesting the censorship apparatus, the regime's interference in publishing, and the lack of freedom to express ideas. Among the themes discussed, they highlighted 'the meaning of freedom, the social stance of the writer, and the necessity of committed literature' (Boroujerdi 1996: 49).

As Stuart Hall aptly argues, 'the organic intellectual cannot absolve himself or herself from the responsibility of transmitting those ideas, that knowledge, through the intellectual function, to those who do not belong, professionally, in the intellectual class' (1992: 281). This transmission of knowledge, at the time of Mohammed Reza Shah and after the coup, was mainly conducted through translation work. Shamlu translated the novel *Barefoot* by Zaharia Stancu (*Pā-berehnegān* 1948), a renowned Romanian socialist realist writer; Behrangi translated (*Mā olāgh-hā* 1965) the work of Aziz Nesin, a famous Turkish leftist writer; Iraj Eskandari translated Marx's *Das Kapital* (first two volumes published in 1970 and 1974 respectively; Sarmayeh), and Shari'ati translated Frantz Fanon (Davari 2014: 89).

For some of the most famous translators in contemporary Iran, the act of translating was a quintessential part of resisting the regime. By way of elucidating what Tymoczko describes as 'translations that rouse, inspire, witness, mobilise, and incite to rebellion' (Tymoczko 2014: 213), we argue that, for Iranian leftist translators, the very act of translation was synonymous with a praxis that in its purest and strongest form aimed at bringing about change and strengthening the articulation of alternative political discourses.

At the same time as these leftist translators were undertaking such work, the Shah's regime was collaborating with FBP, a US-sponsored book translation and publishing program (Haddadian-Moghaddam 2016; Laugesen 2017), to counter any influence from leftist and communist translations. A division developed that separated Iran's committed literati from those who limited themselves to mere formal and aesthetic experiments in translation. For those who worked with FBP and the Shah's regime in this work, translation was theorised as a tool in service of the country's development and progress. For example, Fakhr-al-Din Shadman, a government minister and an intellectual who also undertook some translation, urged that translations be made of both modern and classical Greek and Latin works so that Iranians could become familiar with what he called the 'principles of Western civilization' (Shadman 1948: 109). As we'll see below, the Shah's regime used translation as a means of reinforcing its ties with the US, and hence consolidating its propaganda efforts within Iranian society. We therefore now turn to a discussion of translation and the FBP, followed by a consideration of an important leftist Iranian translator, Behazin, to demonstrate how translation interacted with political power under the Shah.

Franklin Book Programs

FBP was a US-funded book translation and publishing program set up in 1953 (the same year as the overthrow of Mossadegh) to publish American books in translation in a number of different countries, starting with books translated into Arabic produced in Egypt. The books the FBP published complemented translations produced by the United States Information Agency (Cull 2008), but the goal was to produce books with local endorsement and sponsorship and to focus on books that were less stridently anti-communist and more likely to be of greater relevance and interest to local audiences (Laugesen 2017: 2).

The FBP opened an office in Tehran in 1954 to publish books in Persian. Drawing on the expertise of US publishers who helped to negotiate the translation rights and who provided advice and training, the Tehran office was run by an Iranian businessman, Homayoun San'ati. The FBP quickly established itself in the Iranian cultural scene, producing a variety of American books in translation, from textbooks to Louisa May Alcott's *Little Women* (1868) and E.B. White's *Charlotte's Web* (1952). It received the financial support and patronage of the Shah, who used American Cold War strategic concerns to secure US aid in a range of areas (Laugesen 2017: 105). In addition, the FBP assisted in developing a publishing infrastructure, including assisting in the building of a printing plant and training editors, as well as experimenting with bookselling techniques.

By 1961, the FBP's Tehran office had produced 250 translations. According to San'ati, these represented about 50% of all translations into Persian from all sources, and about 25% of all new books published during 1954–1961 (FBP archives, Minutes, Franklin 1961: 4). Translators and intellectuals who worked with Franklin included such notable figures as 'Ali Akbar Siassi (psychologist and former Minister of Education), Muhammad Hejazi (novelist and playwright), Ebrahim Khajenoori (one of Iran's foremost translators), S.R. Shafaq (literary critic), Ehsan Yarshater (historian and linguist), Najaf Daryabandari (writer and translator who later became known for translating William Faulkner), and Mohammed-Ali Jamalzadeh (writer). Texts ranged from American literature, such as Willa Cather's *My Ántonia* (1918), William Faulkner's *Unvanquished* (1938), and John Steinbeck's *The Moon is Down* (1942), to practical non-fiction such as J.R. Gallagher's *Your Children's Health* (1953) and Bertha Morris Parker's *Electricity* (1957), a basic science education book. Politicians often translated (or, more likely, had their names attributed as translators on) a range of texts. For example, Ahmed Mateen Daftari, a former Iranian prime minister, translated Arthur Nussbaum's *A Concise History of the Law of Nations* (1958).

Publications translated and produced by FBP-Tehran shored up the US–Iran diplomatic relationship, while also impacting Iranian culture. Haddadian-Moghaddam has concluded that 'Franklin introduced a narrow form of world literatures into local cultures' (2016: 386), an accurate observation. Importantly, this publishing program guaranteed an increased dominance of American books in translation, as opposed to French, British, or German texts. In 1956, for example, it was noted that an FBP publication had won a prize for the best translation into Persian: George Sarton's *The Life of Science: Essays in the History of Civilization* (1948), translated by Ahmad Birashk. Imperial Court prizes were given to FBP translations of Charles W. Leonard's *Why Children Misbehave* (1952, translated by I. Ahmad Saidi), and B. Pazargad's translation of *Contributions to Political Theory*. Datus Smith, head of the FBP's New York office, notes that he found this

> especially gratifying because the prizes, which attracts as much attention as Pulitzer Prizes do with us, have heretofore reflected the French bias of Persian culture. Only very rarely have they gone to translations from English, and never before to a book of American origin.
>
> *(FBP archives, Smith Memorandum 1956)*

In addition, the FBP's American publishers saw the goal of the organisation's work to be, at least in part, the possibility of future commercial opportunities in the region. The FBP's work in translation was for the Americans thus as much an exercise in cultural and commercial imperialism, as it was in cultural diplomacy.

In the early 1960s, the Shah proclaimed a reform program, including land reform and redistribution, known as the 'white revolution [*Enqelab-e sepid*].' Although the Shah claimed the project was a purely Iranian-motivated endeavor, in reality there was pressure from the US to modernise as a means of undercutting the attractions of communism (Rahnema and Behdad 1996: 21). Titles produced by the FBP often focused on non-fiction works that were considered to reflect the state's modernising agenda. As Ansari argues, the Shah was keen to identify his government with progress, including a focus on programs around education and literacy in which books played an important role (2003: 13). From the US perspective, the relationship with the Shah benefited American strategic interests while promoting a model of modernisation that also transmitted American values and fitted with American interests. Books produced by FBP-Tehran for schools included Raymond F. Yates, *Atomic Experiments for Boys* (1952), Herman Schneider, *Your Telephone and How It Works* (1965), and Ewen Montagu's *Helping Children Develop Moral Values* (1953) (FBP archives, San'ati to Smith 1960). Adult books included books such as *Industrialism and Industrial Man*, by Clark Kerr, John T. Dunlop, Frederick H. Harbison, and Charles A. Myers (all noted professors of economics and/or industrial relations), described by the FBP as 'a clear and informative analysis of the problems of labour management in the industrial societies of the world, and in the societies that seek to industrialize themselves' (FBP archives, Notes). Seyyed Hassan Taqizadeh, president of the Iranian senate (1957–1960), was contracted to translate and write an introduction for Joseph Garland's *The Story of Medicine* (FBP archives, United States Information Agency 1955). In addition, the FBP worked to buttress the Shah's Iranian literacy program, the 'Army of Knowledge [*Sepāh-e dānesh*],' providing reading material for new literates.

Translations also helped to make tangible representations of the American–Iranian relationship: Mohammed Reza Shah's name was attached to a biographical chapter on his father Reza Shah for the Persian edition of Sarah K. Bolton's *The Lives of Poor Boys Who Became Rich and Famous* (an anthology of biographical sketches of historical figures who went from rags to riches), and the Shah's twin sister, Princess Ashraf, was cited as translator of Benjamin Spock's *Baby and Child Care*. The FBP were equally careful not to promote texts that might have success in their other translation programs if they were not appropriate for Iran. For example, in 1955 it was noted by the FBP that while a book such as Hildegarde Hawthorne's biography of American revolutionary Tom Paine might work well in Egypt, it would be unacceptable in Iran because of its anti-monarchical subject matter (FBP archives, Draft Memorandum 1955: 6).

Translated texts were subject to various adaptations to make them more suitable to the needs of the regime. In producing textbooks for the Iranian education system, translations were made of American texts, but parts of the text were substituted with Iranian material produced by a joint American–Iranian team (FBP archives, Smith to James L. Meader 1957). Prefaces and introductions written by notable Iranian intellectuals and political figures also were common. What exact adaptations were made are not easily traceable in the archival record, although there are a few traces. In the case of Bolton's book, mentioned above, biographical sketches deemed to be of less interest to a particular audience were replaced by locally written and relevant choices. More generally, it was noted that FBP adaptations needed 'discretion as well as imagination' (FBP Annual Report 1962: 9).

Ebrahim Khajenoori, deputy to four prime ministers, translated John F. Kennedy's *Profiles in Courage* as Kennedy ran for the White House—for both countries the translation was seen to have value. Kennedy was noted as being interested in the work of the FBP and described as being 'very, very eager to make friends and influence people' (FBP archives, Laughlin 1960). Other books promoted particular political agendas consonant with American perspectives on politics. Najaf Daryabandari, who was employed as an editor with Franklin, worked on the Persian translation of William L. Shirer's *The Rise and Fall of the Third Reich*, which Daryabandari thought

> provided the Persian intelligentsia with a much needed analysis of the Nazi movement which had, before and during the war, its sympathizers in this country too. What pleases me most about the success of the Shirer book is that I think it washes away the residue of the Nazi legend which I am sure has been lurking somewhere in the minds of those who once sympathised with Hitler. This is no small service on the part of Franklin.
>
> *(FBP archives, Daryabandari to Smith 1965)*

The FBP's work, therefore, served to further the goals of the Shah's regime, while also serving the needs and aims of the US during the Cold War. It had the effect of bringing American books in translation into the Iranian cultural sphere, and, perhaps, shaping political, social, and cultural discourse. It also worked to shore up the impression that Iran was open to outside ideas and to culture generally. At the same time, oppositional ideas were suppressed, and opportunities for either Iranian literature or the literature of other countries to find their way into circulation were curtailed. We now turn to discussing an example of a 'committed' Iranian translator who used translation to challenge the Shah's regime.

Mahmoud E'temadzadeh (Behazin)

In order to offer a fuller picture of the politics of translation during the Pahlavi regime, it is essential to highlight the neglected 'committed' translations undertaken by oppositional figures, especially leftist ones. We now take a brief look at the translations of one of the most prominent Iranian translators, whose every translation was intended to raise political awareness among readers. Mahmoud E'temadzadeh (also known as Behazin, 1915–2006) was an Iranian author, translator, and political activist. As one of the most prominent Iranian translators, Behazin's translations were closely linked to his broader agenda of propagating leftist ideals of justice and freedom. Unlike those translators who worked with FBP, and hence were enjoying high rates of payment, foreign travel (such as Daryabandari's nine-month visit to Switzerland on behalf of Iran's Franklin branch—see Mozaffari-Savowji 2009: 90), and book publications, translators on the left who were fighting against the Shah's dictatorship and the suppression of freedom were always on the brink of being sentenced to exile and prison. Referring in his autobiography to the Association of Writers of Iran, known for its oppositional stance against the Shah's regime, Behazin derided FBP as 'the American establishment of Franklin' (Behazin 2008: 34).

Behazin's two-volume book, *Az har dari* (*From Here and There*) (1991), bearing the subtitle *Political-Social Biography* (*Zendegi-nāma-ye siyāsi ejtemā'i*), is in itself a testament to the scope of his political views. Given that European translation scholars during the past three decades have attempted to bring the figure of the translator and his subjectivity to the fore through discussions on, for example, visibility, it may be surprising to see that Iranian translators have published books and commentaries about themselves and their political views. We do not place an anachronistic 'translator as activist' label on to these figures—rather, this was how they thought about themselves and their cultural role and identity.

In a small essay, written in 2010 in *Chista* magazine, Behazin wrote that 'access to French translations of Marxist classics proved to me the necessity of fighting against plunder, injustice, corruption of world capitalism, and Iranian feudalism' (E'temadzadeh 2010: 39). Behazin decided to join what he called the 'vanguard political party of the time': the Tudeh Party. Despite his membership in Tudeh, he insisted on his own agency in what and how he translated, asserting that he never received translation briefs from the party, 'except for one case in the translation of *Strategy of Revolutionary War in China*.' Behazin further reflects,

> the writers that I have been successful in translating, despite all the differences in style and theme of writings, have all looked at the fate of humanity with sympathy and have attempted to find solutions for this fate; they have all called for social justice, freedom, and equality either explicitly or implicitly.
>
> *(E'temadzadeh 2010: 40)*

Behazin clearly asserted that his literary output, including his translations, was not separate from his overall political activism: 'My political-social activities have always gone hand in hand with my literary writings, and there has never been a separation between them' (E'temadzadeh 2010: 44). As one of the main members of the Association of Writers of Iran, Behazin was arrested in 1969 and imprisoned for four months. Later, while recounting the interrogations to which he was subjected, he commented:

> The military prosecutor believes that the concept of enticement to take up arms is not limited only to actual weapons. Rather, any spoken or written statement can provide a context for the opposition because it arms them against the state.
>
> *(cited in Karimi-Hakkak 1985: 202)*

Prison and torture were the cost of Behazin's political activities and translations.

One of the first translations by Behazin was Balzac's *Père Goriot* (1834) (*Bābā goriyo* 1954); as is well known, Balzac has always been a favorite author of Marxist critics as he was a favorite of Marx himself (Prawer 2014: 181). Behazin also translated part of the oeuvre of Romain Rolland, whose works have been among the most widely read and praised translations of all time in Iran. As an example of 'great revolutionary literature,' Rolland's *L' âme enchantée* (1922) (*Jān-e shifteh* 1976) made resistance to fascism central in its narrative, characters, and unifying vision and was the most potent anti-fascist novel of the early 1930s (Fisher 2017: 147, 170). Fisher provides a detailed analysis of the novel and its apparent Marxist themes. He writes: 'The first hypothesis of the novel was the neo-Marxist one that "the entire capitalist regime of this degenerated bourgeoisie" was indissolubly bound up with the origins, popularity, and continuance of fascism' (2017: 171).

Two other famous books belonging to the socialist realist genre and translated by Behazin were Mikhail Sholokhov's *And Quiet Flows the Don* (1928) (*Don-e ārām* 1967) and *Virgin Soil Upturned* (1932). According to one Russian critic, *Virgin Soil Upturned*'s 'strongest point was the presence of a dominant idea—the transformation of a village of small property owners into a socialist village—that gave unity to the novel's form and ideological content' (Ermolaev 1982: 33). In his ten-page preface to the translation of *Virgin Soil Upturned*, Behazin situated the critical issues of the novel within the socio-political order of Iran and emphasised those aspects of the novel that would provide readers with insights and experiences of other people into the mechanisms of fighting and resisting the dominant order:

> For us, Iranian readers, especially at this time of transformation of economic bases and consequently, social ones, and also necessities of evolving along the lines of global pressures that are aimed at tearing apart the traditional forms and replacing them with new modes of production, *Virgin Soil Upturned* could illuminate many issues and therefore, deserves a critical reading.
>
> *(E'temadzadeh 1968: 13)*

As suggested by the above reflections, one of the key features of modern translation in Iran has been this omnipresent paratextual preface, dedicated solely to the thoughts and reflections of the translator. This has been even more the case with translators with political leanings. Behazin, too, harnessed the potential of the preface to draw his readers' attention to ongoing upheavals within Iranian society that came with the dispossession and disorientation that accompanied modernisation and industrialisation.

Behazin's legacy of the 'committed translator' today remains alive within Iran's literary field. In January 2015, *Bokhara* magazine commemorated Behazin's centenary birthday in which prominent figures such as Touran Mirhadi (an Iranian educator and author), Mahmoud Dowlatabadi, and Shams Langroudi (a contemporary Iranian poet) recounted their memories from Behazin and his translations.[1] His life, translations, political activities, and resistance testify to the crucial role played by translator activists like him throughout the Pahlavi dictatorship.

Gramsci's notion of organic intellectuals with its insistence on the existence of clear-cut relations between the intellectuals and the classes they represent or adhere to provided us with the critical sociological perspective to analyse the role of translators as intellectuals in Iranian society. Further studies on whether this analysis could be applied to the role of translators in other societies or not can contribute to a more comprehensive analysis of translation and activism throughout history.

Related topics

The Political Modes of Translation in Iran; Theory, Practice, Activism; Late-Qing Translation (1840–1911) and the Political Activism of Chinese Evolutionism.

Note

1 The video of this gathering can be found here: www.youtube.com/watch?v=Hgi_156FNeQ

Further reading

Laugesen, Amanda (2017) *Taking Books to the World: American Publishers and the Cultural Cold War*. Amherst: University of Massachusetts Press.

This is the first book-length study of the Franklin Book Programs activities, including their work in Iran and in translating and publishing work in various countries during the Cold War period.

Karimi-Hakkak, Ahmad (1985) 'Protest and Perish: A History of the Writers, Association of Iran,' *Iranian Studies* 18 (2–4): 189–229.

This article provides a brief account of the Writers' Association of Iran, and highlights the issues over which intellectuals and the Shah's regime were opposed to each other. BehAzin's role in reviving the association's activities is also discussed.

Francese, Joseph (ed.) (2009) *Perspectives on Gramsci: Politics, Culture and Social Theory*. London: Routledge.

A general collection of papers on Gramsci. The concept of 'organic intellectuals' is employed in some of the chapters. Especially relevant is 'Sinking Roots Using Gramsci in Contemporary Britain' by Kate Crehan.

References

Abrahamian, Ervand (1979) 'The Causes of the Constitutional Revolution in Iran,' *International Journal of Middle East Studies* 10 (3): 381–414.
Abrahamian, Ervand (1982) *Iran between Two Revolutions*. New Jersey: Princeton University Press.
Abrahamian, Ervand (1999) *Tortured Confessions: Prisons and Public Recantations in Modern Iran*. Berkeley, CA: University of California.
Abrahamian, Ervand (2013) *The Coup: 1953, the CIA, and the Roots of Modern US-Iranian Relations*. New York: The New Press.
Abrahamian, Ervand (2018) *A History of Modern Iran*. Cambridge: Cambridge University Press.
Adamiyat, Fereydun (1985) *Ideoloji-ye nehzat-e mashrutiyat-e irān* (The ideology of constitutional movement in Iran). Tehran: Payam.
Adamiyat, Fereydun (1975) *Amir kabir va irān (Amir Kabir and Iran)*, 2 Vols. Tehran: Kharazmi Publishing House.

Adamiyat, Fereydun (1992) *Ide'oloji-ye nehzat-e mashrutiyat-e irān, majles-e aval va bohrān-e āzādi (The Ideology of the Iran's Constitutional Movement, the First Parliament and the Crisis of Freedom)*. Tehran: Rushangaran.

Afshar, Iraj (2003) 'Book Translations as a Cultural Activity in Iran 1806–1896,' *Iran* 41 (1): 279–289.

Alavi, Samad Josef (2013) 'The Poetics of Commitment in Modern Persian: A Case of Three Revolutionary Poets in Iran,' PhD dissertation, UC Berkeley.

Alvandi, Roham (2016) *Nixon, Kissinger, and the Shah: The United States and Iran in the Cold War*. New York: Oxford University Press.

Amanat, Abbas (1993) 'Russian Intrusion into the Guarded Domain: Reflections of a Qajar Statesman on European Expansion,' *Journal of the American Oriental Society* 113 (1): 35–56.

Amanat, Abbas (1997) *Pivot of the Universe: Nasir al-Din Shah Qajar and the Iranian Monarchy, 1831–1896*. Berkeley: University of California Press.

Ansari, Ali M. (2003) *Modern Iran since 1921: the Pahlavis and After*. London: Longman.

Aqa Khan Kermani, Mirza Abdo'l-Hoseyn (1924) *Haftād-o-do melat*. Berlin.

Azadibougar, Omid (2010) 'Translation Historiography in the Modern World: Modernization and Translation into Persian,' *Target. International Journal of Translation Studies* 22 (2): 298–329.

Azarang, Abdolhossein (2015) *Tārikh-e tarjoma dar irān (The History of Translation in Iran)*. Tehran: Qoqnoos.

Bakhtiyar, Mozaffar, and Hoda Arabzadeh (2009) 'Dār-al-tarjoma-ye nāserī va edāre-ye sānsur [Court Translation Center and Censorship Bureau],' *Adab-e Farsi* 1 (2): 16.

Balay, Christophe (1998) *Peydāyesh-e romān-e fārsi (La genèse du roman persan moderne)*. Tr. M. Ghavimi and N. Khattat. Tehran: Moeen.

Baraheni, Reza (1976) *God's Shadow: Prison Poems*. Bloomington, IN: Indiana University Press.

Boroujerdi, Mehrzad (1996) *Iranian Intellectuals and the West: The Tormented Triumph of Nativism*. Syracuse, NY: Syracuse University Press.

Chesterman, Andrew (2009) 'The Name and Nature of Translator Studies,' *HERMES-Journal of Language and Communication in Business* (42): 13–22.

Cholokhov, Mikhaïl (1968) *Zamin-e Noābād*. Tr. Mahmoud E'temadzadeh. Tehran: Nil.

Cull, Nicholas John (2008) *The Cold War and the United States Information Agency: American Propaganda and Public Diplomacy, 1945–1989*. Cambridge: Cambridge University Press.

Davari, Arash (2014) 'A Return to Which Self? 'Ali Shari'ati and Frantz Fanon on the Political Ethics of Insurrectionary Violence,' *Comparative Studies of South Asia, Africa and the Middle East* 34 (1): 86–105.

Delisle, Jean, and Judith Woodsworth (2012) *Translators through History* (revised edition). Amsterdam and Philadelphia: John Benjamins Publishing.

Ermolaev, Herman (1982) *Mikhail Sholokhov and His Art*. Princeton, NJ: Princeton University Press.

Eskandari, Iraj (1970) *Sarmāyeh*, Vol. 1. Liepzig: Tudeh.

E'temadzadeh, Mahmoud (Behazin) (1991, reprinted 2008) *Az har dari (From Here and There)*. Tehran: Dustan pub.

E'temadzadeh, Mahmoud (Behazin) (2010) 'Sokhani az Behazin [A Short Piece by Behazin],' *Chista* 28 (275): 724, 731.

Fisher, David (2017) *Romain Rolland and the Politics of the Intellectual Engagement*. London: Routledge.

Gasiorowski, Mark J. (1987) 'The 1953 Coup d'etat in Iran,' *International Journal of Middle East Studies* 19 (3): 261–286.

Gasiorowski, Mark J. (2013) 'The CIA's TPBEDAMN Operation and the 1953 Coup in Iran,' *Journal of Cold War Studies* 15 (4): 4–24.

Gheissari, Ali (1998) *Iranian Intellectuals in the Twentieth Century*. Austin, TX: University of Texas Press.

Gheissari, Ali (2010) *Iranian Intellectuals in the Twentieth Century*. Austin: University of Texas Press.

Gheissari, Ali, and Vali Nasr (2006) *Democracy in Iran: History and the Quest for Liberty*. Oxford: Oxford University Press.

Gould, Rebecca Ruth, and Kayvan Tahmasebian (forthcoming) 'Translation as Alienation: Sufi Hermeneutics and Literary Modernism in Bijan Elahi's Translations,' *Modernism/Modernity*.

Gramsci, Antonio (1971) *Selections from the Prison Notebooks of Antonio Gramsci*. Ed. Hoare, Quintin and Geoffrey Nowell Smith. New York: International Publishers.

Haddadian Moghaddam, Esmaeil (2011) 'Agency in the Translation and Production of the Adventures of Hajji Baba of Ispahan into Persian,' *Target. International Journal of Translation Studies* 23 (2): 206–234.

Haddadian-Moghaddam, Esmaeil (2014) *Literary Translation in Modern Iran: A Sociological Study*. Amsterdam and Philadelphia: John Benjamins Publishing Company.

Haddadian-Moghaddam, Esmaeil (2016) 'The Cultural Cold War and the Circulation of World Literature: Insights from Franklin Book Programs in Tehran,' *Journal of World Literature* 1 (3): 371–390.

Hall, Stuart (1992) 'Cultural studies and its Theoretical Legacies', *Stuart Hall: Cultural Studies*. Eds. L. Grossberg, C. Nelson, and P. Triechler, New York: Routledge. 277–294.

Jalali, Younes (2018) *Taghi Erani, A Polymath in Interwar Berlin: Fundamental Science, Psychology, Orientalism, and Political Philosophy*. Cham, Switzerland: Springer.

Kamshad, Hassan (2011) *Modern Persian Prose Literature*. Cambridge: Cambridge University Press.

Karimi-Hakkak, Ahmad (1985) 'Protest and Perish: A History of the Writers' Association of Iran,' *Iranian Studies* 18 (2–4): 189–229.

Khojaste Rahimi, Reza, and Maryam Shabani (2010) 'Noqte-ye 'atf frānklin bud na mashruteh : Bāz khāni-ye masir-e tārikhi-ye tarjome-ye irāni bā hozur-e Kamran Fani, Khashayar Deyhimi va Farrokh Amirfaryar [The turning point was Franklin not Constitutional Revolution; A Revision of the historical trajectory of translation in Iran with Kamran Fani, Khashayar Deyhimi and Farrokh Amirfaryar],' *Mehrnameh* 7: 45–51.

Kia, Mehrdad (2001) 'Inside the Court of Naser od-Din Shah Qajar, 1881–96: The life and Diary of Mohammad Hasan Khan Eʿtemad os-Saltaneh,' *Middle Eastern Studies* 37 (1): 101–141.

Kinnunen, Tuija, and Kaisa Koskinen (2010) *Translators' Agency*. Tampere: Tampere University Press.

Laugesen, Amanda (2017) *Taking Books to the World: American Publishers and the Cultural Cold War*. Amherst: University of Massachusetts Press.

Lawrence, Tanya Elal (2018) 'The Iranian Community of the Late Ottoman Empire and the Egyptian 'Crisis' through the Persian Looking Glass: the Documentation of the ʿUrabi Revolt in Istanbul's Akhtar,' *Iranian Studies* 51 (2): 245–267.

Letter, Henry Laughlin to Datus Smith, May 12, 1960, Box 10, Folder 14, FBPR

Minutes of Franklin Board of Directors (January 26, 1961) p. 4, Box 1, Folder 4, FBPR.

Mirsepassi, Ali (2000) *Intellectual Discourse and the Politics of Modernization: Negotiating Modernity in Iran*. Cambridge: Cambridge University Press.

Mozaffari, Nahid (2005) *Strange Times, My Dear. The Pen Anthology of Contemporary Iranian Literature*. New York: Arcade.

Mozaffari-Savowji, Mehdi (2009) *Goftogu bā Najaf Daryabandari (An Interview with Najaf Daryabandari)*. Tehran: Morvarid.

Nakhostin kongera-ye nevisandegān-e irān (1978 [1947]) Tehran: Anjoman-e Ravabet-e. Farhangi-ye Iran va Ettehad-e Jamahir-e Showravi-ye Sosiyalisti.

Odabaei, Milad (2016) 'Shrinking Borders and Expanding Vocabularies: Translation and the Iranian Constitutional Revolution of 1906,' in *Iran's Constitutional Revolution of 1906 and Narratives of the Enlightenment*. Ed. Ali M. Ansari. London: Gingko Library. 98–115.

Parsinejad, Iraj (2003) *A History of Literary Criticism in Iran, 1866–1951: Literary Criticism in the Works of Enlightened Thinkers of Iran—Akhundzadeh, Kermani, Malkom, Talebof, Maraghe'i, Kasravi, and Hedayat*. Bethesda, MD: Ibex Publishers, Inc.

Prawer, Siegbert Salomon (2014) *Karl Marx and World Literature*. London: Verso.

Rahnema, Saeed, and Sohrab Behdad (1996) *Iran after the Revolution: Crisis of an Islamic State*. New York: IB Tauris.

Rastegar, Kamran (2007) *Literary Modernity Between the Middle East and Europe: Textual Transactions in 19th Century Arabic, English and Persian Literatures*. New York: Routledge.

Sandler, Rivanne (1986) 'Literary Development in Iran in the 1960s and the 1970s Prior to the 1978 Revolution,' *World Literature Today* 60: 249.

Shadman, Seyyed Fakhr al-Din (1948) *Taskhir-e tamadon-e farangi (Defeat of Western Civilisation)*. Tehran: Chapkhaneh-ye Majles.

Shafiee Kadkani, Mohammad Reza (2011) *Bā cherāq va āyineh: Dar jostoju-ye risha-hā-ye tahavol-e she'r-e mo'āser-e irān (With the Lamp and the Mirror: In Serach of the Roots of Change in Contemporary Poetry of Iran)*. Tehran: Entesharat-e Sokhan.

Shamisa, Sirus (2006) *Naqd-e Adabi* (2nd ed.). Tehran: Mitra.

Talattof, Kamran (1996) 'Ideology of Representation: Episodic Literary Movements in Modern Persian Literature,' PhD dissertation, University of Michigan, Ann Arbor, MI.

Talattof, Kamran (2000) *The Politics of Writing in Iran: A History of Modern Persian Literature*. Syracuse, NY: Syracuse University Press.

Tymoczko, Maria (2000) 'Translation and Political Engagement. Activism, Social Change and the Role of Translation in Geopolitical Shifts', *The Translator* 6 (1): 23–47

Tymoczko, Maria (2006) 'Translation: Ethics, Ideology, Action,' *The Massachusetts Review* 47 (3): 442–461.

Tymoczko, Maria (2014) *Enlarging Translation, Empowering Translators*: London: Routledge.

Vejdani, Farzin (2014) *Making History in Iran: Education, Nationalism, and Print Culture*. Stanford, CA: Stanford University Press.

Yaghmaee, Eghbal (1970) 'Madrasa-ye Dār-al-fonun [School of Dar-al-funun],' *Yaghma* 23 (264): 361–366.

Documentary data cited

Darybandari, Najaf to Datus Smith. 14 July 1965, Box 239, Folder 10, Franklin Book Program Records, 1920–78, Public Policy Papers, Department of Rare Books and Special Collections, Seeley G. Mudd Library, Princeton University (hereafter FBPR).

Draft Memorandum on Relations between Franklin Publications, Inc and USIA, 15 March 1955, Box 5, Folder 6, FBPR.

Franklin Annual Report for the Year Ending 30 June 1962. FBPR.

Franklin Publications, 'Local Participation by Civic and Intellectual Leaders,' 2 January 1958, Box 5, Folder 4, FBRP.

Notes on Industrialism and Industrial Man, Box 205, Folder 12, FBRP.

Smith, Datus to Franklin Board of Directors. 20 March 1956, Box 5, Folder 5. FBPR.

United States Information Agency, Franklin Publications in Tehran, 14 January 1955, Franklin Book Programs, Box 66, Folder 19.

12

Translating for *Le Monde diplomatique en español*

Disciplinary norms and activist agendas

Tania P. Hernández-Hernández

Introduction

Activists aim at changing the social space. Accordingly, activist media and journalism comprise media and journalism that 'generally engage in some sort of structural analysis concerned with power and the reconstitution of society into more egalitarian arrangements' (Huesca 2000: 31). Activist practices and products revolve around three elements: (1) engaged individuals; (2) defended causes; and (3) activist organisations (Vendramin 2013). News outlets that identify as activist media or that support activist causes offer unique contexts for studying the interaction between these three elements.

This chapter examines the monthly *Le Monde diplomatique* (*LMd* henceforth), a French left-wing periodical established in Paris in 1954. *LMd*'s activist agenda, trajectory and practices have included publishing and translating in-depth articles on issues and world regions that have usually been ignored by the French mainstream press (Harvey 2010, 2014a) as well as the participation of prominent members and contributors of *LMd* in activist forums, associations and publications. Since the late 1970s, *LMd* has consistently launched foreign editions with the aim of disseminating, via translation, the content and editorial line of the French edition. With time, the growing presence of *LMd* in the international journalistic field has positioned translation as an instrumental practice and translators as crucial agents in the international dissemination of its articles.

In this chapter, *LMd* and the four Spanish editions selected are considered as an activist organisation in which translation and the individuals responsible for this practice are essential for the circulation of the causes defended by the French monthly. In particular, I focus on the translators of four foreign Spanish editions of *LMd* published in Mexico City (three) and Buenos Aires (one). As will be illustrated later, some translators have also produced and circulated their own activist causes. I will argue that the profile of the translators as well as their reasons for translating for this periodical have changed from an amateur activism to a more institutionalised one. I selected these editions because they have played a central role in the translation and distribution of the content of the

French edition of *LMd* in the Spanish-speaking Latin American countries. The data analysed has been secured from ten semi-structured interviews conducted by the author of this chapter with translators, editors and chief editors of the editions under scrutiny; and through documentary research conducted in libraries and personal archives.

Le Monde diplomatique: overview of an activist periodical

As communication technologies emerge and consolidate, the production, dissemination and consumption of the news become more international. Tempted by the possibility of widening their audiences, while maintaining the loyalty of their readers abroad and disseminating their editorial line among new readers, some media groups have ventured to launch news media products whose content has been tailored to cater to a new readership. This has been the case of *The International Herald Tribune*—rebranded as *The International New York Times* since 14 October 2013 (Schmemann 2013)—the *Spiegel Online International*, *CNN* (Valdeón 2006) and *LMd* to name a few.

These and other international ventures of different media have propelled the interaction between the local and the global, the use and consolidation of certain languages—e.g. English, French, Spanish and Arab—as linguae franca (Gutiérrez 2006), hence leading to the consolidation of translation as the sine qua non of the global circulation of the news. This, however, is not to say that such status is acknowledged. Moreover, translation and translators are rendered invisible either through the domestication of the source text (Venuti 1995) and, within the context of media, through the assimilation of translation to the practice of journalism (Bielsa and Bassnett 2009). In this regard, Bielsa and Bassnett (2009) argue that the ways in which translation, news and the involved agents interact in news agencies posit a challenge to the traditional concepts of 'translation,' 'text,' 'translated text,' 'translator' and 'authorship.'

Furthermore, Bielsa (2007) contends that news products are inseparable from journalistic practices; and that, more often than not, news agencies specialise in the provision of international news. In this context, translation is not perceived as a separate practice from journalism; accordingly, translation is done mostly by journalists. They are the ones who, along with editors and other journalistic agents, are responsible for translating, editing, selecting and rewriting. News agencies and foreign correspondents are central to the production and circulation of international news. A significant number of these products involve translation, as agencies provide them to different linguistic settings. News agencies are also important as they sometimes are the 'first to approach and describe new realities, creating ways of addressing them and introducing new vocabulary to represent them' (Bielsa 2007: 146). Although news agencies, as well as foreign correspondents, are very visible and active agents in the international news network, other actors may emerge to try to contest both the centrality of agencies and the narratives they circulate. As described in the following section, this was the case with *LMd* and some of the individuals who have participated in its consolidation and international dissemination.

Consolidation and internationalisation of LMd's activism

LMd is a political left-wing French monthly published in Paris since May 1954. As the choice of the word 'diplomatique' might suggest, *LMd* was originally addressed to the diplomatic elites (*LMd* 1954). Thus, the content included diplomatic developments, books and the analysis of issues pertaining to the African, Asian and Latin American regions. Nowadays, *LMd* is defined as a 'French monthly specialising in international politics having a "radical-left wing" editorial line' and that 'has been involved with some activist movements since the 1990s' (Harvey 2010: 298). This idiosyncrasy has been and remains central to *LMd*'s agenda since it was first released. However, the emphasis of these features has varied over the decades, in keeping with the four editors who have directed *LMd*: François Honti (1954–1973), Claude Julien (1973–1990), Ignacio Ramonet (1990–2008) and Serge Halimi (2008– present).

Since its early years, *LMd* has strived to assert its independence from political agents in the French context and as it presents itself as a platform providing extensive and critical scrutiny of socio-political issues (Harvey 2010). To succeed in this goal, *LMd* should strike the right balance between the depth of coverage and the monthly's capacity to keep up to date with events. Being a monthly newspaper, it is necessary to ensure that news stories remained topical until the publication of the next issue. The emphasis on reflection over instant reporting has continued to shape the practices of *LMd*'s contributors and staff—understood as the set of institutional practices they have internalised within *LMd*'s newsroom—up to the present day. Even in the current media landscape, characterised by intense global interconnectedness and the heightening of global consciousness (Bielsa and Bassnett 2009), contributors of *LMd* are more likely to focus on those issues and events that, more often than not, are ignored by mainstream media (Harvey 2009, 2014a).

LMd remains true to its foundational principles as a whole, albeit the publication has changed its agenda and priorities with each president. François Honti, a Hungarian journalist, was the first editor of *LMd*. The truth was that Honti was the only member of the staff of *Le Monde* exclusively dedicated to *LMd*: most of the articles published in *LMd* were written by journalists of the international section of *Le Monde*. On the other hand, the fact that diplomats and foreign affairs officials represented a large percentage of its target audience is mirrored in the vast coverage of diplomatic appointments and events. Additionally, the international events were selected according to their relevance to French political issues. As a result, during Honti's tenure as chief editor, *LMd* echoed the editorial line of *Le Monde* which, at the time, was perceived as Eurocentric and Franco-centric (Harvey 2014). Honti was the head of *LMd* for seventeen years. He retired in 1973 and was replaced by an experienced French journalist at *Le Monde* called Claude Julien.

Julien began working for the international section of *Le Monde* in 1951. He became the editor of this section in 1969. In 1971, Julien took a sabbatical, and when he returned in 1973, instead of re-joining the staff of *Le Monde,* he was appointed as chief editor of *LMd*. In 1982, he became the editor of *LMd*; he held this position until 1990. It was under Julien's tenure that *LMd*'s editorial line acquired its distinctive activist and critical tone, particularly towards the role of mainstream media (Harvey 2010). During his editorship, *LMd* effectively ceased to operate as a supplement of *Le Monde*. The nationalist bias that impregnated the pieces written by the journalists of *Le Monde* was hardly compatible with the type of symbolic capital that Julien was seeking. Julien sought to provide *LMd* with economic and editorial independence and, thus, position it as a leading and autonomous publication in the field of opinion journalism. As part of this positioning strategy, Julien promoted what is currently described as the 'internationalisation' of *LMd* (Vidal 2006).

In *LMd*, internationalisation has been a twofold process. Firstly, the articles of the staff of *Le Monde* were gradually replaced by articles written by foreign contributors, because Julien considered that critical views on specific foreign policies, political actors or events were bound to be more effective and legitimate if they were articulated from the inside, that is, by authors born or based in the country whose policies or issues were being criticised (Harvey 2009). Conversely, in this volume, Shwaikh illustrates how the stories told by Palestinian journalists, activists and translators are modified to conform to a certain editorial line or agenda (see Chapter 8). In this regard, however, *LMd* has consistently utilised foreign contributors; in that way, critical views on specific foreign policies, political actors or events are bound to be more effective and legitimate as they are articulated from the inside, that is, by authors born or based in the country in question. In sum, although the translation of news generally follows 'the pace of global commerce' (Orengo 2005: 171), within the *LMd* editions, translation is paced by a different rhythm.

Secondly, aiming to introduce the content of *LMd* into other countries, Julien also encouraged the launch of foreign editions of *LMd*. The progressive shift of influence from French international correspondents to foreign contributors allowed *LMd* to: (1) gradually become emancipated from *Le Monde*; (2) embrace a more leftist editorial line with a sharper focus on third-world issues; and (3) boost its circulation by presenting itself as an innovative or unorthodox publication. In fact, *LMd* registered a dramatic growth: between 1973 and 1990, its circulation rose from 50,000 to 150,000 copies (Peigne-Giuly 2005). On the other hand, by enlisting the services of foreign contributors across the world, translation soon became a central process in the production and publication of *LMd*, as not all of these contributors were able to write in French. Despite this, the professional identity of the translators, and the fact that the text offered to the reader might be a translation is rarely shown in the print or electronic version of the French edition of *LMd*. Julien's arrival and the subsequent changes were mirrored in a new graphical layout, the reorganisation of the newspaper sections, more diversity in terms of topics (cinema, economics, society) and growing attention to Latin America (Ramonet 2005). The most significant achievements of Julien's tenure—a higher degree of independence and the launch of the internationalisation process—were further endorsed under the presidency of the Spanish journalist and intellectual who would follow Julien, Ignacio Ramonet.

In 1990, Ignacio Ramonet was appointed as editor of *LMd*. Under his editorship, the French monthly entered its most radical and activist period since it was launched, and supported liberation movements that stand against imperialism, neoliberalism, media empires and the dissemination of the 'single thought' (Ramonet 1995) and that contribute to ideological diversity and to the construction of 'a different world' (Ramonet 2003). Nonetheless, other types of activism such as feminism have struggled to access the pages of *LMd* (Harvey 2014b). The Zapatista movement, World Social Forum (WSF) and Association for the Taxation of Financial Transactions and for Citizens' Action (Association pour la Taxation des Transactions financières et pour l'Action Citoyenne, henceforth, ATTAC) have frequently been covered by *LMd* during Ramonet's term. In a few words, the Zapatista movement is a social and armed movement that groups Mexican indigenous people from the South of Mexico to stand against the Mexican government's neoliberal policies and to fight for the recognition of their autonomy, rights and their culture (Rovira 2015). Since its emergence on 1 January 1994, Zapatistas have featured in the pages of *LMd* a number of times. For example, in March 2001,

Ramonet's editorial 'Marcos marche sur Mexico [Marcos marches on Mexico City]' covered the journey of the Zapatista Army of National Liberation to the Mexican capital (Ramonet 2001). Over the years, Zapatismo has lost momentum and, consequently, its news value has also been affected. Nonetheless, *LMd* still devotes at least one article to Zapatismo every year (LMd 2019).

In the late 1990s and early 2000s, Ramonet, along with other editors, translators and contributors of the foreign editions of *LMd*, were also actively involved in the organisation and coverage of the WSF, an annual meeting founded in 2001 to stand against the World Economic Forum. When the first forum was launched, Ramonet was at the head of the French and Spanish editions of *LMd*. The main goal of the WSF has been to provide a space where as many individuals as possible can 'discuss and learn from each other experiences' (Ekman 2011: 31). According to Ramonet, the 1990s were devoted 'to defining globalization,' an essential step 'to figuring out the entity to be fought against' (Sin permiso e Ramonet 2008; my translation). The second phase, once globalisation was defined as a common enemy for activists from both the Global North and South, led to the emergence of the WSF. However, once framed within the limits of the forums, the movement lost visibility in the media and, to a large extent, it also lost momentum. In an interview, Ramonet argued that one of the obstacles standing in the way of the development of social movements, including the WSF, was the difficulties in finding effective ways of creating a 'reticular network' (Sin permiso e Ramonet 2008; my translation) that would facilitate the articulation of common causes. In any case, however, after Ramonet's term, the visibility of the WSF decreased significantly. During his term, *LMd* published a total of 105 articles related to the WSF; from 2009 to 2018, there have been only 35 articles.

The radicalisation of the editorial line of *LMd* during the golden age of the anti-globalisation movement led some members and contributors of *LMd* to establish ATTAC in June 1998. The rationale for the creation of this association dates back to an editorial article published in December 1997 called 'Disarming the Markets' (Ramonet 1997). Financial globalisation, Ramonet argues, has created a supranational state articulated around institutions such as the International Monetary Fund, the World Bank, the Organisation for Economic Cooperation and Development and the World Trade Organization. Therefore, *LMd* readers should organise themselves to oppose the effects of this development (Ramonet 1997).

Bernard Cassen, general director of *LMd* and co-founder of ATTAC, acknowledges that *LMd*'s initiative, i.e. the foundation of ATTAC, allowed the movement against neoliberal globalisation to crystallise in France (Cassen 2003). However, it also led to growing ideological confrontations which were finally resolved when Serge Halimi was unanimously elected as editor in December 2007. Unlike Ramonet, by the time Halimi joined *LMd*, he was already a respected scholar, author and specialist regarding internal and external policy matters in the United States. More widely, his left-left-wing position provided him with a ruthless will to fight against the forces of the neoliberal empire. He also had a well-known critical stance towards print media, as manifested in the book *Les Nouveaux chiens de garde* (*The New Watchdogs*) (Halimi 2005), and his contributions to the French association, Action-Critique-Médias, and political newspapers *and* magazines such as *Pour lire pas lu* (*To Read not Read*), *Plan B* and *Le Canard enchaîné* (*The Chained Duck*). On the other hand, his mother was Gisèle Halimi, a prestigious and feminist militant lawyer, as well as a sporadic *LMd* contributor. When Ramonet decided not to run for another presidential term, a number of candidates were considered. The reputation of Halimi within print journalism might have been perceived as a possibility to reorient the editorial line of *LMd* and overcome the crisis derived from Ramonet's resignation as president of the French edition of *LMd* as well as both the internal ideological turbulences and the economic difficulties of the publication. Although under Halimi's editorship some of the causes pursued by Ramonet have lost momentum, *LMd* maintains its 'radical left-wing editorial line' (Harvey 2010: 298).

The foreign editions of LMd

As indicated in the previous section, Ramonet was a key actor in the development and consolidation of *LMd*'s activist and critical journalism. An endeavour to internationalise their editorial line and to make the content of this monthly available to a non-French readership accompanied this positioning. This internationalisation process led the editors of the monthly to favour the participation of foreign contributors and to encourage the launch of foreign editions worldwide and, as illustrated in the following section, these editions have often been published by journalists or intellectuals who present themselves as activists. The first foreign editions date back to the mid-1970s, and new ones continue to be launched. By 2019, there were 29 foreign editions (LMd 2019)—25 printed and four digital-only editions—and it was translated into 18 languages, including German, English, Arabic, Bulgarian, Esperanto, Finnish, Greek, Hungarian, Italian, Japanese, Korean, Kurdish, Norwegian, Persian, Polish, Portuguese, Serbian and Spanish.

The foreign editions are diverse in terms of format and content; however, their content has been mostly composed of a combination of translated articles of the French edition and of locally produced articles. Inasmuch as the editions of *LMd* analysed in this chapter are published on a monthly basis and comprise an average of 70 per cent of translated texts (Hernández-Hernández and Gabetta 2012), it seems reasonable to posit that the status and roles of both translation and the individuals responsible for carrying it out are different from those observed in other media.

The centrality of translation and translators within *LMd*'s foreign editions is illustrated by the composition of the staff which, depending on the edition, will include a translators' coordinator or a group of translators. This has led to a division of the tasks that is not frequently observed within printed media. Hence, while traditionally, within newsrooms, journalists or editors translate texts without considering themselves as translators (Bielsa and Bassnett 2009), the translators of or for *LMd* are practically devoted to translating the articles produced by the French edition. Selection does occur, as not all the articles published by *LMd* are considered relevant for all the foreign editions. This selection is usually the responsibility of the editor or the editorial board of the foreign editions. In addition to translating, some foreign editions also produce local articles; however, these are rarely published in the French edition. To the best of my knowledge, the English edition of *LMd* is the only foreign edition whose articles are frequently translated and published by the French edition. In any case, however, these articles do not mention the name of the translator, and they only acknowledge the name of the authors and their edition of affiliation. In this regard, it is interesting to mention that a few articles of Carlos Gabetta and José Nathanson (editors of the Argentinean edition of *LMd* from 1999 to 2011 and from 2011 respectively) addressing local political issues have been published in *LMd*. However, most of these articles have been written specifically for the French edition. The circulation via translation of articles within *LMd*'s circuit could thus be considered as a one-way street, which, amongst other things, entails a certain control on both the way certain topics are represented as well as on the topics that are covered by *LMd* and translated by its editions. This differs significantly from other activist translators like those analysed in the chapter on the Sunflower Student Movement in Taiwan (see Chapter 30), where the horizontal structure that characterised their involvement gave these translators the possibility to act with great freedom to select and translate other perspectives that were being neglected or suppressed by the Taiwanese government and the local press.

The translators of the Hispanic Latin American *Monde diplomatique*s: activist agendas versus disciplinary norms

Throughout its process of internationalisation, foreign editions of *LMd* have emerged in various Spanish-speaking countries: Argentina, Bolivia, Chile, Colombia, Mexico, Peru, Spain and Venezuela have each hosted at least one edition of *LMd* in the last 18 years (Hernández-Hernández 2015, 2017). In fact, except for two brief periods (from 1976 to 1979 and from 1990 to 1993), there has consistently been at least one foreign edition of *LMd* translated and published in Spanish. The variety of *LMd* editions available in Spanish opened up ample opportunities for research on *LMd*'s internationalisation in Latin America.

After interviewing a range of participants, it became apparent that studying only those editions that have actively engaged in the translation of the content of the French edition of *LMd* would provide insight on the evolution of translators' trajectories and practices. Thus, a final decision was then made to cover only three Mexican editions: *Le Monde diplomatique en español* (1979–1987, hereafter referred to as *LMd-Spanish 1*), *Le Monde diplomatique en español* (1986–1988, hereafter referred to as *LMd-Spanish 2*), *Le Monde diplomatique edición Mexicana* (1997–2002, hereafter referred to as *LMd-Mexican*); and one Argentinean edition: *Le Monde diplomatique edición Cono Sur, el Dipló* (1999–present, hereafter referred to as *Dipló*); and to explore these editions through semi-structured interviews and documentary data.

The participants were selected based on their participation in the selected editions. Before starting the interview, interviewees were asked to sign a participation consent form. The interviews were conducted face to face, by telephone or via Skype. Likewise, some interviewees were asked further questions via email. As all the interviews were conducted in Spanish, the analysis is based on the Spanish transcription of the conversations. Where appropriate, the analysis includes excerpts from these interviews. To facilitate the reading, I have translated these excerpts into English. Table 11.1 compiles the names of the Latin American editions and the interviewees referred to in this chapter.

Political exiles as translators

According to a draft of the contract between the representatives of *LMd* and *LMd-Spanish 1*, the editor of the Mexican edition was granted 'the exclusive rights to publish *Le Monde diplomatique en español* and distribute it in the Americas, Spain and other countries' (Julien and Fasano 1981). This contract also allowed the Mexican editor to discard the publication of those sections that 'may not be of much interest for the target readership ("Revue des Revues," reviews of books and events …)' (Julien and Fasano 1981) and 'to publish or not, partially or completely, the section "Activities of

Table 11.1 Interviewees per edition and position occupied

Publication period	Full name of the edition	Interviewees and position occupied within the edition
1999–present	*Le Monde diplomatique, edición Cono Sur, el Dipló*	Former editor: Carlos Gabetta Translator and translators' coordinator: Marta Vassallo
1979–1987	*Le Monde diplomatique en español*	Managing editor: Antonio Tenorio Translator: Alejandro Katz Translators' coordinator and contributor: Eduardo Molina
1986–1988	*Le Monde diplomatique en español*	Chief editor: Erasmo Saénz Translator: Pilar Ortiz
1997–2002	*Le Monde diplomatique, edición mexicana*	Editor: Eda Chávez Translators: Irene Selser and Steven Johansson

International Organisations"' (Julien and Fasano 1981). The editor was also permitted to add a Latin American supplement composed of locally produced articles. The supplement, however, was not to exceed six pages. *LMd-Spanish 1* and its supplement, called 'América Latina sección especial de la edición en español [Latin America Special Section of the Edition in Spanish],' were published virtually without interruption from January 1979 to March 1987. In spite of this restriction, the publishing of the Latin American supplement materialised some of the aims of the internationalisation project of *LMd,* such as producing 'a newspaper of opinions, radically committed to the left and favourable towards Third-Worldism' (Harvey 2009: 86; my translation). Given that the contributors of the supplement were natives of the country whose regime was being criticised, their critique could be considered as more legitimate.

The coexistence of translated and non-translated texts in the pages of a foreign edition was a watershed in the internationalisation of the French edition. In this context, the role of translation in enabling the publication to import and export the prestige of *LMd* became less important. But, at the same time, this entailed the strengthening of writing as a tool to achieve autonomy, prestige and, most importantly, legitimacy in the field of Mexican journalism (Hernández-Hernández 2017).

LMd-Spanish 1 was edited by Federico Fasano, a Uruguayan journalist and former political exile. Other Latin American exiles who were living in Mexico to escape dictatorial regimes at the time were also involved in the translation and publication of this edition. For the translators' coordinator, the exiles' participation in *LMd-Spanish 1* was largely based on the editorial line of *LMd* and on the possibility of continuing with their political activities. 'Mexico was an oasis. I mean, it was our chance of survival, it even allowed us to be politically active in relation to our country [...] We could talk about military dictatorship, write, and launch publications' (Hernández-Hernández and Molina 2012). To a large extent, reflection and denouncement of the Argentinean dictatorship concentrated in the 'numerous, irregular and, most of the time, ephemeral periodicals' (Chioccheti 2010: 4; my translation) launched from exile, such as *Argentina. Boletín informativo* (Paris, 1980–1983), *Controversia. Para el examen de la realidad argentina y la revalorización democrática* (Mexico City, 1979–1981) and *Testimonio Latinoamericano* (Barcelona, 1980–1983). Overall, these printed materials were aimed at '"informing" and "disseminating" the Argentinean situation among the exiles and the host society' (Franco 2004; my translation). However, according to Alejandro Katz, former translator of *LMd-Spanish 1*, this publication occupied a somewhat marginal position in the debate about exile, 'when one revisits discussions about exile, about the experience of exile in any shape or form, there are no references to *Le Monde diplomatique* [*LMd-Spanish 1*]. It was very marginal from the point of view of exile' (Hernández-Hernández and Katz 2012).

In the opinion of Antonio Tenorio, managing editor of this edition, the government supported the introduction of *LMd* to Mexico in order to reduce the dependence on the information flow from the United States, rather than to help political exiles:

> At the time, Mexico depended greatly on the news produced in the United States. There were no other media. There were no other newspapers [...]. It [*LMd-Spanish 1*] was also a rich source of information for politicians and intellectuals [...] And, on the other hand, it was in Spanish and this was extraordinary. [...] I think that was the state's role and its interest. That is, to promote an independent outlet, other types of information, another opinion, that was the idea.
>
> *(Hernández-Hernández and Tenorio 2012)*

This excerpt stresses the state's interest in the development of the Mexican journalistic field and the strengthening of its editorial autonomy. In this scenario, it would seem reasonable to assume that the practice of translation, whose role was to import the editorial line as well as the prestige of the French edition, should be more appreciated than that of writing—considering that the Mexican edition was launched as a result of the internationalisation project of *LMd*. Nonetheless, the interview with the former translators' coordinator suggests that this was not always the case: 'In the South American section I had a lot of freedom, I wrote what I wanted, and I chose the contributors I wanted. No one ever told me what to do' (Hernández-Hernández and Molina 2012). This freedom to choose the contributors and the content of the supplement contrasts with the restrictions regarding the translated content, which entailed that even if Molina 'did not agree with everything that *Le Monde diplomatique* published' (Hernández-Hernández and Molina 2012), he had to translate all the articles.

Overall, the interviewees of this edition establish a relation between the writing of original articles and the accumulation of symbolic, social and cultural capitals on the one hand; and between the translation of French articles and the accumulation of economic capital on the other hand. *LMd-Spanish 1* emerged at an early stage of the internationalisation process of *LMd*. The production of its content brings to the fore the extent to which journalistic and translation practices intertwine in the production of news. Therefore, whether the readership was the main reason behind the inclusion of articles originally written in Spanish or not, the fact is that this became a distinctive feature that distinguished the Mexican edition from earlier international editions of *LMd*. In this regard, the first Mexican edition could be considered as a pioneer in a new stage of the internationalisation process of *LMd*. In this 'new' stage the dependence on the practice of translation is reduced by the possibility of producing original content.

Professional and amateur translators

In the second half of 1986, another edition of *LMd* called *Le Monde diplomatique en español* (*LMd-Spanish 2*), also translated and published in Mexico City, was launched by Iván Menéndez, a sociologist and an active member of the party in power. Before being appointed as editor of *LMd-Spanish 2* by the editors of the French edition of *LMd*, Menéndez also worked as chief editor of *LMd-Spanish 1*. The new publication emerged after the editors of the French edition of *LMd* decided to terminate the contract with *LMd-Spanish 1*, arguing that the quality of the translation and its print run were weak.

The translation of the content of *LMd-Spanish 2* was the responsibility of a group of translators who had followed translation training at El Colegio de México, a Mexican institution of higher education renowned for the quality of its teaching and research. Gradually, the discourse of political actions to overthrow authoritarian and dictatorial governments that dominated the Latin American political landscape was replaced by an emphasis on the professionalism involved in the translation and the writing of the articles. The chief editor of *LMd-Spanish 2* explained that translators were hired mostly because they had 'translated some books' (Hernández-Hernández and Sáenz 2012). This means that having relevant work experience was crucial in establishing who could become a translator of the new edition. This editor also mentioned that, in addition to the translators' experience, there were other internal mechanisms regulating the work of translators, such as general guidelines on how to translate the texts and meetings to discuss difficulties in the French texts. While the translator of this edition whom I interviewed, Pilar Ortiz, corroborated the existence of such meetings, she also explained that, due to time pressures, meetings with the chief editors to revise the translations were not very frequent and, more often than not, the discussions revolved around general issues that were not necessarily related to translation. The positive side of the lack of enforcement of a standardised set of rules to define the translators' professional behaviour was that, in the words of the translator, '[t]hey [the editors] had absolute faith in us [the translators]' (Hernández-Hernández and Ortiz 2012).

Although neither of the interviewees mentioned it explicitly, the editors' faith in the translators' competence may well have been the result of the recognition of the latter's capacities. In any case, the conflict between the editions of *LMd* was instrumental in bringing about the hiring of qualified translators. To be considered as a legitimate translator in *LMd-Spanish 2*, it was not enough to have an activist trajectory; instead, it was necessary to have cultural capital consisting of academic education and work experience, specifically as a translator. Hence, there was a need to establish and institutionalise what was considered as adequate in terms of translation practices (Noordegraaf and Schinkel 2011: 68).

On 6 November 1986, Iván Menéndez 'was found dead in the trunk of his car' (Los Angeles Times 1986). National and international media initially treated Menéndez's murder as a political crime, and as proof of the danger of being a journalist in Mexico. However, subsequent investigations suggested that his death was not motivated by Menéndez's involvement in domestic politics (De La Madrid and Lajous 2004). In August 1987, Gerardo Estrada, a Mexican scholar, was appointed as editor of this edition. In November 1988, the publication ceased to be published due to financial difficulties (Casa Editorial Raza Cósmica 1988).

It took almost a decade for a new edition to be published in Spanish in Latin America. Then, in July 1997, a Mexican left-wing journalist called Eda Chávez launched *Le Monde diplomatique edición Mexicana*, which was published until 2002 in Mexico City (Hernández-Hernández and Chávez 2012). In the case of this edition, the translation of the content of *LMd* experienced a significant change. From 1997 to 2000, the translations were carried out by translators based in Mexico City; then, from 2001 onwards, the translations were bought from the Argentinean edition. I interviewed two translators, Irene Selser and Steven Johansson, and the editor of this edition, Eda Chávez. Selser is a journalist, writer and, in her own words, a 'translator without a translation qualification' (Hernández-Hernández and Selser 2012). Born in Argentina, this interviewee studied French because it was part of the basic education curriculum. She arrived in Mexico at the age of 20 because her father Gregorio Selser, a prestigious journalist and historian, was forced into exile due to the dictatorship. As a journalist, she worked for a Nicaraguan news agency, for various Mexican newspapers and television channels and a political magazine called *Cuadernos del Tercer Mundo*. From 1998 to 2001, she worked as a translator of *LMd-Mexican*. She left that job to become the editor of the international section of *Milenio*, a Mexico City-based newspaper, where, for more than ten years, she translated international news and opinion articles published by the French press. She also continued translating literary texts and essays on international politics and joined the Mexican Association of Literary Translators (Asociación Mexicana de Traductores Literarios). During her time at *LMd-Mexican*, she was involved in translating as well as in coediting the monthly issue. Although this interviewee did not mention having any activist affiliation or any activist background before or during her time in this edition, her personal and professional biography indicates a particular penchant for left-wing political issues.

To some extent, Steven Johansson's career path as well as his personal trajectory have some features in common with those of Selser. Johansson is the son of a French academic who relocated to Mexico for work reasons. Born in Mexico City, this translator is bilingual in French and Spanish. He did not have any specific translation training when he joined *LMd-Mexican* as a translator; actually, it was his first job as a translator. He collaborated as a translator for almost three years. In the interview, Johansson mentioned that, due to the quality of the publication and its editorial line, he was not that upset when he was not paid for his job. In this regard, he added that he did not get paid for his first translations, and when he did get paid 'the remuneration did not match the job done, the retribution was something symbolic, very symbolic' (Hernández-Hernández and Johansson 2012). Like Selser, this interviewee did not link his involvement in *LMd-Mexican* with his activist views; in any case, his willingness to support the publication could be considered as evidence of his political commitment—that is, as some sort of left-wing journalistic activism. This interviewee stopped translating for this edition because, besides the irregular payments, *LMd-Mexican* started to buy the Spanish translations of *LMd* from the edition established in Buenos Aires in 1999.

The *Dipló* was directed by the Argentinean journalist and former member of the Ejército Revolucionario del Pueblo (People's Revolutionary Army), Carlos Gabetta, from 1999 to 2010. Gabetta began to collaborate with the French edition of *LMd* when he was exiled in Paris (Hernández-Hernández and Gabetta 2012). Gabetta's social and activist capitals were key for the foundation of an edition of *LMd* in Buenos Aires. Like most foreign editions of *LMd,* the *Dipló* started with a solid team of translators, whose translations have been bought and published by other Spanish Latin American editions such as the ones launched in Bolivia (2009), Chile (2000), Colombia (2002–2013), Honduras (2014–2016) and Peru (2007–2010).

From 2010 onwards the Argentinean journalist and political analyst, José Natanson, has directed the *Dipló*. In the first years of its existence, this edition was under the direction of Gabetta. At that time, the Argentinean writer, journalist, translator and feminist activist Marta Vassallo was responsible for coordinating the translation of the articles of the French edition. Vassallo was also the translator who translated the monthly editorial of *LMd*, and she authored a significant number of articles on different topics such as violence, economic inequality and especially on women's rights (Hernández-Hernández and Vassallo 2012). In 2007, Vassallo left the *Dipló* to coordinate a project on the policies of memory. Since then, the translations have been coordinated by other members of the staff whose trajectories have developed mostly in the journalistic and academic fields. In any case, the interviewee acknowledged that the translators had little or no influence on the edition or the publication of the texts they translate. Likewise, the number of translators who, in addition to translating, contribute with an original article has also reduced; this would suggest that the value attributed to their activist adscriptions or practices has also been affected.

Conclusion

This chapter has chronicled the history of *LMd* from the point of view of its positioning as an activist periodical. This account has brought to the fore the impact of the editors' activist practices and trajectories, particularly those of Ignacio Ramonet, on the editorial line and the position of *LMd* in the French and international journalistic fields. The chapter has also illustrated that the translation into Spanish of *LMd* could be divided into at least two stages. In the first stage, the translation of the articles was carried out by political exiles having an activist trajectory and linguistic resources; thus, in addition to participating in the translation and dissemination of *LMd* in Spanish, they were also able to capitalise on their involvement in the periodical by writing articles criticising the political regimes of their home countries. During the second stage, most of the individuals responsible for the translation still ascribe to the political and activist agenda of *LMd* but do not necessarily link their translation practice in the periodical to any sort of participatory activism. In any case, these different stages account for the diversity of causes that have and are still supported and promoted by the *LMd*'s editions.

Although the assessment of the impact of the activist practices of *LMd*, its foreign editions or, for that matter, of those who, in a more direct or indirect manner, belong to or contribute to this periodical still remains a pending issue; this chapter has illustrated that collective or individual causes are more easily disseminated when they are articulated within an organisation or an institution that identifies as either an activist agent or that subscribes to similar causes.

Related topics

Civil Resistance through Online Activist Translation in Taiwan's Sunflower Student Movement; Translating Mourning Walls.

Further reading

Bielsa, Esperança, and Susan Bassnett (2009) *Translation in Global News*. London: Routledge.

This book examines journalistic translation within international media from a sociological perspective. Thus, it provides insight on the conditions of production and circulation of international news products.

Harvey, Nicolas (2014) *Le Monde diplomatique: Un concept éditorial hybride au confluent du journalisme, de l'universalité et du militantisme*. Paris: L'Harmattan.

Based on his PhD thesis, in this book Harvey examines the evolution of activism within the French edition of *Le Monde diplomatique*. Although it does not directly address translation or translators, it does offer a thorough analysis of the history of this periodical and it also offers insight into the different activist causes that have been supported by this publication.

Matonti, Frédérique, and Franck Poupeau (2004) 'Le capital militant. Essai de définition,' *Actes de la recherche en sciences sociales* 5 (155): 4–11.

Drawing on Pierre Bourdieu's concepts of capital and its various forms, in this paper the authors offer a sound description of the concept of 'militant capital,' a concept that is useful to examine actions of individuals who do not belong to a party, organisation or group socially recognised as part of the political field.

References

Bielsa, Esperança, and Susan Bassnett (2009) *Translation in Global News*. London: Routledge.
Bielsa, Esperança (2007) 'Translation in Global News Agencies,' *Target* 19 (1): 135–155.
Cassen, Bernard (2003) 'On the Attack,' *New Left Review* 9: 41–60.
Champagne, Patrick (2000) 'Le médiateur entre deux *Monde*. Transformation du champ médiatique et gestion du capital journalistique,' *Actes de la recherche en sciences sociales* 131–132: 8–29.
Chioccheti, Magali (2010) 'Exilio, memoria e identidades políticas. La revista *Controversia. Para el examen de la realidad argentina* y la revalorización,' *Question* [online]. Available at: http://perio.unlp.edu.ar/ojs/index.php/question/article/viewArticle/992 [accessed 20 July 2019].
Ekman, Mattias (2011) 'Alternative Media in the World Social Forum,' in *Encyclopaedia of Social Movement Media*. Ed. John D. H. Downing. Thousand Oaks: SAGE. 30–33.
Franco, Marina (2004) 'Testimoniar e informar: exiliados argentinos en París (1976–1983), '*Les Cahiers ALHIM* [online]. Available at: https://journals.openedition.org/alhim/414#tocto1n2 [accessed 20 July 2019].
De La Madrid, Miguel, and Andrea Lajous (2004) *Cambio de rumbo. Quinto año de gobierno*, Vol. 5. Mexico City: FCE.
Gutiérrez, Miren (2006) 'Journalism and the Language Divide,' in *Translation in Global News, Proceedings of the Conference Held in the University of Warwick* [online]. Available at: https://bit.ly/2VjlCJu. 29–33 [accessed 20 July 2019].
Halimi, Serge (2005) *Les nouveaux chiens de garde*. Paris: Liber-Raisons D'Agir.
Harvey, Nicolas (2009) 'L'internationalisation du *Monde diplomatique*: entre 'cosmopolitisation' et homogénéisation éditoriale,' *Pôle Sud* 1 (30): 85–97.
Harvey, Nicolas (2010) 'Le Monde diplomatique (France/Transnational), 'in *Encyclopaedia of Social Movement Media*. Ed. John D. H. Downing. Thousand Oaks: SAGE. 298–299.
Harvey, Nicolas (2014a) *Le Monde diplomatique: Un concept éditorial hybride au confluent du journalisme, de l'universalité et du militantisme*. Paris: L'Harmattan.
Harvey, Nicolas (2014b) 'La difficile féminisation du *Monde diplomatique*. Ouvertures et résistances de la rédacton de 1954 à 2008,' *Politiques de communication* 1 (2): 171–188.
Hernández-Hernández, Tania (2015) 'La traducción y la escritura de *Le Monde diplomatique en español*: agentes, capitales e influencias,' *Mutatis Mutandis Revista Latinoamericana de Traducción* 8 (2): 529–546.
Hernández-Hernández, Tania (2017) 'Translation, a Hybrid Form of Capital: The Translators of *Le Monde diplomatique en español* (1979–1988),' *Perspectives* 25 (3): 509–520.
Huesca, Robert (2000) 'Activist Media,' in *The International Encyclopaedia of Communication*. Ed. Wolfgang Donsbach. Malden: Blackwell. 31–33.

LMd (1954) 'À nos lecteurs,' in *Le Monde diplomatique* [online]. Available at: www.monde-diplo matique.fr/1954/05/A/21148 [accessed 20 July 2019].

LMd (2019) 'Éditions internationales,' in *Le Monde diplomatique* [online]. Available at: www. monde-diplomatique.fr/diplo/int/ [accessed 20 July 2019].

Los Angeles Times (1986) 'Bullet-Riddled Body of Mexican Newspaper Editor Found in Car,' in *Los Angeles Times* [online] 7 November. Available at: www.latimes.com/archives/la-xpm-1986-11-07-mn-15758-story.html [accessed 20 July 2019].

Noordegraaf, Mirko, and Willem Schinkel (2011) 'Professionalism as Symbolic Capital: Materials for a Bourdieusian Theory of Professionalism,' *Comparative Sociology* 10 (1): 67–96.

Orengo, Alberto (2005) 'Localising News: Translation and the 'Global-national' Dichotomy,' *Language and Intercultural Communication* 5 (2): 168–187.

Peigne-Giuly, Annik (2005) 'Mort du journaliste Claude Julien,' in *Libération* [online] 9 May. Available at: http://alturl.com/h654h [accessed 20 July 2019].

Ramonet, Ignacio (2005) 'Claude Julien,' in *Le Monde diplomatique* [online] 12 May. Available at: www.monde-diplomatique.fr/carnet/2005-05-12-Claude-Julien [accessed 20 July 2019].

Ramonet, Ignacio (2003) '*Le Monde* et le *Diplo*,' in *Le Monde diplomatique* [online]. Available at: www.monde-diplomatique.fr/2003/04/RAMONET/10096 [accessed 20 July 2019].

Ramonet, Ignacio (2001) 'Marcos marche sur Mexico,' in *Le Monde diplomatique* [online]. Available at: www.monde-diplomatique.fr/2001/03/RAMONET/6164 [accessed 20 July 2019].

Ramonet, Ignacio (1997) 'Désarmer les marchés,' in *Le Monde diplomatique* [online]. Available at: www.monde-diplomatique.fr/1997/12/RAMONET/5102 [accessed 20 July 2019].

Ramonet, Ignacio (1995) 'La pensée unique,' in *Le Monde diplomatique* [online]. Available at: www.monde-diplomatique.fr/1995/01/RAMONET/6069 [accessed 20 July 2019].

Rémond, Bruno (1990) *Sirius face à l'histoire*. Paris: Presse de la Fondation Nationale des Sciences Politiques.

Rovira, Guiomar (2015) 'From Armed Struggle to Interaction with Civil Society: Chiapas' Zapatista National Liberation Army,' in *Civil Resistance and Conflict Transformation: Transitions from Armed to Nonviolent Struggle*. Ed. Véronique Dudouet. Abingdon: Routledge. 126–153.

Schmemann, Serge (2013) 'Turning the Page,' in *The New York Times* [online] 13 October. Available at: https://nyti.ms/2GMS0kK [accessed 20 July 2019].

Sin permiso e Ignacio Ramonet (2008) 'La crisis política del Foro Social Mundial. Entrevista con Ignacio Ramonet,' in *Sin permiso, república y socialismo, también para el siglo XXI* [online] 25 January. Available at: https://bit.ly/2PrSImw [accessed 20 July 2019].

Valdeón, Roberto (2006) 'The CNN enEspañol NEWS,' *Perspectives: Studies in Translatology* 13 (4): 255–267.

Vendramin, Patricia (2013) 'L'engagement militant: la rencontre entre un individu, une cause et une organisation,' in *L'engagement militant*. Ed. Patricia Vendramin. Louvain: Presses Universitaires. 15–34.

Venuti, Lawrence (1995) *The Translator's Invisibility. A History of Translation*. London: Routledge.

Vidal, Dominique (2006) 'L'internationale du "Diplo",' in *Le Monde diplomatique* [online]. Available at: https://bit.ly/2BLDfc4 [accessed 20 July 2019].

Yankelevich, Pablo (2010) *Ráfagas de un exilio. Argentinos en México, 1974–1983*. Mexico City: FCE-El Colegio de México.

Interviews cited

Hernández-Hernández, Tania, and Eda Chávez (2012) 'Interview with Eda Chávez,' 6 February.

Hernández-Hernández, Tania, and Carlos Gabetta (2012) 'Interview with Carlos Gabetta,' 22 September.

Hernández-Hernández, Tania, and Alejandro Katz (2012) 'Interview with Alejandro Katz,' 12 March.

Hernández-Hernández, Tania, and Steven Johansson (2012) 'Interview with Steven Johansson,' 23 February.

Hernández-Hernández, Tania, and Eduardo Molina (2012) 'Interview with Eduardo Molina,' 19 July.

Hernández-Hernández, Tania, and Pilar Ortiz (2012) 'Interview with Pilar Ortiz,' 15 February.

Hernández-Hernández, Tania, and Erasmo Sáenz (2012) 'Interview with Erasmo Sáenz,' 3 May.

Hernández-Hernández, Tania, and Irene Selser (2012) 'Interview with Irene Selser,' 10 February.

Hernández-Hernández, Tania, and Antonio Tenorio (2012) 'Interview with Antonio Tenorio,' 8 August.

Hernández-Hernández, Tania, and Marta Vassallo (2012) 'Interview with Marta Vassallo,' 3 October.

Documentary data cited

Casa Editorial Raza Cósmica (1988) 'Letter [to the readers, unpublished],' Mexico City, in the personal archive of Gerardo Estrada (editor of *Le Monde diplomatique en español*, 1987–1988).

Julien, Claude, and Federico Fasano (1981) 'Contract between editors of *Le Monde diplomatique* and *Le Monde diplomatique en español*,' 5 August, in the personal archive of Gerardo Estrada (editor of *Le Monde diplomatique en español*, 1987–1988).

Part IV
Bearing witness

13

Written on the heart, in broken English

Ayşe Düzkan

We never drank Coca-Cola at home when I was a kid. Actually, nobody drank soda often then. On special occasions, Mum would buy a local brand. Both my parents were members of the Labour Party. It was late 1960s and anti-USA imperialism was a major part of left-wing thinking. It was in the air.

I took exams for secondary school during the last term of elementary school. As in many countries, there are public and private secondary schools in Turkey. There are also good schools and not-so-good schools and in those times, in order to attend a good school, the student had to take that school's exam and get a good mark. All public schools—no matter how good or bad—were free. For all private schools, the parents had to pay an annual fee. Complicated, isn't it? Being only 11 at the time, I found it dramatically complicated. There were American schools, French schools, a British school, a German and an Austrian school in Istanbul. They were all very expensive, and very hard to get in to.

I took the entrance exams of all of these schools and won the English High School for Girls. It was 1970, a year after the big protests against the USA sixth fleet which had visited Istanbul; my parents were still anti-American but they didn't hesitate to register their daughter at a British school with children of the Istanbul elite. The personal wasn't political back then, at least in Turkey. There were many news and articles about the American war in Vietnam. We supported the Vietnamese. English for us wasn't the language of the occupier but of jazz singers and the hippies who protested against this war. I agreed with my parents then, but I agree with them partially now.

Back then, we didn't use the term 'career.' We wanted to join good professions and speaking English, French and German or any of them would be an important step towards this. And there was no place you could learn Spanish, Chinese or Arabic. Establishing a school that teaches the mother tongue of your people was a privilege that very few states could enjoy.

I attended English High School for Girls (in the building now occupied by the Beyoğlu Anatolian High School). The building was a place fit for shooting a horror movie, but we liked it. The dress code was strict. We had to wear stupid caps with the motto *Post tenebras luxe* ('Light after darkness') outside the school, with our uniforms. The teachers were coming from or going to places in Africa or Asia. In 1971, my first year in high school, a military coup d'état took place in Turkey. My father was arrested; he was released in a few weeks but I had a secret to keep among all those irregular verbs and pronouns. In the coming years, I became acquainted with literature in English. I fell in love with the novels of Jane Austen, Thomas Hardy and the Brontë sisters, but hated reciting Shakespeare's poetry.

After two years of prep and three years of elementary school, we went to English High School for Boys for senior high school. There, thanks to one of our teachers, we had the chance to explore modern literature in English. I became fascinated by Margaret Drabble's novel *The Millstone* (1965), and impressed by Walter Van Tilburg Clark's novel *The Ox-bow Incident* (1940). I felt they were talking about my experiences, which I hadn't lived through yet, but would eventually be living. This was an accurate intuition because later on, I had an experience very similar to Rosamund, the heroine of *The Millstone*. But still, learning and speaking English belonged to a school that I found quite boring. I still enjoyed and felt satisfied by reading in Turkish: political theory and literature, including foreign writers like Simone de Beauvoir, Shulamith Firestone, Kate Millet, Karl Marx, Lenin and also Turkish writers like Orhan Kemal, Yaşar Kemal, Mahir Çayan, Sevgi Soysal, Tezer Özlü, Sevim Burak …

In 1980 came the next coup. A curfew was imposed. I got married to my boyfriend, thinking it would be safer that way. So many friends were being tortured or imprisoned. Political activities that filled my days and evenings were banned. This was when I first began to think of translation. I decided to translate *The Millstone* in 1981. I remember working on a small table in my bedroom, with a typewriter, while my husband held a clandestine meeting in the sitting-room. I needed to fill my days; I wanted my friends who didn't speak English to be able to read a book I loved and identified with. But I wouldn't know what to do with the text even if I could finish the translation. I couldn't, anyway. We had to leave the house, the typewriter, the book and the first few pages of the translation. Life was fast and hard. We didn't have much time. I went into the interrogation room, with Drabble's *A Summer Bird-Cage* (1963) in my bag. I couldn't get the book back when I was released from prison.

I started to work in a translation bureau after I came out of prison. We were translating legal documents and similar materials. The wage was adequate, the office was friendly. I survived, earning my living and learning translation techniques.

In 1984, four years after the coup, I joined a feminist collective. We organised a book club and a publishing house. It was called Women's Circle and was the first second-wave feminist organisation in Turkey. We had never heard of the term NGO. Nobody talked about funding. These were interesting times. Before that, I had been an activist and did some translation. But my first experience with translation as activism was as part of this collective. German feminist Alice Schwarzer had interviewed Simone de Beauvoir and collected these interviews in a book (1984). Some of the interviews in the book were copyrighted and we couldn't afford it but we decided to publish the ones dated before the copyright date, under the title *Ben Bir Feministim* (*I am a Feminist*). We were three women: a physician around her 50s, a friend from high school and myself. Each of us identified with feminism; each of us translated one part of the book. We were of different ages, and didn't use our surnames on the cover that we designed. It is hard to do such a thing—you need to discuss more than using words, and think about meanings and terms. But on the other hand, we learned a lot from each other. This is I think a rule that applies in most fields of activism: working collectively takes more time and is harder than working alone or in a hierarchy but the result is more powerful.

Many people of my generation learned foreign languages by themselves in prisons and started doing translations there. They knew the nuances of English or French but couldn't talk at all! As I learned English from native speaker teachers in a school where it was forbidden to speak Turkish, my spoken English wasn't worse than my reading or writing. But even so, I have never been as fluent as a native speaker or as someone who has spent some time in an English-speaking country. I can joke, write, use metaphors in my mother tongue but I can't do these in English! During the first part of the 1990s, I started working on a women's magazine project with a German feminist foundation called Frauen-Anstiftung (Women Inciting). We were part of the Eastern and Central European Section. The foundation convened conferences, most of which were very interesting for me. There was usually simultaneous translation from a few languages, i.e. the 'official languages' of the conference. On the leaflet of the first conference I attended, I saw that 'Broken English' was one of them! Mind you, not standard 'English'! Seeing those words was such a relief! But then we were there, a bunch of feminists from neighbouring countries. None of us speaking the other's mother tongue and communicating in a language that we had all learned during our formal education. I remember an anthropologist from Croatia who hated everything in English, which she called 'the language of the world's tyrant.' Her perspective was enlightening!

From 1995 until 2002, I worked for the independent feminist magazine *Pazartesi* (the name means Monday in Turkish, the day you start a diet, you decide to get a divorce, and so on), first as an editor, then as the executive editor. I translated articles, news and other material from English for the magazine. In 2002, when the magazine was closed down, I became unemployed. I decided to earn my living by translation. I decided to offer to translate *SCUM Manifesto* by Valerie Solanas (1967)[1] for Sel Yayınevi, a well-known publishing-house. I was lucky—they accepted my offer.

I have loved the *SCUM Manifesto* all my life. I never considered it a real manifesto but rather a critical satire. But even though I am a feminist who would never abstain from being called a man-hater, I thought this brilliant text is prone to being misunderstood. Valerie Solanas, whom I love as an aunt, sister and daughter, is a man-hater of course, but the manifesto does not really offer instructions for getting rid of men. So I decided to write a preface about Solanas, her life and her work. *Erkek Doğrama Cemiyeti Manifestosu* (*Society for Cutting-up Man Manifesto*)[2] is now very popular, especially among young feminists, and has been republished in a few editions. I didn't only translate the text; I also introduced Solanas to Turkish readers. As a translator I believe that I owe loyalty to the text and the writer. If there is an expression I wouldn't use myself for the sake of political correctness, I feel obliged to translate it as it appears in the original. But as a writer commenting on the text, I can express my own views. Translating *SCUM* into Turkish was a form of activism, and other activists have been inspired by the book.

In 2009, I joined BDS Turkey, the Turkish-based division of the global movement to boycott, divest and sanction Israel (Maira 2018). My work as a BDS activist encouraged me to read more about the Palestinian case and the Arab world. In 2014 I translated a book about the Palestinian political activist Leila Khaled (b. 1944): *Leila Khaled: Icon of Palestinian Liberation* by Sarah Irving into Turkish (see Chapter 7 of this volume). I am very proud to be the translator of the biography of the first guerrilla whose name I heard in my teens. I loved the book. I admire Irving's feminist approach to understanding

Khaled as a human being, a woman, and a political leader, but never omitting the history of Palestinian liberation. I learned a lot about history and the present situation from this book and it has been widely read by activists and friends of the Palestinian cause.

But let me say something about the term 'guerrilla.' In 2012 I went to Beirut and visited Shatila refugee camp there. On the wall of an office at the entrance was a photo of Leila Khaled. A young man asked me whether I knew her. I said, 'Of course, she is the first guerrilla I know.' There were three men there. They looked at each other in confusion. 'First what?,' the young one asked. 'Guerrilla?,' I said but the confusion was still there. 'Like Che Guevera,' I insisted. The man said, 'Oh, you mean *fedai*!'

Feda is used for sacrifice in Turkish and *fedai* is in Arabic someone who is ready to sacrifice his life for a cause. But on the other hand, a guerrilla is understood to be a member of an unofficial military group that is trying to change the government by making sudden, unexpected attacks on official army forces. A guerrilla is ready to lose her or his life too but for a *fedai*, this is the primary meaning. Two continents, two different 'meanings' for people fighting for similar causes with similar tools. *Fedai* is a term with familiar roots for Turkish-speaking people. Guerrilla has been adopted from texts in English, French and German.

Arabic is the language of neighbouring countries. Our preference for the term of a non-neighbour term is not a coincidence. Progressive Arab experiences are translated into Turkish from European languages. This also is not a coincidence because there are more schools teaching English than any other language. But it is only the third most spoken language in the world! We use English or French to communicate not only with the French, the British or US citizens, but also with South Asians, Iranians, Arabs, Bulgarians and Greeks. And some of these peoples are our neighbours! Our choice of English is no coincidence. It has a lot to do with British and French colonialism and US imperialism. Turkish intellectuals were Francophone during especially the late Ottoman period but now English is preferred, as in most parts of the world. But this isn't the whole story.

In 2014 a publisher asked me to do consecutive interpretation during a conference for a writer visiting Istanbul. I accepted. The writer was the anthropologist Neil Faulkner, author of *A Radical History of the World* (Faulkner 2018). It was Faulkner's second time in Istanbul. He spoke no Turkish and most of his speech was about Gezi Park occupation. I was translating a speech on what I and all the people in the room had experienced the previous year, by someone who didn't have time to read about it. The audience found nothing surprising in that. They asked him questions about what they have personally lived through. The writer was a Marxist and pointed out even the connection between his wearing shorts and capitalism: there had been a traffic jam because of the lack of public transport and he didn't have time to go to the hotel and change. But he didn't see any connection between his position as a commentator on an event that he hadn't witnessed, in a country where he didn't speak any of the native languages, in the city hosting this event! I wonder if any English-speaking Turkish writer living in London would be invited to comment on Occupy London. This too is no coincidence. And to understand and change these global inequalities, between my country, my country's neighbours and countries distant from Turkey, is part of my activism today.

We are often warned that geography is destiny. But so too is the mother tongue. And the fate of any language is determined by its history. Since 2015, I have been trying to learn Kurdish and Arabic, the languages of my neighbours. I know that I will never be as fluent in Kurdish and Arabic as I am in Turkish or even in English. I will never translate from these languages, but still, I am compelled to take a small step towards changing the destiny that history has written on my life and inscribed in my heart, in broken English.

Related topics

Writing as Hospitality; Feminism in Translation; The Political Modes of Translation in Iran.

Notes

1 Solanas, Valerie (1967) *SCUM Manifesto*. New York: Valerie Solanas.
2 Solanas, Valerie (2002) *Erkek Doğrama Cemiyeti Manifestosu*. Trans. Ayşe Düzkan. İstanbul: Sel Yayınevi.

Further reading

Achcar, Gilbert (2013) *Marxism, Orientalism, Cosmopolitanism*. London: Saqi Books. I don't agree with much of what Achcar says and but this book offers a refreshing perspective on orientalism.

Signs (2014) *Journal of Women in Culture and Society* 39 (3). The special issue of *Signs* offers feminist approaches on translation.

Bozkurt, Sinem (2014) 'Touched Translations in Turkey, A Feminist Translation Approach,' [online]. Available at: www.momentdergi.org/index.php/momentdergi/article/view/32/343 [accessed 29 June 2019].

Sinem Bozkurt's work covers the translation of *SCUM Manifesto* into Turkish, among other feminist texts.

Ergün, Emek, and Olga Castro (eds.) (2017) *Feminist Translation Studies, Local and Transnational Perspectives*. New York: Routledge.

Emek Ergün's work on translation is inspiring for many feminist translators from/to Turkish. The articles in this volume should influence any feminist translating between different languages.

Göl, Damla (2015) 'Türkiye'de 1980 Dönemi Feminist Çeviri Hareketinin Kadın Çalışmaları Dizgesini Oluşturmadaki Rolü,' [online]. Available at: https://tez.yok.gov.tr/UlusalTezMerkezi/tezSorguSonucYeni.jsp [accessed 29 June 2019].

The thesis in Turkish offers detailed information on feminist translation during the 1980s.

References

Drabble, Margaret (1963) *A Summer Bird-Cage*. London: Weidenfeld & Nicolson.
Drabble, Margaret (1965) *The Millstone*. London: Weidenfeld & Nicolson.
Faulkner, Neil (2018) *A Radical History of the World*. London: Pluto Press.
Irving, Sarah (2012) *Leila Khaled: Icon of Palestinian Liberation*. London: Pluto Press.
Irving, Sarah (2014) *Leyla Halid, Filistin Kurtuluşunun Simgesi*. Trans. Ayşe Düzkan. İstanbul: Intifada Yayınları.
Maira, Sunaina (2018) *Boycott! The Academy and Justice for Palestine*. Berkeley: University of California Press.
Schwarzer, Alice (1984) *Simone de Beauvoir Today, Conversations, 1972–1982*. Trans. Marianne Howarth. London: Chatto & Wintus.
Schwarzer, Alice (1986) *Ben Bir Feministim*. Trans. Ayşe, Minu, Sedef. İstanbul: Kadın Çevresi Yayınları.
Solanas, Valerie (1967) *SCUM Manifesto*. New York: Valerie Solanas.
Solanas, Valerie (2002) *Erkek Doğrama Cemiyeti Manifestosu*. Trans. Ayşe Düzkan. İstanbul: Sel Yayınevi.
Van Tillburg, Walter (1949) *The Ox-bow Incident*. New York: Random House.

14

Writing as hospitality

Translating the fragment in Arabic and English

Yousif M. Qasmiyeh

As I negotiate my positionality as a refugee-writer-translator—a place I am still trying to locate in my writing (Qasmiyeh 2016a, 2016b, 2016c, 2017a, 2017b, 2019a, 2019b; Qasmiyeh and Fiddian-Qasmiyeh 2013; Stonebridge 2015, 2018; Stonebridge and Qasmiyeh 2018), I ask: As I write, not knowing which language precedes and follows which, can the two languages in which I write—Arabic and English, or English and Arabic—coexist benignly in the same corpus? Through analysing a selection of my fragmentary writings in Arabic and in English, and ones that are incomplete in either Arabic or English, in this chapter I shed light on the impossibility of locating the origin in these encounters (Kwek 2017). In so doing I reflect on whether translation in its transformative sense, including in contexts of writing refugeeness into literature, is an act of rewriting or simply an alternative to a fragmentariness that is inherent in the origin and is maintained in the form of 'rewriting' in the hosting language. I also consider the implications of these questions for activism, understood in this context as including different forms of resistance to displacement and 'refugeedom' through writing and translation.

In my writing, including in my work before and since my collaboration with the interdisciplinary Refugee Hosts (2016–2020) research project where the notions of hosting, hospitality and hostility towards refugees collide, it is the fragment that I rely on, in its infinite state, in its condensation of the experienced in language. The fragment, as I write and translate it, appears to resemble multiple depictions of the body—my bodies and languages or none—divided and distinguished in direct synergy with my various legal statuses: from refugee in Lebanon, to asylum seeker, refugee and citizen in the UK. Such law-related categorisations of the diverse statuses that I am still living now have formed the dual corpora that I explore in the second half of this chapter.

In response to, but also resisting, these legal statuses, my fragmentary writing may be viewed as part of the burgeoning field of what is denominated 'refugee writing,' in so far as it is a writing not only about but also by and of people who (happen to) have experienced displacement (Qasmiyeh 2019b). However, classifying a piece of writing as refugee writing is a highly complex task not least because of the very meaning of such an artistic correspondence between the refugee as a subject and an author at the same time, and the work of writing in its capacity to embody different forms of resistance and survival. In this chapter I interpret the fragment and its multiple renderings as a mode of writing that escapes categorisations, mirroring my own escape from being interpellated as a refugee writer who must adhere to the rules of either autobiographical enunciations of suffering, exile and testimony, or 'trauma-processing' (Qasmiyeh 2019b; Qasmiyeh and O'Donoghue 2009: 9–10; Stonebridge 2018). In this sense, I foreground my theoretical engagement with the concept of the fragment before turning to my own fragmentary writing, noting that '[f]or clarity's sake, I talk on behalf of no one, let alone myself, my brothers-in-asylum, and my only mother' (Qasmiyeh 2016e: 248).

The chapter is structured as follows: I start by tracing the roots and contours of the fragment and its emergence as a new genre in German romanticism in the 18th century. I focus in particular on the different interpretations and readings of the fragment within and beyond established literary canons. I argue that the fragment's distinction from other genres is that 'in the very same moment and gesture of fragmentation, the fragment both is and is not System' (Lacoue-Labarthe and Nancy 1988: 50). As a form whose system is both existent and non-existent, the fragment is infused with a deconstructionist and even activist potential since 'with writing [meaning] is made and unmade' (Derrida 1979: 21), thereby elucidating, precisely, its potential to disrupt and resist. Resistance is an integral part of activism, and it characterises the condition of the refugee who has to constantly reassert his refugeeness. These interpretations are then juxtaposed, and supplemented with, the varied Arabic equivalences which emerged in the mid–late 20th century, in particular the works of the modernist Lebanese poet Unsi al-Hajj. After briefly theorising the notion of fragment in European and Arabic literatures, I proceed to an exploration of translating of and hosting in the fragment, in its ability to accommodate but also transcend different, at times contradictory, languages, voices and registers. I do so by noting that, since translation is also a host in rewriting, it bears resistant and transformative features which can be traced in the body of the translated and the rewritten. I then situate my fragmentary writing in and between Arabic and English, by drawing comparisons (as well as contrasts) between the original and the translation. In so doing, I highlight the eternal rupture between knowing a language and translating it by stressing the impossibility of locating the origin. I conclude by providing a preliminary delineation of the complexities that govern writing in two languages, including in resisting displacement.

Theorising the fragment

In 'The Fragment: The Fragmentary Exigency,' a seminal attempt to inaugurate the fragment in the specifics of German romanticism in the 18th century, Lacoue-Labarthe and Nancy remind us that 'the fragment is the romantic genre *par excellence*' (1988: 44). Such an assertion establishes the position of the fragment in literature, and further signals Lacoue-Labarthe and Nancy's theoretical awareness that for the fragment to survive its own making it has to move beyond what is deemed canonical in the genre-sense. In depicting the fragment as an anti-canonical model, the self-sufficiency of which is in its own incompleteness, they regard it 'as a determinate and deliberate statement, assuming or transfiguring the accidental and involuntary aspects of fragmentation' (1988: 41). What is anti-canonical and transformative is individuation (1988: 43); as stated in

Schlegel's *Athenaeum* fragment 116, it is a state that 'should forever be becoming and never perfected' (1988: 43). In other words, the writing of the fragment carries within itself the seeds of a movement, not to say a revolution, which is enabling in so far as the directionality of writing becomes that of the language and nothing else. This is not to say that other genres offer nothing in this department, but to view the position of the fragment as one that continuously escapes positions.

In presenting the fragmentary and the fractured in writing as conjoined epithets, Lacoue-Labarthe and Nancy reiterate that

> [i]f the fragment is indeed a fraction, it emphasises neither first nor foremost the fracture that produces it. At the very least, *it designates the borders of the fracture as an autonomous form as such as the formlessness or deformity of the tearing.*
>
> *(1988: 42, my emphasis)*

So 'the borders of the fracture' in the fragment are exactly what are being erected as writing takes place, not in order to constrict the content, but more precisely to ascertain an autonomy whose tenets are those of discursive and conceptual individuality. This is to say that '[t]he fragmentary work is neither nor absolutely the Work. But its own individuality must be grasped, nonetheless, with respect to its relation to the work' and the recognition that '[f]ragmentary individuality is above all that of the multiplicity inherent to the genre' (1988: 43).

Asserting the individual in the fragment equally attests its uninhibited expressiveness without any excess of meaning and without the need to present itself as the representative of other forms but itself. Its amputated status is not there to be pitied since it is the antithesis of exhaustiveness—a constant reminder of the fragment's desire not to seek completion but to roam around it as it is plural and takes multiple shapes (el-Janabi 2015: 30–31). The concept of the fragment thus relies heavily on this organic collision between what is written and what is there to remain as a fragment of the writing itself: '[f]ragments are definitions of the fragment; this is what installs the totality of the fragment as a plurality and its completion as the incompletion of its infinity' (2015: 44). In the context of the romantic fragment, according to Lacoue-Labarthe and Nancy, 'far from bringing the dispersion or the shattering of the work into play, [the fragment] inscribes its plurality as the exergue of the total, infinite work' (1988: 48). In such a friction between the meaning of the fragment and its life beyond writing, it becomes apparent that what is in front of us is a form that is reflective of a tearing or a rupture in life itself exemplified in the fragment's own struggles with form and formlessness (where the tearing and rupture echo Derrida's notion of circumcision and circumfession —see Bennington and Derrida 1993: 3–315). Since writing itself is an act whose function is to be queried later, the fragment seems to have this querying edge at its very genesis. Further, '[t]he fragment closes and interrupts itself at the same point: *it is not a point, a punctuation, or a fractured piece*, despite everything, of the fragmentary work' (Bennington and Derrida 1993: 57–58, my emphasis). In other words, the fragment is never an identifiable location, a sign marked by a fixity or an appearance with limitations. It is, above all, its own system and none.

Fragments, in adopting a no-form, side with the foreign, including, I would argue, with the refugee. This foreignness within literature can also be conceptualised as a revolt for the rereading of literature and its constant battles with the establishment. Highlighting the tendency of the fragment to be set free from other genres conveys a writing whose ultimate goal is to create its own borders through writing and by (using) writing as a forum to deliberate, test, and, above all, contest the manifestations of life and living in modern-day life. This deliberation between the fragment as a concept and the fragmentary nature of life grounds the former theoretically: it becomes a perpetual reminder of the value of writing the instant in a variety of forms which refract in the fragment's soil. Indeed, when a fragment is produced, so are its own laws—the laws that differ with every writing so they continue to reinterpret themselves as marks of renewal.

Why is the fragment there in the first place? What is its capacity and what are the exact parameters, if any, of a fragmentary fragment? These postulates take us knowingly to the question of space and the poetic space, more precisely (as I explore in detail through my fragments below), and the ways in which writing without a destination in mind can become the ultimate destination. Would the fragment be present if it were not for the poetic voice whose struggles as well as aspirations are embedded in language itself—in its willingness (or reluctance) to bend itself for the sake of the new law? If the fragment is out there, it is there to portray with suspicious eyes what is normally deemed visible. Unlike parables, proverbs and reflections, the fragment thrives in its uncertainty and as such never commits to the didactic in speech but negates it to the extent of obliterating it, as if what matters in writing is the question of writing, no more, no less (el-Janabi 2015: 28). Indeed, in the fragment, the writer becomes the language's guest par excellence, the writer is at the language's threshold upon the language's request since it is the absolute giver in its capacity as the custodian of the would-be written.

The Arabic fragment: al-shaqīqa

In articulating the position of Unsi al-Hajj's fragments in the latter's poetic corpus, the Iraqi poet and translator Abdel Kader el-Janabi needed to theorise the fragmentary in al-Hajj's poetry in conjunction with what is perceived as the whole poem (el-Janabi 2015). This incompleteness, inherent in the fragment, evades its physical deficiency to stay whole within itself: 'it has cut the umbilical cord with a previous life of which it was part in a whole so it would become the whole, like a branch which falls [off a tree] to become the tree itself' (el-Janabi 2015: 30).[1] Such an understanding presents the fragmentary as an independent entity but with the potential to neighbour other genres with enough space for its limbs to grow in. The collisional nature of a fragment evokes 'a scar, a deep wound in narration' (el-Janabi 2015: 30). Even though el-Janabi's interrogation of the fragment in al-Hajj's work is not related to translating the fragment into other languages per se, in this case from Arabic into English, he argues for the preservation of the fragmentary beyond its own linguistic habitat. For it is uncertainty that a fragment aims to convey; its habitats become none and many at the same time. Indeed, even though the fragment's ultimate goal is to conclude nothing, the lack of a well-demarcated conclusion in its subsequent translations (one of the facets addressed in this chapter) becomes a new fragment which is independent of its original fragment.

This capacity of the fragment to go beyond itself as it seeks new lives becomes not only a reflection of the fragmentariness of its themes and topics therein, but rather a mechanism whereby meaning as a human condition is engendered, multiplied and reconfigured. Since, in the Arabic tradition, the fragment (al-shaqīqa) carries the state of an offshoot, section, segment, shrapnel, equivalent, ending and a scattering (el-Janabi 2015: 27–33, 111–112; Ibn Manzur 2015a: 387–391), interrogating such equivalences in line with the fragment's organicity, its incessant ability to relate to itself within its own borders, becomes urgent. El-Janabi's analysis of al-Hajj's 'new' writing as the correlative of a new body/corpus is pertinent in understanding the fragment's textuality (el-Janabi 2015: 28). The textuality that el-Janabi alludes to is that of precariousness, of fragments within fragments, of the amputated body, severed from within to reclaim a new form, never a static one. In so doing, el-Janabi develops a new reading: the fragment is also the body proper lying before us awaiting to be scrutinised, anatomised, in order to see beyond the skin, to delve deeply into the flesh of the text in the hope of laying our hands on the fragment which is also the wound (Qasmiyeh 2016c: 119).

This partialness is productive in nature and as such is capable of managing its own survival beyond its concealed origins, as a rhizome which grows downwards in language, seeking a life in the very depths of language and for the language, as if it were a growth that is solely based on the language. While it connotes and generates violence as it moves away from the origin, irrespective of what the origin is, it equally constructs a form that should be read on its own, without pre- or post- (el-Janabi 2015: 30). It may exist without fixity but this fixity should never be conflated with incompleteness in the didactic sense. It is, above all, uncertainty that the fragment is trying to convey. In the poetic fragment, the Arabic origins, as well as the Latin ones, are inherent in the notion of departure: a movement in search of and away from language.

How can a departure in the shape of a fragment which lacks an origin (an ancestral one) continue to survive as a form? Such a question takes us back to the fragment as an articulation located in poetry and philosophy yet independent of both (Lacoue-Labarthe and Nancy 1988: 39–58). This resistance to other genres makes the fragment an interconnection as it scatters, one that connects genres within its body but also has the ability to travel and leave traces on its own (following Derrida 2014).

Hosting in the fragment?

'We are the guests of language,' recounts the Moroccan literary historian and critic, Abdelfattah Kilito (2017: 86), without being able to locate the very source of this saying or its occasion. He grants the reader a saying which is devoid of any past (save its hidden origins) yet which looks to the future. Yet this is not the full story for Kilito since guests, in order to live with relative ease in the said languages, have to become aware of the realms, parameters and secrets of such languages. Such an understanding positions the bilingual speaker as arriving at a totally new prosodic territory, that which would inevitably impinge on the speaker's mother tongue. A day must come when they have to choose one or the other (Kilito 2017: 21–37). In Kilito's words, '[t]ere are no oppressive and oppressed languages; when they "meet on one tongue," each is simultaneously an aggressor and a victim. Their relationship is not built on peaceful coexistence but, to the contrary, on tugging, opposition, and quarrel' (2017: 23). This imbalance takes us back to the question of hosting. Since hosting as a practice is contingent on the host's unconditional acceptance of the Other, it, however, does not forbid the questioning of the foreigner, as Derrida reminds us: 'When faced with questions that are so many demands, and even prayers? *In what language can the foreigner address his or her question? Receive ours? In what language can he or she be interrogated?*' (Derrida 2000: 131, my emphasis).

In what language can the foreigner write or speak when it is their responsibility, as the hosted, to answer the host's questions?

> He has to ask for hospitality in a language which by definition is not his own, the one imposed on him by the master of the house, the host, the king, the lord, the authorities, the nation, the State, the father, etc.
>
> *(Derrida 2000: 15, also see Fiddian-Qasmiyeh and Qasmiyeh 2016)*

By posing the first question in this new language, the guest/the writer who is moving away from their language is announcing a new beginning in the linguistic sense: Here I am declaring in your language my need to speak, write and communicate. With reference to the new language, the one which eternally owns the idiom, in which all communications between the host and the guest are conducted, in which all questions will be asked at the threshold, not necessarily to test the newcomer's knowledge or their ability to articulate their needs in what soon would become their second language, but rather to delineate the limits and limitations of this language to both parties: the host and the guest.

The fragment is a host, in its reflective power as it summons languages over. In my own writing, what I write is what I also translate or semi-write, within the linguistic space that escapes me, which will never be mine in the technical sense. Nor will it allow me to feel completely at home in it since the foreigner, who is both the guest and the enemy, is destined to miss the nuances of the secrets (Kilito 2017: 45). The small (aesthetic) body that is called a fragment has found a crack in language, to spy on writing. This crack consists in its two or multiple languages. It is (n)either Arabic (n)or English. Neither is it a complete literal translation of what is out there. It could be the translation that is yet to be located in the text or more its traces. Since '[a]n act of hospitality can only be poetic' (Derrida and Dufourmantelle 2000: 2) and since it is the new language that possesses all meaning and where the guest submits him/herself to navigate his or her surroundings, the poetic becomes the litmus test for good hosting. Yet if we were to lend, as Derrida suggests, '[h]ospitality, hostility, hostpitality' (Derrida 2000: 45) to the same signification or connotation, that of either/or, that of both states together but with compromised and coined conditions, the poetic could be everywhere and nowhere, at the same time. *Everywhere* insofar as the poetic act between the host and the guest is translated into an embodiment of a becoming relationship, be it linguistic, emotional or hierarchical. *Nowhere* in accentuating the necessity of looking beyond languages in the languages.

Translating the fragment into its selves (in the plural) can be seen as a self-inflicted origin and, in the same vein, a possible return to the language which is never complete to be imposed on the text solely. A perception that clarifies such an abstraction is inherent in the evolution of the Arabic term *lugha* (language): *lugha* in the Arabic language is the evolved version of the archaic word *lughwa* (sharing an etymological linkage through their common root, *l-gh-w*), the latter of which is, according to al-Azhari, an incomplete or deficient noun (al-Azhari, cited in Ibn Manzur 2015b: 183). Another term sharing this root (*l-gh-w*) is *laghw*, which is classically understood as 'the baby camel who is not strong enough, therefore unreliable, in terms of stature and health to be included in blood money' (Ibn Manzur 2015b: 183, my translation). The continual deficiency of language, as a premise to which the beginnings of voice belong—on the one hand, and its fragile corpus, on the other—problematises the very meaning of translation.

The re-inscribed and/or translated fragment in my work

In examining the question of a relevant translation, Derrida indicates how translation '[leaves] the other body intact but not without the other to appear' (Derrida 2001: 175). 'Relevant,' in Derrida's words, 'carries in its body an ongoing process of translation [...] as a translative body, it endures or exhibits translation as the memory or stigmata of suffering [*passion*] or, hovering above it, as an aura or halo' (2001: 177). This somatic interpretation of a relevant translation puts the original and the translation in close (physical) proximity to each other, as two corpora whose fluids are continually shared. In his opinion, what we translate is nothing but the flesh. Literally, it is the flesh that we barter in order to settle down debt, implement a law (irrespective of its illegality at times), or respond to a summons (Derrida 2001: 174–200). To avoid entering into fatalist assumptions à propos the translatability and untranslatability of things, Derrida appeals '[t]o the condition of a certain *economy* that relates the translatable to the untranslatable, not as the same to the other, but *as same to same or other to other*' (2001: 178, my emphasis). So, it is the complete sameness or otherness that lies in the folds of the translatability–untranslatability axiom, a distinction necessary to ensure that these bodies are in constant conversation or coercion until their emergence as a difference.

Before I move into the discursive features of the dual Arabic and English corpora in my writing, I will begin by outlining the ways in which such entities have come to existence in the first place by wedding them (without compromising their authenticity) to the abovementioned legal statuses that I have so far borne and resisted. Rather than viewing them as pointers of change, I see them as borders that include and exclude spaces in the process of their demarcation.

In his oft-cited essay, 'The Task of the Translator,' Walter Benjamin stresses that the comprehension of translation as a mode 'must go back to the original, for that contains the law governing the translation: its translatability' (Benjamin 1968: 70). For such a conditionality to be met, the original has to be identified as such in the strictest sense. In other words, it (that is, the original) has to belong to a language that is not the language of the translation. The idea of a law inherent in the original and only 'activated' à propos the notion of translatability institutionalises translation as a space created by and in the presence of an original—an original that will forever foresee its translations through its own laws. What is at stake in writing is what keeps it grounded in a series of specifics. As noted in the introduction to this chapter, the specific to which I respond in writing belongs to language in the first place, and since it is my eyes that turn me back to Arabic as a language which owns the specific, nothing survives in writing save the language. Since Arabic delineates the archival in my writing (Qasmiyeh 2020), the archival which informs another becoming archive in English or in-between-Arabic-and-English, the processes and spaces of translation and rewriting in this context not merely become entwined but are also at times palpably at variance with one another.

As the act of writing is 'per se already [...] violence' (Blanchot 1995: 46), when translation is brought into this space, precisely as an act of 'rewriting,' the process itself becomes doubly or even triply transformative. It is transformative, or to paraphrase Derrida, it marks both a spiritual as well as a fleshly circumcision (Derrida 2001: 184, 194), in so far as it questions languages: it sets them against one another, and yet also, at times, drags them to the same writing body as an act of coexistence and solidarity and/or collusion. Promised in this conversion is a new religion based on its discourse. It may intersect with the old theologically, '[a]s if the business of translation were first of all an Abrahamic matter between the Jew, the Christian and the Muslim' (Derrida 2001: 184), and yet its newness marked by the new tongue can only be interpreted as a separation that ought to be completed for the sake of the survival of all texts concerned. This survival may not be experienced by all parties as a benign survival.

My conversion, self-inflicted as it is, in the shape of the written (oath), the oath that 'passes *through* language, but it passes beyond human language' (Derrida 2001: 184), can be found, albeit in fragments, in the writing, rewriting and/or translation of my work from Arabic and also in writing and translating from the very same corpus, be it incomplete renderings in Arabic or English. To tie back what follows to the question of the bodily as well as the textual survival: Is it always the case that writing poetry survives itself when it reaches the ultimate goal? That is to say, the arrival of the poem especially à propos the formation of, as well as the response to, fragments in two domains: writing poetry and translating poetry or one of its forms and entities—in this case, fragments. One might argue that the arrival of the poem is achieved, for me at least, when neither Arabic nor English knows its place in the poem. This occurrence, in spite of being unattached to one language, is also a 'poetic bearing witness' (Derrida 2005: 87). We may find signs (or signatures), awkwardness and traces that might allude us to a multiplicity within the sameness or, to be even more radical, the absence of a definite language in the traditional sense.

In highlighting such mutations and/or developmental stages, I am not presenting a fixed chronology of how translation—my translation—has transformed itself and my work, but rather invite alternatives to the ways in which such translations and rewritings have been completed.

My translations of and in my work have moved around and towards two spaces. These spaces lack clear borders: it is impossible to contain them within a particular chronology, in the absolute sense, and yet as these are spaces which have come to existence in direct correspondence between the state and the status of the individual, they can be conceptualised as spaces of traces which can be detected in the language(s) at work, the directness which evades itself and above all the absence of the complete poet/translator.

First space

In this space of entanglement, a distance between the Arabic and English is maintained in order to conceal the former from any tension that may arise if and when both languages start to share the same corpus as if, 'in the original, language and revelation are one without any tension, so the translation must be one with the original in the form of the interlinear version, in which literalness and freedom are united' (Benjamin 1968: 82). The freedom that Benjamin is referring to is the difference in meaning, the form that is consumed in order to be reproduced as a difference that only the translator is able to discern. The translator, to transcend the literalness that is shared across translations, should be free of their literalness without tampering with the unity of the original. Such a process has manifested itself in my writing in translating or transferring the Arabic into English by conveying loyalty to the original's integrity, i.e. the body, the narrative and to a certain extent the form. In this first space, my aim has been to maintain a degree of directness that I have tried to carry from the first language (Arabic) to the second (English) without interfering with the first's wholeness or attempting to impose an English that is not organically part of the original's self. In other words, the traditional claim that a translation has 'occurred' is sustained by accepting the assertion that the 'source' language (Arabic) has evolved into a different language (English) while maintaining its original integrity. For the sake of showing the Arabic and the English side by side and in order to bring them to the space of coexistence and solidarity, I will scrutinise two fragments of my poem, 'Holes', published in *Modern Poetry in Translation*, originally in Arabic, alongside their English renderings (Qasmiyeh 2009: 15, 11):

رَأساً على عَقِبٍ
وَفي نِصْفِ الدَّارِ
وَضَعوا رَسْمَهُ
لَم يُغَيِّروا مَكانَ الإناءِ.
سَيَبْكي
وَتَطْفو الصُّورة
على خَدِّ الإناءِ.
*
كيفَ أَموت وَالجميع يراني؟

Upside down/
And in the middle
Of the yard/
His picture was hung/.
They did not change
The place of the pail/.
He will cry/,
And the image
Will float/ on the
Face of the pail.
*
How will I die
While all
Can see me?

In these fragments, the two jobs (writing and translating one's own writing) are separate acts insofar as they appear to be equivalences that are in direct correspondence with one another not only semantically but above all with reference to syntax, form and tense. Repetition, in the first fragment, is maintained throughout (the, pail and will), with only one shift that is exemplified in changing the word 'cheek' in Arabic into 'face' to ensure a degree of continuity in the long vowel in the words 'place,' 'pail' and 'face.' Changing the positionality of the pail in translation by switching body organs (from 'cheek' to 'face'), from what is part of a face to the face in its entirety, could be interpreted as an act of reconciliation between what is 'part of,' like a fragment, and the 'whole.' Such a product(ion) finds a place in Derrida's acute reading of translation as a survival and a growth: '[t]ranslation augments and modifies the original, which, insofar as it is living on, never ceases to be transformed. It modifies the original even as it also modifies the translating language' (Derrida 1988: 122). These processes engage our perceptions of the original as the bearer of the law since 'translation is also the law' (Derrida 1988: 153). Since translation is something other than a mere transcription, 'it is a productive writing called forth by the original text' (Derrida 1988: 153).

In the second space, this writing continues, but in a state of being that is neither in Arabic nor in English in the complete sense.

Second space

This space exists when neither Arabic nor English is complete or triumphant in the way they have been dealt with throughout the writing process but are mere fragments that respond to, while disavowing, one another in a dynamic that seems to suggest that 'poetry runs ahead of us' (Derrida 2005: 5). Translation itself appears to be a fragment of a fragment; Arabic and English share and compete for the same space. As such, the origin (Arabic) generates a plurality of origins or at times is itself effaced in a space that gathers traces of an Arabic that I knew, I know or will know.

This space represents an engagement with both languages in the same body, not necessarily in equal measure, but in a collaborative (or even collusive) mode that steals from both languages to formulate a certain sense in the fragment that embodies 'a terminus and a destination' (Nancy 2006: 114). This collaboration (or collusion), to a certain extent, has become a corpus, a third body, or even an in-between one, whereby Arabic and English can survive, multiply or die *en masse*.

While I work on the poem, or when offshoots of ideas come to mind, it becomes my task, time and space permitting, to transform a blurry idea (i.e. the blankness that we all face when there is something that may grow into another thing in Arabic (and/or English)) into another thing that has the body of a poem. I do not really know in this *space* which language precedes the other throughout the writing process, but what I am sure of is that English and Arabic never move in parallel, but on the contrary compete and clash at times for the same space.

It is a matter of collision between the two languages; the way they compete for the same space in one's memories, that produce what might be called an 'in-between language.' These are the entanglements that will keep the poem alone (to paraphrase Derrida) for its sake and ours. The following fragments—'If this is my face, so be it' (2016c), 'Thresholds' (2016d) and 'At the Feast of Asylum' (Qasmiyeh 2016e)—which may appear as quasi-translations from Arabic 'claim nothing other than the fragmentary body of the refugee, the corpus that is carrying its corpse and others' (Qasmiyeh 2016c: 119–123). In these pieces, languages are mere signs of bodies at war and may only be entered 'according to one of two opposing logics: the logic of assimilation or the logic of destruction' (Nancy 2013: 83). In these writings, we enter the equivalent of a threshold (corporeal and linguistic); 'a conspicuous marker for residents and foreigners alike to visit whenever they feel like it; a place which suddenly becomes more central in our existence than the house or home itself' (Qasmiyeh 2016d: 67–68).

If this is my face, so be it
Walking alongside his shadow, he suddenly realised that it was both of them who needed to cross the border.
We might also say: the face is a dead God.
Refugees and gods always compete for the same space.
The refugee is only intimate in his death and if there is only one death to ponder, it is that of the refugee.
Refugees, to kill time, count their dead.
Killing time is the correlative to killing themselves.

A death with no place can never happen.

A refugee only returns to bear witness to his own return.

Only those who have never seen a place can describe the place.

In asylum, we borrow our bodies for the last time.

Whenever my mother wanted to leave the house, it was to see God's face. God's face, according to her, was somewhere else.

Man, how is it that your body is intact?

On the threshold, they slaughtered us and time.

Thresholds
Fingerprinting

She did to me what a friend would normally do for a friend or a lover for another lover—she held my hand very tightly. When I looked at her, my fingers were above the scanner—my flesh was scanned and so was the air around us. I thought of looking her in the eye again, pretending that we were in love and in that room where asylum-seekers and suspects gather it was our opportunity to embrace one another while the machine was doing its job. I gave my fingerprints and left. Every time I think of that moment I feel the need to go back to that terminal and ask her what it meant to touch a stranger.

At the Feast of Asylum

How would I not think of them when every being can see them as they drag themselves into the soil, the solid and dry soil of our house. I would even say that they belong to me as much as they belong to her. The cracks in my mother's heels—those symmetrical and orderly beings—have always contributed to the way I see things, in a way that would even allow me to say that through them I can see a place that I cannot see.

It is when absence meets absence, when blindness sees blindness from a distance without recognising itself, and when that which is coming our way stops to catch its breath so we can catch ours, then, and only then, will a good death happen.

Since these fragments lack an equivalence in Arabic and English, equivalences which can be deemed totally present 'since the value of any value is its equivalence' (Nancy 2015: 6), syntactically sound from the onset, or self-inscribing to the extent of claiming the linguistic upper hand, the languages therein may be detected in certain folds or images that look mutated and amputated at times or 'in the discreet tremor of language' (Derrida 1998: 35). In these pieces 'places are dead bodies: their spaces, their tombs, their extended masses and our bodies coming and going among them, among ourselves' (Nancy 2008: 121).

Conclusion or beginnings

In interrogating the processes and the outcomes of these spaces—including the outcome that exists as a translation of fragments of fragments—I am of the opinion that separating languages in our writing, especially those languages which we regularly engage with, is an impossibility that only corroborates itself in the processes of writing and rewriting. Fragments are quintessentially separations and/or ruptures in languages. In effect, interrupting the incessant is 'the distinguishing characteristic of fragmentary writing: interruption's having somehow the same meaning as that which does not cease' (Blanchot 1995: 21). What makes us see through the body of language is a crevice which takes us into another space from an initial space without compromising its intactness as a hole which is separate and yet on the same line of vision as the other hole at the other end. These holes as their languages are as much self-sustaining as open to new possibilities.

'Language, perpetuating itself, keeps still' (Blanchot 1995: 145). Such an assertion becomes more traceable in the fragment: what happens in a fragment is never static. It may suffer from a lack of an identifiable system but this should not allude to a lack of direction. In fact, disowning a precise system which might draw fragments closer to a form of completeness while writing and/or translating a fragment can only be done when such systems are acknowledged in certain traces or ruins within the text but are not reproduced or mimicked. To return again to Blanchot with reference to the fragment's resistance to completion and its persistence on (its) incompletion,

> fragments, destined partly to the blank that separates them, find in this gap not what ends them, but what prolongs them, or what makes them await their prolongation— what has already prolonged them, causing them to persist on account of their incompletion.
>
> *(Blanchot 1995: 58)*

The persistence on such incompletion is also a persistence on its own law when translated: 'a translation touches the original lightly and only at the infinitely small point of the sense, thereupon pursuing its own course according to the laws of fidelity in the freedom of linguistic flux' (Benjamin 1968: 80).

My attempt at referring beginnings to Arabic in my writing, rewriting and translation is also an attempt to include 'the history of the language, the history of the author's moment, the history of the language-in-and-as-translation' which, as an embodiment of agency, 'must figure in the weaving' (Spivak 2009: 209). This is not to claim that English, the language that is persistently seeping out of rewriting what otherwise is incomplete structurally (as is the case in the second space discussed above), is entirely benign or that its inclusion in one's space is not happening at the expense of another space. While languages cannot be possessed and '[t]ranslation remains dependent upon the language skill of the majority' (Spivak 2009: 214), within the folds of this notion of the majority and amidst this bilingual rewriting (Arabic and English), there lies a new writing that can be labelled, to follow Deleuze and Guattari, 'minor literature.' The concept of minor literature can be seen as an instrument of destratification which is affected by a high co-efficient of deterritorialisation and always privileges the connection of the individual to a political immediacy (Deleuze and Guattari 2012: 16–27). That is why '[w]riting has a double function: to translate everything into assemblages and to dismantle the assemblages' (Deleuze and Guattari 2012: 47).

Like fingerprints that we sometimes submit to strangers, at times coercively, so we would have our presence verified in airports, police stations and during financial transactions, we submit our writing, writing the fragment, in languages which are meeting over and for the wound, since it is in the wound that we ponder the value of writing (Ahmed 2000). It is writing as resistance when 'responding to a disaster via writing […] becomes the correlative of presence itself' (Qasmiyeh 2016c: 119). As 'translation is the most intimate act of reading' (Spivak 2009: 204), it becomes doubly intimate when it is a rewriting or a translation of the self. It is the (self-)translation as a gaze whose exposition consists in the body proper. 'But whose body is it? It is that of the refugee. The body that conquers language, noise and, above all, borders to hear itself en route' (Qasmiyeh 2016c: 119).

English is a system to which I 'converted,' not canonically, but in order to preserve my language from itself and for myself, just as Shylock had 'to translate himself (*convertere*) into a Christian, into a Christian language, after having been in turn forced, through a scandalous reversal—he who was entreated to be *merciful*—to implore the doge for mercy on his knees' (Derrida 2001: 189). The vulnerability that is conveyed in the fragility of the body, and in turn the fragility of the language that hides behind its body, prompts languages as they seek places, at times those of domination and coercion, to return to the body, the refugee and the citizen body, and to whomever is waiting to be struck in the real and metaphorical sense by a language. The intellectual and theologian Abu 'Uthman 'Amr ibn Bahr al-Jahiz (776–869 CE) continuously referred his readers to a capable interpreter of the Qur'an, Musa ibn Sayyar al-Uswari, who lectured in the same mosque for thirty-six years, and whose tongue, at his regular gatherings, was split into two halves, Arab and Persian, to address his audience in Arabic to the right and in Persian to the left, without these two groups intermingling in this holy place (al-Jahiz, cited in Kilito 2017: 21–27). In line with this historical event, Kilito reminds us that 'to speak a language necessitates turning to one side. Language is tied to a location on the map or to a given space' (2017: 23). I ask: what is the language and the location of a fragment written in multiple geographies and none?

Related topics

Written on the Heart, in Broken English; Translation in the War-Zone; Thought/Translation.

Note

1 Here and elsewhere, all translations from Arabic are by Qasmiyeh.

Further reading

Cox, Emma, Sam Durrant, David Farrier, Lyndsey Stonebridge, and Agnes Woolley (eds.) (2019) *Refugee Imaginaries: Research across the Humanities*. Edinburgh: Edinburgh University Press.

This volume centralises the increasingly crucial role of the arts and the humanities in proposing, imagining and conceiving of different modes of seeing forced migration and refugeeness in the modern era.

Fiddian-Qasmiyeh, Elena (ed.) (2020) *Refuge in a Moving World: Refugee and Migrant Journeys across Disciplines*. London: UCL Press.

This volume not only combines diverse multidisciplinary readings of migrant and refugee journeys, but above all foregrounds the positionality of the researcher as a refugee and the refugee as a researcher.

Suleiman, Yasir (2011) *Arabic, Self and Identity: A Study in Conflict and Displacement*. Oxford: Oxford University Press.

This book astutely investigates the interconnectedness between the Arabic language, and individual and collective identities under occupation and in displacement.

References

Ahmed, Sara (2000) *Strange Encounters: Embodied Others in Post-Coloniality*. London: Routledge.

Benjamin, Walter (1968) *Illuminations: Essays and Reflections*. Tr. Harry Zohn. New York: Schocken Books.

Bennington, Geoffrey, and Jacques Derrida (1993) *Jacques Derrida*. Chicago: Chicago University Press.

Blanchot, Maurice (1995) *The Writing of the Disaster*. Tr. Ann Smock. Lincoln: University of Nebraska Press.

Deleuze, Giles, and Felix Guattari (2012) *Kafka: Toward a Minor Literature*. Minneapolis: Minnesota University Press.

Derrida, Jacques (1979) *Spurs: Nietzsche's Styles*. Tr. Barbara Harlow. Stanford: Stanford University Press.

Derrida, Jacques (1988) 'The Passage into Philosophy: Reply,' in *The Ear of the Other: Texts and Discussions with Jacques Derrida*. Ed. Christie McDonald. Lincoln: Nebraska University Press. 119–126.

Derrida, Jacques (1998) *Monolingualism of the Other OR the Prothesis of Origin*. Stanford: Stanford University Press.

Derrida, Jacques, and Anne Dufourmantelle (2000) *Of Hospitality: Anne Dufourmantelle Invites Jacques Derrida to Respond*. Stanford: Stanford University Press.

Derrida, Jacques (2001) 'What is a 'Relevant' Translation,' *Critical Inquiry* 27 (2): 174–200.

Derrida, Jacques (2005) *Sovereignties in Question: The Poetics of Paul Celan*. Ed. T. Dutoit and O. Pasanen. New York: Fordham University Press.

Derrida, Jacques (2014) *Cinders*. Tr. Ned Lukacher. Minneapolis: Minnesota University Press.

Donato, Eugenio (1988) 'Spectacular Translation,' in *The Ear of the Other: Texts and Discussions with Jacques Derrida*. Ed. Christie McDonald. Lincoln: Nebraska University Press. 126–129.

el-Janabi, Abd al-Kader (2015) *Unsi al-Hajj: min qaṣidat al-nathr ilā shaqāiq al-nathr (Unsi al-Hajj : From the Prose Poem to Fragments)*. Beirut: Jadawel.

Fiddian-Qasmiyeh, Elena, and Yousif M. Qasmiyeh (2016) 'Refugee Neighbours and Hospitality: Exploring the Complexities of Refugee-refugee Humanitarianism,' *The Critique* 5 January 2016 (originally published on *The Critique*); republished [online] 20 March 2018. Avaialbale at: https://refugeehosts.org/2018/03/20/refugee-neighbours-hostipitality/ [accessed 10 October 2019].

Fiddian-Qasmiyeh, Elena, and Yousif M. Qasmiyeh (2017) 'Refugee-Refugee Solidarity in Death and Dying' (multimedia piece), invited contribution to *The Absence of Paths*, Tunisian Pavillion, Venice Bienalle May 2017.

Kilito, Abdelfattah (2017) *Thou Dost Not, and Shalt Not, Speak My Language*. Syracuse: Syracuse University Press.

Kristeva, Julia (1991) *Strangers to Ourselves*. New York: Columbia University Press.

Kwek, Theophilus (2017) 'In Conversation: Yousif M. Qasmiyeh on Language and Liminality,' *Asymptote* [online]15 February. Available at: www.asymptotejournal.com/blog/2017/02/15/in-conversation-yousif-m-qasmiyeh-on-language-and-liminality/ [accessed 10 October 2019].

Lacoue-Labarthe, Philippe, and Jean-Luc Nancy (1988) *The Literary Absolute*. New York: State University of New York Press.

Levinas, Emanuel (1987) *Time and the Other*. Pittsburgh: Duquesne University Press.

Ibn Manzur (2015a) *Lisān al-'Arab (Tr. The Language of the Arab People)*, Vol 5. Cairo: Dar Ibn al-Jawzi.

Ibn Manzur (2015b) *Lisān al-'Arab (Tr. The Language of the Arab People)*, Vol 8. Cairo: Dar Ibn al-Jawzi.

Nancy, Jean-Luc (2006) *Multiple Arts: The Muses II*. Stanford: Stanford University Press.

Nancy, Jean-Luc (2008) *Corpus I*. New York: Fordham University Press.

Nancy, Jean-Luc (2013) *Corpus II*. New York: Fordham University Press.

Nancy, Jean-Luc (2015) *After Fukushima: The Equivalence of Catastrophes*. New York: Fordham University Press.

Qasmiyeh, Yousif M. (2009) 'Holes,' *Modern Poetry in Translation* 3 (12): 11–15.

Qasmiyeh, Yousif M. (2016a) 'Writing the Camp,' *Refugee Hosts* [online] 30 September. Availabel at: https://refugeehosts.org/2016/09/30/writing-the-camp/ [accessed 10 October 2019].

Qasmiyeh, Yousif M. (2016b) 'My Mother's Heels, in *Being Palestinian: Personal Reflections on Palestinian Identity in the Diaspora*. Ed. Yasir Suleiman. Edinburgh: Edinburgh University Press. 303–305.

Qasmiyeh, Yousif M. (2016c) 'If This is My Face, So Be It,' *Modern Poetry in Translation* 2016 (1): 119–123.

Qasmiyeh, Yousif M. (2016d) 'Thresholds,' *Critical Quarterly* 56 (4): 67–70.

Qasmiyeh, Yousif M. (2016e) 'At the Feast of Asylum,' *GeoHumanities* 2 (1): 248–253.

Qasmiyeh, Yousif M. (2017a) 'Refugees are Dialectical Beings,' *Refugee Hosts* [online] 5 September. Available at: https://refugeehosts.org/2017/09/01/refugees-are-dialectical-beings-part-one/ [accessed 10 October 2019].

Qasmiyeh, Yousif M. (2017b) 'Writing the Camp Archive,' *Refugee Hosts* [online] 1 September. Available at: https://refugeehosts.org/2016/09/30/writing-the-camp/ [accessed 10 October 2019].

Qasmiyeh, Yousif M. (2017c) 'A Sudden Utterance is the Stranger,' *Refugee Hosts* [online] 15 April. Available at: https://refugeehosts.org/2017/04/25/a-sudden-utterance-is-the-stranger/ [accessed 10 October 2019].

Qasmiyeh, Yousif M. (2017d) 'The Camp is Time,' *Refugee Hosts* [online] 15 January. Available at: https://refugeehosts.org/2017/01/15/the-camp-is-time/ [accessed 10 October 2019].

Qasmiyeh, Yousif M. (2019a) 'Writing the Camp: Death, Dying and Dialects,' in *Refugee Imaginaries: Research across the Humanities*. Eds. Emma Cox, Sam Durrant, David Farrier, Lyndsey Stonebridge and Agnes Woolley. Edinburgh: Edinburgh University Press. 311–329.

Qasmiyeh, Yousif M. (2019b) 'Theorising Refugee Writing: Literature about, by and for Refugees,' Paper submitted at the University of Oxford, on file with the author.

Qasmiyeh, Yousif M. (2020) 'Writing the Camp, Writing the Archive: The Case of Baddawi Camp in Lebanon,' in *Refuge in a Moving World: Refugee and Migrant Journeys across Disciplines*. Ed. Elena Fiddian-Qasmiyeh. London: UCL Press.

Qasmiyeh, Yousif M., and Elena Fiddian-Qasmiyeh (2013) 'Refugee Camps and Cities in Conversation,' in *Rescripting Religion in the City: Migration and Religious Identity in the Modern Metropolis*. Eds. Jane Garnett and Alana Harris. Farnham: Ashgate. 131–143.

Qasmiyeh, Yousif M., and Bernard O'Donoghue (2009) 'Holes,' *Modern Poetry in Translation* 3 (12): 9–11.

Spivak, Gayatri C. (2009) *Outside in the Teaching Machine*. New York and London: Routledge.

Stonebridge, Lyndsey J. (2015) '"To be borderline": Poetic Statelessness, Auden and Qasmiyeh,' *Textual Practice* 29 (7): 1331–1354.

Stonebridge, Lyndsey J. (2018) *Placeless People: Writing, Rights and Refugees*. Oxford: Oxford University Press.

Stonebridge, Lyndsey J., and Yousif M. Qasmiyeh (2018) 'The Camp as Archive,' *Politics/Letters Live* [online] 6 February. Available at: http://politicsslashletters.org/features/the_camp_as_archive/ [accessed 10 October 2019].

15

Joint authorship and preface-writing practices as translation in post- 'Years of Lead' Morocco

Brahim El Guabli

The Moroccan 'Years of Lead [*Sanwāt al-raṣāṣ*]' (1956–1999) triggered an impressive testimonial prison literature whose authors recount their kidnapping, disappearance, torture and imprisonment experiences during the reign of King Hassan II (1961–1999). In the last two decades, Moroccan testimonial prison literature has been a site of innovative joint authorship and prefatorial practices that raise crucial questions about the relationship between activism, translation and testimony. Since the publication of Ṣalāḥ al-Wadī''s novel *al-ʿArīs* (*The Groom*) (1998), testimonial prison literature, which testifies to the imprint of politically motivated state violence on individuals, families and communities, has shaped Moroccan people's perceptions about their past and the repressive nature of their state.[1] The publication of survivors' accounts of state violence revealed the state's brutality, but also created joint authorship and preface-writing practices in which these survivors perform their individual and collective histories, ensuring an afterlife for their experiences beyond the mere revelation of the crimes state agents committed during the Years of Lead. Scholarship, however, has not been able to stay abreast of these practices since their significance remains largely untheorised. Therefore, conceptualising joint authorship and preface-writing practices as activist translation allows us to theorise how translation weaves testimony into various levels of signification and resignification in post-state-violence contexts.

This chapter argues that joint authorship and preface-writing practices constitute acts of activist translation. Activism transforms translation into 'an act [that] generally has a very public dimension in postcolonial contexts' (Tymoczko 2010: 16). Collaborations between Moroccan survivors of the Years of Lead and professional authors to transfer the memory of embodied experiences of suffering from the realm of the body into the realm of inscription and writing have deep implications for post-independence Moroccan society. I propose that professional writers who agree to work with former victims of state violence to publish their memoirs are de facto activist translators who negotiate multiple levels of linguistic and paratextual registers to endorse the veracity and collective importance of embodied experience despite the limitations of 'paratext as translation' (Gürçağlar 2002: 45–47). Moreover, preface writers, whether they are co-authors, translators or persons of high moral integrity, are also activist translators who, in agreeing to preface the textual version of a reconstructed experience, engage in multifaceted forms of activist endeavours. In reading joint authorship and preface writing as translation, I reveal how translation as an activist act participates in the process of transformation of survivors' lived experience into activist-driven texts, confirming the truth of testimony, supporting its societal significance and helping the creation of discourses for political transformation. Because testimony presupposes the truth of the experience recounted, translation, whether it is in the form of joint authorship or in the form of a preface, is subordinated to the ethical duty to remain true to survivors' experiences, which are central to the testimonial act, but may not apply to other literary genres. Unlike translation theory's concern with fidelity and the voice in translations of written texts (Apter 2005; Hermans 1996; Schiavi 1996), co-authorship and preface writing as translation foreground the narrativised texts' rendering and interpretation of an embodied experience of state violence into narrative form.

The Years of Lead, joint authorship and prefatorial practices in post-1999 Morocco

The years between 1956 and 1999 were a period of state-inflicted violence in Morocco.[2] Known as the Years of Lead, *sanawāt al-jamr wa-l-raṣāṣ*, or *les années noires*,[3] among others, the forty years between Morocco's independence from the French Protectorate in 1956 and the passing of King Hassan II in 1999 witnessed the kidnapping, forcible disappearance, secret imprisonment and even assassination of political opponents of the monarchy (Kably 2011; Rollinde 2002; Slyomovics 2005). Although the state was the main perpetrator of violence after 1961, both state agents and members of the political parties were involved in the political crimes committed between 1955 and 1960, especially the assassination of political figures, such as 'Abbās al-Msā'dī, a leader of the Moroccan Liberation Army (*jaysh al-taḥrīr al-maghribī*), and the persecution of rank-and-file members of the Democracy and Independence Party (*ḥizb al-shūrā wa-al-istiqlāl*) in the north of Morocco.[4] Members of the Moroccan Liberation Army, who refused to stop their armed struggle against the French and the Spanish occupiers after 1956, were also arrested and mistreated by the state. However, the source of the political struggle shifted to social protests in the 1960s, which caused many more casualties among ordinary citizens. Facing the wrath of the Moroccan people directly was the price the monarchy had to pay for its control of political life. For instance, the eruption of the events of 23 March 1965 in Casablanca was only the first in a series of social uprisings that emanated from the government's unpopular economic and social decisions that weakened the middle classes' buying power and prevented their social mobility. In response to the Ministry of Education's decision to put an age limit on access to high school, which would have deprived many students from humble origins of social mobility, the events of 23 March 1965 started as a student revolt, but the dire economic conditions of Casablanca's population turned them into a city-wide political rebellion. In the next decades, other small rebellions followed in Casablanca (1981), Nador (1984) and Fez (1990). The Equity and Reconciliation Commission (ERC) has written in its final report that its investigations

> established that 325 of the persons, some of whose names were listed among those of unknown fate, had died following the civil disturbances that occurred respectively in 1965 (50 deaths), 1981 (114 deaths) and 1984 (49 deaths distributed as follows:

13 in Tetouan, 4 in Ksar El-Kebir, 1 in Tangier, 12 in Al Hoceima, 16 in and around Nador, 1 in Zaio, and 2 in Berkane), 1990 (12 deaths), due to the excessive and disproportionate use of public force.

(ERC 2009: 67)

In a summary of its findings about the social uprisings ('disturbances' in the language of the report) in 1965, 1981, 1984 and 1990, the ERC reached the conclusion that the state committed 'grave violations of human rights mainly represented in infringement of the right to life of a number of citizens including children and also persons who had no involvement in those events' (ERC 2009: 72).

In conjunction with the repression of these social events, state violence during the Years of Lead also targeted politically active Moroccans. For instance, Mahdi Ben Barka, a co-founder of the National Union of Popular Forces (*al-ittiḥād al-waṭānī lil-quwwāt al-sha'biyya*) in 1959, was kidnapped in Paris on 29 October 1965 to never reappear. Unable to reconcile the combination of authoritarianism with lack of economic opportunity, which increased the potential of socio-political strife, the king declared a state of emergency from 1965 to 1970 (ERC 2006: 44). Despite the state of emergency, the Frontists (*al-jabhawiyyūn*),[5] a group of Marxist-Leninist groups that emerged in the aftermath of the Casablanca events and the failure of the Moroccan Communist Party to defend the interests of the proletariat and uphold a stronger position in support of the Palestinian struggle against the American Roger's Plan, adopted the proletarian revolution as a horizon of their struggle against the monarchy starting from 1970 (Ṣ'īb and Shibārī 2002: 17–20). The Frontists were brutally repressed, and many of them passed through the notorious Derb Moulay Chérif, where they were subjected to unspeakable torture and forcible disappearance. Derb Moulay Chérif was a first step in a long journey through the Moroccan carceral system before the opposition members were transferred to legally recognised prisons to await trial. Although short-lived, because of the arrest of its leadership between 1972 and 1977, the Frontists' mobilisation among students and intellectuals instituted a significant rupture in Moroccan politics. The Frontists worked to overthrow the monarchy through covert action. Despite the failure of the dreamed-of revolution, the Frontists would become the driving force behind the human rights organisations in Morocco in the 1990s. Further complicating the political situation in the 1970s, the two consecutive coups against the king in 1971 and 1972, after he ended the state of emergency, added military victims to the register of state crimes. With the creation of the Tazmamart secret detention centre, where fifty-eight soldiers and officers were held incommunicado for two decades starting from 1973, the Years of Lead became synonymous with inconceivable state crimes and impunity.

The Years of Lead also have a legal aspect. For instance, starting from 1959, numerous trials were held in Morocco to try members of the National Union of Popular Forces, the National Union of Socialist Forces (*al-ittiḥād al-ishtirākī lil-quwwāt al-sha'biyya*) and the Moroccan Communist Party (*al-ḥizb al-shuyū'ī al-mghribī*), as well as trade union leaders (Hay'at al-inṣāf wal-muṣālaḥa 2005; Karam 2005; Ouammou 2005). The January–February 1977 trial of the Frontists was historic both for the abuse of the rudimentary principles of due process and also for the lengthy jail time the revolutionary youth were handed by the judge. Accused and 'found guilty of plotting the violent overthrow of the Government,' one hundred and seventy-eight Frontists were sentenced to prison sentences between five years and life in prison (Amnesty International 1977: 83). The use of the military tribunal to try civilians who were accused of endangering the security of the state was a crucial aspect of injustice during the Years of Lead (Benamro 2005).

However, not all those who suffered the Moroccan state's arbitrary power were directly involved in its opposition. Some of the victims of the Years of Lead were victims by association. Officers and soldiers who, without any prior knowledge or ideological conviction, participated in one of the two coups against Hassan II in 1971 and 1972 were enemies by association (El Guabli 2014). Their loyalty to the monarchy did not absolve these soldiers of the crime of executing military orders during a coup they did not even know was unfolding in their presence. Even if all they did was execute orders, they found themselves embroiled in the broader implications of the two coups against Hassan II. Tried by a military tribunal, their sentences ranged between freedom and expulsion from the army for cadets, and one year to life in prison for soldiers and officers (Marzouki 2015: 58–59). These sentences made a significant difference in where they ended up in 1973. While those who received less than two years served their jail time and were released to resume their civilian lives, fifty-eight others who were serving longer periods were kidnapped in August 1973 and taken to a makeshift jail in a military base in the village of Tazmamart (al-Marzūqī 2015; Al-Rāys 2001; Daure-Serfaty 1992; El Ouafi and Trotet 2004; Serhane 2004).

They would remain in disappearance until 1991, when a massive international campaign fuelled by Christine Daure-Serfaty, Gilles Perrault and the Comité de lutte contre la répression au Maroc (Committee Against Repression in Morocco) forced the Moroccan authorities to release them (Daure-Serfaty 1992; El Guabli 2018b). However, by the time of their release, only twenty-eight of the original fifty-eight soldiers and officers had survived their inhuman detention conditions. Of these survivors, seven have authored or co-authored memoirs in French, which was the language they mastered the most, thus shaping the Moroccan testimonial prison genre (Al-Rāys 2001; al-Talīdī 2009; Chberreq 2014; El Guabli 2017; El Ouafi and Trotet 2004; Marouki 2015; Serhane 2004).

General Mohamed Oufkir's family members were also turned into enemies by association. In a situation that defies logical rationalisation, General Oufkir's entire family was disappeared simply due to their family ties to him. When the 1972 coup took place, General Oufkir was Minister of Defense, and the second most powerful man in Morocco after the king. Immediately after the failure of the first coup in 1971, Hassan II promoted Oufkir and enlarged his powers to protect his throne. Oufkir, however, had his own aspirations to rule Morocco alone. He was not only privy to Colonel Amkrane's plan to overthrow the monarchy in 1972, but recent testimonial literature reveals that he was the mastermind behind the coup (El Ouafi and Trotet 2004: 42; Serhane 2004: 23). Because of Oufkir's betrayal of the king, Oufkir's wife and six children, including three-year-old Abdellatif, and their maid were taken to an unknown location in the south of Morocco, where they would spend the next twenty years being transferred from one secret jail to another. The Oufkirs were denied any presumption of innocence in their father's treason of the king. Within hours of his execution, General Oufkir's house went from being the most powerful household in Morocco after the royal palace to being empty, silent and even erased from existence.

Although I have focused this contextualisation of the Years of Lead on the experiences of the Frontists, Tazmamart disappeared soldiers and the Oufkirs, I hasten to say that the implications of the Years of Lead transcend these cases. In fact, the Years of Lead are rife with stories of individuals, families, communities and entire regions, like the Rīf, that for one reason or another found themselves in direct confrontation with

Hassan II's regime. These traumatic experiences left intergenerational consequences, which have only recently been theorised (El Guabli 2018a). Specifically, as a result of the generalised terror unleashed by the state, Moroccan society in its entirety was traumatised by state violence,[6] thus requiring even more engagement with the collective dimensions of traumatic experiences recovered in these testimonial prison memoirs.

Since 1998, there has been a steady increase in the number of prefaces and jointly authored memoirs about the Years of Lead (Table 15.1).[7] Although Table 15.1 is not exhaustive, it demonstrates that the years between 2000 and 2006 witnessed the publication of at least twelve works in French and Arabic. Six of these works were published between 2000 and 2004, which coincided with the mobilisation of Moroccan civil society around the survivors' demands to establish a truth commission that would investigate the crimes committed in the past (Būdarqa and Binyūb 2017). The activist nature of joint authorship and preface-writing practices during this time was determined by their advocacy for the opening of the questions of the state crimes. Their publication amidst mobilisation for the establishment of survivors' rights and their rehabilitation was an act of activism. The existence of this literature has contributed directly to the establishment of Instance Equité et Réconciliation (henceforth ERC) on 7 January 2004, which King Mohammed VI tasked with the mission of investigating the crimes committed in the past, determining the fate of the forcibly disappeared and making recommendations on ways to resolve the legacy of this past (Hay'at al-inṣāf wal-muṣālaḥa 2004: n.p). Activist translation in the context of ERC's work continues the survivors' desire to establish the truth of their experiences, but also reveals a dogged insistence on providing details about the lived experiences of politically motivated violence, both inside and outside prison walls, in order to ensure the non-repetition of this past. Additionally, activist translation created a multilingual corpus of testimonial prison literature that addressed international readerships and limited the Moroccan state's options in regard to ignoring the demands of its victims.

In addition to showing the publication trends over the years, Table 15.1 gives us the profiles of preface writers and co-authors of Moroccan testimonial prison literature. It shows that co-authors range from highly accomplished writers, such as Abdelhak Serhane and François Trotet, who respectively co-authored memoirs with Tazmamart survivors Salah Hachad and Ahmed El Ouafi and their wives, to social-justice-oriented journalists, like Ignace Dalle, a former director of the French News Agency in Morocco, who wrote the preface to Ahmed Marzouki's bestseller *Tazmamart cellule 10* (*Tazmamart: Cell No. 10*) (2015) as well as Abdelfattah Fakihani's *Le couloir: Bribes de vérité sur les années de plomb* (*The Hallway: Fragments of Truth About the Years of Lead*) (2005). Lawyer Abderrahim Berrada, famous for his defence of the detainees during the Years of Lead, wrote the preface to Aziz Mouride's *On affame bien les rats* (*We Starve the Rats Really Well*) (2000) while Gilles Perrault, known for revealing the crimes of the Moroccan state in his book *Notre ami le roi* (*Our Friend the King*) (1990), wrote the preface to Driss Bouissef-Rekab's *A l'ombre de Lalla Chafia* (*Under the Shade of Lalla Chafia*) (2007a). Abraham Serfaty, a prominent leader of the Marxist-Leninist movement in Morocco, wrote the preface to Jaouad Mdidch's *La chambre noire* (*The Dark Chamber*). Other preface writers include Michèle Fitoussi, a Franco-Tunisian writer, who co-authored and prefaced Malika Oufkir's *La prisonnière* (*Stolen Lives: Twenty Years in a Desert Jail*) (1999). 'Abd al-Ḥamīd al-Jamāhīrī translated and wrote the preface to Muḥammad al-Rāys's *Min Skhirāt ilā Tazmamārt* (*From Skhirat to Tazmamart*) (2000) while Bilāl al-Talīdī compiled and wrote the preface to Mofadel Magouti's memoir *Wa ya 'lū ṣawtu al-'ādhān min jaḥīm*

Table 15.1 A non-exhaustive chart of testimonial prison literature works analysed in this chapter

Title of the memoir	Survivor's name	Co-author	Preface writer	Year	Original language	Co-authors'/preface writers' social status
al-'Arīs	Salāḥ al-Wadī'	No	'Abd al-Qādir al-Shāwī	1998	Arabic	A former Marxist-Leninist prisoner, novelist, translator and essayist
La prisonnière	Malika Oufkir	Yes	Michèle Fitoussi	1999	French	A prominent Franco-Tunisian journalist and novelist
La chambre noire, ou, Derb Moulay Chérif*	Jaouad Mdidch	No	Abraham Serftaty	2000	French	The ideologue of *Ilā al-Amām* and a Jewish former political detainee
On affame bien les rats!	Abdelaziz Mouride	No	Abderrahim Berrada/ Rachid Maaskri	2000	French	Berrada is a lawyer who defended political detainees in the 1970s
Tazmamart: Cellule 10	Aḥmad al-Marzūqī	No	Ignace Dalle	2000	French	A prominent French journalist and former director of l'Agence France-Presse's (AFP's) bureau in Rabat
Kitābāt bada'at min ḥay al-i'dām	Ḥakīmī Bilqāsim	No	Musṭfa Qāssū/ Muḥammad Hafīḍ	2001	Arabic	Prominent journalists
Ḥadīth al-'atama	Faṭna al-Bwīh	No	Fatima al-Zahrā' Azrwīl	2001	Arabic	A sociologist, translator and feminist scholar
Min Skhirat ilā Tazmamart: Tadhkiratu dhahāb wa iyyāb ila-l-jaḥīm	Muḥammad al-Rays	Yes	'Abd al-Ḥamīd al-Jamāhirī	2001	French	A prominent journalist, translator and writer
Opération Borak F5: 16 août 1972 L'attaque du Boeing royal	Ahmed and Kalima El Ouafi	François Trotet	No	2004	French	A French novelist
Kabazal: Les emmurés de Tazmamart	Salah and Aida Hachad	Abdelhak Serhane	Abdelhak Serhane	2004	French	A prominent Moroccan novelist and academic
Le couloir: Bribes de vérité sur les années de plomb	Abdelfattah Fakihani	No	Ignace Dalle	2005	French	A prominent French journalist and former director of AFP's bureau in Rabat
La tyrannie ordinaire: Lettres de prison	Driss Bouis-sef Rekab	No	'Abd al-Qadir al-Shāwī	2005	French	A former Marxist-Leninist prisoner,

(Continued)

Table 15.1 (Cont.)

Title of the memoir	Survivor's name	Co-author	Preface writer	Year	Original language	Co-authors'/preface writers' social status
						novelist, translator and essayist
A l'ombre de Lalla Chafia (second edition)	Driss Bouissef Rekab*	No	Gilles Perrault	2007	French	A prominent French journalist and human rights activist
Dhākirat faynīq: Sira dhātiyya li-wajh min sanawāt al-raṣāṣ	Saʿīd Ḥājjī	No	Tawfīqī Balʿīd	2006	Arabic	A former political detainee and poet
Wa yaʿlu ṣawtu al-ādhān min jaḥīm Tazmamart	Mofadel Maghouti	Bilāl al-Talīdī	Bilāl al-Talīdī	2009	Arabic	An Islamist journalist and political scientist
Le lit de la mort: Chronique d'une grève de la faim au pénitencier de Kénitra	Miloudi El Ktaïbi	Patrick Guès	Denis Pryen	2009	Arabic	Founder of L'Harmatten publishing house
Kāna wa akhawātuhā	ʿAbd al-Kader al-Shawi	No	ʿAbd al-Kader al-Shawi	2010	Arabic	A former Marxist-Leninist prisoner, novelist, translator and essayist
Courbis, mon chemin vers la vérité et le pardon	Mḥammad Lashqar	No	Ḥaṣan Awrīd	2012	French	A former spokesperson for the royal palace, novelist and political scientist
Le train fou: mémoires d'un rescapé de Tazmamart, 10 juillet 1971 au 29 octobre 1991	Driss T. Chberreq	No	Mustapha Bencheikh	2014	French	An academic in French Studies

* My analyses are based on the Arabic translations of these two works.

tazmamart (*Indeed, the Call to Prayer Raises from Tazmamart*) (2009).[8] Saʿīd Ḥājjī, a former prisoner, whose tribulations during the Years of Lead were due to corruption of top administrators, obtained a preface from Tawfīqī Balʿīd, a former political prisoner and poet turned publisher, for his book *Dhākirat faynīq* (*The Memory of a Phoenix*) (2006).

Muḥammad Ḥafīḍ, a university professor, and Mustapha Qāssu, a journalist, co-authored the preface to Ḥakīmī Belqāsim's *Kitābāt bada'at min ḥay al-i'dām* (*Writings Started from the Death Sentence Quarters*) (2001). Fāṭima al-Zahrā' Zriwīl prefaced Fatna El Bouih's *Ḥadīth al-'atama* (*Talk of Darkness*) (2001) in Arabic, but the preface was not included in the English translation.[9] Mustapha Bencheikh, a literary scholar, wrote the preface to Driss T. Chberreq's *Le train fou* (*The Crazy Train*) (2014). *Le train fou* was Chberreq's BA thesis in French under Bencheikh's supervision. Finally, of all preface writers, 'Abd al-Qādir al-Shāwī, a former political prisoner and prominent

243

ideologue of the Marxist-Leninist movement, has written prefaces for Salāḥ al-Wadī's *al-'Arīs* and Driss Bouissef-Rekab's *La tyrannie ordinaire* (*Ordinary Tyranny*) (2005). In 2010, al-Shāwī prefaced the second edition of his novel *Kāna wa akhawātuhā* (*Kāna and its Sisters*) (2010). Beyond their ubiquity, these joint authorship and preface-writing practices point to how their interpretative acts have consequences for Moroccan society as a whole.

Beyond the context of the prefaces and co-authored memoirs, which I address in the next section, I want to underline the fact that these co-authors and preface writers hail from a variety of backgrounds that are representative of the richness of Moroccan society. Straddling different ethnic, national, linguistic, professional and social backgrounds, these co-authors and preface writers open up testimonial literature's multilayered dimensions to interrogations about translation as it relates to democratisation, social justice and citizenship. While there are no tangible criteria why and how specific individuals were solicited to co-author a memoir or pen a preface for one, it is possible to surmise from the published works that those who agree to be involved in these projects have a vested interest in contributing to wider debates about democratisation and political change through memory and rewriting history.

Some of these preface writers have a long history of struggle with the Moroccan authorities, thus, for them, prefacing a testimonial work is another way of continuing their struggle for the Morocco that they have sacrificed for. In lending their voices to those of the survivors of state violence, they attest to the truth of their experiences, support their testimony, become co-witnesses and further contextualise political disappearance in Morocco in contexts that survivors may not be able to do. Their different backgrounds notwithstanding, these activist co-authors of testimonial literature share an unwavering ethical desire to redress the wrongs done to all the victims of state violence and their society at large.

Co-authorship and preface writing as activist translations

In engaging in translation practices that challenge grand narratives, defy institutionalised hegemonies and partake in the ideological struggles in their societies, translation practitioners undertake activist acts (Baker 2010: 23, 27; Tymoczko 2010: 6). In the words of Baker, activist translators 'invest emotionally and intellectually in projects designed to undermine dominant discourses' (2010: 34). Baker, however, warns that accusations of bias and untrustworthiness could jeopardise translator activists' projects, which forces them to mark their translational activism through 'various methods of framing the translation, including paratexts, timing of the release of translations, [and] where translations are placed' (Baker 2010: 35).

Paratexts are particularly crucial for activist translation practices because, for the activist translator, the form is as important as the translation itself. French literary theorist Gérard Genette defined a paratext as that which 'enables a text to become a book and to be offered as such to its readers' (Genette 1997a: 1). Made of 'a title, a subtitle, intertitles; prefaces, postfaces, notices, forwards, etc.,' the paratext is a space of mediation between the in-text and the off-text, between what constitutes the body of the book and what is added to make that body more legible (Genette 1997b: 3). These paratextual constituents of the book are all the more crucial in testimonial prison literature. Because the latter is premised on the truth of the experiences narrated, the paratextual additions, from images to subtitles and prefaces, are ethically bound to confirm the truth of the translated experience. In this sense, the activist translator who participates in the writing of a testimonial prison work becomes a co-witness to the testimony of the experience he elicited from the survivor. It would even be said that total trust of the survivor reflected in the paratext is a requisite for activist translation. Because of the difficulty of proving the veracity of experiences lived during political disappearance, the paratext becomes pivotal to testimonial prison literature's very ability to acquire the stamp of truth.

The survivor's disappeared and battered body is the source of testimonial literature. It is the locus where the suffering endured during disappearance is sedimented, but it is oftentimes the only material evidence that may be left of an undocumented ordeal, which makes its translation all the more crucial. In his work on translation, Roman Jakobson defined three ways in which linguists interpret verbal signs: interlingual, intra-lingual and intersemiotic (Jakobson 1959: 233). Of these three ways, 'intersemiotic translation,' which Jakobson defines as 'an interpretation of verbal signs by means of signs of nonverbal systems' is productive in its reversed version (Jakobson 1959: 233). In a reversed reinterpretation of this Jakobsonian definition of intersemiotic translation in which verbal signs are translated into non-verbal signs, Hron draws on immigrant communities' expressions of suffering to theorise the movement from the realm of the non-verbal (embodied) to the realm of inscription (publication) (Hron 2009: 40). In this reversed paradigm, intersemiotic translation means transferring non-verbal signs—pain, suffering and torment—into written form (Hron 2009: 40). Conveying their pain, Hron argues, requires immigrants 'to identify it, describe it, understand it, but also to transform it' (Hron 2009: 40). Hron's theorisation of this reversed intersemiotic translation opens up a space for us to consider jointly authored memoirs as inscriptive translations of embodied painful experiences, encompassing arrest, torture, interrogation, trial, imprisonment and disappearance.

Translation studies scholars have indeed grappled with the preface as a paratextual constituent of translation (Sanconie 2007; Sardin 2007). Dimitriu, for instance, has defined three functions for translators' prefaces. A translator's preface can fulfil an 'explanatory,' 'normative/prescriptive' or 'informative/descriptive' function (2009: 195). Translators may use the preface to explain their choices, provide advice to their peers and to analyse the translated work. Translators' prefaces or lack thereof have also raised questions about their importance for both the visibility of the translator and the consecration of a translated work as translation (McRae 2012: 66–69; Venuti 1995). Rather than focusing on the status of the translator through the preface, however, a more productive approach in the context of testimonial prison literature is to examine prefaces as acts of testimonial activist translation. While prefaces in testimonial literature and testimonial prison literature specifically are translations that are strongly embedded in ethical and moral considerations, they also entail a high degree of interpretation.

In making this proposition, I follow in the footsteps of Daniel and Aline Patte who distinguished between exegesis as 'the comprehension of the text itself' and hermeneutic, which 'reveals what it means to the interpreter and his contemporaries' (Patte and Patte 1978: 13). Because of the fact that the would-be text is in itself the result of the act of translation, both the meaning of the text and its interpretation happen concurrently. As a result of this simultaneity, co-authors and preface writers' interpretative acts of translation in testimonial prison literature render unproveable experiences into a language that signifies in and of itself and upholds the truth of the survivor's experience. The truth of a testimonial work matters for the survivors as well as for their communities and societies to whose collective experience it bears witness. Beyond bearing witness, however, testimony is 'a model for a new form of politics, which also means a new way of imagining the identity of the nation' (Beverley 2004: xvii). Because one of testimony's aspirations is to build a new polity through the creation of a more inclusive collective memory, the endeavours of co-authors and preface writers' acts of activist translation in testimonial literature are instrumental to achieving this change. Both activist translation and testimony are underlaid by the idea that they can effectuate societal changes (Beverley 2004; Tymoczko 2010: 7), which requires further analysis of the ways in which they operate in the Moroccan context.

This focus on testimony's transformative action reveals testimonial prison literature's and its translators' socio-political impact beyond the mere telling of the truth. Both survivors and their partners—co-authors and preface writers alike—use translation to transform the conditions that allowed the violations recounted to happen. Those who partake in testimonial literature projects make their interventions from clear positions about what society, politics and history should become in order for the past violations not to be repeated. Because it involves revealing silenced acts of systematic violence that remained inaccessible to the citizenry, testimony has the capacity to change a society's perceptions about its history, memory and even polity. It also has the potential to catalyse political change.

The Moroccan Truth and Justice Forum (*al-muntadā al-maghribī min ajl al-ḥaqīqa wal-inṣāf*), which was created in 1999 by survivors of state repression during the Years of Lead, summarises this important question in wondering how the page of state crimes could be turned without it having been fully read, and more importantly, without action to protect society from its sequelae (Būdarqa and Binyūb 2017: 374)—questions which point to the necessity of political change in Morocco. In line with this train of thought, both the survivors and their co-authors build on testimonies' ethical force to transform their present and establish guarantees for a better future. The activist nature of the testimony and the act of transcribing it emanate from these considerations and from the consequences they hold for any given society's social and cultural memory.

Nonetheless, there should be no illusion that the mere publication of activist translations is enough to achieve the transformations the survivors and their co-authors and preface writers seek. Transformation only happens when these translations of the experience are used to perform human rights and memory in the public arena (Slyomovics 2005). The jointly authored testimonial prison texts as well as the prefaces, which are usually solicited from specific individuals, establish their afterlife once they become the object of various usages in social memory. Through public readings of testimonial prison literature, its serialization in newspapers and the different mnemonic and commemorative practices built around these works, testimonial prison literature is thrust into society, where other types of activist struggles draw on its materiality to make political transformation possible. For instance, it was the public unfolding of Muḥammad al-Rāys's memoir *Min Skhirāt ilā Tazmamart* in the daily newspaper *al-Ittiḥād al-Ishtirākī* that submerged Moroccans in details of state violence and transformed their views of their state (El Guabli 2017). 'Abd al-Ḥamīd al-Jamāhīrī's translation and serialization of al-Rāys's memoirs contributed significantly to the ongoing demands for the Moroccan state to acknowledge its wrongdoing in the past. Outside Morocco, Gilles Perrault's book *Notre ami le roi* (1990), which wedded literary accomplishment with interpretations of various disappearance experiences, caught human rights groups' attention and contributed to the liberation of Moroccan political detainees, including the ones disappeared to Tazmamart (Daure-Serfaty 1992; El Guabli 2018b).

Co-authorship as translation: from embodied experience to text

In the following analysis I demonstrate how the co-authors of *Kabazal: Les emmurés de Tazmamart* (*Kabazal: The Prisoners of Tazmamart*) (2004), *Opération Borak F5: 16 août 1972 l'attaque du Boeing royal* (*Borak Operation F5: 16 August 1972, Attack on the Royal Boeing*) (2004), *La prisonnière* (1999), and *Wa ya'lū ṣawtu al-'adhān min jaḥīm tazmamart* (2009) engaged in different levels of translation of embodied experiences through the prism of reversed intersemiotic translation and paratext.

Abdelhak Serhane published *Kabazal* in 2004 based on the testimonies of Salah and Aïda Hachad. In Salah Hachad's words, with 'Aïda, I decided to write our memoirs. I, my struggle inside Tazmamart, and she, her fight in the outside' (Bernichi 2004). Hachad explains further that after writing their memoirs they 'entrusted Abdelhak Serhane with them in order to give them literary force' (Bernichi 2004). Organised in two halves, each half of *Kabazal* is narrated by one of the two survivors. While Salah recounts Tazmamart from within, Aïda depicts the gendered and familial aspects of state violence outside prison (El Guabli 2018a: 121–125). Without realising it, however, Salah Hachad's explanation of the process of their writing of their memoir in a journalistic interview draws attention to the intralingual translation he and his wife asked Serhane to undertake. Hachad reveals that he and Aïda handed their written memoirs to novelist and academic Abdelhak Serhane to infuse them with literary intensity—to transform them into a memoir. In this sense, Serhane was tasked with the sensitive work of transforming lived experience, written in its survivors' unembellished, testimonial style, into something more elaborate, more literary, and even more dramatic. Thus, Serhane has translated the testimonial prison memoir within the same language by rendering it from a rudimentary form of writing into literary language. Rather than having to elicit the embodied experience and transform it into a written work, Serhane was given an already existing text to rewrite into an idiom, another language that is supposedly, in the Hachads' understanding, more sophisticated, because more literary. In this case, however, the survivors exercised their agency to choose that their written text be translated into Serhane's professional idiom, which poses significant challenges to the idea and premise of truth in testimony.

Although Serhane received the manuscript from Salah and Aïda Hachad, he is still listed as the main author of the book. Indeed, the paratext of the memoir is where we find that Serhane's joint authorship of *Kabazal* entailed more than just transposing it from one language register to another within the French language. My analysis of the paratext reveals Serhane's activist inscription of the memoir in reference to texts and discourses that may not even have been of interest to Salah and Aïda Hachad. For instance, the epigraph includes a saying in which King Hassan II expressed his joy at 'having done everything he could to spread happiness around [him], not wronging anyone, having harmed no one' (Serhane 2004: n.p.). Yet, the placement of Montesquieu's truism that it is 'an eternal experience that any man who has power is doomed to abuse it' immediately below Hassan II's words deprives them of any validity (Serhane 2004: n.p.). The paratext also indicates the importance Serhane has accorded to engendering the experience of the Years of Lead. Opening Aïda Hachad's section of the memoir is a paragraph in which Elisabeth Guigou, a former French minister, stresses that what was needed were 'women who dare to transgress the immemorial prohibitions' faced by women (Serhane 2004: 197). Further entrenching this feminist orientation is the inclusion of Guigou's call for 'women to be supportive of each other, not in order to kick men out, but in order to allow each woman, wherever she wishes it, to bring to public life her share of humanity' (Serhane 2004: 197). Combining ideas from a variety of theoretical sources, *Kabazal* is an excellent example of how the translator/co-author reinscribes testimonial prison literature in wider discourses in political philosophy, feminist theory and memory struggles. Clearly conscious of the context in which he was entrusted with the manuscript, Serhane uses the translation authority vested in him to exercise his activist role by giving the manuscript its final shape. The dedication is where Serhane's own voice and authority appear to mark his presence in the testimonial endeavour:

> *To the memory of those who did not survive the torments of the Years of Lead.*
> *To the memory of those who perished under torture in Qal'at M'Gouna, Derb*
> *Moulay Cherif, Dar al-Moqri, Agdz, and other secret detention centres.*
> *To the memory of Morocco, inhabited by the fear of the dark years, in order to say*
> *'enough!'*
> *To today's Morocco in order to reject amnesia, arbitrariness, impunity. This*
> *Morocco is absolutely going to the dogs and to say to those who betray that his-*
> *tory does not forget.*
> *To the memory of all those who never returned from Tazmamart.*
> *I dedicate this book so that the terror does not happen again.*
> (Serhane 2004: n.p., italics in the original, my translation)

Moroccan testimonial prison literature is no different in terms of the theoretical questions related to the visibility or invisibility of the translator (Venuti 1995). For example, while Serhane's co-translator's status is expressed in paratextual markers, François Trotet, the co-author of *Opération Borak F5* has endeavoured to erase his presence from the text. Other than indicating on the cover of the book that he collected the testimonies, nothing reveals the degree of Trotet's intervention in the memoir or the extent of his curatorial endeavours in preparing the text, including the decisions he might have made about language, style, pictures and archival documents included in the memoir. The ambiguity of Trotet's role is made even more intriguing when we read Ahmed El Ouafi's exultation of his wife having 'kindly written [a narra-tive] in order to shed light on the countless trials our families underwent while we were imprisoned' (El Ouafi and Trotet 2004: 6). This sentence from El Ouafi's intro-duction to the memoir indicates that Kalima El Ouafi has written her section to bear testimony to the gendered aspects of political violence outside the disappearance system. Therefore, there is reason to think that both El Ouafi and his wife entrusted a manuscript to Trotet to work from. However, one still wonders whether Trotet's translation of the El Ouafis' experience was intralinguistic or intersemiotic—a question that cannot be adjudicated due to the dearth of information about their collaboration. What is certain is that Trotet contributed to the further translation of the Years of Lead. However, his status as a foreigner may have limited his margin of manoeuvre.

Where Serhane and Trotet are silent concerning the process of their joint authorship of Hachad's and El Ouafi's testimonies, Michèle Fitoussi's and Bilāl al-Talīdī's joint authorship of Malika Oufkir's memoir *La prisonnière* and Mofadel Magouti's *Wa ya'lū ṣawtu al-adhān*, respectively, provides richer information about translation in this con-text. Both Fitoussi and al-Talīdī translate the testimonial text, which they produced as a result of a reversed intersemiotic translation, by underlining their empathy with the survivors and also by inscribing the act of testimony within a bigger ideological project, especially in al-Talīdī's case, or a personal journey, in the case of Fitoussi. For instance, both Fitoussi and al-Talīdī weave their own stories into the stories of the survivors whose experiences of state violence they help reconstruct. Michèle Fitoussi underlines how, after meeting Malika Oufkir at a party, she could immediately see the weight of suffering she carried inside her. Interpreting her own life through Malika's, Fitoussi reflects on how she, a Franco-Tunisian Jewish woman, was able to fulfil her dreams and live her life fully at the same time Malika Oufkir, her peer, was passing her formative years being transferred from one detention centre to another (Oufkir and Fitoussi 2001: 2–3). For Fitoussi, the activist act of jointly writing and translating Malika's disappearance story emanated from deeply personal considerations. Her obsession with Malika's story became a fantasy that 'Malika tell [her] her story, and [she] wanted to write it with her' (Oufkir and Fitoussi 2001: 3). Fully cognisant of her role as a translator of Malika's experience of political disappearance, Fitoussi does not shy away from acknowledging the fact that *La prisonnière* is both Malika's words and emotions and hers. She underlines:

> [w]hat I wanted to convey, what we convey together, with her words and mine, with her sentiments and our shared emotion, is above all the incredible journey of a woman of my generation, incarcerated from earliest childhood, first in a palace and then in prisons, and who is now trying to live her life.
>
> *(Oufkir and Fitoussi 2001: 7)*

The co-author/co-translator here underlines that her voice and the voice of the survivor are commingled to communicate Malika's extraordinary journey. Fitoussi points out the fact that it is not just the experience of survival that is translated in this context, but also the emotions of both the survivor and the translator whose relationship was cemented through their collaboration. Rather than pretend that the book is Malika Oufkir's alone, Fitoussi perceptively signals where her own voice as a translator is present in the final work. Moreover, Fitoussi's effort to empathise with Malika and humanise her must originate from the fact that she is the daughter of General Oufkir—a man who was responsible for many tragedies of the Years of Lead. The activist act of foregrounding Malika Oufkir's qualities as a human being against the demonisation of her father, General Oufkir, required that Fitoussi use her own story to translate Malika's. Beyond this humanisation effort, *La prisonnière* is a crucial intervention in Moroccan history through the eyes of the adolescent that Malika Oufkir was when the events she recounts happened.

Bilāl al-Talīdī, on the other hand, reveals the agenda behind his involvement in the writing of *Wa ya'lū ṣawtu al-ādhān*. His reversed intersemiotic translation of Magouti's experience into a written memoir is rationalised with an Islamist project of memory (El Guabli 2017). After pre-emptively dispelling any criticism that might be triggered by his 'tilling of an already tilled land,' Bilāll al-Talīdī stresses the significance and the novelty of his work in jointly writing Mofadel Maghouti's memoir (al-Talīdī 2009:5). Al-Talīdī writes that *Wa ya'lū ṣawtu al-adhān*

> was a different experience that does not stop at the event as such, but records the moments of weakness and strength and recounts cases of human psychology as it

faces torment. [An experience] that conveys faith-related positions of prisoners who found in clinging to God a way to face slow death. When the matter in question is a unique experience that focuses on the role of the religious factor in this plight and the role of the Quran in fighting death and resisting suicide, frustration, and desperation, then it is difficult not to repeat the writing experience, especially when it is about a prisoner of the stature of Mofadel Magouti.

(al-Talīdī 2009: 3, my translation)

Thus, al-Talīdī has underlined that what distinguishes his rendering of Tazmamart is the faith-infused attempt to reveal the power of the Quran and Islamic faith in the survival of those who managed to survive the notorious prison camp. While he excluded suffering as the main lesson from Magouti's experience, al-Talīdī zeroed in on 'the magnitude of the power of faith, which God deposited in the human heart and to which he gave the ability to confront the absolutism of power and oppression' (al-Talīdī 2009: 4). Unlike the other memoirs, al-Talīdī endeavoured to place Magouti above other survivors of the ordeal of Tazmamart. His approach, however, reveals a disparity between him placing Magouti in a high pedestal as a pious man and the fact that he treated him as a container of an experience that he alone recorded and wrote into a memoir. Where Michèle Fitoussi explains the writing process in a way that foregrounds Malika Oufkir's agency and collaborative involvement in the joint authorship of *La prisonnière*, al-Talīdī foregrounds his own contribution to the genre of testimonial prison literature and the ways in which his translation of Magouti's experience adds something new to the field. Time and again, al-Talīdī reiterates his hope of 'bringing the reader closer to the dimension that has been absent from these [previous testimonial prison] prisons' (al-Talīdī 2009: 5): the religious dimension of testimonial literature. He sees himself as unique in being able to bring this dimension to the fore.

In testimonial prison literature, activist translation, in the form of joint authorship, is a continuous process of negotiation between the survivor, who carries an embodied experience archived in their body and survives to tell the story, and the professional co-author/translator, who mediates the transformation of this lived experience into textual form. From this analysis of paratextual aspects of four jointly authored testimonial memoirs, it could be concluded that not all co-authors engaged in reverse intersemiotic translation. While Fitoussi and al-Talīdī had to sit with the survivors to elicit information from their recollections of their embodied experiences in order to transform them into written memoirs, Serhane and Trotet mediated the transformation of a written version of the embodied experience into a more sophisticated form of writing. Thus, each of the four co-authors engaged in different types of activist translation of testimonial literature.

One of the results of these different approaches is that al-Talīdī and Fitoussi, due to the deeply intersemiotic nature of their translations of Magouti's and Oufkir's experiences, reveal a higher degree of emotional, mental and affective investment in their projects, which is manifested in their empathetic and humanising gestures towards the survivors. Serhane's and Trotet's silences on their own positions vis-à-vis their experiences reconstructed allow us, on the other hand, to also take into consideration the variety of ways in which each translator marks their presence in the final experience midwifed into textual form. These analyses substantiate Tymoczko's argument that translators' activist endeavours are revealed in 'the shift they introduce in the texts they produce, including shifts in content, textual form, and political valences' (Tymoczko 2010: 6)—elements present, in various degrees, in the memoirs analysed in this section.

Preface writing as retranslation of testimony and as co-witnessing

Having demonstrated how various levels of translation interact with each other when embodied experience is written into a testimonial work, I shift my attention in this section to the study of prefaces as acts of activist translation. In the context of struggle against institutional amnesia of state violence, prefaces to testimonial prison literature have major implications for both translation and testimony as activist practices. Activism begins when a person of high moral probity agrees to preface a testimonial text, thus adding their own voice to the voice of the direct witness of experiences of state violence. The preface writer undertakes the risk of confronting the state, and in the process manifests his readiness to deal with the backlash that might be triggered by having lent his voice to the survivor. The prevalence of preface writing during the politically tumultuous period between 1998 and 2006 is particularly significant. During this period, preface-writing practices played a crucial role in bringing attention to the survivors of the Years of Lead's unaddressed social, economic, financial and moral suffering. Although their work is similar to that of independent journalists, who reported on the Moroccan state's past violations of human dignity, preface writers, unlike journalists, support the truthfulness of the accounts they preface and are ready to be part of a larger debate about them.

My survey of the different ways in which testimonial prison works in Morocco were introduced to a broader reading public demonstrates that each preface interprets the experience at hand from the perspective of the author. Ranging between introducing the book, interpreting its significance, highlighting its contributions and supporting its veracity, prefaces were composed as activist translation in open conversation with the socio-political context that was unfolding before the eyes of their authors amid Morocco's transitional justice process. These prefaces also reveal how translation and interpretation function in testimonial prison literature. Although some of these functions overlap in various degrees in different prefaces, my research has revealed a number of ways in which prefaces act as testimonial translations. Accordingly, an activist preface in testimonial literature can be understood in four ways:

1) A confirmative act: Activist prefaces are confirmative statements in which the survivor's experience is validated. More than an act of empathy, confirming the experience is a necessary step towards justice, rehabilitation and non-repetition of the crimes of the past. For instance, 'Abd al-Hamīd al-Jamāhirī underlines the truthfulness of Mohammed al-Rāys's account before discussing the risks involved in giving such a testimony. Al-Jamāhirī indicates that al-Rāys might find himself accused of 'libel, lying and endangering the safety of the state' (al-Rāys 2010: 6). Yet instead of merely granting credence to al-Rāys's testimony, al-Jamāhirī adds a future-oriented perspective in proposing that written experiences about the Years of Lead contain 'elements for the construction of a future temporality' (al-Rāys 2010: 6) in Morocco. Hence, the preface writer confirms the experience, interprets its significance and identifies its uses for the future construction of a different Morocco, thus inscribing it in a project of change.

2) An interpretative act: Most prefaces I have surveyed are interpretative in the sense that they render into theoretical and conceptual language specific aspects of the text at hand. For instance, 'Abd al-Qādir al-Shāwī's prefaces are highly interpretative. His prefaces to his novel *Kāna wa akhawātuhā*, Driss Bouissef Rekab's *La tyrannie ordinaire*, and Ṣalāḥ al-Wadī''s *al-'Arīs* engage in different levels of meta-analysis

251

of the works from a position of political, literary and intellectual maturity. His retrospective reflections on the experiences revisited in these works allow al-Shāwī to engage critically with the importance of the events portrayed. For instance, his conclusion that *al-ʿArīs* 'had to be this way: subjective, revealing even as it avoids reportage, a testimony that confuses those who today extol the virtues of democracy about a time when the brave soul had neither shelter nor safety except in the heart of torment' (al-Wadīʿ 1998: 7) illustrates this interpretative function.

Ignace Dalle's introductions to Ahmed Marzouki's bestseller *Tazmamart: Cellule 10* and Abdelfattah Fakihani's memoir *Le couloir* also contain a great deal of interpretation. Writing in the context of the state's backlash against Marzouki's plans to publish his memoirs, Dalle delivered a defence of Marzouki's endeavour in which he discards revenge as a motive for writing the book. As if to appease the Moroccan state, Dalle foregrounded recovering the truth, fostering reconciliation and rejection of revenge as Marzouki's goals (Marzouki 2015: 6). For Dalle, Marzouki wrote his book 'to inform his compatriots of how life was in Tazmamart so that no such monstrosity happens again' (Marzouki 2015: 7). Dalle continues the same interpretative approach in his preface to Fakihani's memoirs. Rather than focusing on alleviating anyone's fears, this time, however, Dalle stressed the uniqueness of Fakihani's memoir in his 'courage, clarity of mind, and honesty' (Fakihani 2005: 7), which allowed him to critique the experiences of the radical left in Morocco.

3) A critical act: Attempts to rethink the experience and its broader implications are analytical. Abraham Serfaty's provocative preface to Jaouad Mdidch's *al-Ghurfa al-sawdāʾ* is an important example in this regard. Faithful to his feisty revolutionary ideal to overthrow the monarchy based on his Marxist-Leninist convictions of the 1970s, which led to his lengthy imprisonment from 1974 to 1991 and then exile from 1991 to 1999, Serfaty analyses the history of the Moroccan Marxist-Leninist movement, identifying its achievements as well as its failures, all through his reading of Mdidch's testimony (Mdidch 2007: 5–8). Also, ʿAbd al-Qādir al-Shāwī dons the critic's hat in the preface he wrote to Driss Boussouif Rekab's *La Tyrannie ordinaire*. For example, his analysis of the Marxist-Leninist movement focuses on the concepts of history and memory and how they connect to testimonial writing. Al-Shāwī suggested his conviction that 'that writing, in this very precise case, embodies multiple forms of representation, interconnected and complementary with each other' (Bouissef Rekab 2005: 7).

Although imprisoned and mistreated for revealing his state officials' corruption, Saʿīd Ḥājjī, whose crime is non-political compared to those who were actively involved in politics, published a memoir entitled *Dhākiratu faynīq* (*The Memory of Phoenix*). The latter elicited a critical preface from former political prisoner Tawfiqī Balʿīd. Not only did Balʿīd comment on the autobiographical nature of the memoir, but he also used the preface to revisit the broader effects Years of Lead had on Moroccan society. Balʿīd has written that Ḥājjī 'has proven the extent to which political despotism and police repression is connected with the spoliation of the people's resources more to political, intellectual and religious disagreement' (Ḥājjī 2005: 7).

4) A gendering of testimonial prison literature: Translating gendered experiences of disappearance, torture and imprisonment requires its own linguistic regime, as

Fāṭima al-Zahrā' Azrwīl's preface to Fatna El Bouih's *Ḥadīth al-'atama* eloquently demonstrates. Azrwīl underlines the gendered nature of state violence experienced by Moroccan women during the Years of Lead and argues that 'steadfastness (*al-ṣumūd*) could be feminine even if torturers insist on stripping women of it and giving them [women prisoners] male names' (El Bouih 2001: 6). Moreover, the gendered nature of repression transcends the political prisoner to have consequences for society. El Bouih writes that *Ḥadīth al-'atama*

> reveals/exposes the torments of the soul and the bodily violation suffered by the female political prisoner, but also the forms of resistance and steadfastness it catalysed. However, preface writing goes beyond that to embrace aspects of the reality of ordinary prisoners and their suffering.
>
> *(El Bouih 2001: 7, my translation)*

Azrwīl uses the preface to capture the condition of Moroccan women both inside and outside prisons. The gendered nature of victimhood during the Years of Lead also appears in Ignace Dalle's preface to Fakihani's *Le couloir*. This time, however, Dalle directs focuses his attention on Fakihani's description of the underground organisation's deprivation of its members of love by forcing them to forsake their beloved wives and girlfriends in order to protect the secret organisation from police infiltration (Fakihani 2005: 8, 89–96).

A preface in testimonial literature is not an ordinary introduction that eulogises an academic achievement or summarises a novel argument. Its production is an activist act involving multiple layers of translation. There are as many translations of testimonial prison literature as there are preface writers. Each preface writer chooses an angle from which to translate the survivor's experience for the readers, public opinion and people in power. Although each of the functions of testimonial prefaces identified above is crucial, the context of political struggle against the repressive state intensifies their significance. Because of their collective nature and the fact that they enable a process of political reform based on the resolution of the crimes of the past, these testimonial prison writings have piqued the interest of major political, literary and journalistic figures, who agreed to be involved in their co-creation. While their words are published as part of the survivors' memoirs, prefaces are addressed to Moroccan society and its social and cultural memory in general.

Conclusion

I have argued that joint authorship and prefatory practices in post-1999 Morocco function as activist translations on different levels. Because of the context in which they emerge, these practices dissent from the institutional attitude vis-à-vis the past they reopen. The cognitive, narrative and reframing processes involved in making survivors' experiences legible to larger audience have placed them at the heart of debates still taking place about testimony and its centrality to political transition, transitional justice and democratisation in Morocco.

Drawing on theorists' efforts to conceptualise Genette's concept of paratexts as reversed intersemiotic translation, and drawing on the primary texts I analyse, I have demonstrated that activist translation is constitutive of the narrative reconstruction and interpretation of the experiences of survivors of state violence. The paratextual aspects of testimonial prison literature published in Morocco between 1998 and 2017 show that joint authorship and preface writing come with various translation privileges that co-authors use to inscribe the memoir in emotional, ideological, intellectual or analytical realms that may not have occurred to the survivors. Despite the ceaseless translations between the body and experience, memory and writing, involved in joint authorship and preface writing, I have not come across any insinuation that these practices impact the veracity of the accounts.[10] Rather, these practices are wholeheartedly embraced, which further confirms their importance for the consecration of the collective nature of the Years of Lead.

Finally, prefaces are a depository of emotions, which also give a different dimension to our concerns with testimonial literature's engagement with the emotional histories of societies that suffered political violence. Joint authorship and preface writing enable the expression of emotions elicited by reading or listening to stories of political disappearance, torture and the violation of human dignity. They function as loci of emotional histories that await to be probed.

Related topics

Activist Narratives; Rendering Bengali Dalit Discourse as Translational Activism; Translating Mourning Walls.

Notes

1 Although this practice started with the publication of 'Abd al-Qādir al-Shāwī's *Kāna wa akhawātuhā* in 1984, the publication of *al-'Arīs* marked the beginning of the widespread use of prefaces in post-1999 Morocco. Several of al-Shāwī's cellmates wrote an afterword to *Kāna wa akhawātuhā*, which is an important contribution to the genre.

2 Only a few months after its establishment, the Equity and Reconciliation Commission (ERC) received over 20,000 applications for reparations. ERC president Driss Benzekri told Human Rights Watch in an interview that his commission received 'close to 40,000 pieces of correspondence, concerning between 25,000 and 30,000 cases' and predicted that 'when the work is completed, it is likely that only 10,000 to 15,000 of these cases will be determined eligible for compensation' (Human Rights Watch 2005). Commissioners Aḥmad Shawqī Binyūb and Mbark Būdrqa reference over 25,000 applications (2017: 61).

3 Abraham Serfaty, the ideologue of the *Ilā al-Amām* secret organisation, specifically criticises the use of *sanawāt al-raṣāṣ* to refer to a period which, in his opinion, was pitch dark. He told his interlocutor in an interview that the years described as the Years of Lead 'were black while lead is grey [...]. These years were black indeed, complete darkness' (Ḥuzal 2008: 23).

4 For more information about the partisan aspects of this political violence, see al-Tajkānī, A. A. (1987) *Dār Barīshah, aw qiṣṣat mukhtaṭaf*. Ed. Aḥmad Maʿnīnū. Casablanca: Maṭbaʿat al-Najāḥ al-Jadīda.

5 These groups were Ilā al-Amām (Forward!), Linakhdum al-shaʿb (Let's Serve the People) and 23 Mārs (23 March Movement, in reference to 1965 events in Casablanca). Ilā al-Amām and 23 Mārs were created in 1970, but Linakhdum al-shaʿb emerged from a secession within 23 Mārs. The members of Linakhdum al-shaʿb prioritised armed struggle and confrontational tactics over the long-term work on political indoctrination of the proletariat.

6 I use collective trauma in this context following Gilad's definition. According to Hirschberger, the 'term *collective trauma* refers to the psychological reactions to a traumatic event that affects an entire society' (Hirschberger 2018: 1). I use collective trauma in the Moroccan context not to imply that every Moroccan had the same experience of the Years of Lead, but rather to indicate the fact that awareness of state violence had marked generations

of Moroccans and shaped the limitations that condition what many Moroccans today think they could or could not say or do.

7 For all important information about the co-translators, preface writers, the languages in which the books were initially published as well as the social importance of the different co-translators/preface writers, see Table 15.1.

8 Apart from 'Abd al-Qādir al-Shāwī, Fatima al-Zahrā' Azrwīl, and 'Abd al-Ḥamīd al-Jamāhirī, who did professional translation in different capacities, the rest of the co-authors and preface writers included in this study cannot be considered translators in the traditional sense of the term.

9 In an email exchange on 8 October 2018, Fatna El Bouih stated that the preface and a friend's letter that she included at the end of the Arabic version were removed on the recommendation of the editor at her US publisher.

10 The exception is probably Bilāl al-Talīdī's Islamisation of Mofadel Maghouti's memoirs.

Further reading

Davies, Peter (2014) 'Testimony and Translation,' *Translation and Literature* 23 (2): 170–184.

Based on translations of Holocaust testimony, this article probes the ways in which ideas about genre affect translation of Holocaust testimony into different cultures.

Hawker, Nancy (2018) 'The Journey of Arabic Human Rights Testimonies, from Witnesses to Audiences via Amnesty International,' *Translation Spaces* 7 (1): 65–91.

This important article investigates the modalities involved in Amnesty International's translators' translation of Arabic testimonies into English.

Norridge, Zoe (2013) *Perceiving Pain in African Literature*. London: Palgrave Macmillan.

A seminal study of African literature's representations of pain. Combining the study of both fiction and life writings, this book could help translation theorists engage questions of testimony and pain as in translation.

References

Al-Rāys, Muḥammad (2001) *Min al-Skhirāt ilā Tazmamārt tadhkiratu dhahāb wa iyāb ila al-jaḥīm*. Casablanca, Morocco: Afriqia al-Sharq.
al-Rāys, Muḥammad (2010) *Min Skhirat ilā Tazmamart: tadhkiratu dhahāb wa iyyāb ila-l-jaḥīm*. Tr. 'Abd al-Ḥamīd al-Jamāhirī. Casablanca: Afriqiā al-Sharq.
al-Shāwī, 'Abd al-Qādir (2010) *Kāna wa akhwātuhā*. Casablanca: al-Fanaq.
al-Tajkānī, A. Al-Mahdī (1987) *Dār Barīshah, aw qiṣṣat mukhtaṭaf*. Ed. Aḥmad Ma'nīnū. Casablanca: Maṭba'at al-Najāḥ al-Jadīda.
al-Talīdī, Bilāl (2009) *Wa-ya'lū ṣawtu al-ādhān min jaḥīm Tazmamart (And the Call to Prayer Rises from the Hell of Tazmamart)*. al-Ribāt: Manshūrāt al-Tajdīd.
al-Wadī', Ṣalāḥ (1998) *al-'Arīs*. Casablanca: Maṭba 'at al-Najāḥ.
Amnesty International (1977) *Amnesty International Report 1977*. London: Amnesty International.
Apter, Emily (2005) 'Translation with No Original: Scandals of Textual Reproduction,' in *Nation, Language, and the Ethics of Translation*. Eds. Emily Apter, Sandra Berman and Michael Wood. Princeton: Princeton University Press. 159–174.
Baker, Mona (2010) 'Translation and Activism: Emerging Patterns of Narrative Community,' in *Translation, Resistance, Activism*. Ed. Maria Tymoczko. Amherst: University of Massachusetts Press. 23–41.
Benamro, Abderrahman (2005) 'Nadwa ḥawla al-mutāba'āt wal-muḥākamāt dhāt al-ṣibgha al-siyyāsiyya in 1956 ilā 1999: al-Dār al-Bayḍā' 18–19 fibrāyr 2005: al-muḥākamāt al-'askariyya bil-qunaiṭira li-sanat 1973 min ajl al-masās bi-amn al-dawla al-dākhilī–qaḍiyyat 'umar dahkūn

wa man ma'ah (milaf jinā'ī 1748/8754aa), '[online]. Available at: www.ier.ma/IMG/pdf/arti cle_abde_ahman_benamro.pdf [accessed 1 July 2019].

Bernichi, Loubna (2004) 'J'aurais marché avec le colonel Amekrane,' MarocHebdo [online] 9 July. Available at: www.maghress.com/fr/marochebdo/61321 [accessed 1 July 2019].

Beverley, John (2004) *Testimonio: On the Politics of Truth*. Minneapolis: The University of Minnesota Press.

Bilqāsim, Ḥakīmī (2001) *Kitābāt bada'at min ḥay al-i'dām*. Casablanca: Maṭba 'at al-Nashr al-Maghribiyya.

Bouissef Rekab, Driss (2005) *La tyrannie ordinaire: Lettres de prison. Casablanca*: Tarik Editions.

Bouissef Rekab, Driss (2007) *A l'ombre de Lalla Chafia*. Casablanca: Tarik Edition.

Būdarqa, Mbark and Aḥmad Shawqī Binyūb (2017) *Kadhālika kān: Mudhakkirāt min tajribat hay'at al-inṣāf wal-muṣālaḥa*. Casablanca: Dār al-Nashr al-Maghribiyya.

Chberreq, T. Driss (2014) *Le train fou: mémoires d'un rescapé de Tazmamart, 10 juillet 1971 au 29 octobre 1991*. Rabat: El Maarif al-Jadida.

Daure-Serfaty, Christine (1992) *Tazmamart: une prison de la mort au Maroc*. Paris: Stock.

Dimitriu, Rodica (2009) 'Translators' Prefaces as Documentary Sources for Translation Studies,' *Perspectives: Studies in Translatology* 17 (3): 193–206.

El Bouih, Fatna (2001) *Ḥadīth al-'atama*. Casablanca: al-Fanaq.

El Guabli, Brahim (2017) 'Testimony and Journalism: Moroccan Prison Narratives,' in *The Social Life of Memory*. Eds. Norman S Nikro and Sonja Hegasy. New York: Palgrave Studies in Cultural Heritage and Conflict. 113–144.

El Guabli, Brahim (2018a) 'Theorizing Intergenerational Trauma in Tazmamart Testimonial Literature and Docu-testimonies,' *META: Middle East-Topics & Arguments* 11: 120–130.

El Guabli, Brahim (2018b) 'Other-Archives: Literature Rewrites the Nation in Post-1956 Morocco,' PhD dissertation, Princeton University, Princeton. [online]. Available at: http://arks.princeton.edu/ark:/88435/dsp01mw22v816g.

El Ktaïbi, Miloudi (2009) *Le lit de la mort: chronique d'une grève de la faim au pénitencier de Kénitra*. Paris: L'Harmattan.

El Ouafi, Ahmed, and François Trotet (2004) *Opération Borak F5: 16 août 1972, l'attaque du Boeing royal*. Casablanca: Tarik Éditions.

Equity and Reconciliation Commission (ERC) (2009) *Truth, Equity and Reconciliation*. Rabat: The Advisory Council on Human Rights Publications [online]. Available at: www.cndh.org.ma/sites/default/files/ier_final_report_volume_1.pdf [accessed 1 July 2019].

Fakihani, Abdelfattah (2005) *Le couloir: Bribes de vérité sur les années de plomb*. Rabat: El Maarif al Jadida.

Genette, Gérard (1997a) *Paratexts: Thresholds of Interpretation*. Trans. Jane E. Lewin. Cambridge: Cambridge University Press.

Genette, Gérard (1997b) *Palimpsests: Literature in the Second Degree*. Trans. Channa Newman and Claude Doubinsky. Lincoln: University of Nebraska Press.

Gürçağlar, Ş. Tahir (2002) 'What Texts Don't Tell: The Use of Paratexts in Translation Research,' in *Crosscultural Transgressions. Research Models in Translation Studies II: Historical and Ideological Issues*. Ed. Theo Hermans. Manchester: St. Jerome. 44–60.

Ḥājjī, Sa'īd (2006) *Dhākirat faynīq: Sīra dhātiyya li-wajh min sanawāt al-raṣāṣ*. Casablanca: Afriqiā al-Sharq.

Ḥājjī, Sa'īd (2005) *Sīra dhātiyya li-wajh min sanawāt al-raṣāṣ*. Casablanca: Afriqīyyah al-Sharq.

Hay'at al-inṣāf wal-muṣālaḥa (2004) 'Nadwa ḥawla al-mutāba'āt wal-muḥākamāt dhāt al-ṣibgha al-siyyāsiyya in 1956 ilā 1999: al-Dār al-Bayḍā' 18–19 fibrāyr 2005,' [online]. Available at: www.ier.ma/IMG/pdf/rapport.pdf [accessed 1 July 2019].

Hay'at al-inṣāf wal-muṣālaḥa (2006) *Al-taqrīr al-khitāmī: al-ḥaqīqa wal-inṣāf wal-muṣālaḥa*. Rabat, Morocco: Al-Majlis al-Istishārī li-Ḥuqūq al-Insān.

Hay'at al-inṣāf wal-muṣālaḥa (n.d.) 'Hay 'at al-inṣāf wal-muṣālaḥa: al-ṭabī 'a wal-mahām,' [online]. Available at: http://ier.ma/article.php3?id_article=270 [accessed 1 July 2019].

Hermans, Theo (1996) 'The Translator's Voice in Translated Narrative,' *International Journal of Translation Studies* 8 (1): 23–48.

Hirschberger, Gilad (2018) 'Collective Trauma and the Social Construction of Meaning,' *Frontiers in Psychology* 9 (1441): 1–14.

Hron, Madelaine (2009) *Translating Pain: Immigrant Suffering in Literature and Culture*. Toronto: Toronto University Press.

Human Rights Watch (2005) 'Morocco's Truth Commission Honoring Past Victims During an Uncertain Present,' [online]. Available at: www.hrw.org/sites/default/files/reports/morocco1105w cover.pdf [accessed 1 July 2019].

Ḥuzal, 'Abd al-Raḥīm (2008) *Al-kitāba wa-l-sijn: ḥiwārāt wa nuṣūṣ*. Casablanca: Afriqia al-Sharq.

Jakobson, Roman (1959) 'On Linguistic Aspects of Translation,' in *On Translation*. Ed. Reuben Arthur Brower. Boston: Harvard University Press. 232–239.

Kably, Mohammed (2011) *Histoire du Maroc: Réactualisation et synthèse*. Rabat: Éditions L'Institut Royal pour la Recherche sur l'Histoire du Maroc.

Karam, Muḥammad (2005) 'Nadwa ḥawla al-mutābaʿāt wal-muḥākamāt dhāt al-ṣibgha al-siyyāsiyya in 1956 ilā 1999: al-Dār al-Bayḍāʾ 18–19 fibrāyr 2005: 'an muḥākamat 1977 al-ma 'rūfa bimuḥā-kamat al-sirfātī wa man ma'ah,' [online]. Available at: www.ier.ma/IMG/pdf/article_KARAM. pdf [accessed 1 July 2019].

Lachkar, M. (2010) *Courbis, mon chemin vers la vérité et le pardon*. Rabat: Saad Warzazi Éditions.

Marouki [al-Marzūqī], Ahmed (2015) *Tazmamart: Cellule 10*. Casablanca: Tarik Edition.

McRae, Ellen (2012) 'The Role of Translators' Prefaces to Contemporary Literary Translation into English: An Empirical Study,' in *Translation Peripheries: Paratextual Elements in Translation*. Eds. Anna Gil-Bardají, Pilar Orero and Sara Rovira-Esteva. Bern: Peter Lang. 63–82.

Mdidch, Jaouad (2007) *Derb Mūlāy al-Sharīf: al-Ghurfa al-sawdāʾ*. Casablanca: Afriqiā al-Sharq.

Mouride, Aziz (2001) *On affame bien les rats*. Casablanca: Tarik Editions.

Ouammou, Abdellatif (2005) 'Nadwa ḥawla al-mutābaʿāt wal-muḥākamāt dhāt al-ṣibgha al-siyyāsiyya in 1956 ilā 1999: al-Dār al-Bayḍāʾ 18–19 fibrāyr 2005: al-muḥakamāt fī majāl al-tandīm al-jam 'awī wa-l-ḥizbī,' [online]. Available at: www.ier.ma/IMG/pdf/article_abdellati f_ouammou.pdf [accessed 1 July 2019].

Oufkir, Malika, and Michèle Fitoussi (2001) *Stolen Lives: Twenty Years in a Desert Jail*. New York: Hyperion.

Patte, Daniel, and Aline Patte (1978) *Pour une exégèse structurale*. Paris: Éditions du Seuil.

Perrault, Gilles (1990) *Notre ami le roi*. Paris: Seuil.

Rollinde, Marguerite (2002) *Le mouvement marocain pour les droits de l'homme, entre consensus national et engagement citoyen*. Paris: Karthala.

Sanconie, Maïca (2007) 'Préface, postface, ou deux états du commentaire par des traducteurs,' in *Palimpsestes* 20 [online]. Available at: https://journals.openedition.org/palimpsestes/102 [accessed 1 July 2019].

Sardin, Pascale (2007) 'De la note du traducteur comme commentaire: entre texte, paratexte et prétexte,' *Palimpsestes* 20 [online]. Available at: http://palimpsestes.revues.org/99 [accessed 1 July 2019].

Schiavi, Giuliana (1996) 'There is Always a Teller in a Tale,' *International Journal of Translation Studies* 8 (1): 1–21.

Serhane, Abdelhak (2004) *Kabazal: les emmurés de Tazmamart, mémoires de Salah et Aïda Hachad*. Casablanca: Tarik Editions.

Ṣ'īb, Ḥasan, and 'Abd al-Mū'min Shibārī (2002) *Munḍḍamat ilā al-amām: al-nash'a.al-taṭawwur. al-imtidād*. Casablanca: al-Ufuq al-Dimuqrātī.

Slyomovics, Susan (2005) *The Performance of Human Rights in Morocco*. Philadelphia: University of Pennsylvania Press.

Tymoczko, Maria (2010) 'Translation, Resistance, Activism: An Overview,' in *Translation, Resistance, Activism*. Ed. Maria Tymoczko. Amherst: University of Massachusetts Press. 1–22.

Venuti, Lawrence (1995) *The Translator's Invisibility: A History of Translation*. New York and London: Routledge.

16

Activist narratives

Latin American testimonies in translation

Amanda Hopkinson and Hazel Marsh

Introduction

'The overwhelming fact of human language,' argues Cronin (2002: 47), 'has been its orality.' Yet within translation studies, orality is frequently neglected, since the 'hold of literacy on our analytical worldview means that we exaggerate the importance of textual translation' (Cronin 2002: 48). This neglect is to the detriment of spoken, sung and recited words, and the ways these oral forms transmit unwritten knowledge. This chapter calls for greater recognition of the role of orality within translation studies. If translator activists are to effect change in society, they must 'learn from the standpoint(s) of the less powerful' (Ardill 2013: 20), and convey these standpoints across modalities and languages. For marginalised groups, who rarely control the framework of their own representation in dominant textual forms, orality offers an important reservoir for unwritten history which the translator-activist must engage.

This chapter examines two forms of popular culture harnessed to their causes by Latin American activists. In a region where ubiquitous literacy has only become the norm during the past half-century, testimony (*testimonio*) retains a powerful and inspirational presence within oral traditions of song and speech. The printed version is but the often-contested final stage of a process of 'bearing witness' to events, usually those involving direct personal experience, that may motivate the listener to action.

Examples are drawn from North, Central and South America. Hazel Marsh, a specialist in popular song and its connections to revolutionary politics, examines the role of singer-songwriters Judith Reyes (Mexico) and Alí Primera (Venezuela). Amanda Hopkinson, a literary translator and specialist in popular culture, focuses on the effects of the publication of the National [Argentine] Commission on Disappeared People's report, headed by author Ernesto Sábato, in publicising the first-person testimonies of survivors of military persecution, and on the international furore that resulted from the publication of the memoir of Guatemalan peasant leader, Rigoberta Menchú.

While songs may be recorded and repeated in the original Spanish across the Americas and beyond, it was the role of the translator in relaying the words of oral testimonies that drew particular attention to the written texts. What the two genres have in common is that both forms of transmission belong to a tradition of *testimonio* that reverts at least as far as the colonial period in Latin America. A 'collectivist form of discourse' (Avant-Mier and Hasian 2008: 330), *testimonio* presents personal experience as part of a common struggle against oppression. As such, it provides 'a means of reconstructing history and a chance for marginalised voices to be heard, defying dominant official historical accounts' (Reda Nasr 2016). It is these voices that the translator-activist should seek out, since 'undermining existing patterns of domination cannot be achieved with concrete forms of activism alone (such as demonstrations, sit-ins, and civil disobedience) but must involve a direct challenge to the stories that sustain these patterns' (Baker 2006: 471).

Testimonio, in oral, written or sung form, offers counter-narratives that challenge and contest dominant power structures, thereby offering resources for people to imagine an alternative future. This chapter calls for academic research into the dynamics of translation across modalities. It is a call for research into the translation of lived experience into written/oral artistic form, a process undertaken with the aim of effecting social justice.

Testimonial texts

Argentina's 'dirty war [*guerra sucia*]'

The two texts considered here are essentially mediated. They relate the first-hand experiences of witnesses which may become second-hand accounts via the work of an interviewer, who may also be the first of several writers and editors responsible for determining what is included or omitted in the final version. Both texts rely on first-person interviews, one undertaken on behalf of a commission, the other by an individual anthropologist, each raising issues of the ownership of any variation in words between source and target text. The role of the interviewer is a position of responsibility matched by that of the translator-(s), whose target readers are potentially different to those of the witness/participant in the events described. The interviewers/writers and translators share a common and equivalent responsibility to their readership: if the translation is not accessible in the way originally intended, neither audience nor author will be well served.

Those involved in compiling a source text of testimonial writing are likely to seek its translation in order to raise international consciousness. Further, it lends itself to campaigns abroad, increasing the potential for redressing as well as addressing issues of human rights. English is the obvious language of choice, since today it is the world's second language in the many places where it is not the first.

In Argentina, following the fall of General Galtieri, the last of three successive military dictators in power from 1976 to 1983, the election of President Raúl Alfonsín inaugurated the country's return to democracy and the formation of a National Commission on Disappeared People (NCDP). The results of that investigation were published by the University of Buenos Aires in 1984, and the English edition in 1986. Its primary aim was to assist in the re-establishment of the rule of law by conducting a thoroughly documented investigation into the systemic and instrumental involvement of the armed forces in human rights abuses over the previous seven years. This was in order for the perpetrators to be brought to justice, and the victims and their families to receive restitution under the law. President Alfonsín's choice to head up the NCDP was as unanticipated as it came to be applauded. He chose the widely revered veteran writer Ernesto Sábato (1911–2011).

Sábato, a notable physicist and an artist as well as a prize-winning author, was by now aged 73. The report was a radical shift from his literary profile as the author of just three novels, each of which had profoundly marked contemporary Argentine literature. Sábato's novels, like his numerous essays, can be read as metaphorical allegories, earning him equal literary status within (although not outside) Argentina; by coincidence his *Dialogues* with Borges were published in 1976, the year General Videla staged his military putsch. Seven years later, and also—like Borges—afflicted with blindness, Sábato revealed his sense of urgency in focusing on what would be a major publication.

In *Nunca Más* (1984), he sought to expose the horrors witnessed by survivors of the 'dirty war,' waged by the armed forces on the civilian population of his home country. It was instigated by a triumvirate of military generals who seized power in 1976 with the express intention of 'annihilating' the Peronist Montonero guerrilla movement. The programme of 'political cleansing/*limpieza política*' rapidly went far beyond armed targets, to include students and trade unionists, intellectuals and any democratic political opposition. Estimates vary widely, but an Amnesty International report (Amnesty International 1977: 1) calculated that up to 15,000 individuals were murdered, the majority either tortured to death or before being thrown alive from helicopters into the ocean. The revised report (Amnesty International 1995: 1) cites the number of the 'disappeared' as approximately 9,000, noting also that the number of those reported still missing in 1983 could have been three times as many.

In Sábato's words:

> After collecting several thousand statements and testimonies, verifying or establishing the existence of hundreds of secret detention centres, and compiling over 50,000 pages of documentation, we are convinced that the recent military dictatorship brought about the greatest and most savage tragedy in the history of Argentina.
>
> *(Sábato 1986 [1984]: 1)*

The account is given, not in his words, but in the anonymised collective account of the National NCDP. Such a collective voice is also characteristic of *testimonio* as a genre, however relayed. This will be addressed further in the section on Rigoberta Menchú, where her own voice is syncretised with that of her people.

Sábato noted that he was obliged to introduce a new vocabulary to describe new horrors:

> In the name of national security, thousands upon thousands of human beings, usually young adults or even adolescents, fell into the sinister, ghostly category of the *desaparecidos*, a word (sad privilege for Argentina) frequently left in Spanish by the world's press.
>
> *(1986 [1984]: 4)*

In fact, 'the disappeared' was a term initially employed in Central America during the civil wars waged by US-backed armies on the guerrilla movements from the 1960s to 1980s. In the words of US journalist Joan Didion (1983: 57): '*Desaparecer*, or "to disappear" is in Spanish both an intransitive and a transitive verb, and this flexibility has been adopted by those speaking English in El Salvador ... there being no equivalent situation, and so no equivalent word, in English-speaking cultures.' The meaning of this new grammatical construct is 'to abduct and render invisible'—i.e. to do away with—another person.

As the anonymised collective authors of the NCDP go on to explain, there is a 'typical sequence [of events],' consisting in '*abduction–disappearance–torture.* Each of the testimonies included in this report is representative of thousands of cases which tell a similar story. Our selection represents only a tiny fraction of the material collected' (NCDP 1984 [1986]: 9). They emphasise that: 'The cases highlighted were not due to any excesses, because no such thing existed, if by "excess" we mean isolated incidents which transgress a norm' (NCDP 1984 [1986]: 10). Such standardisation is then applied to the testimonies, with witnesses invited to give factual and sequential accounts, without reference to personal or emotional reactions. For the reader, this renders the testimonies the more powerful and chilling.

Sábato could as well have added the particular mention of *milicos*, a slang term of abuse for 'the military [*militares*],' associated with crimes against humanity. 'Impunity' means flagrant disregard for the law by those charged with upholding it and 'extra-judicial execution' is of itself an oxymoron, since the word 'execution,' correctly used, is not applicable to illegal killings but attaches to a death sentence handed down through the courts. Both were used in the description, not of the behaviour of 'subversives,' but of the armed forces themselves. *Subversivo* here has no association with an adjective modifying such nouns as 'humour,' but is uniquely a noun synonymous with 'the enemy.'

There is also the question of the survivors' register or tone when recounting their experiences.

As Sábato himself indicates, it was 'the military' itself that appropriated the term 'dirty war' in order to reverse the blame for its inception. In their inverted world of mirrors:

> [F]ar from expressing any repentance, they continue to repeat the old excuses that they were engaged in a *dirty war*, or that they were saving the country and its Western Christian values, when in reality they were responsible for dragging those values inside the bloody walls of the dungeons of repression.
>
> *(Sábato 1986 [1984]: 5)*

This was an argument Sábato then internationalised, emphasising the legal case for human rights activism in a single quotation. Sábato did this by referring to the kidnapping of Italian Prime Minister Aldo Moro in 1978, and the reply given by General Della Chiesa to the member of the security forces advocating the torture of a suspect: 'Italy can survive the loss of Aldo Moro. It would not survive the introduction of torture' (Sábato 1986 [1984]: 1).

Sábato chose to take the risk of remaining in Argentina throughout the 'dirty war.' On 29 June 1982, the heavyweight daily *La Nación* published his letter protesting against the precipitate exile of a longstanding friend and colleague, Andrew Graham-Yooll: 'As an Argentine, I am ashamed to learn of the cowardly assault on the writer and journalist Andrew Graham-Yooll. And we wonder why we have an abominable image abroad!' (Graham-Yooll 1991: 208). This was taken as an appeal to all to speak out and support victims of the 'dirty war,' particularly to those abroad to offer refuge to the exiles.

Graham-Yooll, an Anglo-Argentine, returned to Britain, where he became editor, first of *South* magazine (1985–9), then of the bi-monthly *Index on Censorship* (1989–94), when he returned to Argentina as editor of the *Buenos Aires Herald* (1995–2007). This too was a means of publicising atrocities committed across the globe through their rendition in English, the global language. He described Sábato as 'a national hero,' adding: 'Through those dark days, Sábato was the moral conscience of decent Argentines' (Graham-Yooll 1991: 206). Yet he well knew that Sábato's reputation was not yet international. It was *Index*'s Latin American editor, Nick Caistor, who organised the publication of the *Report*. He commented on Sábato's appointment to head up the Commission: 'The only person Argentines trusted to get at the truth was a man who wrote fiction. It speaks to their respect for writers and says more about public trust of politicians and judges at that time' (Nick Caistor, personal communication with Amanda Hopkinson, 2018).

In so doing he took charge of the translation and editing of *Nunca Más*, and provided a historical introduction. The NCDP made a number of stipulations. They ranged from insisting that the text be neither cut nor amended—including the retention of its original title **NUNCA MÁS** (capitalised in bold), over its English title (*Never Again*) in italicised and smaller typeface—to the importance of bringing out an English translation as early as possible. Caistor kept to the methodology adopted by the National Commission, which employed a number of interviewers and editors, and recruited eight translators, 'mostly regular contributors familiar with the language of human rights' (Nick Caistor, personal communication with Amanda Hopkinson, 2018). Graham-Yooll himself had previously worked with Amnesty International, self-describing his position as that of an 'informer' from 1971 onwards (Graham-Yooll 2018) on Argentina, and on 'Urgent Actions,' circulating all members to take action and become involved in the press and political campaigns it generated.

In 1985 Caistor brokered the co-publication of *Nunca Más* between the anti-censorship organisation Writers & Scholars International and British publisher, Faber & Faber, where it was championed by editors-in-chief Matthew Evans and Robert McCrum. McCrum was a regular literary contributor to the *Guardian*, and became literary editor of the *Observer*. It was in the pages of the latter that playwright Harold Pinter selected *Nunca Más* as his *Observer* 'Book of the Year' in 1986.

Caistor's foreword introduces the reader to the context in which the Commission conducted its investigations, and elucidates key terms such as 'testimonies on disappearances,' 'secret detention camps' and so forth. It concludes: 'It should be remembered that what follows are the stories of the survivors: one can only speculate as to what accounts of atrocity the thousands of dead took with them to their unmarked graves' (Caistor 1986 [1984]: xvi).

Guatemala: Rigoberta Menchú

Testimonial writing has a long literary pedigree in Latin America, reaching back at least as far as its colonisation. It is, perhaps, ironic that it was Christopher Columbus who, in landing on the Caribbean island he named Hispaniola, claimed to have discovered a new world, a marvellous reality (Hopkinson 2016: 72). The term has been recast as 'magical realism,' perhaps the quintessential Latin American literary form. Yet Columbus' letters home to the Spanish King and Queen were intended to bear witness to his discoveries, however fabricated; it could as well be argued that the letters were an early form of testimonial writing, a genre that has branched and grown at least as far as 'magical realism.'

Rigoberta Menchú's life story belongs to a category that already includes such landmark texts as *The Diary of a Runaway Slave* ((*Biografía de un Cimarrón*, 1966) 1966) by Cuban novelist Miguel Barnet and *Let Me Speak!* (1978), the story of the Bolivian activist and labour leader, Domitila Chúngara with Moema Viezzer. Menchú's story is that of a Maya peasant woman from the Quiché highlands of Guatemala.

In almost every aspect her early life was typical of that of her indigenous compatriots for whom human rights abuses were rife in their daily life. Their working conditions approximated slavery and public health, housing and education services were almost completely absent. Menchú was born in 1959, a year after the introduction of scorched earth policies by a succession of military dictators who, from 1958 to 1983, sought to suppress a predominantly peasant guerrilla insurgency with a violence that included crimes against humanity and genocide.

What is exceptional about Menchú is that, although semi-literate and a native Quiché speaker who acquired Spanish only later in life, she became a national leader and international spokeswoman on indigenous and human rights. Her memoir would go into multiple reprints in Spanish but was outsold by the English edition, which went into sixteen reprints and sold over 250,000 copies. Worldwide, it has sold over 500,000 copies translated into thirteen languages. In 1998 Menchú was awarded the Prince of Asturias Award (for advocating women's rights) and in 1992 she won the Nobel Peace Prize 'in recognition of her work for social justice and ethno-cultural reconciliation based on respect for the rights of indigenous peoples' (The Norwegian Nobel Institute 1992). In 2010, she was further honoured with the Order of the Aztec Eagle Award. The story of her life generated a furore that revolved around authenticity and veracity, but which has never succeeded in dismissing—or even diminishing—Menchú's own voice.

When a text already mediated by the interviewer/transcriber is further mediated by the translator/publisher, further scope for argument arises. In this instance, it begins with the title. The original *Me Llamo Rigoberta Menchú y Así Me Nació la Conciencia* can be glossed as 'My Name is Rigoberta Menchú and This is how my Conscience/Consciousness was born.' Or 'raised,' according to the official Nobel Prize website. In translation, ambiguity arises from a word that, in the source text, can mean either 'conscience' or 'consciousness,' depending on context. It fits Menchú's particular story, for her profoundly Christian conscience informed her growing political consciousness and the work she was to undertake in the cause of human and peasants' union rights. One Latin American edition, published in Buenos Aires, was called simply *Me Llamo Rigoberta* Menchú (1983) and the author given as Elisabeth Burgos, the name of her interviewer.

In the English translation (1984), the title was curtailed to *I ... Rigoberta Menchú*, adding *An Indian Woman in Guatemala* by way of further explanation. 'Indian,' when the book appeared over thirty years ago, was still commonly applied to the indigenous peoples of the Americas. She has subsequently written that 'the change was for dramatic effect ... chosen by the publisher, not by me, but I agreed because I thought it was a strong title' (Wright 2000: 20). In the French edition (1983) it became *Moi, Rigoberta Menchú: Une Vie et une Voix, la Révolution en Guatemala* (which can be glossed as *Rigoberta Menchú, A Life and a Voice. Revolution in Guatemala*); and in German (1992) *Rigoberta Menchú: Leben in Guatemala* (*Rigoberta Menchú: Life in Guatemala*). No title corresponds to another, which may reflect the very different ways in which the text can be read according to differing cultural norms. However too little attention was paid to Menchú's own norms, or that she came from a culture where an individual is so culturally integrated she is empowered to give voice to a whole people. Ironically, the initial word of the English title is unlikely to have been used by a Quiché woman at all, since the usage of first-person singular is socially regarded as an inappropriate and immodest term of self-aggrandisement.

The term Quiché (meaning 'many trees') refers to a place, a people and a language, suggesting their indivisibility. The Quiché people predominantly live in the Guatemalan highlands, and are among the many indigenous peoples of Central America and Mexico. They belong to the Maya, whose civilisation reached its peak in the post-Classic period of CE 950–1539, with the building of the famous cities and high temples at such sacred sites as Tikal, Uxmal, Palenque and Chichen Itza.

Menchú's first interviewer was the Venezuelan anthropologist Elisabeth Burgos-Debray, who was based in Paris and married to the French Marxist philosopher, Régis Debray, who was Professor of Philosophy at Havana University in the early 1960s; in the Bolivian jungle with Che Guevara in 1967; and who published *Revolution in the Revolution?*, a handbook for guerrilla warfare—to supplement Guevara's own manual—in 1967. In October that year Guevara was killed by the US-backed Bolivian army, and a month later Debray was sentenced to thirty years' imprisonment. For a period of one week in January 1982, Menchú stayed in her Paris flat, spending up to twelve hours a day recording her story, preparing meals of Venezuelan beans with maize *tortillas*. Burgos-Debray abandoned her original plan of keeping Menchú to a schematic chronological outline in favour of encouraging her to 'talk freely while [I] tried to ask as few questions as possible' (Burgos-Debray 1984: xix). Defending herself against subsequent accusations that she was driven by a professional and political agenda, Burgos-Debray protested:

> Whatever happens in Paris has worldwide repercussions, even in Latin America. Just as the groups which are or were engaged in America [i.e. the Americas] have supporters who adopt their political line, the Indians too have their European supporters, many of whom are anthropologists. I do not want to start a polemic and I do not want to devalue any one form of action: I am simply stating the facts.
>
> *(Burgos-Debray 1984: xvii)*

In fact, in October 1991, Menchú was indeed accompanied by Danielle Mitterrand, wife of France's then president on the occasion of the Second Continental Meeting to commemorate 500 years of indigenous popular resistance. Mme. Mitterrand stayed a week in Guatemala and joined Menchú at the head of the march of 25,000 indigenous people from across Latin America.

Whether anticipated, polemic was not long in coming. The initial attack was launched by fellow anthropologist David Stoll. On his webpage, he wrote:

> In 1987–91 I did my dissertation research in a Mayan town that, not long before, had given considerable support to the guerrilla movement fighting Guatemala's military dictatorship … Based on what they told me, I decided to challenge the guerrillaphile (sic) interpretation of the war adopted by the human rights movement. This led to two books about the conflict, its antecedents and sequel in Quiché Department: *Between Two Armies in the Ixil Towns of Guatemala* (1993) and *Rigoberta Menchú and the Story of All Poor Guatemalans* (1999).
>
> *(Stoll n.d.)*

Writer Robert Strauss (1999) summarised Stoll's claims thus:

> Menchú fabricated some of the most horrific details in her story, manipulating it to create a work of propaganda that would be useful to the anti-government guerrillas she joined in 1981. Stoll also excoriates American academics for naively buying Menchú's story, an account of villainous soldiers and noble peasants that neatly fit the preconceived notions of many professors.

Stoll is himself now a professor of anthropology at Middlebury, Vermont and has preconceived notions of his own. In the words of Menchú's English translator Ann Wright:

> [Stoll] suggests that Menchú's version of her own life was modified to reflect the organisations she was close to. He claims Menchú was 'fashioned' as a peasant leader after the event, when her potential on the solidarity circuit was recognised and that she inserted/omitted details to help the work of the URNG (Guatemalan National Revolutionary Unity).
>
> *(Wright 2000: 16)*

Stoll's own politics include a defence of General Ríos Montt, whose catch phrase was 'If you are with us, we will feed you. If not, we will kill you.' President from 1982 to 1983, having seized power in a military putsch, Ríos Montt was subsequently sentenced to eighty years of imprisonment for crimes against humanity and genocide. Amnesty International's finding—that he had turned Guatemala into a killing field with the massacre of over 10,000 unarmed peasants in the first five months of his short presidency— makes Stoll's defence of him the more astonishing. Stoll states:

> Consider the thousands of unarmed men, women and children killed by the army while he sermonized about morality, and he is a monster. *Consider the hopes invested in him by many Guatemalans, including poverty-stricken Catholic peasants, and he becomes a hero of mythic proportions.*
>
> *(cited in Kinzer 2018, my emphasis)*

Stoll's insistence on the 'literal' truth in every instance is behind the accusations of deception, lies and worse. Rather than consider the conditions of the times—a country ravaged by civil war; gross atrocities perpetrated by the armed forces against a predominantly Maya peasant population; the trauma of losing seventeen family members, within a culture that may describe cousins or half-sisters as siblings—Stoll demands that every detail punctiliously conform to the norms of modern scholarship. This reductionist approach, by which any confusion as to the precise date or weapon of death would discredit an entire testimony, has itself been subsequently scrutinised by a number of academics and critics.

In 1997, Professor Gordon Brotherston reviewed the ongoing debate. He considered that:

> In terms of [other] testimonies ... [this book] ... stands prominent and raises key issues of interpretation; ... it challenges root assumptions of western literary criticism. This much is clear from the responses it has provoked which, on the one hand, make political commitment the priority or, on the other, stray so far into the supposed sophistication of post-modernism as to render quite null the very concept of *testimonio*.
>
> *(Brotherston 1997: 93)*

Brotherston categorises such an often unconsciously mediated worldview as 'faulty geography' and 'faulty chronology' (Brotherston 1997: 99). He argues powerfully against relegating Menchú's memoir 'to the Third World discourse of dependency, oppression and economic underdevelopment' and distinguishes its perspective 'with respect to other attendant factors as the role of indigenous peoples *vis-à-vis* the nation state, or their robust grounding of political resistance in non-western cosmogony' (Brotherston 1997: 99).

It is there from the start, with the collective 'I' in *I, Rigoberta Menchú*. Ann Wright (telephone interview with Amanda Hopkinson, 18 August 2018) now says she greatly regrets 'agreeing to' a title the publisher suggested, because '[t]he first "I" simply doesn't belong. Rigoberta would never have put herself first: it would have been unthinkably rude. Women always take second place behind men among the Maya.' Yes, atrocities happened to Menchú, but also to her family and to her people. In identifying with them, she trusts that they too identify with her experiences. History is in her story, and in Spanish the word for both is the same, *historia*. Spanish is, of course, not Menchú's mother tongue, which is Quiché. Her father was anxious that formal education should not deprive her of her own culture. For a period, he kept her out of school in order for her not to lose her culture. *Ladinisar*, a term he used to describe the acculturation that goes with being born *ladino*, a person of predominantly white/mixed origin, carries an implicit warning. Indigenous people who seek to *ladinisar* themselves to climb the social ladder run the risk of losing their true heritage (Wright 2018).

In 2001 *The Rigoberta Menchú Controversy* was published (Arias 2001), duly creating further controversy. This was a round-up of thirty-three articles with titles such as '*I, Rigoberta Menchú* and the Culture Wars,' 'The Anthropologist with the Old Hat' or 'A Hamburger in Rigoberta's Black Beans.' Four include reference to 'Rigoberta's Lies.' Six refer to 'Truth/s,' typically amplified as 'Truth, Human Rights and Representation,' 'Teaching, Testimony and Truth,' or 'The Primacy of Larger Truths.' It would be simplistic to divide Latin Americans coming to the defence of their indigenous sister from US academics closing ranks around their own, equally so to consider the two groups as engaged in a mute dialogue, almost literally speaking different languages.

Leading luminaries of contemporary Latin America literature rallied to Menchú's cause. Several expressed a sense of déjà vu. In *The Rigoberta Menchú Controversy* by Arturo Arias (2001), Spanish novelist Manuel Vásquez Montalbán indicts the campaign to discredit political indigenism in Latin America and links Menchú's struggle to that of Bishop Samuel Ruiz in Mexico and Guatemalan Bishop Juan Gerardi, assassinated in 1997, two days after his report on military repression was published. In 'Let's Shoot Rigoberta,' Eduardo Galeano reprises the martyrdom of Bishop Gerardi, and concludes with a Maya proverb: 'It is the tree that gives fruit that receives all the stones' (Galeano 2001: 102). In his contribution Victor D. Montejo criticises both sides for monopolising alternative 'truths'; digresses with a critique of Stoll's appropriation of a cover photograph of Menchú on his book; and ends by answering his own question, posed from his position as Chair of the Department of Native American Studies at the University of California: 'How can we now use the book as a college text?' Rejecting Stoll's proposal 'that the best way to teach it is to treat Menchú's biography as an epic novel' and equally opposing 'binomial appositions, good/bad, left/right,' Montejo concludes: 'The Maya people and their culture are in the middle of this intellectual debate, which has become highly abstract and removed from current Maya reality' (Montejo 2001: 390).

That reality, steeped in the *Popol Vuh* (1985), an indigenous epic described by Carlos Fuentes (2001) as 'the Mayan Bible,' is one to which Menchú repeatedly refers. Within it time does not equate with chronology nor identity with individualism. The irony is that Menchú's own voice, emerging from a collective history and identity, is so unique that it makes itself heard notwithstanding the interventions of interviewers, editors, translators, publishers—even foreign academics. Such a powerful voice cannot be appropriated; not even the author claims ownership. Writers appear to understand its language and, more importantly, so do the hundreds of thousands of her readers.

Latin American popular song as testimony

Rigoberta Menchú's testimony aims to leave not a 'personal record, but instead to document the reality of a whole people, the history of those who before were not allowed to voice their story nor their history' (Gugelberger and Kearney 1991: 8–9). In postcolonial contexts, testimony acts as a powerful form of resistance to official and dominant narratives: it gives voice to the marginalised and the silenced, and reconstructs history from the perspective of the oppressed (Reda Nasr 2016). Testimony aims to affirm and empower, to 'name oppression and to arrest its actions,' and to 'speak for justice against all crimes against humanity' (Blackmer Reyes and Curry Rodríguez 2012: 527). It represents personal experience as part of 'the collective struggle against oppression' (Reda Nasr 2016) and constructs a 'discourse of solidarity' (Blackmer Reyes and Curry Rodríguez 2012: 526) with the aim of achieving justice, healing and social and political change for marginalised communities. But testimonies can take many forms, and are therefore likely to remain 'unidentified' if 'conventional search or categorisation approaches' are employed to find them (Blackmer Reyes and Curry Rodríguez 2012: 526–7).

Songs are a vital element in the activist translator's repertoire. Any translator who converts testimonies and activist texts into other languages in order to communicate the ideas, values and goals of collective struggles and to enhance solidarity must reckon with their force. Songs offer more than entertainment and aesthetic pleasure; they provide resources for producing 'things other than music' in social life (DeNora 2011: 50). Songs create spaces within which personal and public experiences are interpreted and mapped on to non-musical matters (DeNora 2000: 26–7). They achieve what Mona Baker (2016: 6) argues translation in its 'broadest sense' does; they translate symbols and experiences across modalities, without necessarily crossing language boundaries. The processes by which songs are legitimated as translators of social and political experiences and symbols are examined here via two case studies. First, the songs of Mexican singer-songwriter Judith Reyes (1924–88), which chronicled and circulated eyewitness accounts of the Tlatelolco massacre of 2 October 1968. Second, the songs of Venezuelan singer/songwriter Alí Primera (1942–85), which denounced the economic, cultural, political, racial and environmental impact of the oil industry on his country, and which were reinterpreted in the Chávez period as precursors of Bolivarian political thought.

Easily memorised and transmitted, songs play a particularly important public and testimonial role in the predominantly oral cultures of Latin America, where illiteracy remained high well into the twentieth century, and where the official media are widely seen to represent the interests of wealthy elites (Pring-Mill 1990: 76). Latin American modernity diverges sharply from that of Europe and North America. In contrast to these latter cases, Latin American modernity does not require 'the elimination of pre-modern traditions and memories' (Rowe and Schelling 1991: 3). Rather, it arises through premodern traditions, 'transforming them in the process' (Rowe and Schelling 1991: 3). Pre-industrial oral traditions persist, and 'traditional folksong has retained its power and currency largely undiminished by the changes of the twentieth century' (Pring-Mill 1987: 179). This power and currency remain undiminished in the twenty-first century (Fairley 2013; Marsh 2016).

In Latin America, ecclesiastical authorities throughout the colonial period sought to eradicate indigenous and African folk music styles brought by slaves, which they associated with 'primitive' peoples and 'backward' ways of life (Tandt and Young 2004: 238–9). The historical suppression of indigenous and African music forms endowed them with enduring associations of resistance to imperialism and elite political interests. Following independence from Spain and Portugal, official policy encouraged emigration from Northern Europe to 'whiten the race' (Gott 2007; Peloso 2014). Such racist patterns of thought constitute one of the many 'disquieting' features of Latin American life: the predominance of military regimes, the deliberate use of brutality by the military and police, suppression of civil liberties and human rights, the exploitation of workers, poverty and United States imperialism and interference in internal affairs all characterise the region (Pring-Mill 2002: 14). The persistence of economic and social injustice causes Latin Americans to remember and interpret the past in more partisan terms that conflict with the narratives bequeathed by developed countries, which are more likely to be 'constructed unambiguously by history's winners' (Johnson 2004: xvi).

Songs, which appeal to the emotive sensibilities alongside the cognitive faculties, also provide cultural resources that marginalised and oppressed groups can draw on to translate lived experience and history into counter-hegemonic knowledge about the world. Song traditions form part of the collective memory and shared history of a group, and by carrying 'ways of seeing and doing between past and present and between individuals across the generations,' they interpret and reinterpret the world for social movements other than those which originally generated the music (Eyerman and Jamison 1998: 47). However, the meaning of music is not fixed, or inherent to lyrics or sonic properties alone; it is created 'in interaction as people do music' (Roy 2010: 14). Songs function as tools that people draw on to defend and share their own interpretations of the world and their place within it, and to contest the interpretations of others. People actively engage with music and use it to assert, resist and negotiate social and political identities. The section now turns to two committed Latin American singer-songwriters, and the ways in which their compositions have been legitimated and drawn into use over time to interpret and reinterpret social and political experiences.

Judith Reyes: song, testimony and activism

Mexican singer-songwriter Judith Reyes (1924–88) has been described as the 'chronicler of the 1968 Student Movement' (Velasco García 2004: 77). In her *Cronología del Movimiento Estudiantil* (*Chronology of the Student Movement*), a collection of twelve songs she composed during 1968 about the Mexican student movement and its repression, Reyes uses the *corrido* form to 'relate and diffuse [news of] events in the face of the silence imposed on the mass media by political authorities' (Velasco García 2004: 77).

The *corrido* is a ballad form that emerged in mid to late nineteenth-century Mexico. It is typically seen to embody lower-class notions of justice, which often defy the authority of the state, and to act as an archive of popular history that provides insights into the opinions, values, grievances and heroes of common people (Frazer 2006: 131). After the 1930s, with the growth of the Mexican film industry and the commercial recording industry, new *corrido* compositions contained few narratives about contemporary challenges to the status quo. At the same time, many earlier *corridos* celebrating the Mexican Revolution were appropriated by the state and officially interpreted as vehicles of the ideology of the *Partido Revolucionario Institucional* (PRI, Institutionalised Revolutionary Party), the political party that for over seventy years controlled virtually every political office at federal and local levels:

> At the moment of composition, these ballads went beyond expressing alternative values to posit those that were profoundly oppositional. When these historical moments passed, these *corridos* became integrative in relation to elite domination and hegemony ... these *corridos* helped to fashion a lower-class historical memory that encouraged the lower classes to accept elite domination. Yet these *corridos* also contained latent elements of instability, for they implied the legitimacy of rebellion against injustice and bad government.
>
> *(Frazer 2006: 139)*

Reinterpreting and reviving the late nineteenth-century revolutionary *corrido* tradition, Reyes composed and performed songs that functioned as oral 'eyewitness' accounts of grassroots activism and government repression (Marsh 2010). Her songs translate lived experience into cultural resources that embody cognitive and non-cognitive knowledge of the violent 2 October 1968 events of Tlatelolco, when the government ordered police and military forces to clear the Plaza de Tres Culturas in Tlatelolco district, Mexico City, of student protestors. It is not known how many protesters were killed in the massacre (Brewster 2010).

Reyes's *corridos* chronicle the many leftist struggles and movements with which she had links, such as those of railway-workers, guerrilla movements, teachers, doctors, telegraph operators, as well as students.

Reyes actively reinterpreted the *corrido*, reclaiming it and restoring its oppositional qualities in an atmosphere of severe government repression, with political dissent impossible to articulate via the media or electoral politics. In his 1968 memoir (2004 [1991]: 34), Paco Ignacio Taibo II writes of a sense that the press at the time

> was lying ... [but] their lies strengthened our convictions. For our part, we knew the truth; we got our news by word of mouth. Eyewitness accounts were told and retold; everything had been seen by someone, heard by someone, and was recounted by everyone.

Reyes's *corridos* were an important means of circulating such eyewitness accounts in late 1960s Mexico. Although Reyes herself was convalescing following surgery during the latter half of 1968, and her *Chronology of the Student Movement* is largely based on information she received at second hand from witnesses and other participants, by May 1969 she was well enough to give a series of recitals in which she gave musical testimony to state violence. At the Universidad Nacional Autónoma de México (UNAM), she gave two or three concerts a day, and later performed at the universities of Zacatecas and Oaxaca, and at prisons, markets and town squares in Mexico City and throughout the country (Liliana García, written communication with Hazel Marsh, 2008). Reyes's compositions were among those embraced and circulated among urban students and leftist intellectuals as a form of 'oral reporting' with which to counteract the perceived 'lies' of the 'sell-out' press:

> The rupture of official political discourse [caused by events of 1968] paralleled the rise of a new language ... often captured in songs that students sang on buses, on street corners, and at school assemblies.
>
> *(Soldatenko 2005: 123)*

Reyes viewed herself as a chronicler of events rather than a protest singer, and chose to create songs that dealt directly with 'what she saw, what she lived through' (Yelly Alarcón, personal written communication with Hazel Marsh, 15 September 2008). 'I like to write our history in my songs,' she asserted, 'I include statistics as well as the words of my people' (cited in Reyes 2006 [1973]: 3). Indeed, in *corridos* such as '*Tragedia de la Plaza de las Tres Culturas*/Tragedy of the Plaza of Three Cultures,' Reyes records dates, times and numbers, names of individuals and describes military attacks on civilian individuals in a vivid eyewitness account of the student movement and its subsequent repression:

> El dos de octubre llegamos
> todos pacíficamente
> a un mítin en Tlatelolco
> quince mil en la corriente.
> Año del sesenta y ocho
> que pena me da acordarme
> la plaza estaba repleta
> como a las seis de la tarde.
> ...
> Hieren a Oriana Falacci
> voz de la prensa extranjera
> ¡Ya conoció la cultura
> del gobierno de esta tierra!
> On the 2 October we went
> peacefully to a rally in Tlatelolco
> about 15,000 of us, in the year of '68.
> It makes me sad to remember it
> The jam-packed plaza at about 6pm ...
> Oriana Fallaci, voice of the foreign press
> is wounded.
> At last, she met the culture
> of the government of this land.
>
> (translated by Barbara Dane in Reyes
> (2006 [1973]: 13), sleeve notes)

Reyes was frequently prohibited from performing her musical testimonies of local struggles and government repression, and in July 1969 she was arrested and held incommunicado for three weeks before being forced into exile.

The student movement's demands did not lead to greater democratisation but were met with state violence, which provoked the radicalisation of a minority and a retreat from political action by the vast majority (Zolov 1999: 110). Reyes was one of those radicalised by the massacre of 2 October 1968, which signalled the PRI's commitment to one-party rule. After returning to Mexico in 1974, she remained 'marginalised from the mainstream of the left' and dedicated herself to chronicling the lives of the peasants and workers she lived with (Dane 2006). For many urban youths, underground rock music, frequently banned by the government due to its associations with US consumerism and psychedelia, now came to translate feelings of anger, fear and mistrust towards authority. As one participant in the student movement expressed it: 'We fought against a corrupt society, [one] that was suffocating us, that was deceiving us ... and rock [music] helped us scream; rock for me is about that scream, a universal scream' (Zolov 1999: 133). Nevertheless, fifty years after the events of 2 October, the lyrics of Judith Reyes embody both a chronicle of government repression and a vivid testimony of lived experience, thus acting as bridge between past and present.

Alí Primera: song, activism and political change

During his lifetime, Venezuelan singer-songwriter Alí Primera (1942–85) composed and performed what he called *Canción Necesaria* (necessary song). Considered by state authorities to be a dangerous subversive whose music encouraged 'non-conformity,' Primera's songs were widely banned in Venezuela during his lifetime (Marsh 2016). In order to distribute his music and that of other singer-songwriters who like him were vetoed by the state, Primera co-established the cooperative record label, *Cigarrón*, on which he recorded thirteen LPs containing over one hundred original songs, the lyrics of which have never been published in English. These LPs were distributed at live performances and via informal networks of friends and relatives. In his *Canción Necesaria*, Primera reinterpreted the history and dominant narratives of his country, which widely represented Venezuela as an 'exception' in the region due to the purported modernising influence of oil (see Ellner 2005; López Maya and Lander 2005, for more on the 'exceptionalism' thesis). Primera's songs articulated a critique of the environmental, economic, racial, political and social impact of the oil industry. His lyrics celebrated and defended indigenous groups, Afro-Americans, the environment and common people, while they denounced capitalist exploitation, racism and inequality. His language was vernacular and direct:

> ... capitalism [is]
> The cause of every misfortune
> That my people suffer.
> ('Ruperto,' from the album *Adiós en dolor mayor*, 1975. Translated by Hazel
>   Marsh)
> I don't like using pretty words
> To perfume shit.
> ('*Panfleto de una sola nota*/single note pamphlet,' from the album *Cuando nombro
>   la poesía*, 1979. Translated by Hazel Marsh)

Primera sought, as he put it, to use his songs to communicate 'a class ideology in a language which ordinary people will relate to' (1974, cited in Hernández Medina

1991: 64). He intended for his songs to provide tools for the marginalised and impoverished masses to recognise and articulate their condition, and in recognising and articulating it be spurred to 'transform [society], because a people that is unconscious of its own reality, even its own strength, is incapable of mobilising and transforming anything' (1985, cited in Hernández Medina 1991: 248). Illiteracy, said Primera, 'isn't an obstacle to understanding my songs ... my songs are simple, the language of the people' (1985, cited in Hernández Medina 1991: 250).

Primera's music is varied, and based on local Afro-Venezuelan, indigenous and popular forms such as the *tamunangue* from the region of Lara, the *gaita* from Zulia, the *joropo* from the plains and rhythmic forms associated with the *tambor* drum ensembles of Barlovento. Instrumentation includes stringed instruments (harp, guitar, mandolin, *cuatro*) and African and indigenous percussion instruments and drums (maracas, *charrasca* scrapers, *quitiplás*, *mina* and *furruco* drums of African origin).

In spite of the media ban, Primera's fame and influence became widespread through direct and unmediated contact with his audiences (Marsh 2016). Though he maintained strong links with leftist political parties throughout his lifetime, Primera believed, as he said in 1984, that if his song was written to express a party line, then it would 'reach as far as it should. I have come to the conclusion that song comes essentially from the people, but the voice of ordinary people everywhere, every day' (cited in Martín 1998: 100). Throughout the 1970s and early 1980s, Primera faced increasing persecution from state authorities; his flat was broken into and searched, and his wife and mother received threatening telephone calls advising them to buy mourning clothes (Marsh 2016: 85). On more than one occasion, Primera reported attempts to assassinate him (Marsh 2016: 85). He remained defiant and proclaimed in 1985 that he would not be silenced:

> My weapon is song ... my weapon is the desire to always be useful to my country. I don't have the makings of a hero, but nor do I have the makings of a deserter. I prefer to take the risk of using my 'weapons' to confront yours.
>
> *(cited in Hernández Medina 1991: 212)*

On 16 February 1985, Primera was returning home after working on his latest album when an oncoming vehicle collided with his car. He was killed instantly.

When a committed artist dies, they are 'set apart' from other living artists and also above them, 'partly because the dead are no longer fallible ... and partly because their characters and their careers begin to be both simplified and ennobled as they undergo a two-stage process of transformation' (Pring-Mill 1990: 63). The first phase takes the artist out of life and into history. The second phase takes the artist into the realm of legend so that such individuals 'come to stand for things which are of greater importance for those who have survived than the individuals themselves may have been ... in life' (Pring-Mill 1990: 64). Alí Primera, whose songs were not tied to any specific political party line, was reinterpreted after his death and came to stand for resistance and opposition to the dominant *Punto Fijo* (Fixed Point) two-party political system. Between 1980 and 1996, poverty increased in Venezuela much more dramatically than elsewhere in Latin America, rising from 17 percent to 65 percent of the population (Wilpert 2013: 192). Posthumously, Primera's songs were reinterpreted and used to translate the shared lived experiences of hardship and state repression into collective action:

In universities, factories and secondary schools, people are joining the struggle for social change, stimulated by the [necessary song] that Alí Primera created. Protests are preceded by the presence of Alí Primera, otherwise they are not protests. His message echoes … his songs are still relevant. The arsenal that he carried in his throat has not been diluted by the passage of time but it is a living presence at each and every act that people undertake to demand their liberation and well-being.

(Hernández Medina 1991: 6)

In March 1994, on the day the then Colonel Hugo Chávez was released from prison time for his role in a failed coup two years previously, he was asked by a journalist if he had a message for the people of Venezuela. 'Yes,' he replied, 'Let them listen to Alí Primera's songs!' (Marsh 2016: 117). Within five years, having formed a new political organisation and mounted a campaign rooted in these very songs, Hugo Chávez was elected president of Venezuela with 56 percent of the vote, becoming the first head of state without links to the country's establishment *Punto Fijo* parties in over forty years. Alí Primera's songs, and collective memories of his life and death, offered Chávez a means of translating his political thought directly to the Venezuelan public. In public appearances, interviews, speeches and on his TV programme *Aló Presidente*, Chávez reinterpreted Alí's life and songs to create a political persona through which to connect with the masses in a profound way; narratives about Alí's life and songs allowed Chávez to represent himself and his political movement as a definitive break with the old order and as representative of the poor and the marginalised.

In the Chávez period, many Venezuelans saw the official promotion of Alí's legacy as a symbol of a new participatory democracy based on their historical struggles. A community radio worker in a Caracas barrio explained to me in 2008 how she interpreted the government's promotion of Alí Primera's songs:

the people have a sense of belonging now … we have a government we feel identified with … We never stopped listening to Alí. We were the ones who kept Alí alive, we talked about him, distributed fliers, and commemorated him … Alí belongs to the people, and it's the people who are now driving this process.

However, Chávez's interpretations of Primera's songs as precursors of Bolivarianism was not universally accepted; while some opponents of Chávez fought against state association with Primera's songs, others used social media to harness the songs' oppositional qualities in order to attack and resist the Chávez government (Marsh 2016). In the Chávez period, Primera's songs came to act as cultural resources which Venezuelans drew upon to translate their political opinions into symbolic action; they mobilised music to create and share political knowledge, to redefine themselves in relation to the state, and to reach new understandings of their place within a changed society. In the twenty-first century, Primera's songs became tools that Venezuelans reinterpreted in order to assert, defend or contest *chavista* hegemony.

Conclusion

Testimonio is, almost by definition, primarily related to the sung or spoken rather than the written word. While the texts under discussion have been brought to an Anglophone readership by translators, the vocative original involves them in a process often more akin to interpreting. This necessitates a particular understanding of, even affinity with, the political and cultural perspective of the singer or speaker. Testimonies such as these most frequently come from the marginalised or powerless, and may describe (or deplore) their situation while attacking those exercising power over them.

In describing interpreting 'as an oral form of translation,' Cronin argues that 'interpreting predates written translation by millennia ... interpretation studies still remain very much a minority interest in academic studies in general and in translation studies in particular' (Cronin 2002: 45). Having reviewed existing material, he makes an explicit link to power politics in his conclusion:

> The antiquity of interpreting, the continued importance of orality as a feature of everyday life in a multilingual world, the crucial importance of the interpreting transaction in countless situations where questions of power and control are to the fore, show there is a more urgent need than ever to bring a new materialist perspective to bear on interpretation studies to illuminate our translation past, present and future.
>
> *(Cronin 2002: 62)*

There has been considerable research into the transmission of postcolonial oral and literary narrative, often emphasising the importance of the intended audience. The Kenyan postcolonial writer Ngũgĩ wa Thiongo provides a first-hand account of how:

> I came to realise only too painfully that the novel in which I had so carefully painted the struggle of the Kenya peasantry against colonial oppression would never be read by them ... I [therefore] did not think I would continue writing in English: that I knew *about* whom I was writing, but *for* whom was I writing?
>
> *(1993: 9–10; also see Chapter 20 in this volume)*

Ngũgĩ's case is unusual in that he was translating information from within a predominantly oral tradition into his second language (English), one that would not have been spoken by either his fictional characters or the 'peasantry' on which his narrative relied. Yet this second oral language was his first written language. The synergy of having a foot in both worlds meant that he felt his mission to be to self-translate (or rewrite) a narrative conceived in English back to the Gikuyu from whence it came.

It is doubtful whether political activists such as Rigoberta Menchú and Judith Reyes had a specifically Anglophone audience in mind as they spoke or sang their words. Yet it is highly likely that the translation of *I ... Rigoberta Menchú, An Indian Woman in Guatemala.* contributed to the award of the Nobel Peace Prize to Menchú in 1992, just as translators of Latin American songs of resistance such as Barbara Dane are directly involved in spreading political activism abroad.

For marginalised communities with limited access to economic, cultural and political resources, testimonies are a powerful means of constructing and sharing counter-hegemonic perspectives. Spoken, written, read, sung or listened to, testimonies translate across modalities. In doing so, they produce cultural resources that enable resistance. While official discourses neglect or deny injustice, brutality and oppression, testimonies represent the lived experiences of such phenomena with a view to effecting social and political change and enhancing solidarity.

Characteristic of *testimonio* is the collective voice, typical of popular and indigenous communities who share a common experience and identity. The voice may vary in expression and in register, but primarily belongs to an oral rather than literary tradition. This chapter addresses some of the issues that arise from the mediation of transcribers, translators, editors, publishers and music promoters as well as the audience's reception of a campaigning, often directly political, message. Further, it proposes that academic critiques are also political, if less directly so.

The translator who wishes to transmit a deeper understanding of the political goals of social movements alongside a profound sense of empathy with the lived experiences of the oppressed must engage with aural, musical and textual testimonies, while recognising their complex and dynamic roles in social and political struggles. As Baker (2006: 471) argues, via translation 'another narrative' becomes possible, which renders subaltern forms of knowledge accessible across modalities and geographies. Translation of oral languages, spoken and sung, has a vital role to play in global struggles against oppression and injustice.

Related topics

Joint Authorship and Preface Writing Practices as Translation in post-'Years of Lead' Morocco; What Is Asylum?; Translating for *Le Monde diplomatique en español*.

Further reading

Grandin, Greg (2011) *Who Is Rigoberta Menchú?* London: Verso.

Following the publication of both *I, Rigoberta ...* and *Crossing Borders* by Rigoberta Menchú, Grandin examines how she became the target of US anthropologists and historians seeking to discredit her testimony and deny US complicity in the genocidal policies of the Guatemalan regime.

Gugelberger, Georg, and Michael Kearney (1991) 'Voices of the Voiceless in Testimonial Literature,' *Latin American Perspectives* 18 (3): 3–14.

An introduction to identifying the basic themes running through 'a different kind of writing' in Latin America, characterised by an authentic/witness narrative. It addresses representation, collective memory and identity.

Morris, Nancy (1986) 'Canto porque es necesario cantar: The New Song Movement in Chile, 1973–1983,' *Latin American Research Review* XXI (1): 117–136.

A research article that focuses on the encoded meanings embedded within the lyrics and performance of folk-based music in Chile during the Pinochet dictatorship.

Pring-Mill, Robert (1990) *Gracias a la vida: The Power and Poetry of Song.* London: University of London: Dept. of Hispanic Studies.

An extended essay in which Pring-Mill examines the lyrics of Chilean singer/songwriters Víctor Jara and Violeta Parra, and discusses the social and political functions of these within local popular and oral traditions.

Smith, Kathryn M. (2011) 'Female Voice and Feminist Text: Testimonio as a Form of Resistance in Latin America,' *Florida Atlantic Comparative Studies Journal* 12: 21–38.

An examination of key testimonial texts from Argentina and Central America and how 'they rescript history, redefine literary conventions and re-inscribe otherwise ignored stories.' Further, how *testimonio* 'directly challenges the authoritarian powers threatening peace in many countries.'

References

Amnesty International (1977) *Report of an Amnesty International Mission to Argentina, 6–15 November 1976.* [online]. Available at: www.amnesty.org/download/Documents/204000/amr130831977eng.pdf [accessed 27 September 2019].

Amnesty International (1995) *Summary of the Report of the Inter-American Commission on the Human Rights Situation in Argentina.* AI Index, AMR 13.2.

Ardill, Allan (2013) 'Australian Sovereignty, Indigenous Standpoint Theory, Feminist Standpoint Theory: First Peoples' Sovereignties Matter,' *Griffith Law Review* 22 (2): 315–343.

Arias, Arturo (2001) *The Rigoberta Menchú Controversy.* Minnesota: University of Minnesota.

Avant-Mier, Roberto, and Marouf A. Hasian (2008) 'Communicating 'Truth': Testimonio, Vernacular Voices, and the Rigoberta Menchú Controversy,' *Communication Review* 11 (4): 323–345.

Baker, Mona (2006) 'Translation and Activism: Emerging Patterns of Narrative Community,' *The Massachusetts Review* 47 (3): 462–484.

Baker, Mona (ed.) (2016) *Translating Dissent: Voices from and with the Egyptian Revolution.* New York and London: Routledge.

Barnet, Miguel (1966) *The Diary of a Runaway Slave.* Trans. Nick Hill. Illinois: Northwestern University Press.

Blackmer Reyes, Katherine, and Julia Curry Rodríguez (2012) '*Testimonio:* Origins, Terms, and Resources,' *Equity and Excellence in Education* 45 (3): 525–538.

Brewster, Keith (2010) *Reflections on Mexico '68.* Chichester: Wiley-Blackwell.

Brotherston, Gordon (1997) '*Regarding the Evidence in* Me Llamo Rigoberta Menchú,' *Journal of Latin American Cultural Studies* 6 (1): 93–99.

Burgos-Debray, Elizabeth (1984) 'Introduction,' in *I ... Rigoberta Menchú, An Indian Woman in Guatemala.* Ed. Elizabeth Burgos-Debray. New York and London: Verso.

Caistor, Nick (1986 [1984]) 'Foreword,' in *Nunca Más (Never Again).* National Commission on Disappeared People. London: Faber & Faber.

Chúngara, Domitila, and Moema Viezzer (1978) *Let Me Speak! Testimony of Domitila, a Woman of the Bolivian Mines.* Trans. Victoria Ortiz. New York: Monthly Review Press.

Comisión Nacional Sobre la Desaparición de Personas (CONADEP) (1984) Buenos Aires: Editorial Universitaria de Buenos Aires.

Cronin, Michael (2002) 'The Empire Talks Back: Orality, Heteronomy, and the Cultural Turn in Interpretation Studies,' in *Translation and Power.* Eds. Maria Tymoczko and Edwin Gentzler. Amherst: University of Massachusetts Press. 387–397.

Dane, Barbara (2006) 'Sleeve Notes,' in *Mexico: Days of Struggle [CD].* Ed. Judith Reyes. Washington: Smithsonian Folkways Recordings.

DeNora, Tia (2000) *Music in Everyday Life.* Cambridge: Cambridge University Press.

DeNora, Tia (2011) *Music-in-action: Essays in Sonic Ecology.* Farnham, Surrey: Ashgate.

Didion, Joan (1983) *Salvador.* London: Chatto & Windus.

Ellner, Steve (2005) 'Introduction: The Search for Explanations,' in *Venezuelan Politics in the Chávez Era: Class, Polarization and Conflict.* Eds. Steve Ellner and Daniel Hellinger. London: Lynne Rienner Publishers. 7–26.

Eyerman, Ron, and Andrew Jamison (1998) *Music and Social Movements: Mobilizing Traditions in the Twentieth Century.* Cambridge: Cambridge University Press.

Fairley, Jan (2013) '"There is No Revolution without Song": "New Song" in Latin America,' in *Music and Protest in 1968.* Eds. Barley Norton and Beate Kutschke. Cambridge: Cambridge University Press. 119–136.

Frazer, Chris (2006) *Bandit Nation: A History of Outlaws and Cultural Struggle in Mexico, 1810–1920.* Lincoln and London: University of Nebraska Press.

Galeano, Eduardo (2001) 'Let's Shoot Rigoberta,' in *The Rigoberta Menchú Controversy.* Ed. Arturo Arias. Minnesota: University of Minnesota. 99–102.

Gott, Richard (2007) 'Latin America as a White Settler Society,' *Bulletin of Latin American Research* 26 (2): 269–289.

Graham-Yooll, Andrew (1991) *After the Despots*. Ed. Norman Thomas Di Giovanni. London: Bloomsbury.

Graham-Yooll, Andrew (2018) 'So When Will All Rights Be Human?' in *The Buenos Aires Times* [online] 9 Decemeber. Available at: www.batimes.com.ar/news/opinion-and-analysis/so-when-will-all-rights-be-human.phtml [accessed 11 October 2019].

Gugelberger, Georg, and Michael Kearney (1991) 'Voices for the Voiceless: Testimonial Literature in Latin America,' *Latin American Perspectives* 18 (3): 3–14.

Hernández Medina, Jaime (1991) *Alí Primera: 'Huella profunda sobre esta tierra'. Vida y obra*. Maracaibo: Editorial Escritos.

Hopkinson, Amanda (2016) 'Cristobal Colón/Cristoforo Colombo/Christopher Columbus: What's in a Name? Translation and Politics in a Postcolonial World,' in *Discourses of Empire and Commonwealth*. Eds. Sandra Robinson and Alastair Niven. Leiden and Boston: Brill Rodopi. 37–44.

Johnson, Lyman (ed.) (2004) *Death, Dismemberment, and Memory in Latin America*. Albuquerque: University of New Mexico Press.

Kinzer, Stephen (2018) 'Efraín Ríos Montt, Guatemalan Dictator Convicted of Genocide, Dies at 91,' *New York Times* [online] 1 April. Available at: www.nytimes.com/2018/04/01/obituaries/efrain-rios-montt-guatemala-dead.html [accessed 13 September 2018].

López Maya, Margarita, and Luis Lander (2005) 'Popular Protest in Venezuela: Novelties and Continuities,' *Latin American Perspectives* 32 (141): 92–108.

Marsh, Hazel (2010) 'Writing Our History in Songs: Judith Reyes, Popular Music and the Student Movement of 1968,' *Bulletin of Latin American Research*, Special Issue: *Reflections on Mexico '68*. 144–159.

Marsh, Hazel (2016) *Hugo Chávez, Alí Primera and Venezuela: The Politics of Music in Latin America*. Basingstoke: Palgrave Macmillan.

Martín, Gloria (1998) *El perfume de una época*. Alfadil: Caracas.

Menchú, Rigoberta (1983) *Me Llamo Rigoberta Menchú Y Así Me Nació La Conciencia*. Barcelona: Editorial Argos Vergara.

Menchú, Rigoberta (1984) *I … Rigoberta Menchú, An Indian Woman in Guatemala*. Ed. Elisabeth Burgos-Debray. Trans. Ann Wright. New York and London: Verso.

Montejo, Víctor (2001) 'Truth, Human Rights and Representation,' in *The Rigoberta Menchú Controversy*. Ed. Arturo Arias. Minnesota: University of Minnesota. 372–391.

National Commission on Disappeared People (NCDP) (1984 [1986]) *Nunca Más (Never Again)*. London: Faber & Faber.

The Norwegian Nobel Institute (1992) 'Rigoberta Menchú Tum Biographical,' [online]. Available at: www.nobelprize.org/prizcs/peace/1992/tum/biographical/ [accessed 27 September 2019].

Peloso, Vincent (2014) *Race and Ethnicity in Latin American History*. New York: Routledge.

Popol Vuh: The Mayan Book of the Dawn of Life (1985). Tr. Dennis Tedlock. New York: Simon & Schuster.

Pring-Mill, Robert (1987) 'The Roles of Revolutionary Song—A Nicaraguan Assessment,' *Popular Music* 6 (2): 179–189.

Pring-Mill, Robert (1990) *Gracias a la vida: The Power and Poetry of Song*. London: University of London.

Pring-Mill, Robert (2002) 'Spanish American Committed Song: The Growth of the 'Pring-Mill Collection,' in *I Sing the Difference: Identity and Commitment in Latin American Song*. Eds. Jan Fairley and David Horn. Liverpool: Institute of Popular Music. 6–38.

Reda Nasr, Rania (2016) 'Testimonio as Resistance in Alicia Partnoy's The Little School,' *Conference paper* [online]. Available at: www.researchgate.net/publication/314343429_Testimonio_as_Resistance_in_Alicia_Partnoy%27s_The_Little_School [accessed 27 September 2019].

Reyes, Judith (2006 [1973]) *Mexico: Days of Struggle [CD]*. Washington: Smithsonian Folkways Recordings.

Rowe, William, and Vivian Schelling (1991) *Memory and Modernity: Popular Culture in Latin America*. London and New York: Verso.

Roy, William (2010) *Reds, Whites, and Blues: Social Movements, Folk Music, and Race in the United States*. Princeton: Princeton University Press.

Sábato, Ernesto (1986 [1984]) 'Prologue,' in *Nunca Más (Never Again)*. National Commission on Disappeared People. London: Faber & Faber. 1–6.

Soldatenko, Michael (2005) 'Mexico '68: Power to the Imagination!,' *Latin American Perspectives* 32 (4): 111–132.

Stoll, David (n.d.) 'Staff Webpage,' [online] Available at: www.middlebury.edu/academics/es/faculty/node/25831 [accessed 27 September 2019].

Strauss, Robert (1999) 'Truth and Consequences,' in *Stanford Magazine* [online] May/June. Available at: https://alumni.stanford.edu/get/page/magazine/article/?article_id=40702 [accessed 27 September 2019].

Taibo, P.I. II (2004 [1991]) *'68*. New York: Seven Stories Press.

Tandt, Catherine and Richard Young (2004) 'Tradition and Transformation in Latin American Music,' in *The Cambridge Companion to Modern Latin American Culture*. Ed. John King. Cambridge: Cambridge University Press. 236–257.

Thiong'o, Ngũgĩ wa (1993) *Moving the Centre: The Struggle for Cultural Freedoms*. Portsmouth: Heinemann African Series.

Velasco García, Jorge (2004) *El Canto de la Tribu*. México: Consejo nacional para la cultura y las artes.

Wilpert, Gregory (2013) 'Venezuela: An Electoral Road to Twenty-first Century Socialism?' in *The New Latin American Left: Cracks in the Empire*. Eds. Jeffery Webber and Barry Carr. Lanham: Rowman and Littlefield Publications. 152–168.

Wright, Ann (2000) 'The Interpretation of Translation, the Translation of Testimony,' *In Other Words, The Journal for Literary Translators* 15: 13–25.

Wright, Ann (2018) Telephone interview with Amanda Hopkinson, 18 August 2018.

Zolov, Eric (1999) *Refried Elvis: The Rise of the Mexican Counterculture*. Berkeley: University of California Press.

Part V
Translation and human rights

17

The right not to have an interpreter in criminal trials

The Irish language as a case study

Noelle Higgins

Introduction

The right to an interpreter for a defendant in criminal trials is clearly enshrined in international law, and is regarded as a core component of the right to a fair trial. This right is protected under Article 14 of the *International Covenant on Civil and Political Rights* (ICCPR), one of the nine core human rights treaties of the United Nations, which was adopted in 1966, and the right is also protected in regional human rights systems, including by Article 6 of the *European Convention on Human Rights* (ECHR). In addition, numerous national constitutions and human rights bills contain a similar stipulation (Brown-Blake 2006: 391). Indeed, even where human rights statutes and constitutions neglect to specifically provide for the right to an interpreter, other aspects of the right to a fair trial have been interpreted to support such interpretative support (Brown-Blake 2006: 391–392). Furthermore, under the common law, the right to an interpreter is recognised as stemming from the principle of natural justice, because natural justice

> incorporates a raft of principles associated with fair hearing and among other things, it requires that a person be given prior notice of the charge against him and an opportunity to meet that charge. An accused person who does not understand the case against him has no opportunity to raise an appropriate defence. In this context, allowing an accused who does not speak the language of the court to have the trial discourse interpreted arises logically.
>
> *(Brown-Blake 2006: 393)*

Rather than assessing the legal framework on the right to an interpreter, this chapter focuses, rather, on the right to not have an interpreter in certain circumstances. The chapter takes the Irish language as a case study, and analyses the recent case of *Ó Maicín* v. *Éire*, where the question of interpretation from Irish to English in Irish courts was raised.

According to Article 8 of the Irish Constitution (1937), the Irish language (*Gaeilge*) is the 'first official language' of Ireland, with English being recognised as a 'second official language.' Despite the preeminent status accorded to the language, there are fewer than 50,000 native speakers of Irish out of a national population of 4.79 million (www. cso.ie/en/index.html). While many more people have varying levels of proficiency in the language as a result of compulsory Irish lessons in the education system, or of interest in the language, or of nationalist ideals, English is the lingua franca of the vast majority of the population. This disparity between the language's de jure and de facto position has led to a number of difficulties in the legal system, one of which centres on the question of interpretation in the court system. While there is a recognised right to conduct legal proceedings in the Irish language, and also a right to have an interpreter to, and from, Irish (Section 8 Official Languages Act 2003), recent cases have focused on the issue of whether there is a right to a bilingual judge and jury (*MacCárthaigh* v. *Éire* [1999] IR 200 and *Ó Maicín* v. *Éire* [2014] IESC 12), i.e. if a right not to have an interpreter exists in the Irish legal system.

This chapter focuses on practical issues which arise in dealing with the issue of interpretation in a court setting (Berk-Seligson 2017). The use, and translation, of the Irish language was once a manifestation of rebellion and activism against British rule. In an independent Ireland, the use, and translation, of Irish became an important marker of Irish identity, with language rights activists demanding enhanced rights for Irish speakers in various aspects of life, including within the court system. Translation into the native Irish tongue in these contexts was a demonstration of activism. Individual Irish-language activists began taking cases before Irish courts in order to ensure language rights, including the right to use Irish before the courts, which required the right to an interpreter were implemented. This right has subsequently been codified in legislation, by means of the *Official Languages Act* 2003. In more recent times, however, Irish speakers have claimed a right for 'direct access' to a bilingual judge and jury, without the need for an interpreter. The research illustrates how the low standard of interpretation from Irish to English and vice versa, where interpreters may not be able to adequately transmit the meaning of actors in a court case, can lead to injustice. While the case study in this chapter focuses on the use of the Irish language in courts in Ireland, similar issues will arise in other jurisdictions, where foreign, or native but lesser-used, languages are employed in the court system (Hayes and Hale 2010).

The first section of this chapter provides a brief contextual history of the Irish language. The second section analyses the constitutional and legislative status of the language. The third section discusses the right to an interpreter in international human rights law and Irish law. The fourth focuses on interpretation services in Irish courts. In the fifth section I examine the case of *Ó Maicín* v. *Éire*, where the question of interpretation was raised. The conclusion offers normative reflections concerning how the law should develop in this area in the future.

History of the Irish language

Irish has been spoken in Ireland for over 2,000 years, and was, until the beginning of the 17th century, the main language spoken throughout the whole island of Ireland (Cronin 1996: 10). It is a member of the Celtic language family, and is closely related to Scots Gaelic and to Manx, and more distantly to the other Celtic languages, such as Breton, Welsh and Cornish. While the Irish Constitution currently accords the status of 'first official language' to Irish, this does not reflect the reality on the ground in terms of numbers of speakers, or indeed, opportunities to use the language, because the constitutional status has not been adequately concretised by means of comprehensive legislation or language-planning policies (Ní Drisceoil 2016). The language has been regarded by some as an important identity marker, and as a means of ensuring the transmission of Gaelic culture (Cronin 2006; Darmody and Daly 2015: xi; Sakai 2009: 73). Irish history is replete with examples of activism (Warren 2012), with individuals and groups on occasion raising the issue of language rights, including interpretation and translation issues, in Irish courts (Nic Shuibhne 1999).

In the early decades of the 17th century the use of Irish declined sharply, and by the end of the 18th century 'Irish was largely the language of the poor and dispossessed' (Higgins and Ní Uigín 2017: 51). This decline was precipitated by three issues: first, the Great Famine (normally dated from 1845–1849 or up to 1855), caused by the failure of the potato crop, the staple food of the Irish, resulted in the death of one million people and emigration of another million, out of a total population of 8.2 million. The western part of the country, which was mainly Irish-speaking, suffered the most from depopulation due to starvation and emigration (Akenson 1970). The majority of the emigrants went to English-speaking countries (the UK, the USA, Australia and Canada), making knowledge of English necessary in all walks of life. Second, the National Schools System, established in 1831 by the British government, prohibited the teaching of Irish in its institutions, thus leading some to abandon their native tongue (Ó Buachalla 1984: 75). Third, language was used as a tool of colonial rule (Niranjana 1992; Rafael 1988). Because English was utilised by political leaders the language was associated with power, prestige and progression. Meanwhile, Irish was associated with poverty and backwardness. Under colonial rule, the Irish language was prohibited in the legal system by virtue of the *Administration of Justice (Language) Act (Ireland)* 1737, which required that only English be used within the courts, although interpreters were used in court proceedings, when necessary, on an ad hoc and unregulated basis (Brady 1959; Howlin 2010).

A 'Gaelic revival' was initiated in Ireland in the late 19th century, leading to a renewed interest in the Irish language, literature and culture (Hutchinson 1987). Numerous organisations were set up to encourage a return to Gaelic ways, including *Conradh na Gaeilge* (the Gaelic League), established in 1893. Language was recognised as an important tool in the re-Gaelicisation efforts, which gained momentum after independence. A stated aim of early political leaders was that the Irish language should become more widespread as the language of the Irish people once again (de Valera 1943). In the 1920s, post-independence, policies were put in place to revive the language, including the inclusion of Irish as a compulsory subject on the primary and second level education curricula (Ó Murchú 2016). Despite the re-Gaelicisation efforts, Irish never regained her status as the language of the majority. Census figures in 2016 recorded the population of Ireland at 4,797,976. Approximately 1,761,420 could speak Irish, which equates to approximately 39.8% of the population. Of this number, only 73,803 spoke Irish daily, and 111,473 spoke the language weekly, despite the fact that Irish is a mandatory subject at both primary and secondary level (www.cso.ie/en/index.html).

Parts of Ireland are designated as a *Gaeltacht*, a geographic area where the majority of the population have Irish as their first language. In the Gaeltacht 66.3% of people could speak Irish according to the Census (www.cso.ie/en/index.html). Therefore, while everybody in Ireland can understand and speak English fluently and would be able to follow court proceedings in that language to varying levels, a proportion of the population would want to engage with court proceedings through the medium of Irish.

For some, it is important as a marker of identity to engage with all areas of the public service through Irish (Cronin 2006). Others feel more comfortable using Irish in court as it is their mother-tongue, and may be concerned that, although they understand and speak English, something might be lost by engaging with the court system through their second language, thus threatening the fairness of the trial (Grabau and Gibbons 1996; Hayes and Hale 2010; Kahaner 2009).

The legal status of the Irish language

When Ireland gained independence, the government adopted a Constitution in 1922, the Constitution of the Irish Free State, Article 4 of which stated:

> The National Language of the Irish Free State is the Irish language, but the English language shall be equally recognised as an official language. Nothing in this Article shall prevent special provisions being made by the Parliament of the Irish Free State (otherwise called and herein generally referred to as the '*Oireachtas*') for districts or areas in which only one language is in general use.

Ireland's current constitution (Constitution of Ireland 1937) was adopted in 1937, and Article 8 builds on Article 4 of the previous constitution, stating:

1. The Irish language as the national language is the first official language.
2. The English language is recognised as a second official language.
3. Provision may, however, be made by law for the exclusive use of either of the said languages for any one or more official purposes, either throughout the State or in any part thereof.

Also relevant to the Irish language is Article 25.5.4 of the Constitution, which states that in cases of conflict between the English and Irish text of the Constitution, the Irish version is to take precedence (Ó Cearúil 1999). Further, the Constitution requires under Article 25 that an Irish-language version of all pieces of legislation should be made available. However, successive Irish governments have failed to live up to obligations under Article 25, with English-only language versions of pieces of legislation being drafted from the 1980s until relatively recently (Ní Drisceoil 2016). In addition, Irish governments failed to interpret Article 8 as requiring them to act in a pro-active way or to allocate resources to Irish speakers, including in the legal system. Therefore, the constitutional position of the Irish language never really translated into rights for Irish speakers. According to Parry, there was 'a complete disconnection between the declared constitutional principle and its practical implementation. Irish language policy thus descended into a series of empty gestures and ritualistic use in the spirit of tokenism' (2015: 208).

Article 8 was viewed essentially as a description of the status of the language that did not bestow any particular rights on Irish speakers (de Blacam 2014). However, the provision enabled activists to take cases before the courts in respect of the Irish language. A number of individuals succeeded in focusing the judiciary's attention on the Irish language in a series of cases, including *An Stát (Mac Fhearraigh) v. Mac Gamhnia* (High Court, unreported, 1 July 1983), *O'Coleáin v. D.J. Crotty* [1927] 61 ILTR 81, *O'Foghludha v. McClean* [1934] IR 469, *The State (Buchan) v. Coyne*

[1936] 70 ILTR 185, *Ó Monachain* v. *An Taoiseach* (Supreme Court, 16 July 1982, unreported), *Ó Beoláin* v. *Fahy and Others* [2001] 2 IR 279, *MacCárthaigh* v. *Éire* [1999] IR 200 and *Ó Maicín* v. *Éire* [2014] IESC 12 (Nic Shuibhne 1999). One of these rights is the right to an interpreter. In order to understand the context in which this right should be assessed, the following section will discuss the right to an interpreter under international law, and then analyse how this right has been addressed under Irish law.

The right to an interpreter under international law and Irish law

As is stated by Grabau and Gibbons:

> Injustice is doubtless being done from time to time in communities thronged with [linguistic minorities], through failure of the judges to insist on a supply of competent interpreters. The subject is one upon which the profession are in general too callous, for no situation is more full of anguish than that of an innocent accused who cannot understand what is being testified against him [or her].

> *(1996: 231)*

As stated in the introduction, under international law, the right to an interpreter is identified as a central tenet of the right to a fair trial. This right is a guarantee, spanning a number of sub-rights, which seek to prevent an abuse of power during the criminal trial process and to ensure the rights of the accused during this process (Brown-Blake 2006: 391). Article 14(3)(f) of the ICCPR provides that, in the determination of any criminal charge against the accused, everyone shall be entitled to a number of minimum guarantees, including: 'To have the free assistance of an interpreter if he cannot understand or speak the language used in court.' In addition, paragraph (a) of Article 14(3) also provides that a person who is charged as part of the criminal process is entitled '[t]o be informed promptly and in detail in a language which he understands of the nature and cause of the charge against him,' which may also entail the work of an interpreter.

The right to an interpreter is also protected under regional human rights law, e.g. in Article 47 of the *Charter of Fundamental Rights of the European Union* and in Article 6(3)(e) of the ECHR, which both apply to Ireland. Following on from the former, Directive 2010/64/EU of the European Parliament and the Council governs the right to interpretation and translation within criminal proceedings within the EU (Schlesinger and Pöchhacker 2010; van der Vlis 2010). The ECHR provides that a person charged with a criminal offence is entitled, among other guarantees, 'to have the free assistance of an interpreter if he cannot understand or speak the language used in court' (Article 6(3)(e), ECHR 1950). The rights protected by the ECHR have been included in Irish law through the adoption of the *European Convention on Human Rights Act* 2003 (ECHR Act), and thus, the right to an interpreter in criminal trials is protected in Irish law by means of legislation, as well as via the common law, as an aspect of the right to a fair trial. Clearly, the rationale behind including the right to an interpreter centres on the fact that a defendant who does not have complete command of the language cannot adequately engage with the legal process, and so is not afforded a fair trial (Brown-Blake 2006; Grabau and Gibbons 1996).

The right to an interpreter under Irish law

The right to a fair trial is enshrined in both the 1922 and the 1937 Constitutions. Article 38(1) of the current Constitution provides that '[n]o person shall be tried on any criminal charge save in due course of law.' However, this provision does not extend to explicitly include the right to an interpreter, as is the case with the ICCPR and ECHR, discussed above. Following on from the 1922 Constitution, legislation was also adopted in respect of the use of the Irish language in court proceedings. The *Legal Practitioners (Qualification) Act* 1929 required Irish barristers and solicitors to have proficient knowledge of Irish and the *Courts of Justice Act* 1924 required that certain members of the judiciary be proficient in the language. In addition, Section 44 of the 1924 Act required that, as far as practicable, circuit judges with knowledge of the Irish language would be assigned to courts where Irish was generally used, so that cases could proceed without the judge depending on an interpreter (Parry 2015: 214).

In the case of *People (Attorney General)* v. *Joyce and Walsh (Attorney General* v. *Joyce and Walsh* [1929] IR 526) in 1929, the Chief Justice of the Supreme Court (Kennedy CJ) stated that if the language of the defendant differed from that of the Court, then 'means of interpreting … should be provided' ([1929] IR 526, 531). In this case it was held that any party to legal proceedings may use the Irish language on two grounds: firstly, as a case of natural law (in case that one party could not understand English), or secondly, as a result of the constitutional status awarded to the language in Article 4. It is interesting to note that the right to use the Irish language was based not only on the constitutional status, but also on the natural law, which exists outside of any written law. Natural law is thus called

> because it derives from the nature of man as a rational being, a person and an individual in society. It is a moral law which prescribes how men should act according to right reason; it imposes obligations and confers rights on man as regards both himself and his fellow men. In order to fulfil the obligations of the natural law human nature is endowed with certain rights which are anterior to all positive human law and which no human law can abrogate.
>
> *(Costello 1956: 403)*

The case focused on the Irish language, and indeed, in 1929, when the case was heard, it would be very rare to have speakers of languages other than Irish or English before Irish courts. However, the 'natural law' argument accepted by Kennedy CJ would equally apply to speakers of a language other than Irish who did not understand English. In this context, the natural law right would be regarded as an aspect of the right to a fair trial.

Further, in the case of *State (Buchan)* v. *Coyne* in 1936 Chief Justice Sullivan stated that not providing an interpretation of evidence for the defendant 'contravened one of the fundamental principles of the administration of justice' ((1936) 70 ILTR 185, 186), thus focusing on interpretation as a means to ensure that justice is done, rather than a requirement emanating from the constitutional status of the Irish language, again echoing 'fair trial' language. It is important to note that both of these cases were decided well before the right to a fair trial was enshrined in international human rights law in 1966 by means of the ICCPR.

Under the 1937 Constitution, in the case of *Ó Monacháin* v. *An Taoiseach*, the Supreme Court held that '[i]t is a fundamental principle of law—part of natural justice which is not permitted to be set aside—that it is neither just nor lawful to hear a case in any language' ([1986] ILRM Digest 660) which the defendant does not understand. While this case focused on the Irish language, it is clear from the phrasing used by the Supreme Court that the principle of natural justice requires that an interpreter is allowed, and indeed, necessary, in criminal cases where the defendant does not understand the language of the court. These cases illustrate that the right to an interpreter emanates from natural justice principles, which inspire the right to a fair trial, separate from language rights.

The constitutional right to an interpreter emanating from natural justice principles sits alongside the legislative right to an interpreter which is provided for in the ECHR Act, mentioned above, and the *Official Languages Act*. The latter Act was adopted in 2003, in response to pressure placed on the government by Irish-language speakers and activists (Comhdháil Náisiúnta na Gaeilge 1998). *Conradh na Gaeilge* had been campaigning for language legislation since the 1970s. However, the *Official Languages Act* was not adopted until 2003. The primary aim of the Act is 'to promote increased use of the Irish language for official purposes' (*Official Languages Act* 2003). In order to oversee the implementation of the legislation, the Act established the Office of the Language Commissioner (*An Coimisinéir Teanga*) (sections 20–30 *Official Languages Act* 2003).

The Act also bestows a number of rights on Irish speakers, including the right to expect that all Acts of Parliament will be published simultaneously in Irish and English, the right to receive replies in Irish from public bodies, the right to avail of all services in Irish agreed by public bodies in language schemes, the right to expect the Language Commissioner to investigate complaints and give advice, and the right to use Irish in court, including the right to an interpreter. According to the Act, Irish or English may be used in any court, in any court pleading and/or in any document issuing from any court. Irish courts must ensure that a person may be heard in the official language of their choice and that a person has the right to use Irish in court regardless of their role in the proceedings, i.e. as a defendant, witness, a plaintiff or a victim. This right applies in all courts, from the lower regional courts to the higher courts as well as in tribunals. In the Irish legal system, the Supreme Court, the Court of Appeal and the High Court are known as 'the Superior Courts' and are provided for in the Constitution of the State. Other 'lower courts,' e.g. the Circuit Court and the District Court, which deal with less serious legal issues, are also established by law. Importantly, Irish courts may make arrangements, as is considered appropriate, for the interpretation of proceedings. The Act states that a person may not be disadvantaged or inconvenienced, or incur additional expense if they choose to use the Irish language in court and no one may be required to give evidence in a language other than the official language of his/her choice (Sections 5–8, *Official Languages Act* 2003).

Interpretation in Irish courts

Interpretation of court proceedings is fraught with difficulties, given the technical nature of the law and the numerous and varied parties involved in the court case (Cao 2013: 415; Fowler et al. 2013: 402; Mikkelson 2000: 3). Indeed, the participation of interpreters in criminal trials has been regarded as a 'necessary evil' (Waterhouse 2009: 47). Waterhouse states that there is a 'certain lack of enthusiasm around interpreter participation in trials' (Waterhouse 2009: 47), and cites numerous reasons for this claim, including: bilingual trials can take longer than trials without an interpreter; interpretation could provide those with a knowledge of the legal system additional time to think through their answers; there may be an element of distrust of those who need an interpreter; there is a potential of interpreters 'to alter content or intervene on behalf of or against the suspect' (Waterhouse 2009: 47). In addition, the person being interpreted for may feel excluded from the trial process as they depend on others to communicate their thoughts to the court (Waterhouse 2009: 47). Furthermore, research has also highlighted the influence which interpreters have over the trial process which can impact on the outcome of the trial (Berk-Seligson 1990; Hayes and Hale 2010). Alongside all of these problems with the interpretation process in the context of criminal trials, there is also another question which goes straight to the core of the right to a fair trial: is the interpreter skilled enough to adequately relay the sentiments of the defendant? In this context we must question the quality of interpretation, because if the interpretation is not of a sufficient quality, a fair trial may simply not be possible (Hayes and Hale 2010: 125).

Writing in a United States context, Kahaner states that 'the lack of sufficient numbers of qualified interpreters in the courtroom poses a significant threat to the fair, impartial, and efficient administration of justice' (Kahaner 2009: 224–225). As stated above, the right to an interpreter in criminal cases is ensured in Ireland by means of the *ECHR Act* 2003, and in respect of the official languages of the State, by means of the *Official Languages Act* 2003. This right is reiterated in Directive 2010/64/EU, which was transposed into Irish law by Statutory Instrument 564/2013 in respect of the Irish police and Statutory Instrument 565/2013 in respect of the courts, on the right to interpretation and translation in criminal proceedings. However, there is a lack of regulation concerning interpreters in the framework of Irish courts. The Rules of the Superior Courts provide that interpreters should 'be available to attend those Courts as required for the hearing of any cause or matter' (Order 120, 'Interpreters and Translations'), but do not refer to any standard which must be met by interpreters. Directive 2010/64/EU does, however, refer to the quality of the interpretation, and provides in Article 2(8) that

> [i]nterpretation provided under this article shall be of a quality sufficient to safeguard the fairness of the proceedings, in particular by ensuring that suspected or accused persons have knowledge of the case against them and are able to exercise their right of defence.

In addition, Article 5(1) of the Directive states that '[m]ember states shall take concrete measures to ensure that the interpretation and translation provided meets the quality required under article 2(8).' Furthermore, European Court of Human Rights case law suggests that there must be some oversight regarding the quality of the interpretation provided (*Kamasinski* v. *Austria*, 19 December 1989, Series A-168, § 74). All in all, there is a legal consensus that the quality of the interpretation is of central importance in ensuring the right to a fair trial. Unfortunately, in Ireland, and indeed, in a number of other States, no measures have been taken to guarantee the standard of interpreting services and there is no required training or accreditation for court interpreters or obligatory test in order to establish competency in interpretation (Phelan 2011: 547). The problems associated with non-qualified interpreters in the courtroom setting have been documented by a number of authors (Grabau and Gibbons 1996: 236–239; Phelan 2011: 547). In addition, there is no requirement that interpreters understand anything about the legal process, which is deemed to be important so that they may appreciate the context in which they are working and 'anticipate misunderstandings that may arise' (Mikkelson 2000: 34). Hale, who analysed legal interpretation in Australia, highlights that the lack of such standards and requirements means that interpreters 'rely on intuition rather than theory, to make their daily interpreting choices' (Hale 2004: 1), while Grabau and Gibbons underline the role of the judge in ensuring that interpretation services are of a high quality (Grabau and Gibbons 1996: 232–233).

It is clear that the legislature and judiciary should focus on the regulation of interpretation services to ensure that a high standard of interpretation is provided in order to guarantee the right to a fair trial, or that natural justice is observed. If they do not do so, there should be another option open to defendants, i.e. 'direct access' to a bilingual judge and jury, without the need for an interpreter. However, Irish case law regarding interpretation has not centred on the issue of quality of services. Rather, claims made in respect of having a right to 'direct access' to a jury and judge, without the services of an interpreter, have focused mainly on the constitutional status of the Irish language.

Claiming the right not to have an interpreter

The case of *Ó Maicín* v. *Éire & Ors* ([2014] IESC 12) focused on whether a person was entitled to a judge and a jury who could hear the case in Irish without the need for interpreters. The appellant had been charged with offences under section 3 of the *Non-Fatal Offences Against the Person Act* 1997 and section 11 of the *Firearms and Offensive Weapons Act* 1990 for allegedly assaulting another man. He was an Irish speaker, the incident had occurred in an Irish-speaking area of the country and the trial was set to be heard in Galway Circuit Criminal Court, a city situated on the borders of the Gaeltacht, where a large concentration of Irish speakers live.

Ó Maicín wanted to conduct his defence entirely through Irish, a practice which had already been established as a right in Irish courts (*Attorney General* v. *Joyce and Walsh* [1929] IR 526; *The State (Buchan)* v. *Coyne* (1936) 70 ILTR 185; *The State (Ó Conghaile)* v. *Governor of Limerick Prison, The Irish Independent*, 3 February 1937). He made an application to do so to the Circuit Criminal Court with the aid of an interpreter. However, the standard of interpretation was very poor and his counsel had to intervene to aid the interpreter on a number of occasions (Bergin 2015). Therefore, Ó Maicín requested the right to be tried by a bilingual jury and judge in order to dispense with the need for an interpreter during the court proceedings, and made an application to the Circuit Criminal Court to this effect. While the judge held that arrangements could be made to appoint a bilingual judge to the case, the empanelling of a bilingual jury, according to the Court, would be discriminatory, and therefore, unconstitutional, as such a jury would not be representative of the community as a whole in accordance with Article 38 of the Constitution, and following on from previous case law (*de Búrca* v. *Attorney General* ([1976] IR 38) and the *State (Byrne)* v. *Frawley* ([1978] IR 326)).

Ó Maicín sought judicial review of the Circuit Court decision in the High Court, and requested, inter alia, an order directing the Minister for Justice to specify a new 'Gaeltacht jury district,' in addition to a declaration that a bilingual jury would not be unconstitutional. He proposed that the borders of the '*Gaeltacht* jury district' would be drawn in a portion of the Gaeltacht stretching from west of the village of Spiddal, Co. Galway, into Connemara. The use of Irish as an everyday language in this area is very high (over 85%). A jury could therefore be randomly selected, which would be broadly representative of the community as a whole. The suggested creation of a Gaeltacht jury exemplifies what Sakai (2009: 83) calls 'bordering': it would create a border between languages and people, which could generate new problems. The High Court again held that the requirement for a jury to be selected by a random process meant that a jury selected on the basis of linguistic competency was unconstitutional (*Ó Maicín* v. *Ireland* [2010] IEHC 179). Ó Maicín therefore appealed to the Supreme Court, the highest court in Ireland, where this decision was upheld (*Ó Maicín* v. *Ireland* [2014] IESC 12). Ó Maicín's case relied on the constitutional status of Irish under Article 8.1, rather than fair trial arguments. However, this argument was met with the State's reliance on Article 38.5 of the Constitution, which provides for trial by jury in non-minor cases.

In the Supreme Court, Clarke J referred to the earlier case of *MacCárthaigh* v. *Éire* (*MacCárthaigh* v. *Éire* [1999] IR 200), where a similar issue had arisen as MacCárthaigh had wanted to have a bilingual jury, although the case was being heard in a non-Gaeltacht area and the incident which precipitated the original court case also happened in a non-Gaeltacht area. In *MacCárthaigh,* a unanimous Supreme Court rejected the claim to a right to be tried before a jury capable of understanding Irish without the assistance of an interpreter. However, the Court did recognise the inherent difficulties in interpretation. In his judgement/opinion/ruling, Hamilton CJ referred to the work of Michael Shulman, who argues:

> When a defendant testifies in a criminal case, his testimony is critically important to the jury's determination of his guilt or innocence. The first noticeable difficulty in the present system of Court interpretation is that non-English speaking defendants are not judged on their own words. The words attributed to the defendant are those of the interpreter. No matter how accurate the interpretation is, the words are not the defendant's, nor is the style, syntax or the emotion. Furthermore, some words are culturally specific and, therefore, are incapable of being translated. Perfect interpretations do not exist, as no interpretation will convey precisely the same meaning as the original testimony. While juries should not attribute to the defendant the exact wording of the interpretation and the emotion expressed by the interpreter, they typically do just that … Given that juries often determine the defendant's guilt or innocence based on small nuances of language or slight variations in emotion, how can it be fair for the defendant to be judged on the words chosen and the emotion expressed by the interpreter?
>
> *(Schulman 1993: 177)*

While agreeing that there were difficulties with interpretation in the court setting, Hamilton CJ decided the case on a pragmatic basis, stating 'in today's Ireland there is no better solution available' ([1999] 1 IR 200 at 212). Without the assistance of an interpreter, most of the population of Ireland would be excluded from sitting on a jury, and this would be in violation of Article 38.5 of the Constitution.

In *Ó Maicín,* Clarke J noted that MacCárthaigh's trial was to take place in Dublin, whereas Ó Maicín's case was to take place in Galway and the offence was committed in the Gaeltacht and the main witnesses were Irish speakers. He thus considered 'whether this case is different either because of a change in circumstances generally or because of the connection between this case and the Gaeltacht' ([2014]

IESC 12, para. 5.3). However, he did not find a need to depart from the previous approach. Clarke J held that empanelling a jury who were proficient in Irish would result in the exclusion of a large section of Irish society that did not understand Irish. In addition, he further held that even if it were not unconstitutional to empanel a jury of Irish speakers, the limited number of Irish speakers would make it almost impossible to empanel a jury using the current methods provided for by law. The decision was made on practicalities (Ó Conaill 2014), rather than on broader questions of justice and fairness, and to an extent, pushed the creation of a Gaeltacht or Irish-speaking jury back to the legislature.

Hardiman J gave the only dissent in this case. As with the majority, he focused on the issue of language rights, as opposed to the right to a fair trial. In his opinion, Ó Maicín had a constitutional right to be tried before a jury who could understand Irish without the assistance of an interpreter. He cited earlier cases on the Irish language, including Ó Foghludha ([1934] IR 469) and Ó Beoláin ([2001] 2 IR 279), and stated that as a result of Article 8 of the Constitution and these earlier judicial determinations that 'Ireland has thus been constituted as a country with two official languages, the national and first official language and a second official language. *It is thus legally constituted as a bilingual country*' ([2014] IESC 12, para. 18; emphasis in original). He focused on the fact that Ireland had been officially a bilingual country since independence and that this status had repercussions for how the State treated the Irish language, including in the legal field, and suggested that a government minister should exercise a statutory power to order a bilingual jury district. In his opinion, the Connemara Gaeltacht area could be declared a jury district from which a bilingual jury could be summoned.

Parry (2015: 199) suggests that the case of Ó Maicín and the issue of bilingual juries have left the State 'at a crossroads.' He suggests that it either has to abandon its bilingual policy altogether or else to embrace it fully. He points to other bilingual jurisdictions which have to deal with similar issues as the one posed in the above cases, and focused on Canada as an example to which the Irish State should aspire. Canadian provinces have created procedures to form a jury whose members who speak one or both of the official languages, French and English. While the procedures vary slightly between provinces, the general approach is to divide potential jurors by language and to create jury language lists (*Jury Act (Alberta)* 2000; *Jury Act (Saskatchewan)* 1998; *Jury Act (Ontario)* 1990). A jury is then chosen randomly from these lists. In Ontario, for example, the jury register is split into three sections: one section includes those who speak only French; another section includes those who speak only English; and the final section includes those who are bilingual. Jurors are then randomly chosen from the applicable list, depending on the language requirements of the case. If it would be difficult to empanel an independent and impartial jury because the number of those who speak the relevant language is too small, the court can transfer the trial to a different venue where there are more speakers of that language. The percentage of French speakers in some Canadian provinces is very small: in both Alberta and Saskatchewan only approximately 2% of the population are French speakers (Parry 2015: 203). Hardiman J also noted how British Colombia in Canada offers bilingual trials despite the fact that there tends to be a very limited pool of French speakers in the province and highlighted the expert evidence offered by Dr Colm Ó Giollagáin in the case, which noted that empanelling a jury of Irish speakers would not present an insurmountable task, particularly in the Connemara region. Ultimately, Hardiman J felt that, because Ireland is a bilingual State under Article 8 of the Constitution, it was very difficult to come to any other conclusion other than that Ó Maicín was entitled to a bilingual jury. The judge also supported the creation of a jury region in the Gaeltacht to facilitate further trials.

As mentioned above, the argument proffered by Ó Maicín focused on the constitutional status of the Irish language, rather than on natural justice or fair trial rights, and the standard of the interpretation was not addressed. This is despite the fact that Bergin comments that '[i]t is uncontested that the standard of interpretation in that instance [i.e. in the case of Ó Maicín] was very poor, and that the defence counsel was required to assist the interpreter on multiple occasions' (Bergin 2015: 214). The fact that the interpretation was flawed could, without doubt, endanger the fairness of the trial. Clearly, the quality of the trial process in the case of Ó Maicín would have been better if he had appeared before a judge and jury who understood him, without the need for interpretation. It is unfortunate that the arguments made on behalf of Ó Maicín focused on the status of the language, rather than on natural justice or the right to a fair trial and the quality of interpretation, as this may have led to a stronger support among the judiciary for his case.

Conclusion

It can be seen from the above discussion that, although the Irish language has high constitutional status, this has not translated into many concrete rights for Irish speakers. In other States, such as Canada, constitutional protection of languages is seen as requiring bilingual juries to be empanelled, and, effectively, the right not to have an interpreter at trial. According to Parry, '[i]n Canada, the right to be tried by a jury who speak an official language is absolute because the state treats both official languages on a basis of equality, regardless of linguistic demography, in the administration of justice' (2015: 203). As is seen in the case of Ó Maicín, the Irish courts have taken a very different view, and focus on the practical difficulties inherent in creating an Irish-speaking jury.

The Irish government's lack of commitment to bilingualism has led to the situation where there is a right to an interpreter but the quality of interpretation is not guaranteed. Unfortunately, the Irish cases on bilingual juries have not focused on the quality of interpretation. I have argued in this chapter that this is where future attention should be placed, as highlighted by various other works (e.g. Hale 2004; Phelan 2017). Irish judges have mentioned that not providing an interpreter in cases where the defendant does not understand the language of the court contravenes natural law (Ó Monacháin v. An Taoiseach) and impairs the administration of justice (State (Buchan) v. Coyne). However, when the interpretation is of low quality, surely this must also violate these basic legal principles. Furthermore, the right to a fair trial is protected under Irish law in the Constitution (Article 38), as well as in the ECHR Act 2003 (Schedule 1, Article 6), and the Charter of Fundamental Rights of the European Union (Article 47), which is binding on Ireland. While this right requires that those charged with a criminal offence have the services of an interpreter, it is suggested that in order to satisfy this right the level of interpretation must be sound. If the quality of interpretation is low the right to a fair trial is endangered (Hayes and Hale 2010: 119). Because Ireland has not made strides under Directive 2010/64/EU, as it should do, to test the level of its interpreters or to require that they undertake a training course or pass an exam, as is advocated by academics and practitioners in the field of interpretation studies (Hale 2007: 166; Phelan 2011: 78), the right to a fair trial can indeed be endangered when interpretation services are required. In such circumstances, the right to a fair trial requires that there be 'direct access' to a bilingual jury. It follows that a right not to have an interpreter should be recognised by the Irish legal system in situations where the quality of the interpretation service cannot be guaranteed.

Related topics

The Right to Understand and to be Understood; What Is Asylum?; Feminism in Translation.

Further reading

de Blacam, Mark (2014) 'Official Language and Constitutional Interpretation,' *Irish Jurist* LII: 90–114.

Discusses case law on the Irish language and the interpretation of Irish constitutional provisions on the Irish language.

Ó Cearúil, Micheál (1999) *Bunreacht na hÉireann: A Study of the Irish Text*. Dublin: Coiste Uile-Pháirtí an Oireachtais ar an mBunreacht/The All-Party Oireachtas Committee on the Constitution.

Analyses the Irish and English text of the Constitution of Ireland 1937, and the translation of the text from one language to another.

Parry, Richard (2015) 'Is Ireland a Bilingual State?' *Northern Ireland Legal Quarterly* 66 (3): 199–221.

Provides an overview of the case of *Ó Maicín* and analyses Irish bilingual policy since the foundation of the State.

Phelan, Mary (2017) 'A Matter of Interpretation,' *Law Society Gazette* April: 52–55.

Includes a discussion of the quality of interpretation before Irish courts.

Waterhouse, Kate (2009) 'Interpreting Criminal Justice. A Preliminary Look at Language, Law and Crime in Ireland,' *Judicial Studies Institute Journal* 2: 42–75.

Focuses on translation and interpreting in Irish courts, to and from different languages and the Irish government's approach to these matters.

References

Akenson, Donald H. (1970) *The Irish Education Experiment: The National System of Education in the Nineteenth Century*. London: Routledge and Kegan Paul.

Bergin, Hazel (2015) 'Gaeilge Bhriste? Irish Language Rights in Ó Maicín v Ireland,' *Trinity College Law Review* 1: 214–223.

Berk-Seligson, Susan (1990) *The Bilingual Courtroom: Court Interpreters in the Judicial Process*. Chicago: University of Chicago Press.

Berk-Seligson, Susan (2017) *The Bilingual Courtroom* (2nd ed.). Chicago: University of Chicago Press.

Bîrzu, Bogdan (2016) 'The Right to Interpretation and Translation within Criminal Proceedings in the European Union. Comparative Examination. Critical Opinions,' *Judicial Tribune* 6 (1): 137–147.

Brady, John (1959) 'Irish Interpreters at Meath Assizes,' *Ríocht na Midhe* 2 (1): 62–63.

Brown-Blake, Celia (2006) 'Fair Trial, Language and the Right to Interpretation,' *International Journal on Minority and Group Rights* 13 (4): 391–412.

Cao, Deborah (2013) 'Legal Translation Studies,' in *The Routledge Handbook of Translation Studies*. Eds. Carmen Millán and Francesca Bartrina. London: Routledge. 415–424.

Central Statistics Office [online]. Avaiable at: www.cso.ie/en/index.html.

Charter of Fundemantal Rights of the European Union (2000) 2000/C 364/01.

Comhdháil Náisiúnta na Gaeilge (1998) *Towards a Language Act: A Discussion Document*. Dublin: Comhdháil Náisinta na Gaeilge.

Constitution of Ireland (1937) Enacted by the People 1st July, 1937.

Constitution of the Irish Free State (1922) Enacted by the Constitution of the Irish Free State (Saorstát Éireann) Act 1922.

Costello, Declan (1956) 'The Natural Law and the Irish Constitution,' *Studies. An Irish Quarterly Review* 45 (180): 403–414.

Cronin, Michael (1996) *Translating Ireland*. Cork: Cork University Press.

Cronin, Michael (2006) *Translation and Identity*. Abingdon: Routledge.

Darmody, Merike, and Tania Daly (2015) 'Attitudes towards the Irish Language on the Island of Ireland,' Economic and Social Research Institute Report [online]. Available at: www.esri.ie/pubs/BKMNEXT294_Vol-1.pdf [accessed 20 September 2018].

de Blacam, Mark (2014) 'Official Language and Constitutional Interpretation,' *Irish Jurist* LII: 90–114.

de Valera, Éamon (1943) 'Language and the Irish Nation,' Speech broadcast on Radio Éireann, 17 March. (RTÉ Archives).

Edwards, John (1994) *Multilingualism*. London: Routledge.

European Convention on Human Rights (1950) As emended by Protocols Nos 11 and 14 and Supplemented by protocols Nos 1, 4, 6, 7, 12, 13 and 16.

Fowler, Yvonne, Eva Ng, and Malcolm Coulthard (2013) 'Legal Interpreting,' in *The Routledge Handbook of Translation Studies*. Eds. Carmen Millán and Francesca Bartrina. London: Routledge. 402–414.

Grabau, Charles M., and Llewellyn Joseph Gibbons (1996) 'Protecting the Rights of Linguistic Minorities: Challenges to Court Interpretation,' *New England Law Review* 30: 227–374.

Hale, Sandra (2004) *The Discourse of Court Interpreting: Discourse Practices of the Law, the Witness, and the Interpreter*. Amsterdam and Philadelphia: John Benjamins.

Hale, Sandra (2007) *Community Interpreting*. Basingstoke and New York: Palgrave Macmillan.

Hayes, Alejandra and Sandra Hale (2010) 'Appeals on Incompetent Interpreting,' *Journal of Judicial Administration* 20 (2): 119–130.

Higgins, Noelle, and Dorothy Ní Uigín (2017) 'Irish Speakers in the Irish Courts: Is there a Need for, and Right to, an Interpreter?' in *Legal Translation and Court Interpreting: Ethical Values, Quality, Competence Training*. Eds. Annikki Liimatainen, Arja Nurmi, Marja Kivilehto, Leena Salmi, Anu Viljanmaa and Melissa Wallace. Berlin: Frank & Timme GmbH. 49–68.

Howlin, Niamh (2010) 'Fenians, Foreigners and Jury Trials in Ireland, 1865–70,' *Irish Jurist* 45: 51–81.

Hutchinson, John (1987) *The Dynamics of Cultural Nationalism*. London: Allen and Unwin.

International Covenant on Civil and Political Rights (1966) Adopted by the United Nations General Assembly through GA. Resolution 2200A (XXI) on 16 December 1966, and in force from 23 March 1976 in accordance with Article 49 of the Covenant.

Kachuk, Patricia (1994) 'A Resistance to British Cultural Hegemony: Irish Language Activism in West Belfast,' *Anthropologica* 36 (2): 135–154.

Kahaner, Steven (2009) 'The Administration of Justice in a Multilingual Society-open to Interpretation or Lost in Translation?' *Judicature* 92 (5): 224–231.

Kelly, Fergus (1988) *A Guide to Early Irish Law*. Dublin: DIAS.

Mac Giolla Chríost, Diarmait (2012) 'A Question of National Identity or Minority Rights? The Changing Status of the Irish Language in Ireland since 1922,' *Nations and Nationalism* 18 (3): 398–416.

Mac Gréil, Micheál, and Fergal Rhatigan (2009) *The Irish Language and the Irish People: Report on the Attitudes towards Competence in and Use of the Irish Language in the Republic of Ireland in 2007–08.* Maynooth: National University of Ireland.

Mikkelson, Holly (2000) *Introduction to Court Interpreting.* Manchester and Northampton: St. Jerome Publishing.

Moynihan, Maurice (ed.) (1980) *Speeches and Statements by Éamon de Valera 1917–73.* Dublin: Gill and Macmillan.

Ní Drisceoil, Verona (2012) 'Austerity and Irish Language Rights,' *Human Rights in Ireland.* [online]. Avaialable at: http://humanrights.ie/constitution-of-ireland/austerity-and-irish-language-rights/ [accessed 27 September 2019].

Ní Drisceoil, Verona (2016) 'Antipathy, Paradox and Disconnect in the Irish State's Legal Relationship with the Irish Language,' *Irish Jurist* 56: 45–74.

Nic Shuibhne, Niamh (1999) 'First among Equals? Irish Language and the Law,' *Law Society Gazette* 93 (2): 18–19.

Nic Shuibhne, Niamh (2002) 'Eighty Years A' Growing—The Official Languages (Equality) Act 2002,' *The Irish Law Times* 13: 198–203.

Niranjana, Tejaswini (1992) *Siting Translation: History, Post-Structuralism, and the Colonial Context.* Berkeley: University of California Press.

Ó Buachalla, Séamas (1984) 'Educational Policy and the Role of the Irish Language from 1831 to 1981,' *European Journal of Education* 19 (1): 75–92.

Ó Cadhla, Stiofán (2010) 'Tiontú an Chultúir: Affaire Dominici agus Maolra Seoighe,' *Études Irlandaises* 35: 2–12.

Ó Cearúil, Micheál (1999) *Bunreacht na hÉireann: A Study of the Irish Text.* Dublin: Coiste Uile-Pháirtí an Oireachtais ar an mBunreacht/The All-Party Oireachtas Committee on the Constitution.

Ó Conaill, Seán (2014) 'Judicial Pragmatism at the Expense of Language Rights: The Ó Maicín Decision,' [online]. Avaiable at: http://constitutionproject.ie/?p=309 [accessed 27 September 2019].

Ó Cuirreáin, Seán (2016) *Éagóir: Maolra Seoighe agus dúnmharuithe Mhám Trasna.* Baile Átha Cliath: Cois Life.

Ó Murchú, Helen (2016) *The Irish Language in Education in the Republic of Ireland.* Dublin: European Research Centre on Multilingualism and Language Learning.

Parry, Richard (2015) 'Is Ireland a Bilingual State?' *Northern Ireland Legal Quarterly* 66 (3): 199–221.

Phelan, Mary (2011) 'Legal Interpreters in the News in Ireland,' *The International Journal of Translation & Interpreting Research* 3 (1): 76 105.

Phelan, Mary (2017) 'A Matter of Interpretation,' *Law Society Gazette* April: 52–55.

Pinto, Meital (2014) 'Taking Language Rights Seriously,' *King's Law Journal* 25 (2): 231–254.

Rafael, Vicente (1988) *Contracting Colonialism: Translation and Conversion in Tagalog Society under Early Spanish Rule.* Durham: Duke University Press.

Sakai, Naoki (2009) 'How Do We Count a Language? Translation and Discontinuity,' *Translation Studies* 2 (1): 71–88.

Schlesinger, Miriam, and Franz Pöchhacker (2010) 'Introduction,' in *Doing Justice to Court Interpreting.* Eds. Miriam Schlesinger and Franz Pöchhacker. Amsterdam and Philadelphia: John Benjamins Publishing Company. 1–7.

Schulman, Michael (1993) 'No Hablo Ingles: Court Interpretation as a Major Obstacle to Fairness for Non-English Speaking Defendants,' *Vanderbilt Law Review* 46 (1): 175–196.

Smith, John (2004) 'Legislation in Irish—A Lot Done, More to Do,' *Bar Review* 9 (3): 91–94.

van der Vlis, Evert-Jan (2010) 'The Right to Interpretation and Translation in Criminal Proceedings,' *The Journal of Specialised Translation* 14: 26–40.

Venuti, Lawrence (1993) 'Translation as Cultural Politics: Regimes of Domestication in English,' *Textual Practice* 7 (2): 208–223.

Waldron, Jarleth (1992) *Maamtrasna: The Murders and the Mystery.* Dublin: Edmund Burke Publisher.

Walsh, John (2012) 'Language Policy and Language Governance: A Case-study of Irish Language Legislation,' *Language Policy* 11: 323–341.

Walsh, John, and Wilson McLeod (2008) 'An Overcoat Wrapped around an Invisible Man? Language Legislation and Language Revitalisation in Ireland and Scotland,' *Language Policy* 7: 21–46.

Warren, Simon (2012) 'The Making of Irish-speaking Ireland: The Cultural Politics of Belonging, Diversity and Power,' *Ethnicities* 12 (3): 317–334.

Waterhouse, Kate (2009) 'Interpreting Criminal Justice. A Preliminary Look at Language, Law and Crime in Ireland,' *Judicial Studies Institute Journal* 2: 42–75.

Williams, Colin (2013) 'Perfidious Hope: The Legislative Turn in Official Minority Language Regimes,' *Regional and Federal Studies* 23 (1): 101–122.

18

The right to understand and to be understood

Urban activism and US migrants' access to interpreters

Sahar Fathi

Introduction

In 2015 I received notice that President Obama's administration would be recognising my programme, the Refugee Women's Institute, for innovation in government at the Annual City Livability Awards. The programme had strong data showing that it had achieved building trust between refugee communities and the police department, and was gaining momentum and publicity at a rapid pace. A considerable amount of in-depth field work was spent with these refugees, as we tried to support them so that they could attend the programme. I listened as a mother of five and her Oromo interpreter described their housing circumstances with a child in a wheelchair and no elevator in the building. She could not speak directly to the building manager because she had no interpreter at home. After speaking with the refugees, I would spend hours calling services, navigating case managers, bringing in interpreters again and again, and often failing horrifically at getting the refugees the support they needed because of the limitations of the various systems.

Sometimes I would walk with refugees to the bus stop and demonstrate the reusable bus pass we had secured for them so that they could get to class. An Iranian refugee pulled me aside and, since I spoke Farsi, whispered to me urgently, 'But what if I get lost? No one speaks my language. How will I get home then?' She had spent months trying to get dental care for her severely rotted teeth. All of the refugees had children they brought to an on-site makeshift day care that we had provided for them. She would walk in dutifully every class, holding her jaw with one hand and her son's hand with the other. She always smiled.

I had spent several years helping to build Seattle's first Office of Immigrant and Refugee Affairs. I was their first staffer, and I created its initial programmes from scratch. The City of Seattle had nearly 12,000 employees and two staff in this office in 2013. Our mission was daunting: to make the City of Seattle more inclusive for foreign-born individuals and work on language access and integration. At the time, the City of Seattle boasted the most diverse zip code in the country (Seattle Times Staff 2010).

The Office and its programmes would not have been created had it not been for significant grassroots activism at the local level. Urban activists came together to lobby the City Council for the Office and an entry point for immigrants and refugees trying to navigate government. The Office in Seattle was based on other Offices that had popped up in the United States, many of which created programmes and developed political stances in direct opposition to the federal government's practices during the Trump administration. In Seattle, and in other cities, local jurisdictions were confronted with the realities of a detention centre being operated by federal government and the question of jurisdiction over those operations. This chapter traces language access policies in both local government and at the detention centres, and the community-led solutions behind them. The first section of the chapter presents a brief history of the US government, the US Department of Justice and its interactions with limited English-proficient (LEP) populations, and urban activism at the local level of government, particularly in creating local Offices of Immigrant and Refugee Affairs. The second section presents a brief analysis of both government and detention centres, showing the inadequate access to language access in detention centres and then discussing both the role of the interpreter and government challenges in providing better language access. Finally, the last section highlights community-led solutions. It describes how local activism and local government can put pressure on higher levels of government to change standards, local legal defence funds advocated for by urban activists, local language access programmes (including a case study of New York City's programme), and a brief critique of the role of urban activism in interpretation and translation.

The US immigration system

Under the Tenth Amendment to the US Constitution, all powers not granted to the federal government are reserved for the states and the people. All state governments are modelled after the federal government and consist of three branches: executive, legislative, and judicial (The White House n.d.). Most individuals interact primarily with local municipalities because they have jurisdiction over things like most roads, public schools, water, police, libraries, fire services, elections, and zoning. Local governments generally include two tiers: counties and municipalities, or cities/towns. In some states, counties are divided into townships (The White House n.d.).

The Department of Justice was created on 1 July 1870 to handle all criminal prosecutions and civil suits in which the United States had an interest (USDOJ 2016). Under the Obama administration, the heads of both the Department of Justice and the Department of Homeland Security served on the President's cabinet (The White House President Barack Obama n.d.). Immigration and Customs Enforcement (ICE), the agency within the US Department of Homeland Security (DHS) charged with immigration enforcement in the country's interior, has the authority to detain, jail, and prosecute non-citizens for violations of immigration law. The Executive Office for Immigration Review (EOIR), an agency within the US Department of Justice, administers the immigration court system, and these proceedings are considered civil law proceedings (NILC 2016: 3).

President Donald Trump was inaugurated as the 45th US President on 20 January 2017. His election campaign was fuelled by anti-immigrant rhetoric, none of which ended when he took office. By the fall of 2018 he had instituted nine Executive Orders on immigration, ranging from increasing border officers and enhancing border security to the so-called 'Muslim Ban' which banned certain Muslim individuals from entering the country and went through three iterations before it was upheld by the US Supreme Court (Pierce et al. 2018: 3). Trump's policies further demonstrated his draconian stance on immigration. For example, in 2018 he lowered the number of refugees that could be accepted by the United States to the lowest it had been since the current resettlement programme began in 1980 (Pierce et al. 2018: 6). Other policies of note include terminating humanitarian protections for hundreds of thousands of migrants and his current litigation seeking to end the Deferred Action for Childhood Arrivals programme (Pierce et al. 2018: 6–9). Arguably, as discussed later in this chapter, the President's anti-immigrant stances have also prompted a new and energised wave of urban activism (Butler et al. 2017: 8–9).

The immigration legal system in the United States is a complicated hybrid, which at face value seems as though it should be conducted in judicial court; instead, however, the EOIR evolved as a function of the executive branch. As such, many of the constitutional rights guaranteed in a judicial court do not carry over into the legal sphere of immigration (Carson 2017: 2). An overwhelming number of detention centres hold non-citizens and there are not enough resources to keep up with the immigration machine that Congress has created over the last century. In particular, after 11 September 2011, Congress restructured its immigration offices, dissolving the US Immigration and Naturalization Service (INS), citing 'new urgency' in its immigration policies and creating the DHS—beneath which they housed US Citizenship and Immigration Services (USCIS), Customs and Border Protection (CBP), and ICE (USCIS 2017). As of 2017, there were 234 detention centres in the United States (Carson 2017: 2), any one of which a non-citizen could find themselves in, usually without guidance, money, or language ability. In response to a Freedom of Information Act request submitted by the Immigrant Legal Resource Center, ICE revealed that, as of the end of 2017, nearly 40,000 people were being detained in over 1,000 facilities across the US (these facilities included hospitals, hotels, county jails, and so on) (NIJC 2018). Non-citizen defendants in the immigration court system are not guaranteed the same due-process rights or right to appointed counsel as US citizens, which severely limits their chance of successful outcome (Carson 2017: 1). Furthermore, the process is overburdened and often judges are extremey limited in the time they can devote to an individual's case. Under the Trump administration, new standards (which began in October 2018) require that an immigration judge complete 700 cases per year to receive a satisfactory review (Catholic Legal Immigration Network 2018). Prior, the average judge completed 678 cases per year (Frej 2018). This new quota, coupled with both the reality that multiple judges often share one law clerk and that US immigration law is considered only second in complexity to US tax law, renders the immigration court system inadequate to meet the needs of the immigrants and refugees before it.

Congress has been officially legislating around immigration since the Naturalization Act of 1790, which limited naturalisation to immigrants who were 'free White person[s]' of good character (US Naturalization Act 1790). From there, of note, the United States passed the Immigration and Nationality Act (first of 1952 and then of 1965), and the Immigration Act of 1990. In 1996, President Clinton signed the Illegal Immigration Reform and Immigrant Responsibility Act of 1996 (IIRAIRA). Prior to the signing of the IIRAIRA, the system operated primarily on either exclusion (inadmissible upon entry) or, more frequently, deportation (violating a condition of one's visa). IIRAIRA created additional types of cases, such as credible fear review or reasonable fear review.

'Credible fear' and 'reasonable fear' are two different processes applied by asylum officers to the cases of individuals in the United States who wish to apply for asylum. Many consider the IIRIRA to be the cause of the massive deportation occurring in the United States today (Lind 2016). In fact, Kerwin writes:

> IIRIRA set the stage for the growth of the immense US immigration enforcement system by authorizing significant funding for border and interior enforcement and by establishing an interlocking set of enforcement partnerships and programs. It also restricted legal immigration, particularly by low-income applicants.
>
> *(Kerwin 2018:193)*

The Immigration and Nationality Act (INA) confirmed that a defendant in immigration court has the right to counsel so long as it is at no expense to the government (INA 1952).

The US government does not provide free counsel to defendants in immigration court and, consequently, does not manage the provision of counsel to defendants in immigration court. Whether or not this is because of an underlying exorbitant cost is debatable. In 2014 an economic consulting firm was retained on behalf of the New York City Bar Association to analyse a proposal to create a programme entirely funded and overseen by the federal government to provide counsel to every indigent respondent in immigration removal proceedings (Montgomery 2014: 2). The author found that, 'providing publicly funded counsel to indigent immigration respondents would cost the Federal government no more than $4 million per year, with 98% of the cost being paid for by Federal fiscal savings' (Montgomery 2014: 3). He also found that 'representation by counsel can lead to reduced detention expenditures of at least $173 to $174 million per year, and likely considerably more' (Montgomery 2014: 6).

Civil detention for immigrants was first litigated in *Wong Wing* v. *United States* (1896). The case found that the detention or temporary confinement of Chinese non-citizens as a means to exclude or expel said non-citizens from the United States was legally valid. The Supreme Court ruled that the United States could forbid aliens from coming within their borders, and expel them from their territory, but when Congress further promoted such a policy by subjecting the persons to 'infamous punishment at hard labour, or by confiscating their property, such legislation, to be valid, must provide for a judicial trial to establish the guilt of the accused' (*Wong Wing* v. *United States* (1896) at 237). Today, ICE holds non-citizens in detention centres throughout the country, in an immigrant bed in criminal jail, or even in some cases in a hotel until they have their court date. Immigration detention is considered civil detention, and as such, non-citizens do not receive the same rights as citizens might under the US Constitution. By statute, they have the right to retain counsel at private expense and the right to a full and fair hearing (Harvard Law Review Notes 2018: 727). Immigration proceedings around civil detention are unlikely to succeed for the average non-citizen, but there is a higher likelihood of success for defendants who can afford representation (18% versus 3%). All defendants are required to testify and are subjected to cross-examination by government attorneys regardless of language abilities or mental capacity (Carson 2017: 4–12).

Limited English populations and the Department of Justice

As noted above, the DHS is a cabinet department within the US federal government. ICE is an agency within the DHS. Under the US government's own standards, neither the DHS nor ICE has taken reasonable steps to provide LEP immigrant detainees with meaningful access to essential programmes and activities such as medical care and communications with deportation officers (Beck 2017: 21). The Department of Justice provides guidance for LEP individuals and has established a four-factor balancing test to determine whether an agency has taken 'reasonable steps' to provide LEP individuals with 'meaningful access to its programs and activities' (Beck 2017: 26):

> The first factor analyses the number or proportion of LEP individuals that access a particular program or activity. [...] The second factor is the frequency with which LEP individuals contact the program. [...] The third factor examines the nature of the program and its importance to LEP individuals. [...] the fourth and final factor examines the agency or funding recipient's available resources to devote to its programs and activities.
>
> *(Beck 2017: 26–27)*

Beck points to ICE's *Language Access Plan* as proof that they are not adhering to the government's requirements for providing adequate interpretation and translation. The ICE *Language Access Plan* states that ICE's policy is to provide meaningful access to its programmes and activities to LEP individuals, including 'providing timely and effective communication to ... LEP individuals in ICE custody' (Beck 2017: 38). She questions how it is possible for ICE to meet this policy given their additional policy of translating the *Detainee Handbook* into the most commonly used languages nationally, but not into the languages most frequently spoken at the detention centres. The *Enforcement and Removal Operations Detainee Handbook* is produced by US ICE and details one's rights and responsibilities as a detainee (U.S. Immigration and Customs Enforcement (ICE) 2016: 4). In particular, it clearly states that if the rules noted in the handbook are not followed a detainee may be subject to discipline (ICE 2016: 4). The *Detainee Handbook* also notes, 'if you do not read or understand English, you have the right to receive important information in a language or format you understand or to have someone explain it to you in simpler terms' (ICE 2016: 4).

Beck points out that the *Detainee Handbook* is printed in five languages, one of which is Vietnamese. In 2014, of the 315,943 removals of foreign nationals, only 48 were from Vietnam. In 2015, only 32 were from Vietnam. Indigenous languages from Central America and Mexico comprise some of the languages most commonly spoken in immigration detention. The five most common countries of citizenship for the 315,943 removals in 2014 were: Mexico (176,968), Guatemala (54,423), Honduras (40,695), El Salvador (27,180), and the Dominican Republic (2,130). At least 94% of immigrants in ICE detention are Mexican or Central American and indigenous languages are underrepresented (Beck 2017: 43). While Spanish is the primary language of these countries, 'DHS policy does not explicitly recognize indigenous language speakers' right to communicate in their primary languages' (Gentry 2015: 11). In a technical review examining indigenous language-speaking immigrants (ILSIs) and federal LEP policy, the author writes:

> DHS has named Kanjobal, Quiche, Kachiquel, and Mam as Mayan languages, but omitted 25 other Mayan languages spoken in Mexico, Belize, Guatemala, Honduras, and El Salvador [...]. The total number of speakers (not immigrants) in Central America total some 4.25 million indigenous language speakers. [...] Verification of viable LEP practice includes meeting international standards for indigenous language rights.
>
> *(Gentry 2015: 13)*

Beck notes that only 7% of all languages spoken by this group appear on the 'I Speak' card which is designed to assist detention staff in identifying an LEP individual's language (Beck 2017: 43). Beyond this, there are documented cases in which detention staff have either actively ignored the language access needs of detainees or have such a lack of training that they overlooked the needs of detainees. In the United States, urban activists like Disability Rights California illuminated this critical language access issue in a report in which they document a Guatemalan's arrival to a detention centre in 2018 (Fischer et al. 2019: 42). This individual could communicate only in Guatemalan sign language, and yet the staff of the detention centre consistently resisted getting him the interpreter he needed (Fischer et al. 2019: 42). Instead, detention centre staff documented that he did not know how to communicate because they did not recognise Guatemalan sign language and he went without the ability to communicate with anyone for months (Fischer et al. 2019: 42).

Activism and local impact

How then, can we bring about policies and legislation to support the needs of immigrants and refugees? Historically, government in the US has often adjusted its policies and practices in response to urban activists in social movements. The women's rights movement, the labour movement, the civil rights movement, the environmental movement, and other movements have all shaped government policy. Often, these movements promote various campaigns that support their causes. One strategy often used by urban activists is to begin advocating and campaigning at a lower level of government and then work upwards to the federal government.

Urban activists' mobilisation around the misdemeanour statute in Washington State in 2009–2010 exemplifies this strategy. In the United States, a misdemeanour crime is a minor offence and generally requires no more than a fine, a year in prison, community service, or probation. In Washington State, attorneys noticed and vocalised the disproportionate impact of sentencing for the misdemeanour statute in Washington State. Non-citizens who were convicted of a misdemeanour (i.e. property theft, driving under the influence (DUI), resisting arrest), and who were given a sentence of 365 days, were automatically deported. However, if the prosecutor were to recommend 364 days instead of 365 days, then the non-citizen had a chance to go to immigration court and explain the circumstances to try and avoid deportation. Urban activists began campaigning to change the legislation around sentencing for the misdemeanour statute, arguing that it should be capped at 364 days so that both citizens and non-citizens were treated the same under the law and able to go to court. Although this was a provision set at the state level, urban activists launched their campaign in Seattle. In this case both attorneys and urban activists joined together to lobby the Seattle City Attorney instead of beginning with state-level action. The idea was to use local government to show the state that there would be no significant impact to the criminal justice system. Pete Holmes, the City Attorney, was supportive of this strategy. He instructed prosecutors to stop requesting suspended jail sentences totalling 365 days in order to avoid mandatory deportations of documented immigrants convicted of minor crimes (The Seattle Times Opinion 2010). The following year, the City Attorney was one of many elected officials who joined community members to lobby the Washington State Legislature to limit the maximum jail sentence for every misdemeanour in the state to 364 days, thus limiting the reach of dysfunctional federal immigration laws across the state (Sullivan 2011). This is an excellent example of how local activism and local government can then put pressure on higher levels of government to change standards.

One might expect that the immigrant rights movement in the US would be limited to the federal government, but policy has gone through waves of activism at the local level around how immigrants are treated in local prisons or when interacting with local government. Urban activism can be a powerful tool when wielded by the average individual. Through civil disobedience, sending emails, and making phone calls en masse to local elected officials, public comment, rallies, and protests, the magnitude of organising tens of people or tens of thousands of people can have a tremendous impact on those in higher office.

During the Obama era, critics consistently accused the President of deporting exponential numbers of non-citizens (Chishti et al. 2017). Immigrants' rights activists have further noted that the current President's policies are draconian and severe for immigrants and refugees. Indeed, both elected officials and advocates view the Trump administration as intensely more antagonistic toward migrants than President Obama (García Hernández 2018: 1416). Continuous dissatisfaction with the immigration system and the various policies at the federal level being promulgated by elected officials catalysed more work and innovation by local government. Much of this work was organised by community members who felt they could achieve more progress at the local level, as they were disenchanted with the sluggish and often stagnant federal system. In the grand scope of allyship with the immigrant rights movement, a number of action plans were released by advocates detailing how local government could support immigrant rights (see Graber et al. 2016; Tobocman 2015). Allyship here means the building of relationships with marginalised individuals or communities, and an ally's subsequent and consistent support of those marginalised individuals and communities. Among these recommendations for local government were criminal law enforcement measures, language access protocols, legal defence funds, and the creation of offices and departments to support immigrant and refugee affairs (Graber et al. 2016: 18).

Local Offices of Immigrant and Refugee Affairs

At the beginning of 2000, several mayors began creating local Offices or Departments of Immigrant and Refugee Affairs. These were meant to coordinate work at the local level to support immigrant integration and immigrant needs. By 2010 and through 2018, offices were popping up all over the country in New York, San Francisco, Los Angeles, Seattle, Boston, Chicago, Denver, Minneapolis, and more. Some office services ranged in correlation with the needs of that city. For example, Seattle had a unique programme, the Refugee Women's Institute (which later became the Immigrant Family Institute), which was recognised for its innovation by the Obama administration (Campbell 2015; Jones 2015). The programme focused on trust building between immigrant and refugee families and the police. This was in large part because Seattle had been put under a Department of Justice consent decree (long-term reform plans negotiated by federal and local officials and supervised and enforced by a federal judge) for its police department, and the Mayor at the time wanted to invest more money in supporting trust building between police and vulnerable community members, so staff created a programme addressing that need.

The cohort involved 40 women: 20 refugees and 20 police officers. The refugees came from Bhutan, Burma, Eritrea, Ethiopia, Iran, Iraq, and Somalia. Refugees were recruited according to data from Washington State that identified the largest numbers of refugees from the preceding five years that had settled in Seattle (Balk 2015). Refugees and officers attended weekly seminars together, with at least seven interpreters in the room, often more. The seminars were co-facilitated by a professor from Seattle University and a refugee who had recently completed graduate school. Classes ranged in topics. One week, the refugees were given a tour of the 911 emergency call centre (911 is the emergency contact number for the police in the United States). Upon entering the centre, one refugee asked the police officers why there were no documents in her language. The police department realised the importance of providing additional translated materials and recognised the need in these communities. That summer the officers worked to translate all of its in-house materials into additional multiple languages. This was a direct result of the refugee's comments. The Institute also recruited interpreters who could begin using their language skills as contractors for the City. Rather than simply choosing from the list of City-approved language contractors, the Office of Immigrant and Refugee Affairs in Seattle did extensive outreach and found interpreters for these new communities. After interpreters were chosen, they had to be approved by the City of Seattle as contractors. The Office soon recognised that the process for becoming an approved interpreter was difficult for those who lacked the required computer literacy. The Office successfully advocated for those processes to be eliminated. Potential city-contracted interpreters no longer need to go through that complex process (Local and Regional Government Alliance on Racial Equity 2015).

Local Offices of Immigrant and Refugee Affairs are able to apply pressure to bureaucracy from within government. They are a bridge for the community to services that the local jurisdiction provides and often advocate for better interpretation, translation, and language access policies. They also provide technical assistance and look for policy solutions to support their constituents.

Government and detention centres

Inadequate access to language access

The lack of attorney representation for non-citizens in a court of law often results in significant denial of due-process rights. We know that, where an immigrant is detained without an attorney, only 3% prevail in their cases. Where an immigrant is detained with an attorney, 18% prevail in their cases. Even more concerning, immigrants without an attorney and who are not detained only prevail in 13% of their cases, whereas undetained immigrants with an attorney prevail in 74% of their cases (Caplow et al. 2011: 363–364). The system is not built to navigate effectively without an attorney.

In particular, community members and attorneys repeatedly complain about the general lack of adequate interpretation and translation in ICE and DHS (Beck 2017: 19). In 2000, President Clinton signed Executive Order 13166, which requires:

> Federal agencies to examine the services they provide, identify any need for services to those with limited English proficiency (LEP), and develop and implement a system to provide those services so LEP persons can have meaningful access to them. It is expected that agency plans will provide for such meaningful access consistent with, and without unduly burdening, the fundamental mission of the agency. The Executive Order also requires that the Federal agencies work to ensure that recipients of Federal financial assistance provide meaningful access to their LEP applicants and beneficiaries.
> *(Limited English Proficiency (LEP): A Federal Interagency Website 2018)*

Advocates have argued that, in order to adequately meet these requirements, ICE must increase general transparency by maintaining a complete public list of all its detention facilities and it must track language data of its detainees. They have also advocated that DHS and ICE revise their *Language Access Plans* to increase language access uniformity across all ICE facilities (Beck 2017: 21). As of early 2020, ICE has a list of its major detention facilities publicly available, but it is not a complete list of all of the possible places a detainee may be housed temporarily. In addition, ICE does not have any public records available of detainee language data and its publicly available *Language Access Plans* continue to be from 2015.

In short, non-citizens are unable to navigate the complexities of the US immigration system and the government is failing to meet its own self-imposed requirements of interpretation and translation standards in the detention centres. In December 2017, in response to concerns raised by immigrant rights groups and complaints to the Office of Inspector General (OIG) Hotline about conditions for detainees held in ICE custody, the OIG conducted unannounced inspections of five detention facilities to evaluate their compliance with ICE detention standards (OIG 2017: 2). They found that language barriers are still prevalent in detention centres, despite consistent guidance to provide access as needed (Shoichet 2017).

ICE apprehends, detains, and removes aliens who are in the United States unlawfully. ICE Enforcement and Removal Operations (ERO) places apprehended aliens who require custodial supervision in detention facilities (OIG 2017: 3–5). Contracts and agreements with facilities that hold ICE detainees require adherence to the *2000 National Detention Standards*, ICE's 2008 *Performance Based National Detention Standards* (PBNDS), or the 2011 *PBNDS* (OIG 2017: 1). In the 2017 audit, although the PBNDS specifies that language assistance be provided to detainees, the OIG reported that such support was not available in the centres they visited (OIG 2017: 4). They reported that the lack of communication and understanding created barriers between facility staff and detainees (OIG 2017: 4). At some facilities, problems began at intake where facility staff failed to use interpretation services for detainees who did not speak English (OIG 2017: 4).

According to the PBNDS, when detainees arrive, they are supposed to receive the *ICE National Detainee Handbook* and a local facility detainee handbook. These handbooks cover information such as the grievance system, services and programmes, medical care, and access to legal counsel (OIG 2017: 4). The OIG reported that, at three facilities inspected, detainees were not always given handbooks in a language they could understand (OIG 2017: 4). The OIG stated that:

> using interpretation services would be a relatively simple way to improve interaction between staff and detainees and reduce misunderstanding. At times, language barriers prevented detainees from understanding medical staff. Although it might have cleared up confusion, staff did not always use language translation services, which were available by phone, during medical exams of detainees.
>
> *(OIG 2017: 3–5)*

The role of the interpreter

In the United States, as in other jurisdictions (see Chapter 17), an individual in a federal programme has the right to interpretation and translation within that system, as established by numerous federal guidelines. Title VI of the Civil Rights Act of 1964, 42 U.S.C. 2000d et seq. ('Title VI') prohibits discrimination on the basis of race, colour, or national origin in any programme or activity that receives federal funds or other federal financial assistance, and this includes non-citizens. In general, individuals with LEP must be afforded a meaningful opportunity to participate in programmes that receive federal funds (US Department of Health and Human Services 2013). According to the US Department of Health and Human Services, 'policies and practices may not deny or have the effect of denying persons with limited English proficiency equal access to Federally-funded programmes for which such persons qualify' (US Department of Health and Human Services 2013). Further, immigrants can secure their own legal representation in immigration proceedings, but generally at no expense to the government (8 U.S.C. § 1362, cited in Katzmann 2018: 489). In theory, with the right resources, non-citizens should have access to an attorney and an interpreter to support them as they navigate the immigration system (8 U.S.C. § 1362, cited in Katzmann 2012: 489).

Along with the right to an interpreter, there is the question of the role of the interpreter in that setting. Interpreters are expected to be neutral parties interpreting the exact words being stated in a trial or hearing before a judge. However, there are additional formats in which one might use an interpreter. Scholars have found that many interpreters tend to push the boundaries of neutral and direct interpretation in their roles while inserting their personal activist agendas (Barsky 2005: 28–30; Morris 1995). In addition, some interpreters tend to manage the space by playing different roles to support the defendant. For example, in her study of US immigration courts, Zambrano-Paff (2008: 130–1) found that interpreters mitigate the intimidating atmosphere of hearings by adding polite forms when addressing immigration applicants; they similarly add polite forms of address when directing their utterances to judges (e.g. 'sir,' 'judge,' 'your honour'). This might not seem problematic at first, but could convey a more relaxed or respectful atmosphere than actually exists within the court. Some interpreters are more versed in a community interpreting atmosphere given the past agency work they have completed. This means that the interpreting they have done in the public service sphere to facilitate communication between officials and lay people (for example at police departments, immigration departments, social welfare centres, medical and mental health offices, schools, and other institutions) is done consecutively, with the interpreter waiting for the speaker to finish a sentence or an idea before the translation is initiated, rather than simultaneously (Wadensjö 2009: 43).

Community interpreting used largely by local government can be more relaxed in nature. However, it can sometimes communicate the interpreter's personal feelings in addition to the subject at hand, thus drastically changing the relationship between the interpreter and the individual needing interpretation. According to Wadensjö, 'community interpreting seems to be further developing to a number of distinct areas of professional expertise,' including 'legal interpreting' (which includes 'court interpreting, interpreting at police stations and in immigration and asylum hearings') (2009: 43). Community interpreting is generally performed by untrained individuals (Wadensjö 2009: 43), and in the past was (and may still be) performed by volunteers, untrained bilingual friends, and relatives, sometimes including children. It has been used by some governments in a somewhat alarming strategy to reduce costs. Sometimes these community interpreters are also activists in the neighbourhood, and government requests that they bridge their relationships within the neighbourhood to do outreach on their behalf and simultaneously interpret as well further blur the line where professional interpret-ation begins and urban activism ends.

Despite, or perhaps in addition to, this, the federal government has to take steps to ensure the availability of formal training, examinations, and certification systems for court interpreters (Gamal 2009: 66). In the United States, there has been some regulation with the Court Interpreter Act of 1978 and its amendment in 1988. Nevertheless, inter-preters are consistently asked to be neutral parties by legislation or policy, but then expected to go above and beyond this in practice. It has been suggested, for example, that asylum claimants are over-burdened in the application process for asylum status. Asylum claimants are viewed as struggling to reconcile their personal narrative with the expectations of what interviewing officers would want to hear in order to grant asylum status. Further, 'Interpreters may be encouraged [through the asylum interview process] to act as intercultural agents and active intermediaries between applicants and the immi-gration service in order to compensate for both cultural and linguistic gaps in misunder-standing' (Inghilleri 2009: 11; Miller et al. 2005: 28).

Government challenges

There are challenges for government when trying to meet the need of interpretation and translation for hundreds of languages and communities in the US. This section draws on my extensive work experience with immigrants and refugees both in build-ing programmes for interpreters and translators for government and in researching standards across the country for application in the jurisdiction within which I worked. First, many policies and laws require certain levels of qualified interpreters and trans-lators to pass different standardised exams in order to be certified to do this work. Legal interpretation is its own field and it can be costly to both study for the exam and take the exam. Not all jurisdictions provide the exams for smaller lan-guages. For example, it is common to find an exam for a language commonly spoken in the United States (i.e. Spanish), but as the language group grows smaller, so do the options to take the exam. The harder it is to take the exam, the more taxing on the individual registering to take it. Exams require training and practice, even if the person is completely fluent in the language, because a wide range of words and phrases need to be reviewed in any field.

In addition, many interpreters do this work as a second, or sometimes third, job. The rarer the language, the less consistent work there is, and therefore the harder to build a full career on legal interpretation for that specific language. As with any career, time is needed to build a reputation and to find the connections needed to do the work full time. Alternatively, for larger language groups, there can be a surplus of interpreters and trans-lators. Finally, not all agencies fulfil their duties of providing quality interpretation and translation for all of their LEP clients. Many LEP clients do not know to ask for the service and often an agency will have a policy that they will provide interpretation when asked for it, but not necessarily in anticipation of the need for it.

Another challenge articulated by government is that quality interpretation costs money. Interpreters deserve to be paid well for their time providing a needed and unique service. Yet many agencies are operating on an already tight budget that does not include funding for interpretation and translation. Alternatively, it simply is not a priority of the agency's head or the elected officials who are appointing those heads. There are also a multitude of languages and poorly developed policies around best practices to provide access. Some policies require key documents to be translated into the twelve most spoken languages of the local jurisdiction, regardless of whether those communities are expected to access those key documents and regardless of whether those language populations live in the targeted neighbourhood. Alternatively, some policies explicitly call for the translation of documents only when a certain population threshold is met, the absence of which creates no paramount duty to translate and thus misses the objective.

The government also experiences challenges in assessing quality control and identifying strategies for meeting the need. There are a number of different kinds of interpreters and different standards for interpretation. Many jurisdictions still struggle with determining what kind of interpreter is needed for their specific body of work and/or what level of certification. Some jurisdictions do not ask for certification at all, relying instead on a constituent's own family members or local community members who assure the agency that they are qualified. In addition, it is difficult for a small jurisdiction to test whether the interpreter is skilled, outside of a formal exam. So, for example, if an individual needs interpretation in a small language group and the agency cannot find a qualified interpreter, is it better for them to rely on a community interpreter who has assured them of their skillset, or provide no interpretation until they secure someone skilled? What if it takes hours to find that interpreter and the need is urgent?

Urban activists have worked hard to force different levels of government to require language access plans and interpretation/translation policies. These are laudable achievements. And yet, there are challenges in effective implementation in a large bureaucracy.

Community-led solutions

Legal defence funds

So-called 'sanctuary cities' are 'local jurisdictions that have decided to limit local enforcement agencies' role in immigration enforcement, leaving immigration enforcement to the federal government' (Martinez et al. 2018: 271). They are not truly 'sanctuary cities' forever, as non-federal entities do not have the power to guarantee freedom from immigration imprisonment and deportation (García Hernández 2018: 1400). Since President Trump took office, cities have found themselves at odds with the administration's immigration policies and have declared themselves 'sanctuary cities,' echoing the sanctuary movement of the 1980s, when cities declared that they would be a refuge for Central American refugees fleeing war and persecution (Deslandes 2017). As cities like New York, Los Angeles, and Chicago declared themselves 'sanctuary cities' in protest against Trump's policies, the Trump administration retaliated, attempting to cut off federal funds in these sanctuary cities, a step ultimately ruled unconstitutional in federal court (Phillips 2018).

In 2014 an exponential number of unaccompanied minors and families, mainly women with small children, began arriving at the Southwest US border, seeking refuge from rising levels of violence in Mexico and Central America by way of Honduras, El Salvador, and Guatemala. Immigration courts nationwide were requested to create special dockets—otherwise known as 'rocket dockets' or 'surge dockets' (Srikantiah and Weissman-Ward 2014)—for these unaccompanied children and families. They moved at an expedited pace to process the deportations swiftly. Hundreds of unaccompanied children and families appeared before immigration judges in the first several weeks alone and most were unrepresented. In the United States, children who are citizens are entitled to an attorney in court, but the federal government has maintained that a child in a deportation hearing is only entitled to this same right if he or she can pay for it (Arulanantham 2018; Good 2014).

In response to the growing case docket of children in immigration court, the Mayor of San Francisco and the Board of Supervisors allocated $2.1 million to support these unaccompanied minors with legal services. The funding was renewed in 2016. In this instance, 13 legal service provider organisations from the San Francisco advocacy community formed a new organisation to advocate for these funds, provide needed legal services, and continue to support non-citizens with legal services that included strong interpretation and translation services (SFILDC 2016; Think Immigration 2016). Other cities have also created similar legal defence funds, including Los Angeles ($10 million), New York ($6.3 million), and Chicago ($1.3 million), through the activism of community members and in order to provide strong interpretation and translation services with their legal support (Rosen 2016; Seattle City Council 2017).

In 2017 and 2018, the City of Seattle created a legal defence fund in response to the mass deportations by the Trump administration. The City of Seattle partnered with King County and distributed $1.5 million in grants to non-profits as part of their legal defence fund work (Office of the Mayor 2017). Seattle awarded funds both to non-profit legal providers who provide direct services and to 'community navigator' organisations that are trusted in the local immigrant and refugee community to help answer questions and then refer community members in need of legal services with the appropriate language support to the non-profit legal providers (Office of the Mayor 2017).

In addition to relying on non-profits, the City of Seattle employs community interpreters and has used them in several large 'legal clinics,' provided by the City for non-citizens in need of legal support. Seattle is unique in that it also has a Department of Neighborhoods, which is charged by the Mayor to coordinate outreach and engagement efforts across the City. The Department runs a programme, called the Community Liaisons, which in 2018 had approximately 80 contractors from immigrant and refugee LEP communities (Barnett 2017).

Language access programmes

In addition to providing funding for attorneys to represent non-citizens in immigration court, one major common thread across the various Offices of Immigrant and Refugee Affairs is a language access programme. As alluded to earlier in this chapter, all levels of government—local, state, and federal—struggle with similar challenges around language access and the administration of interpretation and translation services. They struggle to determine which department or office of the agency will be externally facing to the public to administer these services, what types of documents the public will need to access in language, design, and visual formatting for different cultures, the number of languages that all documents should always be translated into, and the costs associated with these interactions (e.g. completion of forms, interviews with caseworkers, public hearings), in spite of competing demands for funding for public health, safety, and equitable access (McHugh 2015).

San Francisco is widely considered to have the most robust language access programme in the country, with an actual ordinance that dictates how funding for the City's interpretation and translation needs will be raised and spent across departments. In 2009, San Francisco amended legislation to create the Language Access Ordinance. That is then paired with in-house employees in various languages and language access plans that each department creates, highlighting where they intend to do this work going forward (Office of Civic Engagement and Immigrant Affairs 2017). New York City has a similarly robust programme, with their language access initiative and, in fact, New York City is credited for being the first city to release an Executive Order mandating translation into the six most widely spoken languages in 2008 (Santos 2008). The New York City Office of Immigrant Affairs is also credited with requiring pharmacy chains to provide free oral interpretation and written translation of vital documents (Gambetta and Gedtrimaite 2010: 33). New York City's work has expanded the language access plan from within government, to pushing external companies within the city to provide stronger standards as well.

Case study: New York City

In New York City, a group of attorneys and urban activists launched the New York Immigrant Representation Study in 2010. Their aim was to document the areas with the most urgent needs for non-citizens facing deportation (Katzmann 2018: 491). This strategy was intended to advance recommendations about possible resources and strategies, which were published in a report on the need in 2011 and a report with solutions in 2012. The work was viewed as crucial; a recent study found that detained immigrants with attorneys were 500% more likely to win their cases than those without (Rinaldi 2016). Just over five years after the New York Representation Study, the New York Immigrant Family Unity Project (NYIFUP) became the nation's first public defender system for immigrants facing deportation (Katzmann 2018: 491). This project was unique in ensuring universal representation, with screening for income eligibility only, as well as providing basic support services such as translation and interpretation services, social work, and mental health services (Katzmann 2018: 492). It became the gold standard of providing good language access services with legal representation for non-citizens.

Having a programme funded by the City for free lawyers enables immigrants and refugees to access the services they need, regardless of specific legal status. Generally, in the United States undocumented immigrants are ineligible for programmes funded by federal dollars, and restrictions continue until the immigrant has achieved legal permanent status (having been legally in the country for at least five years). Even legal permanent residents are restricted from a number of federally funded programmes (National Immigration Forum 2018). The City programme provides comprehensive wrap-around services, including interpreters and translators, and the programme would provide for universal representation of detained individuals, with screening only for income eligibility. It operates through a small group of institutional providers with capacity to handle the full range of removal cases and in cooperation with ICE and EOIR. It provides basic legal support services such as experts, translators/interpreters, social workers, investigators, and mental health evaluators. The programme has a dedicated funding stream and is overseen by a coordinating organisation (NILC 2016: 16).

New York City is unique in that the State of New York also provides free legal assistance for non-citizens through the Liberty Defense Project (not all cities also have a similar programme at state level). Ten million dollars were allocated by the New York State Governor in his 2018 budget for this work (Blanco 2017).

Paths forward for translational activism

Traditionally, translators and interpreters are expected to be neutral parties. And in fact, government and the courts often expect an unbiased interpreter when conducting their work. Barsky argues that 'activist translators' ought to be involved and engaged and that it is appropriate to inform the general public, through whichever intermediary, as to what is going on, and inform immigrants of their rights. Further, he argues that translators are often the best intermediaries in this sense (2005: 30). He centres his argument around the national detention system and the extent to which there is a developed legal rights education system around the facility in which interpreters are expected to support the language needs of a non-citizen. In the United States, non-citizens are often held in more than one facility—particularly if they have been arrested in a place without a detention centre and need to be transferred. Barsky states that often these non-citizens are asked to make a number of legal decisions without the advice of counsel or any legal support and uses this reality to argue for the elevated role of the interpreter (2005: 36).

This leads to the question of whether language access plans and legal defence funds are meeting their due diligence. Both require that the government identify funding for the glaring need for these services, and force the system to provide a roadmap for government agencies who complain about unexpected cost. When these functions are advocated for in various Offices of Immigrant and Refugee Affairs, then there is generally a programme or policy staff who couple this work with ongoing education and outreach in the community.

One specific area where local Offices could be more proactive is in meeting the need for interpreters and translators in new and emerging languages. For example, in the United States, recent immigrant groups from Nepal, Burma, Venezuela, Afghanistan, and Saudi Arabia have experienced higher rates of growth from 2010 to 2017, with the number of Nepalese immigrants alone increasing 120% in that time period (Zong and Batalova 2019). Local Offices could meet the need for more interpreters and translators by supporting them with government-funded training or financial support to pursue this training on their own. This would be a way for the government to support living-wage jobs and simultaneously fill a gap in services.

The legal system in the United States is inequitable and a convoluted maze for non-citizens. Beyond that, detention centres are not following federal protocols in implementing language access and providing interpretation and translation services. However, local attorneys and urban activists have been leveraging the immigrant rights movement to ask for better standards and begin providing these standards at the local level. Better standardisation across the role of interpreter at the local government level would support more advocacy at the federal level. Some jurisdictions have had the opportunity to be creative and advocate for funding for LEP individuals and, with that funding, to provide better services. Such examples should become a template for providing these services when non-citizens need them the most.

Related topics

The Right not to Have an Interpreter in Criminal Trials; What Is Asylum?; Feminism in Translation.

Further reading

Abel, Laura (2011) 'Language Access in Immigration Courts,' *Brennan Center for Justice at New York University School of Law* [online]. Available at: www.brennancenter.org/sites/default/files/legacy/Justice/LangAccess/Language_Access_in_Immigration_Courts.pdf.

The Brennan Center for Justice at New York University School of Law is a non-partisan public policy and law institute. This paper was written to provide the Department of Justice's Executive Office of Immigration Review (EOIR) with guidance as it reviews the Immigration Courts for language accessibility and updates its language assistance plan.

Barsky, Robert F. (2005) 'Activist Translation in an Era of Fictional Law,' *TTR: traduction, terminologie, rédaction* 18 (2): 17–48.

This article proposes that activist translators be involved and engaged in those legal realms, such as the treatment of undocumented migrants, because this is an area in which translators can act as true intermediaries. However, this form of activism, like other discretionary activities, needs to be directed to lofty causes, such as upholding the human rights of those most excluded by our society.

Harvard Law Review Notes (2018) 'The Right to Be Heard from Immigration Prisons: Locating a Right of Access to Counsel for Immigration Detainees in the Right of Access to Courts,' *Harvard Law Review* 182 (2): 726–747.

This note outlines how the constitutional right of access to courts provides a useful framework for immigration detainees to bring claims to access their counsel. In particular, of relevance to this chapter, this note includes a description of an immigration detainee's need for access to counsel and the failure of current doctrinal frameworks. It also outlines the right of access to courts.

Katzmann, Robert A. (2018) 'Symposium: A Decade of Advancing Immigrant Representation,' *Fordham Law Review* 87 (2): 485–502.

This article transcribes a speech given by Judge Katzmann, which provides a brief overview of the attorney-led endeavour in New York City that focuses on: (1) increasing pro bono activity of firms, especially at the outset of immigration proceedings; (2) improving mechanisms of legal-service delivery; and (3) rooting out inadequate counsel and improving the quality of representation available to non-citizens. The endeavour, which included a study, provided key data on these issues.

Morris, Ruth (1995) 'The Moral Dilemmas of Court Interpreting,' *The Translator* 1 (1): 25–46.

This article discusses the legal distinction between translation and interpretation and illustrates some of the moral dilemmas that confront court interpreters. It argues for a more realistic understanding of their role and a major improvement in their professional status; as recognised professionals, court interpreters can more readily assume the latitude they need in order to ensure effective communication in the courtroom.

References

Arulanantham, Ahilan (2018) 'Immigrant Children do not have the Right to an Attorney Unless They Can Pay, Rules Appeals Court,' in *ACLU* [online] 6 February. Available at: www.aclu.org/blog/immigrants-rights/deportation-and-due-process/immigrant-children-do-not-have-right-attorney [accessed 27 September 2019].

Balk, Gene (2015) 'What King County's Refugee Populations Look Like—Interactive Map,' in *The Seattle Times* [online] 19 November. Available at: www.seattletimes.com/seattle-news/what-king-countys-refugee-populations-look-like-interactive-map/ [accessed 27 September 2019].

Barnett, Erica C. (2017) 'City of Seattle Building Stronger Connections with Community Liaisons,' in *Next City* [online] 14 February. Available at: https://nextcity.org/daily/entry/seattle-public-outreach-community-liaisons [accessed 27 September 2019].

Barsky, Robert F. (2005) 'Activist Translation in an Era of Fictional Law,' *TTR: traduction, terminologie, rédaction* 18 (2): 17–48.

Beck, Katherine L. (2017) 'Interpreting Injustice: The Department of Homeland Security's Failure to Comply with Federal Language Access Requirements in Immigration Detention,' *Harvard Latinx Law Review* 20: 15–50.

Blanco, Octavio (2017) 'New York to Provide Lawyers for Immigrants Facing Deportation,' in *CNN Business* [online] 13 April. Available at: https://money.cnn.com/2017/04/13/news/economy/new-york-immigrant-legal-defense-fund/ [accessed 15 October 2019].

Butler, Martin, Paul Mecheril, and Lea Brenningmeyer (2017) 'Coming to Terms—On the Aim and Scope of this Volume,' in *Resistance: Subjects, Representations, Contexts*. Eds. Martin Butler, Paul Mecheril, and Lea Brenningmeyer. Bielefeld: Transcript Verlag. 7–16.

Campbell, Alexia Fernandez (2015) 'How Some Refugees in Seattle Learned to Trust the Police,' in *The Atlantic* [online] 16 June. Available at: www.theatlantic.com/politics/archive/2015/06/how-some-refugees-in-seattle-learned-to-trust-the-police/432138/ [accessed 27 September 2019].

Caplow, Stacy, Peter L. Markowitz, Jojo Annobil, Peter Z Cobb, and Nancy Morawetz (2011) 'Accessing Justice: The Availability and Adequacy of Counsel Removal Proceedings: New York Immigrant Representation Study Report,' *Cardozo Law Review* 33: 357–416.

Carson, Anna Paden (2017) 'Justice for Noncitizens: A Case for Reforming the Immigration Legal System,' in *VA Engage Journal* 5, article 4 [online]. Available at: http://scholarship.richmond.edu/vaej/vol5/iss1/4 [accessed 27 September 2019].

Catholic Legal Immigration Network, Inc. [CLINIC] (2018) *DOJ Requires Immigration Judges to Meet Quotas* [online]. Available at: https://cliniclegal.org/resources/doj-requires-immigration-judges-meet-quotas [accessed 27 September 2019].

Chishti, Muzaffar, Sarah Pierce, and Jessica Bolter (2017) 'The Obama Record on Deportations: Deporter in Chief or Not?' in *Migration Policy* [online] 26 January. Available at: www.migrationpolicy.org/article/obama-record-deportations-deporter-chief-or-not [accessed 27 September 2019].

Deslandes, Ann (2017) 'Sanctuary Cities are as old as the Bible,' in *JSTOR Daily* [online] 22 March. Available at: https://daily.jstor.org/sanctuary-cities-as-old-as-bible/ [accessed 27 September 2019].

Fischer, Aaron J., Pilar Gonzalez, and Richard Diaz (2019) 'There is No Safety Here,' in *Disability Rights California* [online] March. Available at: www.disabilityrightsca.org/system/files/file-attachments/DRC_REPORT_ADELANTO-IMMIG_DETENTION_MARCH2019.pdf [accessed 27 September 2019].

Frej, Willa (2018) 'DOJ Slaps Quotas on Immigration Judges to Speed Deportations,' in *HUFFPOST* [online] 3 April. Available at: www.huffpost.com/entry/doj-quotas-on-immigration-judges-to-speed-deportations_n_5ac346cbe4b04646b645d061 [accessed 27 September 2019].

Gamal, Muhammad Y. (2009) 'Court Interpreting,' in *Routledge Encyclopedia of Translation Studies* (2nd ed.). Eds. Mona Baker and Gabriela Saldanha. London and New York: Routledge. 63–67.

Gambetta, Ricardo and Zivile Gedtrimaite (2010) 'Municipal Innovations in Immigrant Integration: 20 Cities, 20 Good Practices,' [online]. Available at: www.nlc.org/sites/default/files/municipal-innovations-immigrant-integration-20-cities-sep10.pdf [accessed 27 September 2019].

Gentry, Blake A. (2015) 'Exclusion of Indigenous Language Speaking Immigrants in the U.S. Immigration System, A Technical Review,' in *AMA Consultants* [online] 26 May. Available at: www.amaconsultants.org/uploads/Exclusion_of_Indigenous%20Languages_in_US_Immigration_System_19_June2015version_i.pdf, archived at: https://perma.cc/W7WY-YPFD [accessed 27 September 2019].

Good, Benjamin (2014) 'A Child's Right to Counsel in Removal Proceedings,' *Stanford Journal of Civil Rights and Civil Liberties* 10: 109–157.

Graber, Lena, Angie Junck, and Nikki Marquez (2016) 'Local Options for Protecting Immigrants: A Collection of City & County Policies to Protect Immigrants from Discrimination and Deportation,' [online]. Available at: https://static1.squarespace.com/static/55ea05f0e4b0c34b506fd8c6/t/5a7a29554192028e23de17df/1517955419308/ILDC+local+options+protecting+immigrants-20170208.pdf [accessed 15 October 2019].

Harvard Law Review Notes (2018) 'The Right to be Heard from Immigration Prisons: Locating a Right of Access to Counsel for Immigration Detainees in the Right of Access to Courts,' *Harvard Law Review* 182 (2): 726–747.

García Hernández, César Cuauhtémoc (2018) 'Immigrant Defense Funds for Utopians,' *Washington and Lee Law Review* 75 (3), Article 7: 1393–1425.

Immigration and Nationality Act [INA] (1952) *8 U.S.C. §1362* [online]. Available at: www.law.cor nell.edu/uscode/text/8/1362 [accessed 15 October 2019].

Inghilleri, Moira (2009) 'Asylum,' in *Routledge Encyclopedia of Translation Studies* (2nd ed.). Eds. Mona Baker and Gabriela Saldanha. London and New York: Routledge. 10–13.

Jones, Liz (2015) 'Team of Women: Female Cops and Refugees Work on Trust,' in *KUOW* [online] 25 June. Available at: https://kuow.org/stories/team-women-female-cops-and-refugees-work-trust/ [acessed 27 September 2019].

Katzmann, Robert A. (2018) 'Symposium: A Decade of Advancing Immigrant Representation,' *Fordham Law Review* 87 (2): 485–502.

Kerwin, Donald (2018) 'From IIRIA to Trump: Connecting the Dots to the Current Immigration Policy Crisis,' *Journal on Migration and Human Security* 6 (3): 192–204.

Limited English Proficiency (LEP) A Federal Interagency Website (2018) *Executive Order 13166* [online]. Available at: www.lep.gov/13166/eo13166.html [accessed 27 September 2019].

Lind, Dara (2016) The Disastrous, Forgotten 1996 Law that Created Today's Immigration Problem,' in *Vox* [online] 28 April. Available at: www.vox.com/2016/4/28/11515132/iirira-clinton-immigra tion [accessed 27 September 2019].

Local and Regional Government Alliance on Race and Equity (2015) *Seattle's Women's Refugee Institute: Transforming Community-Police Relations* [online] 12 May. Available at: www.raciale quityalliance.org/2015/05/12/seattles-womens-refugee-institute/ [accessed 27 September 2019].

Martinez, Daniel E., Ricardo D. Martinez-Schuldt, and Guillermo Cantor (2018) 'Criminalization of Immigration,' in *Routledge Handbook on Immigration and Crime*. Eds. Holly Ventura Miller and Anthony Peguero. New York: Routledge. 270–283.

McHugh, Margie (2015) 'It is Time for Federal Agencies to do More to Improve the Provision of Language Access Services,' in *Migration Policy* [online] October. Available at: www.migrationpo licy.org/news/it-time-federal-agencies-do-more-improve-provision-language-access-services [accessed 27 September 2019].

Miller, Kenneth E., Zoe L. Martell, Linda Pazdirek, Melissa Caruth, and Diana Lopez (2005) 'The Role of Interpreters In Psychotherapy with Refugees: An Exploratory Study,' *American Journal of Orthopsychiatry* 75 (1): 27–39.

Montgomery, John D. (2014) 'Cost of Counsel in Immigration: Economic Analysis of Proposal Providing Public Counsel to Indigent Persons Subject to Immigration Removal Proceedings,' in *NERA Economic Consulting* [online] 28 May. Available at: https://perma.cc/K57F-NPE2 [accessed 27 September 2019].

Morris, Ruth (1995) 'The Moral Dilemmas of Court Interpreting,' *The Translator* 1 (1): 25–46.

National Immigrant Justice Center [NIJC] (2018) *ICE Released Its Most Comprehensive Immigration Detention Data Yet. Its Alarming* [online]. Available at: https://immigrantjustice.org/staff/blog/ice-released-its-most-comprehensive-immigration-detention-data-yet [accessed 27 September 2019].

National Immigration Forum (2018) *Fact Sheet: Immigrants and Public Benefits* [online]. Available at: https://immigrationforum.org/article/fact-sheet-immigrants-and-public-benefits/ [accessed 27 September 2019].

National Immigration Law Center [NILC] (2016) *Blazing a Trail* [online]. Available at: www.nilc.org/wp-content/uploads/2016/04/Right-to-Counsel-Blazing-a-Trail-2016-03.pdf [accessed 27 September 2019].

Office of Civic Engagement and Immigrant Affairs (2017) *Language Access and English Language Acquisition—Keys to Engagement and Participation* [online]. Available at: https://sfgov.org/ oceia/language-access [accessed 27 September 2019].

Office of Inspector General (Homeland Security) [OIG] (2017) *Concerns about ICE Detainee Treatment and Care at Detention Facilities* [online]. Available at: www.oig.dhs.gov/sites/default/files/assets/2017-12/OIG-18-32-Dec17.pdf [accessed 27 September 2019].

Office of the Mayor (2017) *City of Seattle, King County Announce Legal Defense Fund Awardees* [online]. Available at: http://murray.seattle.gov/city-seattle-king-county-announce-legal-defense-fund-awardees/ [accessed 27 September 2019].

Phillips, Amber (2018) 'Why the Trump Administration's "Sanctuary Cities" lawsuit against California could backfire,' in *Washington Post* [online] 7 March. Available at: www.washingtonpost.com/news/the-fix/wp/2018/03/07/why-the-trump-administrations-sanctuary-cities-lawsuit-against-california-could-backfire/?noredirect=on&utm_term=.902a629e4d2a [accessed 27 September 2019].

Pierce, Sarah, Jessica Bolter, and Andrew Selee (2018) 'U.S. Immigration Policy under Trump: Deep Changes and Lasting Impacts,' in *Migration Policy Institute* [online] July. Available at: www.migrationpolicy.org/research/us-immigration-policy-trump-deep-changes-impacts [accessed 27 September 2019].

Right to Counsel. 8 U.S.C. §1362 (1952) [online]. Available at: www.law.cornell.edu/uscode/text/8/1362 [accessed 27 September 2019].

Rinaldi, Tiziana (2016) 'In New York City Lawyers Make All the Difference for Immigrant Detainees Facing Deportation,' in *KUOW* [online] 20 September. Available at: http://archive.kuow.org/post/new-york-city-lawyers-make-all-difference-immigrant-detainees-facing-deportation [accessed 27 September 2019].

Rosen, Ben (2016) 'L.A. vs. Trump: City Unveils $10 Million Legal Defense Fund for Immigrants,' in *The Christian Science Monitor* [online] 20 December. Available at: www.csmonitor.com/USA/2016/1220/L.A.-vs.-Trump-City-unveils-10-million-legal-defense-fund-for-immigrants [accessed 27 September 2019].

San Francisco Immigrant Legal Defense Collaborative [SFILDC] (2016) *Why We're Here* [online]. Available at: https://sfildc.org/ [accessed 27 September 2019].

Santos, Fernanda (2008) 'Mayor Orders New York to Expand Language Help,' in *New York Times* [online] 23 July. Available at: www.nytimes.com/2008/07/23/nyregion/23translate.html [accessed 27 September 2019].

Seattle City Council (2017) 'Legal Defense for Immigrants and Refugees: Councilmember Gonzalez's Statement on Legal Defense Fund Awards,' [online]. Available at: www.seattle.gov/council/issues/past-issues/legal-defense-for-immigrants-and-refugees [accessed 27 September 2019].

Seattle Times Staff (2010) 'Seattle's Rainier Valley: One of America's "Dynamic Neighborhoods",' in *Seattle Times* [online] 20 June. Available at: www.seattletimes.com/opinion/seattles-rainier-valley-one-of-americas-dynamic-neighborhoods/ [accessed 27 September 2019].

Shoichet, Catherine E. (2017) 'Surprise Inspections find "Significant Issues" in Treatment of ICE Detainees,' in *CNN.com* [online] 14 December. Available at: www.cnn.com/2017/12/14/politics/immigrant-detainee-treatment-report/index.html [accessed 27 September 2019].

Srikantiah, Jayashri, and Lisa Weissman-Ward (2014) *The Immigration 'Rocket Docket': Understanding the Due Process Implications* [online]. Available at: https://law.stanford.edu/2014/08/15/the-immigration-rocket-docket-understanding-the-due-process-implications/ [accessed 27 September 2019].

Sullivan, Jennifer (2011) 'New State Law Protects Legal Immigrants' Rights,' in *The Seattle Times* [online] 22 July. Available at: https://infoweb-newsbank-com.ezproxy.spl.org/apps/news/document-view?p=WORLDNEWS&t=favorite%3ASEATTLE%21Seattle%2Btimes%2Bcollection%2Bwith%2Bhistorical%2Barchives&sort=YMD_date%3AD&fld-base-0=alltext&maxresults=20&val-base-0=pete%20holmes%20365%20misdemeanor&docref=news/138A9A41232B2C80 [accessed 27 September 2019].

The Seattle Times Opinion (2010) 'Legal Tweak Brings Fairness to Noncitizens,' in *The Seattle Times* [online]. 17 July. Available at: https://infoweb-newsbank-com.ezproxy.spl.org/apps/news/document-view?p=WORLDNEWS&t=favorite%3ASEATTLE%21Seattle%2Btimes%2Bcollection%2Bwith%2Bhistorical%2Barchives&sort=YMD_date%3AD&fld-base-0=alltext&maxre

sults=20&val-base-0=pete%20holmes%20365%20misdemeanor&docref=news/
13114E7277356858 [accessed 27 September 2019].

The United States Department of Justice [USDOJ] (2016) *About DOJ* [online]. Available at: www.
justice.gov/about [accessed 27 September 2019].

The White House President Barack Obama (n.d.) *The Cabinet* [online]. Available at: https://obama
whitehouse.archives.gov/administration/cabinet [accessed 27 September 2019].

The White House. State & Local Government (n.d.) [online]. Available at: www.whitehouse.gov/
about-the-white-house/state-local-government/ [accessed 27 September 2019].

Think Immigration (2016) 'A City on the Hill: San Francisco Protects the Rights of Refugees and
Their Families,' [online] 31 May. Available at: https://thinkimmigration.org/blog/2016/05/31/
a-city-on-the-hill-san-francisco-protects-the-rights-of-refugee-children-and-their-families/
[accessed 27 September 2019].

Tobocman, Steve (2015) 'Guide to Immigrant Economic Development,' in *Welcoming Economies
Global Network* [online]. Available at: www.welcomingamerica.org/sites/default/files/WA_Immi
grantEconomicDevelopment_FINAL_web.pdf [accessed 27 September 2019].

U.S. Immigration and Customs Enforcement [ICE] (2016) 'Enforcement and Removal Operations
National Detainee Handbook,' [online] April. Available at: www.ice.gov/sites/default/files/docu
ments/Document/2017/detainee-handbook.PDF [accessed 27 September 2019].

United States Citizen and Immigration Services [USCIS] (2017) *Post-9/11* [online]. Available at: www.
uscis.gov/history-and-genealogy/our-history/agency-history/post-911 [accessed 27 September 2019].

United States Department of Health and Human Services (2013) *Civil Rights Requirements- A. Title
VI of the Civil Rights Act of 1964, 42 U.S.C. 2000d et seq. ('Title VI')* [online]. Available at:
www.hhs.gov/civil-rights/for-individuals/special-topics/needy-families/civil-rights-requirements/
index.html [accessed 27 September 2019].

United States Naturalization Act of 1790, Sess. 2. Ch. 3 (n.d.) [online]. Available at: http://legis
works.org/sal/1/stats/STATUTE-1-Pg103.pdf [accessed 27 September 2019].

Wadensjö, Cecilia (2009) 'Community Interpreting,' in *Routledge Encyclopedia of Translation Studies* (2nd ed.). Eds. Mona Baker and Gabriela Saldanha. London and New York: Routledge.
43–48.

Wong Wing v. United States (1896) 163 U.S. 228.

Zambrano-Paff, Marjorie (2008) 'Cortesia y Conversacion: De lo escrito a lo oral,' in *Proceedings of
the 3rd Colloquium of the EDICE Program*. Eds. Antonio Briz, Antonio Hidalgo, Marta Albelda,
Josefa Contreras, and Nieves Hernandez Flores. Valencia: Universidad de Valencia/PROGRAMA
EDICE. 366–380.

Zong, Jie, and Jeanne Batalova (2019) 'Immigrants from New Origin Countries in the United
States,' Migration Policy Institute [online] 17 January. Available at: www.migrationpolicy.org/art
icle/immigrants-new-origin-countries-united-states [accessed 27 September 2019].

19

Feminism in translation

Reframing human rights law through transnational Islamic feminist networks

Miriam Bak McKenna

Introduction

With the adoption of the United Nations (UN) Charter (1945), and its commitment to the promotion of 'universal' human rights and fundamental freedoms, 'without distinction on the basis of, inter alia, sex', women's rights gained a new prominence in international legal discourse.[1] A new era of human rights and equality in which women were to be granted full legal and civil capacity sought to provide a decisive break with the oppressive legacies of the past. While the subsequent development of international human rights law has provided positive advancement in the promotion of women's rights and gender equality, given the still precarious and fraught conditions of women's existence in the world, its limitations have also been made clear.[2]

The lack of political will arguably presents the greatest obstacle to women's full inclusion in the human rights regime; however one of the most pernicious barriers has been the creation and re-production of gendered and cultured subjects within the discourse and framework of human rights (Gaer 1998; Fraser 1999; Engle 2005). As various accounts have underlined, a central paradox of international human rights law is its reliance upon the construction of a universal 'human subject,' which unavoidably 'reproduces hierarchies, including those of [gender], race, culture, nation, socio-economic status and sexuality' (Otto 2005: 105–106). For women in particular, the language of human rights has a propensity to reproduce conceptions of women that reinforce gender and cultural essentialism, thereby (re)producing unequal relations of power. The result, as Dianne Otto notes, 'is the continued naturalization of gender identities that normalize women's secondary status,' and which fail to constitute women as fully human (Otto 2013: 197). These subjectivities are produced along multiple axes (race, class, religion, culture, and so on), leading to a situation of 'double jeopardy' of marginalisation and victimisation for 'Third World' women (Kapur 2002: 2) who are caught within broader debates over relativist and universalist approaches to human rights (Donnelly 1984; Oloka-Onyango and Tamale 1995). The tension among gender, culture, and rights and the often essentialist and antagonistic depictions of culture which have emerged further highlight the need to engage with the deeper discursive and normative concerns that shape and structure women's rights.

At the same time, however, rights discourse also contains important opportunities for contestation and change. Women's rights activists have engaged various approaches to push against the masculinist and imperialist underpinnings of human rights discourse and mobilise them in the pursuit of women's rights. This chapter focuses on the use of translation practices by activists seeking to reframe human rights law 'on the ground' in order to counter the (re)production of problematic gender and cultural subjectivities. Drawing on the work of anthropologists Sally Merry and Peggy Levitt and their approach to the translation of human rights as a process that combines both appropriation and transformation—a process they call 'vernacularisation'—the chapter examines how the language of rights and the gender expectations they contain has been interrogated and strategically deployed by feminist rights advocates in local contexts in order to realise the emancipatory potential of human rights law (Levitt and Merry 2009, 2011; Merry 2006a). The concept of vernacularisation calls our attention to critical practices of translation and the ways in which normative ideas or practices move from one social context to another and are made meaningful within—or rejected on the basis of—local realities. As Levitt and Merry note, 'human rights vernacularisation is a process of translation within context' (Levitt and Merry 2017). This approach has revealed the myriad ways in which gender and cultural essentialisms are contested—not through the import of 'Western' ideas of human rights, but through the local idiom.

In this chapter, I consider the productive contribution of 'vernacularisers,' in the case of women's human rights activists working in Muslim communities. Specifically, I examine the work of the activists of the Women Living Under Muslim Laws (WLUML) and Sisterhood Is Global Institute (SIGI) groups. In line with the work of Merry and others, an analysis of these groups reveals the ways in which activists seek to translate women's rights into Muslim contexts without either reinforcing gender and cultural stereotypes or falling back into well-worn and unhelpful binaries of us and them, here and there, universality and cultural relativism. Since their creation, WLUML and SIGI have sought to formulate workable strategies for change, according to their own priorities, and relevant to their own specific national or community contexts, by destabilising the universal category of woman and its problematic relationship to culture.

I begin by examining the representations of sex/gender and the field's asymmetrical commitment to 'women's rights,' showing how these tropes are implicated in the persistence of stereotypical representations of women, particularly for Muslim women. Yet, as I argue, there are also opportunities, already present in the law, to challenge these exclusions by refusing both dualism and asymmetry. Then, I examine the process of vernacularisation and the efforts over the last two decades, by feminists and others, to reimagine sex/gender in the context of international human rights law in order to achieve change for women. Next I explore the ways in which transnational Islamic women's activist networks have translated and fused universal ideas of rights into their work to usher in new forms of change for women's rights. This confrontation brings to view a more discursive relationship between formal human rights law and the strategic and normative claims of human rights practice. In this context, the categories of law, culture, and gender are not conceptualised as monolithic and unchangeable, but as subject to transformation and reinterpretation.

Gender, culture, and the discourse of rights

Like any discourse, law plays a powerful role in the processes that (re)produce and naturalise dominant social norms, categories, and subjectivities. Human rights law is no different. Behind human rights law's appeal to universality lies a complex web of material, social, and power relations, which intersect to create subjects 'that bear the markings of complex histories of subjugation and resistance' (Otto 2006: 319). As Douzinas has observed, human rights 'construct humans,' rather than the reverse (2002: 457). Within theories of rights, the subject of human rights is a divided one. Although striving for unity, it is plagued by tensions, between 'autonomy and nurturance, independence and bonding, sovereignty of the self and relations to others,' prone to privileging one side of these dichotomies and marginalising the other (Benhabib 1994: 86). This tension is perhaps nowhere more evident than in debates over women's human rights. Women's historic struggle to be recognised as human, both universally and with specific attributes and wants, has continuously met the challenge of creating a space for 'women's rights' against the backdrop of the multiple hierarchies, including those of race, culture, nationality, socio-economic status, sexuality, and gender, which are disguised by its claims to objectivity and neutrality, while at the same time grappling with the fact that there exists no universal woman, nor a universal notion of womanhood itself (Smart 1989: 21).

Decades of campaigning by feminist activists against the peripheral status of women in human rights regimes have underlined that, while rights may attenuate the subordination and oppression to which women are vulnerable, they do not fundamentally challenge the discursive reproduction of women as premised upon subordination, nor the regimes and mechanisms which underlie female oppression (Fraser 1999). As Wendy Brown has explored, when women speak of their experiences through rights claims, they are not protected or freed through this discourse, so much as their very identity is created through it —that is, 'rights produce the subjects they pretend only to presuppose' (2000b: 231). The paradox, as Brown notes, drawing on Foucault, is the more highly specified rights are as rights for women, the more likely they are to solidify the image of the subordinated female subject: 'To have a right as a woman is not to be free of being designated and subordinated by gender' (2000b: 231). The framework of women's rights, in Gayatri Spivak's weary formulation, is 'that which we cannot not want' (Spivak 1988).

Feminist critiques of rights have centred on the mechanisms of exclusion and disempowerment associated with legal texts in three key areas: (1) the dis-embedded and disembodied subject of rights; (2) the validity of rights claims grounded on a universal legislating reason; and (3) the ability of a universal, legislating reason to tackle the multiplicity of contexts and life situations with which practical reason is always confronted (Benhabib 1994: 26). Particular attention has been focused on the dualistic or oppositional hierarchies of gender contained in rights instruments, which adopt the 'male' sex as standard, along with a number of recurring female subjectivities which are produced in opposition to the male representations they sustain: as mothers and wives who need 'protection' by the law; as 'formally equal' with 'comparable' men; and as vulnerable 'victims,' assuming women's vulnerability and dependency (Otto 2006: 320).

As Otto explains, international law has historically operated under the assumption of a male/female dichotomy, according to which women were categorised, along with colonised people, as dependent subjects in need of protection (2006: 322–323). The Laws of War, for example, required an occupying power to respect 'family honour and rights,' treating women as part of (male) family property and reputation to be protected by the law, whilst evading any explicit mention of wartime sexual abuse of women.[3] Early international labour law prohibited women's employment in certain occupations, like night work and mining, that were deemed to be too dangerous for women or too disruptive of their domestic responsibilities,[4] while early treaties prohibiting trafficking in women for the purposes of prostitution denied women the capacity to 'consent' to sex work.[5]

The shift towards the full legal equality and rights of women in the UN Charter did not signify an automatic shift in these attitudes. While the Charter's prohibition of 'sex' discrimination (Article 1(3)), rather than discrimination against women, opened the possibility that gender asymmetry would not be automatically presumed, new footholds of protectionism also emerged. In the 1948 Universal Declaration of Human Rights (UDHR) the principle of equality was reiterated in the context of suffrage (Article 21) and marriage (Article 16(1)), while 'special care and assistance' (not parental rights) were granted to mothers with young children (Article 25(2)). As Otto notes, including women by granting 'special' treatment to the specificities of their lives constructs women's experience as non-universal, which has the effect of buttressing the masculinity of the universal (2006: 324). The description in Article 16(3) of the family as 'the natural and fundamental group unit of society' also enforces a similar hetero-normative description of women's roles, while Article 25, which recognises that everyone has the right of an adequate standard of living for 'himself and his family,' reiterates the masculine figure of the household head and breadwinner. Similarly, the *International Covenant on Economic, Social and Cultural Rights* (ICESCR) and the *International Covenant on Civil and Political Rights* (ICCPR), adopted in 1966, also treat women protectively in the context of parenting (ICESCR Article 10(2)) and in the 'natural' family unit (ICCPR Article 17(1) and 23(1), ICESCR Articles 7(a)(ii), 10(1) and 11(1)).

A woman-centred approach

The move towards a 'woman-centred' approach in the 1970s, as a means of recasting the universal subject as a woman and challenging the conceptual boundaries of human rights law, brought with it its own conceits. The drafters of the Convention on the Elimination of All Forms of Discrimination Against Women (CEDAW) sought to expand both the definition of discrimination against women as well as substantive human rights in line with the female subject, for example, by expanding unfair dismissal to include dismissal on the grounds of pregnancy, maternity leave, or work, and including child care in social service supports provided for workers. While making great leaps in the cause for women's equality, CEDAW's continuing reliance on a comparison with men, the lack of reference to violence against women, the assumption of normative married heterosexuality, and its limited acknowledgement of the multiple and intersectional forms of discrimination women face have been critiqued as re-entrenching difference (Rosenblum 2011). As Frances Olsen has observed, CEDAW does little to challenge the 'hierarchisation' of sexed activities (Olsen 1990: 202–203), addressing the discrimination suffered by only one sexed identity group (women), but not the rigid assignment of gendered roles, which paint women as natural caregivers in the domestic sphere. Moreover, men are mentioned only implicitly, mostly as a standard of reference or as the putative discriminators, reinforcing traditional stereotypes of both women and men (Otto 2013: 202).

Particular attention has been drawn to the problems contained within the universalist or universalising discourse of the 'women's rights as human rights' platform adopted at the 1995 Beijing Conference. Black feminists and critical race feminists have taken the lead in underlining the dangers of false universalism contained within reliance upon shared identity contained within the unitary category of 'woman' (Mohanty 1984: 333; Engle 1992: 1509, 2005: 47). Given the wide array of women's concerns and experiences, criticisms of the appeal to gender essentialism have revealed that treating gender difference as the primary concern of feminism has had the effect of reinforcing gendered categories and collapsing differences among women. As Kapur argues:

the emphasis on the commonality of women's experience in a woman-centered approach to gender equality places the analysis on a slippery slope where it can easily slide into the essentialist and prioritizing category of gender; it can blunt rather than sharpen our analysis of oppression.

(Kapur 2013: 276)

Class, cultural, religious, and racial differences between women are collapsed under the category of gender through women's common experience of sexual violence and object-ification by men, obscuring the multiple ways in which women—particularly women in minority and disadvantaged communities—experience multiple forms of subordination. Critics have in particular argued that early feminist descriptions of women's experience focused on white, middle-class, educated, heterosexual women (Alarcon 1995: 357). Consequently, the political priorities of the women's movement (e.g. equal access to edu-cation and employment, abortion rights) have reflected the most urgent concerns of women who do not experience other forms of subordination, such as religious, ethnic, or caste subordination. These various forms of subordination are, as Kapur argues, 'not sep-arate and discrete, but rather, intricately connected' (2013: 277).

The increasing focus on patterns of male violence against women in more recent fem-inist activism has also given rise to one of the most frequently recurring problems in the gendered discourse of human rights: the reinforcement of women's victim status in striv-ing for rights. Increasingly, in human rights settings women are defined primarily by their vulnerability to men's violence (Scully 2001: 113–23), justifying protective responses that deny women's (sexual) agency and autonomy, and that have little to do with promoting women's rights (Miller 2004: 7). The trope of 'woman as victim of vio-lence' has been particularly pernicious in the revival in the Global South of protective stereotypes of women who are painted as 'victims' of culture. The tendency to depict these women through a neo-colonial frame as naïve, backward, helpless, tradition-bound, and in need of rescue from their 'uncivilised' cultures (Abu-Lughod 2015), as Kapur has argued, drives a wedge between 'Western' women and those native 'others' who still need the 'West' to speak for them (Spivak 1988). The textual construction of the 'Third World Woman,' as Mohanty has argued, represents a return to feminism's discursive col-onisation and the self-justificatory identification of groups that needed to be saved (Mohanty 2003). Mani gives the example of British colonialist concerns to save the Indian woman from the 'barbarism' of *sati* (the practice in which a widow sacrifices herself by sitting atop her deceased husband's funeral pyre), for example, which rever-berate with contemporary concerns about female genital cutting in Africa, and forced marriage and so-called 'honour' killings in the Middle East and Asia (Mani 1998).

Particularly problematic are the negative implications which seem to arise from refer-ences to 'culture' as the source of stereotyped gender attitudes in CEDAW, which paint culture and cultural diversity primarily as a negative and subordinating aspect of women's lives. In human rights discourse more generally, culture has arisen as one potentially suspect variable in rights practice, arising in relation to the extremely polaris-ing debate over universalism and cultural relativism. Gender and sexuality remain central to the antagonisms between culture and rights, and cultural relativism continues to be the most discussed issue in the theory of human rights. As Kapur explains,

culture continues to be invoked in ways that demonise the culture of the 'Other' and represent women, especially Muslim or 'Third World' women, as exploited, violated, and abused primarily in and through barbaric cultural practices which stand in contrast to the more civilised treatment of women in non-Islamic Western societies.

(2013: 279)

Although violence against women has been identified as a universal phenomenon, the tendency within human rights discourse has been to condemn certain 'uncivilised' practices in developing countries, such as dowry murders, which produces anew the 'native victim' (Otto 2013: 357). This works not only to replicate assumptions about non-Western culture and the women who inhabit these spaces in ways that are totalising of a culture and its treatment of women, but it also silences women's history of engagement with culture and tradition as a source of empowerment and fails to capture the complex ways in which women's experiences are mediated by their religious and cultural identities. This oppositional relation between culture and rights narrates the ascendancy of one as always and inevitably undercutting or damaging the integrity of the other—that is, culture prevents rights and rights destroy cultures. Culture is reduced to a problem, a 'set of cultural practices deemed violent for women' (Visweswaran 2004: 484), or, put more bluntly, representing women's plight as 'death by culture' (Narayan 1997: 81). Kapur gives the example of the practice of veiling amongst Muslim women, which she says has invariably been assumed to be an oppressive and subordinating practice that typifies Islam and its degrading treatment of women, a view that subsumes the multiple meanings of the veil in different cultural and historical contexts (2013: 279).

Vernacularisation: translating the language of human rights law

These tensions have polarised feminist approaches to human rights, generating both hostility and creative attempts to overcome these problems. Drawing on one of the early lessons from the struggle for women's rights, that 'more legal rights for women will not, by itself, achieve gender equality' (Otto 2012), efforts have focused on the politics of discourse as a key element of social transformation (Foucault 1980). The adoption of a dynamic understanding of law, as a site of discursive struggle over how gender is conceived, and human possibilities are shaped, has become central to feminist engagement with human rights law. In particular, the shift towards multicultural dialogue, 'vernacularisation' and 'contextualisation' rather than universal value as the key to contesting the gendered, heterosexed, and imperial legacies embedded in the language and structures of law, has gained increasing traction.

Scholars and activists focus increasingly on the intersection of formal rights—whether international human rights conventions, constitutional rights, or national legislation—with the everyday realities of women, particularly in settings in which diverse cultural norms and plural legal systems may complicate rights claims. This scholarship underscores the importance of pushing back against the tendency to essentialise local culture or religion and oversimplify the complexity and fluidity of local practices, suggesting that these sites of struggle can create new possibilities and meanings through a politics animated by demands for social and gender justice.

Coomaraswarmy has explored the way in which women situated in the 'Third World,' or in minority and indigenous groups, can fight for their rights without becoming complicit in the legacies of racism and prejudice sponsored by colonialism (2002–2003: 483–513). Coomaraswarmy stresses the importance of 'learning from below' by forging links between global campaigns and locally developed strategies for women's rights, as does Andrews in her discussion of the utility of international human rights law in addressing violence against Aboriginal women (Andrews 1997). Stivens has drawn attention to the many long-term political contests among women's groups and scholars outside of European and North American contexts in general, and specifically in Asia, around the translation and use of the imported term 'gender' and the issue of the subject of feminisms—woman/women/gender. Such contests have been acute for women of the Global South as they seek to navigate the shifting and highly contested meanings of gender, posed in terms of a purportedly universal woman 'reeking of Eurocentric neo-colonialism' (Stivens 2001: 25).

What emerges is the great diversity of sites in which women's rights have been advanced (or resisted), as they are re-articulated, framed, and claimed according to differing notions of womanhood. As in the realm of language, vernacularity derives its communicative and combative power from familiarity (as a mode of speech that requires no explanation and is known by the natives). In the field of human rights, vernacularisation sheds light on the multiple ways women in cultures deemed problematic by some engage in protests, actions, and negotiations in demand of their rights, by translating them into local terms. In doing so, vernacularisation recasts the traditional oppositional logic between culture, gender, and rights by focusing on how, in local contexts, human rights vocabulary concepts and technology are remade in the vernacular—that is, how putatively universal tropes are contested through local idioms (Pardy 2013: 34). Vernacularisation challenges the 'existing scripts' (academic and popular) of gender and culture and disrupts the problematic subjectivities which arise from human rights discourse, particularly that of the passive woman oppressed by traditional culture (Volpp 2011: 90–110).

Merry's work on women's organisations looks at how ordinary women and the local organisations serving them make sense of global ideas and norms, and how the global is transformed in response. In Nigeria, for example, she observes that references to women's rights under *shari'a* are more likely to be accepted than human rights arguments (Merry 2006b). Thus, women's human rights become women's rights under *shari'a*. She also illustrates how activists in India translate and explain international human rights ideas into local terms, and then situate them within local structures of the community and the family, to counter issues such as gender violence. Merry's work demonstrates that women actively constructing and re-imagining the human rights movement from a local perspective, whether in New York or Lima, do so in local terms in order to alter existing social hierarchies.

While vernacularisation contains a number of inbuilt paradoxes, the most significant being the problematic nature of the division between the global and the local that it presupposes (Pardy 2013: 35), it nonetheless challenges the notion of globalisation as a flow of ideas and meanings from the global to the local and back again, unmarked by imbalances in power (Goodale 2007). Merry's argument for vernacularising human rights norms and principles relies on 'the role of activists who serve as intermediaries between different sets of cultural understandings of gender, violence and justice' (Merry 2006b: 56). Rather than assuming a linear top-down hierarchy by which the Global North gives 'developing nations' the gift of human rights, Merry contends that even the concept of human rights is a cultural phenomenon, and the process of articulating and negotiating human rights standards and norms is a multifaceted cultural process (Merry 2006b: 55). The separation between 'us' and 'them' fails to describe the reality of women's rights movements, demonstrating how the oppositions between gender, culture, and rights acquire new meanings when situated in new contexts.

Transnational Islamic feminist networks

Some of the most innovative strategies to vernacularise the language of human rights come from women scholars and activists in Muslim-majority contexts. Over the last three decades, feminist activists and scholars working in Islamic settings have developed strategies that enable women to claim freedom and equality within their communities, without accepting the dichotomies of universalising human rights discourse. The work of groups such as WLUML and SIGI has sought to counter reductive contemporary constructs of 'Muslim women' and construct with differentiated understandings of Islam, gender, and rights as contested and transformed in the context of social movements. In underlining the agency of Muslim women as remaking international law, not simply receiving it, they have also confronted Gayatri Spivak's famous formulation: 'Can the subaltern speak?' (Spivak 1988) in the affirmative, disrupting the image of the 'Third World' female victim, and the dichotomous relationship between Islam and human rights (see also Spivak 2004).

Drawing on the realisation that unmediated rights discourse will not adequately address their interests, particularly as it relates to freedom within identity, activists have sought to forge their own strategies and theories that allow for both culture and change. As Afkhami explains in an interview with Madhavi Sunder, this new approach to thinking about rights emerged out of Muslim feminists' frustrations with traditional conceptions of women's human rights (Sunder 2003: 1451). Caught between the colonial discourse of 'white men are saving brown women from brown men' and the nativists' argument, 'The women actually wanted to die,' women's rights activists in Muslim communities insist on making room for both culture and rights (Spivak 1988: 271). Sunder notes that, in

> turning traditional legal understandings of the 'right to religion' and the 'right to culture' on their heads, these activists are rejecting law's deference to religious authority and demanding an individual right to construct one's identity, not just outside the religious and cultural community but, most particularly, also within it.
>
> *(2003: 1412)*

Women Living Under Muslim Laws

Founded in 1984 in response to rising fundamentalism and identity politics in Algeria, WLUML is characteristic of human rights vernacularisation in that it seeks to facilitate the re-articulation of international human rights standards within Muslim communities and to bridge the gaps in formal legal analysis that currently complicate the realisation of women's rights for women living under Muslim laws. Over the years, WLUML has expanded to include women from over 70 countries, serving as an international solidarity network that provides information, support, and a collective space for women whose lives are shaped, conditioned, or governed by laws and customs said to derive from Islam. The group is unique in that it provides a forum for solidarity and action in a broad range of political contexts. These include countries where Islam is the state religion, secular states with Muslim majorities or political groups demanding religious laws, women in migrant Muslim communities, non-Muslim women who may have Muslim laws applied to them, and women born into Muslim communities who do not identify as religious. At the core of its strategies lies an attempt to diversify the image and social construction of the Muslim woman and foster a recognition that the status of women in Muslim contexts is diverse and shaped by a complex web of customary traditions and legal frameworks.

The network has identified as one of the main challenges to the implementation of human rights concepts in Islamic states, the tension between the secular nature of human rights, and the central role religious identity plays in the construction of women's identity (Sunder 2003: 1434). In addition, the lack of knowledge about rights, and the assertion—made by fundamentalists and some cultural relativists—that human rights are incompatible with Islam, mean that women believe they are faced with a choice between religion and rights. Rather than advocating for 'purely secular strategies' in achieving women's rights, therefore, WLUML employs strategies that seek to reconcile religion and rights, making it possible for women to have both (Shaheed 1994: 999). In this regard, the two key elements of WLUML's work have been, firstly, the use of networks as a means of critiquing the fundamentalist claims about women's religious identity, and, secondly, empowering women to shape religious identity in more egalitarian terms.

WLUML's early work endeavoured to underline the political and historical contingency of practices thought to be essential to Islam as a means of contesting the fundamentalist depictions of religious law emerging in Algeria. The network provided information and resources about women's rights in alternative legal systems in Muslim communities in order to assist activists in advancing progressive interpretations of the Qur'an and the *hadiths*.[6] In line with the work of other transnational human rights networks (Keck and Sikkink 1998), WLUML's approach also focused on solidarity and support for activists, by connecting women with other Muslims. This provided both practical support as well as countering the fundamentalist insistence that feminism and human rights were 'Western' and 'un-Islamic' (Hoodfar 1998: 7). The core of WLUML's approach continues to be the provision of information about the diversity of laws and customs and alternative systems of justice within Muslim contexts that may empower women to contest dominant interpretations of Islamic law. In 2010, it launched an online peer-review publication, *Contestations*, in order to provide a platform for engaging in discussions and analysis of gender justice, women's rights, and sexuality.

This exchange of information seeks to disrupt the fundamentalist claim that certain practices are essential to religious belief, for example, by showing that practices such as female genital mutilation are not essential to Islam but, rather, vary by time and location. Similarly, exposing diversity in the areas of reproductive rights and family law has also 'enabled women to disentangle the complex threads of religion, custom, and law' (Balchin 2002: 128). As one WLUML member, Margot Badran, observes, seeing the variety of Muslim laws for themselves helps women to distinguish between patriarchy and religion (Badran 1988). To strengthen transnational solidarity, WLUML also provides training for activists, as well as support for 'shared lived experiences through exchanges,' promoting 'face-to-face interaction between women from the Muslim world who would normally not have a chance to travel and meet with women from other, culturally diverse, Muslim societies' (Shaheed 1994: 8). These exchanges aim to break women's isolation and undermine the claims of fundamentalists that there is just one way of being Muslim.

WLUML aims to challenge not only a fundamentalist view of religion, but also law and the international community's tendency to defer to a 'homogeneous view of Muslim laws' and of Muslim identity (Hélie 2000). For example, in its third Plan of Action (1986), WLUML condemns the media for giving 'a platform to fundamentalists as the sole representatives of Muslims' (WLUML 1997) WLUML challenges dichotomous and monolithic views of religion and culture and their relationship to rights and bridges the deficiencies of the strategies and choices offered by traditional human rights law. In underlining the centrality of rights and culture to the achievement of rights, WLUML also stresses that religion and culture are plural and contested, and contingent on the constructions individual members themselves forge.

The second key element of WLUML's work focuses on encouraging women to construct their own identities as women and claim their own interpretations of religion and law, based on an exchange of information with people inside and outside the Muslim world. In its report, *Laws, Initiatives in the Muslim World* (1998), WLUML explains that 'the essential issue is who has the power to define what women's identities should be ... It is time to challenge—both politically as well as personally—those who define what the identity of women should be as Muslims' (WLUML 1998: 24). To this end, WLUML seeks to provide resources for women to 'create [their] own identity,' prompting them to engage critically in both religious and secular norms, and building networks so that other women may function 'as alternative legitimising reference points for each other' (WLUML 1998: 46). One effort towards disrupting essentialising constructions of Muslim women has been to collect and share historical examples of women's rights activism in the Muslim world. According to one activist, this was based on the idea that 'it was very important for women from the community to claim feminists from their own culture, and from their personal lives (stories about grandmothers and so on)' (Hélie, cited in Sunder 2003: 1438)

At the core of WLUML's platform for action is the disruption of a reductive depiction of Muslim women's identity, both in fundamentalist and secular terms, and the claim that women must be empowered to shape their own identity and cultures. By refuting the dichotomous separations of rights and religion, private and public, WLUML's confrontation with human rights law centres on the claim that, in order to have more freedom in all aspects of their lives, women must have the right to articulate freedom and equality within the context of a normative (i.e. religious and/or cultural) community, and to vernacularise rights on their own terms.

Sisterhood Is Global Institute and the Claiming Our Rights *manual*

For many Muslim activists and scholars, the major obstacle to the diffusion of the concepts and development of women's human rights is 'a lack of work on identifying and developing culturally relevant language' to convey to Muslim women the message of international human rights documents (Afkhami and Vaziri 1996: 11). On this basis, SIGI, an international women's rights non-governmental organisation with consultative status to the UN and founded in 1984 by feminists Robin Morgan and Simone de Beauvoir, began to develop a resource that would 'utilize indigenous ideas, concepts, myths and idioms to explain and support the rights contained in international documents' (Afkhami and Vaziri 1996: 1). Following on from a meeting of representatives from sixteen Muslim countries regarding strategies for improving women's human rights in their regions in 1995, *Claiming Our Rights: A Manual for Women's Human Rights Education in Muslim Societies* aimed to facilitate the transmission of international human rights law to women in Muslim communities. As Sunder explains, the Manual's goals were both strategic and normative. Strategically, *Claiming Our Rights* sought to facilitate the transmission of international human rights law to local Muslim communities, while effectively answering the claim that universal rights are not relevant to Muslim women. Normatively, the Manual would challenge the supposed 'incompatibility of religion and rights.'

(Sunder 2003: 1445)

The *Manual's* approach to rights translation is premised on the understanding that 'universal human rights are consonant with the spirit of Islam' (Afkhami and Vaziri 1996: 3) Like the work of WLUML, the *Manual* reconceives rights as also relevant in religious and cultural spheres, not just in the public sphere. Drawing on stories, texts, idioms, folklore, and other examples from Islamic cultural and religious life, along with specific religious texts, international human rights texts are brought into dialogue with Islamic cultures. This approach aids in translating the abstract content of international rights to a local idiom. The right of equality, for example, as contained within international human rights texts, is engaged through reflection on a *hadith* from the Prophet Muhammad, which states that '[a]ll people are equal, as equal as the teeth of a comb' (SIGI 1996: 16). Women consider the meaning of equality through discussion of the Prophet's recorded statement that '[t]here is no claim of merit of an Arab over a non-Arab, or of a white over a black person, or of a male over a female' (SIGI 1996: 16). On the issue of domestic violence, the *Manual* offers a verse from the Qur'an that states that '[i]f a wife fears cruelty or desertion on her husband's part, there is no blame on them if they arrange an amicable settlement between themselves' (SIGI 1996: 27).

Rather than providing literalist translations without further commentary, the *Manual* emphasises both the contestability of religious laws and interpretations along with their complexity and multiplicity, in order to engage women in discussing and critiquing the discourses of rights, culture, and religion (Sunder 2003: 1448). To this end, the *Manual* juxtaposes texts that support women's human rights with religious and cultural texts that challenge women's equality and the rights expressed in international law. On the subject of women's right to choose whom to marry, for example, the *Manual* juxtaposes an international legal text stating that '[m]arriage shall be entered into only with the free and full consent of the intending spouses' with conflicting religious texts (SIGI 1996: 19). Women are encouraged to discuss how these contests relate to rights, in light of these multiple and often conflicting texts, alongside their own needs and aspirations (Sunder 2003: 1445).

Like WLUML's documents/dossiers, the *Manual* emphasises the importance of Muslim women's ability to construct identity and conceptions of rights on their own terms. As Sunder explains, 'the Manual's approach is premised on this notion: Individuals are not taught "truths" written in international law, but rather are empowered to construct their own version of the truth—be it in a cultural, religious, or public context' (Sunder 2003: 1452). It therefore takes rights claims and makes them relevant to women's lives, both private and public. The *Manual* uses hypotheticals, role playing, and storytelling to enable women to construct a dialogue and negotiate the tensions between Muslim traditions, international human rights concepts, and evolving notions of gender equality. These exercises are intended to empower women to engage in dialogue and create their own meanings and interpretations regarding the 'relationship between a woman's basic human rights and her culture' (SIGI 1996: 12).

The *Manual* seeks to help individuals participate in 'defining the relevance and validity of ideas regardless of their source or age,' and states that the 'function of a human rights education model...is to promote "rights" by facilitating individuals' participation in the definition of law or truth' (Sunder 2003: 4). Co-author Afkhami says of the *Manual*:

> It's radical ... it is a new way of going the furthest that one can in allowing people to make choices and to have autonomous definitions of their identity, both spiritual and otherwise ... It allows people—for many, many millions for the first time—to think that it is possible to relate to God directly, to relate to culture directly, and to make their own sense of what it means.
>
> *(cited in Sunder 2003: 1453)*

Under this approach, rights are not imposed from outside or above a community, but rather are derived from the process of conflict negotiation by women within the community. In short, women's human rights are reconstructed through dialogue and participation—within one's cultural community and in the legal world of international human rights itself. It is only when women 'reclaim their own cultures, interpreting texts and traditions in self-empowering ways ... [that] women may truly claim their rights' (SIGI 1996: 9).

Conclusion

Despite the problems and paradoxes intrinsic to the discourse of human rights as outlined above, the utilisation of human rights in the pursuit of women's equality has also facilitated considerable gains. The language and law of rights have become an important resource for women throughout the world to demand justice on issues such as violence, sexual and reproductive health, sexuality, and discrimination. This chapter has examined how the rights-based efforts of transnational women's networks in the Muslim world have used translation practices to challenge gender and cultural essentialism, and the problematic dichotomy between gender and culture. Pushing against the masculinist and imperialist underpinnings of human rights discourse, these activists have navigated the discursive problems within rights discourse and re-framed rights through a local idiom in order to mobilise their potential. Utilising a diverse, inclusive approach to gender and culture to free it from the limitations of international rights discourse, Muslim women's activists are contesting fundamentalist and contemporary constructs of Muslim women's identity, transforming these constructs in the context of social movements. In so doing, advocacy for women's rights in the Muslim world signals a fundamental change in the conception of identity itself and stakes a new normative claim in the context of human rights: the right of women to define their identity themselves.

Related topics

Resistant Recipes; Citation and Recitation; Activist Translation, Alliances and Performativity

Notes

1 *Charter of the United Nations* (1945), articles 3, 10, 13(1)(b), 22, 55, 56, 58 and 62(2).
2 Despite some improvements, the grim reality is that women fare considerably worse than men on almost every indicator of social well-being, while discriminatory practices continue to 'put women at the risk of being subjected to abuse, violence and oppression, both inside and outside their homes' ('Statement by Louise Arbour, UN High Commissioner for Human Rights, on the occasion of the 8 Session of the Human Rights Council,' Meeting on Human Rights of Women, Geneva, 5 June 2008).
3 See, for example, *Convention Respecting the Laws and Customs of War on Land* (Hague Convention II), 29 July 1899, article 46.
4 See, for example, International Labor Organization, *Convention Concerning Night Work of Women Employed in Industry*, 1919 (Convention 4); International Labor Organization, *Convention Concerning the Employment of Women on Underground Work in Mines of All Kinds* 1935 (Convention 45); International Labor Organization, *Maternity Protection Convention* 1919 (Convention 3).
5 See, for example, *International Convention for the Suppression of the Traffic in Women and Children* 1921, 9 LNTS 415; *International Convention for the Suppression of White Slave Traffic* 1910, 1912 Gr Brit T S No.20 at 267.
6 *Hadith*s are a collection of the traditions or sayings of the Prophet Muhammad, revered and received as a major source of religious law and moral guidance, second only to the authority of the Qur'ān.

Further reading

Abu-Lughod, Lila (2015) *Do Muslim Women Need Saving?* Cambridge: Harvard University Press.

Addresses the potential of transnational advocacy networks for the diffusion of norms such as 'equality in the family' on a national as well as international basis.

Derichs, Claudia (2010) 'Transnational Women's Movements and Networking: The Case of Musawah for Equality in the Family,' *Gender, Technology and Development* 14 (3): 405–442.

Examines the assumptions and misconceptions about the role of Islam in women's lives in Muslim-majority countries.Explains how the negative and positive aspects of globalisation have helped to create transnational networks of activists and organisations with common agendas.

Kapur, Ratna and Brenda Cossman (1996) *Subversive Sites: Feminist Engagements with Law in India*. Thousand Oaks, CA: Sage Publications.

Provides a feminist analysis of the legal regulation of women in India, examining both the limitations and possibilities of the role that law can play.

Moghadam, Valentine M. (2005) *Globalizing Women. Transnational Feminist Networks*. Baltimore: Johns Hopkins University Press.

Explains how the negative and positive aspects of globalization have helped to create transnational networks of activists and organizations with common agendas.

References

Abu-Lughod, Lila (2015) *Do Muslim Women Need Saving?* Cambridge: Harvard University Press.
Afkhami, Mahnaz, and Haleh Vaziri (1996) *Claiming Our Rights: A Manual for Women's Human Rights Education in Muslim Societies*. Bethesda, MD: Sisterhood Is Global Institute.
Alarcon, Norma (1995) 'The Theoretical Subject(s) of This Bridge Called My Back and Anglo-American Feminism,' in *Making Face, Making Soul: Creative and Critical Perspectives by Feminists of Colour*. Ed. G. Anzaldua. San Francisco: Aunt Lute Press. 28–39.
Andrews, Penelope (1997) 'Violence against Aboriginal Women in Australia: Possibilities for Redress within the International Human Rights Framework,' *Albany Law Review* 60: 917–941.

Badran, Margot (1988) 'Islam, Patriarchy, and Feminism in the Middle East,' in *Women Living Under Muslim Laws* [online]. Available at: www.wluml.org/node/249 [accessed 12 August 2019].

Balchin, Cassandra (2002) 'The Network 'Women Living Under Muslim Laws': Strengthening Local Struggles Through Cross-Boundary Networking,' *Development* 45: 126–131.

Benhabib, Seyla (1994) 'Deliberative Rationality and Models of Democratic Legitimacy,' *Constellations* 1(1): 26–52.

Brown, Wendy (2000a) 'Suffering Rights as Paradoxes,' *Constellations* 7 (2): 208–229.

Brown, Wendy (2000b) 'Revaluing Critique: A Response to Kenneth Baynes,' *Political Theory* 28 (4): 469–479.

Coomaraswamy, Radhika (2002–2003) 'Identity Within: Cultural Relativism, Minority Rights and the Empowerment of Women,' *George Washington International Review* 34: 483–512.

Donnelly, Jack (1984) 'Cultural Relativism and Universal Human Rights,' *Human Rights Quarterly* 6 (4): 400–419.

Douzinas, Costas (2002) 'The End(s) of Human Rights,' *Melbourne University Law Review* 26: 445–465.

Edwards, Alice (2010) *Violence against Women under International Human Rights Law* Cambridge: Cambridge University Press.

Engle, Karen (1992) 'Female Subjects of Public International Law: Human Rights and the Exotic Other Female,' *New England Law Review* 26: 1509–1526.

Engle, Karen (2005) 'International Human Rights and Feminisms: When Discourses Keep Meeting' in *International Law: Modern Feminist Approaches*. Eds. D. Buss and A. Manji. Portland: Hart. 517–610.

Foucault, Michel (1980) *Power/Knowledge: Selected Interviews and Other Writings, 1972–1977*. Ed. and Tr. Colin Gordon. Brighton: Harvester Press.

Fraser, Arvonne (1999) 'Becoming Human: The Origins and Development of Women's Human Rights' *Human Rights Quarterly* 21 (4): 853–906.

Gaer, Felice D. (1998) 'And Never the Twain Shall Meet? the Struggle to Establish Women's Rights as International Human Rights,' in *The International Human Rights of Women: Instruments of Change*. Eds. C.E. Lockwood, D.B. Magraw, M.F. Spring and S.I. Strong. Washington DC: American Bar Association. 4–89.

Goodale, Mark (2007) 'Human Rights at the Crossroads' in *The Practice of Human Rights: Tracking Law between the Global and the Local*. Eds. M. Goodale and S. Engle Merry. Cambridge: Cambridge University Press. 111–121.

Hélie, Anissa (2000) 'Feminism in the Muslim World Leadership Institutes,' Center for Women's Global Leadership and Women Living Under Muslim Laws [online]. Available at: www.wluml.org/sites/wluml.org/files/import/english/pubs/pdf/misc/fmw-institute-eng.pdf [accessed 11 October 2019].

Hoodfar, Homa (1998) 'Muslim Women on the Threshold of the Twenty-First Century,' Center for Women's Global Leadership and Women Living Under Muslim Laws [online]. Availabel at: www.wluml.org/node/237 [accessed 11 October 2019].

Kapur, Ratna (2002) 'The Tragedy of Victimization Rhetoric: Resurrecting the 'Native' Subject in International/Post-colonial Feminist Legal Politics' *Harvard Human Rights Journal* 15 (1): 1–37.

Kapur, Ratna (2013) 'Unveiling Equality: Disciplining the 'Other' Woman through Human Rights Discourse' in *Islamic Law and International Human Rights Law*. Eds. A. Emon, M. Ellis and B. Glahn. Oxford: Oxford University Press. 265–290.

Keck, Margaret, and Katherine Sikkink (1998) *Activists beyond Borders. Advocacy Networks in International Politics*. Ithaca: Cornell University Press.

Levitt, Peggy, and Sally E. Merry (2009) 'Vernacularization on the Ground: Local Uses of Global Women's Rights in Peru, China, India and the United States' *Global Networks* 9 (4): 441–461.

Levitt, Peggy, and Sally E. Merry (2011) 'Making Human Rights in the Vernacular: Navigating the Culture/rights Divide' in *Gender and Culture at the Limit of Rights*. Ed. D. Hogdson. Philadelphia: University of Pennsylvania Press. 81–100.

Levitt, Peggy, and Sally E. Merry (2017) 'The Verncularisation of Women's Humans Rights,' in *Human Rights Futures*. Eds. S. Hopgood, J. Synder and L. Vinjamuri. Cambridge: Cambridge University Press. 213–236.

Mani, Lata (1998) *Contentious Traditions: The Debate on Sati in Colonial India*. Berkeley: University of California Press.

Merry, Sally E. (2006a) 'Transnational Human Rights and Local Activism: Mapping the Middle,' *American Anthropologist*, 108 (1): 38–51.

Merry, Sally E. (2006b) *Human Rights and Gender Violence: Translating International Law into Local Justice*. Chicago: University of Chicago Press.

Miller, Alice (2004) 'Sexuality, Violence against Women, and Human Rights: Women Make Demands and Ladies Get Protection' *Health and Human Rights* 7 (2): 16–47.

Mohanty, Chandra (1984) 'Under Western Eyes: Feminist Scholarship and Colonial Discourses' *Boundary 2* 12 (3): 333–358.

Mohanty, Chandra (2003) '"Under Western Eyes" Revisited: Feminist Solidarity through Anti-Capitalist Struggles,' *Signs* 28 (2): 499–535.

Narayan, Uma (1997) *Dislocating Cultures: Identities, Traditions, and Third-World Feminism*. New York: Routledge.

Oloka-Onyango, J., and Sylvia Tamale (1995) 'The Personal Is Political' or Why Women's Rights are Indeed Human Rights: An African Perspective on International Feminism,' *Human Rights Quarterly* 17 (4): 691–731.

Olsen, Frances (1990) 'Feminism and Critical Legal Theory: An American Perspective,' *International Journal of the Sociology of Law* 18: 199–224.

Otto, Dianne (2005) 'Disconcerting "Masculinities": Reinventing the Gendered Subject(s) of International Human Rights Law,' in *International Law: Modern Feminist Approaches*. Eds. D. Buss and A. Manji. Oxford: Hart. 105–129.

Otto, Dianne (2006) 'Lost in Translation: Re-Scripting the Sexed Subjects of International Human Rights Law,' in *International Law and Its Others*. Ed. A. Orford. Cambridge: Cambridge University Press. 318–356.

Otto, Dianne (2012) 'Gender Issues and International Human Rights: An Overview,' University of Melbourne Legal Studies Research Paper No. 606. [online]. Available at SSRN: https://ssrn.com/abstract=2154770 [accessed 18 August 2019].

Otto, Dianne (2013) 'International Human Rights Law: Towards Rethinking sex/Gender Dualism and Asymmetry,' in *The Ashgate Research Companion to Feminist Legal Theory*. Ed. V. H. Munro. London: Ashgate Publishing. 197–211.

Pardy, Maree (2013) 'Under Western Eyes Again? Rights Vernacular and the Gender Culture "Clash",' *Australian Journal of Human Rights* 19: 31–53.

Rosenblum, Darren (2011) 'Unsex CEDAW, or What's Wrong with Women's Rights,' *Columbia Journal of Gender and Law* 20(2): 1–65.

Scully, Pamela (2001) 'Vulnerable Women: A Critical Reflection on Human Rights Discourse and Sexual Violence,' *Emory International Law Review* 23 (1): 113–123.

Smart, Carol (1989) *Feminism and the Power of Law*. New York: Routledge.

Spivak, Gaytri (1988) 'Can the Subaltern Speak?' in *Marxism and the Interpretation of Culture*. Eds. C. Nelson and L. Grossburg. Urbana: University of Illinois Press. 271–315.

Spivak, Gaytri (2004) 'Righting Wrongs' *The South Atlantic Quarterly* 103 (2/3): 523–581.

Stivens, Maila (2001) 'Introduction: Gender Politics and the Reimagining of Human Rights in the Asia Pacific,' in *Human Rights and Gender Politics: Asia Pacific Perspectives*. Eds. A. Hilsdon, V. Mackie, M. Macintyre and M. Stivens. London: Routledge. 1–35.

Visweswaran, Kamala (2004) 'Gendered States: Rethinking Culture as a Site of South Asian Human Rights Work,' *Human Rights Quarterly* 26 (2): 483–511.

Volpp, Leti (2011) 'Framing Cultural Difference: Immigrant Women and Discourses of Tradition,' *Differences* 22 (1): 90–110.

Sunder, Madhavi (2003) 'Piercing the Veil,' *Yale Law School* 112: 1399–1472.

Shaheed, Farida (1994) 'Controlled or Autonomous: Identity and the Experience of the Network, Women Living under Muslim Laws,' *Signs* 19: 997–1019.

WLUML (1986) *Aramon Plan of Action*. London: Center for Women's Global Leadership and Women Living Under Muslim Laws.

WLUML (1997) 'Dhaka Plan of Action,' Center for Women's Global Leadership and Women Living Under Muslim Laws [online]. Available at: www.wluml.org/node/451 [accessed 11 October 2019].

WLUML (1998) *Laws, Initiatives in the Muslim World*. London: Center for Women's Global Leadership and Women Living Under Muslim Laws.

Part VI
Translating the vernacular

20

Against a single African literary translation theory

Mukoma Wa Ngũgĩ

Introduction: limiting the infinite in African translation

Given the number of languages and cultures, different histories either before or after the advent of colonialism, and uneven support of African languages in individual countries such as Kenya and Tanzania, anything loosely termed African translation will have to flow in a myriad of ways. We must not have an African theory of translation but rather a plethora of translation theories that are particular in part or in whole to African languages. Nevertheless, as with anything of infinite possibilities, it is crucial to capture or frame some foundational principles that make discussion possible, that serve as a starting point.

The first principle, which will help make the debate manageable, is that at a minimum three kinds of translation exist in relation to African languages: where the African language is the source and therefore translation flows outwards; where the African language is the target and the source a language outside of the continent; or where the act of translation is between African languages. Translating into and between African languages suffers from the worst kind of neglect— very few translators are translating into and between African languages, and even fewer have attempted to particularise translation theory to African languages.

The second of these principles, closely interacting with the first, is that each act of African translation will have a set of problems that are universal to any translator no matter what language or flow of translation. This is to say that there are problems a translator between French and Italian faces and the African translator in any of the above three configurations will also face. For example, lack of equivalents, or in the case of poetry, lack of corresponding form—the questions of whether to engage in a metaphrase, a literal phrase-for-phrase translation, and when do what John Dryden calls an *imitation*,[1] 'where the translator … assumes the liberty not only to vary from the words and sense but to forsake them both as he sees occasion' (2000 [1680]: 146).

The third principle is that a target language related to but distinct from the source language will behave differently in an act of translation than when it is not related to the source language. Each act of translation will raise a different set of problems and call for different solutions. When translating between Kiswahili and isiXhosa, the problems and solutions will be different from those faced when translating between isiXhosa and English. This is to say that linguistic features such as morphology are very much at play.

Due to Africa's historical relationship to the world, there is a fourth organising principle. Translating, in a situation where one language has a history of imperial domination and the other of resistance, is also a political act. African translation theory has to look at questions of language power relations in this age of globalisation, the question of imperial versus resisting languages. In short, translation is a dynamic act in which the living historical questions determine what is being translated, into what language, and the process, which is to say the nature of the act of translation itself.

Knowledge production and translation

The theory that underpins Walter Rodney's *How Europe Underdeveloped Africa* also informs African translation. European languages in the African continent and in Europe developed at the direct expense of African languages—and knowledge produced by Africans has traditionally flown one way—Africa to Europe, through translation. Novels, philosophies, and systems of thought are translated into European languages. But seminal European philosophers, writers, and scientists are not translated into African languages; their ideas remain sealed in languages that only the African elite have access to. The majority of the African population in this exchange has served as a laboratory for others: cultures studied and quantified, needles poked into bodies to extract medical data, and labour and raw materials converted into European goods.

Language was used by colonialism to discipline. By divorcing the African from his or her culture, access to the world through one's own lens was also lost. In the colonial framework, African languages had no political, scientific, or economic function. The only participation possible in the political, scientific, and economic colonial worlds was through mastering the colonising language. As European languages became the containers of new scientific and philosophical knowledge, African languages were in an agonising process of atrophy. They became social languages spoken in the privacy of homes and at social events. As the relationship between African and European languages continued through neocolonialism and now globalisation, African languages found that the world had left them behind. Therefore translating, let's say, a science fiction novel that uses pedestrian physics on time travel into Gikuyu will require much more invention and coinage of new words than it would if I was translating it into a European language which has from the beginning kept up with scientific debates—to put it simply, quantum physics as a discipline simply does not exist in the Gikuyu language. This is not an immutable condition: Gikuyu language, as a result of history, and a carefully designed policy that promoted English over African languages, is behind existing knowledge.

Therefore, the magnitude of the problem facing African translators should not be hidden behind the argument that the lack of equivalents is a problem that exists between all languages. If I want to translate Stephen Hawking's rather accessible physics book, *A Brief History of Time* (1988), having never read a physics, chemistry, or philosophy book in Gikuyu, I will run into problems that a translator of the text into German will not. The German language has been keeping up with new theories and inventions.

Gikuyu has not—new knowledge, say about quantum computers, for the Gikuyu speaker is stored in the English language.

Again, this is not to suggest that African languages do not have the capacity to carry scientific knowledge, but to point out that translating into an African language will require more than fluency and the target-language dictionary. Some words and concepts, depending on the text, simply do not exist. Every translator, no matter the language, faces this problem. But for the translator translating into an African language, the gaps will be much larger and, perhaps in this regard, the African translator should ideally have a community of other translators and native speakers to constantly fall back upon. The whole colonial enterprise wanted to fossilise African languages—it did not quite succeed—and therefore the translator has much to work with. But nevertheless, out of languages whose speakers have been convinced they cannot carry physics or medical terms, the translator must convince them that it is indeed possible.

In the coinage and invention of words, an act that languages naturally perform as they engage the world around them, an act that is constantly undermined when it comes to African languages for any number of reasons, the translator has to make sure the translated text is intelligible. The translator's mandate is not to create a new language, but rather have the translated text fit intelligibly in the target language. The translator therefore has to keep checking with others. Can *kahinda gakunje* (literally 'folded' time in Gikuyu) mean 'time warp' or is it too much of a stretch? Would it in fact sound ridiculous to the Gikuyu ear? Are there philosophical concepts that perhaps can convey the idea of time warp? Conversely it will require updating words in the African language to carry multiple meanings. In Kiswahili the word *mtandao* means 'internet' as well as 'spider web.' Here, a word with one meaning now has another.

The will, and it is nothing if it is not first a will, to do justice by African languages, to pour new wine into old skin by giving old words new meanings, to improvise and to learn through trial and error, to hold up the least-spoken languages to imperial languages, is a political act.

The politics of translating inter-African languages

For most peoples, the idea that you can have a national literature expressed in the former coloniser's language is strange, to say the least. The Chinese would laugh at the idea of a national literature in Japanese. But not only has the idea of a national literature in English or French been accepted, writing in an African language is actively resisted. Therefore, an African translator translating into an African language has to fight the same battles and counter the same arguments as a writer who is writing in an African language. That is, translating into an African language makes for a small market and promotes ethnic chauvinism while the European language promotes national reconciliation (if one forgets colonialism and global imperialism), and the arguments continue. Translating between African languages ironically requires fewer resources since most Africans speak more than two languages. African translation as a literary field will not lack for candidates.

This resistance to working in African languages has an immediate and pragmatic problem. In a continent that intellectually mimics Europe, a translator who takes the leap might find a publisher who is willing to publish a translated work of Shakespeare or Wordsworth, itself an important accomplishment. But a translation from, let's say, a text in Spanish, Hindi, or Chinese into Kiswahili or Kikuyu will not find a publisher. Neither will the African translator translating between two African languages. The works of Masizi Kunene, the late South African poet, will not exist in Gikuyu, for example, because no publisher will touch such a translation. By the same token there is very little literary criticism being produced in African languages. Thus, the writer, the critic, the reader, and the publisher, the educational and political system are all complicit in the atrophying of African languages. Yet, just like the few writers, literary critics, publishers, and starved readers who are slowly expanding the playing field for African languages, the translator simply has to jump in with both feet. The translator makes possible what the African writer or critic cannot. African translators translating a single text across multiple languages make possible conversations across multiple African cultures.

Translating between African languages involves concerns that are shared by all translators. But these concerns become peculiar by virtue of taking different shades depending on which of the three political acts (from, to, and inter-African languages) of translating the African translator engages in. One concern might diminish while another is heightened. In order to highlight the often glossed over differences, let us look at how these principles interact with one another in the translating of two well-known poems, '*Titi La Mama*' (1947) by the Kiswahili poet, Shaaban Robert, from Kiswahili into English, and Kiswahili into Gikuyu, and 'Harlem' (1951), by African American poet Langston Hughes from English into Gikuyu (Mazrui 2007). These two poems—short, deceptively simple, accessible, and aesthetically beautiful—are widely popular in their respective orbits. Following the analysis are the original poems and their translations as well as literal translations (trots).

Translating three ways—Kiswahili into Gikuyu and English into Gikuyu and Kiswahili into English

A superficial separation between the social context that produces the poem (what for the duration of this essay I will call the *under-text*) and the language and words contained in the text allows us to tease out the differences in the three types of African translation outlined at the beginning. A poem does not exist in and of itself; the times the poem is written in and the times in which the poem is read shape its meaning. Therefore, the culture that produces the poem and the culture into which the poem is translated will influence the choices the translator makes. Anyone in the United States reading Langston Hughes's 'A Dream Deferred' (1951: Hughes 2020) today will not help but hear echoes of Martin Luther King Junior's 'I Have a Dream' (2013) speech, even though it was delivered seventeen years after the poem was written (King 2013). The poem and the speech have become intertwined in a common tapestry of continuing African American marginalisation—the continued deferment of freedom. Time has added another layer of complexity to the poem. Time and space are therefore factors that will influence the choices the translator makes.

In a move that appears counter-intuitive, to translate the poem into Gikuyu the translator does not need Vladimir Nabokov's mountain of footnotes to carry the history and social context in which the poem was written. The poem resonates with the same collective tragedy in Gikuyu. The trials and tribulations of Kenyans with colonialism and neocolonialism make the poem immediately accessible. A shared history of radicalised oppression in the forms of colonialism and segregation has made Gikuyu and African American cultures mutually intelligible. However, for the same poem in a European language, where this historical context is remote, where African/African American suffering isn't part of that society's undercurrent, footnotes might be needed in order for the reader to grasp or tap into the full tragedy of the poem.

But what happens to the under-text, the living history of '*Titi La Mama,*' when I translate it from Kiswahili into Gikuyu? A contemporary poem in that it was written in the 1960s, the main worry for the translator becomes the question of sound. Because both languages live next to each other, are close together in the Bantu family of languages, the task of the African translator will have more to do with the internal workings of the poems as opposed to the under-text that informs the original. An example will suffice: When translating into English, the word *mbwa* (in the context of the poem meaning female dog) becomes 'sow.' The translator does not want the word 'bitch,' the correct translation, for obvious reasons. In the Kiswahili original, dog is used to show that even in the lowliest and dirtiest of animals, puppies will love the mother's milk. But in an English context, where dogs are loved as pets, the contrast loses its power. When translating the poem into Gikuyu, *mbwa* becomes *ngui*, in Gikuyu thus keeping the shock entailed in/evoked by the contrast alive. This is because to call someone a dog in both languages is to insult them—that is to see them as subhuman, beggarly, and a strain on society.

In the Gikuyu translation of the Kiswahili poem, the under-text, much like in the case of 'A Dream Deferred,' is not lost. Readers who have not lost a language might not grasp the extent of the tragedy. A culture that is imperialist will not allow the poem in without wanting to ingest it and spit out a translation that has at least been made palatable. The English language resists the Kiswahili poem because the historical context is lost, and it can only be impervious to it. The poem in the original language does not need to mention colonialism, or the civilising missions that denigrated African cultures, that loved the caricatures it produced; the poem's edifice is this history itself.

A good Gikuyu translation will not need to hit the reader over the head with living history, colonialism, and the psychosis of it. The psychosis of loving someone else's mother is the template. Immediately I mention language and mother, a history of loss has been tapped. Thus, the title of the Gikuyu translation, *Iria ria Ma itu* ('The milk of our truth,' and at the same time, 'My mother's milk'), is a choice made purely because *Runyondo rwa Nyina/Maitu* (A/My Mother's Breast) sounds terrible even when it conveys the same meaning as '*Titi La Mama.*' The English translation, in order to carry the politics, has to do more work. Hence the title changes from *A Mother's Breast* to 'Kiswahili' in order to hint at the politics of language. Words like 'salve' and 'wounds' are used to contain this history. Because history has done this work for it, the poem can go on to do other things, like create beauty through intricate sound patterns.

In translating the poem from Kiswahili into English, sound is sacrificed for meaning. However, because both Kiswahili and Gikuyu share the same phonology, alliteration, cacophony, or other manipulations of sound are easy to maintain. In terms of sound, the Gikuyu translation is more faithful than the English translation. In fact, once the Kiswahili original establishes the history of colonialism and the politics of language, it runs on the beauty of sound. In this regard, it is not a cerebral poem: you do not think of its meaning, you hear it first. From the very start, with the high conga sounds of *Titi la mama litamu hata*, beauty is being woven through sound.

It is this beauty that the English version loses with the awkward but necessary 'a mother's breast.' The Gikuyu translation might sound harsh to the English ear, perhaps even to the Kiswahili ear. But standing alone, it does weave intricate sounds as a result of the linguistic features that flow with Kiswahili—such as concord noun agreements. In both languages, the linguistic features contribute to the overall meaning of the poem—beauty and intricacy of language.

There are other things that the Gikuyu translation can do better than the English translation—it can borrow and easily own Kiswahili words. The Gikuyu word for perfume is *maguta magutaririka*, which would be too heavy for this translation. But there is another Gikuyu word that was borrowed from Kiswahili which is commonly used for perfume—*maraci*. Because of the linguistic structure, Kiswahili lends itself more easily to being owned by Gikuyu.

Because the complexity of the poem lies in the under-text of a complex social world, and the words that are on the surface weave beauty through sound, translating in English risks either fossilising the poem or infantilising it. In short, translating the words on their surface without translating the roots infantilises the poem. There is a difference here between simplicity and regressing the poem. Both poems, '*Titi La Mama*' and 'A Dream Deferred,' run on simplicity—the words are easily accessible, the images are practically everyday. But they are also very complex poems that use the familiar to defamiliarise the reader into looking at the world anew. Yet in the English translation, the following line—'A mother's breast is the sweetest, a sow it may be'—risks becoming something other than the first line in the Kiswahili original. In the Gikuyu translation of '*Titi La Mama*,' even if some of the grace is inevitably lost, the complexity is not lost. Whereas the Hughes poem does not lose its grace of simplicity or get transposed into another historical era when translated into Gikuyu because it finds an equally complex if different social under-text, '*Titi La Mama*'s translations into English border on being terrible—some use 'thou' and 'thee' when addressing the language, thus turning the poem into a biblical relic.

The point here is not to suggest that the Kiswahili poem is not translatable into English—far from it. For the non-African English speaker, the poem stands on its own. It will have its own aesthetic and political beauties. The English translation does in some instances defamiliarise such a reader with ideas and concepts such as 'sow's breast' or milk. By the same token it challenges the English reader to think about other languages and English itself. And that is as it should be. Chaucer wrote the *Canterbury Tales* against the high tides of Latin and French. English in the 13th and 14th century was the sow's milk, unwanted, bitter, disgusting, uncivilised to drink, but writers like Chaucer insisted that it was sweeter to the native speaker than French and Latin. English did not come into its own until Romanticism and, even then, it still had its own share of detractors who wistfully looked back to the days of Latin and French.

The point then is not to value one kind of translation over another, or one language over another, which has indeed been the colonial project, but rather to value all languages through translations that flow freely from and into multiple languages. This also calls for welcoming translation theories that recognise different cultures are at the end of the day mutually intelligible and that translation is an act that allows us to tap into that mutuality. Consequently, such theories will recognise the universality and peculiarities of the translator's task depending on the languages in conversation. To put it differently, if for Walter Benjamin (2000), 'translation's ultimate purpose is to express the innermost relation between languages,' translators of African literature have the ultimate duty of translating the innermost relations between cultures.

The task of the African translator

The task of the African translator, which is to contribute to the growth of African languages, at minimum, can therefore be seen as setting out to accomplish four main tasks:

1) Translating between African languages. In translating inter-African languages, there must be a recognition that different African languages will call for different approaches. In addition to universal questions such as those of equivalence and compensation, there will be other sets of questions depending on how close, linguistically and socially, the source language is to the target language.
2) Putting African languages in conversation with other languages that offer a historical and political solidarity, e.g. Spanish, Kannada, Hindi, Urdu, Chinese, or Vietnamese. For example, there is no reason why Gabriel García Márquez's *One Hundred Years of Solitude* should not be translated into Kiswahili or Gikuyu.
3) Translating from European languages into African languages—so that other forms of knowledge are stored and accessed in an African language. There is of course a crucial point here which relates to how we choose what to translate and what not to translate. A translator who relies on a British or United States literary canon that sidelines black and brown voices means that translated works and theories that emanate from that will carry the biases. And be less historically and political useful to African readers. Thus, the translator will translate different peoples' literatures, including those of African Americans (say, Toni Morrison or James Baldwin), Native Americans (Louise Erdrich or James Welch) and women writer-activists (Angela Davis or Audre Lorde).
4) Contributing to the growth of African translation theories. The African translator should also consider while translating how the choices he or she is making are applicable outside the work at hand—and how they can be systematised. For example, Jalada Collective, a group of young African writers, took a short story, 'Ituĩka Rĩa Mũrũngarũ,' (2019) written by African writer Ngũgĩ Wa Thiong'o in Gikuyu and had it translated into 85 languages, half of them African. This is a treasure trove for translators as two questions immediately emerge—in this digital age, what does this project add to our understanding of translation theory? And how is translating between African languages different from translating from African language into European or Asian languages?

The act of translating African literature is a political act. The task of the African translator is therefore political.

Poems: originals and translated[2]
Titi la Mama
Shaban Robert
Titi la mama litamu, hata likiwa la mbwa,
Kiswahili naazimu, sifayo iliyofumbwa,
Kwa wasiokufahamu, niimbe ilivyo kubwa,
Toka kama mlizamu, funika palipozibwa,
Titile mama litamu, Jingine halishi hamu.
Lugha yangu ya utoto, hata sasa nimekua,

Tangu ulimi mzito, sasa kusema najua,
Ni sawa na manukato, moyoni mwangu na pua,
Pori bahari na mto, napita nikitumia,
Titile mama litamu, jingine halishi hamu.

Kiswahili

A mother's breast is sweet to her young. Even a sow's!
My mother-tongue I declare—I will sing of your brightness
to the blind and those who have long forgotten you. Mother,
feed, flow, salve our wounds and unclog our choking veins.
A mother's breast is sweet, another simply will not fulfil
Mother, as a child my tongue was weighed down. Now
that I can speak I see you were all around me, a perfume
to my heart and senses. Whether through the wilderness,
the river Nile or the Indian ocean—Mother, you carry me across.
My mother's breast is sweet, another won't satisfy my longing

Iria ra Maitu

Runyondo rwa maitu rwi-cama. Ona rwi rwa ngui
Githweri nindatua, ndoiga kuri matarakuriririkana
nguina uria uwega muhithe, uria wi munene
Maitu tiririka, uma tari mukiha uhature kuria kuhingikite
Runyondo rwa maitu, rwi muriyo rungi rutininaga thuti
Kuma rurimi rwakwa rwi rurito ndi mwana, nginyagia riu
ndakurire na kwaria ni njui, ruthiomi rwakwa nita
maraci magicanuka kana magitararika ngoroini
Weruini kana gatagati ka iria, ningithagio ni we.
Runyondo rwa maitu rwi muriyo, rungi rutinginina thuti

Harlem

Langston Hughes
What happens to a dream deferred?
Does it dry up
like a raisin in the sun?
Or fester like a sore—
And then run?
Does it stink like rotten meat?
Or crust and sugar over—
like a syrupy sweet?
Maybe it just sags
like a heavy load.
Or does it explode?

Mwihoko Wa Gwitiriria

Mwihoko ungiitererithio ri
Ni kii gikikaga?

No kuma na kugoda
ta thabibu riyuaini?
Kana ni kuhoha ta kironda
nginya ukoimia mahira?
Utararikaga ta nyama buthu
Kana umaga kuma
Ta ngogoyo nduru?
Kana mwihoko uhohaga
Ta murigo muritu?
Kana, ni ututhukaga?

Kiswahili/Gikuyu/English trots: 'A Mother's Breast' and \'A Dream Deferred'
Titi la Mama
Runyodo rwa nyina
A mother's breast
Titi la mama litamu, hata likiwa la mbwa,
Runyondo rwa nyina rwi-cama ona rwi rwa ngui
Breast of mother is sweet even if a dog's
Kiswahili naazimu, sifayo iliyofumbwa,
Githweri nindatua wega waku muhithe
Kiswahili I have decided wellness yours hidden
Kwa wasiokufahamu, niimbe ilivyo kubwa,
Kuri matarakuririkana, nguina uria wi munene
To those not remember you sing how it is big
Toka kama mlizamu, funika palipozibwa,
Uma tari mukiha kunika kuria kuhithe
Come like vein close/undo where it is covered
Titile mama litamu, Jingine halishi hamu.
Runyondo rwa nyina rwi muriyo rungi rutininaga thuti
Breast of mother is sweet, another does not finish desire
Lugha yangu ya utoto, hata sasa nimekua,
Ruthiomi rwakwa ndi mwana ona riu ndimukuru
Language mine of child even now I am old
Tangu ulimi mzito, sasa kusema najua,
Kuma rurimi rurito riu kwaria ni njui
Since tongue heavy now speak I know
Ni sawa na manukato, moyoni mwangu na pua,
Ni undu umwe/na ngoroini yakwa na maniuru
Same as perfume heart in mine and nose
Pori bahari na mto, napita nikitumia,
Weruini kana mayini, niingaga ngikuhuthira
In the wilderness or ocean I cross using you
Titile mama litamu, jingine halishi hamu.
Runyondo rwa nyina rwi muriyo rungi rutininaga hamu
Mother's breast is sweet, another does not finish longing

A Dream Deferred

Mwihoko Wa Gwitiririo
What happens to a dream deferred?
Nikii gikikaga kwi kiroto/mwihoko murarie/mwitiririi
Does it dry up
Ni kuma umaga
like a raisin in the sun?
ta thabibu riyuaini?
Or fester like a sore—
Kana ni kuhoha ta kironda
And then run?
Arabu gigateg'era?
Does it stink like rotten meat?
Kana gitararikaga ta nyama buthu?
Or crust and sugar over—
Kana kiumaga kuma
like a syrupy sweet?
Ta ngogoyo nduru
Maybe it just sags
Kana kihohaga
like a heavy load.
Ta murigo muritu
Or does it explode?
Kana ni gituthukaga?

Related topics

The Single Most Translated Short Story in the History of African Writing; Theory, Practice, Activism; *Okyeame Poma*

Notes

1 Dryden, John (2000) 'Preface to *Ovid's* Epistles,' in *The Translation Studies Reader*. Ed. Lawrence Venuti. London: Routledge. 144–159.
2 All translations by Mukoma Wa Ngũgĩ.

Further reading

Bandia, Paul (2008) *Translation as Reparation: Writing and Translation in Postcolonial Africa*. Manchester: St. Jerome Publishing.

Bandia's contribution to the literary criticism of Europhone African literature from a translation perspective offers a ground-breaking exploration into African literatures and cultures and an important case study of the theory and practice of translation beyond Eurocentric models.

Inggs, Judith, and Libby Meintjes (eds.) (2009) *Translation Studies in Africa*. London and New York: Continuum.

This collection of essays on translation and interpreting in African contexts discusses the importance of translation in shaping African culture and history.

Jalada (2019) 'Jalada Translation Issue 1: Ngũgĩ Wa Thiong'o,' *Jalada* [online] 20 January. Available at: jaladaafrica.org/2016/03/22/jalada-translation-issue-01-ngugi-wa-thiongo/ [accessed 11 April 2019].

This first special issue from the literary journal *Jalada* gathers together translations of Ngũgĩ Wa Thiong'o's story, 'The Upright Revolution: Or Why Humans Walk Upright,' originally written in Gikuyu in 2012, into 88 mostly African indigenous languages. It offers an impressive example of African languages talking to each other through translation.

Ngũgĩ, Mukoma Wa (2018) *The Rise of the African Novel: Politics of Language, Identity, and Ownership*. Ann Arbor: University of Michigan Press.

This book situates African-language literatures of the late 1880s through the early 1940s in relation to the literature of decolonisation that spanned the following three decades. The author challenges the narrowing of the identities and languages of the African novel and writer that has affected writers in previous generations.

Thiong'o, Ngũgĩ Wa (2011 [1986]) *Decolonising the Mind: The Politics of Language in African Literature*. London: J. Currey; Portsmouth: NH: Heinemann.

Ngũgĩ Wa Thiong'o's best-known and most-cited collection of essays theorising linguistic decolonisation and stressing the importance of writing in indigenous languages for African writers.

References

Benjamin, Walter (2000 [1923]) 'The Task of the Translator,' in *The Translation Studies Reader*. Ed. L. Venuti. London: Routledge. 15–23.

Dryden, John (2000 [1680]) 'Preface to *Ovid's* Epistles,' in *The Translation Studies Reader*. Ed. L. Venuti. London: Routledge. 144–159.

Hawking, S. W. (1988) *A Brief History of Time: From the Big Bang to Black Holes*. Toronto: Bantam.

Hughes, Langston (2011) 'Harlem,' in *Selected Poems of Langston Hughes*. Ed. L. Hughes. Vintage. 46.

Hughes, Langston (2020) *The Collected Poems of Langston Hughes*. Vintage. 46.

King Jr, Martin Luther (2013) *The Essential Martin Luther King, Jr.: "I Have a Dream" and Other Great Writings*. Vol. 9. Beacon Press. 185–194.

Mazrui, Alamin M. (2007) *Swahili beyond the boundaries: Literature, language, and identity*. No. 85. Ohio University Press. 27–28

Ngũgĩ, Thiong'o Wa (2019) 'Jalada Translation Issue 01: Ngũgĩ Wa Thiong'o.' *Jalada Africa*, Jalada, 18 Dec. 2019, jaladaafrica.org/2016/03/22/jalada-translation-issue-01-ngugi-wa-thiongo/.

Robert, Shaaban (1947) 'Titi La Mama,' in *Pambo La Lugha*. Johannesburg: Witswatersrand UP.

Rodney, Walter (1974) *How Europe Underdeveloped Africa*. Washington: Howard University Press.

21

The single most translated short story in the history of African writing
Ngũgĩ wa Thiong'o and the Jalada writers' collective

Moses Kilolo

The story

'Ituĩka Rĩa Mũrũngarũ: Kana Kĩrĩa Gĩtũmaga Andũ Mathiĩ Marũngiĩ,' translated into English as 'The Upright Revolution: Or Why Humans Walk Upright,' is the single most translated short story in the history of African writing. It is a fable in the Kenyan language of Gikuyu about the human body, a contest between the parts of the human body, and why humans walk upright on their two feet instead of four limbs. The story has attracted many thematic analyses, from politics, philosophy, and psychology. However, Ngũgĩ wa Thiong'o once said that, beyond his fascination with dialectics, from Plato to Hegel, he simply wrote the fable 'Ituĩka Rĩa Mũrũngarũ' or 'The Upright Revolution' to be enjoyed as a story and not a treatise on politics and philosophy (Thiong'o 2016).

The fable begins by describing the rhythmic coordination and the cordial relationship between the legs and arms of the human body. Soon, other body parts begin to envy this union. The tongue suggests a wrestling match between the arms and the legs, a contest that is witnessed by the other creatures of the forest. Following this duel, the other body parts cannot determine who the winner is. In the end, they all decide they were a part of the same body, and united, they are stronger. It is this unity of the body parts that made man more human, compared to his animal cousins that rejected the upright revolution.

When he wrote the story in 2012, Ngũgĩ did not imagine that it would one day become the single most translated short story in the history of African writing. He wrote it only as a gift to his daughter for Christmas, and after it was read, the story was momentarily forgotten. Ngũgĩ first spoke about it on stage at the Moderna Museet auditorium during the 2016 Stockholm Literature.[1] When in 2015 he received a request from a group of young writers in Nairobi for a short story in Gikuyu for a possible pan-African translation project, he spent many sleepless nights crafting the perfect story. After many failed attempts, he remembered that he had stashed away 'The Upright Revolution,' a work written as a gift, as an act of unconditional love, and as part of a family tradition—the gift that would soon give him and millions of others so much joy.

I watched him and his family on Kenyan television in early 2015. While he shared many ideas on language and freedom, my mind drifted in and out of the Jalada Language and Translation project that we had been deliberating on. That night, on 6 June 2015, and after hurried contributions from members of the Jalada Collective, I wrote to his son Mukoma wa Ngũgĩ, asking him to pass a word to his father, about contributing to the issue. A few months later the translation issue was published.[2]

In those early days someone told me it was an exceptional achievement for a short story to be translated into a dozen languages. We had translated the story into 33 languages.[3] I do not come from a long tradition of scholars of literary translation, and so I could not assess the accuracy of his statement at the time. I could only say without a doubt that my activism for African languages with the Jalada Collective and beyond was beginning to take shape. Those words were a major compliment, and an encouragement given the work that we at Jalada had done around language, translations, and the use of digital resources. Following this breakthrough, Ngũgĩ himself said, 'I see your Jalada project as a literary melting pot where African languages meet in dialogue among themselves and with other languages including European and Asian ones. From our base we converse with the world' (N. Thiong'o, personal communication, 29 March 2016).

Jalada

Jalada is a pan-African collective of young African writers from across the African continent. I am a founding member and the immediate former managing editor. I conceived and birthed the inaugural Languages and Translations Issue, with contribution from the collective, and remain the project lead for the Jalada Language and Translation project.

The word *jalada* is a Swahili word for an archive or a case or folder for documents. To the collective, Jalada is a digital archive of stories. The seeds of what became Jalada were first planted in 2013, on the sidelines of a workshop convened at the British Council in Nairobi by renowned editor, Ellah Wakatama Allfrey. At the time, Ellah was the deputy editor of *Granta* magazine. She has since left *Granta* but became one of the board members of the Jalada Africa Trust. In that year, she ran the workshop alongside Adam Foulds and Nadifa Mohamed. The latter were featured in the 2013 spring issue of *Granta* magazine, dubbed 'Best of Young British Novelists.'[4]

It began as a conversation among participants about what we as young African creatives drawn from different geographical locations, including South Africa, Zimbabwe, Uganda, Nigeria, and Kenya, could do with the resources we valued: language, creativity, knowledge, and our web of connections. Thus, Jalada was born. In its early days it was largely a Google group, a kind of a virtual office linking voices across the continent. All you needed to do was post a message, and another member would take action. The internet became an enabler of collaboration and a resource in the production process of a digital *Jalada* magazine. It was the beginning of active involvement in both practical work and activism for pan-African interactive spaces for writing and translation.

Our first thematic issue tackled the underexplored subject of mental health within the African context. Titled *Sketch of a Bald Woman in the Semi-Nude and Other Stories*,[5] the e-anthology appeared on what was then jalada.org and has since been changed to jaladaafrica.org. It went live at midnight on 27 January 2014 and featured twelve short stories written and edited exclusively by the Jalada Africa founding members.

Our second anthology, *Sext Me Poems and Stories*,[6] was published on 10 June 2014 and focused on stories of fictionalised sexual experiences in ways that broke the implicit modesty of fictional boundaries for many African storytellers. We also did an anthology on Afrofutures, a publication that allowed us, as Africans, to capture multiple and alternative ways of imagining futures. Titled simply as *Jalada 02: Afrofuture(s)*,[7] it appeared online on 14 January 2015.

The translation issue

In December 2015, we embarked on a translation project with the aim of having one short story translated into as many languages as possible. Since March 2016, when we first published Ngũgĩ wa Thiong'o's story 'Ituĩka Rĩa Mũrũngarũ: Kana Kĩrĩa Gĩtũmaga Andũ Mathiĩ Marũngiĩ,'[8] the story has been translated into 92 languages. The story was originally written in Gikuyu, the most widely spoken language in Kenya after English and Kiswahili. In my introduction to the issue I wrote[9]:

> Following Jalada's ground-breaking emphasis on translation in African Languages in its 2015 Language Issue,[10] we reached out to Ngũgĩ wa Thiong'o who graciously agreed to send us a previously unpublished story for our inaugural Translation Issue. Professor wa Thiong'o is uniquely placed to be the first distinguished author and intellectual featured in our periodical translations issue. He has, for many years, been the most vocal proponent in publishing in African languages.

Ngũgĩ, who is Kenya's best-known author and a contender for the Nobel Prize in Literature, not only believed in the vision from the beginning but has continued to be its most vocal activist. In his seminal essay, 'The Politics of Translation: Notes Towards an African Language Policy,' Ngũgĩ described the work as astounding, and a rare feat. 'It is indeed rare for the publication of a story to become news, but several newspapers carried reports on the *Jalada* translation feat' (Thiong'o 2018). He observed that the issue, in a

> practical sense, made the arguments that … African languages have been and still are legitimate sources of knowledge; that thought can originate in any African language and spread to other African languages and to all the other languages of the world.
>
> *(Thiong'o 2018)*

The Jalada initiative has also been critically lauded as one of the most essential projects in fostering communication amongst readers and speakers of different languages across the globe. In the introduction to their book, Tendai Rinos Mwanaka, Wanjohi wa Makokha, and Upal Deb described the initiative as an important landmark in postcolonial studies that goes 'against the mainstream translation tendencies of working with European versus African languages only, it breaks and provides a fertile ground for academic inquiry and literary experimentation' (Mwanaka et al. 2018: xxi). Indeed, for the first time, a story originally written in an African language was appearing in translation into over 50 other African languages, as well as tens of others from around the world. The same sentiment was captured by Mukoma wa Ngũgĩ in his essay 'A Revolution in Many Tongues,' in which he stated:

> Translation between African languages has yet to be practiced and theorized into critical and popular acceptance. *Jalada* is undertaking both theory and practice and saying that African languages can talk with each other. Its call and answer send out a challenge to writers, scholars and publishers who see African languages in the service of the more useful English. Or conversely, those who understand translation as most desirable when coming from superior European languages into anaemic African languages desperately in need of Anglo-aesthetics transfusion.
>
> *(Ngũgĩ 2016; see Chapter 20)*

The translation did not take shape without its fair share of teething problems. As earlier stated, translation between African languages is still in its formative stages in the most part. Few people in target languages could use the Gikuyu original. Perhaps only the translation into Kimeru by Njagi Brian, edited by Ngartia J. Bryan, made direct reference to the Gikuyu original. Cognisant of this fact, we requested Ngũgĩ to give us an authoritative English translation. It was from this English translation that most other translations were done. However, also I reached out immediately to one of Jalada's dear friends, Edwige Renée Dro, an Ivorian writer, editor, and English-to-French translator for an authoritative French translation as well. French became an intermediary language between the English language and the translators from French West Africa. Ismaila Samba Traoré, the Bamanankan (Bambara) translator, made use of the French translation. The Lingala translation, done by the award-winning Congolese writer Richard Ali A Mutu, was also done from the French. In a similar vein, Khaloudy Mohamed Sa'eed and Abdillahi Raage from Somaliland preferred to translate the story from the Arabic translation. Neither was confident in their English but they were highly proficient in Arabic.

As the story travelled, challenges of orthography were also witnessed. A case that stood out was the Ewe translation. Though the translators did a commendable job, the editor noted some inconsistencies with the approved Ewe orthography. Not only did he meticulously edit the work, but he also shared the Ghanaian font with us. Without this special font, the work could not open properly on my computer. We were also forced to upload either a jpeg or PDF version of the translation. Several other languages did not have Roman scripts. Among these were Amharic, Arabic, Russian, Nepali, Kannada, Kazak, Marathi, Kurdish, Persian, and Malayalam. We were forced to publish some of these in PDF to maintain the integrity of the text which might have been distorted by html.

Under the umbrella of the powerful magic of storytelling, online publishing enabled different languages and cultures to find expression and converse with each other. The Jalada website (http://jaladaafrica.org/), where the story and its translations are published, acts as a portal to a multiplicity of languages wherein you can find languages about which you may never have heard. Because for us at Jalada we are keen on multiple narrative modes of textual and visual storytelling, the story is also made available in the form of podcasts and live multilingual dramatisations.

We conceptualised the *Jalada* translation issue with a specific focus on African languages. Each language represents a specific culture on the continent. From my own Kikamba language, largely spoken in eastern parts of Kenya, to Lingala in the Congo, Ngambai in Chad, Tamazight in Algeria, Wolof in Senegal, XiTsonga in Southern Africa, and many others from all parts of the continent, we brought together a beautiful mix that is representative of hundreds of millions of native speakers. Taken together, our continent is infinitely rich in its cultural resources. Over 2,000 languages exist across 54 nations. Imagine the monumental impact of a story in all these languages. Ngũgĩ's short story is only in 88 languages as of now, yet it stands as an immovable symbol. In history and in scholarship, it will stand as a testament to the fact that all languages are equal. The origins, the colour, and the number of people who use any specific language, and the standardisation of such a language or the lack thereof should not limit or determine our engagement with them. The coming together of all those languages, as was done by the *Jalada* translation issue, destroys any doubt that in our diversity immense beauty can be created with a great and lasting impact.

The *Jalada* translation issue was born from the firm faith that one day, whether during my lifetime or in the generations to come, one short story will exist in all African languages. I want to imagine that over the years the spill-over effect of this will transform our attitudes towards the use of our mother tongues and the languages that we learn from our neighbours through our daily interactions. I want to imagine the impact it might have on the access that our children have to texts written in all languages, especially the marginalised languages, such as Suba, El Molo, Sabaot, and tens of others in Kenya alone. We continually learn to reap from the resources that we have. One such irrefutable resource is the language of our mother tongues.

The illusion of a unifying language

Some of the distinctive African languages represented in the translation issue have suffered many years of non-representation in written form. There are worrisome statistics of the number of books or articles that have been published in these languages. Whenever I want to read a novel in my first language, Kikamba, for instance, it is almost impossible to find one in Nairobi bookstores. In many cases I turn to the Kamba Bible, perhaps the only most authoritative publication in that language, but telling stories that are alien to my culture. Indeed, across many countries and regions within the continent, this is the reality for thousands, tens of thousands, or millions of people, even though they use these languages every day. They transact businesses, they pray, they love, and dream of love and life in these languages, yet so little is written in them. Even more worrying is the small number of people who have access to these written resources. Most written material in African bookstores and libraries is in European languages—English, French, and Portuguese—as well as a few dominant African national languages such as Kiswahili, Hausa, and Zulu.

The illusion of unifying a nation through a single language is widespread, especially in Kenya. This has led to a deliberate marginalisation of African languages and an almost fierce emphasis on the spread and dominance of English or other European languages. We feed on that illusion instilled in us by our education systems, which were designed by European colonialists to serve their empires and then continued as desirable norms by postcolonial governments. There is a daily struggle from many quarters and initiatives to effect change in our school systems. As Hutchison (2006) argues, perhaps the most effective weapon against African-language marginalisation is African-language literature. More writing, more publishing, more teaching, and increased emphasis on education that is rich in maternal and first languages for young readers.

Although there is much cause for concern, the situation is changing for the better. Today, one does not need to go to a well-equipped library to see texts in other languages. You only need to log on to social media, and you will see the flow of conversations in all manner of languages, albeit unevenly. We do not have to look at that with suspicion. We do not have to feel hate and resentment for the existence of the other or feel burdened by the colonial idea that this is divisive. Over the years, I have noted how many young Nairobians flood institutions to learn European languages. Foreign cultural institutions such as Alliance Française and the Goethe-Institut dominate the field, teaching French and Germany respectively. Local centres in Nairobi such as Language Connections College, Kenya Institute of Foreign Languages, and the Language School all seem to be more focused on European languages. We marvel at the possibility of acquiring what is not necessarily ours. That in itself is a beautiful thing; all knowledge is power. However, most individuals learning these languages will never go to France or Germany. They will use that resource amongst themselves in a very small circle, or for employment purposes, such as to serve the occasional tourist or to work at one of the multinationals. Even worse, sometimes such a language is never used by the person who has studied it. It exists merely as a placeholder in a CV or for prestige, such as when someone mentions that they have studied this or that European language.

In their minds, these young Kenyan students are psychologically arrested by the desire to acquire foreign languages. They continually gravitate towards the European home of the new learned language. They will interact occasionally with speakers of other Kenyan languages, sometimes feeling at a loss if they cannot speak to one another without resorting to English and Kiswahili. What if that beautiful desire to learn and appreciate a foreign language was also directed towards other African languages? Only the ACK Language and Orientation School, according to its website,[11] offers language courses in almost all of Kenya's major languages. In the absence of adequate systems to facilitate this kind of interest, the online publishing of stories in different languages, multilingual performances, and podcasts done by Jalada makes a small but vital contribution. Not just for readers who want to read other languages, but also for Africans who have grown up with limited exposure to written texts in their mother tongue.

Practical vision

Ngũgĩ wa Thiong'o used the term 'practical vision' to describe the fresh opportunities for disseminating African literature that the digital age makes possible. Practical vision is about activating dreams in the present; it is about translating a vision that at first seems distant into a doing that makes the vision into a reality. We as the Jalada Collective envision building a multilingual future rooted in pride as regards our past and connections that know no boundaries among writers, publishers, and readers. We are able to move beyond mere conversations towards the execution of ideas because of our access to and connectivity with the internet, but this requires grit and a lot of help from all corners.

If we had edited the translation issue in the pre-internet age, it would have taken us decades and huge financial resources to put it together. The web of translators grew because of my colleagues and interested participants who encouraged others to contribute to the bringing together of 92 languages into one volume. The volume bears the hallmark of conversations among cultures, languages, and people of the world. Thanks to the generosity and time invested by the writers and translators we were able to do this work efficiently in less than a year.

Our ways of consuming information have changed radically since oral literature was shared around a bonfire in early evenings. As a publisher, the Jalada Collective therefore tries to understand the changing nature of communication and the resultant structures. We seek to take full advantage of digital technologies as this is the reality of our generation and of those to come.

Among the founding members of the Jalada Collective, Richard Oduor Oduku contributed a translation in Dholuo. The contribution was one of the most shared and read translations. Dholuo is a language largely spoken in the Lake Victoria region, in Kisumu County, Kenya. People from this area take immense pride as the ancestral home of Barack Obama and Lupita Nyong'o among other global icons. There was also a collaboration between two other founding members. Idza Luhumyo translated the story into Kiswahili, and Okwiri Oduor, winner of the prestigious Caine Prize in 2014, edited the translation. Abdul Adan worked closely with Marat Pussurmanov from Kazakhstan to realise the Kazak translation, a language that he was learning. In 2015, Adan had moved to Kazakhstan to teach English and learn Kazakh.[12] Mwangi Mahugu translated and recorded an audio into Sheng, an urban creole, originating among the urban lower class of Nairobi. Other founding members of the Jalada Collective, including Novuyo Tshuma, Richard Ali, Kate Hampton, Anne Moraa, Alexander Ikawah, Zak Waweru, and Kiprop Kimutai, either reached out to me with suggestions of translators or took to social media to make sure everyone in their networks knew about the exciting project. Wanjeri Gakuru, a Kenyan writer, film maker, and the current managing editor, who is not a founding member but joined us in the earlier years, also helped to spread the word. Marziya Mohammedali, Jalada's long-serving creative director, conceived and designed the flame images for the cover and constituent artwork (Figure 21.1). These have become almost synonymous with the translation issue.

Beyond the founding members, the inaugural Jalada translation issue saw hundreds of people participate as translators, editors, or even proofreaders. We knew that the translators who were part of the translation issue put themselves in the company of other translators making history. After we brought the translators together, their individual translational activism was amplified across the globe. Following the publication of the translation issue, we made a conscious decision to publish each translation on a single page. The language, name, and biography of the translators are listed in the credits. We do not discriminate according to age or background, nor require advanced experience in literary translation. The only requirement is the desire to produce authentic and verifiable translations that can communicate a story in one's own language. However, we check that translators are fluent in source and target language. In instances where new or younger translators struggled, we paired them up with experienced readers and editors for the best outcome. While translating the story to Lwisukha-Lwidakho, a dialect of the Luhya language in Western Kenya, Lutivini Majanja worked closely with her father as editor and proofreader. Neelofer Qadir, a PhD candidate in the Department of English at the University of Massachusetts Amherst, also worked closely with her mother and father to realise the Urdu translation. Collaborations in translating, editing, and proofreading were not only among family members, but also among friends and students with their teachers. And while we do not compensate financially for now, we are looking into funding possibilities and seeking to develop a financial model that would make our work sustainable. As we engage more and more translators, the network grows, and opportunities are spread across the team for the benefit of diligent translators.

Figure 21.1 Cover of the Jalada translation issue. Design by Marziya Mohammedali.
© 2016.

We continue to experiment with many more ways to tap into these digital technologies to share stories in all manner of African languages. Our current challenge is how to facilitate translations that allow a conversation between the languages of Africa and those of the world. Can we create digital publications that capture the infinite resources in our languages and cultures? To meet this challenge, we decided to select one short story of 3,000 words or less, short enough to ensure that the work involved in terms of translation would be feasible. The story had to be powerful enough to speak across multiple cultures. Our vision is to have each story translated into as many of the over 2,000 African languages as possible. One day, in the not so distant future, Jalada will have an online archive of stories and translations in all manner of languages. What we have now are anthologies and audio versions of stories that total up to 92 languages. More must be done to cover most of Africa.

When we started, our ambition was to have a translation issue every year. We would then allow continued translation of the story until we reached all the languages of the world—something that would have stretched the process long after we are dead and gone, a revolving project that would capture and retain the interests of those who come after us. While the second part—that is, the continued contributions—is working perfectly, the annual uptake of stories has yet to materialise. First, it requires a tremendous amount of work to get the translation project done. That is not a problem. Most of the work done in the inaugural translation project was based on volunteer efforts, including my own. Volunteer effort is neither sustainable nor appealing in the long term. We hope to raise funds for the second translation issue. In addition, the writers from whom we requested stories have, despite agreeing, not yet sent them. Now in our third year, we are still working on the first short story. This is neither a complaint nor a regret, for we have had the advantage of many wonderful lessons that have made our process even more effective. With time, of course, we find ourselves revising the plan, thinking of what works best.

Such a vision is not easy to implement. There are a great many misconceptions about African languages and their place in our personal and communal intellectual discourse. For instance, it is commonly held that Kenyans, and Africans in general, do not do much reading for pleasure. It is worse when it comes to reading literature in African languages. These notions fuel the misconception that a publisher would never put its resources into publishing a novel in an African language, for it would be a financial loss. The writer, in return, believes that wasting a few years writing a novel that would not find a publisher, and which in return would not find readers, is an injustice to themselves. What if we believed that we can simply write in the language we want? What if publishers took the risk, published these books, and marketed them among African-language speakers with as much zeal as English novels? What if parents read books in their mother tongues to their children? What if these parents bought these books, and encouraged those children to read? What if African governments put in more resources in the publishing, distribution, and teaching of books in African languages? Would we still believe that there are no readers?

In our contribution to improving the publication, as well as encouraging readership of works in African languages, we needed to lay a firm foundation for the future. First, we recognise that there are voices that have come before us that have already done a great deal to fight for language rights: writers and activists such as the Nigerian academics Abiola Irele, Charles Nnolim, Obiajunwa Wali, and Gabriel Ruhumbika as well as South Africa's Mazisi Kunene and Kenya's Abdilatif Abdalla who went against the trends and stood for African languages (Ukam 2018). Our selection of a story by Ngũgĩ wa

Thiong'o was done in deference to these men and women who had taken responsibility for our African languages. While everyone else was keen on writing in English and other European languages in order to access a global audience, Ngũgĩ and these phenomenal writers and activists decided that they would not sit and passively watch the death of African languages (Thiong'o 1986). As practical visionaries interested in turning ideas into actions, the Jalada Collective fully acknowledges what has come before. We take into consideration the conversations that have been held on the subject, and develop these further by pursuing our translation work in ways that examine the barriers of the past and find ways to overcome them in the present.

Just as we have created and continue to create a database of literary translators, we aim to establish a base of devoted readers. Earlier in the process, someone was quick to ask me, rather sceptically, what happens after we have published the translations? Who will read them? Once the first translation issue was published, the translators and our most devoted readers started sharing the work on Facebook, Twitter, and blogs while expressing their excitement at seeing such a publication. People tweeted links and shared specific languages on their timelines.[13] A Twitter user in Ethiopia, @LindaYohannes, tweeted, 'Reading Ngũgĩ in #Amharic! This feels so right!' Digital technologies helped us tap into greater and faster possibilities whereas the mere exhaustion of putting together the volume in print form would have forced us to store the print copies in the warehouse for a month or two before venturing into marketing and distribution. The exhaustion of the production process has often meant that people get stuck in conversations and never reach the stage of doing.

The work of Jalada supports and is especially supported by literary translation activists. The most beautiful conversations about the issue were held in Vienna among scholars and activists when Ngũgĩ wa Thiong'o visited as a guest of the African studies department at the University of Vienna. The department held its annual conference 'Schnittpunkt Afrika,' which in May 2017 was on 'Strategies for the Promotion of African Language Literature in the Era of Social Media.' The 'Exposition of the Upright Revolution' was conceptualised by Martina Kopf, a senior lecturer at the University of Vienna. It was a year-long exposition of the project, which lined the corridors of the African studies department with excerpts of translations in 17 languages, photographs of the translators, and a brief description of each language. The languages featured were Gikuyu, Kiswahili, Dholuo, Luganda, Somali, Amharic, Lingala, Shona, isiNdebele, isiZulu, Hausa, Bamanankan, Igbo, Dagaare, Kusaal, Ewe, and English. I also attended a digital Africa conference in Amherst College in 2017 that gathered scholars on Africa and African languages. In addition to my presentation of the earliest conception of this chapter, there was a panel conversation that explored the work beyond our translation project.

On 17 and 19 October 2017 I went on to deliver a presentation in Cornell University upon invitation by the English department through Professor Mukoma wa Ngũgĩ. I introduced the idea of horizontal translations as democratising the meeting between languages to his classes. Through the Jalada translation project I also showed the students that dreams do not have to be scaled down, that dreams for social change can be the basis for practical theory. On 24 October 2017, Professor John Mugane invited me to speak about the translation issue and our work at The African Language Program at Harvard. For the rest of my stay in Cambridge, Massachusetts, I was a guest of the Hutchins Center for African and African American Research at Harvard University alongside my colleague Novuyo Rosa Tshuma. We spoke about the journey of Jalada,

Jalada 05/Transition 123, a collaborative issue with *Transition*, and our work in translations at Professor Alejandro de la Fuente's History of Transition Seminar. We also participated in a public event at the Harvard bookstore on 27 October 2017.[14]

Since then, my desire to see African languages communicating one with another has increased my activism, making this work the single most recurrent conversation I have had in the festivals, seminars, and workshops that I have attended in my country and abroad. I am also now a practising translator from English and Kiswahili into Kikamba, my mother tongue. A translation of one of my short stories, 'An Immortal Precariat Goes into the Night,' first published by *Saraba* magazine (Kilolo 2016), was published on January 15th in the 26th issue of *Absinthe*, VIBRATE! Resounding the Frequencies of Africana in Translation (https://quod.lib.umich.edu/a/abs).

Creating digital networks for translation

The connection formed between the writer and publisher is quite important, but the connection formed with the reader is also crucial. We know by now that there are people across the African continent and in the diaspora who believe in the importance of work in a variety of African languages. Perhaps in their love for the translated stories and the process of translation, they too will be inspired to write and translate. In practice, the Jalada Collective effort will call for a continuous and growing engagement with multilinguistic storytelling practices. Vigorous social media campaigns and the sharing of the work across all possible media will enhance such reciprocal relations. Concurrently, collaboration with universities and other institutions dedicated to learning can help to integrate the idea of African languages in research and teaching practices. It is particularly crucial that African children grow up with multilingual access to content and digital technology. For this reason, we will make access possible at no cost. We believe that a generation of young people with a passion for their languages, whatever these languages may be, will be here to hold this vision together for a very long time. To grow that generation, we must continue our activism and encourage those among us who have access to the necessary technologies and relevant experience to participate in projects such as the *Jalada* translation issue. New translators will receive the space to experiment with their abilities. And those who have already translated for prior translation issues will have the opportunity to continue in a supportive environment that allows their talents to grow.

An important step in executing such a practical approach in the area of translations is to keep a good connection between different players: writers interested in different languages, translators who value the power of the stories, and publishers who have demonstrated their willingness to disseminate these works further and further. East Africa Educational Publishers in Kenya, Mkuki na Nyota in Tanzania, and Cassava Republic in Nigeria are excellent examples of publishers that include African languages in their lists of publications. The inclusion of African languages would not be possible without the collaborative processes many continue to put in place. At the heart of our practical vision lies a growing network of connections, in the absence of which our vision would remain merely an idea. Incorporating the structure of digital media—as a web of connections—into our way of working allows for the preservation and sharing of our most valuable resources: African languages and the knowledges, histories, and memories that they carry.

One story, many paths

Despite the crucial importance of digital technology, we have seen that the work can grow beyond the digital platform once it has reached a wider audience. From its digital space, Ngũgĩ's story has been adapted for the stage on several occasions. On 10 November 2016, a group of performers led by Ngartia J. Bryan, a leading thespian in Nairobi, staged a multilingual dramatisation called 'Musicality of Language, a Multilingual Performance of the Upright Revolution,' that included seven languages (Gikuyu, Dholuo, Ikinyarwanda, Kiswahili, Sheng, Kimeru, and English). Other languages have since been included in subsequent performances. Each dramatisation celebrates the role of cultural diversity in imagining better worlds. In 2019, the Centre de Cultura Contemporània de Barcelona in Spain assembled a choir that recorded and performed the 'all-body anthem,' a song within the story that sums up the central theme of unity in the story. Their performance can be seen on YouTube.[15]

Ngũgĩ's story has also entered into print. In Sweden, it was translated by Jan Ristarp into Swedish and published as a children's book titled *Den upprätta revolutionen*[16] by the publishing house Modernista in 2017. It was a bestseller there. The story would later be translated into three Gambian languages: Mandinka by Lamin Yarbo, Wolof by Cornelius Gomez, and Fula by Abdoulaye Barry. These three translations were published in one volume by Sable Publications, based in the Gambia. The multilingual Gambian book was published on the occasion of the Mboka Festival of Arts Culture and Sport, which Ngũgĩ attended as a guest of honour in 2017. In Spain, Ngũgĩ's publisher, Laura Huerga from Rayo Verde Editorial, led a collaborative publication project that resulted in a volume with translations of the story into six different languages—Aranese, Asturian (Bable), Castilian, Catalan, Basque (Euskera), and Gallego. Four other publishers participated in this project: Pages Editors, txalaparta, Editorial Galaxia, and Raig Verd Editorial. Each produced the publication in print, using similar illustrations done by d'Agustin Comotto. The illustrations also appear in the promotional video that accompanied the release of the Spanish translations, which can be seen on YouTube.[17]

From digital to stage, to print and then back into the digital realm: in Bangalore India, on 10 April 2016 the Indian magazine *Kannada Prabha* carried a translation of Ngũgĩ's story into Kannada, a Dravidian language. This translation, alongside an interview with Ngũgĩ, was received with popular acclaim and reached three million readers (Thiong'o 2018). In the United States, the story was nominated for a project that aims to make short digital ebooks available on the subway for a year. According to the New York Public Library website,[18] the initiative for the Subway Library was a joint venture between the New York Public Library, Brooklyn Public Library, and Queens Library, the MTA, and Transit Wireless. Any New York City subway rider could now access ebooks, excerpts, and short stories so that they would read while they were in transit.

The most recent and interesting development in the travels of the story was in the form of an art exhibition at Los Angeles's Jean Deleage Art Gallery. It was curated by Los Angeles-based artist Jimmy Centeno and featured the visual interpretations of Ngũgĩ's story by eleven artists of Latin-American origin and a Nigerian painter. The idea was to have the artists express the 'Upright Revolution' through art, mainly paintings. The inclusion of diverse interpretations allowed one of the artists, Mario A. Hernández, to merge his creative interpretation of the story with Mesoamerican deities and religious practices.

The show opened on 2 May 2019 and was visited by many guests, including Ngũgĩ himself. Ngũgĩ lives nearby and is distinguished Professor of English and Comparative Literature at the University of California Irvine. He lauded the artists for their imaginative but very personal interpretation of the story.[19] In email correspondence to myself and the curator, he said that 'the work put Africa and Latin America into a conversation. [That] the exhibition was phenomenal, presenting deeply felt and carefully crafted visual interpretations in the form of paintings and sculpture' (N. Thiong'o, personal communication, 3 May 2019).

The artists also prepared personal statements about the unexpected ways in which the story and the work of Ngũgĩ inspired them to create artworks that connected holistically. In her statement, Laura Vazquez Rodriguez, one of the painters, said that 'like the story, [her] painting—Enlightened or Awakening or Rise—is a celebration of man's life song. Fashioned uniquely but united in purpose we must rise up and stand together to protect and serve one another in love' (Figure 21.2).[20]

Figure 21.2 'Rise Up!,' by Laura Vazquez Rodriguez. Acrylic on canvas, 20 × 20 inches.
© 2019.

Mario Avila, who contributed four pieces of artwork conceptualised and titled in Spanish, wrote a moving letter to Ngũgĩ to express how the process of creating this visual interpretation reinforced in him the sense of unity between Africa and Latin America. In his letter, he recalled his imprisonment in Guatemala during the military junta and the fact of his two brothers disappearing. In 1976, he spent three months in a maximum-security prison and his sons were tortured, a significant parallel to Ngũgĩ's own life story. On 31 December 1977, Ngũgĩ was arrested and detained at the Kamĩtĩ Maximum Security Prison in Nairobi for close to a year (Serpell 2017). His arrest came after the Ministry of Housing and Social Services withdrew the licence for performances at the Kamĩrĩĩthũ Community Education and Cultural Centre, effectively banning his play in Gikuyu. Titled 'Ngaahika Ndeenda,' or 'I Will Marry When I Want,' the play was co-authored with Ngũgĩ wa Mĩriĩ, who also later fled Kenya. Ngũgĩ's family was at this time subjected to constant harassment. In her chapter for a book written to celebrate Ngũgĩ's 80th birthday, Professor Rhonda Cobham-Sander, with her husband Reinhard Sander, reflects on what it was like for Ngũgĩ's children when he was arrested. The family hosted Ngũgĩ's eldest son, Thiong'o (Tee) Ngũgĩ, and Sander reflects:

> International campaigns in support of political detainees can transform them into saints or romantic heroes, but it was a source of persistent distress for Ngũgĩ that he had been unable to protect the son who carried his name from the inferno of hostility that his political stances had ignited in Kenya. During the six weeks in 1983 that Thiong'o spent living with us, I got a glimpse of the grim realities of what detention and exile actually meant for children affected by their parents' political decisions. Thiong'o talked about what it had felt like at 14 years to suddenly lose access to not just his father, but also the kind of creature comforts most children of academics take for granted—food on the table, reliable transportation; unfettered access to homes of other university children; visits from writers and intellectuals from around the world whose conversation sparked curiosity and enlightenment; cordial relationships with adults in high places who valued a parent's scholarly or creative work.
>
> *(Sander and Sander 2018: 84)*

Beyond introspection into their personal lives, Ngũgĩ's 'The Upright Revolution' also challenged the artists whose work was exhibited in the gallery to experiment with different approaches in their work. Such is the case for Nolan Fansler, whose canvas was a long strip measuring 9 foot × 12 inches. An abstract painter, Fansler found it excessively laborious to express his response to the story through abstract painting. So challenged, he was late for the opening, but this did not prevent him from creating the excellent piece he eventually titled 'Unity is Beauty.' The creative crisis led him to a wonderful new experience, during which he realised that he could incorporate the body/space relation in his creative process. He could paint with his feet, aware of the movement of his body as he takes each step.

While working on his long strip of canvas, Fansler realised that he was an element of something larger than himself—a member of the human family. The final piece was aptly titled 'New Direction.' During a personal interview with Centeno, Fansler acknowledged that this project had inspired him, and had taught him that he did not have to confine himself to working only with framed canvases. He said 'I could now work directly with a canvas on the floor. I allowed my body to participate in its entirety in the creation of the piece' (J. Centeno, personal communication, 3 May 2019).

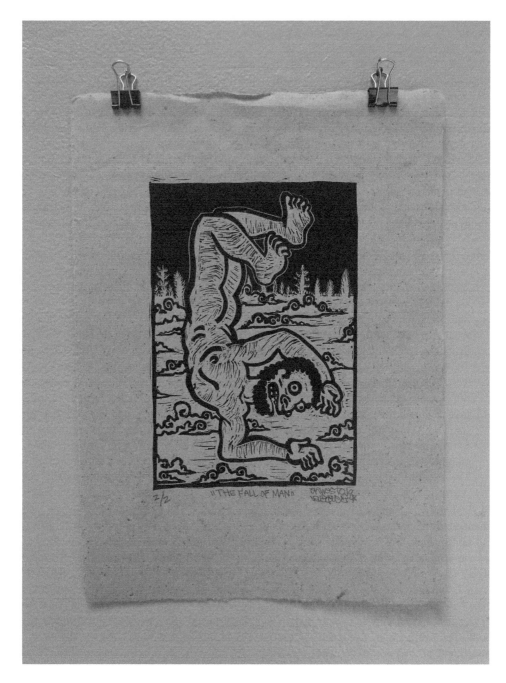

Figure 21.3 'The Fall of Man,' by Ernesto Vazquez. 2019.

Ernesto Vazquez created his work, 'The Fall of Man' (Figure 21.3), as a warning to the inevitable dysfunction that human beings will suffer if they ignore the message of the Upright Revolution. To walk upright, to be well coordinated, and to aid each other through life, the different parts of the body must be united, and the same is true for people despite their cultural backgrounds.

Many of the artists' personal statements, published alongside the visual interpretations by *Jalada Africa*, celebrate the resilience and potential of the human body, while stressing the need for unity if humanity is to remain strong and continue to rise above individual limitations. The exhibition 'The Upright Revolution: A Visual Exhibition' took its title in part from that of the story.

The future is multilingual

With more than 6,900 more languages across the world, Ngũgĩ's story will continue to travel. In the future, we hope to see the younger translators with whom we work move on to bigger challenges. Perhaps then, they will undertake the translation of fiction and non-fiction books and we will have developed the capacity to publish them. While shorter works can be read more easily online, books may require print publication. In this respect, the digital and the analogue co-exist, mutually benefitting each other.

Over the course of the next few decades, we envision having ongoing translations of tens of different stories. Once each story is translated into a hundred or more languages, we will have made it a normal practice to write and translate into and among African languages. With this practice comes the idea of conversation among the languages as they appear alongside each other. The beauty is in the capacity to use any known language anywhere in the world with confidence and the faith in the good of what is your own, something that the Jalada project makes possible for African readers and writers. It is also about respecting the faith and confidence of the other in using and celebrating their linguistic and literary heritage.

And this is the future for African literature: a place for practical visionaries. A time of pride rooted in our multilingual past and connections that know no boundaries among writers, publishers, and readers. When we act out our ideas, the future will overcome difficulties of access to digital technologies; the exclusion of languages through translations; and the limitations of opportunities through the growth of collective work. We will wake up one day soon and feel the light of possibility shine upon our faces. And because the 'Upright Revolution' (so aptly inspired by Ngũgĩ's story) of digital innovation is inevitable, the publisher, the writer, the translator, and the reader—who wants the works to survive and remain relevant—must find ways of taking advantage of the digital technologies at their disposal for multilingual storytelling.

Related topics

Against a Single African Literary Translation Theory; The Dialectics of Dissent in Postcolonial India; Rendering Bengali Dalit Discourse as Translational Activism.

Notes

1 https://sli.se/apps/sli/prodinfo.php?db=3&article=UR198671 [accessed 18 September 2019].
2 https://jaladaafrica.org/2016/03/22/jalada-translation-issue-01-ngugi-wa-thiongo/ [accessed 18 September 2019].
3 www.theguardian.com/books/2016/mar/29/jalada-africa-short-story-ngugi-wa-thiongo-translated-over-30-languages-publication [accessed 18 September 2019].

4 https://granta.com/issues/granta-123-best-of-young-british-novelists/ [accessed 18 September 2019].
5 https://jaladaafrica.org/2014/01/27/sketch-of-a-bald-woman-in-the-semi-nude-and-other-stories/ [accessed 18 September 2019].
6 https://jaladaafrica.org/2014/06/10/sext-me-poems-and-stories/ [accessed 18 September 2019].
7 https://jaladaafrica.org/2015/01/14/jalada-02-afrofutures/ [accessed 18 September 2019].
8 https://jaladaafrica.org/2016/03/22/ituika-ria-murungaru-kana-kiria-gitumaga-andu-mathii-marun gii-3/ [accessed 18 September 2019].
9 https://jaladaafrica.org/2016/03/22/introduction-beyond-the-languages-i-claim-as-my-own/ [accessed 18 September 2019].
10 https://jaladaafrica.org/2015/09/15/jalada-04-the-language-issue/ [accessed 18 September 2019].
11 www.acklanguageschool.org/ [accessed 18 September 2019].
12 https://milesmorlandfoundation.com/abdul-adan-2016/ [accessed 18 September 2019].
13 https://brittlepaper.com/2016/04/twitter-reactions-jalada-translation-revolution/ [accessed 18 September 2019].
14 www.youtube.com/watch?v=9VifFWvEwEA&fbclid=IwAR2JCWsBrv8YqNKrZBh7al5Sd0_IYr HEoTQFkGgd_fWj9FeeZue9s-dRsTU [accessed 18 September 2019].
15 www.youtube.com/watch?v=XHlA2XH0DXs [accessed 18 September 2019].
16 www.modernista.se/bocker/den-uppratta-revolutionen [accessed 18 September 2019].
17 www.youtube.com/watch?v=l0qVwDE7KuU [accessed 18 September 2019].
18 www.nypl.org/blog/2017/06/08/subwaylibrary [accessed 18 September 2019]
19 www.youtube.com/watch?v=ImU9k4wHooM [accessed 18 September 2019].
20 https://jaladaafrica.org/2019/06/13/text-to-mixed-media-a-visual-interpretation-of-the-upright-revolution/ [accessed 18 September 2019].

Further reading

Thiong'o, Ngũgĩ wa (2012) *Globalectics: Theory and the Politics of Knowing*. New York: Columbia University Press.

This book delves deep into the politics of language in African writing, but is grounded in the author's journey as one of the foremost activists in the writing, publication, and reading of work in African languages.

Mugane, John (1997) 'Learning African Languages with Evolving Digital Technologies,' *Africa Today* 44 (4): 423–441.

This article, written before most of the social media platforms emerged by one of the foremost scholars on African languages, is a definitive account of how these digital technologies can play a vital role in African language instruction.

Gikandi, Simon, and Wachanga Ndirangu (2018) *Ngũgĩ: Reflections on His Life of Writing*. London: James Currey.

This book brings together the work of friends, family, scholars, and the many people who have interacted with Ngũgĩ wa Thiong'o in his many years of writing, in which they celebrate the legacy of the man whose influence in literature, language, and cultural criticism has been phenomenal.

References

Hutchison, John (2006) 'African Language Literature as a Weapon against African Language Marginalization,' in *Selected Proceedings of the 35th Annual Conference on African Linguistics: African Languages and Linguistics in Broad Perspectives* [online]. Available at: www.lingref.com/cpp/acal/35/paper1293.pdf [accessed 21 August 2019].
Kilolo, Moses (2016) 'An Immortal Precariat Goes into the Night,' in *The Crime Issue*. Ed. Dami Ajayi. Lagos: Saraba. 18–23.

Mwanaka, Tendai Rinos, Wanjohi Makhoha and Upal Deb (2018) *Writing Language, Culture, and Development: Africa Vs Asia*. Harare: Mwanaka Media and Publishing.

Ngũgĩ, Mukoma (2016) 'A Revolution in Many Tongues,' in *Africa is a Country* [online]. Available at: https://africasacountry.com/2016/04/a-revolution-in-many-tongues [accessed 21 August 2019].

Sander, Rhonda Cobham and Reinhard Sander (2018) 'Professor, You are in Ngũgĩ's Book,' in *Ngũgĩ: Reflections on His Life of Writing*. Eds. Simon Gikandi and Wachanga Ndirangu. London: James Currey. 84.

Serpell, Namwali (2017) 'Kenya in Another Tongue,' in *The New York Review of Books* [online] 12 April. Available at: www.nybooks.com/daily/2017/04/12/kenya-in-another-tongue-ngugi-wa-thiongo/ [accessed 9 September 2019].

Thiong'o, Ngũgĩ (2016) 'Translations Enable Creative Dialogue among African Languages,' in *This is Africa* [online]. Available at: https://thisisafrica.me/arts-and-culture/translations-enable-creative-dialogue-among-african-languages/ [accessed 21 August 2019].

Thiong'o, Ngũgĩ (2018) 'The Politics of Translation: Notes towards an African Language Policy,' *Journal of African Cultural Studies* 30 (2): 124–132.

Thiong'o, Ngũgĩ (1986) *Decolonising the Mind: The Politics of Language in African Literature*. London: Heinemann.

Ukam, EI (2018) 'The Choice of Language for African Creative Writers,' *English Linguistics Research* 7 (2): 46–53.

22

The dialectics of dissent in postcolonial India

Vrishchik (1969–1973)

Khushmi Mehta

Introduction

In January 2018, I sat across from Gulammohammed Sheikh in his brightly lit studio in Baroda, Gujarat (a state in western India). A collection of in-progress ceramic sculptures lay meticulously arranged in the corner. He brought out a stack of old periodicals—his collection of *Vrishchik*. Carefully flipping through its yellowed pages, he narrated the histories behind each print, article and poem.

Vrishchik was an artists' periodical published in Baroda, co-edited by the artists, Gulammohammed Sheikh and Bhupen Khakhar. In its short span from 1969 to 1973, this periodical emerged as an active forum for Indian artists, providing a platform for them to voice literary expression and socio-political concerns. A trilingual publication with writings published in Hindi, Gujarati and English, the question of language was critical to the issues that *Vrishchik* engaged with. The periodical's emergence in the midst of India's postcolonial trajectory further heightened the implications of its content, at a moment when the production of art and literature was directly linked to the development of a visual culture for the nation. Through this chapter, I use the case study of regional Indian literatures published in *Vrishchik* to discuss the implications of English translations when disseminated in the context of a postcolonial society, viewing cultural and linguistic multiplicities as a form of resistance to a totalising national culture in the precarious state of a newly post-independence nation.

Situating *Vrishchik*: historical precedents and context

Recognising a need for a channel of communication between artists from disparate backgrounds across a multilingual country, Gulammohammed Sheikh and Bhupen Khakhar collaborated with a group of artists/writers working in Baroda, such as Jeram Patel, Jyoti Bhatt, Vivan Sundaram and Geeta Kapur, to publish *Vrishchik*. *Vrishchik* was named after the astrological sign Scorpio, which nearly all the members of the group shared. Sheikh jokes that, in hindsight, the name was fitting—'it did do some work of stinging'

(Hyman and Sheikh 2010) in its challenging of institutional norms. *Vrishchik* was started as an independent endeavour, and all steps to publish the periodical, from writing, creating visuals and disseminating, came from the group of friends (Thakkar 2008). Working under a restricted budget, dependent only on 'contributions of well-wishers' (*Vrishchik* 1969, 1 (1)),[1] the periodical was printed on inexpensive brown paper. It was initially founded as a monthly periodical; over the years its issues were published quarterly or according to the funding available. Yet, the members remained generous with their contributions, supplementing each edition with a print insert, allowing readers to literally own an original artwork, and thereby offering them closer engagement with the issues that the artists were concerned with.

Over a period of four years, the members published a total of twenty-nine issues, including special editions like a compilation of Geeta Kapur's series of essays, *In Quest of Identity* (1973). The format of the editions remained consistent to an extent, with prose and poems interspersed with prints and drawings. The layout of each page was unique, individualised to the thematics of each issue. The content too varied between editions, with each issue usually focusing on a specific theme. In their inclusion of texts ranging from Indian folk songs to European short stories, translation appeared as an overarching narrative. English translations sought to increase accessibility to outsider art, and their very admission of canonically marginalised works stood as an act of resistance to the expected iterations of a national visual culture. While the individual contributions were personal, they attempted to speak to broader issues impacting artists across the nation through issues like 'The Social Context of Contemporary Art,' edited by Geeta Kapur (*Vrishchik* 1973, 4 (4)). Although operating out of a niche community in Baroda, the editions addressed a discourse around transnational issues. They primarily featured artworks by Indian artists, and while they avoided blindly following the trends of movements in Euro-America, they acknowledged the need to remain in conversation with such trends.

Publishing regional literatures and works by artists who were institutionally unrepresented, *Vrishchik* was one of the many manifestations of the little magazine movement that emerged in various Indian languages in the post-independence period after 1947. Nerlekar expounds on the subculture of little magazines, admitting to the challenges of assigning a definition that fit the multitude of mutations that these magazines took, terming it 'the quintessential never-to-be-caught snark of literary publishing—without a home, without a form, undefinable, and therefore unknowable' (2016: 43). However, in spite of the elusive nature of the genre, Nerlekar suggests that the little magazines, along with the translations that they encouraged, instituted locus-specific practices that kindled new questions regarding the identity of both English and vernacular literatures in the modern, post-independence context (2016: 40). The subculture of the little magazine itself, often associated with the birth of modernism, spread across countries around the world, and although it served as a vehicle to transmit modernist texts from Euro-America, it continued to belong to postcolonial communities. *Vrishchik*, in its low production costs, lack of subscription charges and brief publication span, followed the conventions of other little magazines.

However, the texts published in *Vrishchik* stand apart in their unequivocal voicing of issues of national importance, amplified by its establishment in Baroda amidst a volatile cultural and political climate following the 1969 Gujarat riots. In the months of September and October 1969, large-scale communal violence broke out across the state of Gujarat, involving looting, arson and massacre that resulted in over 600 deaths, and was known as the deadliest Hindu–Muslim violence since the 1947 partition of the subcontinent (Jaffrelot 2010: 377). Against this background, *Vrishchik*'s situating in Baroda compelled its members to be directly engaged in a discourse of socio-political significance. In an article titled 'Against Communalism,' published in *Vrishchik*, the members called for readers to 'come forward and condemn the discrimination and atrocities' (*Vrishchik* 1969, 1 (7–8)). They further drew attention to their accountability as artists, stating that 'arts and literature too are not free from it' (1969, 1 (7–8)), seeking to use their positions of influence to call out discrimination in other forms of institutional representation.

Serving as a platform for activism and institutional critique, *Vrishchik* provided a space for artists to fight for autonomy in opposition to the singular authority of institutions like the Lalit Kala Akademi (National Academy of Art). Buried under problematics of bureaucracy and inter-party disputes, the Akademi was criticised for its inability to keep up with the contemporary conditions of Indian schools of art and for its recurring composition of nominated members. In response, the members of *Vrishchik* came together to join the All India Protest Committee, the functioning body of protest, and further supported the formation of the Council of Indian artists, a move by artists to reclaim the power to steer the narrative of Indian art and call for democratic representation within national institutions. In March of 1971, a group of artists boycotted the Lalit Kala Akademi on the occasion of India's second Triennale of Contemporary World Art, an international exhibition organised by the Akademi. In spite of the refusal of nearly two-thirds of the invitees to participate, the Triennale took place on schedule, opening with expected speeches by dignitaries. The protesting artists were present—donning large plaster cast medals printed in gold, with 'Boycott Akademi' inscribed on them. The participating members considered this silent protest to be a response to the rumours of artists partaking in more active demonstrations—believing it to be a 'peaceful yet highly significant protest' (*Vrishchik* 1971, 2 (4–5)). The success of the protest reflected to the group the impact they could have in creating a new identity for Indian art, one that reflected the realities of the artists of the nation, not just that of the few chosen by the Akademi. Kapur describes *Vrishchik* as a project that attempted to place its members at the forefront of the national social and political discourse of the time (2011). *Vrishchik*, through its defiant editorials and critical essays, addressed issues of exclusivity of institutions, offered a space for marginalised narratives between its pages and kindled a discourse around the agency of artists in their representation.

Multilingualism, hybridity and cultural difference: translations of vernacular literatures in *Vrishchik*

Salvador, accounting for the centrality of translation in India, explains that in multilingual societies, 'pluralism is organic and translation is an inevitable way of life' (2005: 189). Mirroring the multiplicity of the social and cultural spheres in India, translational practices therefore find their way in the daily chain of communication. Taking into consideration the fragmentary nature of postcolonial development, translations become part of a larger picture, including the economic and political framework in which ideas are circulated. The binary polarisation of power relations—the colonised and coloniser, East and West, Third World and First World—that enable structures of oppression is weakened by the hybridity of contemporary cultures (Simon and St-Pierre 2000: 17). In this regard, it is no longer sufficient to view translation through a lens of the dichotomy between English and the vernacular. What needs to be centred is the position of hybridity in postcolonial translation—one that allows for a recognition of interstitial spaces between linguistic boundaries.

Wolf extends this discourse to locating interventions from a 'third space,' arguing that translation 'no longer means bridging a gap between two different cultures but rather, producing meanings which are created through the encounter of cultures that are already characterised by multiculturality' (2000: 141). This is especially amplified in a multilingual nation like India, located in an interstitial space between the First and the Third Worlds, with all the characteristics of a capitalist country but one that has its colonial past nostalgically rehashed periodically through various channels of media (Ahmad 1987: 7). As an act of resistance to the continued hegemony of English in postcolonial contexts, this hybridity manifests in the form of Indian writers reclaiming English, altering the very language itself to express the nuances of an Indian context. Dingwaney expands on this phenomenon, stating that the colonised deliberately (mis)translate the colonial script, alienating and undermining its authority, proceeding from an awareness of the Other's agency and own forms of subjectivity, which returns the Other to a history from which they were violently wrenched (1995: 9). This transmutation of language is evident in the Indianised English adopted by the writers of *Vrishchik*, with the embedding of various colloquialisms and frequent use of Hinglish (an amalgamation of English and South Asian languages, involving code-switching between the two within a sentence). For example, *Vrishchik* 1 (3) included a note condemning the state of national institutions of art and literature:

> The art tamashas in the forms [of] annual exhibitions organised by the central or state akademies, without the slightest feeling of shame, that many artists have stopped participating in them since years, continue. The central Lalit Kala Akademi has demonstrated the height of inefficiency by not being able to handle the Indian contingent at the Sao Paulo Bienalle. Gujarat Lalit Kala Akademi has unashamedly pocketed the protest of most of the important artists of Gujarat and its secretary has the audacity to doubt the integrity of all these artists! And at the literary conferences, the same parrot talks, digging graves of old foggies …
>
> (Vrishchik *1970, 1 (3)*)

Their use of Hinglish words like *tamashas* (spectacle) in the first line, used without a translation, and Indianised idioms like 'parrot talks' add a tone of satire to their criticism and further speak to the intended audience of their publication—an Indian reader, aware of the nuances of these colloquialisms.

On the other hand, the writers of *Vrishchik* further critiqued the perception of Indian literature and art criticism being targeted towards a Euro-American readership, in a manner of looking west for approval and justifying the worth of Indian writing. In an article titled, 'Miniature Purana,' published in *Vrishchik* 1 (9–10), they criticise Indian art historians and critics for continuing to emulate Euro-American culture, especially when writing during a critical period of the nation's postcolonial development. They use the example of renowned Indian scholars and philosophers, Swami Vivekananda, Rabindranath Tagore and Ananda Coomaraswamy, all of whom played a key role in introducing Indian art and culture to Europe and America during the colonial era, to highlight the contradictions prevalent in the colonial period, when Indian culture was upheld in some instances and desecrated in others.

Writing on art in India seems to have begun with the view of explaining to the world (or 'west' in this context) that we too are capable of producing a culture and art of our own. Thus, accepting the premise of 'replying' [to] that Englishman who did not hesitate to call Ajanta as [a] specimen of barbaric art, or of certain miss Meyo's views that we are an uncivilised race, we seem to have pleaded in the world court of culture about our worth. At times we did this with our head high like Vivekananda and Tagore or Coomaraswamy, at other times, with our knees touching the earth.

(Vrishchik 1970, 1 (9–10))

'Miniature Purana' argues that the flaw in writing on Indian art lies in the motivations of the authors of postcolonial histories. Writers at the forefront of the revival of the nation's visual culture had been those whose minds were shaped by colonial diplomacy, such that even in the act of freeing Indian art from adhering to European cultural norms, they continued to appeal to the same European authorities for recognition (1970, 1 (9–10)). Translations of regional Indian poetry to English are then considered to be primarily for European consumption, turning it to a one-way process rather than a reciprocal act of exchange (Bassnett and Trivedi 1999: 5). The perceived hegemony of English texts then relegates the translated vernacular literatures to the position of an imitation, mirroring the very asymmetrical power relations that colonialism operates under. A translation as a copy of the original text reflects the notion of the colony as a copy of the coloniser. If the assumption that something is lost in translation is to be accepted, the colonised is inherently viewed as lesser than the coloniser. Tymoczko contrarily, argues for postcolonial literature written in the coloniser's tongue to be a form of intercultural transfer. She claims that postcolonial texts as translations are 'communicative agents with powerful resonances, having the capacity to mediate between languages and cultures in radical and empowering ways.' In this regard, postcolonial literatures, like translations, in their ability to straddle between cultures, hold tremendous revolutionary potential in themselves (Tymoczko 2000: 148).

'Miniature Purana' also raises the issue of a nuanced reading of the original text being essential to a true translation. The authors suggest that medieval Indian poems are often translated into English without an understanding of the medium of the poetry, translated by those with little authority over the subject matter.

Moreover, snobbish interpretations of themes (every Nayak compared with Krishna) with miles long list of footnotes and bibliography have obscured the possibilities of better appreciation. Thus, the said writers have created an imaginary territorial line of what they call an area of authoritative research. Any one who happens to speak about these paintings without having qualifications designed by the authorities in question, is either ignored or frowned upon. That [may be why] until today writing on Indian art has remained a lifeless academic exercise.

(1970, 1 (9–10))

Bassnett and Trivedi, similarly using the example of anthropological footnotes accompanying English translations of Indian or Arabic texts, argue that textual practices of editing and cutting original texts and supplementing them with insider notes to European readers only served to establish the subordinate position of the original writing. Certain literatures, while successfully translated from the original, were considered to rise to the status of 'art' only when read in English, and successful translation was premised on the cultural superiority of the language of the coloniser over that of the colonised (1999).

The authors of 'Miniature Purana' further include a comment on what they consider inaccurate translations of medieval Indian poetry into English:

> One more thing worth noting is the translations of texts into English which accompany many a picture. These texts, usually some of the best of mediaeval poetry, are translated into English without much sensitivity and understanding of the medium of poetry.
>
> *(Vrishchik 1970, 1 (9–10))*

Their criticism reflects what P. Lal, a poet, translator and publisher known for his promotion of Indian-English literature in the post-independence era, termed as 'transcreation' (Lal 1996). 'Transcreation' was defined as the method of translation of seeking maximum readability, within the confines of a faithful rendering. Lal believed that the quality of the translator's engagement, or rather their 'empathy,' was reflected in the quality of the translation, and that the significance of the work of the translator lay in their ability to comprehend the spirit of the text, understand the effect that the author was attempting to create, and finally, communicate that within the resources of the English language (Salvador 2005). His practice therefore combined interpretation with translation in an endeavour to modernise a historical text.

Translational approaches to India's 'moment' of modernism

Zecchini argues that modernism in India was reinvented through a constant flux of translational and transnational transactions between English and other Indian languages (2014: 15). She suggests that both canons of the postcolonial and the modern can productively alter and decentre each other, but are equally inflected by heterogeneous voices. At the same time, she describes modernism and modernity as 'unstable categories that exceed rigid space, time and national boundaries' and that the moment of modernism varies from one country to another, taking different forms depending on its context (2014: 5). This discourse was taken up by art historian and one of the members of *Vrishchik*, Geeta Kapur, in her seminal text, 'When was Modernism in Indian Art?' (2000), where she attempts to locate this 'moment' of modernism in India, and the contexts that enabled it. In postcolonial societies like India's, the modern occurred simultaneously with anti-colonial struggles, creating grounds for deep politicisation and potential for resistance. While it was equally desired and abhorred throughout the nationalist period, it was also continually contested in the post-independence era. Kapur claims that it was only then, at the time of her writing this text in 2000, that Indian artists became fully modern in what could be considered the postmodern age, defining modernity in the sense of 'being able to confront the new without flying to the defence of tradition' (2000: 299).

The period during the 1960s and 1970s was, as a result, still characterised by waves of transition in all realms—the shift from orature to print culture being the primary one that impacted translation studies at the time. As writer and translator A.K. Ramanujan pointed out, Indian culture was distinctly organised along the principle of contextualisation, along the lines of both caste and class (1999: 96–114). In a previously largely non-literate society, where the culture had been primarily oral-performative, this progression was significant as it translated to a shift from a culture of speaker–listener to one of reader–writer. This transition itself resulted in an erosion of the principle of contextual-isation, with the modern writer no longer addressing a specific community or familiar audience but rather an anonymous mass of dispersed readers (Ramanujan 1999). This de-contextualisation was especially evident in the several translations of medieval *bhakti* (devotion) poetry in the 1960s and 1970s, published in little magazines that were inter-ested in offering a space for recreations of the past in order to better comprehend the present. With these translations, medieval poetry, once targeted towards a niche reader-ship, was made accessible to a wider, more disparate audience. The shift in the reader-ship of Indian poetry from a limited private sphere to a public one in turn meant a transition in the very content of the poetry that was translated—from highly stylised, metaphoric poetry with a limited subject matter to those with broader socio-political themes (Zecchini 2014).

Vrishchik played a key role in this movement, with a special issue published in Sep-tember 1970, featuring English translations of *bhakti* poetry, including poems by Mukta-bai, Janabai and Namdev, translated from Marathi by Arun Kolatkar, 'Recastings from Kabir,' translated from Hindi by Arvind Krishna Mehrotra, and the poems of Vasto, translated from Gujarati by Gieve Patel. These iconic poems, translated and interpreted numerously over the years, are renewed in these simplified translations imbibed with a modernist sensibility. Here, I focus on Mehrotra's series of translations of Kabir's poems, eventually published as a book in 2011, to illuminate the significance of these translations as interventions into the nation's modernist trajectory.

The poems of Kabir held immense social, political and religious value in their original context, in their defiance of rigorous societal traditions. Kabir, a 15th-century saint and poet, used his writings to critique Brahmanical practices of the caste system, and the rites and rituals of both Hinduism and Islam. Rather than serve as a synthesis of Hindu and Muslim traditions, Kabir's poems condemn the rigidity of both (Pande 1985). Kabir, like other medi-eval poets including Namdev, Tukaram and Nanak, belonged to a lower caste and class. These poets' voices emerging from the margins of communities were themselves symbols of dissent against societal structures, and of the activist potential of translation from vernacular languages. While the political and economic state was characterised by feudal oppression, the social state was encumbered by Brahmanical authority. In order to maintain their position of privilege in society, the upper caste enforced complex rituals, and those who did not fit into the established *varnas* (castes) were termed *chandalas* (outcastes) (Pande 1985: 232–233; also see Chapter 23). In the act of defying the practices of elaborate ceremonies, and strict rites and rituals, in exchange for direct devotion to God, Kabir was also implicitly revolting against social hierarchies. The excerpt below from 'Recastings from Kabir,' identi-fied as a translation of the poem KG85 in Parasnath Tiwari's 1961 *Kabir Granthavali* (McDonald 2017: 239), exemplifies this sentiment.

> You be the pauper or prince,
> or the mendicant-saint,
> once you have come
> you must then end
>
> riding his throne
> one reaches the grave,
> the other is in iron bound
> and limps towards it.

The kings shall go, so will their pretty queens,
courtiers and all the proud ones shall go.
Pundits chanting the Vedas shall go,
and go will those who listen to them.

Masochist yogis and bright intellectuals shall go,
go the moon and sun and water and wind.
Thus says Kabir only those can remain
whose minds are tied to the rocks.

(*Vrishchik* 1970, 1: (11–12))

Through this poem, Kabir represents a radical dissent against the divisive notions of social hierarchy, equalising all—irrespective of caste and class—in death. In choosing to translate this specific poem, Mehrotra inserts himself into a continued discourse of social stratification. 'Recastings from Kabir' stands apart from previous English translations of Kabir's poems, such as those by Rabindranath Tagore (Kabir 1915), in Mehrotra's minimalistic use of heavy expression and jargon, and their fidelity to the constant rhythm and simplicity of Kabir's language. Accepting the responsibilities of interpreting medieval poetry amidst a modernist development, Mehrotra's translations grappled with the tensions intrinsic to catering to a modern readership while maintaining the colloquialisms embedded in the originals. In their opposition to the caste system, feudal oppression and other ingrained social norms, Kabir's poems were symbols of a political stance in themselves. Mehrotra's translations of Kabir's writings therefore carried with them not only literary weight, but also critical historicity.

The *bhakti* poems published in *Vrishchik*, although translations of works that were widely accepted in the literary canon, were revisionary in their anti-establishment stance. As Nerlekar explains, 'the language that was employed in the translations was radically disruptive of the canonical expectations of the text so that the translating act represented rebellion even in the midst of popular or institutional backing' (2016: 128). Zecchini, illustrating the importance of these translations in shaping Indian modernism, states: 'these translations illustrate the fecund tension between rupture and filial attachment, disownment and recovery, exile and homecoming, which defines Indian modernity' (2014: 75). It was these very juxtapositions that represented a secular Indian sensibility. By translating poems that were once a part of a religious canon, these translators on the one hand rejected the realms of oppression and superstition that these poems were adopted into, while also asserting the presence of this literature in a renewed national culture. Acknowledging the historical importance of these translations, Mehrotra includes an afterword following his translations in *Vrishchik*:

The Afterword: I hope there's a scholar/reviewer who is already snooping around these recastings, smacking his lips, all set for the kill. I hope someone rushes excitedly to Kabir's oeuvre and comes back with the headline *These damn things don't exist there*. In all probability they don't. Yet. Between Kabir and me stand five centuries, and any number of vulgar translations of his poetry—mainly Tagore's and Banke Behari's. All these and more had to be melted, purified, and cast again. So Kabir began living in the nineteen seventies, I in the fourteen hundreds.

(1970, 1 (11–12))

The sharp satire in Mehrotra's words indicates his awareness of the positionality of his writing in the history of translations of medieval Indian poetry. Rather than an attempt to mirror the characteristics of dissent of Kabir's original writings, Mehrotra's translations register their location in a vastly different social context. Here, his terming of these translations as 'recastings' is significant in that it points to the multitude of transmutations that these poems have undergone over time, with each permutation a reflection of its contemporary context. According to Mukim, Mehrotra's translations have the potential to unsettle not only older translations, but also older readings of the text. His translations, and those of his contemporaries, must be therefore seen as more than mere imitations of their originals (Mukim 2014). Mehrotra's translations stand as original poems in their own right, while also accumulating the influence of the histories they lived through. They neither distance themselves from their ancestry, nor hide Mehrotra's presence as one their several authors.

In this regard, Mehrotra's original poems reflect similar motivations as his translations in their attempt to dismantle the elusiveness of modern poetry. In the short poem below with the same brevity of lines, rhythmic movement and uneven syllables as his translation of Kabir, Mehrotra expresses the very simplicity and accessibility that modern poets now strived for.

> Just two days ago
> the poet traded all
> the rare lines
> in his collection
> for common ones. (Mehrotra 1976: 46)

These poets now combined elements of their lived experiences to reflect the palpability of their world, with a linguistic rejection of poetic conventions to suit their content (Nerlekar 2016). Rather than approach larger themes of the nation's postcolonial development, they attempt to break down and de-complicate the monumentality of contemporary modernity.

Decentring the nation: confronting institutional boundaries

The Lalit Kala Akademi was inaugurated on 5 August 1954 in New Delhi, funded by the Ministry of Culture. With its primary goal of supporting visual artists in India, the Akademi was responsible for organising exhibitions and publications to represent Indian artists both nationally and internationally. The Akademi was established by the Government of India 'in pursuance of the dream of the first Prime Minister of independent India, Pandit Jawaharlal Nehru for a cultural and national identity' (Lalit Kala Akademi 2018). In this context, the institution stood as a symbol of the formation of a national culture for a newly independent India. Nehru, now entrusted with the task of restructuring the postcolonial nation, stood at the forefront of those who believed an assimilative nation-state to be the correct model for constructing a modern India. He represented a dichotomy of opinions of embracing India's history as its cultural identity, while also being a profound believer in Euro-American rationalism as the only path to achieving a modern and economically progressive India (Spitz 1993). Nation building and national integration became sacred for new states, and the Lalit Kala Akademi served to further these efforts in building a visual culture for the subcontinent.

Over the years, the Akademi came under fire for its inefficiency and partiality towards art forms that conformed to an established iteration of the modern. *Vrishchik* emerged as an active platform for artists to protest the national institutions' interpretation of contemporary Indian art and literature. An article published in the *Vrishchik* 2 (4–5) titled, 'Triennale and the Implications of Internationalism,' by Indu Jaisingh (1970), evaluated the works that the Akademi continued to privilege—the art of the 1950s that mirrored the movements of Euro-America that they were influenced by. Jaisingh states that obsolete art forms continued to dominate the institutions, calling it 'a hangover from colonialism mixed with rising bourgeois values' (1970). On the other hand, artists from the 1960s now placed emphasis on 'Indian' identities expressed through modern art. The artists participating in the protest against the Akademi represented a heterogeneity of art styles, united in their need for social expression. Yet, the Akademi's continued favouring of a single art style, one that emulated the techniques of the colonial schools of art, spoke to their inability to meet the needs of the current generation.

The rift within a postcolonial nation because of a displacement of a totalising national culture exemplifies what Homi Bhabha identifies as 'cultural difference' (Bhabha 1994: 162–164). Outlining the contrast between cultural diversity and cultural difference, Bhabha emphasises the necessity of the autonomy of the people against a homogeneous culture emerging in the spaces of modernity. He defines cultural difference as a recognition of the unequal and uneven forces of cultural representation involved in the contest for political and social authority within the modern world order (Bhabha 1994: 34). His interpretation dissects the apprehensions of a new nation with a vacant space for contending cultural forces, causing a rift within the community, such that the coloniser is no longer the only authoritative power. He argues that cultures are never unitary in themselves and that a dualistic understanding of Self to Other within a culture entails simplification (148). He suggests turning the lens from the boundary outside to the boundaries within, thereby eliminating the notion of cultural difference as a problem of 'other' people and instead emphasising the otherness of the people-as-one (150). Bhabha is explicit in distinguishing the field of cultural difference from that of cultural diversity, implying a focus on merely cultural diversity to be reductive.

The recognition of a multiplicity of regional literatures through the channel of *Vrishchik* resisted the single narrative encouraged by national institutions. In *Vrishchik* 1 (3), a note by the editors, Gulammohammed Sheikh and Bhupen Khakhar, critiqued institutions like the Gujarati Sahitya Parishad (Gujarati Literary Council) for their literary conferences, 'where except one or two speakers, all literary men busied themselves in everything but literature, be it mysticism or falling at the feet of politicians' (*Vrishchik* 1969, 1 (3)). They perceived this as a reflection of the apathy and indifference exhibited by institutions towards the discipline, holding them accountable for the forms of art and literature that they continued to perpetuate. They further critiqued state institutions for their social discrimination in the form of patronage awarded to artists from Scheduled Castes (officially designated groups of historically disadvantaged people), when singled out as a separate category based on caste or class rather than literary merit. The practice of the Parishad in categorising caste as a criterion was condemned as breeding 'segregation in the literary community and [succeeding] in defeating the remotest ideals of literature' (*Vrishchik* 1970, 1 (7–8)).

Gulammohammed Sheikh, writing in a 2004 essay titled, 'Our Literature, Their Literature?' in the aftermath of the 2002 communal riots in Gujarat, state-wide violence that resulted in over a thousand deaths, extends this resistant discourse to the agency of communities in directing the reception of their literature. He critiques the categorisation of 'minority literature' in sectarian terms, challenging whether the social fissures caused by a communal divide are reflected in their vocation as writers. He asks, 'have we examined our literature to gauge our perception of the "other" through history?' (Sheikh 2004). Referring to the ostracisation of certain literatures based on the religion, caste or class background of the author or community portrayed, Sheikh questions the acceptance of majority literature in non-sectarian terms. This polarisation of two categories of Indian vernacular literature allows the majority literature to extend to the terrain of the 'other,' whereas Dalit, feminist or Muslim literatures are expected to locate themselves within the confines of their own terrain, without challenging the stereotypes that they are cast into (Sheikh 2004).

Visibility as protest: translating non-canonical narratives

Vrishchik's antidote to the aforementioned forms of segregation was to shift the narrative from the agendas of institutions to the visibility of communities whose histories mattered. As Heredia writes, the task of the translators has been to make comprehensible what seems not translatable, to unveil the information that the writer transmits in a veiled manner, and that it is 'part of the job of translators, that, thus, become "unveilers" of silenced contents' (2004: 167). By featuring translations of vernacular poetry and prose that national institutions tended to overlook, little magazines like *Vrishchik* sought to increase visibility for regional literatures. For example, *Vrishchik* 1 (2) was dedicated to translations of the poetry of Ravji Patel, a Gujarati poet and novelist (1939–1968). An article by Suresh Joshi, a Gujarati writer and translator, entitled 'Life Against Death: The Poetry of Ravji Patel,' evaluated the significance of Patel's poetry in the context of India's post-independence history.

Early modernist literature emerging amidst India's freedom struggle attempted to give a sense of homogeneity to literary productions, neutralising the individual voice in the process. Joshi argues that the revolutionary fervour of the anti-colonial movement was detrimental to the evolution of socially relevant works, stating that their dissent expressed through colloquial speech 'though colourful in parts, did not lend itself easily to the expression of righteous indignation whether simulated of genuine' (Joshi 1969). The romantic naïveté of Gandhian idealism of pre-independence (and pre-partition) literature characterised by ideals of *satyagraha* (truth) and *ahimsa* (non-violence) failed to convey the agonising experiences of artists who had lived through the violence of the 1947 partition of the nation. The development of a newly post-independence state now compelled a modernist revision of the linguistic structure of vernacular writing. Joshi writes:

> Gone are the jingling rhymes and the dulcet tones. Instead, we have words forced into shapes and sounds which resemble the hard contours of life itself. Figures of speech cease to be mere decorative appurtenances and acquire new salience through an unconventional syntactical arrangement. The ironic tone, apart from lending distance and objectivity, becomes a characteristic and objective force, giving a new muscular quality to the words, animating the whole poetic vision.
>
> (Vrishchik *1969, 1 (2))*

Joshi's translations of Patel's poetry are therefore critical to the visibility of emerging poets, striving to make their voices heard from the margins of their communities. Not only expected to convey the underlying meaning of cultural codes, translators were now also accountable for reflecting the rhythm and tone integral to the recitation of folk songs. Undoing meters and conventions of compositions that early modernist poets adhered to under the guise of decorum, poets now sought to revive the zeal of folk poetry in search of a new socio-political identity. Patel's poetry, while rooted in his cultural milieu, remained free of the burden of traditional norms. His work, incorporating colloquial idioms and rhythms, seemed to have discovered a balanced convergence of a modern and native sensibility (1969). This new significance afforded to traditional Indian imagery is evident in Patel's poem, મારી આંખે કંકુના સૂરજ આથમ્યા (*Maari aankhein kankuna suraj aathamya*), translated by Joshi as 'Kumkum suns went down my eyes today.' Joshi's transliteration of the word *kumkum* in his translation of the poem speaks to the impossibility of translating the cultural connotations embedded in folk literature. *Kumkum* refers to the vermillion mark worn by a Hindu woman on her forehead as a symbol of her marriage, and the setting of *kumkum* suns indicates the death of her husband, evoking notions of tragedy, departure and loss.

House highlights the influence of language on the lived experiences shared by members of a social group, stating that language acts as a means of categorising cultural experiences and reflects cultural codes shared by its speakers. Concurrently, linguistic relativity implies the very opposite, that the lexicon and structure of language influence the speaker's thought processes and perceptions (House 2002: 95). In either instance, the retention of symbolic words like *kumkum* remains crucial to a collective cultural imaginary. An English translation of a poem such as this, ripe with references to familial and marital traditions of Gujarat, may therefore lose its specificity so deeply rooted in the cultural consciousness. Patel's poetry invited a re-envisioning of the literary and visual culture for the nation—one that resisted carrying forward conventions of European writing as well as the reverting to an expected homogenous Indian tradition. What a cultural revival for a developing Indian identity called for was not the centring of a nation or nationality but that of a community that could extend beyond the conventional nation-state model and could admit a multiplicity of ethnicities, religions and cultures within and without.

Translation across mediums: interdiscplinary approaches to visuals and words

In keeping with the interdisciplinary practices of the Baroda artists, the works included in *Vrishchik* spanned a range of genres and mediums, linking to an outlying form of translation—that of shifts between disciplines. Using examples of works produced in Baroda at the time, I discuss translations of mediums in the form of illustrations supplementing written text, and narratives expressed through text and illustration concurrently.

Sheikh's work as a writer and artist reveals his ease in shifting between disciplines, with his work taking forms of prose, paintings and poetry to meet the needs of his expression. In 1968, returning from a three-year stay in England, he began a series of free-form text in Gujarati, titled *Gher Jatan* (Returning Home). He writes: 'they articulated both a conflict and convergence of the worlds we live in. The world that was given to us, the world that came to us, the world that we created and the world that we yearned for' (Hyman and Sheikh 1968). Although describing a nostalgia and longing for a return to his hometown of Kathiawad, Gujarat, Sheikh's words also speak to the transitory condition of postcolonial societies wherein the inherited culture of the nation is often displaced by a search for an identity of its own. Sheikh's awareness of the inadequacy of the 'world that was given to us' is further translated to a search for 'the world that we yearn for' (Sheikh 1968). His text can be seen in the context of the separation between the culture that is expected of the artists and writers of the time and the one that they aspire to create.

Sheikh's narrative paintings from the 1970s and 1980s echo similar notions, extending his exploration of the cultural matrix of postcolonial India. His works placed value on representational ambiguity, focusing on how multiplicity could be experienced temporally with shifts in historical periods (Zitzewitz 2014: 103). To Sheikh, living in India meant living simultaneously in several times and cultures. His paintings reflect his gradual adoption of a cosmopolitan perspective, returning to India as a trained artist after a three-year fellowship at the Royal College of Art in London. His paintings, *Returning Home* (1969–1973)*, Revolving Routes* (1981), and *Speaking Street* (1981), create a sense of temporal difference within a single plane. Incorporating a jumble of figures, colours and landscapes, the composition of these paintings reflects the visual language of the free-form verse of *Gher Jatan*.

Visual Notes, a poem by Bhupen Khakhar published in the first issue of *Vrishchik*, takes this notion of a translation of words to images a step further through his use of visual imagery. Reflective of his narrative paintings, Khakhar is unapologetic in his descriptive observations of the postcolonial space unfurling around him. Juxtaposing ambitious visuals of Nehru's Five-Year Plans with whimsical advertisements of Badhshahi soap '(what a magic!)' (Khakhar 1969), Khakhar seems to address the multiplicity of Indian society through the integration of modernity in the everyday, by invoking and satirising the looming monumentality of it. His approach normalises the elusive celebrity of certain sections of the masses while also conflating the importance of others, therefore unifying a range of disparities within the people. Khakhar's writing style further coalesces a range of cultural signifiers. *Visual Notes*, neither divided into verses nor comprised of complete sentences, gives the impression of a continuous chain of observations, none more immediate than another. His utterance of a multitude of related/unrelated objects—'photographs of the British Raj with Viceroys' and 'photographs of family groups in front of Taj Mahal'—seemingly in a single breath, lends contrasting experiences equal attention (Khakhar 1969). Khakhar's visual representation is articulated in Homi Bhabha's question: 'How does one write the nation's modernity as the event of the everyday and the advent of the epochal?' (Bhabha 1994: 141). This was an issue that all the members of *Vrishchik* grappled with: how could they represent the temporality of a nation by creating timelessness in a work of art? Khakhar's poem surpasses the need for a visual translation of these abstract concepts expressed through text, rather than a figurative painting, by blurring the boundaries between the disciplines.

Arvind Krishna Mehrotra's original poems in English, featured in *Vrishchik* 2 (6–7), took a parallel approach to this form of interdisciplinary translation. Mehrotra's unique poems expressed meaning through their layout and typography, with indents resembling tidal waves in one, or isolating single words on each line in another. 'Culture and Society' (1970), the first poem of this issue, stands out for its visual layout. Nerlekar categorises this poem as concrete poetry, a movement started simultaneously with Ernst Gomringer in Europe and the Noigandres groups in Brazil in 1955 (Nerlekar 2016), in which the letters and words on the page coagulate to become solid, thereby creating literal visuals by themselves. Comprised solely of onomatopoeias formed primarily of vowels, 'Culture and Society' reads as a continuous chain of sounds of laughter, shouts and shrieks. The words themselves are laid out in the form of a monument with individual alphabets repeated vertically in each row. Combined with its title, 'Culture and Society,' and its references to modernist architecture, this poem appears to allude to the postcolonial anxieties of a newly developing nation. Artists at the time stood at a challenging crossroad, between presenting as being rooted in tradition, while ushering in a new mode of modernist revival.

In a postcolonial nation, modernism was perceived to be an offspring of former colonial powers and modern Indian artists writing in English were often met with hostility and accused of being un-Indian. The very practice of writing in English, especially in the case of bilingual poets and translators who had an 'Indian' language at their disposal to go back to, was seen as an act of cultural betrayal (Zecchini 2014: 8). In this regard, these writers' decision to continue to employ English was a political choice. They recognised the power of the languages they operated in, and chose to have their voices heard beyond the borders of the nation. It was in the adoption of the otherness of English that Indian writers were able to reinvent their own iteration of the modern. As A.K. Ramanujan explains, 'English has distorted our traditions, but it has also made us look at our traditions. English has been the "other" through which we have returned to ourselves' (2001: 79).

Vrishchik's role in the postcolonial development of a visual art and literature for a newly independent India was critical in expanding the boundaries of a national culture to works produced from the margins. In the act of dissenting against a homogeneous visual culture, they admitted a multiplicity of artworks, coalescing artists in a linguistic and culturally disparate nation. The discourse surrounding institutional critique in *Vrishchik*, while one that was tethered to the development of a national culture, created a space for narratives that reached beyond the conventional nation-state model. *Vrishchik*'s attempts at restructuring the canon relied on the autonomy of the communities represented in these institutions. By addressing strategies of cultural identification, they made *people*, rather than institutions, the immanent subjects of social and literary narratives. *Vrishchik* held artists accountable in situations which institutions were not equipped to handle, calling for an active participation in issues that they were directly implicated in.

Related topics

Rendering Bengali Dalit Discourse as Translational Activism; Resistance, Activism and Marronage in Paul Bowles's Translations of the Oral Stories of Tangier; The Single Most Translated Short Story in the History of African Writing.

Note

1 All *Vrishchik* entries cited in this chapter are referenced with the year of publication followed by the year number, and issue number in parentheses. *Vrishchik* was published for a span of four years in twenty-nine issues.

Further reading

Sheikh, Gulammohammed (2004) *Our Literature, Their Literature?* Asia Art Archive. Courtesy of Gulammohammed Sheikh. Source: Gulammohammed Sheikh and Asia Art Archive (Unpublished).

This essay (part of a collection of Sheikh's writings digitised by the Asia Art Archive) was written in the aftermath of the 2002 communal violence in Gujarat. Sheikh invokes his position as a Gujarati writer, calling upon the literary fraternity to reflect upon their responsibility in addressing perceptions of the 'other' in the nation's history.

Kapur, Geeta (1970) *In Quest of Identity.* Masters of Art Dissertation. Royal College of Art, London.

This essay, written during Kapur's stay in London between 1968 and 1969, is an exploration of her ideas on the relationship between art and 'indeginism,' which she defines as 'a contemporary's concern for the unique features of [the] nation's history and tradition.'

Iyer, Nalini, and Bonnie Zare (eds.) (2009) *Other Tongues: Rethinking the Language Debates in India.* New York: Rodopi.

Iyer and Zare expand on the ongoing debate among Indian authors on the role of the English language in Indian literature, problematising the hegemony of the language and challenging the binary divisions of English/vernacular and diaspora/native.

References

'Against Communalism,' (1969) *Vrishchik* 1 (7–8). Courtesy of Gulammohammed Sheikh. Gulammohammed Sheikh and Asia Art Archive.

Ahmad, Aijaz (1987) 'Jameson's Rhetoric of Otherness and the "National Allegory",' *Social Text* 17: 3–25.

Bassnett, Susan, and Harish Trivedi (eds.) (1999) *Post-colonial Translation: Theory and Practice.* London: Routledge.

Bhabha, Homi (1994) *Location of Culture.* London: Routledge.

Dingwaney, Anuradha (1995) *Between Languages and Cultures: Translation and Cross-Cultural Texts.* Pittsburgh: University of Pittsburgh Press.

Heredia, Goretti López (2004) 'African Literature in Colonial Languages: Challenges Posed by "Minor Literatures" for the Theory and Practice of Translation,' in *Less Translated Languages.* Eds. Albert Branchadell and Lovell Margaret West. Philadelphia: John Benjamins Publishing Company. 165–176.

House, Juliane (2002) 'Universality versus Culture Specificity in Translation,' in *Translation Studies: Perspectives on an Emerging Discipline.* Ed. Alessandra Riccardi. London: Cambridge University Press. 91–109.

Hyman, Timothy, and Gulammohammed Sheikh (2010) *Web of Stories: Vrishchik and Lalit Kala Akademi* [online]. Available at: www.webofstories.com/play/gulammohammed.sheikh/1 [accessed 15 October 2019].

Jaffrelot, Christophe (2010) 'The 2002 Pogrom in Gujarat,' in *Religion, Caste and Politics in India.* Ed. Christophe Jaffrelot. Delhi: Primus Books. 376–396.

Jaisingh, Indu (1970) 'Triennale and the Implications of Internationalism,' *Vrishchik* 2 (4–5). Courtesy of Gulammohammed Sheikh. Gulammohammed Sheikh and Asia Art Archive.

Joshi, Suresh (1969) 'Life against Death: The Poetry of Ravji Patel,' *Vrishchik* 1 (2). Gulammohammed Sheikh Archive. Courtesy of Gulammohammed Sheikh and Asia Art Archive.

Kabir, Das (1915) *Songs of Kabir: Translated by Rabindranath Tagore.* New York: Macmillan Company.

Kapur, Geeta (1973) 'The Social Context of Contemporary Art,' *Vrishchik* 4 (4). Gulammohammed Sheikh Archive. Courtesy of Gulammohammed Sheikh and Asia Art Archive.

Kapur, Geeta (2000) *When was Modernism in Indian Art?.* New Delhi: Tulika.

Kapur, Geeta (2011) 'Signatures of Dissent,' *The Art News Magazine of India* 6 (2): 78–81.

Khakhar, Bhupen (1969) 'Visual Notes,' *Vrishchik* 1 (1). Gulammohammed Sheikh Archive. Courtesy of Gulammohammed Sheikh and Asia Art Archive.

Lal, Purushottama (1996) *Transcreation: Seven Essays on the Art of Transcreation*. Kolkata: Writers Workshop.

Lalit Kala Akademi (2018) *Lalit Kala Akademi: About* [online]. Available at: http://lalitkala.gov.in/showdetails.php?id=39 [accessed 12 May 2018].

McDonald, Peter D. (2017) *Artefacts of Writing: Ideas of State and Communities of Letters from Matthew Arnold to Xu Bing*. London: Oxford University Press.

Mehrotra, Arvind Krishna (1970) 'Culture and Society,' *Vrishchik* 2 (6–7) Gulammohammed Sheikh Archive. Courtesy of Gulammohammed Sheikh and Asia Art Archive.

Mehrotra, Arvind Krishna (1970) 'Recastings from Kabir,' *Vrishchik* 1 (11–12). Gulammohammed Sheikh Archive. Courtesy of Gulammohammed Sheikh and Asia Art Archive.

Mehrotra, Arvind Krishna (1976) *Nine Enclosures*. Bombay: Clearing House.

'Miniature Purana,' (1970) *Vrishchik* 1 (9–10). Gulammohammed Sheikh Archive. Courtesy of Gulammohammed Sheikh and Asia Art Archive.

Mukim, Mantra (2014) 'Mantra Mukim Reviews Arvind Krishna Mehrotra's Collected Poems 1969–2014,' *Asymptote Journal* [online]. Available at: www.asymptotejournal.com/criticism/arvind-krishna-mehrotra-collected-poems-19692014/ [accessed 15 October 2019].

Nerlekar, Anjali (2016) *Bombay Modern: Arun Kolatkar and Bilingual Literary Culture*. Evanston: Northwestern University Press.

Pande, Rekha (1985) 'The Social Context of the Bhakti Movement: A Study of Kabir,' in *The Forty-Sixth Session, Indian History Congress*, Guru Nanak Dev University. 230–235 [online]. Available at: www.researchgate.net/publication/236003005. [accessed 15 October 2019].

Ramanujan, A. K. (1999) *The Collected Essays of A. K. Ramanujan*. Ed. Vinay Dharwadker. Delhi: Oxford University Press..

Ramanujan, A. K. (2001) *Uncollected Poems and Prose*. Eds. Molly Daniels-Ramanujan and Keith Harrisson. Delhi: Oxford University Press.

Salvador, Dora Sales (2005) 'Translational Passages: Indian Fiction in English as Transcreation?' in *Less Translated Languages*. Eds. Albert Branchadell and Lovell Margaret West. Philadelphia: John Benjamins Publishing Company. 189–205.

Sheikh, Gulammohammed (2004) *Our Literature, Their Literature?*. Gulammohammed Sheikh Archive. Courtesy of Gulammohammed Sheikh and Asia Art Archive.

Simon, Sherry, and Paul St-Pierre (eds.) (2000) *Changing the Terms: Translating in the Postcolonial Era*. Ottawa: University of Ottawa Press.

Spitz, Douglas (1993) 'Cultural Pluralism, Revivalism, and Modernity in South Asia,' in *The Rising Tide of Cultural Pluralism: The Nation-state at Bay?* Ed. Crawford Young. Madison: University of Wisconsin Press. 242–264.

Thakkar, Piyush (2008) 'Gulammohammed Sheikh and Many Literatures,' *The Guild* [online]. Available at: www.guildindia.com/artjournal/BooksMuseumsandlibraries-Nov07/Gulammohammed%20Sheikh%20and%20Many%20Literatures.htm [accessed 15 October 2019].

Tymoczko, Maria (2000) 'Translations of Themselves: The Contours of Postcolonial Fiction,' in *Changing the Terms: Translating in the Postcolonial Era*. Eds. Sherry Simon and Paul St-Pierre. Ottawa: University of Ottawa Press. 147–163.

Vrishchik (1969) 1 (1) Gulammohammed Sheikh Archive. Courtesy of Gulammohammed Sheikh and Asia Art Archive.

Vrishchik (1970) 1 (3) Gulammohammed Sheikh Archive. Courtesy of Gulammohammed Sheikh and Asia Art Archive.

Vrishchik (1971) 2 (4–5) Gulammohammed Sheikh Archive. Courtesy of Gulammohammed Sheikh and Asia Art Archive.

Wolf, Michaela (2000) 'The *Third Space* in Postcolonial Representation,' in *Changing the Terms: Translating in the Postcolonial Era*. Eds. Sherry Simon and Paul St-Pierre. Ottawa: University of Ottawa Press. 127–143.

Zecchini, Laetitia (2014) *Arun Kolatkar and Literary Modernism in India*. London: Bloomsbury.

Zitzewitz, Karin (2014) *The Art of Secularism*. London: Oxford University Press.

23

Bengali Dalit discourse as translational activism
Studying a Dalit autobiography

Bidisha Pal and Partha Bhattacharjee

Introduction

Dalit literature is a minor and non-canonised Indian literature. 'Dalit' is derived from the Sanskrit word 'দলন' or 'দলিত,' that means 'crushed' or 'broken down to the ground.' According to Hindu cosmology and traditional Indian political divisions, Dalits are situated at the lowest stratum of the five-fold caste structure. Dalits are identified as the *panchamvarna*; the other four are *brahmin, kayastha, vaishya* and *sudra*. Dalits are often designated as 'অস্পৃশ্য' (*asprishya*) or 'untouchable,' 'অচ্ছুত' (*acchuta*) or 'outcast,' 'হরিজন' (*harijan*) or 'children of God,' 'পারায়াহ' (*pariah*) or 'the other,' 'জল-আচল' (*jal-achal*) or 'untouchable to water' and so on, terms that are derogatory and clearly indicate their distant position from the rest of the society. Hailing from different regional states of India including Maharashtra, Karnataka, Tamilnadu, Kerala, Andhra Pradesh, Punjab, Gujarat, Odisha and Bengal, Dalit literature has not been able to shed its regional affiliations. Translation of Dalit literature has enabled a generative transformation that enables us to attend to 'local suffering and [which] folklorises transnational discourses of rights, dignity and agency' (Nayar 2011: 25).

Bengali Dalit literature comprises further layers within the shifting literary history of India. It is comprised of various genres. Dalit autobiographies and autobiographical narratives tend to champion the assertion of the marginalised selves. Dalit autobiographical writing serves a distinct role in the Dalit movement for human rights and socio-political equality as 'a rich and expressive medium of Dalit personhood' (Ganguly 2009: 429). Bengali Dalits are a sub-subaltern category dominated by a caste–class dichotomy and the politics of middle-class Bengali 'ভদ্রলোক' (*bhadrolok*)[1] intelligentsia. The translation of autobiographical narratives helps to expose and critique the suffering that the Bengali Dalits face.

This chapter analyses the Bengali autobiography of the Dalit writer Manoranjan Byapari, namely ইতিবৃত্তে চণ্ডাল জীবন (*Itibritte Chandal Jiban*) (2012), a work translated under the title *Interrogating My Chandal[2] Life: The Autobiography of a Dalit* (2018) by Sipra Mukherjee, an academician and critic who has been actively engaged in the study of Dalit literature for decades and has ventured into literary translations of several other Bengali Dalit poems and novels. As the first Dalit autobiography in Bengal, Byapari's *Itibritte* often deviates from the norms of conventional autobiography while engaging in socio-political activism and bearing testimony to a number of tumultuous waves of the history of India. 'Byapari is placed relentlessly in the margins of caste and class, but this is a margin which weaves in and out of the erstwhile familiar majoritarian discourse of history,' writes Mukherjee (2018). Byapari admits himself, 'আত্মজীবনীর এই এক মস্ত অসুবিধা-কোনো আড়াল থাকে না' (Byapari 2012: 14), ['This is a great difficulty with autobiographies—that there is no veil that I can draw around me'] (Byapari 2018). The translation of Byapari's autobiography aids in expressing the marginality and marginal voice(s).

Mukherjee has an interesting take on translating Byapari's autobiography. She admits:

> I believe my own Bengal background with a grandfather who arrived here from East Bengal, my years of growing up in the suburbs, and my entering the city as a young woman who knew nobody, allowed me some immediacy of understanding the many nuanced ways in which hegemony works to marginalise and control.
>
> *(Mukherjee 2018)*

As such, the translation confirms the thesis of Bassnett and Trivedi, that 'translations are always embedded in cultural and political systems, and in history ... the strategies employed by translators reflect the context in which texts are produced' (1999: 6). Apart from Byapari, Manohar Mouli Biswas' *Surviving in My World: Growing up Dalit in Bengal* is the sole Dalit autobiography to have been translated into English, in 2015. Translation aids in bridging the local and the global together; it provides shape to the critical disjuncture that is embedded within the textuality of the autobiography.

Sharankumar Limbale, the Marathi Dalit author and critic who was born in 1956 and penned several major works, including the autobiography *The Outcaste* (2003), a critical essay *Towards an Aesthetic of Dalit Literature: History, Controversies and Considerations* (2004), the short-story anthology *The Dalit Brahmin and Other Stories* (2018) and the novel *Smouldering Horizons* (2019), has also laid focus upon the important roles that the translators of Dalit literary texts play within society which are extremely effective. The author and the translator both hail from a particular social atmosphere and so the translation develops a specific commitment to the cause of the marginalised ethos and suffering. In his analysis of the nature of the translation of testimonial prison literature, El Guabli shows how activist translation acts as joint authorship to negotiate between the survivors and the co-author or the translator who 'mediates the transformation of this lived experience into textual form' (2020: 23). Translators of Dalit writings also act as mediators in transforming the lived experience of the marginalised community into a textual form linguistically distinct yet similar in tonality and essence to the original.

The chapter offers a detailed corpus analysis of Byapari's autobiography in both the original Bengali and the translated English. We ask how translation of marginalised narratives advances the activist cause against hegemonic mainstream history, how literary translation becomes a socio-political instrument of change in the process of its transmission, and how the very act of translation becomes translaboration, a process where and by which both the translator and the author together contribute to the Dalit discourse of marginalisation.

Activism against the hegemonic mainstream

Literary products that cater to society and its socio-political condition acquire a particular identity. The literature of Dalit writers emerges from a marginalised discourse. In the writing process, the social movement gets merged with the literary movement. Chatterjee points out that, while minorities and the Dalits may have been incorporated into India's political society by law, they are not yet a part of its civil society (2004). Dalit autobiographies and autobiographical narratives give vent to the exploration of a particular resistance towards the hegemonic *Homo hierarchicus* society (Dumont 1966: 69). The mode of representation is determined by a counter-public culture in discord with the mainstream. As Gouanvic notes, 'marginalised writers and artists … are the maroons of the source culture, as they attempt to remove themselves from the hold of legitimacy' (2000: 107).

Through their literary outputs, Dalits unleash accumulated expressions of anger and give voice to the suppressed and subsumed history that objectifies them. Their literary forms are steeped in local regional languages and cultures. The translation of the literary texts tends to re-assert and broaden the scope of emancipation because translation, as Tymoczko points out, is 'a means of shifting discourses, a means available for the purposes of identity formation' (2000: 31). The act of translation de-contextualises the source texts of marginalised Dalit culture.

Narrated from the perspective of a member of that particular group which resides at the fringes of society and revealing the hypocrisy and nepotistic policies of that particular society, Manoranjan Byapari's ইতিবৃত্তে চণ্ডাল জীবন (*Itibritte Chandal Jiban*) (*Interrogating My Chandal Life*) holds some significance. It is written by a person who is not an author by profession. Byapari currently serves as a cook in a school for the mute in the Jadavpur region of Kolkata. He has never had a formal education. In his book he discusses how his involvement in his youth with the Naxals and the Naxalite movement of central India puts him behind bars for a brief period, and his introduction to letters is initiated within those four corners of the Alipur Central jail at a very later stage of life. Byapari's narrative revolves around the struggles for existence and sustenance of an impoverished Dalit who was born in Turuk-khali near the village Pirichpur of the Barisal district of then East Pakistan (now called Bangladesh). After partition, he came to West Bengal to spend the later part of his life. The first part of the narrative depicts the tragic and helpless condition of Byapari's family—consisting of his parents and brothers and sisters—who endure a failed struggle for the basic amenities of life.

In spite of being a non-fiction *Bildungsroman*,[3] the book is more than a mere representation of a personal story; it serves as a testimony to the contemporary socio-political upheavals, post-partition trauma and suffering of the refugees of then East Pakistan, the horrific conditions of camp life and the hypocrisy and unabashed cruelties of upper-caste society. The lucidity of expression and strident tone of the narrative correspond to the tragic candour of poverty. The original Bengali story garners critical attention and reviews, as Byapari mentions in the preface:

বহু স্বনামধন্য সন্মানীয় মানুষ যখন তাদের শক্তিশালী কলমে তার কথা লেখেন-যুগান্তর, বর্তমান, আনন্দবাজার, প্রতিদিন, আজকাল, EPW, কথাদেশ, নতুন খবর, দিনকাল, স্টেটসম্যান, টাইমস অফ ইন্ডিয়া, মেইনস্ট্রিম আরেক রকম, দৈনিক জাগরণ, যুগশঙ্খ, হিন্দুস্তান টাইমস, এই সব পত্রিকায় তার নাম পরিচয়, প্রকাশিত হয়, দূরদর্শনের জনপ্রিয় প্রোগ্রাম 'তারা নিউজ' এর 'তারার নজর', ২৪ ঘন্টা, ইটিভি এর সংবাদ এ যখন তাকে দেখানো হয়, RSTV চ্যানেল তথ্যচিত্র বানায় তখন সে ভাবতেই পারে-জীবন সার্থক।

(Byapari 2012: 14–15)

[When the powerful pens of many famous writers, critics, write about the literature that he has created in famous journals and newspapers—*Jugantar*, *Bartaman*, *Anandabazar Patrika*, *Pratidin*, *Aajkal*, *The Hindu*, *EPW*, *Kathadesh*, *Natun Khabar*, *Dinkal*—publishing his name and his life's details—when popular television shows like Doordarshan's 'Khash Khobor', Akash Bangla's 'Sadharon Asadharon', 'Khojkhobor', or 'Tarar Nazar' or Tara News talk about him, then his belief that life has been fulfilling may be understandable.]

(Mukherjee 2018)

Translating the minority culture helps in re-establishing the identity against the majoritarian culture (Venuti 1998; Tymoczko 2000; Cronin 2006). The translation of Byapari's autobiography takes place nearly six years after and is indeed a necessary move to convey the suppressed history of a Bengali Dalit to the broader audience. As the translator confesses, 'I needed to translate Manoranjan Byapari's autobiography because it was the other half of the story that I had known existed' (Mukherjee 2018). Published by the respected Delhi-based publishing house Sage-Samya, the translation made Byapari a household name within a couple of months. He featured as the invited speaker in a number of leading Indian literary festivals, including World Book Fair, Delhi 2018, Jaipur Literary Festival 2018, Apeejay Kolkata Literary Festival 2018, Times Lit Fest, Kolkata Literature Festival, national and international academic seminars in major universities of West Bengal, including Presidency University, Rabindra Bharati University, University of Kalyani, discussion panels and book fairs in Kolkata and Delhi.

There have been critical commentaries and reviews in leading journals and newspapers as well because the translation makes a valuable contribution to the slender corpora of Bengali Dalit literature in translation. Author Souvendra Sekhar Hansda comments in the *National Herald*: 'from the original Bengali to the English translation, Byapari's autobiography—or memoir—gathered one identity after the other. Quite like how Byapari himself gathered several identities through his lifetime' (8 April 2018). In another interdisciplinary journal, *Rupkatha*, Pal argues that 'the book paves the way for the opportunities of more translation endeavours to come that would be able to contribute a significant lot in near future to the existing corpora of Dalit literature in English translation' (2018: 269). In 2018 the translated autobiography also received the Hindu Literary Prize, one of India's most prestigious literary accolades for non-fiction. Translation, thus, mainstreams the source text's ideology to further impact critics and readers.

The narrative of *Interrogating My Chandal Life* is rich in detail about the suffering and resistance of Byapari. At various stages of his life, the protagonist has to fight with a number of enemies: poverty, caste affliction, economic crisis, hunger, penury, sexual abuse, the hypocrisy of the upper-caste people in his journey. Evacuated as a refugee from his homeland Turuk-khali of then East Pakistan (or East Bengal) in the wake of the partition of Bengal (1947), Byapari's life is awash with uncertainties until he meets author Mahasweta Devi, who inspires him to write and introduces him as the 'Rickshaw-wallah' (Mukherjee 2018: 215) writer to the world. This particular event cuts a new course in Byapari's life; he gradually becomes an indispensable part of West Bengal's literary mainstream. Byapari tends to unravel the aestheticism of fictional representation by pointing out the sordid realism where he launches a movement with his particular manner of contextualising things.

As the lingua franca of modern South Asian literature, English acts as a bridge within the linguistic plurality and multilingual ambience of India. English helps to globalise the vernacular Dalit discourse to make a source of transnational solidarity that 'can connect people around the globe to the Dalit experience' (Prasad 2005). Limbale, in a conversation with Arun and Alok Mukherjee, shares his experience about the effective role of translation: 'Translation has given me a name and international recognition. My books are now included in university syllabi. Academics read and do research on my books. Translation has contributed to disseminating my thinking processes' (2015). Limbale focuses on how English destroys language barriers and strengthens the Dalit movement and language of human rights.

Byapari's autobiography delineates contexts where power and politics play an intertwined role in shaping the shifting narrative frames. It records a tumultuous period of history and expresses suppressed anger against the hegemonic society that has silenced Dalit voices for millennia. Being translated into English by a member of the dominant society and into a target language marked by cultural hegemony, the autobiography enables constructive activism that reverberates across the narrative. Firstly, it carves a specific provision among the mainstream. As Zubillaga notes, 'in order to aspire to be translated into hegemonic languages, minority language texts almost always need to be first translated into a/the hegemonic language/s with which the minority language coexists' (2017: 12). Secondly, by entering into the very hegemonic mainstream society, the translation pays back the society in its own coin. Dalit literature is a 'literature of action' (Valmiki 2003: xxxv). While the writer initiates a movement against the hegemonic society, the translation arrests the particular contexts of the narrative, the terms, sentences and phrases that denote the myriad ways of movement.

A close study of the text reveals where the contexts of movement are built within the narrative. The example from the text cited in Table 23.1 in both original and translated forms echoes the feelings of the author.

Here the Bengali words 'ছেঁড়া ফাটা বেসুর বেতাল ঢাক' in the original Bengali source text convey the jarring tone that Byapari uses in order to introduce the unfavourable circumstance he has been subject to. However, the translator's choice of words poses a stark contrast to the literal rendering presented in the third column. 'ঢাক' is the Bengali musical instrument used during festivities; it has no recognisable link to activism or to a political movement. Besides, 'ঢাক পেটানো' or 'beating the drum' in Bengali connotes the tendency to brag about oneself. The use of 'drum' evokes an association with activism (as soldiers and army men carry drums while marching and drums are

Table 23.1 Comparison of the established translation and an attempted translation of the original Bengali line denoting an activist frame of mind

Original Bengali	Established translation	Literal translation (translation ours)
আমার ছেঁড়া ফাটা বেসুর বেতাল ঢাকের বাজনা (Byapari 2012: 14).	The sound of my cracked, splintered and pitted drum (Byapari 2018).	The beating of my tattered, burst out, unmelodious, and unrhythmic cylindrical musical instrument.

used in wars). Hence, the rough cacophonous sound like that of a prostrated drum serves as a figurative metaphor for venting anger at the hypocrisy of the hegemonic society against which Byapari launches his tirade. Again 'splintered,' 'cracked' and 'pitted' denote the harshness that the translator has constructed; these words do not correspond with the literal rendering that has been provided. The chosen words in the translation tend to modify the text to constitute the active marching of a marginalised writer of Bengal who no longer wants to remain silent; however hard to the ear it may be, beating the drum of protest in the translated narrative builds a path towards activism. Thus, equivalence is established with the intended sense and intention of the original text, if not with the words. The translator makes the political meaning of the text more visible in translation.

There are similar examples in various phases of the narrative where the transference of words from the Bengali original to the translated text constructs an activist writer to a wider circle of readers who might not be aware of the original Bengali words but who can nonetheless make a connection to the scenario (Table 23.2).

Notably, in the above examples, the translation often modifies the original and tends to differ from the literal rendering. The conscious choices that the translator makes here depict and re-present the socio-political journey of Byapari. The translation is informed by a revolutionary attitude and constructs a political agenda that accords with this attitude. Each phrase conveys the translator's activist orientation.

The first translated phrase provides an additional word—'victim'—which is lacking in the original and which changes its meaning. The translation tends to project Byapari as a physically and mentally strong personality who can exercise his power in order to defeat his equally powerful enemy. The manner of translating the text

Table 23.2 Comparison of established and attempted translations of the original Bengali lines denoting the activist frame of mind

Original Bengali	Established translation	Literal translation (translation ours)
সবল **সশস্ত্র প্রতিপক্ষ** (Byapari 2012: 55).	My victim, my armed enemy (Byapari 2018: 50).	The strong-armed enemy.
উগ্র বল **প্রয়োগের** দ্বারাই (Byapari 2012: 127).	Have had to take recourse to violence (Byapari 2018: 128).	It can be successful through the application of extreme force.
আগুনখোর নকশালদের সাথে ছিলাম (Byapari 2012: 167).	I had worked with the fiery Naxalites (Byapari 2018: 176).	I had remained with the fire-engulfing Naxalites.
যাদের **মৃত্যু** কামনা **করি** (Byapari 2012: 454).	Those whom I detested as oppressors of the human spirit and humanity (Byapari 2018: 344).	Those whose death I desire.
আমার গল্পো তাকে মেরে ফেলি (Byapari 2012: 454).	I waged awar against them through writing (Byapari 2018: 344).	I killed them in my stories.
এতেই পাই **মানসিক তৃপ্তি** আর **বেঁচে** থাকার রসদ (Byapari 2012: 454).	[Omitted.]	I get mental satisfaction and the purpose of living.

thus suggests the individuality of the translator. The second translated phrase contains the term 'violence,' which is absent from the literal rendering. Violence is an extreme form of unleashing power; using such a word implies the translator's attempt to make the marginalised man fight back with utmost rage and anger. In the third example, the translator uses the word 'worked' instead of 'stayed' or 'remained.' 'Work' is an active term compared to the 'stayed' or 'remained' of the literal meaning that denotes passivity; the translator uses it to suggest socio-political tumultuousness. The very next phrase furthers this agenda with the words 'oppressors of human spirit and humanity,' which however do not exist in the original. This is also a translational invention and it conveys the ideology of the translator who takes part in the author's revolt against the mainstream. The invention does not maintain the word-to-word correspondence with the literal meaning; the translator modifies and develops the sense. In the fifth phrase, 'মেরে ফেলি' has been replaced with 'waged a war,' whereas the literal meaning it connotes is 'killed.' This again is a translational modification where 'waged a war' connotes the very revolutionary activist mindscape.

Notably, in the final column, the phrase 'এতেই পাই মানসিক তৃপ্তি আর বেঁচে থাকার রসদ' is omitted in the translated piece for the sake of sophistication. Emotive expression knows no bound when a Bengali writer writes in Bengali, but emotional overflow sometimes resists being translated into a culturally dissimilar context. The phrase is not given its literal meaning but the omission creates a gap here; not contextually, but it certainly meddles with the progress of the narrative.

From a literary journey to a socio-political journey

Literary translation becomes effective as socio-political translation when it addresses particular aspects of the social milieu. Dalit autobiographies are community biography; they serve not only personal selves but also the social and socio-political selves of the community. Byapari's autobiography offers a socio-political testimony of an unfavourable time for the oppressed people whom he represents and with whom he shares a common cause. As Byapari states, 'As a Dalit myself, I harboured a weakness for people of my community, believing that whatever ills we may have, we were not like the self-seeking and corrupt upper castes and upper classes' (2018: 346). The narrative of his life converges with many scintillating events, without which translation would be unheard and unseen.

Along with corresponding to the linguistic or syntactical transference of the literary narrative, the translation of Byapari's autobiography transposes the text's social context and thereby enables societal change. 'Micro-perspectives' embedded in the texts

> attempt to examine issues related to resistance and activism (e.g. Tymoczko 2010) and explore translations as records of cultural contestation and ideological struggle … translations are then seen as a form of ethical, political, and ideological activity rather than merely as a communicative act or a creative literary activity.
> *(Hrystiv 2017: 32)*

According to Tymoczko:

> Translators must make choices, selecting aspects or parts of a text to transpose and emphasize. Such choices in turn serve to create representations of their source texts,

representations that are also partial … indeed partiality is what differentiates transla-tions of the same or similar works, making them flexible and diverse, enabling them to participate in the dialectic of power, the ongoing process of political discourse, and strategies for social change.

(2000: 24)

The translation, thus, is not a blind replica of the source text or target text; the translator is a social agent fortifying Dalit discourse into a particular socio-political context. The translator has to select which parts of the text will be emphasised for the sake of narra-tive flow. The texts provide the social context and constitute the intersection of the liter-ary and the socio-political horizons.

Byapari's autobiography becomes an astute analytical socio-biography when he talks about the *Namasudra*[4] community, its particularities and the role of casteism and casteist politics in society. The translated portions retain some of the Bengali words 'নমোশুদ্দুর' (a fond colloquial way of addressing the Namasudra people), 'নমশূদ্র' (the community regarded as the outcaste in certain parts of Bengal), 'কাশ্যপ গোত্র' (a Hindu lineage or clan believed to be originated from the ancient sage Kashyapa), 'চণ্ডাল' (a Hindu lower-caste community associated with handling corpses and considered untouchable), 'চাঁড়াল' (a fond way of addressing a member of the 'Chandal' caste), 'জল-আচল' (not able to touch water), 'বাঙাল' (inhabitants of former East Pakistan (now East Bengal or Bangladesh) who came to West Bengal after the partition of Bengal and India), 'নমঃ' (another fond colloquial way of addressing the Namasudra people) and 'বাগ্দী' (the lower scheduled caste[5] fisherman community of Bengal considered as untouchables). Notably, these words have no exact equivalent in English; retaining them illuminates local textures of Byapari's world. The translator's decision to retain such words alerts the reader to the presence of the vernacular (Table 23.3).

Table 23.3 Comparison of the established and attempted literal rendering of the Bengali word steeped in the social context

Original Bengali	Established translation	
ভারতীয় সমাজ ব্যবস্থায় বঙ্গভূমির বাঙালি মননে, বিশেষ করে কলকাতা মহানগরীর মধ্যবিত্ত ভাবনায়, ছোটজাত, ছোটোলোক, কায়িক শ্রম এই তিনটি শব্দ অঙ্গাঙ্গিভাবে জড়িত যারা ছোটজাত তারাই ছোটোলোক (Byapari 2012: 122).	In the Indian social system, and in the minds of the Bengalis, especially the urban-resident Bengalis, three words are inextricably linked with each other: lowly folk, lowly caste, physical labour. All who are of the low caste are lowly (Byapari 2018: 120).	
Original Bengali	*Established translation*	*Literal translation (translation ours)*
ছোটোলোক (Byapari 2012: 122)	Lowly folk (Byapari 2018: 120)	A slang used to insult one regarding one's social status

In the example given in Table 23.3, one particular word—'ছোটোলোক'—creates confusion as it connotes different interpretations. Using 'lowly folk' for 'ছোটোলোক' does not seem to be a convincing translation. The term 'ছোটোলোক' is slang in Bengali society; it is used as a form of insult and is associated with feelings of inferiority. Someone can be a 'ছোটোলোক' irrespective of status, caste and class. But here, in the translated version, the word has been given a substitute, 'lowly folk,' without regard for the context and inherent meaning which it carries. It thus loses the flavour of the original. The translator here takes the theorising method to aim at the target audience. The translation here makes a compromise with the socio-political background of Bengal owing to the lack of an exact equivalent for 'ছোটোলোক.'

In general, however, the translation of Byapari's autobiography provides the associative sense and sensibility of the original and does not differ much except when the translator seeks to develop the latent socio-political aspects of the text. The modernity of Byapari's language assists the translator in choosing the proper terms that show the acquired fidelity of the target text to the source text.

Translation as translaboration: collaboration of the author and the translator

'Translaboration' is a neologism, combining the words 'translation' and 'collaboration,' which has been used in connection with 'the sociological turn or activist turn in translation studies' (Wolf 2007). Cordingley and Manning (2017) focus on the collaborative role of translation from the standpoint of relational sociology where the translator and the author are in a relationship of embedded authorship in social structures. The activity of translation is a collaborative activity of the translator and the author. A translator performs the role of 'human bridging' (Bush and Basnett 2006: 2) in carrying across the author's emotive intentions. 'Like an author, the translator has to make the reader laugh and cry, and feel a whole range of emotions,' argue Schwartz and De Lange (2006: 10). An effective translation requires a sufficient amount of vested interest on the part of both the writer and the translator. Wolf notes that 'the act of translating is incorporated through, and at the same time influenced by, the translator's habitus, which can be identified by reconstructing the translator's social trajectory' (2007: 19). Indeed, as social agents living within particular social scenarios, translators aim to project their own views on to the narrative that they intend to translate. Thus, the sociological turn 'broadens our understanding of the relationship between political institutions, ideological struggles and discursive practices' (Delisthati 2011: 219).

Zielinska-Elliott and Kaminka (2017) advocate three types of collaboration in the process of translation: collaboration between a translator and the author; collaboration between the author and a group of translators, each working in a different language; and collaboration between two or more translators working on the same text and translating into the same language. In translating marginalised texts, translators become cultural gatekeepers in the process of transposing one cultural environment to a target environment that differs from that of the source text. Dalit texts are steeped in a unique representation of history from below, which sociologists and historiographers often overlook in the course of mainstream history. Wolf has critically noted:

Within the wider range of cultural politics, translation has been associated with the worldwide struggles for decolonization and for political rights, and translators have been engaged in promoting the emancipation of marginalized and discriminated groups and in creating a balance between languages and cultures.

(2014: 18)

A text like **ইতিবৃত্তে চণ্ডাল জীবন** (*Itibritte Chandal Jiban*), full of socio-political and activist discourses, demands an equal apportioned thinking from the translator, as Mukherjee et al. state: 'if a Dalit writer is an activist, I would say that the translator is also an activist' (2006: 6). In this way, the translator and the writer act together in a collaborative manner to generate a transnational Dalit culture.

Throughout the text of *Interrogating*, the author's and the translator's collaboration is visible. In some passages, the author and the translator give choric commentaries and invite the reader to take part in those and create a continuum for establishing an associative bond with the text. Hersant notes that 'collaboration is also an experience of writing, the effects of which are sometimes felt not only on the translation currently taking place but also on the work to come' (2017: 106). Byapari's autobiography offers the means of seeing and knowing the world in which we live, which has nurtured a sabotaging binary of 'us' and 'them' politics. The translation of such a text enables further change by deterritorialising the local into global as the translator plays the role of an active agent in serving the marginalised cause.

The remainder of this chapter focuses on the collaborative association or translaboration, described above. The translation process reveals the lack of demarcation between the writer and the translator when both act as active collaborators in providing commentaries and reflective views from marginalised perspectives.

The lines in Table 23.4 are mostly reflective; there is perfect coordination between the original and the translated lines. Mukherjee retains the vernacular texture of the original in the translated phrases.

In the first example, the translator has chosen to omit the original phrase, again for the sake of sophistication. The literal rendering of the phrase conveys the sense; it appears to have been omitted in the translator's version due to the shame of the hypocritical society, who are compared to creatures worse than the animal or who bear the

Table 23.4 Comparison of established and attempted literal rendering of the original Bengali lines that contain reflective thoughts

Original Bengali	Established translation	Literal translation (translation ours)
মানুষ হয়ে ওঠার *গর্ব* করা এক জানোয়ার পৌঁছে গেছিলো সেই ভূমিকায় যা দেখে জানোয়ার ও ঘৃণায় থুতু দেবে (Byapari 2012: 105).	[Omitted.]	One who boasts of being a human, he reached the state of being an animal to the extent that an animal would detest out of shame.
নরপিশাচ (Byapari 2012: 223).	Monsters (Byapari 2018: 232)	Human demons.

quality of an animal. The second example, in which the translator chooses the word 'monster' in place of 'নরপিশাচ,' is an attempt to modify the text. These different renderings reflect a hierarchical society that diminishes the existence of those situated at the lowest rung of the ladder.

The translator's move in Table 23.4 is that of an active collaborator who co-creates a target text which does not blindly imitate the original while the translated text becomes an activist text itself. The translator's choices leave open spaces for unconstrained discussions regarding marginalised people, society and views regarding it. Like other activist translations, the English version of Byapari's autobiography reflects the collaborative work of the translator and the author. The translator, as stated earlier, is well acquainted with the socio-political changes within her society. The translator co-habits with the author in the text as an activist; its views and commentaries are as much her own as that of the writer. Translation thus gains a move within itself and the process of translating becomes an activist performance in the English version of Byapari's autobiography. Translation, thus, offers no 'afterlife' production, as Benjamin (1996 [1923]: 254) earlier stated in his theory of literary translation, but both the original and the translation make a simultaneous move in that direction.

Conclusion

The chapter has examined the activist and social turn of literary translation with respect to the Bengali Dalit writer Manoranjan Byapari's autobiography ইতিবৃত্তে চণ্ডাল জীবন (*Itibritte Chandal Jiban*). We have shown how the translation of the autobiography of this marginalised writer has facilitated translational activism for Dalit communities. Translation resuscitates suppressed voices and reasserts the identity of a Dalit writer within a hegemonic mainstream. Whether in the original or in translation, Byapari serves as the spokesperson for those occupying the lowermost rung of society's hierarchical ladder. Translation of the text involves contextual transmission as much as it does textual transfer for both the translator and the author who share a particular socio-politico-historical habitus. Translation, in this case, functions as a sociological instrument that promulgates the social change that Byapari's autobiography advocates. At the same time, translation becomes a collaborative act: the translator transposes marginalised discourse into a hegemonic language while the translator and the author both contribute to Dalit discourse through shared activism.

Related topics

The Dialectics of Dissent in Postcolonial India; Resistance, Activism and Marronage in Paul Bowles's Translations of the Oral Stories of Tangier; Joint Authorship and Preface Writing Practices as Translation in post-'Years of Lead' Morocco

Notes

1 A class of gentry or gentleman that emerged in the British colonial Bengal (1757–1947). This class consists of the Bengali upper castes or middle-class merchants, mainly *baidyas, brahmins, kayasthas,* and later *mahishyas* (see Bhattacharya, Tithi (2007) *The Sentinels of Culture: Class, Education and the Colonial Intellectual in Bengal*. New York: Oxford University Press).

2 A Sanskrit word for someone who deals with disposal of corpses, and is a Hindu lower caste, traditionally considered to be untouchable (see Viswanath, Rupa (2014) *The Pariah Problem: Caste, Religion, and the Social in Modern India*. Columbia University Press. 268).

3 Coined in 1819, the term *Bildungsroman* denotes a coming-of-age story that depicts the moral and psychological growth of a person from youth to adulthood. The character undergoes several changes during the journey.

4 *Namasudra* is an Indian *avarna* (or casteless) community who lived outside the four-tier Hindu *varna* or caste system and were considered outcastes and thus treated as untouchables within society. The *Namasudra* community was earlier known as *Chandala* or *Chandal*, an extremely derogatory term. The community was primarily engaged in fishing and boatmen occupations. Later they turned into agricultural peasants (see Bandopadhyay, Sekhar (2004) *Caste, Culture and Hegemony: Social Dominance in Colonial Bengal*. New Delhi: Sage Publications).

5 The term 'scheduled caste' is used for the disadvantaged communities of India or those who fall outside the four tier *varna* or caste system of Hindu society and hence they are known as untouchables. In the British regime the communities were designated as depressed classes. They came to be regarded as Dalits or the marginalised communities. The 2011 census has shown a record where nearly 16.6% of the total Indian population was comprised of scheduled caste community people (see 'Scheduled Caste Welfare- List of Scheduled Castes,' *Ministry of Social Justice and Empowerment* [online]. Available at: http://socialjustice.nic.in/userview/index?mid=76750 [accessed 9 October 2019]; '2011 Census Primary Census Abstract,' [online]. Available at: Censusindia .gov.in [accessed 9 October 2019])

Further reading

Baker, Mona (2006) 'Translation and Activism: Emerging Patterns of Narrative Community,' *The Massachusetts Review* 47 (3): 462–484.

This essay provides a narrative framework within which the work of communities of translators and interpreters who are actively involved in social or political agendas may be explained and critiqued. It presents an argument that narratives are about shared language and values. The essay thus mobilises numerous individuals with very different backgrounds and attributes around specific political, humanitarian or social issues.

Fedirici, Federico M., and Dario Tessicini (eds.) (2014) *Translators, Interpreters, and Cultural Negotiators: Mediating and Communicating Power from the Middle Ages to the Modern Era*. New York: Palgrave Macmillan.

The book broadly enquires into the intellectual, social and professional identity of translators and interpreters and their roles and contributions in different periods of time and locations when they are involved in negotiating a relationship with political powers and cultural authorities.

Hermans, Theo (ed.) (1985) *The Manipulation of Literature Studies in Literary Translation*. London and New York: Routledge.

The essays in this edited collection introduce a descriptive and systematic approach to the study of literary translation. They bring together theoretical thinking and practical research carried out by an international group of scholars. They vouch for the need for a rigorous scientific approach to translation and argue for the importance of the discipline of Comparative Literature as a way of linking the study of particular translated texts with a broader methodology.

Song, Zhongwei (2014) 'The Art of War in Retranslating Sun Tzu: Using Cultural Capital to Outmatch the Competition,' in *The Sociological Turn in Translation and Interpreting Studies*. Ed. Claudia V. Angelelli. Amsterdam: John Benjamins Publishing Co. 57–71.

'The Art of War in Retranslating Sun Tzu' adopts cultural capital to the study of translation. In this paper, Zhongwei Song explores how the two American translators, Griffith and Gagliardi, use their cultural capital in retranslating the classical Chinese text *The Art of War* (sixth century BC). The strategies and methods adopted by the two translators are analysed by Song and he also shows how Gagliardi challenges Griffith's translation.

Tymoczko, Maria (2010) *Translation, Resistance, Activism*. Massachusetts: University of Massachusetts Press.
The essays in this volume explore ways to study translations as sites of cultural contestation and ideological struggle and as a means of fighting censorship, physical coercion, cultural repression and political dominance. They also show how the ways of studying translation as texts foster a wide variety of goals, from cultural nationalism to armed confrontation. The forms of translation are regarded as ethical, political and ideological activity and not mere communicative transactions or creative literary exercises.

References

Bassnett, Susan, and Harish Trivedi (1999) 'Introduction: Of Colonies, Cannibals and Vernaculars,' in *Postcolonial Translation: Theory and Practice*. Eds. Susan Bassnett and Harish Trivedi. London and New York: Routledge. 1–18.

Benjamin, Walter (1996 [1923]) 'The Task of the Translator,' in *Selected Writings Vol. 1, 1913–1926*. Eds. Marcus Bullock and Michael W. Jennings. Harvard: The Belknap Press of Harvard University Press. 253–263.

Bhattacharya, Tithi (2007) *The Sentinels of Culture: Class, Education and the Colonial Intellectual in Bengal*. Oxford: Oxford University Press.

Bush, Peter, and Susan Basnett (2006) 'Introduction,' in *The Translator as Writer*. Eds. Susan Basnett and Peter Bush. London and New York: Continuum. 1–8.

Byapari, Manoranjan (2012) *Itibritte Chandal Jiban*. Kolkata: Deys' Publishing.

Byapari, Manoranjan (2018) *Interrogating my Chandal Life: The Autobiography of a Dalit*. Trans. Sipra Mukherjee. [Kindle ebook]. Kolkata: Sage and Samya. (Original work published in 2012).

Chatterjee, Partha (2004) *The Politics of the Governed: Reflections on Popular Politics in Most of the World*. New York: Columbia University Press.

Cronin, Michael (2006) *Translation and Identity*. London and New York: Routledge.

Cordingley, Anthony, and Céline Frigau Manning (2017) 'What Is Collaborative Translation?' in *Collaborative Translation: From the Renaissance to the Digital Age*. Eds. Anthony Cordingley and Céline Frigau Manning. London and New York: Bloomsbury. 1–30.

Delisthati, Christina (2011) 'Translation as a Means of Ideological Struggle. Translation and Ideological Struggle; a Case Study of the Translations of the Communist Manifesto into Greek, 1919–1951,' PhD thesis, Middlesex University, London.

Dumont, Louis (1966) *Homo Hierarchicus: The Caste system and its Implications*. Chicago: University of Chicago Press.

El Guabli, Brahim (2020) 'Co-writing and Prefatory Practices in Moroccan Testimonial Literature as Translation,' in *The Routledge Handbook of Translation and Activism*. Eds. Rebecca Ruth Gould and Kayvan Tahmasebian. London and New York: Routledge. 237–257.

Ganguly, Debjani (2009) 'Pain, Personhood and the Collective: Dalit Life Narratives,' *Asian Studies Review* 33: 429–442.

Gouanvic, Jean-Marc (2000) 'Legitimacy, Marronnage and the Power of Translation,' in *Changing the Terms: Translating in the Postcolonial Era*. Eds. Sherry Simon and Paul St-Pierre. Ottawa: University of Ottawa Press. 101–112.

Hansda, Souvendra Sekhar (2018) 'The Writer's Journey,' in *National Herald* [online] 8 April. Available at: www.nationalheraldindia.com/reviews-recommendations/a-dalit-writers-journey-of-multiple-identities-and-struggles [accessed 10 July 2019].

Hersant, Patrick (2017) 'Author-translator Survey: A Typological Problem,' in *Collaborative Translation: From the Renaissance to the Digital Age*. Eds. Anthony Cordingley and Céline Frigau Manning. London and New York: Bloomsbury. 91–110.

Hrystiv, Nataliya (2017) 'Translating from Mariupolitan Greek, a severely Endangered Language, into Ukrainian: Historiographic and Sociological Perspectives,' in *Moving Texts, Migrating People and Minority Languages, New Frontiers in Translation Studies*. Eds. Michele Bordo, et al. Singapore: Springer Nature. DOI 10.1007/978-981-10-3800-6. 31-40.

Limbale, Sharankumar (2015) 'In Conversation with Alok Mukherjee and Arun P. Mukherjee,' in *Dalit Literature In/And Translation: An International Conference*, British Centre for Literary Translation, University of East Anglia, Norwich.

Mukherjee, Arun, Alok Mukherjee, and Barbara Godard (2006) 'Translating Minoritized Cultures: Issues of Caste, Class and Gender,' *Postcolonial Text* 2 (3): 1–23.

Mukherjee, Sipra (2018) 'Translator's Note,' in *Interrogating My Chandal Life: The Autobiography of a Dalit*. Trans. Sipra Mukherjee. Kolkata: Sage and Samya (ebook).

Nayar, Pramod Kumar (2011) 'Subalternity and Translation: The Cultural Apparatus of Human Rights,' *Economic and Political Weekly* 46 (9): 23–26.

Pal, Bidisha (2018) 'Book Review: Interrogating My Chandal Life: An Autobiography of a Dalit by Manoranjan Byapari, Translated by Sipra Mukherjee,' in *Rupkatha Journal on Interdisciplinary Studies in Humanities* 10 (2). DOI: 10.21659/rupkatha.v10n2.27 [accessed 10 July 2019].

Pandey, Gyanendra (2006) 'The Subaltern as Subaltern Citizen,' *Economic and Political Weekly* 41 (46): 4735–4741.

Prasad, Chandra Bhan (2005) 'Dalit Writing Makes its Mark,' [online]. Available at: www.csmonitor.com/2005/0815/p15501-lire.html [accessed 4 March 2019].

Schwartz, Ros, and Nicholas De Lange (2006) 'A Dialogue: On a Translator's Interventions,' in *The Translator as Writer*. Eds. Susan Basnett and Peter Bush. London and New York: Continuum. 9–22.

Tymoczko, Maria (2000) 'Translation and Political Engagement,' *The Translator* 6 (1): 23–47.

Valmiki, Omprakash (2003) 'Introduction,' in *Joothan: A Dalit's Life*. Trans. Arun Prabha Mukherjee. New York: Columbia University Press. xvii–xlviii.

Venuti, Lawrence (1998) 'Introduction,' in *Translation and Minority*. Ed. Lawrence Venuti. Special Issue of *The Translator* 4 (2). 135–144. New York: Routledge.

Viswanath, Rupa (2014) *The Pariah Problem: Caste, Religion, and the Social in Modern India*. New York: Columbia University Press.

Wolf, Michel (2000) 'The Third Space in Postcolonial Representation,' in *Changing the Terms: Translating in the Postcolonial Era*. Eds. Sherry Simon and Paul St-Pierre. Ottawa: University of Ottawa Press. 127–146.

Wolf, Michela (2007) 'The Emergence of a Sociology of Translation,' in *Constructing a Sociology of Translation*. Eds. Michel Wolf and Alexander Fukari. Amsterdam: John Benjamins. 1–36.

Wolf, Michaela (2014) 'The Sociology of Translation and its "Activist Turn",' in *The Sociological Turn in Translation and Interpreting Studies*. Ed. Claudia V. Angelelli. Amsterdam: John Benjamins Publishing Co. 7–21.

Zielinska-Elliott, Anna, and Ika Kaminka (2017) 'Online Multilingual Collaboration: Haruki Murakami's European Translators,' in *Collaborative Translation: From the Renaissance to the Digital Age*. Eds. Anthony Cordingley and Céline Frigau Manning. London and New York: Bloomsbury. 167–191.

Zubillaga, Naroa (2017) 'Translating from and into Basque: The Case of Children's Literature,' in *Moving Texts, Migrating People and Minority Languages, New Frontiers in Translation Studies*. Eds. Michael Borodo, et al. Singapore: Springer Nature. 3–14. DOI: 10.1007/978-981-10-3800-6. [accessed 4 March 2019].

Part VII
Translation, migration, refugees

24

What is asylum?

Translation, trauma, and institutional visibility

Aria Fani

What is asylum? The definition of asylum has preoccupied the minds of diplomats, judges, lawyers, legal institutions, immigration rights advocates, and asylum seekers since its codification in the Convention Relating to the Status of Refugees in 1951 in Geneva. The Refugee Convention of 1951 defined the term 'refugee' as a person with a 'well-founded fear of persecution for reasons of race, religion, nationality, membership of a particular social group or political opinion' and outlined certain rights that pertain to such persons (UNHCR 1951, 1967). In 1967, the Protocol Relating to the Status of Refugees removed time limits (initially defining asylum 'as a result of events occurring before January 1, 1951') and expanded the document's geographic scope beyond Europe. These changes notwithstanding, the legal category of asylum, along with its legal lexicon, has remained at the core of a transnational practice since the second half of the twentieth century.

This chapter does not revisit the definition of asylum, no less at a time when long-standing precedents regarding asylum are being unravelled by nativist governments worldwide. Instead, I aim to illustrate how the legal category of asylum assumes a degree of both institutional literacy and visibility in the process of making a viable and credible asylum claim. I understand institutional literacy as familiarity with a set of assumptions and norms within any given legal system in any given period that validates certain refugees as asylum-worthy and denigrates others as unworthy of protection. To have institutional literacy means being able to present one's claim in a style that is viewed as credible, in a way that fits certain legally codified criteria for asylum, and overall to navigate the invasive and lengthy process of seeking asylum from start to finish (which may take 4–5 years or even more). In many cases, it means having the skills to make your client visible within institutionally recognised categories of persecution. And for many asylum seekers, particularly those who do not speak the language of their host country, it means ceding agency to others to tell their story and establish their credibility.

This chapter draws from my experience working with Central American asylum seekers as an immigration rights advocate at the East Bay Sanctuary Covenant (EBSC) in Berkeley, California, since January 2017. Through conducting asylum interviews,

I have mainly served EBSC as a translator. My primary training is in literary and translation studies; I have no specific background in immigration law. I have lived and travelled extensively in Latin America and speak Spanish, particularly its Mexican and Central American variations. My linguistic and writing skills have helped me to conduct preliminary asylum interviews and present my clients' declaration in a manner that both stays true to their experience of trauma and speaks to legal criteria outlined in asylum forms. My training in literature may seem irrelevant at first, but in the course of volunteering at EBSC I realised that my analytical and language skills translated well into the field of immigration rights advocacy. Earning a doctoral degree in the humanities has placed me among an extremely privileged group. Advocating for the rights of a particularly vulnerable community has helped me better understand the extent and power of that privilege.

Given that the majority of my clients have come from El Salvador and Guatemala, it is necessary to briefly delve into the history of immigration from Central America into the United States (US) and explain EBSC's role in pioneering what came to be known as the Sanctuary Movement in the early 1980s. In 1960, civil war erupted in Guatemala and in El Salvador it began in 1980. These conflicts consumed the lives of hundreds of thousands of people. Under the banner of eradicating communism, Central American states brutally targeted dissidents and vulnerable communities. In El Salvador, the war mainly affected union members and leaders, students, farmers, catechists, and Catholic monks, nuns, and church delegations who denounced state violence. In Guatemala, the war took more than three decades (as opposed to 12 years in El Salvador, which is much smaller in size) and mainly affected the country's indigenous communities that speak more than twenty Mayan languages (as opposed to the Salvadoran population, which is predominantly Spanish-speaking). Between 1980 and 1983 half a million Salvadorans and Guatemalans fled military and political persecution by crossing into the US (Lesser and Batalova 2017). Asylum, at the time, was primarily granted to refugees fleeing from the Soviet Union (Goodman 2018).

On 11 December 1981, the Salvadoran Army, trained and sponsored by the US Army (some soldiers were trained within El Salvador while others had received training in Panama and the US state of Georgia), massacred close to a thousand Salvadorans, many of them women and children, in the town of El Mozote and surrounding villages (Maslin 2016). It has been characterised as the worst massacre in contemporary Latin American history. The US State Department repeatedly lied about the massacre—initially it even denied that it happened (Danner 1993). After the massacre, US President Ronald Reagan continued to fund the 'friendly' government of El Salvador (Danner 1993). Reagan equally ignored atrocities unfolding in Guatemala. When he met with the Guatemalan president, Efraín Ríos Montt, on 5 December 1982, Reagan praised him as 'a man of great integrity' and 'totally dedicated to democracy' as the latter was committing a genocide of indigenous Mayans (Grandin 2013). His administration deliberately mischaracterised what was happening in Central America with the objective of turning away Salvadoran and Guatemalan asylum seekers. Of all Central American asylum seekers in the US, only 2 percent of Salvadorans and 1 percent of Guatemalans were granted asylum (Gzesh 2006). To put this into perspective, 40 percent of Afghan and 32 percent of Polish refugees who had fled from the Soviet Union, a political adversary, were granted asylum in the US.

The majority of US Americans were uninformed of what was going on in Central America. That changed with the assassination of Óscar Romero. During a sermon on

23 March 1980, Romero, the Archbishop of El Salvador, the country's highest-ranked religious and cultural figure, demanded an end to violence in Central America. He was gunned down the next day during a mass at the chapel of the Divina Providencia Hospital in San Salvador. In response to military repression, people's insurgency began the day after Romero's killing in El Salvador. For most of his career, Romero had been a politically conservative figure. But in 1977, he had a change of heart after the assassination of Rutilio Grande, a Jesuit priest and Romero's close friend, after which he fully devoted himself to the cause of social justice for indigenous communities. Grande's murder was part of a brutally systematic effort by the Salvadoran state to silence any legitimate dissent. This effort included killing tens of peaceful students from the National Autonomous University of El Salvador who were marching for social and economic justice on July 30, 1975. The news also reverberated far beyond El Salvador, with services held in the San Francisco Bay Area and in other major cities across the US.

On 24 March 1982, on the second anniversary of Romero's assassination, five congregations in Berkeley, California and one in Tucson, Arizona formed a national coalition with the mission of providing advocacy for asylum seekers who were denied protection by the US government. Under the leadership of Reverend Gustav Schultz, immigration rights advocates in Berkeley and Tucson risked arrest by giving refuge to asylum seekers. Their activism marked the birth of the Sanctuary Movement which was built on transnational solidarity (Mineiro 2019). It defied inhumane immigration policies in the US and drew its inspiration from the Latin American discourse on Liberation Theology. Formed in the 1950s and 60s in South America, Liberation Theology set out to bring Christian theology into alignment with the experience of marginalised indigenous peoples and amplify their demand for social dignity and economic egalitarianism across Latin America. The most prominent thinkers of Liberation Theology include José Comblin, Helder Câmara, Leonardo Boff (all three from Brazil), Jon Sobrino (Spain/El Salvador), Óscar Romero (El Salvador), and Gustavo Gutiérrez (Peru), whose book *Teología de la Liberación* (*Liberation Theology*: 1973) has become the movement's seminal text.

Founded in 1982, the EBSC has been a pioneer in the Sanctuary movement in the US. The organisation, currently located in the humble basement of a church near the campus of the University of California, works with seven lawyers, sixteen paralegals, and more than thirty volunteers. Our volunteer translators, such as myself, often work from the office while interpreters usually work off-site by going to asylum hearings in San Francisco. EBSC has taken on more than two hundred cases of affirmative asylum every year (cases that take place in a non-courtroom setting as opposed to cases of defensive asylum which take place in court on the order of removal). Of all cases that EBSC has undertaken over the years, 97 percent have been granted asylum. The organisation works with asylum seekers from around the world, but it specialises in El Salvador and Guatemala. The organisation has kept an extensive database of Guatemalan villages that were attacked and destroyed in the 1980s. This database has helped to reunite brothers and sisters, parents and children, now residing in the US years after their traumatic separation. Today, EBSC has adopted a broader mission to combat widespread hostility and misunderstanding about immigrants by educating the public about why immigrants flee to the US. For instance, the project *Amplifying Sanctuary Voices* (2018–present) gathers stories of asylees who have settled in the San Francisco Bay Area with the aim of presenting them to the general public, releasing these narratives from the confines of immigration records.

Many of EBSC's clients today are the children of those who experienced the violent turmoil of the 1980s in Central America. Peace treaties may have been officially signed in El Salvador (1992) and Guatemala (1996), but war has left in its wake a pervasive ecology of abuse and criminal impunity. Until recently, survivors of genocide that took place during the Civil War feared disclosing what they had witnessed and were instead forced to believe in false narratives forged by their governments, narratives that were validated by the US government. In the course of the Civil War, US-sponsored governments in Central America brutally cracked down on what they viewed as elements of communism or any progressive grassroots organisation; this led to a violent counter-insurgency. First-hand accounts such as *I, Rigoberta Menchú: An Indian Woman in Guatemala* (1983), written by the Nobel-winning human rights activist, the reporting of US American journalists, and most importantly, the oral accounts of asylum seekers who bravely fled to the US clearly illustrate that the indigenous population in Guatemala was the most vulnerable target of an ethno-racial war that masked itself as a western front against socialist ideology (Nairn 1982).

Thanks to increasing international pressure, certain government officials have since then faced trials but the prospect of real accountability has remained distant. In 2013, Efraín Ríos Montt became the first statesman charged with genocide in his own country; he was sentenced to eighty years in prison. The ruling was met with a sense of closure in Guatemala and its diaspora. But the ruling was overturned ten days later by the country's Supreme Court, to the profound dismay of Mayan communities who survived Montt's crimes against humanity (Malkin 2013). The children of Salvadoran and Guatemalan refugees, most of whom had been denied asylum in the 1980s, were deported in the 1990s by the Bush and Clinton administrations to a country virtually foreign to them. Some of them took to Central America a certain type of gang organisation from Los Angeles which overwhelmed legal institutions and civil society and led to the formation of *maras*, or gangs, such as MS-13 in El Salvador. *Maras* kept growing in the following years, posing a daily threat to the life and livelihood of Guatemalans and Salvadorans (Denvir 2017; Restrepo 2018). My clients at EBSC are survivors of this abusive and crime-infested ecology.

Unsurprisingly, women and members of the LGBTQ community are among the most vulnerable people in Central America, where rampant misogynistic and homophobic hate crimes face little to no legal consequences. In 2017, I interviewed a mother who, along with her teenage daughter, had been gang-raped in a coffee field in Guatemala. The mother was pregnant at the time. María (not her real name) had a miscarriage and had to head north the next day to protect her daughter from being killed or kidnapped. Here, it is necessary to describe the mechanics of preliminary asylum interviews. María had heard about EBSC through word of mouth, as with most of our clients. She walked into our office with no prior appointment and inquired about seeking asylum. Like most of our clients, she did not know what the asylum process entailed or, if granted, exactly what type of status it offered.

I introduced myself to María in Spanish, offered her a glass of water, and walked with her to a private office. I emphasised that I was not a lawyer and could not give her legal advice. I said I was there as an immigration rights advocate to obtain her declaration and submit her request to be represented by EBSC. I explained that a declaration is a person's story about why they cannot return to their own country and why they are seeking protection from the US government. I briefly went over EBSC's four-page preliminary asylum interview form designed to obtain basic information about asylum seekers, their family, how and when they came to the US, whether they have been a victim of a crime in the US, and finally, why they are seeking asylum. Before I began the interview, I put the form aside and told María that, regardless of the outcome, on a human level I valued her story and courage. I shared with her that there are no right or wrong answers and that I was deeply sorry she had to relive her trauma today and possibly again in an asylum hearing.

Once María began telling her story in Spanish, I began to take notes. I stayed silent so she would work through long pauses without any interruption. When she would choke on her tears, I asked if she would like to take a short break. After forty-five minutes, I had a broad sense of her narrative: María's parents escaped to the mountains in order to flee persecution during the Civil War. She was left at her grandparents' house where she grew up in extreme poverty and suffered from malnutrition. As a child, she worked on the field to help her grandparents put food on the table. She left her grandparents when she met her partner. She started a small business by selling clothes and almost immediately faced threats of extortion from *maras*. She could not manage to pay them and keep the business open, so she closed her shop. Meanwhile, her elder daughter was being coerced by *maras* to join their gang. Fearing that her daughter would get abducted, María pulled her from school and sent her to live with relatives in a different part of town. But the *maras* managed to find her. After the horrific incident, María was given twenty-four hours to leave Guatemala or have her daughter forced into sexual slavery.

Once I heard her story, I began to ask pointed questions to document specific dates and establish a clear timeline. Whenever I would run into a question, I would consult with our asylum director who was not present in the same room. For instance, María had a hard time remembering exactly what year her parents returned from the mountains. It was the director who shared with me that calendar years may not mean much to rural Guatemalans and suggested that I reframe the question through María's life. So, I asked María if her parents returned before or after the birth of her daughter, and I received a more reassuring answer. Once our asylum director had no more follow-up questions and certain details had been outlined, I thanked María for telling her story and reassured her that EBSC would get in touch with her soon. Then, I sat down to weave all my notes, written in Spanish and English, into her final declaration to be submitted to our director as part of María's application.

While writing María's declaration, the role of translation and many of its social and cultural valences became clearer to me. From the outset, María had to have some degree of faith that I would retell her story in a culturally sensitive and linguistically accurate manner. By now, it is hardly contentious or novel to suggest that translators and interpreters are far more than 'transmitter of words' and should be seen as 'agents of culture' (Barsky 1996: 46). In context, it means that after chatting with María I would have understood her level of access to educational institutions and her unique cultural background. María grew up in a Mam–Maya household and did not know much Spanish before moving to the US. During her ten years of residence in California, she learned Spanish from Mexican friends and co-workers. Many indigenous Guatemalans are ridiculed for not understanding Spanish. Given the conflicted relationship María had with the Spanish language, I was very careful not to move on to the next question even if she nodded affirmatively or answered briefly. I would rephrase questions multiple times to get a fully clear answer.

For instance, there is a section in the first part of the preliminary asylum interview that outlines different types of persecution. The categories that more closely applied to her included *la etnia* (ethnicity) and *el género* (gender). Past experience had taught me that relying on a transnational social-scientific vocabulary, as exemplified by the question of whether she had experienced persecution based on her ethnicity or gender (*¿Usted ha sido objeto de persecución basado en su origen étnico o género sexual?*), would have led to silence, or upon insistence, a very brief answer. The term '*persecución*,' outlined in the legal document of the Refugee Convention of 1951, had no meaning for someone like María. Given that I do not speak or understand the Mam language, the least I could do was to tap into a linguistic register attentive to María's lived experiences, as opposed to using a generalised Anglophone lexicon with no roots in her local realities. With that in mind, I asked her the following questions: When you would walk on the street, would people ever make fun of your clothing? (*¿En la calle, la gente no se burlaba de su traje típico?*) or, When you would speak Mam on the street, would people call you names? (*¿Cuando hablaba Mam en la calle, que le decía la gente?*). This turn to a vernacular, non-imported lexicon proved to be the cultural-linguistic register through which María accessed the depth of her trauma. I no longer received silence or brief answers; instead she opened up and gave detailed answers about how she was regularly called 'worthless [*no vales nada*]' on the street and was told people 'like her' were not wanted in Guatemala (*aquí no queremos a gente así*).

Sahar Fathi's chapter in this volume (Chapter 18) highlights the challenges asylum seekers face in the courtroom without an interpreter. Fathi shows how the US immigration system has failed to meet its own requirements regarding interpretation standards and identifies speakers of indigenous Latin American languages as among the most vulnerable communities in the US today. Later in this chapter, I will outline the implications of my work as a translator for the practice of interpretation. The success of a claimant's institutional visibility may often rest on a particular iteration of their story produced in the process of translation. For instance, given María's ethnic background, our asylum director advised me to ask if her rapists said anything before, during, and after the horrific incident that indicated she and her daughter were raped because they are indigenous or perceived to be so. I returned to María from the director's office, again apologised that she had to relive her trauma, and asked: when they were raping you, did any of them make fun of your looks or way of speaking? (*¿Cuando le violaban, uno de ellos se burló de su idioma o vestimenta?*). Yes, she responded, 'one of them kept saying that you are Indian, you shouldn't be here [*eres una india, no deberías estar aquí*].' With that response, my line of questioning gained an entirely different angle.

Establishing the fact that María and her daughter were targeted *because* they were indigenous (or perceived as such) helps to make her case more visible within asylum criteria and practices today. The Trump administration has attempted to make it extremely difficult, if not impossible, for survivors of gang and domestic violence to seek asylum in the US. In a ruling, the former Attorney General Jeff Sessions argued that gang and domestic violence is not grounds for asylum (Benner and Dickerson 2018). The question of history seems to be all but elided from discussions on asylum. The 1970s and 1980s may be seen as bygone decades by the US legal system, but the history of Central American civil wars and their aftermath provides a key in understanding the psyche of Guatemalan and Salvadoran asylum seekers today.

Most survivors of violence in Central America are just beginning to come to terms with its personal, emotional, and cultural impact. For instance, in El Salvador there exist many support groups today that provide a platform for people to finally speak publicly about what they witnessed as children or adults during the Civil War. For years, their governments denied any wrongdoing and heavily punished those who challenged its narrative (Danner 1993). The US government has still not apologised for or acknowledged its military and political support for dictatorial regimes, its facilitation of their genocide, and for criminalising legitimate and credible asylum cases in the 1980s. Political figures such as Elliott Abrams, responsible for providing cover for crimes against humanity, have not even been reprimanded, let alone charged (Abrams was charged only for lying to Congress, but was pardoned by George H. W. Bush in 1992). In fact, Abrams was named a special envoy to Venezuela by the Trump administration in January 2019. Given this background, it is entirely unsurprising that most lawyers and immigration rights advocates who have worked with Central Americans tell of these refugees' deeply internalised lack of self-worth and value in their lived trauma. That is why I begin every interview with a personal note: 'I value your story regardless of any outcome.' Accessing the depth of one's trauma and establishing credibility in order to achieve institutional visibility requires placing a degree of value in one's story.

Members of the LGBTQ community in Central America have been a particularly vulnerable target of gang violence and rampant homophobic acts. In 2017, I interviewed Julio (also not his real name) who was born and raised in San Salvador, El Salvador. He has lived in the US as an undocumented immigrant for the past eighteen years. He heard about EBSC through a friend who has an ongoing case with us. Today, Julio identifies as gay. As a child and young adult, he was perceived as effeminate and was subject to verbal, physical, and sexual abuse as a result. During the preliminary asylum interview, I asked Julio if he had been a victim of verbal or physical abuse. Julio had finished high school in El Salvador so I translated the question on the English-language form word by word and without modifying its register: *¿Has sido la víctima de acoso verbal o físico basado en tu orientación sexual?* He answered yes, and elaborated on how such treatment made him feel.

Asylum declarations need to be detailed, mainly to establish credibility. Julio was extremely embarrassed to divulge any details of his abusive treatment in El Salvador. Given that I was still establishing my own trustworthiness to him, I did not insist further. After an hour, I took his declaration to EBSC's managing attorney. She had a number of questions regarding the nature of certain encounters and asked for more details concerning verbal abuse. So, I returned to Julio, sitting by himself in a separate office, and explained why those details would matter to his case. It was clear the idea of repeating abusive terms pained him a great deal, so I said: 'I know how deeply upsetting this must be for you and I am terribly sorry you have to hear them again, but would it be OK if I read you some of those terms and you could tell me if you have been called by such labels at home, work, or school?' He agreed. At EBSC, I had learned about homophobic attitudes and behaviours in Central America and Mexico, so I was familiar with a number of pejorative terms unique to that region (for instance, the word '*hueco*' in Castilian Spanish merely means 'hole,' but in Central America it is also a homophobic term).

Several weeks later, EBSC decided to take on Julio's case. I was assigned to work with him to produce a more extensive version of his declaration, one that EBSC would ultimately submit as part of his petition for asylum. One of the areas in which our attorney needed more clarity was Julio's experience with sexual abuse. When he was ten years old, Julio had been regularly raped for three years by his older cousin. During our second meeting, I noticed that Julio did not use terms like *abuso sexual* (sexual abuse) and *violación* (rape) to characterise his experience. I was less wedded to any single term and more committed to creating a space wherein Julio could describe his trauma on his own (linguistic) terms. He was deeply conflicted about it and was thinking through what it did to him then and how it impacts him now. He said, 'I feel like it took away my innocence [*me quitó la inocencia*].' I asked, 'What do you mean by that?' He replied, 'I didn't know what [act] was good or bad [*no sabía si estaba bien o estaba mal*].' He then shared that he had never disclosed his story to anyone before.

In another session, he talked more about how 'feeling different [*me sentía diferente*]' as a child and being 'perceived as different [*me veían diferente*]' shaped his relationship with his parents and extended family. He shared that his father regularly told him 'you are not from God [*no eres de Dios*]' and his uncle, their family barber, refused to ever cut his hair because that required touching him. So, I asked him 'What would it mean to see what your cousin did to you as rape?' He replied, 'Yes, it was [*Sí, era*],' followed by a long silence. But he still did not feel comfortable uttering the term '*violación*.' I asked, 'do you think the reason he raped you was because he saw you as different?' He said, 'yes,' but did not elaborate. I had to dig deeper by tapping into his experience with homophobic attitudes and behaviour. I said, 'When he was in bed with you, would your cousin ever make fun of your appearance or way of walking or speaking?' 'Yes,' he said, 'he would often tell me to "behave like a man [*compórtate como hombre*]."' Julio's answer offered me a new angle with which to explore his trauma, specifically his experience with rape.

At the end, EBSC made Julio's case visible within what is enshrined as 'discrimination based on sexuality' in asylum laws. But simply asking Julio whether he had been a victim of homophobic acts would not have activated the details of his trauma, blocked by his survival instincts. Doing so necessarily requires speaking in a register that is attentive to a claimant's lived experience and that highlights the importance of translators and interpreters whose linguistic knowledge goes beyond books and classrooms and is complemented by knowledge of culture and history. In my first encounter with Julio, I took him to an office space with a poster of Óscar Romero on the wall. It was an attempt at making him feel more welcome, letting him know he was in a space where the suffering and resilience of his people were acknowledged. Julio referred to our sessions as therapy and at the end of each one he would tell me, 'Thank you for listening [*Gracias por escuchar*].' In September 2018, Julio was granted asylum in San Francisco.

Translators and interpreters have played a formative role in the Sanctuary Movement. Translators afforded legal institutions access to a host of key documents in the evaluation of an asylum claim, including birth certificates, police reports, testimonies, psychological evaluations, and medical records. Interpreters played a vital role by giving asylum officers and judges access to stories of suffering and survival. Both translators and interpreters cultivated an inclusive and trustworthy space wherein asylum seekers opened age-old wounds and in so doing facilitated their ability to tell their full story with dignity and respect. By making thousands of first-hand testimonies available in English at a time when Central American and US governments were actively silencing them, translators and interpreters helped to create a 'counter-narrative' that later guided international investigators to uncover the extent of atrocities committed in Guatemala and El Salvador (Baker 2006).

In 1982, EBSC was established in response to an urgent humanitarian crisis in Central America. Very few people who got involved then thought that the Sanctuary Movement would be alive and well in 2020. Today, EBSC does much more than represent cases of affirmative asylum. It has fostered a community of lawyers, advocates, immigrants, and asylum seekers who seek to create more 'counter-narratives.' It understands that the questions of history, cultural visibility, and social empowerment are necessarily interconnected. EBSC has worked with a population that has been told by their government that they did not matter, then they were told by the US government that they were unworthy of protection, and finally they were made invisible within a legal system that ignored their struggles and the resilience it took to overcome them.

Given these hostile conditions, it is unsurprising that so many Central American asylum seekers feel ashamed of coming forward to seek asylum. They have been told by different US administrations that their stories are unworthy of being heard. Like all translators and interpreters at EBSC, I have understood my task as more than translating from Spanish into English with accuracy but also remain attentive to the historical, social, ethnic, and cultural power dynamics that are embedded in our mode of encounter. On the record, I attempted to tell a story that closely reflected asylum seekers' cultural and linguistic registers. It was my job to convey to them that their story meant more than just a 'declaration in support of a petition for asylum.' What enabled me to do this was the context in which I had learned Spanish, and was able to effectively understand oral statements, while translating them into written documents. I studied Spanish in Mexico, where I personally witnessed how xenophobic attitudes negatively affected indigenous Mexicans. I noticed how indigenous languages with their own distinct literary tradition, like Zapoteco, are often dismissed as dialects (*dialectos*). Bringing an awareness of language politics into asylum interviews helped me to better connect with my clients on a cultural level and speak to them with a more familiar social register.

Finally, what does the Central American case teach us about the role of translation and interpretation and their interplay in immigration rights advocacy? To make a credible and compelling asylum claim is to be made visible within a legal category. The asylum lexicon used by legal institutions worldwide may pose as universal, but it is entirely detached from linguistic, cultural, and historical realities in Guatemala, El Salvador, and many other countries. When it comes to the practice of interpretation, fluency and grammaticality should be seen as far less ideal than the ability to form questions that asylum seekers would understand by speaking directly to their lived trauma without using any legal jargon. In fact, interpreters should be given more leeway by courts and asylum hearings in ignoring institutionally imported terms like 'persecution' or 'ethnicity' and rendering them intelligible within a specific cultural, socio-economic, and linguistic context. Unlike interpreters, translators are less constrained by time and can delve deeper into questions of translation through the process of give-and-take with asylum seekers whom they interview. In fact, translators with a literary background can enrich the field and practice of interpretation from which it is often separated. Ultimately, I understand both translation and interpretation in the context of social activism to be a work of empathy.

As I began writing this chapter in December 2018, a large group of Central Americans headed toward the US on foot, most of them asylum seekers, women and children. Their exodus represents the failure of the state as a political institution in Honduras, Guatemala, and El Salvador. The Trump administration responded by equating asylum seekers with MS-13, blocking their access to legal ports of entry, separating children from their parents, and placing them in woefully crowded facilities and conditions (Amnesty International 2018). These unlawful policies have again summoned a group of translators and interpreters, from organisations like EBSC, to advocate for their rights. Unlike the 1980s, there is now a significant community of Central Americans in the US who are demanding to be part of the national debate on immigration and asylum laws. In February 2019, three thousand holders of Temporary Protective Status (TPS), most of them from El Salvador, marched in front of the White House with a single dignified slogan: Nothing about us, without us (Lang 2019).[1]

Related topics

Activist Narratives; The Right to Understand and to be Understood; Resistant Recipes; Citation and Recitation.

Note

1 Acknowledgement: I am grateful to Sr. Maureen Duignan, Lisa Hoffman, Manuel De Paz, Kaveena Singh (managing attorney), Michael Smith (asylum director), and Amelia Mineiro at the East Bay Sanctuary Covenant.

Further reading

Bau, Ignatius (1985) *This Ground Is Holy: Church Sanctuary and Central American Refugees.* New York: Paulist Press.

Bau examines the role that the University Lutheran Chapel in Berkeley and Rev. Gustav Schultz played in the formation of the Sanctuary Movement.

Crittenden, Ann (1988) *Sanctuary: A Story of American Conscience and the Law in Collision.* New York: Weidenfeld & Nicolson.

Ann Crittenden, a noted investigative journalist, delves into how the US government dealt with the civil disobedience of Sanctuary activists in Arizona.

Davidson, Miriam (1988) *Convictions of the Heart: Jim Corbett and the Sanctuary Movement.* Tucson: University of Arizona Press.

Davidson tells the story of how Jim Corbett mobilised communities of faith to address the plight of Central American refugees at the Arizona–Mexico border.

Bonnín, Eduardo (ed.) (1982) *Espiritualidad y Liberación en América Latina.* San José, Costa Rica: El Departamento Ecuménico de Investigaciones.

Published at the same time as the rise of the Sanctuary Movement in the US, this is an anthology of theological writings by notable Latin American liberation theologians.

Golden, Renny and Michael McConnell (1986) *Sanctuary: The New Underground Railroad.* Maryknoll: Orbis Books.

Golden investigates how church groups came together in the 1980s to help Central American refugees who were fleeing brutal civil wars.

References

Amnesty International (2018) 'US Government Endangers Asylum Seekers with Unlawful Policies,' [online] 26 November. Available at: www.amnesty.org/en/latest/news/2018/11/americas-us-gov ernment-endangers-asylum seekers-with-unlawful-policies/[accessed 29 June 2019].
Baker, Mona (2006) 'Translation and Activism: Emerging Pattern of Narrative Community,' *The Massachusetts Review* 47 (3): 462–484.
Barsky, Robert F. (1996) 'The Interpreter as Intercultural Agent in Convention Refugee Hearings,' *The Translator* 2 (1): 45–63.

Benner, Katie, and Caitlin Dickerson (2018) 'Sessions Says Domestic and Gang Violence Are Not Grounds for Asylum,' in *The New York Times* [online] 11 June. Available at: www.nytimes.com/2018/06/11/us/politics/sessions-domestic-violence-asylum.html [accessed 29 June 2019].

Danner, Mark (1993) 'The Truth of El Mozote,' in *The New Yorker* [online] 6 December. Available at: www.newyorker.com/magazine/1993/12/06/the-truth-of-el-mozote [accessed 28 June 2019].

Denvir, Daniel (2017) 'Deporting People Made Central America's Gangs. More Deportation Won't Help,' in *The Washington Post* [online] 20 July. Available at: www.washingtonpost.com/news/posteverything/wp/2017/07/20/deporting-people-made-central-americas-gangs-more-deportation-wont-help/?utm_term=.f70814b49a45 [accessed 28 June 2019].

Goodman, Carly (2018) 'Like Donald Trump, Ronald Reagan Tried to Keep out Asylum Seekers. Activists Thwarted Him,' in *The Washington Post* [online] 2 July. Available at: www.washingtonpost.com/news/made-by-history/wp/2018/07/02/line-donald-trump-ronald-reagan-tried-to-keep-out-asylum-seekers-activists-thwarted-him/?utm_term=.5b34142a7089 [accessed 28 June 2019].

Grandin, Greg (2013) 'Guatemalan Slaughter Was Part of Reagan's Hard Line,' in *The New York Times* [online] 21 May. Available at: www.nytimes.com/roomfordebate/2013/05/19/what-guilt-does-the-us-bear-in-guatemala/guatemalan-slaughter-was-part-of-reagans-hard-line [accessed 28 June 2019].

Gzesh, Susan (2006) 'Central Americans and Asylum Policy in the Reagan Era,' in *Migration Policy Institute* [online] 1 April. Available at: www.migrationpolicy.org/article/central-americans-and-asylum-policy-reagan-era [accessed 28 June 2019].

Lang, Marissa J. (2019) 'Hundreds Protest in Washington to Support Immigrants with Temporary Protected Status,' in *Washington Post* [online] 12 February. Available at: www.washingtonpost.com/local/hundreds-protest-at-white-house-to-support-immigrants-with-temporary-protected-status/2019/02/12/7a4757f8-2e34-11e9-813a-0ab2f17e305b_story.html?utm_term=.cfdcb5062cc6 [accessed 28 June 2019].

Lesser, Gabriel, and Jeanne Batalova (2017) 'Inmigrantes centroamericanos en los estados unidos,' in *Migration Policy Institute* [online] 27 April. Available at: www.migrationpolicy.org/article/inmigrantes-centroamericanos-en-los-estados-unidos [accessed 28 June 2019].

Malkin, Elisabeth (2013) 'Former Leader of Guatemala Is Guilty of Genocide against Mayan Group,' in *The New York Times* [online] 10 May. Available at: www.nytimes.com/2013/05/11/world/americas/gen-efrain-rios-montt-of-guatemala-guilty-of-genocide.html?module=inline [accessed 28 June 2019].

Maslin, Sara Esther (2016) 'Remembering El Mozote, the Worst Massacre in Modern Latin American History,' in *The Nation* [online] 13 December. Available at: www.thenation.com/article/remembering-el-mozote-the-worst-massacre-in-modern-latin-american-history/[accessed 28 June 2019].

Mineiro, Amelia (2019) 'Transnationalism of Liberation Theology in the Rhetoric of the East Bay Sanctuary Covenant,' Undergraduate Thesis, University of California, Berkeley.

Nairn, Allan (1982) 'Guatemala Can't Take 2 Roads,' in *The New York Times* [online] 20 July. Available at: www.nytimes.com/1982/07/20/opinion/guatemala-cant-take-2-roads.html [accessed 28 June 2019].

Restrepo, Lider (2018) 'A Gang that Was Made in the USA,' in *SocialistWorker* [online] 12 February. Available at: https://socialistworker.org/2018/02/12/a-gang-that-was-made-in-the-us [accessed 28 June 2019].

Stock, Stephen, Rachel Witte, and Jeremy Carroll (2018) 'Data Points to Wide Gap in Asylum Approval Rates at Nation's Immigration Courts,' in *NBC* [online] 10 May. Available at: www.nbcphiladelphia.com/investigations/national-investigations/Data-Points-to-Wide-Gap-in-Asylum-Approval-Rates-at-Nations-Immigration-Courts-482182911.html [accessed 28 June 2019].

Tymoczko, Maria (ed.) (2010) *Translation, Resistance, Activism.* Amherst and Boston: University of Massachusetts.

UNHCR (1951, 1967) 'Convention and Protocol Relating to the Status of Refugees,' in *United Nations High Commissioner for Refugees* [online]. Available at: www.unhcr.org/3b66c2aa10.html [accessed 29 June 2019].

25

Citation and recitation

Linguistic legacies and the politics of translation in the Sahrawi refugee context

Yousif M. Qasmiyeh and Elena Fiddian-Qasmiyeh

Introduction

This chapter examines the roles played by citation and recitation, as part of a broader politics of translation which are intimately related to sustaining international solidarity networks in support of the self-determination of the inhabitants of what is commonly referred to as 'Africa's last colony.' We start by introducing the contours of the history of the territory now known as Western Sahara (formerly the Spanish Sahara between 1884 and 1975) and the establishment of the Sahrawi refugee camps in south-west Algeria in 1975. Subsequently, we set out the cross-lingual, multi-source, and interdisciplinary research underpinning our chapter, and outline our conceptualisation of the roles of citation, recitation, and translation both within the context of academic research vis-à-vis this protracted refugee situation, and the transnational solidarity networks that support Sahrawi refugees' political quest for self-determination and their material survival in the camps. By drawing on a range of sources—from Sahrawi historiographies of the conflict, to primary data derived from multisited ethnographic research in and about the Sahrawi camps—we develop a close reading of the terms *naṣārā* and *milḥafa* which have simultaneously become invisible and hyper-visible in transnational accounts of the camps. In so doing, we argue that translation and activism in this context are mutually constitutive.

A history of the Western Sahara

The inhabitants of the North African territory now known as the Western Sahara were historically members of nomadic tribes with 'mixed ethnic origins' (including Arab and Berber), who spoke Hassaniya Arabic, shared a series of cultural practices, and followed the Maliki school of Islam (Hodges 1983: 8–9; Fiddian-Qasmiyeh 2014). Arab populations first arrived in north-west Africa towards the end of the seventh century, interacting with, and often conquering, the local Berber populations which had, in turn, arrived during the first millennium BC. Between the late-fourteenth and late-fifteenth centuries, a group of tribes known collectively as the Banu Hassan migrated from Yemen to the region, enforcing the Arabisation and Islamisation of the area's Berber groups (Diego-Aguirre 1991: 104–107). These processes of migration and conquest were accompanied by intermarriage and alliances, giving rise, by the end of the seventeenth century, to 'a new Arabic-speaking people, known to us today as the "Moors," a people of mixed ethnic origins' (Hodges 1983: 8–9).

It is now widely recognised that the inhabitants of the territory of Saguíat el-Hamra y Río de Oro (now identified as the Western Sahara) all shared 'broad commonalities' with Berbers in southern Morocco and with *al-bayḍān* or *maures* in northern Mauritania, all of whom were camel-herding nomads with a selection of cultural practices in common, and who often spoke Hassaniya (a name derived from Banu Hassan) (Hodges 1987: 33). Hassaniya is a spoken register of Arabic (commonly known as a dialect), and, just like other spoken registers of Arabic across the Middle East and North Africa, Hassaniya has absorbed, accepted, and rejected diverse terms from other languages and dialects.

While the term *ṣahrāwī* in Arabic refers to any inhabitant of the desert (*ṣahrā'*), this identifier is now most frequently used to refer to the people who traditionally lived in and moved throughout the Western Saharan territory. Through this linguistic association, the term *ṣahrāwī* serves a clear function of tying people to a specific place. This usage of the term *ṣahrāwī* is relatively recent, emerging as a key identifier in the anticolonial movements which developed in the 1960s and 1970s, towards the end of the Spanish colonial occupation of what was then referred to as the Spanish Sahara.

In 1964, the territory was placed on the UN Decolonisation Committee's agenda and, after the birth and suppression of a number of anticolonial movements, the Popular Front for the Liberation of Saguíat El-Hamra y Río de Oro (known by its Spanish acronym Frente POLISARIO, henceforth Polisario) was established in 1973. Polisario gained popular support as it firstly resisted Spanish colonialism, and later Moroccan and Mauritanian claims over the territory. Although Spain conducted a census of the population in December 1974 to prepare for a referendum for self-determination, Spain withdrew from its colony without holding a referendum in late 1975, and the territory was then occupied by Morocco and Mauritania, which claimed historic rights over this area. Following Franco's death in November 1975, the conflict between Morocco, Mauritania, and Polisario intensified, with a mass exodus of Sahrawis firstly being displaced to other parts of the territory, and later to the nascent Algerian-based refugee camps near these countries' common border (for a more detailed overview of the history of the camps, see Fiddian-Qasmiyeh 2014). Mauritania withdrew from the conflict soon after, while Morocco and the Polisario continued to engage in armed conflict until 1991, when a ceasefire was brokered by the African Union. To this date, the Western Sahara remains on the UN's list of non-self-governing territories pending decolonisation, and the camps continue to be home to both Sahrawi refugees and the Polisario.

Since the mid-1970s, Polisario has governed and administered the Sahrawi refugee camps and its refugee population via the state in exile (the Sahrawi Arab Democratic Republic, SADR) which it constituted on 27 February 1976, one day after Spain officially withdrew from its colony. The Polisario and its SADR state have developed their own constitution, camp-based police force (and prisons), army, and parallel state and religious legal systems.

Although the camps are almost totally dependent upon externally provided aid, since the 1980s the camps have been heralded as 'unique' and even 'ideal' (contrasting the Sahrawi with other refugee populations; see Fiddian-Qasmiyeh 2014) due to the Sahrawis' self-management and administrative, bureaucratic, and professional self-sufficiency (see Harrell-Bond 1981: 1–4; Mowles 1986: 8–9); as such, analysts and pro-Sahrawi activists alike identify the camps as 'models of efficient local government' and even claim that they are 'the best run refugee camps in the world' (Brazier 1997: 14). As we argue below, these are amongst the assertions and descriptors that are regularly 'cited and recited' by academics and activists who play a key role in constituting knowledge about, and modes of responding to, the unresolved conflict over the Western Saharan territory and its associated protracted refugee situation.

Indeed, Appadurai has stressed that 'every major refugee camp … is a trans-locality' (2003: 339), hinting at the multiple ways in which refugees may be implicated in international or transnational networks, including the presence of UN agencies and international non-governmental organisations (NGOs), the role of remittances, and transnational livelihood strategies (Hyndman and Walton-Roberts 2000; Crisp 2003). The Sahrawi refugee context is characterised by these and other transnational dynamics, in particular a specific dependence on a range of non-Sahrawi state and non-state actors which offer the Polisario/SADR different forms of humanitarian aid and political support. We argue, drawing on Fiddian-Qasmiyeh (2014), that this dependency has led to the development of particular strategies designed to ensure the continuation of support which keeps the camps, their inhabitants, and the Sahrawi cause alive, of which linguistic and translational strategies are an integral part.

Citation, recitation, and the politics of 'knowing' the Sahrawi refugee situation

Most reports on the Algeria-based Sahrawi refugee camps written and published by NGOs, journalists, and academics have typically been based on analyses conducted solely in European languages, mainly Spanish, French, and English (see Fiddian-Qasmiyeh 2014). Only rarely—and relatively recently—have accounts drawn on primary research conducted directly in the Hassaniya dialect of Arabic spoken by Sahrawi refugees. This is despite the fact, as highlighted by Edward Said, that

> [i]t would be impossible to be taken seriously as a reporter or expert on Russia, France, Germany, Latin America, perhaps even China and Japan, without knowing the requisite languages, but for 'Islam' no linguistic knowledge seems to be necessary since what one is dealing with is considered to be a psychological deformation, not a 'real' culture or religion.
>
> *(1997: xxxvi)*

Despite the limited nature of research conducted directly in Arabic, Arabic terms and their translations are nonetheless habitually used by non-Arabic speakers in accounts of the Sahrawi camps, even when little attention has been given to the precise meaning and linguistic functions of these words. Rather, external observers have typically relied on previous authors' transliterations and translations of Arabic terms; these, in turn, have usually been provided by Sahrawi interpreters who are closely associated with the Sahrawi's official political representatives, the Polisario Front. In part, this reflects the 'citational' nature of much research, not only of the Sahrawi context, but across many fields of study (see Said, discussed by Abu-Lughod 1989: 269), and evidently fails to address the politics of translation and naming in such contested spaces. Beyond the citational nature of such research, however, in this chapter we argue that many analysts have systematically and uncritically 'recited' terminology and discursive representations presented by the Polisario, resulting in what we refer to as the strategic activation of 'travelling lexicons' which are cited and recited by Sahrawis and non-Sahrawis across time and space.

These travelling lexicons can be understood as forming part of what Fiddian-Qasmiyeh has elsewhere identified as an official 'travelling discourse' (following Said's notion of 'travelling theory'; 1983: 226–247), with the mainstream representation of the Sahrawi refugee camps having travelled both across time—from the old to the new generation of Sahrawis—and across space—from camp-based Sahrawis to Sahrawis around the world, and simultaneously to non-Sahrawi observers (Fiddian-Qasmiyeh 2013, 2014). As we argue below, the rigidity of understanding embodied in the unequivocal acceptance and reproduction of these terms and their translations epitomises the ways in which official Sahrawi renderings of key words, phrases, and concepts have in effect displaced the original, popular script. These translations have thus not only substituted the popular meaning of terms, often enacting a 'dissolution' of the prototypal or archetypal meaning (following Bachelard 1994: 161), but have created an alternative social pattern (canonical formations) whereby researchers and reporters no longer refer to the original script, but rather recite that which has previously been cited.

Challenging such an approach, we examine the absence of the construct *naṣārā* in English-language sources, before turning to the ways in which one key term, *milḥafa*, has been interpreted and utilised in European languages. Throughout, we contrast these mainstream interpretations with a socio-linguistic analysis of these terms. This chapter therefore queries the roles of constructs which have been embraced and re-produced in, or erased and marginalised by, accounts produced in European languages without critical engagement with these as individual terms and as discursive constructs per se.

We argue that engaging critically with the nuances of the Arabic terminology used in interviews, daily life, and official non-Sahrawi and Sahrawi accounts of the colonial era and life in the camps is imperative, simultaneously, to understand the Sahrawi refugee context and its historical backdrop. Rather than relying upon research completed either with specific groups of Sahrawis who have previously had access to Spanish- and/or English-speaking environments, or through interpreters associated with the Polisario, this article draws upon interviews conducted by Fiddian-Qasmiyeh in Hassaniya Arabic, Fuṣḥa (modern standard Arabic), English, French, and Spanish with Sahrawi refugees in the Sahrawi refugee camps in Algeria, Cuba, South Africa, and Syria between 2004 and 2010, and Qasmiyeh and Fiddian-Qasmiyeh's analysis of relevant Arabic and European-language texts. Throughout the chapter, all translations from Arabic and Spanish are by Qasmiyeh and Fiddian-Qasmiyeh respectively.

Amongst the Arabic-language texts we refer to are a trilogy written by the former Polisario representative to Syria (Mustafa al-Kuttab), whose accounts of the colonial and refugee eras provide a unique approach to a history of the Sahrawi conflict. Given the extent to which al-Kuttab's novels largely draw on, and are supported by, historically validated facts, we propose that it is possible to use his works as an official historiography of the conflict. Indeed, al-Kuttab's stated aim has been to document the colonial and refugee periods and indicate the specificities of the Sahrawi experience (Ghazawi

2002: 8–11). Essentially, al-Kuttab's texts and other Sahrawi sources not only present insights into the context being discussed; rather, 'authorial intention' (Darby 1997: 16ff) emerges as a central concern to be examined, in particular when considering Polisario officials' accounts of the refugee situation. Simultaneously, Darby reminds us that literary sources are, 'of course,' invaluable since they 'themselves are part of the process of international exchange, and the critical debate which they engender represents a new form of enquiry into the relationship between different peoples' (1997: 8).

It is precisely the politics underlying the re/presentation, mobilisation, monopolisation, and magnification of specific images and interpretations of the history and present of the refugee context (whilst sidelining or silencing others) that demands analysis (Fiddian-Qasmiyeh 2014). Through analysing the roles played by Sahrawi authors and translators, we reveal the centrality of particular conceptualisations of the Sahrawi self and other on the local, popular level, and elucidate the ways in which certain Sahrawis have enacted linguistic interventions in this protracted conflict situation by strategically (mis) translating certain terms, ignoring the classical connotations of these constructs, and simultaneously dynamising a range of mainstream postcolonial understandings.

We propose that this cross-lingual, multi-source, and interdisciplinary approach mitigates many of the limitations which have characterised research based upon interviews with members of the Sahrawi elite, or with Spanish-speaking individuals employed by Polisario. We show how, in addition to enabling insightful and reliable research, linguistic and literary modes of engagement elucidate the discourses which surround this conflict, and which have yet, until now, remained unexamined. Beyond presenting linguistic or etymological discussions per se, these terms yield a new understanding of how the Polisario, as a North African liberation movement, functions on popular and international levels, and the extent to which it has variously magnified and minimised the significance of certain classical and postcolonial terms. The ways in which these terms have evolved, and occasionally been devolved (in the sense of being transferred to a new discursive agent as in the representation of the *milḥafa*, explored below), indicates that the postcolonial epoch has not only resuscitated both a range of classical concepts and their translations, but has also centralised the latter in a mode which serves the official discourse, rather than popular conceptualisations and understandings (Fiddian-Qasmiyeh 2014).

This article is structured around an analysis of two key terms: *naṣārā* and *milḥafa*. While the first construct (*naṣārā*) has been entirely absented from Western accounts of the camps, the second one (*milḥafa*) has played hyper-visible roles in demonstrating the uniqueness and the difference of the Sahrawi people. We start by discussing the miniaturisation of the term *naṣārā*, thereby examining the religious dimension of both the Spanish colonial and refugee eras. In turn, we explore the ways in which the *milḥafa* has been discursively distanced from the veil (hijab) and centralised as a *sine qua non* of Sahrawi womanhood by Sahrawis and Spaniards during the refugee era.

Naṣārā: bright bonds and blurred boundaries

Throughout fieldwork in and about the Algerian-based Sahrawi refugee camps, and throughout Arabic texts analysed, the word *naṣārā* (masculine broken pl.) has emerged as a pivotal descriptive term used to refer to the Sahrawi's former colonisers: Spaniards. In spite of this centrality, this term has remained unexamined in the literature on the colonial history of the Western Sahara and the Sahrawi camps.

While *naṣārā* is a Quranic term which refers to 'Christians' (see Ibn Manzur 2015b: 156–158; also see al-Baalbaki 1985: 352, 606), it has in the past been translated by Sahrawi researchers as meaning 'Europeans.' Indeed, in a series of interview transcripts pertaining to the colonial era, *naṣārā* was translated by Sahrawi researchers into Spanish as follows: 'and they fought with the *Naṣārā* (Europeans)' and 'they sold it to the Europeans (*Naṣārā*) as well as to Muslims' (cited and analysed in Fiddian-Qasmiyeh 2014: 75). This rendering leads us to ask not only why al-Kuttab and Sahrawi interviewees decided to use this particular word to refer to the colonisers, but also why Sahrawi translators should have opted for this label, hiding its religious meaning from contemporary observers.

An analysis of the relevant Quranic references and al-Jaberi's in-depth overview (in Arabic) of Christian and Muslim scholars' diverse interpretations of this term reflects the complexity of the concept in theological and historical senses (2006: 37–39), since describing former colonisers as *naṣārā* underscores their religious otherness. Such a recognition suggests some reasons why Sahrawi translators might have distanced themselves from the religious connotations of the term *naṣārā*, leading them to purposely present it as meaning 'Europeans.' Nonetheless, in the second example quoted above it is clear that by contrasting the term *naṣārā* with the latter term, 'Muslims,' the speaker's intention was precisely to use the word as a religious marker, rather than simply referring to the people's origin (from Europe). Indeed, references in al-Kuttab's historiography highlight the religious significance of the term, mentioning the debate around whether it was haram (forbidden) or halal (permitted) to make the pilgrimage to Mecca relying on *māl an-naṣārā* ('the Christians' money') (2002: 185), and including references to the *naṣārā* in relation to the existence of brothels and bars in colonial Aaiun (Al-Kuttab 2002: 158; on the latter, also see Fiddian-Qasmiyeh 2011a).

Until now, the religious dimensions of the colonial encounter and the general animosity towards the Spanish colonial presence in the territory have been largely excised from popular Spanish and Sahrawi histories of the colonial era, for reasons explored in detail elsewhere (Fiddian-Qasmiyeh 2014). Nonetheless, the frequency with which this term appears in Arabic-language narratives pertaining to the colonial era indicates the extent to which the colonial encounter was a religious one, and suggests that the colonised population was resentful of their Christian occupiers, who are presented as homogenised religious Others and as holders and transmitters of Islamically forbidden goods and services.

Equally, despite official (Polisario and Spanish) claims to fraternity, sisterhood, and friendship between Sahrawi refugees and Spaniards, and the systematic depiction of the camps to European and North American audiences as secular spaces in spite of religious identity and practice being central to popular scripts and both individual and communal priorities (see Fiddian-Qasmiyeh 2011b, 2014), research conducted in Arabic in the camps and in South Africa reveals that Spaniards continue to be referred to as *naṣārā* in offstage contexts by Sahrawi refugees.

An important note at this stage is as follows: during Fiddian-Qasmiyeh's research in South Africa in 2006 it became apparent that Black South Africans, many of whom are Christians, were not described using this term, but rather through other—often racial, rather than religious—descriptors. This highlights the limitations of a definition of *naṣārā* as 'a general term for "foreigner" (non-Muslim) and especially for tourists,' as claimed in passing by Casciarri (2006: 407, footnote 14). The connotations of the term are, rather, more clearly defined through equating *naṣārā* primarily with white, European, and North American Christians, leading us to note that the term *naṣārā* has evolved to carry not only a religious dimension but also a racial identification: despite the classical origin of this term, in the contemporary context it has become synonymous, in popular spheres, with the White European or American Christian.

As such, although Spaniards are referred to directly (for external use) as 'brothers' and 'sisters,' they are conceptualised and described by Sahrawis on an unofficial level (offstage) as *naṣārā*. In this context *naṣārā* is specifically a term designed for internal consumption and comprehension. Although this term is not fundamentally derogatory, it highlights religious difference and religious otherness. It could therefore be identified as a key marker of 'bright boundaries' (Alba 2005) between Sahrawis and European observers, with Europeans being conceptualised not as 'official sisters' but as the 'popular Other' amongst Sahrawi refugees (Fiddian-Qasmiyeh 2014: 178–181). Such an analysis both confirms the importance of religious identity and difference in the refugee camps, and suggests some reasons why certain discursive markers must be concealed from outsiders.

The contemporary backstage or offstage usage of this term must be viewed in the context of a protracted conflict situation in which Sahrawi refugees are entirely dependent upon humanitarian and political support offered by European audiences, and in particular by members of Spanish civil society. In such a situation, the question of external relations, and therefore how one presents one's impressions regarding the Other, becomes a matter of the Sahrawi's 'politics of survival' (Fiddian-Qasmiyeh 2014). In direct contrast with public declarations of Sahrawi secularism designed to blur boundaries in order to establish 'bright bonds' with European observers (following Alba 2005), the public usage of the term *naṣārā* has the potential to accentuate the 'brightness' of these boundaries between aid providers and recipients by demonstrating both the differences between these groups, and the continued importance of religious identity and identifiers in daily interactions in the camps. Consequently, protecting official bright bonds with European observers has required a strengthening and policing of linguistic boundaries which cannot, and must not, be transcended in this context.

Indeed, dependence on aid providers is often characterised by ambivalence or animosity towards different sectors of the international community, although the Polisario's official discourse projected to European observers efficiently eliminates traces of such responses. In this context, we propose that *naṣārā* could be understood as a term of resistance, or a 'weapon of the weak' (Scott 1985), reproduced amongst, by, and for refugees who are thereby enabled to channel these unequal power dynamics away from the gaze of their aid providers (Hyndman 2000: 156; Scott 1990: 3). The widespread usage of this term in offstage settings points to the reality of historically rooted and ongoing resentment towards Spanish civil society which is not expressible in public in this protracted refugee context.

Veiling and 'veiling' the milḥafa

Alongside the religious marker *naṣārā* having been strategically smothered by the national discourse presented to European audiences, other religiously charged symbols have also been rendered invisible in mainstream accounts of the refugee camps (on this dynamic in the Sahrawi camps, also see Fiddian-Qasmiyeh 2011b, 2015). In particular, the mainstream discourse projected by the Polisario to Western observers with regard to

Sahrawi women is permeated with claims that, unlike other Arab/Muslim women, they did not veil during, before, or after the colonial era. Hence, discussing Sahrawi women during the colonial era, al-Kuttab states that 'she does not veil [*hiya lā tatahajjab*, where *hajaba* is the Arabic root of the verb "to conceal" or "to veil"]' (2002: 63). Equally, like other visitors to the refugee camps, Harrell-Bond was told by informants throughout her visit in the early 1980s that '[o]ur women were never veiled and they always worked' (1999: 156; also see Feo 2003). Such accounts of Sahrawi women 'not veiling' either in the past or in the present lead us to explore the distinguishing role of the *milhafa*.

The *milhafa* is a long piece of fabric worn by Sahrawi women over an existing layer of clothing, loosely wrapped around their bodies and head. Derived from the verb *lahafa*, meaning 'to cover,' the *milhafa* is literally a dress/layer (as per *Lisān al-'Arab* by Ibn Manzur 2015a: 222–223) that is worn over another dress/layer. Although it has been used by varied groups of Muslim women throughout the Arab world (Fernández-Puertas 1994: 379; Stillman 2003: xxv, 14, 149; Rouse 2004: 230; Harvey 2005: 72; Taylor 2005: 10, 32), such widespread usage is resolutely ignored in accounts of the Sahrawi refugee camps, with the *milhafa* remaining one of the main identifiers, a *sine qua non*, of Sahrawi womanhood and consequently a quintessential symbol of Sahrawi nationhood. Just as the term 'Sahrawi' has come to be synonymous with those who originate from the Western Sahara (Fiddian-Qasmiyeh 2014), so too has the *milhafa* become a unique signifier, which distinguishes Sahrawi women from all Other Arab women (see below).

Whilst the *milhafa* is a traditional item which fulfils mainstream interpretations of the Islamic requirements of veiling/covering, and therefore should be understood as a veil (Fiddian-Qasmiyeh 2014), conventional Sahrawi representations of this item of clothing to Europeans purport to distance the *milhafa* from religious obligations or connotations, even overtly declaring that Sahrawi women 'do not veil.' However, not only do Sahrawi refugee women veil, but the typical assumption in the camps is that all Muslim women are *Islamically obliged* to wear some sort of veil, and that if they are Sahrawi women, they should specifically wear the *milhafa* (Fiddian-Qasmiyeh 2014). Complementing the introductory discussion of the strategic translation of the term *nasārā* in the context of the transnational solidarity network, in part to maintain an official distance with Islam, what is of interest in this section is the separation created, for a European audience, between 'the veil' and the *milhafa*.

The identifiers 'veil,' 'veiling,' and 'unveiling' are omnipresent throughout analyses of women in the Middle East, and yet these terms' meanings often remain unexplored or undefined, despite authors referring to the heterogeneity of practice and significance given to veiling by women themselves and by the communities they live in. Lewis and Mills' anthology (2003) contains a section specifically dedicated to the 'Harem and the Veil,' and yet only one of the six contributors, El-Guindi, explicitly differentiates between 'veiling in two feminisms,' thereby exploring alternative forms of both veiling and unveiling. In the remaining pieces, however, authors make reference to 'the veil,' 'veiling,' and/or 'unveiling' without defining precisely what it is that they are describing. In so doing, it appears that the authors assume that their readers will automatically know what the veil is, understand its multifaceted purposes, interpretations, justifications, and regulations, as well as its physical nature, including what it covers or leaves exposed.[1] The Sahrawi claims that 'they do not veil' whilst wearing the *milhafa* merit closer scrutiny (also see Fiddian-Qasmiyeh 2015).

In the five articles mentioned above, by simply using the term 'veil' rather than explaining whether the author is referring to a *chador, niqāb, jilbāb*, or hijab, not only are the various types of veils worn by different Muslim women elided, but so too is the significance of the terms 'veiled' and 'unveiled.' El-Guindi's discussion of the significance of the veil in two case studies of Muslim feminism is particularly relevant at this point. With reference to a 'public political feminist act' in which the founder of the Egyptian feminist union, Huda Shaʿrawi 'unveiled ceremonially,' El-Guindi reminds us that

> The phrase used in the discourse surrounding the context of lifting the 'veil' was *rafʿ al-higab* (the lifting of the *hijab* [pronounced 'higab' in the Egyptian vernacular]). Ironically, what secular feminists lifted was the traditional face veil (*burquʿ*), which is rooted in cultural tradition and history rather than Islamic sources, not the *hijab* … When Huda Shaʿrawi dramatically cast off the veil in 1923, it was the face veil she removed, not the *hijab*.
>
> *(2003: 596)*

As Shaʿrawi's example clearly demonstrates, it is possible to remove the veil and yet remain veiled, since there are different degrees and forms of veiling which Muslim women may don. Such insights are absent from Graham-Brown's usage of the term 'unveiled' in the caption that accompanies a late-nineteenth-century photograph of three women in Egypt:

> *The unveiled woman* in the foreground, gazing directly at the camera, is contrasted with the *two veiled women* in the background … However, *she draws her head-veil slightly across her face* in the presence of the man behind the camera.
>
> *(2003: 507, our emphasis)*

As indicated in the caption itself, 'the unveiled woman' is in fact wearing a head veil, and the briefest examination of the photograph demonstrates that the term 'unveiled' refers solely to the absence of a face veil, since the three women are all wearing a loose piece of cloth which covers their bodies, necks, heads, and foreheads.

It is thus precisely through recognising the different ways in which veiling (being *muhajjabāt)* and unveiling can be conceptualised, and by asking who and what Sahrawi women and the *milhafa* are being *compared with* when analysts declare that they 'did not [or do not] veil,' that we can best understand mainstream representations of veiling in the camps. Hence, if *compared* with those Bedouin women who wear face veils or Muslim women who wear the niqab or burqa (*al-munaqqabāt*, El-Guindi 1999:144), it might be valid to note that Sahrawi women did not, and do not, cover their faces (major exceptions being when women protect their faces from the sun or the sand). Such an understanding is offered by one Cuban-based Sahrawi student interviewed by Fiddian-Qasmiyeh in Havana, who claimed that the only Arab women who 'do not cover their faces or hands' are Mauritanian and Sahrawi women who wear the *milhafa* (Fiddian-Qasmiyeh 2014). He continued by further stating that 'in other places in the Arab world, you can only see the woman's eyes.' As these words suggest, if one considers face veiling to be veiling *per se*, one might reach the conclusion that Sahrawi women did not veil in the past and do not veil in the present.

Conclusion

While the *milḥafa* may, as a matter of fact, be a traditional item of clothing, and whilst it is admittedly neither a hijab (*qua* headscarf) nor a niqab or burqa, the *milḥafa* is nevertheless a 'veil' in the traditionally Islamic sense. The determination with which Polisario spokespeople have distanced themselves from the veil as a visible sign of Muslim identity in their portrayals of Sahrawi womanhood, alongside the concealment—or the *representation* (see Fiddian-Qasmiyeh 2016)—of religious identifiers such as *naṣārā*, demonstrates that in this context, as elsewhere, 'representation becomes nothing but a body of expressions with which to communicate our own images to others' (Bachelard 1994: 150). Indeed, the very survival of Sahrawi refugees, their refugee camp-homes and broader quest for self-determination, is dependent upon such processes of communication and indeed translation. The selective processes of representation underpinning the modes of citation and recitation explored throughout this chapter demonstrate the extent to which the translation of *naṣārā* and *milḥafa* has been undertaken in order not to disrupt the status quo, precisely by presenting them as apolitical (and areligious) and devoid of the complex colonial history of the territory and its inhabitants. In this regard, these terms and their renderings have evolved to become part of a discourse that is simultaneously independent from Sahrawi refugees and European observers, and yet is cited and recited by both.

The process of translating, citing, and reciting these constructs by and for specific audiences—including different generations of Sahrawis and non-Sahrawis alike—is an essential part of the past–present nexus that is always moving into the future, with the transnational activist networks being, at their core, committed to securing a particular outcome for Sahrawi refugees. In this sense, both translation and activism are processes that, in order to take place, can only be completed in the future, but rely upon a re-inscription of the past. An independent Sahrawi future is only viable, or at least imaginable, when the past and present have been selectively translated in ways that suppress or dilute key identifiers associated with the colonial encounter.

Reflecting the complexities of the relationship between (forced) movement and immobility experienced in the Sahrawi context, these terms have thus simultaneously become part of a 'travelling discourse,' and yet are static in nature. As such, they are both characterised by and result in a definite set of linguistic parameters that in turn emerge as a prerequisite to protecting the Sahrawi national cause in the international arena, with the *milḥafa*-qua-non-veil as one of its key nationalist symbols, and the dilution of religious identifiers such as *naṣārā* an essential component that sustains the complex solidarity networks that support the camps and their residents, with a view to creating a new future. Echoing Derrida's assertion that '[t]ranslation is writing; that is, it is not translation only in the sense of transcription. It is a productive writing called forth by the original text' (1985: 153), we can identify the power and significance of these processes of translation, as both a *product* and, more pertinently in this context, as a *prerequisite* for a 'productive' relationship between Sahrawi refugees and various activist groups, today and in the future.

Related topics

Resistant Recipes; Translation in the War-Zone; Translator, Native Informant, Fixer

Note

1 The same suras (24: 30, 31 and 33: 53 and 59) and examples from the hadith are habitually drawn upon by members of contemporary Islamic movements when they defend the Islamic bases for specific dress and behavioural codes (El-Guindi 2003: 588–589; Küng 2007: 621 ff), and yet the religious requirement to veil remains a debated issue within Muslim communities, and in part explains the variety of veiling practices around the world.

Further reading

Ahmed, Sara (2004) *The Cultural Politics of Emotion*. Edinburgh: Edinburgh University Press.

This nuanced study examines the relationship between emotions, languages, and bodies, providing insights into the way that these relate to politics on different levels.

Fiddian-Qasmiyeh, Elena (2014) *The Ideal Refugees: Gender, Islam and the Sahrawi Politics of Survival*. New York: Syracuse University Press.

A multisited and multilingual study of the ways that Sahrawi refugees and their political representatives interact with and mobilise different audiences, from civil society groups, to academics and journalists.

Said, Edward W. (1983) *The World, the Text, and the Critic*. London: Vintage.

An essential text and treatise exploring the significance of critique, including through the motifs of travelling, repetition, and the notion of originality.

References

Abu-Lughod, Lila (1989) 'Zones of Theory in the Anthropology of the Arab World,' *Annual Review of Anthropology* 18: 267–306.

Alba, Richard (2005) 'Bright vs. Blurred Boundaries: Second-generation Assimilation and Exclusion in France, Germany, and the United States,' *Ethnic and Racial Studies* 28 (1): 20–49.

al-Baalbaki, Munir (1985) *Jane Eyre*. Beirut: Dar al-Ilm lil Malaayiin.

Al-Jaberi, Mohammad A. (2006) *Madkhal ila al-Qur'ān al-Karīm. Al juz' al-awwal fī al-ta'rīf bil-Qur'ān* (Trans. *An introduction to the Noble Qur'an. Volume one of introducing the Qur'an*). Beirut: Markez Dirasat.

Al-Kuttab, Mustafa (2002) *Riwāya min al-Ṣahrā' al-Gharbiyya: Awtād al-'Arḍ* (Trans. *A Novel from Western Sahara: The Pegs of the Earth*). Damascus, Syria: Muasasat al-Tibaa al-Taswiria.

Almond, Ian (2007) *The New Orientalists: Postmodern Representations of Islam from Foucault to Baudrillard*. London: I.B. Tauris.

Appadurai, Arjun (2003) 'Sovereignty without Territoriality: Notes for a Postnational Geography,' in *The Anthropology of Space and Place. Locating Culture*. Eds. Setha M. Low and Denise Lawrence-Zuniga. Oxford: Blackwell Publishing. 337–350.

Bachelard, Gaston (1994) *The Poetics of Space*. Boston: Beacon Press.

Brazier, Chris (1997) 'Special Edition: War and Peace in Western Sahara,' *The New Internationalist* 297.

Casciarri, Barbara (2006) 'Coping with Shrinking Spaces: The Ait Unzar Pastoralists of South-Eastern Morocco,' in *Nomadic Societies in the Middle East and North Africa: Entering the 21st Century*. Ed. Dawn Chatty. Leiden: Brill. 393–430.

Crisp, Jeffery (2003) *No Solution in Sight: The Problem of Protracted Refugee Situations in Africa*. San Diego: University of California Press.

Darby, Phillip (1997) 'Postcolonialism,' in *At the Edge of International Relations: Postcolonialism, Gender, and Dependency*. Ed. Phillip Darby. London: Pinter. 12–31.

Derrida, Jacques (1985) *The Ear of the Other: Otobiography, Transference, Translation*. Trans. P. Kamuf. New York: Schocken.

Diego-Aguirre, José Ramon (1991) *Guerra en el Sáhara*. Madrid: Ediciones Istmo.

El-Guindi, Fadwa (1999) *Veil: Modesty, Privacy and Resistance*. Oxford: Berg.

El-Guindi, Fadwa (2003) 'Veiling Resistance,' in *Feminist Postcolonial Theory: A Reader.* Ed. Reina Lewis, and Sara Mills. Edinburgh: Edinburgh University Press. 586–609.

El-Hamel, Chouki (1999) 'The Transmission of Islamic Knowledge in Moorish Society from the Rise of the Almoravids to the 19th Century,' *Journal of Religion in Africa* 29 (1): 62–87.

Feo, Pilar (2003) 'Hijas de la Arena,' *Diario de Avisos* [online] 2 February. Available at: www. elguanche.net/hijasdelaarena.htm.

Fernández-Puertas, Antonio (1994) 'Sobre los relieves en la predela de los retablos de la Capilla Real de Granada,' *Anales de la Historia del Arte* 4: 373–384.

Fiddian-Qasmiyeh, Elena (2016) '*Repress*entations of Displacement in the Middle East,' *Public Culture* 28 (3). doi:10.1215/08992363-3511586

Fiddian-Qasmiyeh, Elena (2015) 'The Veiling of Religious Markers in the Sahrawi Diaspora,' in *Religion in Diaspora: Cultures of Citizenship*. Eds. Jane Garnett and Sondra L. Hale. London: Palgrave Macmillan. 181–201.

Fiddian-Qasmiyeh, Elena (2014) *The Ideal Refugees: Gender, Islam and the Sahrawi Politics of Survival*. New York: Syracuse University Press.

Fiddian-Qasmiyeh, Elena (2013) 'Transnational Childhood and Adolescence: Mobilising Sahrawi Identity and Politics across Time and Space,' *Journal of Ethnic and Racial Studies* 36 (5): 875–895.

Fiddian-Qasmiyeh, Elena (2011a) 'Histories of Displacement: Intersections between Ethnicity, Gender and Class,' *Journal of North African Studies* 16 (1): 31–48.

Fiddian-Qasmiyeh, Elena (2011b) 'The Pragmatics of Performance: Putting "Faith" in Aid in the Sahrawi Refugee Camps,' *Journal of Refugee Studies* 24 (3): 533–547.

Ghazawi, Zuhair (2002) 'Introduction,' in *Riwāya min al-Ṣahrāʾ al-Gharbiyya: Awtād al-ʾArḍ* (Trans. *A Novel from Western Sahara: The Pegs of the Earth*). Ed. Mustafa al-Kuttab. Damascus, Syria: Muassasat al-Ṭibāʾa al-Taṣwīriyya. 8–11.

Graham-Brown, Sarah (2003) 'The Seen, the Unseen and the Imagined: Private and Public Lives,' in *Feminist Postcolonial Theory: A Reader*. Eds. Reina Lewis and Sara Mills Edinburgh: Edinburgh University Press. 502–519.

Harrell-Bond, Barbara E. (1999) 'The experience of Refugees as Recipients of Aid,' in *Refugees: Perspectives on the Experience of Forced Migration*. Ed. Alastair Ager London: Pinter. 136–168.

Harrell-Bond, Barbara E. (1981) *The Struggle for the Western Sahara* Hanover: American Universities Field Staff.

Harvey, Leonard Patrick (2005) *Muslims in Spain, 1500 to 1614*. London: University of Chicago Press.

Hodges, Tony (1983) *Western Sahara: The Roots of a Desert War*. Westport: Lawrence Hill & Co.

Hodges, Tony (1984) *The Western Saharans*. London: Minority Rights Group.

Hodges, Tony (1987) 'The Origins of Saharawi Nationalism,' in *War and Refugees: The Western Sahara Conflict*. Eds. R.I. Lawless and L. Monahan. London: Pinter. 31–65.

Hyndman, Jennifer (2000) *Managing Displacement: Refugees and the Politics of Humanitarianism*. London: University of Minnesota.

Hyndman, Jennifer, and Margaret Walton-Roberts (2000) 'Interrogating Borders: A Transnational Approach to Refugee Research in Vancouver,' *The Canadian Geographer* 44 (3): 244–258.

Ibn Manzur (2015a) *Lisān al-ʾArab* (Trans. *The Language of the Arab People*), Vol 5. Cairo: Dar Ibn al-Jawzi.

Ibn Manzur (2015b) *Lisān al-ʾArab* (Trans. *The Language of the Arab People*), Vol 3. Cairo: Dar Ibn al-Jawzi.

Küng, Hans (2007) *Islam: Past, Present and Future*. Oxford: Oneworld Publications.

Lewis, Reina (2003) 'On Veiling, Vision and Voyage: Cross-Cultural Dressing and Narratives of Identity,' in *Feminist Postcolonial Theory: A Reader*. Eds. Reina Lewis and Sara Mills Edinburgh: Edinburgh University Press. 520–541.

Lewis, Reina, and Sara Mills (eds.) (2003) *Feminist Postcolonial Theory: A Reader*. Edinburgh: Edinburgh University Press.

Muhibbu-Din, Murtada A. (2000) 'Ahl Al-Kitab and Religious Minorities in the Islamic State: Historical Context and Contemporary Challenges,' *Journal of Muslim Minority Affairs* 20 (1): 111–127.

Mowles, Chris (1986) *Desk Officer's Report on Trip to the Sahrawi Refugee Camps near Tindouf, Southern Algeria, June 16- 21, 1986*. Oxfam: Refugee Studies Centre (RSC) Grey Literature Collection, University of Oxford.

Rouse, Caroline M. (2004) *Engaged Surrender: African American Women and Islam*. London: University of California Press.

Said, Edward W. (1983) *The World, the Text, and the Critic*. London: Vintage.

Said, Edward W. (1997) *Covering Islam: How the Media and the Experts Determine How We See the Rest of the World*. London: Vintage.

Scott, James C. (1985) *Weapons of the Weak: Everyday Forms of Peasant Resistance*. London: Yale University Press.

Scott, James C. (1990) *Domination and the Arts of Resistance Hidden Transcripts*. New Haven: Yale University Press.

Stillman, Yedida K. (2003) *Arab Dress, a Short History: From the Dawn of Islam to Modern Times* (2nd ed.). Leiden: Brill.

Taylor, Jeffery (2005) *Angry Wind: Through Muslim Black Africa by Truck, Bus, Boat, and Camel*. Boston: Houghton Mifflin Harcourt Books.

26

Resistant recipes

Food, gender and translation in migrant and refugee narratives

Veruska Cantelli and Bhakti Shringarpure

Introduction: food and migration

During a field trip to a shelter in Northern Italy, anthropologist Cristiana Giordano recalls the misunderstandings between the migrant foreigners and the volunteers of a Catholic non-governmental organisation regarding appropriate behaviour at the table (Giordano 2014). Giordano points out that, when the Senegalese migrants prepared a dish called *mafe*, the members of her research group followed the Senegalese way of eating with their hands from a communal bowl and noticed the uneasiness of the Catholic volunteers who deemed the custom unhygienic, and readily introduced plates and silverware. This event prompted Giordano to question whether the shelter was actually moved by a spirit of support and solidarity or whether it was providing not recognition but a form of conversion to translate what would be otherwise considered 'indigestible' (Giordano 2014: 3–4). Giordano describes such a practice of 'translation' in her study of therapeutic practices in ethno-psychiatry in Italy as one founded on fundamental classifications by assigning 'scripts, roles and stories that represent the foreigner and translate her alterity into its own language' (2014: 3–4), a language that can ultimately fulfil the state's necessity to pin the foreigner as 'the other.' In her work on postcolonial and transnational feminism, Chandra Talpade Mohanty has highlighted the ambiguity of benevolence against the framework of 'objectification' (2003: 23–24), an observation often echoed in the dynamics of giving and charity, and of which the Giordano story becomes an example.

Giordano's work exposes food as a tool for conduct; when food is denied, controlled and rationed, the act of giving begins to transform into discipline. And, indeed, one does not have to go far to connect these events with the dehumanising practices instituted by histories of colonisation: 'Animalisation forms part of a larger, more diffuse mechanism of naturalisation: the reduction of the cultural to the biological, the tendency to associate the colonised with the vegetative and the instinctual rather than the learned and cultural' (Shohat and Stam 1994: 138). Regulating food and rituals around food is yet another way in which subjects come to be dominated, restrained and branded. Institutions designed to provide service relief to refugees operate under the seeming necessity to identify and categorise individuals for the purpose of channelling the appropriate legal path.

Additionally, the above anecdote illustrates the complicated and troubled relationships between migration, refugees, food and translation. The precarity of migrant and refugee lives is emphasised in pressing issues such as the poor conditions in camps and detention centres and legal battles over resettlement and asylum. Questions of food allotment and food shortages in refugee and migrant spaces have also become increasingly more urgent. Images and narratives emerging from the media have fabricated reducible, dehumanised identities of migrants and refugees as culturally associated with starvation and scarcity. In the contexts of dislocation and detention, food enters back into the realm of the politics of sustenance through expressions of loss and the desire for autonomy. Images of food lines in refugee camps in Europe (Dinham 2017) and the banning of meals as a tactic for keeping migrants from settling (Gentleman 2017), which led to the arrest of volunteers in the Italian town of Ventimiglia (Dearden 2017), are just two examples in which food in the current migrant crisis is being turned into a weapon of control.

As discourses about migrants and refugees proliferate in news and media outlets, a whole new genre of writing that unearths, promotes and disseminates refugee recipes has emerged simultaneously. One approach involves bringing about food relief through books such as *Soup for Syria: Recipes to Celebrate our Shared Humanity* that accumulated soup recipes from celebrity chefs (Abdeni Massad 2015) or the #CookForSyria and #BakeforSyria campaigns and books (Boy and Gruen 2018). Proceeds from all these books are donated to organisations such as United Nations High Commissioner for Refugees (UNHCR) for food relief efforts. A second food-centric approach involves initiatives that organise dinners and supper clubs for refugees in various locations, emphasising community integration and supportive environments for refugees (*Refugees Welcome, Displaced Dinners* and *Syria Supper Club* 2018). Yet another approach, explored in this chapter, foregrounds refugee women, their cooking and their recipes with an eye towards understanding communal solidarities, national nostalgias and the archiving of historical memory. Though there has been a strong emphasis on Syrian refugees and Syrian cuisine in the past few years, our chapter examines the wider context of translating refugee women's recipes as evidenced in food-related works coming out not just from Syria but also Palestine, Western Sahara, Somalia and Eritrea.

We have chosen four contemporary works that illustrate that not only can a collection of recipes become works that resist dehumanisation, compression and a univocal narrative, but that translating these works firms up the interwoven nature of gender, culture, memory and activism. These works include *Dining in Refugee Camps: The Art of Sahrawi Cooking* by Robin Kahn (2010), *The Gaza Kitchen: A Palestinian Culinary Journey* by Laila El-Haddad and Maggie Schmitt (2013), two recipes published on *Mediterranean* by Shringarpure et al. that originally appeared in the collection *Cum-panis: Storie di fuga, identità e memorie, in quattro ricette* (Papa and Mollo 2014) by Associazione culturale 'La Kasbah Onlus' and *Cooking a Home: A Collection of the Recipes and Stories of Syrian Refugees* by Pilar Puig Cortada (2015). The recipes included here are not simply journeys into food nostalgia but also an exploration into the fear of its disappearance. They are accompanied by stories bearing witness to ruptured histories and violent cartographies which also insist on honouring communities that were established in the aftermath, and to centralise the women who were responsible for the labour of rebuilding. At the outset, we encounter a double gendering when it comes to the translation of recipes. Food and recipes have traditionally been stereotyped as the domain of women and have been consistently pushed out of the domain of feminist work. Furthermore, translation itself has been perceived as a gendered gesture—a reproduction or an adaptation, never original, never a source. In order to make this work productive, urgent and activist-oriented, and to counter the pernicious gendering of food studies as well as translation studies, we elaborate upon and build a *feminist food translation studies framework*. Through this framework, we argue that the creative, caring and dynamic ways in which these recipes were gathered and translated prove that the translation of these recipes can facilitate and nurture the work of disseminating collective memory, provide a space for revisiting history, offer a chance to express and mourn displacement and trauma, and also for creating physical and virtual communities that resist against distorted and decontextualised narratives.

Food as a site of paradox

Food functions as a site of paradox in discourses about migration and refugeedom. On the one hand, food can function as a mode of control managed by the state and on the other hand, stories and narratives about food are employed by migrants themselves to express belonging, community and loss, and to reframe historical memory. Migrant and refugee experiences are saturated with contradictory and humiliating food-related imagery. Images of overabundance and scarcity are frequently juxtaposed: the amount of a scoop or the frugality of a lunch consumed from a plastic plate can manipulate us into believing in dynamics of deficit, overpopulation and the impossibility of aiding excessive numbers of migrants. The video from a reception centre in Hungary shows police deliberately throwing sandwiches at refugees (Walker 2015). Such imagery illustrates the extent to which desperation is objectified and exploited for amusement.

When Cantelli interviewed Mary Bosworth, author of *Inside Immigration Detention*, a study on the everyday life of migrants in British detention centres, and Director of Border Criminologies, she underlined that

> [t]he politics of food in detention revolve around the issue of choice and culture. Those who observe particular diets, e.g. halal, vegan or vegetarian, are very suspicious about the claims of the institution that the food is appropriate. They do not like being forced to eat at particular times.
>
> *(Shringarpure et al. 2018: 30–31)*

The control exercised through food is manifested in scheduling, issues of choice, quality of food and restrictions as well as in the exclusion from its preparation. Bosworth also points out that the micromanaging of meals goes as far as prohibiting fresh produce in the rooms in which migrants are housed, essentially driving them to live off packaged food that can be made in the microwave or with a kettle (Shringarpure et al. 2018: 30–31). Conviviality in these circumstances is not the spontaneous, deliberate instance of bonding but a practice artificially managed by the staff. Almost all women's centres in the UK now have cultural kitchenettes, a space that a group of people can book to prepare food and eat it together. Meanwhile 'in the men's institutions, the centres are run a little differently' (Shringarpure et al. 2018: 30–31). Bosworth speaks about how in Colnbrook, for instance, one man usually works alone, with some officers monitoring him, to cook for a small group of friends who are then allowed to enter and eat together. In each center the staff are concerned about access to knives and sharp objects.

(Shringarpure et al. 2018: 30–31)

The differentiations between the genders is taken for granted here, with kitchen implements, cooking spaces and domestic spheres relegated to women while the same aspects are framed as dangerous and heavily surveilled when it comes to men.

As in any situation of surveillance, meal sharing excludes workers. Detainees and those who supervise them remain segregated. This separation is reflected even among the migrants. 'Socially, food plays an ambiguous role in the centers,' says Bosworth (Shringarpure et al. 2018: 30–31). In some institutions like Campsfield House, outside Oxford, and Tinsley House, near Gatwick airport, detainees and staff eat together in a dining hall with the men grouping themselves by nationality and the staff sitting separately. Such patterns of segregation build on the pervasive pairing of migration with criminality. People seeking relocation from war-torn countries are quickly turned into potentially violent individuals in such spaces. Examining migrant experiences through the prism of food reveals the dehumanising and degrading ways in which migrants and refugees are treated, and systematically closed off from certain spaces. In the following section, we articulate strategies and expressions that are employed by women migrants in order to repossess discourses around food and reframe questions of belonging, memory, community and power; and of course, the processes of translation that make these projects possible.

Paradoxically, migrant narratives have attempted to resist inhumane experiences and hegemonic classifications by asserting and reclaiming heritage through discourses of food itself. Stories and narratives expressed through a variety of genres from novels to essays to cookbooks subvert degrading modes of domination via food. These narratives do more than simply evoke cuisines and recipes that are personal and communal; they also emphasise the act of making a meal together or eating together, and attempt to recreate the conversations that take place over meals. This also allows for an unofficial and spontaneous archiving of the cultural memories from which migrants may have been uprooted. Anita Mannur coins the term 'culinary citizenship' to describe a type of

affective citizenship which grants subjects the ability to claim and inhabit certain subject positions via their relationship to food. Within such narratives, official and traditional models of national definition become reinterpreted so as to hint towards the multiplicity of definitional possibilities.

(Mannur 2007: 13)

Ripped from their homes and flung far from families and communities, food whether in the form of stories, cookbooks or recipes becomes a way to 'negotiate the pangs of migratory displacement' (Mannur 2007: 13). At the same time, recipes can also become tools of resistance that subvert the degradation that has come to be part and parcel of the migration and refugee experience. Here, food is not simply the act of self-identification but also the assertion of refugee humanity. It becomes a resistant claim that counters the dehumanisation which marks migratory journeys and refugee spaces.

In the limbo of detention centres, migrants' physical and psychological condition often gets worse not only because of the precarious conditions but also from the poor quality of the food being meted out, and 'as people's health deteriorates in detention, they often long for fresh fruit and vegetables, and for home cooking and conviviality' (Shringarpure et al. 2018). Bosworth's extensive work has put her in touch with the many stories of escape. She emphasises that food and cuisine 'often come up in interviews. Men and women miss their local dishes. They often describe particular recipes they used to make and the diverse ingredients that exist in their countries' (Shringarpure et al. 2018). A kind of lost conviviality, the warmth of belonging and an affective bond of citizenship can spring up through recipes and cookbooks, facilitated by processes between translators, editors and the cooks and the community that interact extensively during the creation of the books. For example, El-Haddad and Schmitt emphasise the importance of what might be banal, domestic conversations in their introduction to *Gaza Kitchen*. They write that 'to talk about food and cooking is to talk about the dignity of daily life, about history and heritage in a place where these very things have often been disparaged or actively erased' (El-Haddad and Schmitt 2013: 12). This shared experience is an opportunity to create what Roy calls 'gastrophilic histories' (2002: 472), stories and narratives that evoke national histories and idioms of national belonging for those displaced from their place of origin.

It is important to distinguish the many forms that such gastrophilic histories might take. While novels of diaspora tend to emphasise food and cooking rituals, and certain cookbooks aim to keep national cuisines alive, the texts we have chosen are not necessarily framed by the same concerns. They do not always display a diasporic subject's nostalgia 'for foods that are unfamiliar and untasted or for a homeland that one may desire precisely because one wishes never to return to it' (Roy 2002: 489), nor is there any sort of 'self-exoticizing' gesture (Roy 2002: 489). For example, Um Rami, one of the cooks featured in *Gaza Kitchen*, lost her husband and mother-in-law from the shock of the 2009 assault on Gaza. She explains that when she visited her father after returning from Saudi Arabia to get married in Gaza she took him some *khobeiza* (a type of green vegetable that grows in Gaza) wrapped in newspaper. She says,

> The first thing I did when I got there was cook this dish for him. He told me 'this is the best gift ever' because the poor thng hadn't eaten it for so long. It was so simple, but he really appreciated it, it tasted like home.
>
> *(El-Haddad and Schmitt 2013: 71)*

The women presented in these works are, undoubtedly, conscious of their desire to recreate a connection to home. The women are victims of dislocations often caused by conflicts, and their recipes resist the misrepresented and distorted identity that denies them an origin, an origin that is not lost or reinvented, but rather kept alive. The recipes become a site of resistance that is grounded in a political struggle and which may not necessarily involve a redefinition of group identity. Rather, the recipes become a strategy to resist the normalisation of uprooted-ness, the psychological violence of being forgotten and the anguish of becoming victims of racist othering and being unjustly criminalised.

Towards a feminist food translation framework

The four gastrophilic texts explored in this chapter are written by or orally narrated by women. They have all been translated by women too. A double gendering marks these acts of narrating, gathering and translating these collections. Food and recipes have traditionally been stereotyped as the domain of women and have consistently battled for legitimacy within the domain of what counts as feminist theory and praxis. In their ground-breaking theorisation of feminist food studies, Avakian and Haber claim that '[f]eminists organised around housework and women's studies scholarship addressed domesticity, but cooking was ignored as if it were merely a marker of patriarchal oppression and, therefore, not worthy of attention' (2005: 3). However, food as a site of feminist expression and feminist resistance has a long and rich history. Avakian and Haber take the reader through a long lineage that emerges from the food shortages of World War II to the sporadic appearance of works outlining the importance of food and feminism right until the late 1990s, which witnessed a sudden flowering of books and articles on women and food. Feminist food studies call for an intersectional perspective that recognises the agency intrinsic to all expressions around food and which aims to theorise and historicise the entangled and inextricable relationships between women and food as forms of feminist resistance.

Similarly, the act of translation has also been seen as gendered work, with the translated work *submitted* to the original, as being less than the original and as secondary to the original text. For the most part, such debates have largely been dismantled thanks to Jacques Derrida's argument that

> the idea that original and translation are hierarchically equal, with no dependence or submission, and that the translator (normally a woman), like the author, writes, she does not rewrite. Derrida favours the woman translator and the translation in relation to the man and the original text, his aim being to put an end to textual and sexual subordination.
>
> *(Godayol 2013: 173–182)*

Doing away with the gendered paradigms and embedded hierarchies, several sets of scholars have called for a productive intersection between translation studies and feminist studies since the 1990s (Godayol 2013). Feminist translation studies have a three-part agenda: to recover a history of women translators, to generate a theory of translation and gender as imbricated projects and to produce translation criticism that emphasises paratextual materials generated during translation practice (Godayol 2013).

We propose a feminist food translation framework which takes seriously the work of gastrophilic histories being narrated or written by women, and the politically engaged women translators who attempt to make these works visible and legible to a transnational audience. Along the way, such works foreground women as producing resistance against the extraordinary violence of occupation, war, displacement, detention and sexual assault. Food becomes the most corporeal and immediate site to explore the particularities of the plight of women caught in the throes of these crises. Women's work with food and in domestic spaces as well as the gendered work of translation ends up being rendered invisible and it is often unpaid and underacknowledged. In our case, the connections between and the significance of the relationship between food and migration are easy to classify but the role of translation in clarifying this relationship has not been explored in particular depth.

A feminist food translation framework would involve a fundamentally collaborative methodology which gives impetus for women to build networks across class, nation and race lines. If we apply black feminist geographer Katherine McKittrick's provocative argument that the history of black women is a 'geographic story' (2006: x) and that black women's geographies 'signal alternative patterns that work alongside and across traditional geographies' (2006: xiv), then a feminist food translation framework indeed brings about new imaginative and epistemological geographies created by marginalised and racialised women. It allows for a re-calibrating and rebuilding of existing spaces of cooking and domesticity, spaces of patriarchal domination and the gendered and second-ary roles relegated to translators and editors. To that end, recipe collections and the translations that allow them to circulate become geographic stories that contain within them new forms of citizenship and belonging, and remappings of borders and national identities.

Our four texts are ideal examples for promoting the feminist food translation frame-work. They deploy resistance in several different ways. First, they foreground food and rituals around food as a feminist practice. Second, they build an archive to counter material, historical and cultural loss and devastation through gastrophilic forms of memory making. Third, they forge communities within the migrants and refugees as well as with a transnational readership. Fourth, their stories, woven into the recipes, con-vert food narratives into a form of witness and testimony against rights violations.

Resistant recipes

Published in 2010 by an anarchist collective called Autonomedia (www.autonomedia. org/), *Dining in Refugee Camps: The Art of Sahrawi Cooking/Cenando en los Campa-mentos de Refugiados: Un Libro de Cocina Saharaui* (2010) is a bilingual work curated, translated and edited by Robin Kahn. The book was gifted to this chapter's co-author Bhakti Shringarpure by Fatima Mehdi, secretary general of the National Union of Sah-rawi Women during an interview with Mehdi in hopes that the book would offer insights into the cause for Western Sahara's independence, and to emphasise the role that women play in fighting for rights and standing up against the Moroccan occupation. Located in the Sahara Desert and squeezed between Morocco, Algeria and Mauritania, Western Sahara has had a long colonial historical and was a Spanish colony from 1884 until 1975. The United Nations (UN) demanded that Spain relinquish control of Western Sahara but, instead of making room for self-determination and autonomous rule, Spain decided on joint administrative control with Morocco. Spanish still remains one of the more widely spoken languages in the region and Kahn's book curates Spanish and Eng-lish, side by side, in the recipe collection. Kahn, who describes herself as a 'feminist artist' (Kahn 2010: 5), stayed in a Saharawi refugee camp for a month, and participated in the life of a group of women. Using a collage technique that seems to symbolise frag-ments of all the women's stories coming together, the book offers a short colloquial his-tory of Western Sahara's struggles along with introductions to women's role in government and civil life. 'Sahrawi women hold property rights and control over house-hold and livestock. They are in charge of the family, the cooking, the provisions and the cleaning,' Kahn explains. 'With the help of their friends and children, they carry all sup-plies from the centre to their home as it is the man's role to supply the money for extra necessities' (Kahn 2010: 12). The recipes follow soon after, along with an explanation of the ways in which food has been determined by food rations that come from places like Mauritania, Spain, Italy, the UN and Algeria. There are also rations for water and electricity. Micro-histories populate the book through narratives about a few select women who provide the reader with an intimate lens into the ingredients, implements and rituals that are part and parcel of the cooking. Kahn assembles the book bilingually with English on one side and Spanish on the other, even though the images for the translated texts are always different. Though not much insight has been provided into the process of assembling the book, it immediately establishes itself as a collaborative work that has involved numerous translations from the original Arabic and Spanish, and then into English.

The community of women and the communality around food are openly framed as a mechanism of resistance to the occupation and the ways in which it has erased Saharawi history. Kahn writes:

> Sharing is a peaceful means to communicate a common history of tragedy and struggle. There is little infighting because everyone endures the same hardship and *one* unified dream to regain their right to self-determination and to live once more in their own unoccupied land.
>
> *(Kahn 2010: 16)*

The act of sharing a meal together is presented as an overarching metaphor for unity and a shared political agenda. Memory making during the meal through the enunciation of common histories of tragedy is imbricated with the desire and demand for the right to land and self-determination. Additionally, the feminist underpinnings of this book rise to the surface again and again as Kahn works to narrate the lives of the women who seem to become symbols of the particularity of the struggle for self-determination as it plays out within the sphere of intimacy and family, and thus transforms itself into a women's struggle. A textured background for each image seems to suggest tapestries and quilts, artefacts that have a long history of framing women's worlds and the intimacy that characterises them. The reader is invited into that intimate space through the welcoming visual of the tapestry and we have a sense of having become part of the intimate space of a diary, a handmade, homey collection of recipes. It is to Kahn's credit that she conceives of this book through the lens of the ordinary and the intimate, assembling the work in a way that mimics the frugality of life in these camps and the inherent dignity that seems imbued in the sparsely available resources.

Gaza Kitchen, in a way, furthers the type of work that Kahn puts into motion. Multidisciplinary at the core, cuisine from Gaza forms only 'one component in a book that maintains an exquisite choreography between ethnographic document, feminist storytelling, land and agricultural politics, developmental economics and Gaza's troubled history' (Shringarpure 2013). *Gaza Kitchen* exemplifies the feminist food translation framework. In an interview with Shringarpure, co-author Maggie Schmidt, in fact, claims that she

> quickly got totally hooked on food as a point of entry, a way of talking about all kinds of other things—history, politics, economy, social change, aesthetics … Writing from a food perspective got me thinking about different methodologies, too—ways of telling. I started doing what I called 'kitchen anthropology.'
>
> *(Shringarpure 2013)*

Gaza Kitchen brings a food perspective to the long duration of the Israeli–Palestinian conflict and sheds light on staggering, endlessly debilitating quality of daily struggles whether in the form of electricity cuts, water shortages, unappetising food aid, the restrictions on movements and the drawing and redrawing of borders that make it impossible for Palestinians in Gaza to fish or grow food. For each recipe, prepared slightly differently in various households, we are given a context that goes from the particular household to the genesis and transformations of the ingredients. Each context has a direct connection with a political rupture that may have accompanied it. Within this landscape, 'the girls continue to cavort on the rooftop, and the rabbits need to be fed, and somehow the sheer vitality of the household pushes onward' (El-Haddad and Schmitt 2013: 20).

The book also contests the cliché that food is the domain of women. Here, the line between the public, political actors in the struggle for Palestinian liberation and those relegated to the traditional, intimate space of domesticity is blurred. This happens due to El-Haddad and Schmidt's exploration of foodways, the study of socio-political and economic forces that drive food production, whether it is the journey from the farm to factory to table or micro-economies that may circumvent restrictions. Gaza is a rich site for understanding the intricate foodways that conflict and occupation generates, and the ways in which it transforms the original inhabitants of the land into refugees without resources and without rights. The book takes us inside Palestinian homes but it also delves deep into small factories where dishes like *tahina* are produced with sesame seeds arriving from India, Somalia or Sudan (El-Haddad and Schmitt 2013: 31) or where Jamal keeps the art of the *qidra* oven alive (El-Haddad and Schmitt 2013: 84) or offers a portrait of farmer Mohammed Ahmed Al-Soltan, who lost all his crops to Israeli bulldozers but keeps trying to till the land (El-Haddad and Schmitt 2013: 76). 'Indeed, like small manufacturers all over Gaza, the Al Manar factory is anxiously watching the borders,' El-Haddad and Schmidt recount.

> Israel is currently allowing manufactured goods (like *tahina*) to enter the Strip, where they compete with local products, and at the same time limiting the entry of raw materials (like sesame seeds). This means higher operating costs and small market manufacturers, and could mean the end of the few industries still operating in Gaza.
>
> *(El-Haddad and Schmitt 2013: 31)*

A staple sauce such as *tahina* is connected to the restrictions put in place by the conflict. Significantly, men are shown here engaged in not just producing and supplying produce but also preparing the Palestinian food staples. These juxtapositions shatter the representation of food spaces as women's spaces, with men, women, youth and children shown as participants in the hyper-connected and complex units of food production and food consumption. Just as men are active in the space of food, women are active in the space of politics, thus allowing for a reclamation of a feminist food politics that is rigorous in the voice, empowerment and agency that Palestinian women exercise.

Gaza Kitchen and *Dining in Refugee Camps* produce complex political texts that engage a range of fields and disciplines while pioneering a feminist methodology that translates the stories of the members of these refugee communities, and adapts them from oral narration to written texts. A similar translation and adaptation process is deployed by *Cum-panis: Storie di fuga, identità e memorie, in quattro ricette* (roughly translated as 'Breaking bread: Stories of escape, identity and memory through four recipes'), produced by Associazione Culturale Multietnica 'La Kasbah onlus' and *Cooking a Home: A Collection of the Recipes and Stories of Syrian Refugees* by Pilar Puig Cortada. These two works are more invested in a feminist approach to memory work, a concept that aims to facilitate a 'process of exploring the past, which has multiple meanings, references and methods of communication' (Fraser and Michell 2015: 322). Memory work indeed privileges memories in order to produce histories but the process is neither scientific nor predictable. 'Time and place affect the formation, recall and representation of memories. Autobiographical memories are often episodic, reflecting particular characters, times, places and events. Specific images, sounds, smells and/or feelings are often referenced when people recount memories' (Fraser and Michell 2015: 323). A feminist iteration of memory work engages new imaginative frameworks to be taken into consideration and in fact, it is 'based on the premise that remembered narratives provide a window into, or a bridge between, the personal and political' (Fraser and Michell 2015: 323). Such memories offer a glimpse into women's lives, often obfuscated by overly dominant patriarchal figures. Often these involve unofficial, oral accounts by women with little or no access to education or institutional support of any kind.

The translation and adaptation process used by *Cum-panis* is supported by an Italian non-profit initiative that promotes integration and dialogue in a country politically divided on the rights of refugees and migrants arrived from the Mediterranean Sea. The book brings together four accounts accompanied by recipes by four women from Somalia, Eritrea, Palestine and Syria. As the title suggests, 'cum panis,' the idea of breaking bread together, is a gesture of sharing in order to cut through the tensions generated by the shattering of familiar life, the efforts at rebuilding and the desire to anchor oneself in the certainty of the past. It is also an invitation to sit at the table of memories and partake in the joy of sharing and storytelling. The book opens with a translation of the poem '*La Cucina* [The Kitchen]' by Syrian writer Maram al-Masri, where the space of cooking is presented as

> a narrow space
> for scattered souls
> vast
> for laughs and memories
> secrets told in confidence/to the saucepans.
>   (*Cum-panis* 2014: 5)

Women thus spend their life recreating the cries and joys of families that used to be together that are now re-rendered, but only as fragments, in the recipes of the book. Dissonances, whether in time or in space, become an important aesthetic element in several of these books, perhaps above all *Cum-panis*. They appear as moments of non-recognition for those recounting the recipes and where the women's cooking turns into distant and alienated encounters due to the new realities that have been thrust upon them. For the Palestinians in *Gaza Kitchen*, a dissonance of time is always recorded in food, 'for many elders, food—real food—is always in the past tense' (El-Haddad and Schmitt 2013: 58). Food becomes a site where time is experienced as non-linear and disorienting.

The stories in *Cum-panis* become an example of memory work, further articulating those moments of dissonance. Hamdi from Somalia teaches the reader how to make *sambus*, a fried triangle pastry stuffed with ground meat, onion, curry and cumin. The recalling of the recipe merges with the story of her migrant journey, the past she left behind and the communal meals that she misses so much. She recounts:

I miss my mother very much. I hear her voice while I make *sambus* for my family, I see her joking and immediately I become very sad and revisit everything I went through. Often, I cook and eat by myself and cry. In Somalia, it is inconceivable that a person eats by herself. We always eat together three times a day for breakfast, lunch, and dinner, and we also talk a lot, we tell each other about our day and sometimes we argue. I call my mother every day. Usually she laughs, blesses me and tells me not to be worried. But then there are days when she cannot hold her tears because she is afraid she will never see me again. I reassure her and tell her that she will see her grandchildren soon. I make sure to sound cheerful, but as soon as I hang up …

(Shringarpure et al. 2018: 82)

The excerpt above reveals the ways in which the making of *sambus* merges with the concatenation of memories that simultaneously disrupt, unify and fragment. Additionally, the format of weaving recipes with a testimonial narrative ensures in *Cum-panis* that women who have been excluded from official accounts of these historically significant events are given an opportunity to tell their story. The collaborative process of translation here is crucial as these women narrate their experiences and stories in their native languages (Somali, Tigrinya and Arabic in this instance). These are transcribed, rendered into Italian for a primarily European readership. Excerpts have now been translated into English for an American audience in the Warscapes 2018 publication *Mediterranean*. The four accounts assembled in one book allow for a cohesive understanding of a specifically women's migration experience. In this text, translation becomes a resistant act of activism because it forces the Euro-American readership into a dialogue with their governments' attitudes and policies towards migration. The feminist food translation paradigm here manages to activate a radical politics of food as well. Readers are reminded that the consumption and enjoyment of foreign foods are not neutral acts and that there is a story and a struggle that must be taken into consideration, one that is punctuated by suffering, violations, humiliations and deprivation.

Cortada compiles her collection of recipes by collaborating with Syrian refugees seeking asylum in Jordan. Each chapter is a portrait of an individual, all of whom have been rendered refugees because of the war in Syria. Cortada starts by explaining how and where she met them, translates their stories and moulds them into a linear narrative charting their lives from before and after the war. The preparation of the food and the recording of recipes are interwoven through the portrait and short biography of the subject. Here, once again, unofficial accounts of memory are privileged. 'My family, whose homes were destroyed under shelling, lost most of the family photos, including the ancient ones in black and white' (Cortada 2015: ix), Afra Jalabi writes in the foreword to the book: 'But the recipes survive. They sneak through borders and are smuggled in the despairing hearts of the migrating ones' (Cortada 2015: x). The act of sneaking through borders highlights the unofficial, oral and memorised nature of these recipes and ways in which they sustain even though the official history preserved in photographs has been lost forever. In her introduction, Cortada offers an intimate glance into the process of compiling these recipes and the relationships she was able to build along the way:

Some recipes I learned from people who invited me into their homes, into their kitchens, and took the time to teach me how to make their chosen dish. Others were scribbled down in the notebook I took with me everywhere, in Arabic, in Spanish, in English … hurriedly annotated in the waiting room of a clinic set up for refugees, or while bidding goodbye at the end of an interview. In these cases, though I have done my best to provide complete and accurate recipes, certain steps of ingredients may have been lost.

(Cortada 2015: xvii)

Cortada's admission that little aspects of the recipes might even have been lost in translation is revealing. The recipes offer a point of entry for reconnecting with the past and for an evocation of memory as the now displaced Syrians linger over their cooking and recount their experiences. It is Cortada insisting that these men and women be given a space to speak, to mourn, to linger and to archive their personal and national heritages. At its core, this work intervenes at the level of collective and individual memory employing translation, transcription and adaptation to create an ethos of national and communal belonging.

In attempting to prove a historical overview of the genre of cookbooks, Black writes that, while literary representations of food and consumption have received much attention, cookbooks, much like personal diaries, have been elided because of their reputation as a feminised genre and activity (2010: 3–4). Domesticity and cooking become associated with maternal practices, as 'practices performed by and upon the female body' are 'pressured to uphold traditional notions of cultural integrity' (Black 2010: 4). Black underlines the binding effect that domestic cooking and consequently cookbooks often cover as narratives that can formulate identities and tie entire communities together. Borrowing from Benedict Anderson's theories of nation and nationalism, Black classifies cookbooks as 'imagined communities' that 'mediate between oral and written traditions, often in structure and voice seeking to recreate communities of cooks who share experiences and expertise' (Black 2010: 3). They are also often endowed with the inspirational role to recruit a new generation who can assure continuity in the life of traditional practices. Black underlines that 'cookbooks often work to conceal their own modernity' (2010: 4) in an effort to evoke a universal, timeless and unchanging tradition around food and, by extension, of culture. Black's ideas foreground the connection between gastrophilic texts and cultural-national identity formation. Cookbooks and recipe collections, spurred by nostalgia, can generate a complex negotiation between issues arising from migrant national identity such as multiculturalism, cosmopolitanism, questions of assimilation and diaspora. While readers may find an inviting performance toward cosmopolitanism and multiculturalism in cookbooks, our texts rarely intend to incite 'culinary experimentations' or 'imagined' social bonds (Black 2010: 5). Rather, they seek to authorise recipes rooted in stories of dispossession. What we end up partaking in, in the end, is not conviviality but dissonance, not nostalgia but resistance.

However, for these concerns and agendas to rise to the surface, it becomes imperative to put a feminist food translation framework into motion. The four texts we explored engage such a framework in meaningful, challenging and ethically productive ways. All of the works inscribe food as a feminist practice that pushes for women's work in the domestic and public spheres to be acknowledged as indispensable, rigorous and deeply political. Additionally, memory work is a motivating force in each of these texts. The ways in which translators listen, retell, narrate, adapt and translate the stories ensure that these unofficial, marginalised, feminised and racialised discourses can be made visible and can be counted as historical archive. Finally, the process of recounting and translation allows for the creation of communities, shattering the isolation and alienation that plague migrant lives; not only do the subjects of the books come in contact with the translators, they also have the opportunity to meet their fellow migrants and forge relationships grounded in common experiences.

Conclusion: beyond 'suppliers of stories'

As we promote and explore the possibilities offered by a feminist food translation framework when applied to recipe collections and cookbooks, it is also important to engage the possible pitfalls that tend to accompany such projects. In a cross-disciplinary roundtable initiated by Richa Nagar, the politics of women's encounters through translations are examined and challenged (Castro and Ergun 2017: 111–135). Highlighting translation as a fundamentally feminist epistemological process charged with the capacity to order and reorder feminist knowledges, the participants confirm that translation is 'essential to feminist activism' (Castro and Ergun 2017: 112). Their argument extends Judith Butler's idea as expressed in Castro and Ergun's symposium, that there cannot be global solidarity without translation (Castro and Ergun 2017:113). Nagar points out that ethical translation 'across languages of difference' should be at the centre of the work; she asks: 'how do vernaculars (literal and metaphoric) of expert knowledge shape our uneven landscapes of modernity, violence, empowerment and dispossessions?' (Castro and Ergun 2017: 118)

Translation is never neutral; it is always attended by the capacity to 'reproduce colonial or imperial logics' (Castro and Ergun 2017: 118). As we looked closely at the translated gastrophilic texts selected for this chapter, we kept an eye out for this particular danger. We wanted to make sure that the stories and lives represented appeared to be more than 'raw materials' (Nagar 2018: 119). Nagar expands on this question in her article 'Hungry Translations: The World Through Radical Vulnerability' (Nagar 2018), where she confesses her concern about those invisible and inaudible ideas and feelings that cannot be captured on a regular print page. Here, she is specifically referring to the translation of real bodies into academic research papers and the ways in which linguistic transference can silence and further obliterate a subject.

Against these problematic translational processes, she proposes 'radical vulnerability,' a practice whereby 'the individual ego must surrender to a politics of co-travelling and co-authorship [...] a tool to repositioning the subject in the world and in history' (Nagar 2018: 19). Through her work with the Sangtin Kisaan Mazdoor Sanghathan (SKMS, roughly translated from Hindi as 'Sangtin's Agricultural Labourers' Association') movement, comprised of 8,000 farmers and labourers in Sitapur District of Uttar Pradesh and a performance project with a group of twenty amateur and professional actors in Mumbai interrogating caste, patriarchy and issues such as hunger and death, Nagar illustrates how global representations of hunger occupy a central role in defining and redefining peasants and farmers in a global context. Nagar notes that poverty experts 'have no trouble recognizing that those who live with hunger of underfed bellies are also hungry for justice' (2018: 10). She adds that 'the same experts participate in epistemic nihilation of the "poor" by refusing to appreciate their hunger for justice as a ... governed by a social imaginary that is often unthinkable or unintelligible through dominant frameworks' (2018: 10).

There is no doubt that food discourses immediately allow for an entry on to the agendas around global hunger, food shortage and development. For example, Colombian anthropologist Arturo Escobar's extensive work on the massive post-war development campaign in the so-called Third World offers a detailed explanation on how development created 'perceptual fields' (Escobar 1994: 41) through linguistic classifications such as abnormalities, the illiterate, the underdeveloped, the malnourished, small farmers and landless peasants. These categories were part of a larger programme to 'treat and reform' (Escobar 1994: 41). Escobar points out that discourses of development have created a 'perceptual field structured by grids of observation' (1994: 42) as spreadsheets, algorithms and economic models to compress and simplify complicated and affective realities. Similarly, in his book on postcolonial translation studies, Lefevere identifies two distinct grids in translation which he calls the conceptual and the textual grid, both of which exercise a level of ideological pressure on the decisions made by the translator (Lefevere 1999). Conceptual grids might redefine what is acceptable and not acceptable in a given society, while textual grids might be related to a level of faithfulness and reproduction of a given genre. Lefevere concludes that the interplay of these two grids 'may well determine how reality is constructed for the reader, not just of the translation, but also of the original' (1999: 77). The damage of such methodologies is the construction of a type of translation that is ontologically loaded. From their original domain in the expert reports and papers, this language inevitably has the potential to be filtered into cultural representations and our mainstream perception of the now well-crafted Third World. By introducing the concept of 'radical vulnerability,' Nagar wants to resist the perceptual field/grid system by advocating for a methodology and a language 'without guarantees.' Following this vision, translation becomes less a system of transference or colonisation (sameness), but one that is destabilising and that destabilises 'authorising practices' (Nagar 2018: 4).

Returning to food, stories of food and the translations of stories of food, one can recognise that a single perceptual field or grid may reproduce multiple versions in cultural translations and that ethnic food can become a mirror of development's grids. Moving forward, we want to conclude with a set of provocations for the translator-activist engaged in the work of transcribing, adapting and translating food narratives: how does one make sure that food as a cultural paradigm does not enter into the dichotomies of victim and agent, saviour and saved and masculine and feminine? How can a cookbook question and destabilise the rhetoric of expert-dom and authority? How do these works resist compression and commodification? Cookbooks have the potential to become decorative coffee-table objects and aesthetic trophies of cosmopolitan tastes. At the same time, they can also be resistant mediums that break free from expert-oriented representations and allow the encounters of the sensorial and the practical to be historically and politically situated. We insist on a feminist food translation studies paradigm becoming an analytical gauge that guides future projects that aim to translate the stories of women and food, and inscribing these women and their domestic labour within overarching discourses of language, belonging, identity and nation. To echo Nagar's brilliant metaphor, recipes are simply creative variations of our hunger for justice (2018: 9).

Related topics

Feminism in Translation; Citation and Recitation; Written on the Heart, in Broken English

Further reading

de Lima Costa, Claudia, and Sonia Alvarez (2014) 'Dislocating the Sign: Toward a Translocal Feminist Politics of Translation,' *Signs* 39 (3): 557–563.

This article puts forward a range of important questions for unpacking the apparatus of feminist theories in translation: citations, textuality, mediums. It is an invitation towards a decolonisation of knowledge not only through analysis of mistranslated theories, but also through a study of the cultural responses and adjustments such translated feminist theories present with academic and non-academic text.

References

Abdeni Massad, Barbara (2015) *Soup for Syria: Recipes to Celebrate our Shared Humanity*. Northampton: Interlink Pub Group.

Associazione culturale 'La Kasbah onlus' (2014) *Cum-panis: Storie di fuga, identità e memorie, in quattro ricette*. Edizioni Erranti.

Avakian, Voski Arlene, and Haber Barbara (eds.) (2005) *From Betty Crocker to Feminist Food Studies: Critical Perspectives on Women and Food*. Boston: University of Massachusetts Press.

Black, Shameem (2010) 'Recipes for Cosmopolitanism: Cooking across Borders in the South Asian Diaspora,' *Frontiers: A Journal of Women Studies* 31 (1): 1–30.

Boy, Clerkenwell, and Serena Gruen (2017) *Cook for Syria Recipe Book*. London: Suitcase Media International.

Castro, Olga, and Emek Ergun (eds.) (2017) *Feminist Translation Studies Local and Transnational Perspectives*. New York: Routledge.

Cortada, Puig Pilar (2015) *Cooking a Home: A Collection of the Recipes and Stories of Syrian Refugees*. Bloomington, IN: AuthorHouse.

Dearden, Lizzie (2017) 'British Man among Aid Volunteers Arrested for Giving Food to Refugees Stranded in Italy,' in *Independent* [online] 24 March. Available at: www.independent.co.uk/news/world/europe/british-man-refugee-volunteer-food-arrest-ventimiglia-italy-gerard-bonnet-roya-citoyenne-group-a7648661.html [accessed 27 September 2019].

Dinham, Paddy (2017) 'Food Queue with Echoes of Europe's Dark Past: Freezing Migrants Wait for Aid in Belgrade Today in Pictures Chillingly Similar to Those from the Second World War,' in *Mailonline* [online]. Available at: www.dailymail.co.uk/news/article-4107102/Belgrade-migrants-wait-food-pictures-similar-Second-World-War.html [accessed 27 September 2019].

Displaced Dinners [online] Available at: https://komeeda.com/series/3 [accessed 15 October 2019].

El-Haddad, Laila, and Maggie Schmitt (2013) *The Gaza Kitchen, A Palestinian Culinary Journey*. Charlottesville: Just World Press.

Escobar, Arturo (1994) *Encountering Development: The Making and Unmaking of the Third World*. Princeton: Princeton University Press.

Fraser, Heather, and Dee Michell (2015) 'Feminist Memory Work in Action: Method and Practicalities,' *Qualitative Social Work* 14 (3): 321–337.

Gentleman, Amelia (2017) 'Calais Mayor Bans Distribution of Food to Migrants,' in *The Guardian* [online]. Available at: www.theguardian.com/world/2017/mar/02/calais-mayor-bans-distribution-of-food-to-migrants [accessed 27 September 2019].

Giordano, Cristiana (2014) *Migrants in Translation*. Oakland: University of California Press.

Godayol, Pilar (2013) 'Gender and Translation.' in *The Routledge Handbook of Translation Studies*. Eds. Carmen Millán, and Francesca Bartrina. London and New York: Routledge. 173–185.

Jalabi, Afra (2015) 'Fast Forward to a Peaceful Delicious Syria,' in *Cooking a Home: A Collection of the Recipes and Stories of Syrian Refugees*. Ed. Pilar Puig Cortada. Bloomington, IN: Author House. ix–xii.

Kahn, Robin (2010) *Dining in Refugee Camps: The Art of Sahrawi Cooking*. Autonomedia.

Lefevere, André (1999) 'Composing the Other. Post-Colonial Translation Theory and Practice,' in *Postcolonial Translation: Theory and Practice*. Eds. Susan Bassnett, and Harish Travedi. London: Routledge. 75–95.

Mannur, Anita (2007) 'Culinary Nostalgia: Authenticity, Nationalism, and Diaspora,' *MELUS* 32 (4): 11–31.

McKittrick, Katherine (2006) *Demonic Grounds: Black Women and the Cartographies of Struggle*. Minneapolis: University of Minnesota Press.

Nagar, Richa (2018) 'Hungry Translations: The World through Radical Vulnerability,' *Antipode: A Journal of Radical Geography* 51 (1): 1–22.

Nagar, Richa, and Roozbeh Shirazi (2019) 'Radical Vulnerability,' in *The Antipode. Keywords in Radical Geography: Antipode at 50*. Eds. Tariq Jazeel, Andy Kent, Katherine McKittrick, Nik Theodore, Sharad Chari, Paul Chatterton, Vinay Gidwani, Nik Heynen, Wendy Larner, Jamie Peck, Jenny Pickerill, Marion Werner, and Melissa W. Wright. Hoboken, NJ: Wiley-Blackwell. 236–242.

Papa, E., and F. Mollo (2014) *Cum Panis, Storie di Fuga, Identita e memorie in Quattro Storie*. Edizioni Erranti.

Refugees Welcome [online] Available at: http://refugeeswelcometodinner.com/faq/ [accessed 27 September 2019].

Roy, Parama (2002) Reading Communities and Culinary Communities: The Gastropoetics of South Asian Diaspora *Positions: East Asia Cultures Critique* 10 (2): 471–502.

Shohat, Ella, and Robert Stam (1994) *Unthinking Eurocentrism: Multiculturalism and the Media*. New York: Routledge.

Shringarpure, Bhakti (2013) 'Kitchen Anthropology in Gaza,' in *Warscapes* [online] 1 June. Available at: www.warscapes.com/retrospectives/food/kitchen-anthropology-gaza [accessed 27 September 2019].

Shringarpure, Bhakti, Michael Bronner, Veruska Cantelli, Michael Busch, Jessica Rohan, Melissa Smyth, Jason Huettner, Gareth Davies, and Noam Scheindlin (eds.) (2018) *Mediterranean*. Warscapes magazine and UpSet Press.

Simon, Sherry (1996) *Gender in Translation: Cultural Identity and the Politics of Transmission*. London and New York: Routledge.

Talpade Mohanty, Chandra (2003) *Feminism without Borders: Decolonizing Theory, Practicing Solidarity*. Durham: Duke University Press Books.

The Syria Supper Club [online] Available at: www.theunitedtastesofamerica.org/ [accessed 27 September 2019].

Vanilli, Lily, Boy Clerkenwell, and Serena Gruen (2018) *Bake for Syria Recipe Book*. Guildford: Suitcase Media International.

Walker, Peter (2015) 'Refugees Forced to Scramble for Food by Police in Hungary,' in *The Guardian* [online]. Available at: www.theguardian.com/world/2015/sep/11/refugees-roszke-hungary-police-food-camp [accessed 27 September 2019].

Part VIII
Translation and revolution

27

Late-Qing translation (1840–1911) and the political activism of Chinese evolutionism

Kuan-yen Liu

This chapter analyses interconnections between the task of translation and the agendas of reform and revolution in late-Qing (1840–1911) Chinese political and intellectual culture. I begin by offering in the first section an overview of how translation was connected with enlightenment projects and political agendas in each stage (1840–1860, 1860–1894, and 1894–1911) of late-Qing China. I then examine translation in post-1894 China in the second section with an emphasis on the role of translation in the shaping of intellectual culture, the appropriation of translation for political actions, and the identity and self-assumed duty of the translator. The third section uses the transformative translation of evolutionism in post-1894 China as a case study to reveal how political mobilisation in nationalist, reformist, and revolutionist agendas served as a filter through which Western ideas were selected and re-created. I conclude by re-evaluating the strong implication of political activism in post-1894 translation and Chinese evolutionism in terms of Talal Asad's theory of 'cultural translation' (1986), Lydia H. Liu's theory concerning the 'agency' of the host language (1995), and Godfrey Lienhardt's theory pertaining to the 'further potentiality' of the translator's language and thought (1954) in the fourth section. By linking translation history, textual studies, intellectual history, and political history, this chapter aims to contextualise and theorise the agency of the Chinese language to transform Western thought in the meaning-making process of translation. At the same time, I develop a framework for Chinese conceptions of political activism that provides crucial historical context for related chapters in this volume (see Chapter 28).

The history of translation in Chinese history can be divided into three phases: (1) the translation of Sanskrit texts of Buddhism from the second century to the eleventh century (Tso 1990); (2) the translation of Latin texts of European canons from the seventeenth century to the eighteenth century (Tsien 2009: 2–6; Zou 2011); and (3) the translation of European and North American texts from the mid nineteenth century to the present. The second phase was terminated owing to the ban on Catholicism and the expulsion of Jesuit missionaries from China. It was after the Opium War between Britain and China in 1840 that the Chinese re-started to accept what they deemed as '*Xixue* [西學 Western Learning].'

The beginning and early developments of the third phase of translation correspond to the ideals of political reforms triggered by a series of foreign intrusions from 1840 to 1911. When China, which was once the so-called Celestial Dynasty, was coerced to open its previously closed gate to Europeans and dragged into the modern and global world by imperial empires, the translation of European texts and ideas played an increasingly important role in the intertwined projects of enlightenment and saving the country. This chapter aims to demonstrate the close connection between political purposes and translation tasks in the late-Qing period (1840–1911) and focuses particularly on how the Chinese translation in the wake of the First Sino-Japanese War (1894) was informed by a strong sense of political mobilisation.

In existing research, scholars have investigated the interplay between politics and translation in late-Qing China from the perspective of intellectual history (Schwartz 1964; Pusey 1983), the history of books and publication (Tsien 2009; Pan 2014), the history of institution and education (Ji and Chen 2007b; Zhang 2017), and textual and theoretical analysis (Liu 1995; Cheung 2010). Cheung's chapter, entitled 'Rethinking Activism: The Power and Dynamics of Translation in China during the Late Qing Period (1840–1911)' (2010), is most relevant to the discussion of activism in my chapter.

Cheung gives an overview of the principal translations in each stage of the late-Qing period by introducing major historical figures who translated or appropriated European ideas, like Lin Zexu, Wei Yuan, Hong Xiuquan, Liang Qichao, Yan Fu, and Lin Shu (2010: 242–252). Besides, borrowing the theoretical model in Aberle's (1991) evaluation of the locus and extent of change which social movements aim at, Cheung evaluates the activist projects of late-Qing translation in terms of the following categories: 'transformative activism' (a total change of supra-individual systems), 'reformative activism' (partial change of supra-individual systems), 'redemptive activism' (total change of individuals), and 'alterative activism' (partial change of individuals) (2010: 240–241). Cheung's evaluation demonstrates a transition from reformative and alterative activism to transformative and redemptive activism in the purpose of translation from 1840 to 1911 (2010: 242–252).

While Cheung's approach to the study of the type and scope of activist projects in late-Qing translation is theoretical, my chapter integrates the approaches of textual and contextual studies and further investigates how the intertwined projects of enlightenment and salvaging the country filtered how European texts and ideas were selected, translated, and transformed from 1840 to 1911. Particular attention will be paid to the purpose, style, and meaning-making process of translation in relation to the intellectual and political history of late-Qing China. In addition, I examine the nuanced or apparent difference between the significance of a transplanted idea in the late-Qing Chinese language and context and its significance in the original text and context with an eye to investigating how political activism contributed to the translation, reinterpretation, and transformation of a foreign idea.

An examination of political activism is important to the study of late-Qing translation. From 1840 to 1911, the significance of transplanted ideas and thoughts was constructed not just through textual translation but also through political agendas and actions. For instance, as I shall further discuss in the third section, Darwin's ideas of evolution and natural selection were widely accepted and appropriated in nationalist discourse when there was still not a translation of *The Origin of Species* (1988 [1859]) in the 1890s. Moreover, Ma Junwu 馬君武 (1881–1940), an engineering scholar who obtained a PhD in Germany, translated some chapters of Darwin's *The Origin of Species* in 1903, 1904, and 1906 (1957 [1919]: 1–2), but his work did not attain much attention from the public while Darwinian ideas were quite popular at that time. In the late-Qing Chinese language, the literal translation of Darwin's chapters did not contribute to the meaning making of Darwinian ideas as much as Yan Fu's reinterpretative appropriation of the ideas of natural selection and evolution.

The above-mentioned importance of political agenda and patriotic mobilisation to the meaning-making process of translation also holds true for the acceptance of many other European ideas in the late-Qing period, especially in the post-1894 era. Late-Qing translation of foreign ideas should be studied in a wider context of political and intellectual history, and the meaning of 'translation' should be defined in a broad sense rather than limited to literal and textual translation. Thus, seminal political writings, important newspaper articles, as well as other documents that contributed to Chinese interpretation of European ideas, should not be neglected in the study of the meaning-making process of late-Qing translation.

The picture of late-Qing Chinese translation is complicated in that British and American institutions in China also engaged in the Chinese translation of European texts. It is beyond the scope of this chapter to include Christian missionaries' religious, educational, and political motivations in their tasks of translation in China. My study of the interconnection between the task of translation and the agendas of reform and revolution in the context of late-Qing Chinese political and intellectual culture will deal mainly with translation by Chinese intellectuals or Chinese institutes.

As noted above, late-Qing Chinese intellectuals situated the foreign sources that they received and translated within a canon of *Xixue* [西學 Western learning].' In their conceptualisation and categorisation of knowledge, all works from Europe, Britain, and America, like the Greek text of Euclid's *Elements* (c. 300 BCE), the British text of Darwin's *The Origin of Species*, and the American text of Wheaton's *Elements of International Law* (1836), belonged to 'Western learning.' Even Japanese translation and reinterpretation of European works belonged to 'Western learning.' The '*xi*' in the term '*Xixue* [Western learning],' which late-Qing intellectuals used, meant 'Western.' From their perspective and worldview, all of the above-mentioned thoughts and works came from the 'Western' world. They paid attention to the political use of 'Western' thoughts without differentiating between the 'Western' sources written in different languages, areas, and periods. For instance, when Sun Yat-sen used the ideas of 'rights' and 'democracy' in political proclamation, he did not try to specify different versions and meanings of these ideas in various European, British, and American sources (1905, 1906, 1954 [1927]).

Late-Qing translation in three phases

The late-Qing period can be subdivided into the years 1840–1860, 1860–1894, and 1894–1911. Both translation and political change were largely triggered by the intrusions of imperial powers, that is, the Opium War between China and Britain in 1840–1842, the Second Opium War between China and the military alliance of Britain and France in 1856–1860, and the First Sino-Japanese War in 1894–1895. As part of the project of political reformation, the translations of various European, British, and American works were intended to enlighten the Chinese about the global world, especially about imperial countries' colonial, technological, industrial, scientific, and economic powers as well as their socio-political systems and thoughts. The choice of European texts and the style of translation vary across the three main phases of the late-Qing period and reflect the changes in political and intellectual culture.

1840–1860: knowing the global world for military defence

Before the Opium War in 1840, Chinese intellectuals were quite ignorant of the European world. Under such circumstances, when viceroy of two Guang provinces Lin Zexu (林則徐) (1785–1850) arrived in Guangzhou in 1839 to deal with British merchants and suppress the opium trade, he employed people to collect information about the global world and translate Hugh Murray's (1779–1846) *An Encyclopaedia of Geography* (1834). This effort resulted in *Gazetteer of Four Continents* (*Sizhou zhi* 四州志). Lin Zexu later gave this document to Wei Yuan (魏源) (1794–1856), who added new materials and reorganised it into *Illustrated Treatise on the Maritime Kingdoms* (*Haiguo tuzhi* 海國圖志). Neither *Gazetteer of Four Continents* nor *Illustrated Treatise on the Maritime Kingdoms* was a 'translation' in a strict sense. Instead, on the basis of Murray's work as well as various sources, Lin Zexu and Wei Yuan excerpted, abridged, reorganised, and compiled the information they needed about other countries with an eye to gaining and distributing knowledge about the wider world and defending Chinese territories.

A closer look at Murray's work reveals the discrepancy between the original work in English and its adaptations in Chinese. Murray's *An Encyclopaedia of Geography* includes three parts. The first part concerns the history of the study of geography from the ancient period (including Hebrew and Greek geography) to the modern period. The second part considers geography as a discipline that relates to the status of earth in the solar system and the study of physical elements, animals, plants, and the human race. The third part treats the 'natural features … political constitution, the industry and wealth, the civil and social condition of its inhabitants' of each country with 'a local and topographical survey of its districts, cities, and towns' (Murray 1834: 1). The historical development of geographical study and the scientific knowledge of the earth in Murray's original work were not translated in its Chinese adaptations. With no particular interest in scientific knowledge of geography, Lin Zexu and Wei Yuan just wanted to introduce the basic and general knowledge about the world to their Chinese contemporaries, most of whom were quite ignorant of Europe, America, and Africa as well as some countries in Asia.

The intention of Lin Zexu and Wei Yuan to understand the global world differs from Murray's. In his preface, Murray argued that geographical study of climes and regions 'enlarges and enlightens the human mind' and 'gratif[ies] … a liberal curiosity' (1834: iii, iv). In the introduction, he pointed out that '[g]eography, [which] consists in the description and delineation of Earth, … enables the navigator, the merchant and the military commander, to carry on their respective operations' (1834: 1). By contrast, Lin Zexu and Wei Yuan compiled gazetteers not for curiosity about remote regions or academic interest in geographical sciences, but mainly for the strategic purpose of defending the Chinese domain against Western naval power. As Wei Yuan put it, 'There are two ways of attacking barbarians: One is to make the enemy of barbarians attack them, and the other is to learn the expertise of barbarians to control them' (Wei Yuan 1999 [1852]: 75). The 'barbarians' in this context referred to Europeans, and the 'expertise of barbarians' referred to modern technology and industry. Wei Yuan was eager to push the Chinese and the Qing Dynasty to confront European powers through diplomatic strategy and modern military technology in that his Chinese compatriots still sensed neither the backwardness of China in military and industrial technology nor the intensified interactions of countries around the global world.

Murray and nineteenth-century British people considered the global world from the standpoint of a colonial and global empire that founded colonies, formed political relations, and opened commercial intercourse with remote regions (1834: ii). By contrast, Lin Zexu and Wei Yuan tried to promulgate the knowledge of geography for the sake of the internal defence of the Chinese domain rather than an external exploration of the unknown world. In this regard, Lin Zexu and Wei Yuan transferred the geographical knowledge in Murray's geographical encyclopaedia from its original contexts of European science and British international politics into the late-Qing context of military defence of the Chinese coast against the invading powers coming from the ocean.

While the information in Lin Zexu's work was still closer to the original information in Murray's work, Wei Yuan added many more Chinese sources when he transformed Lin Zexu's translation into *Illustrated Treatise on the Maritime Kingdoms*. Both of them intended to collect and compile all information useful for military defence and diplomatic interactions. Although their works were far from line-by-line translations, Lin Zexu and Wei Yuan still captured and 'translated' both the intention to know more about remote regions as well as the connection between geographical knowledge and cross-continental international politics in Murray's work.

The circulation and influence of the above-mentioned two Chinese works were very limited at the time of their publication. The effort of Lin Zexu and Wei Yuan to awaken their Chinese compatriots concerning the rise of European powers was fruitless. It was not until the Second Opium War in 1856–1860 that the Qing government and Chinese intellectuals started to pay more attention to the importance of European knowledge and the needs of translation.

1860–1894: the study of European languages and knowledge in reformist agenda

In the 1860s, after the devastating Taiping Rebellion (1850–1864) and the intrusion of the military alliance of Britain and France into the capital Beijing, the Qing government needed to rebuild the order of society and politics. Certain officials called for a reform, which was called the Movement of Self-Strengthening 自強運動 (*Ziqiang yundong*), with an eye to strengthening the national power of China. The 'self-strengthening' project included the education of foreign languages, which was necessary to learn European knowledge and technology as well as diplomatic interactions in international relations.

In the Self-Strengthening Movement, Prince Gong (1833–1898) established an institute for the study of foreign language and knowledge in Beijing, and Li Hongzhang (1823–1901) founded another one in Shanghai and still another one in Guangzhou (Ji and Chen 2007b). This was a great step in the acceptance of European languages and knowledge. As Ji and Chen indicate, before 1860, in the Qing government, the 'Institute of Barbarians on Four Directions [*Siyi guan* 四夷館],' responsible for the reception of embassies from foreign countries or minority ethnic groups, just translated the languages of Asian peoples which had interaction with the Qing court (2007b: 17–18). As to European languages, there were the Institute for Russian and the Institute for Latin, but the linguistic proficiency of translators was quite limited (Ji and Chen 2007b: 20–32). The Second Opium War and the subsequent Treaty of Tianjin forced the Qing government to develop the education of foreign languages and train translators for diplomatic interactions.

The institute for foreign language and education which Prince Gong established in Beijing was called Tongwen Guan (同文館), the literal meaning of which was 'to make the language the same,' that is, translation. Tongwen Guan offered education in European language and knowledge and it also published Chinese translations of European works. Under the supervision of William Alexander Parsons Martin (1827–1916)—an American Presbyterian missionary with a Chinese name, Ding Weiliang (丁韙良)—Chinese teachers and students translated works on science and mathematics such as *Advanced Chemistry*, *Mathematical Physics*, *Physiology*, and *Elements of Astronomy* (Li and Li 2000: 160–163). Besides, the translators trained in Tongwen Guan translated European works for Chinese journals concerning technology (Li and Li 2000: 163). The translation of Tongwen Guan also included works on international law as well as the geography and history of foreign countries, like *International Law*, *History of Russia*, and *Outlines of World History* (Li and Li 2000: 161–162). The scope of translation reflects late-Qing officials' attempts to accept European knowledge and advanced technology and to cope with international affairs.

The task of education and translation in Tongwen Guan did not result in a wide acceptance of European languages and knowledge in China, but triggered a surge of severe criticism from conservative officials. There was a conflict between Western learning and Chinese learning (Zhang 2017: 248–278). Wo Ren 倭仁 (1804–1871), the teacher of Emperor Tongzhi, resorted to the orthodoxy of Chinese value and culture, contending that the acceptance of Western technology would result in 'the never-ending transformation of the Chinese into barbarians' (2008 [1867]: 2010). Besides, Wo Ren argued that 'the fundamental blueprint [of the country] depends on people's mind rather than on techniques' (2008 [1867]: 2009). Wo Ren's criticism of efforts to study European knowledge and technology struck a chord in the circle of Chinese intellectuals and officials (Zhang 2017: 264), and the education of European knowledge faced setbacks owing to a perceived conflict between European and Chinese cultures and values.

Another reason why the study of European knowledge and languages was not widely promoted from 1860 to 1894 is that, for the Qing court, the command of foreign languages meant a power in the communication between the Qing Dynasty and foreign countries. At the beginning, Tongwen Guan recruited students only from the Manchu people, an ethnic group that ruled China from 1644 to 1911, for the study of foreign languages (Zhang 2017: 130–131). This also happened in the Tongwen Guan in Guangzhou (Li 2016: 67). Even though the Han people, who constituted the majority population of China, were later allowed to study at Tongwen Guan, the student number was still limited. From the 1860s to the 1890s, around five hundred students graduated from the Beijing Tongwen Guan (Li 2016: 32). The number of graduates from the Tongwen Guan in Shanghai and the Tongwen Guan in Guangzhou could not be specified owing to the limitation of historical records, but we do know that the number of students enrolled in these two language institutes was as limited as that of the Tongwen Guan in Beijing (Li 2016: 53–54, 66–70). Instead of trying to promote the study of European languages and knowledge, the Qing court just wanted sufficient officials with expertise in foreign languages to deal with international interactions as requested by foreign embassies, who insisted that any treaty should be based on the English version and that the Qing government should be responsible for Chinese translation (Ji and Chen 2007b: 32–33).

By 1894, the political career of graduates from the above-mentioned language institutes was limited. Most of them served as tutors or translators in governmental institutions at home and abroad, and it was mainly after 1894 that several graduates became high-ranked officials (Li 2016: 33–39, 54–61, 70–71). In terms of the governmental system and opportunity for promotion from the 1860s to the 1890s, the command of European languages and knowledge was still far less useful and important than a degree in the Civil Service Examination, the scope of which was traditional Chinese classics. Thus, influential and intellectual families were reluctant to send their children to study at the institutes for foreign language and knowledge (Ji and Chen 2007b: 469).

Foreign knowledge was not completely neglected in the circle of the literati during this period. European works attracted the attention of certain Chinese intellectuals and officials and became their readings (Pan 2014). However, it was only after the First Sino-Japanese War in 1894 that European languages and knowledge gained wide acceptance in China and fundamentally transformed Chinese political culture and intellectual thought.

1894–1911: search for European knowledge and thought

In the wake of the débâcle of China in the First Sino-Japanese War (1894), for Chinese intellectuals, the success of Japan in modernisation contrasted with the bumbling of the Qing Dynasty. This disjuncture goaded Chinese intellectuals to rethink the institution of the government as well as Chinese culture in general. They called for 'Bianfa [變法],' which literally meant 'changing the law,' and broadly referred to the reformation of the governmental institution. The national crisis which Chinese sensed after the war led to the unsettling of the beliefs, values, and socio-political order (Chang 1987). Many leading Chinese intellectuals and officials searched European sources for a means of salvaging China from downfall and a method to reform or revolutionise Chinese society and politics.

The Historical Documents Concerning Chinese Translation of Science (*Zhongguo kexue fanyi shiliao* 中國科學翻譯史料) shows that many officials put forward proposals to establish institutes for translation and to promote the study of European languages and knowledge (Li 1996). In a memorial to Emperor Guangxu (1871–1908), Prince Qing (1838–1917) and other officials argued that the translation of European works would be fundamental to the agenda of reformation (1996 [1898]: 75). As to the regional government, Viceroy of Huguang Provinces Zhang Zhidong (張之洞) (1837–1909) reported that, in the Self-Strengthening Academy (a new-style school), the learning of foreign languages would be the foundation for the study of new European knowledge (1996 [1898]: 79). In the post-1894 era, the craving for fundamental reform changed Chinese views of European languages and knowledge.

Thanks to their aspiration for 'law-changing,' reform-minded officials and intellectuals started to rethink what kind of European knowledge and work should be translated into Chinese. Prince Qing and other officials contended that the previous translation of European works was limited to the fields of military technology and medicine and therefore not conducive to the 'changing of the law' (1996 [1898]: 75). Kang Youwei made a similar point:

> The Western books translated into Chinese under the guidance of Fu Lanya 傅蘭雅 [John Fryer 1839–1928] were works on military technology and medicine, which were unimportant for [political reform]. As to the study of politics, there are many new Western theories which are not translated into Chinese. Thus, the most important issue is to establish an institute for translation.
>
> *(1996 [1898]: 95–96)*

In post-1894 political culture, the translation of European social and political thoughts was connected with a reformist agenda.

As a matter of fact, unlike what Prince Qing and Kang Youwei contended, European works translated into Chinese before 1894 were not limited to military technology and medicine. Instead, there were also works on international law and world history. However, after the War in 1894, the then-existing translated European works could no longer meet the demand for European thought that was directly concerned with society and politics. There was a call for more translations of European social and political works; Chinese officials and intellectuals were of the opinion that European thought would guide the transformation of Chinese politics and society.

Reform-minded Chinese intellectuals were enthusiastic about reading the works of European thought which were translated into Chinese directly from original European works or mediately from Japanese translation and interpretation of European works. Prince Qing suggested that the Chinese could learn Japanese and read Japanese translations of the major works of European knowledge (1996 [1898]: 75). Besides, Kang Youwei, one of the leading intellectuals and reformers, put forward a plan to establish an Institute for Translation and translate into Chinese Japanese translations of European works (1996 [1898]: 95–96). As Wang Fan-sen indicates, the amount of Chinese translation of Japanese books after the First Sino-Japanese War exceeded the amount of Chinese translation of European books before 1894 (2003: 183). Since Japan became a model of Westernisation and it was much easier for the Chinese to learn Japanese than European languages, Chinese students went to study in Japan and learned the European thought filtered through the lens of Japan, which underwent the restructuring of politics and reformation of society from 1868.

In the last few years of late-Qing China, the translation of European works and the acceptance of European knowledge became a project of enlightenment and this project was put into practice through institutional reformation. In 1905, European knowledge finally replaced traditional Chinese classics in the nationwide system of education after the Civil Service Examination, through which intellectuals could get a degree and became officials in the government, was abolished. Besides, according to the proposal for a new nationwide system of education, the study of European languages and knowledge became an integral part of the school curriculum (Ji and Chen 2007b: 528–570). It is also worth mentioning that the years following 1894 witnessed the displacement of Chinese science and medicine and the acceptance of European science and medicine (Elman 2005: 396–421). In post-1894 China, there was a shift from the traditional Chinese model of knowledge and education to the modern European model.

Translation and transformation of European thought in post-1894 political discourse

The years after 1894 witnessed the rise of Chinese nationalism and the formation of the nationalist discourse of evolutionism in China. In addition, there were two main factions of political activists: constitutionalists and revolutionists. Constitutionalists, like Kang Youwei and Liang Qichao (梁啟超) (1873–1929), aimed to transform the Qing court into a government of constitutional monarchy in emulation of Meiji Japan or Victorian Britain. Revolutionists like Sun Yat-sen 孫中山 (1866–1925) and Zou Rong 鄒容 (1885–1905) launched uprisings in order to overthrow the Qing Dynasty and to found a republic without monarchy. These developments were integrally linked to the transla-tion and transformation of European works and ideas.

Yan Fu: the identity and task of the translator in political enlightenment and action

In late-Qing China, the most representative translator was Yan Fu (嚴復) (1854–1921). After the First Sino-Japanese War, he utilised Darwinian ideas of 'natural selection' and 'evolution' to awaken his Chinese compatriots to the survival crisis which the Chinese nation confronted. In 1895, as his son Yan Qu indicated,

> [The Treaty of Shimonoscki] kindled my father's anxiety and, from then on, he con-centrated on the task of translation. He began with the translation of Huxley's *Evo-lution and Ethics* and completed his translation in several months.
>
> *(1998: 9)*

In his translation of Huxley's *Evolution and Ethics* into *Tianyan lun* (天演論) (*The Operation of Heaven*), Yan Fu transformed Huxley's ethical ideal of preserving each member of industrial capitalist society into a nationalist discourse of saving the race from extinction in international competition (Liu 2020a). He also translated Adam Smith's *The Wealth of Nations*, Herbert Spencer's *The Study of Sociology*, John Stuart Mill's *On Liberty* and *A System of Logic*, Edward Jenks's *A History of Politics*, and Montesquieu's *The Spirit of Laws*. As Schwartz argues in *In Search of Wealth and Power: Yen Fu and the West*, the works which Yan Fu selected for translation were those which he thought would be conducive to the search for national power and wealth even when these works did not really concern this topic (1964). In particular, Yan Fu's translation and transformation of British evolutionism, which situated the biological prin-ciples of struggle for existence, natural selection, and survival of the fittest within an international competition for the survival of a given race, contributed to the discursive formation of Chinese nationalism.

The wide acceptance of Yan Fu's works in post-1894 China reflected the change in the social status of the translator. The translator had previously been called '*Tongshi* [communicator]'; it was not a highly respected role and job in Chinese society (Ji and Chen 2007a). Furthermore, those who knew English were despised for their connection and interaction with foreigners (Li 2016: 75–76). Before 1894, European languages and knowledge were still devalued, and students recruited to the institutes for foreign lan-guages were mainly from poor families (Ji and Chen 2007b: 469). After the death of his father, Yan Fu chose to receive European education at the Naval Academy of Fouzhou in 1867 because his study at this school would be financially supported by the government.

From 1877 to 1879, sent by the Qing government to Britain, Yan Fu studied at the Royal Naval College of Greenwich. He usually 'discussed the difference between Chinese and Western academics and institutions' with Chinese ambassador Guo Songtao (郭嵩燾) (1818–1891), who spoke highly of this talented and overweening young man (Wang 1977: 5). Nevertheless, Yan Fu's command of English and European knowledge did not benefit his political career after he returned to China and served as an instructor in the Northern Naval Academy in Tianjin from 1880. Only after the First Sino-Japanese

War did he start to draw the attention of Chinese officials and intellectuals through his translation and knowledge of European thought.

Yan Fu's self-assumed obligation of translation and enlightenment (Huang 2005; Chen 2011: 89–91) shaped the identity and task of the translator. In his letter to his friend Zhang Yuanji 張元濟 (1866–1959), Yan Fu argued that

> even though the [Qing] court does not do anything or just does wrong things, the Yellow Race may not be destined to downfall if [intellectuals] without official positions in the government and talented young people know about the reality of China and Western countries.
>
> *(1998 [1899]: 183)*

He aimed to 'enlighten the people' (*Kai minzhi* 開民智) and considered the task of translation to be a matter of priority and urgency (1998 [1899]: 183). He also mentioned to Laing Qichao that 'the task of translation' aimed to 'distribute civilized thought to the people' (1998 [1902]: 284). When he translated a work, he had a clear purpose. For instance, after he translated Spencer's *The Study of Sociology* into *Qunque yiyan* (群學肄言 *The Study of the Group*), he argued that this work opened the path for 'the study of the group' (群學 *Qunxue*) (1998 [1903] a: 299). Besides, he wrote a proposal for the establishment of an institute for translation in the Academy of Beijing (*Jingshi daxue tang* 京師大學堂) (1998 [1903] b: 300–305). Yan Fu considered the task of translation as a patriotic obligation to save the Chinese nation (Chen 2011: 90) and, therefore, imbued his translation of European works with a strong sense of political action and mobilisation.

Kang Youwei and Liang Qichao: the task of translation in constitutionalist reform

Translation also played an important part in the shaping of Chinese constitutionalist thought and the agenda of the Hundred Day's Reform in 1898. The advocates of monarchical constitutionalism established the Datong Publication House for Translation (*Datong yishu ju* 大同印書局). Liang Qichao pointed out that the major purpose of this publication house was to translate and publish works concerning successful or ongoing cases of law change in various countries and he contended that the effort of reform in China would become fruitless if the above-mentioned works were not translated (1996 [1897]: 469).

Liang Qichao also promoted the translation of foreign political fiction. In '*Yiyin zhengzhi xiaoshuo xu* [譯印政治小說序 Preface to the translation and publication of political novels],' he argued that the political idea in fiction could change people's view and spirit and that the political progress of America, England, Germany, France, Italy, Austria, and Japan depended largely on political novels (1898). To him, it was important to select and translate foreign political fiction to enlighten the Chinese people for the purpose of political reform (1898).

Kang Youwei, the master of Liang Qichao, compiled *Political Transformation in Japan* (*Riben bianzheng kao* 日本變政考) and *Peter the Great's Political Transformation in Russia* (*Eluosi dabide bianzheng ji* 俄羅斯大彼得變政記) and presented these works to the reform-minded Emperor Guangxu during the Hundred Days' Reform in 1898. Even though he did not know foreign languages, Kang Youwei tried to translate the successful models of reformation and modernisation in Meiji Japan and Peter the Great's Russia in his political works and actions.

Sun Yat-sen: European thought and Chinese revolutionary discourse

As to the political camp of revolutionists, Sun Yat-sen utilised Euopean ideas to promote revolution. Born in Guangdong, Sun Yat-sen studied in Hawai'i during his teenage years, earned his degree in medicine from the Hong Kong College of Medicine for Chinese in 1892, and stayed in Britain from 30 September 1896 to 1 July 1897 (Huang 2007: 3). During his stay in England, Sun Yat-sen read widely about European works in the library of the British Museum and became familiar with a variety of European thought.

The ideas in Sun Yat-sen's magnum opus *Three Principles of the People* (*Sanmin Zhuyi* 三民主義), published in 1927, had their early gestation during his travel in Europe (Huang 2007) and firstly appeared in the first issue of *People's Newspaper* (*Minbao* 民報), a journal which the revolutionary alliance Tong Menghui (同盟會) launched in 1905. In 1906, Sun Yat-sen delivered a speech on 'The Three Principles of the People and the Future of the Chinese Nation' (*Sanmin zhuti yu zhongguo zhi qiantu* 三民主義與中國民族之前途) in Tokyo.

'Three Principles of the People' referred to 'Nation, People's Rights and People's Livelihood [*Minzu, minquan and Minsheng* 民族、民權、民生],' which derived from European thoughts. In his revolutionist propagandas, Sun Yat-sen borrowed European discourses of Darwinism and nationalism to draw the attention of his compatriots to the survival crisis of the Chinese nation in international competition. He used the ideas of rights, constitution, and democracy as well as nation to emphasise the necessity to overthrow the Manchu-ruled Qing Dynasty and to promulgate the ideal of a republic without monarchy (Sun Yat-sen 1905, 1906).

From 1894 to 1911, the translation and transformation of European thought were interconnected with various political agendas. What mattered for Chinese intellectuals in their interpretative reading and political transformation of European texts was the appropriation of European ideas for political actions. They 'translated' and 'adapted' European ideas into nationalist, reformist, or revolutionary propaganda. In the late-Qing Chinese language, political actions and agendas shaped the meaning of European ideas and thoughts. The transplanted ideas of evolution, natural selection, constitution, rights, and democracy were endowed with nationalist, patriotic, and activist significance in post-1894 Chinese intellectual and political culture.

Chinese evolutionism as a case study of 'political mobilisation' in post-1894 translation

Since the late-Qing Chinese accepted European ideas and works due to political exigency, they did not really try to understand European knowledge and thought within their original knowledge systems and intellectual contexts. The meaning of 'translation' in late-Qing studies should be defined in a broad sense in that most translations of European thought were partial, distortive, creative, and transformative. Not only literal translation but also interpretative translation, radical transformation, and selective appropriation contributed to the meaning-making process in the acceptance of European ideas and knowledge.

This section uses the translation of European evolutionism as a case study to reveal how political agendas influenced the selection and transformation of European texts and ideas in the task of translation from 1894 to 1911. In *China and Charles Darwin*, Pusey has delineated the ramifications of evolutionism on the social and political thought of late-nineteenth-and-early-twentieth-century China. In this section, I will analyse the nuanced meaning of the text to reveal how the intersection between nationalism and evolutionism motivated Chinese intellectuals to pursue an activist agenda.

Yan Fu's nationalist translation of evolutionism

In the wake of the First Sino-Japanese war in 1894, Yan Fu published articles which introduced Darwin's and Spencer's thoughts. In '*Yuanqiang* 原強 (On strengthening [the country]),' Yan Fu described Darwin's theory of evolution as a nationalist discourse:

> Two chapters of Darwin's book [*The Origin of Species*] are particularly renowned. All Western intellectuals know these chapters. The first one is 'Competition for Self-Existence' ['Struggle for Existence'] and the other is 'Procreation of the Fittest Race' ['Natural Selection']. 'Competition for Self-Existence' means that living things or people coexist in the world, and share the natural resources of the heaven and the earth. They encounter each other, and compete with each other for self-existence. In the beginning, a species competes with another species. Afterwards, societies and countries are formed; societies compete with one another, and countries compete with one another. The weak fall prey to the strong. The foolish will be the slave of the intelligent.
>
> *(1998 [1895]: 34–35)*

Yan Fu 'translated' the ideas of Darwinism and connected the phenomena of struggle for existence in living things with the phenomena in international competition. Darwin did not directly argue about the competition between human races or between countries in terms of biological theory in *The Origin of Species*, *The Descent of Man*, and other seminal works, but Yan Fu, in his interpretation of Darwin's theory, compared the competition among animal species to the war between nations and countries—a theme that Darwin did not engage with. While the main point which Darwin aimed to make in *The Origin of Species* was that the transformation and evolution of species resulted from the accumulation of advantageous features in struggle for existence and natural selection, in his introduction of Darwinism Yan Fu tried to indicate that struggle for existence was fundamental to national survival.

The most exemplary illustration of Yan Fu's transformation of European thought was the above-mentioned *Tianyan lun*, an interpretative translation of Huxley's work. In *Evolution and Ethics* (1989 [1893]), Thomas Huxley disputed the attempt of Social Darwinism to apply the biological principle of struggle for existence to political and social problems. In order to defend his ethics against the naturalistic criticism of the disunity between nature and society, Huxley contended that the removal of intensified competition from the community could also be an advantage in natural selection, as exemplified in the societies of bees and ants (Liu 2020a). In his translation, Yan Fu paid attention to the idea of 'outside competition,' which was actually not Huxley's major concern. He used the example of the bee society to argue that the solidification of the community by removing internal competition would be conducive to victory in its competition with other communities (Liu 2020a). Yan Fu twisted the logical line of thought that connected ideas in Huxley's thinking about evolution and ethics and thereby imbued these ideas with a strong significance of nationalism.

The following textual analysis further reveals how Yan Fu imbued Huxley's text with a significance of nationalist sentiments and patriotic mobilisation. In the beginning of *Evolution and Ethics*, Huxley described the struggle for existence among plants:

> The native grasses and weeds, the scattered patches of gorse, contended with one another for the possession of the scanty surface soil; they fought against the droughts of summer, the frosts of winter, and the furious gales. … One year with another, an average population, the floating balance of the unceasing struggle for existence among the indigenous plants, maintained itself.
>
> *(1989 [1893]: 1–2)*

In his translation, Yan Fu added words and ideas that did not appear in the original text:

> All exuberant [grasses and vines] exert their utmost natural capabilities to sustain their races. Within several acres of land, the war is intense. The weak perish earlier, and the strong die later. Year in and year out, some [species] exist and remain.
>
> *(1998 [1901]: 181)*

In the Chinese language, the term for 'race,' *zhongzu* (種族), was used to refer to a group of men. By inserting the aforesaid passage, Yan Fu drew an analogy between plants and races and therefore personified plants. The implication was that, just as 'angry grasses and entwined vines compete to dominate' (1998 [1901]:181), so human races struggle for existence with one another. By adding some words, Yan Fu changed the nuanced significance of the original text and implied that his Chinese compatriots should struggle for the existence of their race.

The following passage of Hu Shi (1891–1962) comes from a recollection of his life in Shanghai during 1904 and 1910 and illustrates how European ideas were filtered through the lens of Chinese nationalism in post-1894 China:

> A few years after its publication, *Tianyan lun* (On the operation of Heaven) gained its nationwide popularity. It even became the textbook for high-school students. Most people who read this book did not understand Huxley's contribution to the history of science and to the history of thought. What they could understand was just the significance of the formula of 'the survival of the fittest, and the extinction of the unfit' in international politics. In the wake of China's continuous fiascos in the war, not least the gigantic national shame during 1900 and 1901, this formula, like a goad hitting somebody in the forehead, awakened numerous people to an immeasurable extent. In several years, this kind of thought, spreading like wildfire, kindled the heart and blood of the youth. The terminologies 'evolution,' 'competition,' 'extinction' and 'natural selection' appeared as catchphrases in the newspaper, and gradually became the popular phrases for aspiring patriots.
>
> *(Hu Shi 1993 [1933]: 48–49)*

Hu Shi's contemporaries did not understand Huxley's text and Darwin's biology in their own terms. Instead, for intellectuals and patriots, Darwinian terminologies like 'evolution,' 'struggle for existence,' 'extinction,' and 'natural selection' became a warning against the extinction of a race and a prescription to struggle for national survival. In the spirit of national competition, late-Qing intellectuals and translators accepted Spencerian ideas of 'the fit' and 'the unfit.' The principle of social policy in Spencer's theory was to make the fit prosper and leave the unfit extirpated for the purpose of social evolution and human progress (Spencer 1874: 344–346), but late-Qing intellectuals and translators understood Spencer's principle as the survival of the fittest race and the extinction of the unfit race. In Chinese translation, Darwinian terminologies and Spencerian ideas became patriotic catchphrases. As Hu Shi indicated, a series of fiascos of China in the war, particularly the defeat of China by the Alliance of Eight Nations in 1900, kindled among the Chinese an anxiety over the downfall of the Chinese nation.

In the post-1894 era, Chinese intellectuals and patriots endowed the above-mentioned evolutionist terminologies, which derived originally from Darwin's theory of biology and Spencer's social theory, with a strong meaning of 'activism' in the sense that these ideas became imbued with an implication that the Chinese ought to struggle for national survival in international politics. Both Yan Fu's nationalist translation of evolutionary thought as well as the widespread acceptance of evolutionism among intellectuals and patriots increased the patriotic significance of Darwinian terminologies and ideas for post-1894 China.

Evolutionism and women's rights in the agenda of reform

When Chinese nationalism crystallised during the last years of the late-Qing dynasty, not only evolutionary biology but also other kinds of European thought were endowed with a sense of patriotism in the meaning-making process of translation. One example was the evolutionist and nationalist reinterpretation of nineteenth-century European ideas concerning the education and rights of women in the late-Qing discourse of 'the mother of citizens [國民之母 Guomin zhimu],' which emphasised the importance of the mother to the nation (Chou 2010; Judge 2010).

As part of his project of political reform, the leading constitutionalist Kang Youwei connected women's intelligence with the survival of the nation:

> The race procreated by incarcerated women is inferior to the race procreated by women who study and travel, and the former will lose to the latter and collapse. ... If mothers are stupid and uneducated, ... the race produced by them will be a great failure.
>
> *(2002 [1901]: 195–196)*

Kang Youwei believed that education and travel could improve women's intelligence. To him, if Chinese women were not intellectually and physically emancipated, their children would be intellectually and physically feeble and thus China would lose in the war against imperial countries. He advocated the education of women not for women's sake but for the evolution and survival of the Chinese race in international competition.

Like his mentor Kang Youwei, Liang Qichao connected the education of women with the preservation of the race in his agenda of reform:

> 'Fetal education' is the primary concern of Western research on the race. They [Westerners] try various ways to make their races evolve. In all [Western] countries, those who are concerned with the strengthening of their military power require

women to take physical education. They assert that only through physical education can women procreate healthy and strong offspring. Thus, physical education is important to women's schools. … How can we preserve the race? We should make the race evolve in order to preserve it. … The preservation of the race starts from the education of women.

(2002 [1896]: 93)

Liang Qichao believed that the physical education of woman could be conducive to improving the physical quality of children. The logic in this argument was that what a woman has done would affect her embryo—a belief of 'fetal education' in traditional Chinese medicine. In the late-Qing period, the traditional idea of fetal education was connected with the British theory of evolution. To Liang Qichao, fetal education was not just for the cultivation of children but also for the evolution of the whole race. He promulgated the physical education of women with a focus on strengthening military power and the preservation of the Chinese nation rather than for the sake of women.

Lü Bicheng (1883–1943), a female disciple of Yan Fu and an advocate of women's rights, also accepted the connection between the education of women and 'the strengthening of the race and the country' in her explication of the goal of the education of women (2007 [1904]: 127). The logic implied in her argument was also that the effect on women's bodies would affect their offspring. Thus, she attacked the practice of footbinding women. In traditional China, women's feet were bound and kept to a small size. To Lü Bicheng, the foot-binding of women would influence the bodies of their children, and this was why 'the race of Chinese was notorious for its inferiority' (2007 [1904]: 127). It was also for the 'strengthening of the country and the race [強國強種]' that Lü Bicheng encouraged women to receive physical education and ameliorate their physical quality (2007 [1904]: 127).

In her book chapter 'History, Nation, and Female Talent,' Judge argues that the Chinese ideal of 'mothers of citizens' is the sinicisation of the Japanese idea of 'good wives and wise mothers' put forth by Utako Shimoda (1854–1936), who returned from Britain to Japan in 1895 and emphasised the importance of maternal education and female physical education for the purpose of bringing up strong, healthy, and intelligent citizens (Judge 2010: 110–122). Before Shimoda tried to convey her ideas to Chinese readers in the early twentieth century (Judge 2010: 111–114), Kang Youwei and Liang Qichao developed their nationalist and evolutionist thoughts about the education of women from the middle of the 1890s. No matter whether they drew inspiration from Shimoda's thoughts, their translation and appropriation of European ideas about the education of women illustrated that a variety of ideas, coming directly from European texts or filtered by Japanese reinterpretation, were accepted through the lens of Chinese nationalist evolutionism.

The discourse concerning women's education and rights varied between late-Qing China and Victorian Britain. In *The Subjection of Women*, John Stuart Mill criticised 'the legal subordination of one sex to the other' and argued for 'perfect equality that does not allow any power or privilege on one side or disability on the other' (1869). While Mill pointed out the contribution of gender equality to the improvement of society, he also paid attention to the problem of gender equality itself. By contrast, in late-Qing China, intellectuals did not argue for women's rights to education for the sake of women. Instead, the proposal of women's intellectual and physical education in Kang You's and Liang Qichao's agendas of reform was focused on the evolution and survival of the Chinese race in international competition. Even the female intellectual Lü Bicheng buttressed her argument about the emancipation from foot-binding and the necessity of the education of women through the rhetoric of evolutionism and nationalism.

Racial classification in Zou Rong's revolutionary manifesto

The Qing Dynasty (1644–1911), the last monarchical dynasty in Chinese history, ended in 1911. In their attempts to overthrow the Manchu-ruled Qing Dynasty, revolutionists not only disseminated Western ideas that were directly relevant to the founding of a democratic republic, such as 'liberty' and 'rights,' but also appropriated those ideas irrelevant to the type and institute of the government to promulgate revolution. For instance, Zou Rong incorporated European ideas of 'evolution' and 'racial classification' into his discourse of revolution in *Revolutionary Army* (*Geming jun* 革命軍). The role of this pamphlet by Zou Rong in the 1911 revolution and the shaping of Chinese national identity was comparable to that of Thomas Paine's *Common Sense* during the American War of Independence (Xu 2005:42).

In *Revolutionary Army*, Zou Rong defined the Chinese race by differentiating it from other races in the section entitled 'The Requisite for Revolution is to Distinguish Different Races' (*Geming bi poqing renzhong* 革命必剖清人種) (1983[1903]: 62–66). In his classification of races, the yellow race in Asia included two sub-categories: the Chinese race and the Siberian race. The Chinese race included three sub-races: the Han race (the major ethnic people in China in terms of population), the Tibetan race and the Vietnamese race (1983 [1903]: 62–63). It should be noted that, for Zou Rong, Koreans and Japanese originated from the Han race, and the Siberian race included three sub-races: the Mongolian race, the Tungusic race (including the Manchu people), and the Turkish race (1983 [1903]: 62–63).

As Yang Jui-sung indicates, Zou Rong rearranged the classification of human races in Japanese scholar Kuwabara Jitsuzo's work by bringing the Japanese and Koreans nearer to the Chinese than the Manchu people in order to promulgate anti-Manchu revolution (2012: 50–52). In *Revolutionary Army*, Zou Rong foregrounded the distinction between Han Chinese and the ruling Manchu people: 'There is no interracial marriage between the Manchu people and us. We are the pure Descendants of the Yellow Emperor' (1983 [1903]: 66). The national identity of 'Descendants of the Yellow Emperor' was constructed in late-Qing China, and revolutionists excluded the Manchu people from this national community (Shen 2001: 286–321). In this sense, the classification of races in Zou Rong's *Revolutionary Army* was to target the enemy of Han Chinese, that is, the Manchu people (Yang 2012). As he put it, 'I lamented the situation of the Han race and thus intended to use the concept of "race [*Zhongzu* 種族]" to awaken the Han race' (1983 [1903]: 65). In his revolutionist manifesto, Zou Rong transformed and appropriated the knowledge of 'racial classification' to make the Han people aware of their 'racial' difference from the Manchu people, and therefore pushed the Han people to overthrow the Manchu-ruled Qing Dynasty.

For Zou Rong, Han Chinese were at once tortured by the Manchu people at home and assailed by foreigners from various countries (1983 [1903]: 71). He pointed out,

> The Yellow Race and the white race are endowed by Heaven with equal intelligence, capability and militancy. These two races make the most of these qualities and fight with each other in the Heaven-operated world, which is always an arena

of power and intelligence competition and has been a gigantic stage for the competition and evolution of things from the time immemorial.

(1983 [1903]: 62)

He intertwined the nationalist discourse of 'racial classification' and the Darwinian discourse of 'natural selection and evolution' to solidify the national identify of the Chinese and awaken them to the survival crisis of the Chinese nation in international competition.

In the late-nineteenth and early-twentieth centuries, the interaction between the theory of evolution and the knowledge of racial classification varied between Europe and China. For instance, the classification of races in Victorian Britain was an attempt to prove the superiority of the White race (not least the British people) over other peoples and races in terms of evolutionary theory and the allegedly scientific investigation of human races (Lorimer 1988: 406; Claeys 2000: 235–240). By contrast, the system of racial classification in Zou Rong's revolutionist manifesto was not informed by a sense of racial pride, but by Chinese Darwinist anxiety over the extinction of the race or the downfall of the nation.

In late-Qing political culture, intellectuals and politicians had an inclination to find certain European sources and ideas to justify their political ideals. They explicitly referred to European thought in their reformist and revolutionist propagandas or implicitly translated and incorporated European ideas into their socio-political statements. Since they accepted and distributed European ideas for their political agendas, the transplanted European ideas like evolution, racial classification, and women's rights became tools to advance an activist agenda and were used to mobilise the people for political actions.

The 'agency' and 'potentiality' of the Chinese language in post-1894 translation

With the rise of the theory of cultural translation, which originates from anthropology and influences the study of literature and culture, the meaning of the term 'translation' is not confined narrowly to the line-by-line translation of words; rather, it is extended to the translation of elements from other cultures (Asad 1986; Liu 1995: 23). Borrowing Tylor's concept of 'culture,' Asad points out the 'culture' in translation … includes knowledge, belief, art, morals, law, custom, and any other capabilities and habits' (Tylor 1920: 1; Asad 1986). According to this definition, late-Qing translation can also be considered as cultural translation: not only texts and ideas but also institutions and governmental types from European culture were translated into various political actions, agendas, reforms, and revolutions.

The wide acceptance of European thought and the ultimate abolition of the Civil Service Examination in post-1894 China caused traditional Chinese knowledge to be increasingly replaced by European knowledge. However, as Lydia H. Liu argues, the power relationship between European culture and Chinese culture cannot always be reduced to that of 'native resistance and Western domination' (1995: 23–25). Lydia H. Liu pays attention to the agency of the Chinese language to transform European ideas in the meaning-making process of translation (1995: 29). My previous discussion shows that, when European ideas such as evolution, women's rights, and racial classification were used to justify an argument or express a statement in post-1894 Chinese political culture, the transplanted ideas were endowed with Chinese nationalist concerns. In this regard, the Chinese language manifested its agency as it transformed European ideas according to Chinese concerns and contexts.

The agency of the Chinese language and culture to transform European ideas can be understood in terms of Lienhardt's account of the understanding of foreign ideas in the process of translation (1954). In his discussion of anthropologists' translation of primitive culture, Lienhardt argues that 'when we try to contain the thought of a primitive society in our language and categories, without also modifying these in order to receive it … it begins in part to lose the sense it seemed to have' (1954: 97–97). For Lienhardt, Western anthropologists use the categories in European languages and culture to understand the thought of a primitive society, and the primitive thought filtered through European modes of thought loses its original sense in the process of translation. Lienhardt also points out that 'it is not finally some mysterious primitive philosophy that we [anthropologists] are exploring, but the further potentialities of our own thought and language' (1954: 96). 'Potentiality' refers to something that can be actualised. In the process of translation, trans-lators actualise the 'potentiality' of the categories and thoughts from their own language and culture when they try to use them to understand foreign elements.

In late-Qing translation, the Chinese language also demonstrates the potentiality of the categories and thoughts of Chinese culture. When Yan Fu understood and translated the British concept of 'evolution' through the lens of Lao Zi's concept of the Dao, he actualised the potentiality of Lao Zi's thought so that that the concept of the Dao could take shape and reveal its potentiality in the interpretation of the evolution of man and society (Liu 2020b). While Lienhardt deals with the translation of a dominated culture into a domineering culture, his theory also holds true for the translation of elements from a domineering culture to a dominated culture, like the translation of British evolu-tionary theory into Chinese thought.

While Lienhardt mainly focuses on the encounter between the 'modes of thought' of two cultures in translation, the 'further potentiality' of the translator's language also appears in other elements and aspects of culture. When Chinese intellectuals and states-men turned to European knowledge for solutions to the problems of China, they used the patriotic concerns in late-Qing Chinese political culture to contain and reinterpret European thought. What late-Qing intellectuals explored in their cultural translation was not just European knowledge but also their own concerns with the project of enlighten-ment, national survival, and socio-political reform. The 'potentiality' of these Chinese concerns was actualised when they took shape in the reinterpretation of European ideas like survival of the fittest, women's rights, and racial classification.

The mediation between European and primitive cultures in anthropologists' translation is largely one-sided—that is, the dominance of the host language over the guest lan-guage. By contrast, the mediation between Chinese and European cultures in late-Qing translation was more 'interactive' in that the above-mentioned Chinese concerns with national survival, enlightenment, and socio-political reform were responses to European power, knowledge, and thought. For instance, in late-Qing Chinese political culture and thought, the idea of national survival was triggered by European power and evolutionary theory and then became a filter through which a variety of European ideas like women's rights and racial classification were selected, interpreted, and transformed.

Related topics

Translating Marx in Japan; Thought/Translation; 'The Pen is Mightier than the Sword'

Further reading

Cheung, Martha P.Y. (2010) 'Rethinking Activism: The Power and Dynamics of Translation in China during the Late Qing Period (1840–1911),' in *Text and Context: Essays on Translation & Interpreting in Honour of Ian Mason*. Eds. Mona Baker, Maeve Olohan, and Maria Perez Calzada. Manchester: St. Jerome Publishing. 237–258.

Cheung gives a broad overview of the use of translation in political agendas from 1840 to 1911 and evaluates the different stages of late-Qing translation in terms of Aberle's theoretical model concerning the scope and level of the influence which a movement aims at.

Liu, Lydia H. (1995) *Translingual Practice: Literature, National Culture, and Translated Modernity —China, 1900–1937*. Stanford: Stanford University Press.

An important work that revisits the power relation between European and Chinese languages in translation, examines the 'agency' of the Chinese language and culture to receive and transform European works and ideas, and bridges the study of translation theory and the study of Chinese translation.

Liu, Kuan-yen (forthcoming 2020a and 2020b) 'Yan Fu's Xunzian-Confucian Translation of Thomas Huxley's *Evolution and Ethics*' & 'Yan Fu's Daoist Reinterpretation of Evolutionism,' in *Asian Religious Responses to Darwinism: Evolutionary Theories in Middle Eastern, South Asian, and East Asian Cultural Contexts (Sophia Studies in Cross-cultural Philosophy of Traditions and Cultures)*. Ed. Mackenzie Brown. Cham: Springer. Chapters 11 and 12.

By focusing on Yan Fu's translation and thought, Kuan-yen Liu's book chapters demonstrate how the traditions of ancient Chinese philosophy interacted with British scientific and socio-political thoughts in the discursive formation of late-Qing Darwinism.

Pusey, James Reeve (1983) *China and Charles Darwin*. Cambridge: Harvard University Press.

Pusey provides rich information about how the theory of evolution infiltrated into various fields of Chinese culture and interacted with a variety of socio-political thoughts, like revolutionism, constitutionalism, and anarchism, during the late-Qing and early-Republican period.

Schwartz, Benjamin (1964) *In Search of Wealth and Power: Yen Fu and the West*. Harvard: Harvard University Press.

Schwartz's influential work in the study of Yan Fu and Chinese Darwinism deals with how Yan Fu translated and transformed the works and thoughts of major European authors like Thomas Huxley, Herbert Spencer, Adam Smith, Montesquieu and John Stuart Mill into Chinese works that concerned the search for national power and wealth.

References

Aberle, David F. (1991) *The Peyote Religion among the Navaho*. Oklahoma: University of Oklahoma Press.
Asad, Talad (1986) 'The Concept of Cultural Translation in British Social Anthropology,' in *Writing Culture: The Poetics and Politics of Ethnography*. Eds. James Clifford and George E. Marcus. Los Angeles, CA: University of California Press. 141–164.
Chang, Hao (1987) *Chinese Intellectuals in Crisis: Search for Order and Meaning, 1890–1911*. Los Angeles: University of California Press.
Chen, Gukang 陳福康 (2011) *Zhongguo yixue shi 中國譯學史 (The History of Chinese Study of Translation)*. Shanghai: Shanghai waiyu jiaoyu chuban she.
Cheung, Martha P.Y. (2010) 'Rethinking Activism: The Power and Dynamics of Translation in China during the Late Qing Period (1840–1911),' in *Text and Context: Essays on Translation & Interpreting in Honour of Ian Mason*. Eds. Mona Baker, Maeve Olohan, and Maria Perez Calzada. Manchester: St. Jerome Publishing. 237–258.
Chou, Chun-yen 周春燕 (2010) *Nuti yu guozu: Qiangguo qiangzhong yu jindai zhongguo de funu weisheng 女體與國族: 強國強種與近代中國的婦女衛生, 1895 ~ 1949 (The Female Body and the Nation: The Hygiene of Women in Relation to the Strengthening of the Country and the Race in Modern China: 1895–1949)*. Gaoxiong: Fuwen.

Claeys, Gregory (2000) '"Survival of the Fittest" and the Origins of Social Darwinism,' *Journal of the History of Ideas* 61 (2): 223–240.

Darwin, Charles (1988 [1859]) *On the Origin of Species*. New York: New York University Press.

Darwin, Charles (1989 [1877]) *The Descent of Man, and Selections in Relation to Sex* (2nd ed.) (Revised and Augmented). New York: New York University Press.

Elman, A. Benjamin (2005) *On Their Own Terms: Science in China, 1550–1900*. Cambridge: Harvard University Press.

Hu, Shi 胡適 (1993 [1933]) *Sishi zishu*四十自述 *(Autobiography at the Age of Forty)*. Beijing: Wenlian.

Huang, Ko-wu 黃克武 (2005) 'Zouxiang fanyi zhilu: beiyang shuishi xuetang shiqi de yanfu 走向翻譯之路:北洋水師學堂時期的嚴復 (Beginning a New Career in Translation: Yan Fu at the Northern Naval College),' *Zhongyang yanjiu yuan jindai shi yanjiu suo jikan* 49: 1–40.

Huang, Yuhe 黃宇和 (2007) *Sun yixian zai lundun 1896–1897: sanmin zhuyi sixiang tanyuan*孫逸仙在倫敦, 1896–1897: 三民主義思想探源 *(Sun Yat-sen in London, 1896–1897: On the Origin of Three Principles of the People)*. Taipei: Lianjing.

Hugh, Murray (1834) *An Encyclopaedia of Geography: Comprising a Complete Description of the Earth, Physical, Statistical, Civil, and Political*. London: Longman.

Huxley, Thomas (1989 [1893]) *Evolution and Ethics, and Other Essays*. New Haven: Yale University Press.

Ji, Yaxi 季壓西 and Chen, Weimin 陳偉民 (2007a) *Yuyan zhangai yu wangqing jindai hua licheng: zhongguo jindai tongshi* 語言障礙與晚清近代化歷程: 中國近代通事 *(Language Barrier and the Modernisation Process of Late-Qing China: Translators in Modern China)*. Beijing: Xueyuan.

Ji, Yaxi 季壓西 and Chen, Weimin 陳偉民 (2007b) *Yuyan zhangai yu wangqing jindai hua licheng: cong tongwen sanguan qibu* 語言障礙與晚清近代化歷程: 從同文三館起步 (Language Barrier and the Modernisation Process of Late-Qing China: Starting from Three Tongwen Institutions of Translation). Beijing: Xueyuan.

Judge, Joan (2010) *The Precious Raft of History: The Past, the West, and the Woman Question in China*. Stanford: Stanford University Press.

Kang, Youwei 康有為 (1996 [1898]) 'Guangyi riben shu sheli jingshi yishu ju zhe 廣譯日本書設立京師譯書局折 (A Memorial Concerning a Plan to Establish a Translation Institute in Beijing and Translate a Wide Variety of Japanese Books),' in *Zhongguo kexue fanyi shiliao*中國科學翻譯史料 *(The Historical Documents Concerning Chinese Translation of Science)*. Ed. Li Nanqiu. Hefei: University of Science and Technology of China Press. 95–97.

Kang, Youwei (2002 [1901]) *Datongshu* 大同書 *(Book of Great Harmony)*. Beijing: Huaxia.

Kang, Youwei (2011 [1898]a) *Riben bianzheng kao*日本變政考 *(Political Transformation in Japan)*. Beijing: China Renmin University Press.

Kang, Youwei 康有為 (2011 [1898]b) 'E bide bianzheng ji 俄彼得變政記 *(Peter the Great's Political Transformation in Russia)*,' in *Riben bianzheng kao* 日本變政考. Eds. Jiang Yihua and Zhang Ronghua. Beijing: China Renmin University Press. 327–340.

Li, Nanqiu 黎難秋 (ed.) (1996) *Zhongguo kexue fanyi shiliao*中國科學翻譯史料 *(The Historical Documents Concerning Chinese Translation of Science)*. Hefei: University of Science and Technology of China Press.

Li, Nanqiu 黎難秋 (2016) *Tongwen sanguan: wanqing fanyi jia waijiao jia de yaolan* 同文三館: 晚清翻譯家外交家的搖籃 *(Three Tongwen Institutes of Translation: The Cradle of Late-Qing Translators and Diplomats)*. Wuhan: Wuhan University Press.

Li, Yashu 李雅舒 and Li, Nanqiu 黎難秋 (2000) 'Zhongguo kexue fanyi shi 中國科學翻譯史 *(The History of Chinese Translation of Science)*.' Hunan: Hunan jiaoyu chuban she.

Liang, Qichao 梁啟超(1898) 'Yiyin Zhengzhi xiaoshuo xu 譯印政治小說序 (Preface to the Translation and Publication of Political Novels),' *Qingyi bao*清議報1: 24.

Liang, Qichao (1996 [1897]) 'Datong yishu ju xuli' 大同印書局敍例 (An Illustration of the Datong Publication House),' in *Zhongguo kexue fanyi shiliao*中國科學翻譯史料 *(The Historical Documents Concerning Chinese Translation of Science)*. Ed. Li Nanqiu. Hefei: University of Science and Technology of China Press. 468–470.

Liang, Qichao (2002 [1896]) *Bianfa tongyi* 變法通議 *(General Discussion of Reform)*. Beijing: Huaxia.

Lienhardt, Godfrey (1954) 'Modes of Thought,' in *The Institutions of Primitive Culture*. Eds. Edward Evan Evans-Pritchard, et al. Oxford: Basil Blackwell. 95–107.

Lin, Zexu 林則徐 (2018 [1841]) *Sizhou zhi* 四洲志 *(The Record of Four Continents)*. Beijing: Zhaohua.

Liu, Kuan-yen (forthcoming 2020a) 'Yan Fu's Xunzian-Confucian Translation of Thomas Huxley's *Evolution and Ethics*,' in *Asian Religious Responses to Darwinism: Evolutionary Theories in Middle Eastern, South Asian, and East Asian Cultural Contexts (Sophia Studies in Cross-cultural Philosophy of Traditions and Cultures)*. Ed. Mackenzie Brown. Cham: Springer.

Liu, Kuan-yen (forthcoming 2020b) 'Yan Fu's Daoist Reinterpretation of Evolutionism,' in *Asian Religious Responses to Darwinism: Evolutionary Theories in Middle Eastern, South Asian, and East Asian Cultural Contexts (Sophia Studies in Cross-cultural Philosophy of Traditions and Cultures)*. Ed. Mackenzie Brown. Cham: Springer.

Liu, Lydia H. (1995) *Translingual Practice: Literature, National Culture, and Translated Modernity —China, 1900–1937*. Stanford: Stanford University Press.

Lorimer, Douglas (1988) 'Theoretical Racism in Late-Victorian Anthropology, 1870–1900,' *Victorian Studies* 31 (3): 405–430.

Lü, Bicheng呂碧城 (2007 [1904]) 'Lun tichang nuxue zhi zongzhi 論提倡女學之宗旨 (On the Goal of the Promulgation of the Education of Women),' in *Lü Bicheng shiwen jianzhu* 呂碧城詩文箋注 *(Annotation on Lü Bicheng's Poetry and Prose)*. Ed. Li Baomin. Shanghai: Shanghai guji. 125–132.

Ma, Junwu 馬君武 (1957 [1919]) Trans. *Daerwen wuzhong yuanshi* 達爾文物種原始 *(Darwin's The Origin of Species)*. Taipei: Zhonghua shuju.

Mill, John Stuart (1869) *The Subjection of Women*. London: Longman, Greens, Reader and Dryer.

Pan, Kuang-che 潘光哲 (2014) *Wanqing shiren de xixue yuedu shi (1833–1898)* 晚清士人的西學閱讀史 *(The History of Late-Qing Intellectuals' Reading Western Knowledge)*. Taipei: Academia Sinica.

Pusey, James Reeve (1983) *China and Charles Darwin*. Cambridge: Harvard University Press.

Qing, Prince (Yi Kuang奕劻) (1996 [1898]) 'Zongli geguo shiwu yikuang deng zhe 總理各國事務奕劻等折 (The Memorial from the Institute for Foreign Affairs: Yi Kuang and Other Officials),' in *Zhongguo kexue fanyi shiliao*中國科學翻譯史料 *(The Historical Documents Concerning Chinese Translation of Science)*. Ed. Li Nanqiu. Hefei: University of Science and Technology of China Press. 75–77.

Rong, Zou 鄒容 (1983 [1903]) '*Geming jun* 革命軍 (Revolutionary Army),' in *Zourong Wenji* 鄒容文集 *(A Collection of Zou Rong's Works)*. Ed. Zhou Yonglin. Chongqing: Chongqing chuban she. 40–74.

Schwartz, Benjamin (1964) *In Search of Wealth and Power: Yen Fu and the West*. Harvard: Harvard University Press.

Shen, Sung-chiao 沈松橋 (2001) 'Woyi woxie jian xuanyuan: huangdi shenhua yu wanqing de guozu jiangou 我以我血薦軒轅: 皇帝神話與晚清的國族建構 (I Sacrifice My Blood to Yellow Emperor: The Myth of Yellow Emperor and the Construction of Nation in the late-Qing Period),' in *Xingbie zhengzhi yu jiti xintai* 性別、政治與集體心態 *(Gender, Politics and Collective Thought)*. Ed. Lu Jianrong 盧建榮. Taipei: Maitian. 286–321.

Spencer, Herbert (1874) *The Study of Sociology*. New York: Appleton.

Sun, Yat-sen 孫逸仙 (1905) 'Minbao fakan ci 民報發刊詞 (The Opening Announcement in the First Issue of *People's Newspaper*)'.

Sun, Yat-sen (1906) 'Sanmin zhuti yu zhongguo zhi qiantu 三民主義與中國民族之前途 (The Three Principles of the People and the Future of the Chinese Nation)' http://sunology.culture.tw/cgi-bin/gs32/s1gsweb.cgi?o=dcorpus&s=id=%22SP0000000586%22.&searchmode=basic

Sun, Yat-sen (1954 [1927]) *Sanmin zhuyi*三民主義 *(Three Principles of the People)*. Taipei: Zhengzhong.

Tsien, Tsuen-hsuin 錢存訓 (2009) *Dongxi wenhua jiaoliu luncong*東西文化交流論叢 *(Collection of Essays on the East-West Cultural Exchange)*. Beijing: Shangwu.

Tso, Sze-bong 曹仕邦 (1990) *Zhongguo fojiao yijing shi lunji*中國佛教譯經史論集 *(Collection of the Essays on the History of Translation in Chinese Buddhism)*. Taipei: Dongchu.

Tylor, Edward Burnett (1920) *Primitive Culture*. London: John Murray and Albemarle Street.

Wang, Fan-sen 王汎森 (2003) *Zhongguo jindai sixiang yu xueshu de xipu* 中國近代思想與學術的系譜 *(A Genealogy of Modern Chinese Thought and Scholarship)*. Taipei: Lianjing.

Wang, Quchang 王蘧常 (1977) *Yan jidao nianpu*嚴幾道年譜 *(The Chronology of Yan Fu's Life)*. Taipei: Shangwu.

Wo, Ren 倭仁 (2008 [1867]) '*Qingba tongwen guan yong zhengtu renyuan xi tiansuan zhe* 請罷同文館用正途人員習天算折 (A Petition to Prevent the Officials in the Tongwen Guan from Learning [Western] Arithmetical Astronomy),' in *Chouban yiwu shimo: Tongzhi chao* 籌辦夷務始末: 同治朝 *(The Management of Foreign Affairs during the Reign of Emperor Tongzhi)*. Ed. Bao Yun. Beijing: Zhonghua Shuju. 2009–2010.

Xu, Guoqi (2005) *China and the Great War: China's Pursuit of a New National Identity and Internationalization*. Cambridge: Cambridge University Press.

Yan, Qu 嚴璩 (1998) 'Xian fujun nianpu 先府君年譜 (The Chronological Biography of My Father),' in *Yanfu heji XVII: Houguan yanshi pingdian laozi* 嚴復合集 17: 侯官嚴氏評點老子 (The Collected Works of Yan Fu XVII: Commentary on *Lao Zi* by Mr. Yan of Houguan). Ed. Lin Tsai-Chueh. Taipei: Gugongliang wenjiao jijin hui. 1–18.

Yan, Fu 嚴復 (1998 [1895]) 'Yuanqing 原強 (On Strengthening),' in *Yanfu heji I: Yanfu wenji biannian yi* 嚴復合集1: 嚴復文集編年一 *(The Collected Works of Yan Fu I: The Chronological Collection of Yan Fu's Works I)*. Ed. Lin Tsai-Chueh. Taipei: Gugongliang wenjiao jijin hui. 34–47.

Yan, Fu (1998 [1899]) 'Yu zhang yuanji shu 與張元濟書 (A Letter to Zhang Yuanji),' in *Yanfu heji I: Yanfu wenji biannian yi* 嚴復合集1: 嚴復文集編年一 *(The Collected Works of Yan Fu I: The Chronological Collection of Yan Fu's Works I)*. Ed. Lin Tsai Chueh. Taipei: Gugongliang wenjiao jijin hui. 182–184.

Yan, Fu (1998 [1901]) *Yanfu heji VII: Tianyan lun huikan sanzhong* 嚴復合集7: 天演論匯刊三種 *(The Collected Works of Yan Fu VII: Three Versions of the Operation of Heaven)*. Taipei: Gugongliang wenjiao jijin hui. (Interpretative and creative translation of Thomas Huxley's *Evolution and Ethics*).

Yan, Fu (1998 [1902]) 'Yu liang qichao shu 與梁啟超書 (A Letter to Liang Qichao),' in *Yanfu heji I: Yanfu wenji biannian yi* 嚴復合集1: 嚴復文集編年一 *(The Collected Works of Yan Fu I: The Chronological Collection of Yan Fu's Works I)*.' Ed. Lin Tsai Chueh. Taipei: Gugongliang wenjiao jijin hui. 284–287.

Yan, Fu (1998 [1903]a) 'Qunxue yiyan yiyu zuiyu 《群學肄言》譯餘贅語 (Redundant Remarks after the Translation of *The Study of Sociology*),' in *Yanfu heji I: Yanfu wenji biannian yi* 嚴復合集1: 嚴復文集編年一 *(The Collected Works of Yan Fu I: The Chronological Collection of Yan Fu's Works I)*. Ed. Lin Tsai Chueh. Taipei: Gugongliang wenjiao jijin hui. 297–299.

Yan, Fu (1998 [1903]b) 'Jingshi daxue tang yishu ju zhangcheng 京師大學堂譯書局章程 (The Charter of the Institute for Translation in the Beijing Academy),' in *Yanfu heji I: Yanfu wenji biannian yi* 嚴復合集1: 嚴復文集編年一 *(The Collected Works of Yan Fu I: The Chronological Collection of Yan Fu's Works I)*. Ed. Lin Tsai Chueh. Taipei: Gugongliang wenjiao jijin hui. 300–305.

Yan, Fu (1998 [1903]c) *Yanfu heji X: Qunxue yiyan* 嚴復合集10: 群學肄言 *(The Collected Works of Yan Fu X: Remarks on the Study of the Group)*. Taipei: Gugongliang wenjiao jijinhui. (Interpretative and creative translation of Herbert Spencer's *The Study of Sociology*).

Yang, Jui-sung 楊瑞松 (2012) 'Dazao gongtong ti de xinchou jiuhen: zourong guozu lunshu zhong de "tazhe jiangou"' 打造共同體的新仇舊恨: 鄒容國論述中的「他者建構」 (The Construction of the Collective New Enemy and Old Hatred: "Othering" in Zou Rong's Discourse of the Chinese Nation),' *Guoli zhengzhi daxue lishi xuebao*. 37: 43–72.

Yuan, Wei 魏源 (1999 [1852]) *Haiguo Tuzhi* 海國圖志 *(Illustrated Treatise on the Maritime Kingdoms)*. Zhengzhou: Zhongzhou guji.

Zhang, Meiping 張美平 (2017) *Jingshi tongwen guan waiyu jiaoyu yanjiu* 京師同文館外語教育研究 *(The Education of Foreign Languages in Beijing Tongwen Institution of Translation)*. Hangzhou: Zhejiang University Press.

Zhang, Zhidong 張之洞 (1996 [1898]) *Ziqiang xuetang gaike wuguo fangyan zhe* 自強學堂改課五國方言折 (The Memorial Concerning the Teaching of Five Foreign Languages in the Self-Strengthening Academy),' in *Zhongguo kexue fanyi shiliao* 中國科學翻譯史料 *(The Historical Documents Concerning Chinese Translation of Science)*. Ed. Li Nanqiu. Hefei: University of Science and Technology of China Press. (79–80).

Zou, Zhenhuan 鄒振環 (2011) *Wanming hanwen xixue jingdian: bianyi quanshi liuchuan yu yingxiang* 晚明漢文西學經典·編譯、詮釋、流傳與影響 *(Chinese Translation of Western Canons in the late-Ming Period: Compilation, Translation, Interpretation, Distribution, and Influence)*. Shanghai: Fudan University Press.

Zou, Zhenhuan (2012) *Shutong zhiyi shi* 疏通知譯史 *(The History of Communication and Translation)*. Shanghai: Shanghai renmin chuban she.

28

'The pen is mightier than the sword'

Exploring the 'warrior' Lu Xun from 1903 to 1936

Min Gao

Introduction

Since the cultural turn of the 1990s, research on translators' agency has been a focus for scholars of translation studies. The translator's neutrality is questioned; the positive role of the translator is investigated in terms of 'rewriting,' 'manipulating,' and 'mediating.' Theorists such as Bassnett and Lefevere (1990), Lefevere (1992), Venuti (1995), and Hatim and Mason (1997) are among the early contributors to the discussion. In contemporary translation studies, the translator's active role is further explored, and key words like 'intervention,' 'resistance,' and 'activism' frequently appear in translation studies research (see, for example, Tymoczko (2002, 2010), Baker (2005, 2006), Boéri and Maier (2010)).

In this chapter, I discuss Chinese translator Lu Xun (Zhou Shuren, 1881–1936) and his roles as activist and leading literary figure in China's turbulent twentieth century. As both a writer and translator, Lu Xun believed that the translation of foreign literature into Chinese would help promote domestic social change (2014a: 6326). As a translator, Lu Xun used his pen as a 'sword,' beginning in the late Qing Dynasty (1840–1912), through the New Culture Movement (1915–1923),[1] and into the transition period to the New Democratic Revolution (1919–1949). For over thirty years, from the completion of his first translated work in 1903 to his last publication in 1936, Lu Xun translated 244 works by 110 writers. While primarily focusing on texts in German and Japanese, Lu Xun translated works by authors from Russia and the Soviet Union, Japan, England, the Czech Republic, France, Germany, Spain, Austria, Hungary, Romania, Bulgaria, the Netherlands, Poland, the United States, and Finland. As for translation from languages that he did not know, he employed what he called 'indirect translation.' Due to his tremendous literary contributions, Lu Xun has long garnered interest from academics both in China and abroad. Nevertheless, according to Luo (2007: 42), 'few [studies] have discussed Lu Xun's ideas on translation,' despite the fact that 'Lu Xun started and ended his literary career as a translator.' Recently, Wang (2016: 1) has argued that 'Lu Xun as a translator has not received a sufficient study that he deserved.' This chapter fills the gap by exploring Lu Xun's role as a translator amidst large-scale societal change, and in a context replete with political and ideological conflicts.

The cataclysms in the period of Lu Xun included the 1911 Revolution, the May Fourth Movement,[2] the Chinese Civil War fought between the Kuomintang (KMT: the Nationalist Party of China) and the Communist Party of China (CPC), and the Anti-Japan War. Both Lu Xun's writing and translation revealed his ideological shifts, which moved from anti-imperialism to antifeudalism and literary revolution, from social Darwinism to Marxism. This chapter distances Lu Xun's approach to translation from aesthetics that treat art as an end in itself. Over the long course of his literary endeavours, Lu Xun constantly positioned himself as an activist translator and revolutionary; his translations went beyond the text and became tools for resisting European imperialism, feudalism, and, later, the KMT regime. He carried through the notion of 'hard translation [*ying yi* 硬译]' to promote social and cultural reform, as well as to serve his political agenda.

This chapter uses Mona Baker's narrative theory to investigate how Lu Xun as translator uses translation as a means of resistance and positions himself as a revolutionary. First, I expound on Lu Xun's translation activities for resistance in different social contexts, such as the linguistic revolution and the first KMT–CPC civil war (1927–1937). Then, I establish his notion of 'hard translation' as a means of social activism and as a stimulus to revolution. Finally, I offer a few conclusions about Lu Xun and his translation work.

Lu Xun as an activist translator and revolutionary

Lu Xun's revolutionary translation activities can be divided into two. Part of his translational activism was dedicated to resistance to feudalism, imperialism, and the KMT regime, which opposed Marxism and insisted that China should take the capitalist road. The other part was developed by his concept of 'hard translation' for language reform, social change, and his political aspirations. In other words, Lu Xun's revolutionary interests are reflected both in his resistance to the old social system and foreign invasions on one hand, and his advocacy for building a democratic and later a socialist society on the other. As a chief contributor to the New Culture (*Xin wenhua yundong*) and May Fourth movements (*Wusi yundong*), along with intellectual revolution and socio-political reform in China between 1917 and 1921, Lu Xun's translation activities intended to awaken the Chinese nation to seek changes through a cultural revolution. As Wang (2014) notes, 'Chinese intellectuals waged the New Culture Movement, questioning the relevance and validity of the Confucian tradition while searching for new ideas from abroad.' Lu Xun's activities reflect Baker's findings that 'translators and interpreters can make use of various other routines that allow them to inject the discourse with their own voice (in other words to actively frame its narrative)' (Baker 2006: 110).

In his later years, Lu Xun emerged as a leader of the Progressive Writers League (*Zuoyi Zuojia Lianmeng*), an organisation whose advocation of Marxism challenged the KMT. Lu Xun translated Marxist works against the social backdrop of the conflict between the KMT and the CPC from 1926 to 1936. The civil war witnessed the KMT suppression of the communist movement with the aim of seizing political power across China. Lu Xun's translation of Marxist literary theory in this period can be perceived as his way of resisting the KMT as an activist translator and revolutionary. Furthermore, his notion of 'hard translation' illustrates his political stance through years of turmoil, defining his identity as a revolutionary, which is expounded in the latter half of this chapter.

Lu Xun did not often directly involve himself in the actual revolutionary movements. At the same time, he called himself a spiritual warrior (精神界之战士)—an activist during a tumultuous political period. As Chou (2012: 51) argues with reference to Lu

Xun, it is not only the battlefront that defines a fighter, but also their everyday life. Lu Xun's cutting of his pigtail in the early years, his use of fiction and poetry to awaken the Chinese, and his connections with young artists and writers during his last years are all part of his profile as a fighter (2012: 51).

Translation as resistance

This section divides Lu Xun's activities as an activist translator and revolutionary into three distinctive periods: 1903–1917, 1919–1926, and 1927–1936. Lu Xun's ideological development as a translator can be organised into these three periods. Lu Xun's translations during these years reveal different beliefs about the main task of the Chinese people and the proper direction for the nation.

1903–1917: Conflict, aggression, short stories/novels, social change, reform

Known colloquially as the 'late Qing and early Republic [*Qing mo Min chu*],' the period from 1903 to 1917 saw China's transition from the Qing Dynasty to the Republic of China. At the end of the nineteenth century, especially following its defeat in the First Sino-Japanese War (1894–1895) resisting Japan's invasion, China's progress towards semi-colonisation accelerated. According to the Treaty of Shimonoseki (1895), which ended the war, China made territorial concessions and paid indemnities to the Japanese Empire. Afterwards, other imperialist countries made aggressive moves against China. For example, France, Russia, and Germany successively built railways, and operated mines in China for profit. It could be said that the late Qing Dynasty, under the rule of its eleventh Emperor Guangxu, had been in the process of rapid decline since it seized power from the Ming Dynasty in 1644.

Against this backdrop, led by the Confucian scholars Kang Youwei and Liang Qichao, officials initiated the Hundred Days' Reform in 1898, which gained the support of the Guangxu Emperor. The movement aimed to save the nation from subjugation. However, it only lasted from 11 June 1898 to 21 September 1898 before ending in failure, and was opposed by the Queen Mother Ci Xi, who disapproved of the reformist efforts to change China's feudal system in particular. Reformists sought to learn from Europe by reforming China's political and educational systems and promoting scientific and cultural development. The Queen Mother Ci Xi (1835–1908), a representative of the conservatives, staged a coup in 1898 to stop the reform. As a result, the Guangxu Emperor was taken captive and the initiators of the reform were either beheaded or forced to flee abroad to escape persecution.

Although the reform movement ended in vain, the Qing government continued to send students abroad to study in Europe, the United States, and Japan, a practice reflected in the Self-strengthening Movement (1861–1895) that aimed to achieve economic, educational, and military reform by learning from European methods and technology. Due to its closeness to China, Japan was an ideal destination for Qing students to study at comparatively low cost. This was especially the case after the Meiji Restoration in 1868, when the revolution dissolved Japan's feudal system of government and returned power to imperial rule under the Meiji Emperor. The success of the Meiji Restoration and rapid development reinforced the image of Japan as an ideal destination where one could learn how to incorporate European methods to rise as a global power.

Lu Xun arrived in Japan in 1902 to study medicine as a member of a group of students supported financially by the Qing government.

In the same year, Liang Qichao, a social activist, who moved to Japan to escape persecution after the failure of the 1898 reforms, started the magazine *Xin xiaoshuo* (*New Novel*). In the initial issue, Liang wrote his article 'Lun Xiaoshuo Yu Qunzhi Zhi Guanxi [On the relationship between novels and the control of the masses].' According to Liang, novels have great power for promoting social change. He argued that 'Political reform starts from new novels [*Yu xin zhengzhi, bi xin xiaoshuo*]' due to 'their immense power for governing the masses [*Xiaoshuo you bukesiyi zhili zhipei rendao gu*]' (Liang 1992: 3).

Lu Xun shared Liang's views. He was a loyal reader of *Xin xiaoshuo*, which introduced Victor Hugo to a Chinese readership by publishing translations of works such as *Bug-Jargal* and *Les Misérables*. It was from reading *Xin xiaoshuo* that Lu Xun developed an interest in Hugo's works and decided to translate Hugo into Chinese in order to influence Chinese readers by using the power of the novel. Lu Xun embarked on his translation career, internalising Liang's belief in the power of literature to bring about revolution. He began to read and translate Victor Hugo and other authors engaged in struggle, resistance, and revolution. In his first translation, '*Ai chen* [Mourning Dust],' Lu Xun indirectly translated the Japanese version of Hugo's 'Origine de Fantine.' Lu Xun readily acknowledged his reliance on the Japanese version and wrote two articles advocating the necessity and advantages of indirect translation (Lu Xun 2006a, 2006b).

'Origine de Fantine' was a short story written by Victor Hugo in 1841 based on his own experience. It was originally included in *Choses Vue* (Things Seen), published in 1887. Later, Hugo developed the story, on the basis of which he published his masterpiece *Les Misérables* in 1862, with *Fantine* as the first volume. The 'Origine de Fantine' was about a poor woman who was unfairly treated by police officers after she became involved in a fight with a rich young man. In spite of her innocence, the police arrested the woman and imprisoned her for six months. The translation of 'Origine de Fantine' into *Ai chen* served the function identified by Baker (2006: 129), who writes of how 'titles of textual and visual products such as novels, films, and academic books' that 'are not normally part of a rival system in which they compete [with] each other [...] can be used effectively to (re)frame narratives in translation.' '*Ai* [mourning]' is associated with 'sadness' in Chinese while '*chen* [dust]' signifies 'insignificance' and 'lowliness.' The title alone helped rebuild the protagonist in the story, a fragile image with a miserable fate, echoing the contemporaneous image of China trampled by imperialist powers. In spite of the weak image of the protagonist faced with a young man, she struck him back with a snowball right after she was bullied. Later, when the police side with the young man, the woman appears to be even more overpowered, confronted as she is with a group of strong men. However, even under such circumstances, 'the unfortunate woman [nonetheless] struggled with them' (Hugo 2009: 44). She shouted and defended herself throughout the conflict. Through the translation, Lu Xun tried to awaken the Chinese people to the fact that the only way to escape from destruction was to stand up and resist Tsarist Russia's refusal to withdraw troops from northeast China.

In 1903, Lu Xun indirectly translated another story from Japanese—'Si ba da zhi hun [The Ghost of Sparta]' (Lu Xun 1903a, 1903b). The author of this story is unknown. Lu Xun wrote in the preface of his work *Ji Wai Ji* that he could not recollect the source of *The Ghost of Sparta* even though he exerted himself to do so (2002a: 474). Japanese researcher Tarumoto Teruo has argued that Lu Xun probably translated from the stories of *The Histories* written by Herodotus in 440 BCE, originally in ancient Greek (2001: 38). Lu Xun used an adaptive translation method by mixing and translating from several sources. Lu Xun's translation described how 300 Spartan soldiers, led by King Leonidas of Sparta, fought with Persian invaders. Lu Xun regarded it as a glorious defeat and praised the 'Spirit of Sparta,' which he deemed as 'the best medicine that China needs' (Huang 2012: 46).

The Ghost of Sparta was published during Russia's invasion of northeastern China and its demands for the Qing government to cede territory. Russian actions triggered fervent protests among Chinese students in Japan. They called on the Qing government to resist on 29 April 1903 'with a letter briefly quoting the story of the "Ghost of Sparta"' (Huang 2012: 46). Later in June, Lu Xun translated the same story of *The Ghost of Sparta* as well as *Ai Chen* and published them in the same issue of the journal *Zhejiang Tide* (*Zhe Jiang Chao*). Lu Xun's translation of this story's framed narratives uses what Baker calls 'temporal and spatial framing' (Baker 2006: 112). This involves the selection of a particular text (source narrative), embedded from a different temporal and spatial framework. Such narratives are then highlighted and connected with contemporary narratives. In other words, the narrator uses source narratives to accentuate similar circumstances in contemporary narratives. Through such temporal and spatial framing, Lu Xun associated the narratives of resisting invaders in the source text with China's situation. In the preface to *Ji Wai Ji*, he noted that he translated *The Ghost of Sparta* in order to encourage a military spirit among his Chinese readers (Lu Xun 2002a: 474). Therefore, the translation served to introduce similar narratives of resistance within a larger anti-imperialist framework.

The translation of *Yu wai xiao shuo ji* (A Collection of the Foreign Stories) (1909), completed in collaboration with his brother Zhou Zuoren,[3] fulfilled a similar function. According to comments on the volume's contents by Zhou (2012: 249), three of the translated stories were originally from the UK, US, and France, seven were from Russia, one was from Poland, and two were from Bosnia. This selection illustrates their focus on translating Slavic works and the literature of oppressed nations. The translation of works from oppressed nations generated proximity between translation and readers, or what Baker calls 'the repositioning of participants' (Baker 2006: 132). As individuals (participants) who are embedded in constructing the various narratives, 'none of us is in a position to stand outside any narratives' (Baker 2006: 5). Through the translation of Lu Xun, when readers or the audience were led to interact with the source narratives (constructed by the participants/fictional characters), they may 'become potential participants in movement actions' (Cunningham and Browning 2004: 348). In short, the depiction of the source text and participants helped socially contextualise a similar narrative for participants during Lu Xun's time. Lu Xun's own words confirm this: 'I want to use the novel to change society ... my focus is not on writing, but introducing or translating, especially those works from the oppressed nations' (Lu Xun 2005: 71).

Noteworthily, although Russia was not considered to be among the oppressed nations, Lu Xun thought 'Chinese literature [could] learn something from Russian literature, learn the kind soul of the oppressed ... and understand there are two kinds of people in the world: the oppressor and the oppressed' (Lu Xun 2014b: 2502). Hence, Russian works are also included in forming his narrative of resistance. After all, 'the Russian opposition movement [reflected in Russian literature] became best known by the method of resistance' (Gamsa 2008: 18). Accordingly, translations of Russian literature, as 'instructions for action,' have the end result of the successful achievement of a political or military target (Gamsa 2010: 101). In *Yu wai xiao shuo ji* (A Collection of the Foreign Stories), Lu Xun translated from the German version of three Russian works, including 'Hypocrisy [*man*]' and 'Silence [*mo*],' written by Leonid Andreev, and 'Four Days [*siri*],' by Vsevolod Mikhailovich Garshin.

The 1917 Russian Revolution had a great impact on China in general, and on Lu Xun in particular, as an activist translator and revolutionary. The two revolutions in Russia respectively broke out in February and October of 1917, when the imperial government was overthrown and the Bolsheviks seized power, leading to the formation of the Soviet Union. Lu Xun welcomed the Russian Revolution, calling it 'a tempest that howled and engulfed anything that is decayed' (Lu Xun 2002b: 443). He believed in the power of revolution and rebellion as well as the changes they brought about. It is probably for this reason that Lu Xun favoured Russian works reflecting resistance and advocating for revolution.

During his first period of translational activism, from 1903 to 1917, Lu Xun also attributed great importance to the translation of science fiction, thinking that science would help enlighten the ordinary people of China to get rid of their ignorance. He hoped that science would '[help] China become powerful enough to escape from aggression' (Huang 2012: 48). With this expectation, he translated two books by the French writer Jules Verne, indirectly from Japanese. The first book, *Yue jie lü xing* (*Voyage to the Moon*) (1903) was translated from *De la terre à la lune*, and the second book, *Di xin you ji* (*Voyage to the Centre of the Earth*) (1903) was translated from *Voyage au centre de la terre*.

When he translated these two works of science fiction, Lu Xun made significant additions and deletions, for reasons that are justified by his adapted translational method. According to Baker (2006: 114), 'selective appropriation of textual material [aims to] suppress, accentuate, or elaborate particular aspects of a narrative encoded in the source text or utterance, or aspects of the larger narrative(s) in which it is embedded' by means of frequent addition and deletion. Lu Xun's selective translation of works from oppressed nations, as well as from science fiction, accentuates a larger narrative of standing up to resist invaders and promoting anti-imperialist actions through frequent addition and deletion, which highlights the theme of resistance. The appropriation of the plots or functions in the translated works helps establish a connection between these works and what happened in the political sphere. His frequent use of adapted translation through omission or addition further facilitates the framing of the master narrative: resistance.

1919–1926: New Culture Movement, antifeudalism, enlightenment, revolution

In 1910, the bank consortium of the UK, US, France, and Germany forced the Qing government to sign a treaty, in accordance with which the Qing government had to borrow a large amount of money from the banks to construct two railways in China. In this way, the four countries attempted to take ownership of the Chinese railways away from Chinese shareholders, including landowners, merchants, landlords, and farmers. This led to the 'Railway Protection Movement' in June 1911, when the working class launched a series of rebellions against the Qing government. In 1911, the Xinhai Revolution successfully overthrew the feudal system that had governed China for over 2,000 years. Following the failure of the revolution to establish a republican government, the New Culture Movement (1915–1923) emerged to continue the struggle against feudalism by learning from Europe.

Lu Xun actively involved himself in the movement. He was one of the chief contributors to *New Youth* (*Xin Qingnian*), an influential magazine founded by the revolutionary socialist Chen Duxiu in 1915 to publicise science, democracy, and new literature. *New Youth* initiated the New Culture Movement to attack traditional Confucian thought as well as classical Chinese. The movement promoted the use of vernacular Chinese. 'To tear down the iron house [of feudalism] that suffocated the people within,' Lu Xun started to write for *New Youth* (Lu Xun 2014c: 320–321). In 1918, Lu Xun published the first short story written in vernacular in modern Chinese literary history: 'Diary of a Madman,' to 'attack the culture and history of feudalism' (Zhang 2010: 153). During this period, Lu Xun's translational activities reveal a desire for 'enlightenment,' reflecting the sufferings and resistance of his fictional protagonists (Lu Xun 2014d: 2553).

Take his translation of *Worker Shevyrev* (*gongren suihui lüefu*) (1909): Lu Xun once commented on the protagonist Shevyrev that 'taking bombs and guns with all his strength and will, he [Shevyrev] plunged himself into the war, to resist till death' (Lu Xun 2002c: 192). Lu Xun's translation reflects 'the general predicament of reformers, and of those taking upon themselves the task of acting or speaking for the people' (Gamsa 2008: 157). Lu Xun translated this novel in 1921, in the midst of the New Culture Movement, to serve his political agenda of enlightening and awakening the masses to resist feudal rule.

Lu Xun's translation of Artsybashev's 'Schast'e' (Happiness, 1907) also revealed his hope for enlightening the public through his depiction of the story's protagonists, who were easily divided into the oppressor and the oppressed. In the Chinese translation of the short story, entitled '*Xingfu*' [happiness] and published in 1920, Lu Xun depicted a scene between a prostitute named Sashka and a man. Out of survival instinct on a cold winter's night, Sashka accepts a male passerby's offer of five roubles on the condition that she receives ten blows from his cane while standing naked outside. While, on the one hand, this novel reflects the suffering of the female Russian protagonist, the depiction of the miserable fate of the prostitute indirectly attacked an occupation regarded as legitimate within tradition Chinese society: prostitution. This was in line with one of the tasks of the New Culture Movement: to abolish prostitution and fight for liberty, equality, and natural rights. Social activists like Li Dazhao and Wang Shunu deemed prostitution as a form of exploitation that deprived women of their human rights, symbolising the inequality between men and women, and as a holdover from the harmful marriage system of the old feudal society (Yin 2005: 97–98).

In this period, Lu Xun translated with the same goal as in the latter part of his initial translation phase: he deemed changing the thinking of the Chinese people through novels and short stories to be his top priority. Again, Baker's concepts of 'temporal and spatial framing' and 'repositioning of participants' also help explain Lu Xun's selection of works for translation in this period. He hoped that the Chinese people could recognise their own sufferings in the works he translated, and thereby achieve enlightenment through reading his translations. After Russia's October Revolution of 1917, Lu Xun began to translate more Russian literary works, particularly proletarian literature, in the hope that they would inspire the Chinese people.

1927–1936: Civil war, Marxism, proletarian literature

From 1924, the KMT and CPC initiated the National Revolution (1924–1927) by forming a united frontline, under the leadership of which the Chinese people pursued an anti-imperialist and antifeudalist agenda. However, the nationwide success of the revolutions violated the interests of the imperialist countries in China, especially Japan, UK, and the US. In April 1927, supported by the imperialist powers, Jiang Jieshi, the leader of the KMT, launched an anti-revolutionary coup in Shanghai to consolidate the absolute leadership of the KMT and maintain its military dictatorship. The coup was mainly targeted at the CPC. In such circumstances, the collaboration between the two parties fell apart. After the anti-revolutionary coup of 12 April 1927, the KMT government was established at Nanjing. In December of the same year, General Zhang Xueliang, who had governed northeast China, declared that he had joined the KMT camp under the leadership of Jiang Jieshi. So far, the KMT government united China in general. It established its regime across the country and started to further suppress the CPC by persecuting its members.

Thus, the KMT–CPC civil war began in 1927. Having experienced the counter-revolutionary coup which involved mass slaughter and the persecution of leftist activists, Lu Xun underwent substantial ideological changes. His beliefs shifted from Darwinism to the form of Marxism advocated by the CPC (Ren 1982: 47).

Due to the ideological differences between the KMT and CPC as to what kind of path—capitalist or socialist—China should take, Lu Xun translated to declare his support for the CPC and to guide its struggle with the KMT. During this period, Lu Xun developed the idea of making use of literature to serve the CPC's struggle with the KMT, commonly identified as revolutionary literature, visible in his translation activities. Gamsa notes that 'Lu Xun's impressive translation output from mid-1928 to 1932, shows a decisive turn: first towards Russian Marxist theoreticians, then to the new Soviet literature' (Gamsa 2008: 186). He translated large amounts of Soviet literary theory, including Anatoly Lunacharsky and Georgy Plekhanov, from published Japanese translations (Davies 2013: 109). Such translations belonged to the corpus of proletarian literature, defined as 'literary writing by or about working-class people with anticapitalist or prosocialist themes' (Mullen 2013) that was affiliated with the CPC.

Lu Xun's selective translation and promotion of proletarian literary works frame a narrative to support the CPC against the KMT. Representative translations of Lu Xun in this respect include *Yishulun* (On Literature and Art) (1929), *Wenyi Yu Piping* (Literary Criticism) (1929), *Wuchanjiejiwenxue De Lilun Yu Shiji* (The Theory and Practice of Proletarian Literature) (1929), and *Wenyi Zhengce* (Literature and Art Policy) (1930). Furthermore, Lu Xun crafted Chinese-language versions of literary works from the Soviet Union by translating from Japanese. Two representative translated works were the novel *Shiyue* (October), written by Alexander Iakovlev, as well as Fadeev's novel *Huimie* (Rout). Even on his death bed in 1936, Lu Xun continued to indirectly translate from the German version of *Dead Souls*, written by the Russian writer Nikolai Gogol (Wu and Lian 2014: 22). Likening his translation of revolutionary literature to Prometheus stealing the fire from the peak of Mount Elbrus (Lu Xun 2014e: 2064), Lu Xun thought that Soviet literature could shed light on the road that China should follow in its path towards revolution.

Moreover, situated within the social context of KMT–CPC strife, Lu Xun's translation and promotion of Soviet proletarian literary works framed a narrative to uphold the political beliefs of the CPC. As Baker (2006: 20) has noted, 'the awareness that every acceptance of a narrative involves a rejection of others makes the issue politically and personally vital. In a critical sense the differences among competing narratives give all of them their meanings.' More specifically, the ideological differences between the CPC and KMT placed them in two opposing camps, which were associated with two opposing narratives. The CPC represented the proletariats while the KMT represented the capitalist class. This contrast in narratives generated the following question: should China take a socialist road led by the CPC or a capitalist path led by the KMT?

Lu Xun selected for translation proletarian literary works and Marxist theories as part of his effort to side with the CPC and reject the counternarrative from the opposing party, the KMT. In his view, only through a proletarian revolution could China find a way out of its dire situation. This was reflected in his two articles about the proletarian literature in China (Lu Xun 2014i, j). He also joined the Progressive Writers League (左翼作家联盟) in order to publicise proletarian revolutionary literature. In short, Lu Xun positioned himself as an activist translator and revolutionary against the KMT and opposed its political ideology for leading China towards capitalism.

'Hard translation' as activism and revolution

The above section illustrates how Lu Xun's ideology evolved in different social contexts. These changes influenced his selection of works to translate for promoting social change and delineating his political stance. In the following section, I further explore how Lu Xun's notion of 'hard translation [yingyi]' embodied his socio-political engagement and defined him as an activist translator and revolutionary.

In early 1929, Lu Xun first put forward the term 'hard translation.' According to Lu Xun, 'hard translation' is the only choice in his translation of Lunarcharsky's works due to the translator's inadequacy and the limitations of the Chinese language (Lu Xun 2002d: 215). On the one hand, it is commonly assumed that 'hard translation' is a key way of retaining 'the flavour of the source language in the target language in both form and content' (Luo 2007: 43), or of assigning 'equal importance on the semantic and syntactic properties of the [original] text' (Davies 2013: viii). On the other hand, Lu Xun's 'hard translation' contains different voices. Some scholars have argued that the concept of fidelity in his 'hard translation' places more emphasis on the level of grammar rather than on the content of the original (Xia 2009: 65). Nevertheless, others have questioned the possibility of producing the same content because most of Lu Xun's translations are indirect translations from intermediate languages (Gould 2018: 202; Wang 2013: 325).

Although Lu Xun did not coin the term until 1929, the 'hard translation' approach permeated his translation activities beginning with the translation of *Yu wai xiao shuo ji* (Stories from Abroad) in 1909. The work marked a watershed for Lu Xun's translation methodology as it shifted from *gaiyi* (rewriting) to *bianyi* (adapted translation) to 'hard translation.' In other words, the translator changed his approach from large amounts of rewriting, copious additions and deletions, to word-to-word translation and increased faithfulness to the source text. During the New Culture Movement, Lu Xun further developed the notion when promoting the use of vernacular Chinese to replace classical Chinese in translation. According to the authoritative Xinhua Dictionary (*xinhuazidian*) (Han 2009: 24), vernacular Chinese (*baihua*) by definition was the written language of the Mandarin Chinese. It was developed based on the Mandarin spoken in North China since the Tang and Song Dynasties (618–907 CE and 960–1279 CE respectively). Before the New Culture Movement, however, Chinese prose was written in classical Chinese. In feudal China, it had limited use among the literati and officialdom, and was inaccessible to the masses who could not afford the time and expense required to learn this extremely difficult language (Lu Xun 2014f: 3152). In short, it could be said that classical Chinese was the symbol of the elite, while vernacular Chinese represented the lower class.

After the autocratic monarchy system was overthrown in 1911 by the Xinhai Revolution, the New Culture Movement called for replacing classical Chinese with vernacular Chinese. A group of scholars who had studied abroad initiated the language reform, and advocated for the use of written vernacular Chinese. The main contributors were scholars like Hu Shi, Lu Xun, and Chen Duxiu. Their promotion of vernacular Chinese aimed to facilitate the dissemination of European concepts of science and democracy among the masses through the medium of simple language forms. As one of the pioneers in the linguistic revolution, Lu Xun published the first short story written in vernacular Chinese, 'Diary of a Madman' (1918). Later, in his translation of Marxist-Soviet literary criticism beginning in 1929, the development of 'hard translation' peaked, triggering a heated debate with radicals from the Crescent Moon Society,[4] such as Liang Shiqiu and Zhao Jingshen, who claimed that art should be regarded as an end in itself.

The use of 'hard translation' in vernacular Chinese signified the dual aim of this methodology: to promote language reform and to resist feudal culture. By introducing new vocabulary like *zixuzhuan* (autobiography), as well as punctuation marks that were previously non-existent in Chinese, Lu Xun aimed to enrich the new vernacular Chinese language. For Lu Xun, the ultimate objective was to empower the Chinese people to use accurate expressions that were consistent with oral speech. In his view, Chinese people's way of speaking would also benefit from improvement of written Chinese since speech and writing would be brought into greater proximity. Language reform alone, however, could not suffice to achieve this goal. Lu Xun also 'kept harping on the importance of importing ideas from "foreign countries" because Chinese ones were no good' (Sun 1986: 479). According to Lu Xun (2014g: 2198–2199), 'hard translation' must 'use the correct form of vernacular Chinese.'

In essence, language reform through 'hard translation' is tantamount to what Lawrence Venuti termed resistant translation (through 'foreignisation'). Although it differs from Venuti's paradigm in certain respects, the function is similar. Myskja (2013: 6) develops Venuti's concept of domestication and foreignisation by arguing that domestication tends to maintain the structures of the target texts while foreignisation may potentially revise them. Venuti's concept of resistance is pertinent to postcolonial studies to the extent that it enables us to use translation to resist cultural hegemony. It is an outward and intercultural resistance developed by the peripheral culture against the dominant one. According to Venuti (1998: 88), English has been the most translated language but one of the least translated into since the World War II. This asymmetry ensures that the United States and United Kingdom enjoy a hegemony over other foreign countries, politically and economically, as well as culturally. By the same token, colonisers often make use of translation to maintain their ideologies pertaining to the colonised, thus establishing a hierarchical relationship with the latter.

Within colonised countries, translators can act provocatively to revise the dominant values of the hegemonic others in order to resist cultural hegemony. In other words, there exists a bidirectional relationship of assimilation and anti-assimilation between the colonisers and the colonised by way of translation. The case is different in the New Culture Movement, in which context hegemonic Anglo-American values were reinforced in China rather than resisted by Chinese reformers of an earlier generation, most of whom had studied abroad in Europe, the US, or Japan. They advocated the assimilation of dominant values from imperialist cultures. The reformist assimilation went one step further when it was used by the peripheral ideology in China to resist the dominant (hegemonic and feudal) ideologies within the same cultural system. In this complex cultural context, resistance through Lu Xun's 'hard translation' constitutes an intra-cultural resistance from the new vernacular Chinese to classical Chinese and to the class-based oppression intrinsic to the feudal system.

Through introducing the vocabularies as well as values from the hegemonic cultures, Lu Xun and other initiators aimed to subvert the dominant domestic ideologies. On the one hand, the replacement of classical Chinese with vernacular Chinese breaks the hierarchy of power that structured the feudal system since the classical Chinese differentiated the elite class from the ordinary people. On the other hand, the substitution of the classical Chinese by the vernacular opened up Chinese culture and facilitated the dissemination of European ideas within China. In this way, Lu Xun's 'hard translation' framed a narrative for combating social inequality and class-based exploitation while promoting values like equality, liberty, and democracy. In short, resistance and revolution through 'hard translation' or 'foreignisation' take many different forms, and vary according to the political contexts and histories of the literatures and languages under discussion. 'Hard translation' exists between both a dominant culture vis-à-vis a peripheral culture, and within a single cultural system between marginal and mainstream ideologies.

Ultimately, Lu Xun's aspiration for 'hard translation' reached far beyond language reform. Lu Xun tried to make use of 'hard translation' in hopes of remoulding what he regarded as the muddled thinking of the Chinese people. Corresponding with his close friend Qu Qiubai, who opposed 'hard translation' and instead aimed to produce a smoothly readable translation in the target language, Lu Xun attributed the masses' muddled way of thinking, which he regarded as illogical, to imprecision within the Chinese language. Consequently, he deemed language reform the only way to cure the malaise. As Davies perceives, vernacular Chinese was 'conceived first and foremost as an instrument of nation-building' (2013: 9). Hence, by rooting his 'hard translation' in the New Culture Movement, Lu Xun's 'final purpose was to reform the semi-feudal and semi-colonial society of China and cure the mentality of his people' (Luo 2007: 49). By embracing cultural enlightenment and new language and throwing off the constraints 'that held back people's minds' by importing 'cultural others' (Xia 2009: 63–64) through 'hard translation,' Lu Xun positioned all the members of Chinese society—and most notably the masses—within the narrative for pursuing a democratic society. That is also one of the aims of the New Culture Movement.

The third period of his career as a translator is displayed more evidently in Lu Xun's engagement in the political arena, when his concept of 'hard translation' initiated a long-drawn-out debate with 'radical leftist writers' (Wang 2013: 324). Lu Xun's most representative statement can be found in correspondence with his critic Liang Shiqiu in 1930. In one letter, entitled '"Hard translation" and the "class character of literature",' Lu Xun insisted on the impossibility for writers and translators of escaping from the ideological restraints associated with their respective classes. He wrote:

> Literature has a class nature. In class society, literary writers think they can transcend their own class ideologies. However, the fact is that they are dominated by their class ideology. Their writings, correspondingly, do not reflect the culture of other classes.
>
> *(Lu Xun 2014e: 2058)*

In other words, translators are agents of their class and disseminate classist ideology to the public through literature. Their literary writings are bound by their class ideology to serve the class they represent. Thus, these utterances form a narrative, which, as Baker might argue (2006: 132), put Lu Xun 'in certain ideological positions.' This is further revealed through the justifications he provides for 'hard translation' as a translational method linked to activism and revolution.

In discussing 'hard translation,' Lu Xun distinguished two opposed groups of readers: critics who read proletarian literature for sheer enjoyment vis-à-vis those who strive to understand proletarian literary theory. In '"Hard translation" and the "class character of literature",' Lu Xun revealed his views on the intended readership of his articles. On the one hand, Lu stated that '我的译作, 本不在博读者的"爽快", 却往往给以不舒服, 甚而至于使人气闷, 憎恶, 愤恨' (My translation is not for readers' enjoyment. Rather, it often discomforts them, generating a feeling of suffocation, abhorrence and resentment)[5] (Lu Xun 2014e: 2046). On the other hand, he claimed,

> 究竟为什么而译的呢? …我的回答, 是: 为了我自己, 和几个以无产文学批评家自居的人, 和一部分不图'爽快', 不怕艰难, 多少要明白一些这理论的读者 (I translated for myself, for several self-proclaimed proletarian literary critics, and those who are willing to exert their efforts to understand these theories rather than for enjoyment).
>
> *(Lu Xun 2014e: 2063)*

For Lu Xun, the incompatible groups of readers follow two competing narratives, which are mutually incommensurable. He denounces one group in order to justify his support for the other. Lu Xun argues that it is not his approach of 'hard translation' but the laziness and muddled mind (Lu Xun 2014e: 2051) of the accusers that bears responsibility for their failure to understand proletarian literature. By criticising literary critics who read proletarian literature for pleasure and in order to achieve 'a quick and undeserved fame for themselves' (Davies 2013: 138), Lu Xun positioned himself with the camp seeking to understand proletarian literary theory for the good of China's future.

By means of 'hard translation,' Lu Xun facilitated the introduction of a precise and original proletarian literary theory, rather than its readability. Differing translation requirements created a conflict between revolutionaries and their opponents. As one of the main contributors from the Progressive Writers League, Lu Xun thought that literature served the ideology of a class. Art for politics' sake is his conviction. Therefore, he advocated for the introduction of proletarian literary theories and Marxist theories through 'hard translation.' To ensure accessibility to the original theories, Lu Xun put faithfulness at the top of other criteria, even at the cost of fluency. By contrast, his rivals from the Crescent Moon Society claimed that literature had no class nature. They were committed to a concept of art for the sake of art alone. Liang Shiqiu, one of Lu Xun's chief opponents, argued that 'art is the voice uttered deep from the heart of a writer. It is therefore narrow and superficial to deem that literature is bound by the ideology of a class' (Liang 1996a: 591). With this belief, members from the Crescent Moon Society claimed that fluency and readability were the most important aspects of a successful translation. Zhao Jingshen, another main opponent of Lu Xun, even argued that it was better 'to be smooth than faithful' (Lu Xun 2014g: 2199); he was proposing an inversion of Lu Xun's dictum, 'rather to be faithful than smooth' (Lu Xun 2014h: 2215). Lu Xun's notion of 'hard translation' was criticised by such rivals as 'dead translation' (Liang 1996b: 598–599).

The KMT–CPC conflict is a microcosm of a larger narrative. While the critics from the Crescent Moon Society flirt 'with the Nationalist Party' (Wang 2013: 326), Lu Xun's opposition to these critics positioned him in the political camp of the CPC. Since 1927, Lu Xun 'allied himself with the Communist Party,' (Chou 2012: 15) for 'promoting the left-wing cause and the advent of a "proletarian literature" [until his death]' (Cheng 2013:169).

Translators as revolutionary activists

As I have shown, Lu Xun's translations reveal that activist translators can be defined by both their extra-textual involvement (the selection of works to translate, his joining the Progressive Writers' League, debate with opponents) and intra-textual manipulation (through 'hard translation,' the use of vernacular Chinese in substitution for classical Chinese in translation, and the translation of proletarian literary theories). Going further, one may search activist roles within the field of translation studies. The *Oxford English Dictionary* (Simpson and Weiner 1989) defines 'activist' as 'a person engaged in or advocating vigorous political activity; an active campaigner.' 'Activist' refers to someone who acts vigorously to cause social or political changes. According to Tymoczko (2010: viii), an 'activist cannot simply oppose or resist social and political constraints: they must also be able to initiate action, change direction, construct new goals, articulate new values, [and] seek new paths.'

When associated with translators, 'activist' highlights the active role in shaping society or making changes. It may accentuate the translator's agency, as advocated by numerous theorists in translation studies, including, among others, Venuti (1995, 1998), Bassnett and Bush (2006), and Baker (2006). The translator's agency is not only demonstrated through the linguistic manipulation of the text. Rather, translators use their work as tools and go beyond the text to influence readers, to 'promote peace,' 'fuel conflicts,' or even 'subjugate entire populations,' as Baker (2005: 4) argues.

The translator's agency or activism can take the form of an ideological defence for or subversion of adversaries. According to Lefevere (1992: vii), rewriting associates translation with power relations and ideology: 'Translation is, of course, a rewriting of an original text. All rewritings, whatever their intention, reflect a certain ideology and a poetics and as such manipulate literature to function in a given society in a given way.' Chen (2014: 66), however, argues that Lefevere's theory of rewriting 'did not adequately account for the interactive relationship between ideology and translation as well as how ideology functions during translation.' Furthermore, Chen contends that the translator's ideological position has long been neglected and research on the translator's agency merits more discussion. In contemporary translation studies, scholars increasingly agree that translators do more than reflect ideology through translation; they make use of translation to transform ideology.

The translator's activism also manifests itself in resisting cultural hegemony. Venuti (1995) first proposed using 'foreignisation' in translation for resisting Eurocentrism, cultural narcissism, and imperialism. Tymoczko (2010: vii) noted that 'Venuti's writing on translation as a mode of resistance and his calls for action addressed to translators were central in motivating discourses about translation, ethics, ideology, and agency in translation studies.' Moreover, translators actively participate in promoting social changes, as evidenced by the case of Lu Xun as an activist translator. Mona Baker argues that translators should make their voices heard and actively participate in 'creating, negotiating, and contesting social reality' (Baker 2006: 105). Objecting to the long-held neutrality of translators, Baker states that 'whether professional translators or scholars, we do not build bridges nor bridge gaps. We participate in decisive ways for promoting and circulating narratives and discourses of various types' (Baker 2005: 12). By the same token, Tymoczko denies the impossibility of the translator's position 'in between' (Tymoczko 2002: 197). She argues that translators can be activist agents of social change. Her viewpoint regarding the function of translation indirectly reveals her position: 'In peace as in war, translation always has an […] activist edge, that it is driven by ethical and ideological concerns, and it participates in shaping societies, nations, and global culture in primary ways' (2010: 19–20).

During the past two decades, multiple books have dealt with the theme of translation and activism (Baker 2006; Tymoczko 2010; Baer and Kaindl 2017). The First International Forum on Translation/Interpreting and Social Activism held in the University of Granada, Spain in 2007 expanded further on the concept of activist translator. In the forum, scholars proposed that translators can influence practice, by for example 'refus[ing] to interpret in wars of occupation' (Boéri and Maier 2010: 1). The collected volume resulting from this event, edited by Boéri and Maier (2010), explores issues pertinent to the relationship between translation and social activism. It argues that translation should be regarded as a tool for both resistance and dominance. This understanding should be disseminated not only in academic circles but also 'in the field of political engagement and social action' (2010: 1). The volume effectively shows that 'many translators are political and social activists playing a role in these [political and social] struggles' (Skrandies 2012: 230). The forum called for the establishment of a community of activist translators and interpreters and to use translation as a driving force for change (Boéri and Maier 2010: 3).

Lu Xun anticipated these developments by nearly a century. Stylistically and politically, he pioneered the path of a translator who could effect social change. Through translation, 'hard translation' in particular, Lu Xun became involved in anti-imperialist and anti-feudalist causes and promoted linguistic revolution. In his final years, Lu Xun translated proletarian literary theories and Marxist theoretical writings to combat the KMT regime and its ideology. Taken together, these activities defined him as a revolutionary activist.

Conclusion

This chapter has delved into Lu Xun's translational activities while focusing in particular on his notion of 'hard translation.' In order to clarify how we can understand Lu Xun as an activist translator and revolutionary, I have divided Lu Xun's translation activities into three distinctive periods, highlighting his translation works in each period according to the forms of resistance that dominated each period. To investigate how Lu Xun framed his translation narratives to uphold his ideological beliefs, I have used the narrative theory of Baker (2006) in my analysis of Lu Xun's involvement as an activist translator. I scrutinised Lu Xun's concept of 'hard translation' to reveal his socio-political engagement and his political stance during the KMT–CPC conflict that spanned the last ten years of his life.

During the first period (1903–1917), Lu Xun embarked on his career as a translator while studying in Japan. At that time, imperialist powers invaded China. During these years, Lu translated to encourage the Qing government and the Chinese people to fight against the invasion by Tsarist Russia and other European imperialist countries. In the second period (1919–1926), Lu Xun actively involved himself in the New Culture and May Fourth movements and translated Russian literary works. These years saw his ideology shift to embrace anti-imperialism, anti-feudalism, and the cause of literary revolution. Against the backdrop of the initial years of the KMT–CPC civil war, in the third period (1927–1936), Lu Xun further developed his ideology, shifted his beliefs from social Darwinism to Marxism, and advocated for the new democratic revolution led by the CPC. He selected literary works from the Soviet Union for translation and translated large amounts of proletarian literary theory to promote Marxism.

Lu Xun's translational activities across the three periods illustrated above reveal his ideological shifts. These shifts show how Lu Xun used translation to promote social change and language reform as an activist translator and revolutionary. His socio-political engagement as a revolutionary is also visible in his notion of 'hard translation' as a tool for linguistic and social reform, and later for introducing proletarian literature that advanced his political agenda, which permeated most of his career as a translator. In sum, I reiterate my findings that translators' activism and revolutionary involvement are manifested both in their intra-textual manipulation and in their extra-textual involvement, for the cause of peace or for war, on an everyday basis.

Related topics

Thought/Translation; Theory, Practice, Activism

Notes

1 New Culture Movement (1915–1919; 1919–1923): A cultural reform initiated by a group of scholars who once received education abroad in Japan, the US, and Europe. The aim of the reform was to attack Confucian ideas and feudal traditions as well as classical Chinese and exalted democracy and science. The leaders of the reform included Hu Shi, Chen Duxiu, Lu Xun, and Li Dazhao.
2 May Fourth Movement (1919): a patriotic movement opposing Japan, European imperialism, and feudalism. It is part of the New Culture Movement.
3 Zhou Zuoren: younger brother of Lu Xun; writer, poet, and translator, who collaborated with Lu Xun in translating many literary works.
4 Crescent Moon Society: a Chinese literary society founded by the Chinese scholar Hu Shi and the poet Xu Zhimo in 1923 for the exploration of new poetry writing and theory; it was dissolved in 1931 following the death of Xu Zhimo. Crescent Moon (*Xinyue*) is named after *The Crescent Moon,* an anthology of the poetry of the Indian poet Tagore. The society once entered into debate with the left-wing Writers' League, an organisation affiliated to the CPC.
5 All translations are by the author.

Further reading

Lu Xun (2011) *Na Han (Outcry)*. Tianjin: Beijing Yan Shan Chu Ban She.

A collection of translated essays from Lu Xun's representative works, written during his second translation period. These essays provide an indirect revelation of his personal ideologies as a translator and writer across different social contexts.

Lu Xun (2008) *Lu Xun Yi Wen Quan Ji (Complete Translated Works of Lu Xun)*. Fuzhou: Fujian Jiao Yu Chu Ban She.

These are eight volumes of Lu Xun's translations. The chronological organisation of the volumes reflects Lu Xun's selection of works during different periods. His translation strategies, especially 'hard translation,' are portrayed throughout the collection.

Rosa, Alexandra, Hanna Pięta, and Rita Maia (2019) *Indirect Translation: Theoretical, Methodological and Terminological Issues*. London: Routledge.

The collected volume was edited based on publications from a special issue of *Translation Studies*. The book focuses on the conceptual, terminological, and methodological issues on indirect translation. It challenges the current binary paradigms permeated in translation studies and explores the new research avenues of the future.

References

Baer, Brian, and Klaus Kaindl (2017) *Queering Translation, Translating the Queer* (1st ed.). New York: Routledge.

Baker, Mona (2005) 'Narratives in and of Translation,' *SKASE Journal of Translation and Interpretation* 1 (1): 4–13.

Baker, Mona (2006) *Translation and Conflict: A Narrative Account*. London and New York: Routledge.

Baker, Mona (2010) *Critical Readings in Translation Studies*. New York: Routledge.

Bassnett, Susan, and André Lefevere (1990) *Translation, History, and Culture*. London: Pinter.

Bassnett, Susan, and Peter Bush (2006) *The Translator as Writer*. London: A&C Black.

Boéri, Julie, and Carol Maier (2010) *Compromiso social y traducción-interpretación*. Granada: ECOS.

Cao, Yinghua, and Liu Jin (2005) 'Lu Xun Fanyi Zhi Xuanze [The Choice of Lu Xun for Translation],' *Journal of Inner Mongolia University* 4: 8–12.

Chen, Lang (2014) 'Xinshiji Yilai de Yishixingtai Fanyi Yanjiu [On Ideological Research in the Translation Studies since the 21st Century],' *Journal of Foreign Languages* 37 (6): 65–73.

Cheng, Eileen (2013) *Literary Remains: Death, Trauma, and Lu Xun's Refusal to Mourn*. Honolulu: University of Hawai'i Press.

Chou, Eva (2012) *Memory, Violence, Queues: Lu Xun Interprets China*. Ann Arbor: Association for Asian Studies, Inc.

Cunningham, David, and Barb Browning (2004) 'The Emergency of Worthy Targets: Official Frames and Deviance Narratives within the FBI,' *Sociological Forum* 19 (3): 347–369.

Davies, Gloria (2013) *Lu Xun's Revolution: Writing in a Time of Violence*. London: Harvard University Press.

Gamsa, Mark (2008) *The Chinese Translation of Russian Literature: Three Studies*. Leiden: Brill.

Gamsa, Mark (2010) *The Reading of Russian Literature in China: A Moral Example and Manual of Practice*. New York: Palgrave.

Gould, Rebecca (2018) 'Hard Translation: Persian Poetry and Post-national Literary Form,' *Forum for Modern Language Studies* 54 (2): 191–206.

Hatim, Basil, and Ian Mason (1997) *The Translator as Communicator*. London: Routledge.

Han, Zuoli (2009) *Xinhua Zidian (Xinhua Dictionary)*. Beijing: The Commercial Press.

Huang, Qiaosheng (2012) *Lu Xun Tu Chuan (Biography of Lu Xun)*. Beijing: Zhong Yang Bian Yi Chu Ban She.

Hugo, Victor (2009) '1841. Origin of Fantine,' in *Things Seen*. Cabin John: Wildside Press. 42–47.

Lefevere, André (1992) *Translation, Rewriting, and the Manipulation of Literary Fame*. London: Routledge.

Liang, Qichao (1992) 'Lun Xiaoshuo Yu Qunzhi Zhi Guanxi [On the Relationship between Novels and the Control of the Masses],' in *Liang Qichao Wenxuan Xiaji* (2nd volume of selected works of Liang Qichao). Ed. Xia Xiaohong. Beijing: China Broadcasting and Television Press. 3–8.

Liang, Shiqiu (1996a) 'Wenxue Shi You Jiejixing De Ma? [Does Literature Have Class Nature?],' in *Lu Xun He Ta De Ludi Wenxuan: Xiajuan* (Selected essays of Lu Xun and his opponents in the debate: Volume two). Eds. Li Fugen, and Liu Hong. Beijing: China Today Publication. 588–597.

Liang, Shiqiu (1996b) 'Lu Lu Xun Xiansheng De Yingyi [On Mr. Lu Xun's 'Hard Translation'],' in *Lu Xun He Ta De Ludi Wenxuan: Xiajuan* (Selected essays of Lu Xun and his opponents in the debate: Volume two). Eds. Li Fugen, and Liu Hong. Beijing: China Today Publication. 598–600.

Lu, Xun (1903a) 'Si ba da zhi hun [The Ghost of Sparta],' *Zhejiang Chao [Zhejiang Tide]* 12 (5): 159–164.

Lu, Xun (1903b) 'Si ba da zhi hun [The Ghost of Sparta],' *Zhejiang Chao [Zhejiang Tide]* 12 (9): 123–127.

Lu Xun (2002a) 'Ji Wai Ji Xu Yan [Preface of Ji Wai Set],' in *Xin Ban Lu Xun Za Wen Ji: Ji Wai Wen Ji (Xia)* (The new edition of Lu Xun's essays: Jiwwai Set: 2nd volume). Eds. Chen Fangjing and Zhang Zhongliang. Hangzhou: Zhejiang People's Publishing House. 473–476.

Lu Xun (2002b) 'Shi'er Ge Houji [Postscript of the Twelve],' in *Xin Ban Lu Xun Za Wen Ji (Shang)* (The new edition of Lu Xun's essays: 1st volume). Eds. Chen Fangjing and Zhang Zhongliang. Hangzhou: Zhejiang People's Publishing House. 443–447.

Lu Xun (2002c) 'Yi Le *Gongrensuilvefu* Zhihou [After Translating Worker Shevyrev],' in *Xin Ban Lu Xun Za Wen Ji (Shang)* (The new edition of Lu Xun's essays: 1st volume). Eds. Chcn Fangjing and Zhang Zhongliang. Hangzhou: Zhejiang People's Publishing House. 188–193.

Lu Xun (2002d) 'Wenyi Yu Piping Houji [Postscript of 'Literary Criticism'],' in *Xin Ban Lu Xun Za Wen Ji (Xia)* (The new edition of Lu Xun's essays: 1st volume). Eds. Chen Fangjing and Zhang Zhongliang. Hangzhou: Zhejiang People's Publishing House. 213–218.

Lu Xun (2005) *Lu Xun Zishu [Autobiography of Lu Xun]*. Beijing: Jinghua Publishing House.

Lu Xun (2006a) 'Lun Chongyi [On Inirect Translation],' in *Huabian Wenxue (Fringed Literature)*. Ed. Wang Haibo. Beijing: People's Literature Publishing House. 38–40.

Lu Xun (2006b) 'Zailun Chongyi [Rediscussing Indirect Translation],' in *Huabian Wenxue (Fringed Literature)*. Ed. Wang Haibo. Beijing: People's Literature Publishing House. 69–71.

Lu Xun (2014a) 'Lüeli [Examples],' in Mr. Lu Xun Memorial Commission. *Yu Wai Xiaoshuo Ji [Short Stories from Abroad]: Lu Xun Quan Ji: Dishiyijuan* (Complete works of Lu Xun: 11th volume). Beijing: Tong Xin Chu Ban She. 6325–6328.

Lu Xun (2014b) 'Zhu Zhong E Wenzi Zhijiao [Celebrating the Literary Exchange between China and Russia],' in Mr. Lu Xun Memorial Commission. *Nanqiangbeidiaoji (Mixed dialects) of Lu Xun Quan Ji* (Complete works of Lu Xun). Beijing: Tong Xin Chu Ban She. 2500–2506.

Lu Xun (2014c) 'Nahan Zixu [Preface of Call to Arms],' in Mr. Lu Xun Memorial Commission. *Lu Xun Quan Ji: Diyijuan* (Complete works of Lu Xun: 1st volume). Beijing: Tong Xin Chu Ban She. 314–322.

Lu Xun (2014d) 'Wo Zeme Zuoqi Xiaoshuo Lai [Why I Started the Novels],' in Mr. Lu Xun Memorial Commission. *Lu Xun Quan Ji: Diwujuan* (Complete works of Lu Xun: 5th volume). Beijing: Tong Xin Chu Ban She. 2552–2557.

Lu Xun (2014e) 'Yingyi Yu Wenxue De Jiejixing [Hard Translation and the Class Nature of Literature],' in Mr. Lu Xun Memorial Commission. *Er Xin Ji (Two hearts): Lu Xun Quan Ji: Disijuan* (Complete works of Lu Xun: 4th volume). Beijing: Tong Xin Chu Ban She. 2042–2069.

Lu Xun (2014f) 'Qiejieting Zawen [Demi-concession Studio Essays],' in Mr. Lu Xun Memorial Commission. *Lu Xun Quan Ji: Diliujuan* (Complete works of Lu Xun: 6th volume). Beijing: Tong Xin Chu Ban She. 3065–3278.

Lu Xun (2014g) 'Guanyu Fanyi De Tongxin [Letters of Translation],' in Mr. Lu Xun Memorial Commission. *Er Xin Ji (Two hearts): Lu Xun Quan Ji: Disijuan* (Complete works of Lu Xun: 4th volume). Beijing: Tong Xin Chu Ban She. 2196–2211.

Lu Xun (2014h) 'Huixin [A Letter of Reply],' in Mr. Lu Xun Memorial Commission. *Er Xin Ji (Two hearts): Lu Xun Quan Ji: Disijuan* (Complete works of Lu Xun: 4th volume). Beijing: Tong Xin Chu Ban She. 2211–2221.

Lu Xun (2014i) 'Zhongguo Wuchanjieji Gemingwenxue he Qianqudexue [The Chinese Proletarian Revolutionary Literature and the Blood of the Pioneers],' in *Er Xin Ji (Two Hearts): Lu Xun Quan Ji: Disijuan (Complete Works of Lu Xun: 4th volume)*. Beijing: Tong Xin Chu Ban She. 2106–2108.

Lu Xun (2014j) 'Heian Zhongguo de Wenyijie de Xianzhuang: Wei Meiguo Xinqunzhong Zuo [The Status of the Art and Literary Circles in the Dark China: for the New Masses of America],' in *Er*

Xin Ji (Two Hearts): Lu Xun Quan Ji: Disijuan (Complete Works of Lu Xun: 4th volume). Beijing: Tong Xin Chu Ban She. 2108–2114.

Luo, Xuanmin (2007) 'Translation as Violence: on Lu Xun's Idea of Yi jie,' *Amerasia Journal* 33 (3): 41–52.

Mullen, Bill (2013) 'Proletarian Literature,' in *Oxford Bibliographies* [online] 29 October. Available at: www.oxfordbibliographies.com/view/document/obo-9780199827251/obo-9780199827251-0130.xml [accessed 30 June 2019].

Myskja, Kjetil (2013) 'Foreignization and Resistance: Lawrence Venuti and His Critics,' *Nordic Journal of English Studies* 12 (2): 1–23.

Ren, Fangqiu (1982) *Lu Xun San Lun (Scattered Essays of Lu Xun)*. Xi'an: Shaanxi Renmin Chubanshe.

Simpson, John, and Edmund Weiner (1989) 'Activist,' in *Oxford English Dictionary*. Eds. John Simpson and Edmund S. Weiner. Oxford: Oxford University Press.

Skrandies, Peter (2012) 'Compromiso Social y Traducción/Interpretación- Translation/Interpreting and Social Activism,' *JoSTrans: The Journal of Specialised Translation* 18: 230–232.

Sun, Lung-Kee (1986) 'To Be or Not to Be "Eaten": Lu Xun's Dilemma of Political Engagement,' *Modern China* 12 (4): 459–485.

Teruo, Tarumoto (2001) 'Guanyu Lu Xun de Sibadazhihun [About Lu Xun's *The Ghost of Sparta*],' Tr. Yue Xin. *Lu Xun Research Monthly* 6: 38–46.

Tymoczko, Maria (2002) 'Ideology and the Position of the Translator: In What Sense is the Translator 'In Between'?' in *Apropos of Ideology: Translation Studies on Ideology-Ideologies in Translation Studies*. Ed. María Calzada Pérez. Manchester: St Jerome Publishing. 181–201.

Tymoczko, Maria (2010) *Translation, Resistance, Activism*. Amherst: University of Massachusetts Press.

Venuti, Lawrence (1995) *The Translator's Invisibility: A History of Translation*. London: Routledge.

Venuti, Lawrence (1998) *The Scandals of Translation: Towards an Ethics of Difference*. London and New York: Routledge.

Wang, Edward Q. (2014) 'May Fourth Movement,' in *Oxford Bibliographies* [online] 25 February. Available at: www.oxfordbibliographies.com/abstract/document/obo-9780199920082/obo-9780199920082-0077.xml?rskey=XXSA65&result=3&q=New±Culture±Movement#firstMatch [accessed 1 April 2019].

Wang, Yougui (2016) *Fanyijia Lu Xun [The Translator Lu Xun]*. Tianjin: Nankai University Press.

Wang, Pu (2013) 'The Promethean Translator and Cannibalistic Pains: Lu Xun's "Hard Translation" as a Political Allegory,' *Translation Studies* 6 (3): 324–338.

Wu, Yuming, and Yajian Lian (2014) 'Lu Xun dui E'su Wenxue Zuopin Yijie Chengjiu [A Review of Lu Xun's Translation of the Soviet Russia's Literary Works],' *China Publishing Journal* 12 (5): 20–22.

Xia, Tian (2009) 'On Lu Xun's Un-fluent Translation,' *Cross-cultural Communication* 5 (4): 60–70.

Yin, Danping (2005) 'Xinhuawen Yundong Shiqi Guanyu Feichu Changji De Sikao [Thinking on the Abolition of Prostitution in the New Culture Movement],' *Jianghan Luntan (Jinaghan Tribune)* 11: 97–100.

Zhang, Tierong (2010) 'Zhoushi Xiongdi Yu Wusi Xinwenhua Yundong [The Zhou Brothers and the May Fourth New Culture Movement],' *Guangdong Shehui Kexue (Social Sciences in Guangdong)* 6: 150–156.

Zhou, Zuoren (2012) 'Guanyu Lu Xun Zhi Er [About Lu Xun],' in *Gua Dou Ji (Melon and Bean Collection)*. Ed. Zhi An. Beijing: Beijing Shiyue Wenyi Publishing House. 243–256.

29

The political modes of translation in Iran

National words, right sentences, class paragraphs

Omid Mehrgan

In reflecting on the relation between translation and radical politics in Iran since the 1979 revolution, I will work with two sets of concepts—one set, comprising nation, class, rights, stems from politics, and the other, words, sentences, paragraphs, from translation. If there is any necessary relation between the two sets, it must be sought in a concrete historical framework that constitutes the specific form and content that the politics of translation has taken in Iran. The political modality of the Iranian translation style should be understood in this historical and conceptual configuration. In order to make its argument about the politics of translation in post-revolutionary Iran, this chapter adopts an interpretive view on the Iranian practice of translation during the twentieth century on two premises. The first premise is that the formation of modern Iran since 1905 pursued the project of building a nation-state (Katouzian 2003; Marashi 2008). The second premise states that the 1979 revolution meant both a break with and a decisive continuation of that project. This double character of the revolution introduced, in the words of the Marxist scholar and an important figure around 1979, Ehsan Tabari, a dichronism or double temporality—resorting to the past in a religious mode and moving towards the future in a modernist, constitutionalist mode (Tabari 1981: 14). I will argue that this dichronism in respect of Europe as a phenomenon and as a force symbolised by the former regime accompanied the practice of translation and determined its politics through and through (see Chapter 11). In conclusion, I will draw on my own experience as a translator in Iran in order to point out one way of overcoming the dichronism and of resolving its contradiction as best manifested in the practice of translation.

Between nothing and no comment

An interpretive incident occurred at a key moment in the 1979 Iranian revolution while the Air France plane was carrying Ayatollah Khomeini to Tehran following his fifteen years in exile. A foreign correspondent for ABC News, Peter Jennings, solicited the ayatollah's companion Sadegh Ghotbzadeh to ask him how he felt about returning to Iran. This exchange followed:

'Ayatollah, would you be so kind as to tell us how you feel about being back in Iran?'
'*Hichi*,' the ayatollah replied. 'Nothing.'
'*Hichi*?' Ghotbzadeh asked him. Even he seemed incredulous at the response.
'*Hich ehsasi nadaram*,' the ayatollah said for emphasis. 'I don't feel a thing.'

(Sciolino 2011: 55)

Sciolino is right when she adds that decades later 'Iranians are still debating what Khomeini meant' (2011: 55), even though the consensus leans towards suggesting his utter indifference. What she fails to relay is the translator's answer to the reporter. Ghotbzadeh—who incidentally became one of the first censors as the head of the state television in the new government—seemed too shy or shocked or simply afraid to render faithfully the ayatollah's response. In fact, the *nothing* for the Persian *hichi* (a colloquial form of *hich*) is Sciolino's own addition for the readers of her memoirs and not what was actually said to the eager reporter. As an existing clip of the scene reveals, the ayatollah's translator indeed answers: 'He doesn't make any comment,' a clear mistranslation.

A *no comment*, to be sure, implies a *nothing*, a *hichi*, but on two fundamentally different levels. One indicates that there is no answer to the question whatsoever and the other offers the nothing *as* the answer. The reporter does hear the person interviewed utter something in a foreign tongue, a something which comes to nothing in the translator's words. The interpreted message, or the very no-message, in other words, was the sought-after answer itself. It is this interpretive or translational moment in the exchange that Sciolino's account suppresses, an innocent suppression because the sole matter at hand had to be what the ayatollah said in answer to the question about his feeling and not the translator's choice of answer. As regards this answer, the translator's response is bound to become a matter of indifference. But, one could argue, the translation itself reclaims its significance as an integral part of the entire scene, not merely a vanishing mediator.

The mediator does not vanish for two reasons (Mason and Stewart 2001). The manifest reason is that he mistranslates or refuses to translate what the ayatollah said. Once we realise this, we start noticing his role. The latent reason pertains to the political content of this refusal. The charismatic leader of the revolution not feeling anything about this epochal moment while millions are eagerly waiting to welcome him back home just ten days before the ultimate collapse of the Pahlavi monarchy would probably send no good message to the watching world. A religious explanation of this *hichi* is also possible. The ayatollah was a self-sufficient, profoundly pious man who did all this not for his personal gain and fame but for the sake of Islam. Showing or having private passion would run counter to the ascetic virtues of a devout revolutionary. Opposed to this disposition in our scene are two statements common to the modern discourse of journalism: 'How do you feel?' and 'He makes no comment.' The content of the scene can then be best characterised as what Michel Foucault called 'political spirituality' with regard to the 1979 revolution (Afari and Anderson 2005: 134).

Ghotbzadeh's mistranslation of Khomeini's message and Sciolino's suppression of it emerge as attempts to cope with the complex ambiguity buried in the political-spiritual *hichi* of a revolutionary Iran. Prefigured by this scene, translation remained an unresolved tension from 1979 and imposed itself with peculiar stubbornness on the political and intellectual scene with each decade to come. The peculiar way in which translation relates to politics is already latent in the famous dictum, *tradutore, traditore*, or 'the translator is the betrayer.' It becomes manifest, however, when, following Roman Jakobson, we rephrase it by posing the double question: 'Translator of what messages? Betrayer of what values?' (1987: 435). These are questions with which Jakobson closes his short essay on translation and linguistics, which is hardly accidental. Jakobson's linguistic standpoint cannot answer both questions, but only the first one. 'Message' is well within the preview of his discipline, formal linguistics, whereas 'value' surpasses linguistics as a discipline that, in its traditional form, falls short of what lies beyond sentences (Barthes 1982: 254–258). A proper treatment of the relation between translation and politics ought to deal with the relation between sentences and what goes beyond them (Evans and Fernandez 2018). At stake is what links 'the translation of messages' to 'the betrayal of values,' the rewriting of a text in a foreign language that is bound up to an entire context of connotations, practices, agents, problems, and positions vis-à-vis those problems. Value is owned by a 'concrete living totality' that does not allow for formal rules of combination and substitution (Bakhtin 1984: 181; Finch 2000: 116). A linguistic account of translation understood as an essentially political practice can surpass the limitations of linguistics (Chilton and Schäffner 1997). A shift to discourse analysis in recent years has provided better tools to employ linguistic categories in understanding translation (Schäffner 2004; Munday 2007).

A dichronism since 1979

In a small volume of articles titled *Motarjemān, kha'enān* (*Translators, Traitors*) (2007), the Iranian translator Hasan Kaamshaad implies a straightforward answer to the questions posed by Jakobson, and yet one that is limited to the mechanics of rendering messages and the ethics of this rendering. Translator, for him, betrays the original texts, be it in Persian or English, primarily by committing misunderstanding, misreading, imprecision, ellipses, redundancies, and literalness, and adopting inadequate or ineloquent equivalents. What is betrayed, therefore, is the very practice of faithful translation through particular acts of bad translation. At issue here is the technique of interpreting messages. Much of what has been said by established translators about translation in contemporary Iran deals solely with this technique. A notable name in this respect is Karim Emami (1994), and most recently, though with a much more acute political and self-conscious tenor, Saleh Najafi (2015). The underlying moral maxim of such a criticism rightfully holds that there ought to be no false promise in a translation. If, for instance, a book bears the name and the title of Jean-Paul Sartre's *La nausée* (*Nausea*: *tahavvo'* in Persian), then it is carrying the promise of offering that book to the Persian-speaking world. If it breaks that promise, then it will betray that maxim, a traitor to the practice. Deciding if there is a betrayal entails knowing the message in its original context. A bad translation, where there is no equivalence of any sort between two different verbal systems of signs with regard to a particular text, resembles less a lie than a broken promise.

The promise of translation can be broken at several levels, each bringing about its own politics: words, sentences, paragraphs. These make up the basic units of translation variously discussed in the decision making of translators (Reiss 1971; Nord 1997). In rendering a text, the translator constantly faces choices between the three levels: should she stick to the words and reproduce their arrangement? Should she read an entire sentence and then rearrange it in accord with the syntactic demands of

Omid Mehrgan

the target language? Or ought she to read an entire paragraph and rewrite it in her mother tongue according to the concept of the paragraph? To this trio one can add the issue of style, which poses further choices for translators (Boase-Beier 2006; Parks 2007).

Let us place the levels of difficulty in translation from the standpoint of messages in the concrete context of Iran during the late 1980s and 1990s. Here we reach the level of values. Those who came of age in the aftermath of the Reformist Era in Iran during the mid-nineties through the mid-noughties—when Mohammad Khatami was the president and a series of political reforms were attempted and partially succeeded —tend to recoil in boredom, if not in horror, at the threadbare topic of 'the conflict of tradition and modernity [*taqābol-e sonat va moderniteh*].' At issue here are two sets of tensions: one between religious-traditional and secular-liberal strata of Iranian society, and the other between a growing civil society and a religiously oriented mode of legislation and governing since 1979. The *taqābol* approach then casts these tensions in the form of a sweeping conflict between modernity and tradition as independent wholes (for an example of a best-seller, see Zibakalam 2001). For all its intensity, no resolution has been offered to the conflict. No consensus has ever been reached regarding any of the two terms, especially modernity. Even naming the debate has given rise to disparity. Ever since the debate became the order of the day for the intelligentsia, three different terms have been used to refer to 'modernity': *moderniteh*, *moderniyat*, and *tajadod*. Ideologically and politically, they are different terms even though their shades of meaning are generated by exposure to the same source of light, the West. The first was used by more secular voices (Jahanbegloo 1994; Ahmadi 1998), the second by a small group who showed linguistic sensitivities but were still on the left (Ashouri 1997), and the third, an Arabic word, by the centrist or reformist camp who mainly identified themselves as the 'religious intellectuals [*rowshanfekrān-e dini*].' A similar translational political nuance has determined the discourse around democracy since the 1979 revolution. The official discourse and segments of the Reformist movement tend to use the Farsi term *mardom-sālāri*, a literal rendering of the original Greek *demos-krasy*. Other segments, mostly secular and leftist, opt for *demokrāsi* (democracy). The choice of words carries with it implicit political positions.

However abstractly it surfaced in much of public debates in newspapers, interviews, and books, the *taqābol* topic had a historical content tracing back to the early twentieth century. The ways in which translation relates to politics in Iran pertain to this multifaceted historical content and its unresolved conflicts. A chronology of this trajectory in a series of key years runs thus: 1906 and the Constitutional Revolution; 1921 and the British-backed coup that installed the Pahlavi dynasty and marked the beginning of Iran's modern state; 1941 and the ousting of Reza Shah leading to the reign of his son; 1953 and the coup that toppled Mosadegh's national government; the 1979 revolution that led to the establishment of the Islamic Republic; 1988–1989 and the end of the Iran–Iraq war, the death of Ayatollah Khomeini, and the beginning of liberalisation of the economy; 1997 and the Reformist Era; 2009 and the Green Movement following the presidential elections.

In a speech delivered about two years after the 1979 revolution, the Marxist scholar and prominent Tudeh Party member Ehsan Tabari summed up the historical framework within which Iran has had to move as a *dichronism* (*do-zamānegi*):

One of the most important peculiarities of our society from a cultural and civiliza-
tional perspective is a sort of 'dichronism.' On the one hand, we have not yet left
our 'Middle Ages.' On the other hand, from a global standpoint we live in an age
described as that of transition from a system of exploitation and domination to
a system of work and cooperation [...], that is, we live in a world in which both the
relations of production and the productive forces are undergoing an amazing transformation. This dichronism has at times agonizingly reflected itself in all our affairs.
This dichronism has found expression even in our Islamic revolution.

(Tabari 1981: 14)[1]

Careful not to indulge too much in Marxist terminology that would soon to be violently
suppressed, Tabari nevertheless recasts Iran's situation with the concept of mode of production. Note that he wrote those words at a turning point in European and North
American capitalism when social democracy, welfare state, and the New Deal era began
to make room for an aggressive turn to the right, opening up what became known as
neoliberalism. Thus, even though he was right about an imminent 'amazing transformation,' he proved too optimistic with regard to the direction and content of that transformation. Still, even as a member of a communist party that had declared its allegiance
to the nascent Islamic Republic, and thus not shying away from calling the revolution
Islamic, he had insight into the incurably double character of 1979: the revolution was
a call both for returning to the past and for opening up a free society beyond the political repression and economic inequality of the Shah's regime, although his recourse to
the European concept of 'Middle Ages' fails to point out the specificity of the kind of
return to the past that characterised what was Islamic in the revolution. Dichronism is
a far more accurate designation of Iran after the revolution than 'fundamentalism' or
anachronism, that is, being out of step with the contemporary world (Abrahamian 1993:
13–38).

The insight into the double character of post-revolutionary Iran, into its dichronistic
state, provides an avenue for thinking about the status of translation. So far as translation
goes, its temporality allies with European time, as it were. Translation in Iran has
always meant rendering texts from traditions north or west of Iran and seldom from
southwest or east. For all the profound debt that Iranian Islam carries to Arabic, translation as a social practice looking toward Europe transpires essentially as a secular modernist practice performed by intellectuals not necessarily committed to religion. But, it
finds itself immediately entangled with the other time, namely, that of the early Shi'ite
period of holy Imams (or of the 'medieval' past, in Tabari's language), which is force-
fully at work in the Persian modes of saying and signifying. By 'medieval' or *ghorun-e
vostāyi* Tabari might be alluding to the reactionary aspects of the new regime since the
1979 revolution with the re-introduction of Shari'a, despite the fact that his communist
party did align itself with the Islamic Republic. Translators in Iran know very well what
a double temporality means. Exploring this dichronism, however, requires a more concrete account of what makes up the double character of the Iranian situation as Tabari
characterises.

I propose to account for the political substance of the transformative shifts leading up
to and permeating post-revolutionary Iran with three concepts: nation, class, rights. What
imposed itself as 'Western civilisation' appeared as a powerful force for building
a modern nation-state in Iran. Both the nascent intellectuals and the statesmen and bur-
eaucrats took part in defending a national state devoid of religious superstitions,

uncivilised conduct, unregulated language, all the way down to public education, dress code, and hygiene. This movement generated both extreme nationalism and a people's political movement to cut off the hands of the foreigners in oil production and its revenues. It resurfaced in the slogan of *esteqlāl* (independence) in the 1979 revolution and later on in a variety of calls for politically engaging national unity since the Reformist Era.

While nation or *melat* (originally meaning a religious community) designated an internal state-backed unity in opposition to external forces, class introduced a differentiation within that unity itself. As a contested political category, *melat* can be argued to have signified as a unity distinct from the state, not including the state (Katouzian 1981: 16) or a unity that paved the way for the formation of the nation-state or the modern state proper (Sharifi 2013: 32). From the early twentieth-century Social Democrats (*ejtemā'iyun 'āmiyun*) north and northeast of Iran and the sporadic labour movements coupled with it in the Caucasus to communist trends culminating in the Tudeh (Masses) Party, at stake were the struggles within a presupposed national space. The Social Democrats participated in the struggles leading to the Constitutional Revolution in 1906, which proved instrumental in the emergence of national unity (Yazdani 2013). The flourishing of translation as a pedagogical and political tool owed much to the socialist imaginaries of the 1930s and 1940s (Khalili and Khazaeefar 2015; Matin-Asgari 2018: 155–157). Along with ideas such as nation, law, and constitution, others emerged: materialism, working class, evolution, production, practice (Shakeri 1974). Mohammad Reza Shah Pahlavi (ruling from 1941 to 1979) saw communists as his main enemy. Many of the key Marxist-socialist terms found their ways not only in the Islamicist Marxism of the pre-revolutionary radical groups but in the post-revolutionary Islamic Republic that had established itself by 1981 by widely suppressing all leftist groups. Thanks to Ali Shari'ati's readings of Marxist terms into the Qur'an and early Islamic history of first Shi'ite Imams, 'proletariat,' 'imperialism,' and 'unity' became *mostaz'afīn* (the weakened), *estekbār* (imperialism), and *towhid* (monotheism). The official discourse of the post-revolutionary government assimilated the socialist lexicon in disguise. The real repression of the left corresponded to its symbolic integration in the new system.

The nineties and the noughties, of course, saw the undisturbed translation of Marxian and Marxist works. Much of this were reprints of 'white-cover [*jeld sefīd*]' translations of socialist literature, from Lenin, Trotsky, and Ernest Mandel to Althusser and Poulantzas during the immediate years and months preceding and succeeding the 1979 revolution. Even so, the political force of translation would require nearly two decades in order to show its relevance. In the meantime, and especially during the Reformist Era, the tension between class and the nation had yielded its place to frictions between 'civil society [*jāme'a-ye madani*]' and a partly democratic, partly authoritarian government always harassing minority and dissident voices. The substance of what the reformists longed for, that is, the 'political opening [*goshāyesh-e siyāsi*],' can be captured by the idea of rights. Being recognised as a citizen enjoying fundamental human rights, as groups previously unrepresented, from women to religious minorities, thus particularly the right to freedom of conscience and speech constituted the core of the reformist politics. Rights-based political activism reached its fullest, bloody expression in the 2009 social movement, with its central slogan being, 'Where is my vote?'

The political and the translational

In the second half of this chapter I consider the relation between translation and politics in the Iranian context in an immanent manner. That is, rather than discuss the politics of translators or the sociological function of translation from a political perspective, I focus on the politics of those translational choices in connection with right, nation, and class under concrete historical conditions. These three pairs are treated in isolation for heuristic reasons; in historical reality they are intertwined. Such a path promises to shed a different light on the proverbial translator as traitor; it liberates translation from the dominant technical and ethical implications of messages and opens it up to the political and historical dimensions of values.

National words

The breaking of the promise of translation may occur at the level of words, that is, when the equivalence of words in source and target languages may fail to be achieved so that, say, *revolution* is rendered as *coup d'état*, or *nothing* as *no comment*. This makes for a paradigmatic failure and thus a betrayal, especially when, in a hypothetical case, a translator deliberately changes 'revolution [*enqelāb*]' to 'coup [*kudetā*]' when interpreting the news of the 1979 Iranian revolution for a BBC correspondent. Words make for the immediate level at which foreignness and translation reveal themselves to the speakers of a language. Words were the first site where the crisis of Persian in modern times showed itself. In the polemical play *Ja'far-Khan Has Returned from Europe* (*Ja'far-khān az farang bargashteh*), written in 1922 by the young playwright Hassan Moghaddam (1898–1925), which depicts the passions and troubles of a Europe-educated man returning to his traditional hometown only to find trying incompatibilities with his own ways, the protagonist keeps dropping French words when talking to his family about the most mundane matters in daily life. Annoyed by this habit, his traditional family resists Ja'far-Khan's informed or naively reformist instructions about using the bathroom and eating at the table. He clearly comes across as a pathetic and altogether ridiculous figure in the context of native manners and practices.

In the face of the countless concepts flooding into Persian, two extreme responses have been offered: admitting foreign words and resorting to archaic words as their equivalents. As Theodor W. Adorno stated with regard to the German language,

> every foreign word contains the explosive material of enlightenment, contains in its controlled use the knowledge that what is immediate cannot be said in unmediated form but only expressed in and through reflection and mediation [...], only what is translated back into foreign words from the jargon of authenticity says what this jargon means to say. Foreign words teach us that language can no longer cure us of specialization by imitating nature; it can do so only by assuming the burden of specialization.
>
> *(translation modified; 1991: 190)*

Adorno wrote these words as a sharp critique of what he called the jargon of authenticity, that is, the language of fundamental ontology worked out by Martin Heidegger and other German phenomenologists and existentialists since the First World War, such as Otto Friedrich Bollnow, Ulrich Sonnemann, and Karl Jaspers.

Foreign words, mainly from European languages, have emerged both as the most omin-
ous enemy agents and as the most precarious non-citizens in the countries of the Persian
language since the late nineteenth century. Even so, foreign words have undertaken to perform much of the work that Persian words could not do: *rofuzeh* (refusé), *budjeh* (budget),
kelasik (classique or classic), *fāmil* (family). The politics of translation in Iran has always
paid obsessive attention to the presence of these lexical foreigners, sometimes accepted and
assimilated amicably as guest workers, at other times frowned-upon undocumented illegals
that need to be expelled in order to restore the purity of the mother tongue. Much labour
has been expended, and at times lost, by the state, academia, and by independent translators
in order to find equivalents for the flood of French, English, and Arabic words that found
their ways into Persian in virtue of a variety of practices: science, technology, statecraft and
bureaucracy, progressive politics, and religion. The state-sponsored *farhangestān* or the
Academy of Persian Culture (language and literature), founded in 1935, employing a legion
of prominent literary figures of the time, coined and legally enforced by 1941 a massive
amount of words, many of which have found currency in the decades to follow until
this day. Successful examples include *āgahi* for *avis* or *advertisement*, *āludegī* for *souillure*
or *pollution*, and *daryānavard* for *marin* or *marine*, replacing the formerly common Arabic
word *bahri*. Many of these words proved misfires, such as *hāl-bān* for *goalkeeper*, or more
recently, *kesh-loghmeh* for pizza (see Kianoush 2002)

An immense systematic effort was made during the 1980s by the prominent Iranian
translator Mirshams-al-Din Adib-Soltani to find pure Persian equivalents for modern philosophical terms. His magnum opus in this regard is his syntactically flawless translation of
Kant's *Critique of Pure Reason* (*Sanjesh-e kherad-e nāb*) (1983). His impressive undertaking in this project reveals a contradictory principle: while he offers archaic, bizarre equivalents instead of using existing equivalents, loans, or calques for standard philosophical
concepts such as 'dialectic,' 'object,' and 'subject,' he radically adheres to the German
syntax of Kant's text. In this syntactic imitation of foreign language, Adib-Soltani uncovers
possibilities in philosophical Persian that would have been lost if he had wanted to recreate
or rewrite the text. And yet, his syntactic literalism goes hand in hand with a paradigmatic
reaction or repressiveness: his Kantian vocabulary is hard to decipher without the glossary
he provided at the end of the book, for there are no examples of their usage either in colloquial or in academic language. Still a reliable translation, his *Critique of Pure Reason* trains
Persian thinking historically and philosophically while at the same time renders it, termino-
logically, ahistorical and severed from the traditions of theoretical Persian. A millennium
ago, efforts by Ibn-Sina and Abureyhan Birnui to make philosophy and science, metaphys-
ics and astronomy speak eloquent Persian by ingeniously finding equivalents in ancient or
colloquial Persian of the time proved highly influential and to a remarkable extent effective
(Moeen 1998: 67–73). Centuries later, purist, archaistic intellectual trends such as the six-
teenth-century Iranian-born Zoroastrian priest Azar Kayvan and his followers in India took
a more extreme step in the same direction, with mixed results (Tavakoli-Targhi 2003).
Adib-Soltani seems to have followed in the same footsteps.

Words are the last refuge for the homely and the familiar, the traditional or the
inherited, in the face of the foreign culture's subjugation of all corners of a nation.

Right sentences

At a second level, the combination of words or the syntagmatic character in the original
sentence fails to find the proper equivalence in translation. The most conspicuous

mistakes such as rendering negation as affirmation aside, the syntagmatic failure may take a variety of forms. The standard English translation of the title of Freud's short book *Das Unbehagen in der Kultur* to *Civilization and its Discontents*, instead of *The Discontent in Culture*, is a case in point (Mobasheri 2013). Moreover, a paradigmatic decision is on display, too: 'civilization' instead of 'culture,' which is not as decisive as 'coup d'état' for 'revolution,' and yet equally of a political nature (Mehrgan 2003). It is at this level that translation can become most conservative, preserving the dominant modes of combining words to form sentences in Persian and resisting foreign syntax as stubbornly as possible. The syntagmatic is the key battlefield in the politics of translation. The most systematic campaign against the capitulation of the Persian language to foreign syntax and to foreign lexicons was waged by the prominent Iranian translator and linguist Abolhasan Najafi's famous 1991 lexicon of Persian common mistakes, *Let's Not Write Incorrectly* (*Ghalat nanevisim*).

Najafi's immensely influential book draws on a wealth of examples or witnesses from classical Persian letters in order to offer suggestions for resisting unjustified, lazy, or hasty admissions of foreign words, idioms, and sentence structures. Those returning from *farang* (France in particular, but Europe or the West generally) are responsible for ruining Persian in their unfettered and careless use of foreign expressions. In the preface to his book, where Najafi states the goal of the books thus, he highlights what he regards as the unfortunate phenomenon of *garteh-bardāri* or calque:

> The word-by-word translation of foreign phrases and expressions that primarily in recent years have found currency in press and radio and television and many books, and which disagrees with the spirit and the nature of Persian. This has been the result of news agencies' hastiness and of translators' carelessness and the linguistic shortcomings of the students who have returned from *farang*.
>
> *(Najafi 1988: 4)*

This implicit defence of the authenticity of Persian as against its historical malformation by European discourses has a political dimension. Najafi's lexicon was composed a year before the end of the Iran–Iraq war and two years before the death of Ayatollah Khomeini. It had already undergone three reprints in three years by 1991, which marked the dawn of what is called the Thermidor of Iranian Revolution, when a wave of economic liberalisation and foreign investment began to shape a new middle class and more prosperous and diverse civil society in the succeeding decades. The more removed Iranian society was from the grey-on-grey years of the war, the more relevant the lexicon became. Its call for return to tradition and to rules meant to oppose the frivolity of new television talk shows, tasteless and ungrammatical reporting on soccer, gaudy, kitschy, ever-growing commercial language, and the tacky pomposity of official speeches. In a word, it was a linguist's critique of a post-war bourgeois society. For all its usefulness and rigor, this critique, however, remained torn between a petty-bourgeois sentiment and an aristocratic claim (see Abazari 2009).

Najafi's project to a great extent conformed to the eminent translator and writer Jalal Al-e Ahmad's (1923–1969) critique of occidentosis (*ghrabzadegi*). The eponymous pamphlet, which turned out to be his most famous non-fiction piece of prose, though not his best, offers a sharp polemic in a political key and on historical premises of two aspects of the Pahlavi's top-down modernisation project. In one fold, it places this project within colonialist and imperialist subjugation of the Orient by the Occident, whereas in another it presents a critique of the cultural and social manifestations of that project, most notably in the figure of *gherti* (dandy). A most conspicuous symptom, the *gherti* mimics the European style in speaking, dressing, and gesturing on the superficial, pathological side, and thereby participating in the hollowing out of, not only native culture, but ultimately national industry and independence. Both Najafi and Al-e Ahmad regarded Persian as an organism plagued by the foreign as a form of disease, although the latter's critique was played in a much more emphatically political key. In so far as translation is working on language as a whole, it is directly implicated in contracting the disease known as the West.

Two responses have been offered to this petty-bourgeois defence of the essence of Persian against the foreign. From a liberal standpoint, the prominent linguist and lexicographer Mohammad-Reza Bateni criticised Najafi for failing to recognise the ever-changing nature of language. In his article called 'Please Let us Write Incorrectly [*Ejāza bedahīd ghalat benevisim*],' written just a year after Najafi's book was published (1988), Bateni departs from the basic assumption that borrowing, be it in words or in syntax, from foreign languages has enriched Persian:

> In most cases, what infuriates these people [like Najafi] and make them rage furiously against any kind of novelty or modernism in language, accusing others of illiteracy and ignorance, hardly bothers the linguists, because they mainly regard these 'mistakes' as correct and in accord with the evolution of language.
>
> *(Bateni 1988: 27)*

An affirmation of change, these words prefigure what was to come in the aftermath of the Iran–Iraq war, which saw an outburst of newspapers in colour, books, and new TV series, leading up to the impressive political and cultural opening of the Reformist era when Mohammad Khatami won a presidential election in 1997 in a landslide victory. At the heart of Bateni's sharp attack on Najafi's lexicon lay a call for accepting the new period of liberalisation soon to come.

In both Najafi and Bateni's cases, the talk of translation and language remains at the level of words and sentences. It is all about the message and not the value, about the technique of rendering the messages correctly and not about the politics of transferring values. The politics of translation was yet to assert itself properly about a decade later when economic liberalisation necessitated a political one. Much of the political force of translation in post-revolutionary, post-war Iran was expended on introducing and advocating a variety of liberal-democratic agendas, translating and assimilating works by Karl Popper, Richard Rorty, Jürgen Habermas, John Rawls, and others. The intellectuals such as the revolutionary-turned-reformist dissident Akbar Ganji began moving towards a rights-based politics as their key concern in nascent civil society (Ganji 2011). From the Constitutional Revolution (1906) through the early years after the 1979 revolution, nation and class became operative concepts in political movements. Analogously, the post-war liberalisation of the economy and subsequent opening up of political space facilitated the emergence of the right of the individual as person. The concept of right has a structural affinity to translation.

As the very space in which freedom of individuals is to be a real possibility, right has two aspects, particular and universal. A particular individual is entitled to see her specific needs, wants, and interests in her capacity as a person met insofar as they do no encroach upon those of others. What protects these particular needs is the universal system of laws enforced by the state. Similarly, translation deals with a particular text with its specific verbal, lexical, syntactic, and stylistic demands to be rewritten in a different language. These specific aspects of the text, however, need to be organised in translation in such a manner as to fit into the demands of the target language, in order to settle down, as it were. But just as not all individual desires are recognised as their rights by the existing laws (the rights to gay marriage, to strike, to vote for women took time and struggle to become the law), so are aspects of a foreign text not acknowledged as valid when translated into a language other than the original language of the text. The foreign in a translation, whether it be the words, the syntactic structure, the concepts, need to fight its way into the target language.

Class paragraphs

The third level in the study of translation, namely paragraphs and whole texts, goes beyond the substitutable words or their combinations in a sentence as the primary site of translation. It is only in the paragraph that a topic manifests itself. It is impossible to pin the political problematic of translation only on one of words or sentences, just as the modern study of translation has persistently eluded scientific taming by means of linguistics or rhetoric or discourse analysis. Translation as a linguistic activity is recalcitrant to the extent that translation studies as a discipline is bound to claim a strong independence. If the core of translation as a necessary practice is linguistic difference, or the fact of differences between many languages, then words, sentences or paragraphs as given units of a verbal composition cannot exhaust that difference.

Value, as proverbially betrayed by the translator, goes beyond messages as supposedly transmitted by translation, finding its home in paragraphs. The rhetorical and poetic aspects of translation appear here. Of the first three parts of rhetoric in classical division, namely, invention, arrangement, and style (the other two, memory and delivery, pertain to speech), invention offers the essential materials for a textual construction: the topics, proofs, commonplaces, even fallacies. It puts forward an argument, at least in deliberative or forensic discourses. Arrangement decides how parts of the text are to sit together. Here is the relationship between paragraphs, introductory remarks, narrative, and the unfolding of the idea articulated. The most abstract part, style, decides the very direction of the text, whether it aims to warn, instruct, reject, agitate, preach, or manifest a revolutionary will. In its style, the text may employ figures as means of enhancing the meaning (see Lanham 1991: 164–176).

All three already leave behind the level of words and sentences, and are thus unattainable by linguistics alone. But it is in particular the case with the third part involving the text's relationship with its context, including its conditions of arising, types of audience, and the entire social or political circumstances in which the text finds itself. This level determines what a text actually does. It claims the text's intervention in the ways tropes, topics, images, metaphors, arguments, and beliefs are distributed and organised in the symbolic sphere or in the body politic, for that matter. Although the style of a work finds its proper analysis in poetics, the tradition of rhetoric teaches us that the most self-sufficient, stylistically boastful works have a rhetorical character in a specific sense: they have something to say about issues that are of public interest. If rhetoric is designated as the art of persuasion, then it must orient itself towards a public, whether this public be a jury, prospective customers, or the revolutionary masses. Translation reveals this orientation most explicitly. Owing to its relationship both to a public and to the whole of a language, it is profoundly invested in politics.

If we take the logical syntactic arrangement of words in successive sentences, the re-organising of which in accordance with the syntax of the target language would be the task of the translator, then the rhetorical does something different:

> Logic allows us to jump from word to word by means of clearly indicated connections. Rhetoric must work in the silence between and around words in order to see what works and how much. The jagged relationship between rhetoric and logic, condition and effect of knowing, is a relationship by which a world is made for the agent, so that the agent can act in an ethical way, a political way, a day-to-day way; so that the agent can be alive, in a human way, in the world. Unless one can at least construct a model of this for the other language, there is no real translation.
>
> *(Spivak 1992: 399)*

Spivak's articulation of the key problematic in translation is helpful, but her emphasis on rhetoric takes us back to what Benjamin calls the 'mode of signification [*Art des Meinens*]' of a language, which is impossible to convey by any act of recreation as it is specific to each language (Benjamin 1968: 77, 78). Languages' modes of signification constitute their very difference from one another. Connotations and shades of meaning belong to this mode as their rhetorical aspects. Instead, what can be safely translated from any language to another, as Jakobson argues, are the logical aspects or the concepts of a foreign text: 'All cognitive experience and its classification is conveyable in any existing language' (1987: 431). Spivak's thesis on 'rhetoricity' makes most sense with regard to translating non-Western literatures into English by subjecting them to the

> law of the strongest: This happens when all the literature of the Third World gets translated into a sort of with-it translatese, so that the literature by a woman in Palestine begins to resemble, in the feel of its prose, something by a man in Taiwan.
>
> *(400)*

Her thesis defends that which remains different and resistible once exposed to the whirlwind of an imperialistic and colonialistic English. It says nothing about the politics of translation in the non-European language itself. The recent expression of this position can be found in Apter's defence of the untranslatability of 'world literature' (2013). Moreover, the untranslatability and its 'rhetoricity' deprive the transformative power of the non-English text of the dominant language itself, precisely through the power of literary form and forms of narrative, as Gould argues (2018), and not by a political or moral commitment to the otherness qua otherness.

Whether the text at issue is deliberative, forensic, or poetic, its rhetorical character appears once the translator starts making decisions about the words' equivalents, the structures of the sentences, and the stylistic modes of conveying the meanings. All along, the translator makes the decisions in tight relation to the modes of signification and expression in the target language. The translator looks at what Najafi calls the 'spirit and nature [*ruh va tabi'at*]' of mother tongue from the outside, from which perspective the mother tongue appears as a body or a body politic with its paradigmatic, syntagmatic, and stylistic rules and habits. Because of the role of what is foreign to this body, what a translation does to the body of the language differs even from the most avant-garde literary productions within the target language itself:

> Once the virus of foreign authorship, infused into the body politic through translation, has spread, the resistance to it residing in the bureau of censors, the guardians of ideological purity, inevitably breaks down. Soon the native author may replicate the new virus. The foreign form of the disease, already infecting the language and morals of the country, grows widespread through the courier of translation. The re-creative transfer of the translation virus is thereby complete and blissfully spreads its invisible message of literary liberation.
>
> *(Barnstone 1993: 123)*

Barnstone's position contains a dialectical core that he does not disclose. The virus of the foreign spreads through translation only when the latter ceases to domesticate it, to rob it of its poison, or to boost the immunity of the translated product by blocking all lexical, syntactical, and stylistic imitation. Translators can actively serve as the guardians of the mother tongue by stopping the foreign contaminating the 'spirit and nature' of the language. In this regard, the ideal of *recreating* a text in the target language, of rewriting a literary work in, say, Persian in such a manner as if the foreign author would have done if they had written in Persian, would prove conservative, a measure against being contaminated by the virus.

On the other hand, Barnstone's talk of literary liberation can imply or accompany colonial capitulation through language. The power relations between national languages determine the nature of the literary liberation. Take the example of Algeria in relation to France, the coloniser. The double character of being contaminated and being liberated literarily once exposed to the virus of the foreign—a dialectic that retains its force in Barnstone's words only at the level of rhetoric—generates an in-between space for both translators and writers in the colonised country. The politics of such a double space involves a struggle on two fronts. In Mehrez's words on Algerian experience:

> The challenge of such space 'in between' has been double: these texts seek to decolonize themselves from two oppressors at once, namely the western ex-colonizer who naively boasts of their existence and ultimately recuperates them and the 'traditional,' 'national' cultures which shortsightedly deny their importance and consequently marginalize them ... It was crucial for the postcolonial text to challenge both its own indigenous, conventional models as well as the dominant structures and institutions of the colonizer in a newly forged language that would accomplish this double movement ...
>
> *(1992: 121, 122)*

In the case of the Moroccan writer Abdelfatah Kilito, she adds: 'the language of the Other can serve a double purpose: it may be the arena for confrontation, for resistance to the Other, but it may also be a means of self-liberation' (123). How this double character of authorship through translation manifests itself in the rhetorical and poetic aspects of particular texts remains to be investigated individually. Mehrez sheds light on what is dialectical in Barnstone's one-sided characterisation of the virus of the foreign. Even so, this position fails adequately to describe the politics of translation in Iran. For Iran has never been a fully colonised country in modern times—particularly in Iran since the 1979 revolution with its two key slogans: independence (*esteqlāl*) and freedom (*āzādi*). The colonialist in-between space changes its character when the official discourse loudly proclaims anti-imperialism and anti-Western as official policies (notwithstanding the strong presence of modern European institutions from the parliament to the constitution and the division of power) (see Abrahamian 1993: 13–38).

If historical comparison is possible, then Iran's case resembles more that of Egypt. Notes Jacquemond, 'in Egypt the split between national and imported cultures was never complete, so that Western intellectual production could be integrated through and by the national language' (1992: 142). Owing to economic, political, and military influence, Iran received a European value system in a similar manner. Yet, this account remains abstract if we do not take into account the two aspects of the reception. That is, first, the European value system was itself deeply conflicted and contradictory: both constitutional liberal democracy with its capitalist mode of production and socialist counter-forces belonged to that system. Secondly, in the case of Iran, the 1979 revolution introduced a national and regional interruption in the very self-understanding of the 'Occidentalized elite,' in Jacquemond's terms (142),

In the concluding words of his brief preface to his Persian translation of a key philosophical work on twentieth-century Marxism, the Iranian leftist translator Mohammad-Jafar Pooyandeh writes:

> On a final note, I continued translating the book [Georg Lukács's] *History and Class Consciousness* under utmost class pressures and worst material and psychological circumstances, and it was perhaps the sum of those pressures that aroused in my existence the urge to finish the translation of this book. And indeed, what better consolation than rendering into Persian one of the most important books in the world?
>
> *(Pooyandeh 1998: 10)*

These words were written about seventeen years after the 1979 revolution, a few months after the beginning of the Reformist Era, when Mohammad Khatami won the presidency in 1997. Less than a year before, the forty-four-year-old Pooyandeh had been murdered during the December 1998 killings of several Iranian dissident intellectuals and writers (Gheissari and Nasr 2006: 111–112). Bemoaning the damning conditions of translation, especially among those who have chosen translation as a vocation, is not uncommon in Persian translators' prefaces. Even so, it is not easy to find a case in which the personal, the political, and the conceptual dimensions of a translation merge so completely as in the above passage. This, however, was in a decade in post-revolutionary Iran when the revolutionary Marxist left had been pushed to the margins, giving way to a nascent liberal-democratic discourse spearheaded by former revolutionary-turned-reformist intellectuals. Pooyandeh presents class struggle as the unifying moment in the relation of the West and Iran. He alludes, therefore, to a revisiting of the *taqābul*, or conflict between 'tradition' and 'modernity.'

The second case makes for the most reflective form of turning translation into a problematic in modern Iran. In a collection of essays, in Persian *'Aql-e afsordeh* (*Depressed Reason*), the Iranian leftist philosopher and translator Farhadpour (featured in the present volume: see Chapter 4) writes:

> Not only is the motivation and origin of these essays translation, but so also is their rule and mode of writing. One dare say that there is no idea, thought, or

opinion in them that has not already been said somewhere else and in a better way. This judgment stems not from humility, nor does it express any lack of self-confidence or 'occidentosis.' The writer of these lines over the past years has repeatedly stressed that in the present epoch—roughly starting with the Constitutional Revolution and probably ending in a not too-near future—translation in the broadest sense of the word is the only true form of *thinking* for us. My own personal experience in translating and authorship, and the achievements of others in these two realms no less, testify to this view ... Today, in order to defend thinking one must justify and defend translation.

(Farhadpour 1999: 10)

Depressed Reason hardly deals with the concept of class directly. The key to the essays, however, is the notion of contradiction permeating major intellectual endeavours in modern German thought: from Hegel's phenomenology of spirit and Nietzsche's aesthetics to Weberian sociology, Husserlian phenomenology, and Benjamin's theory of history. One cannot overestimate the significance of the *Depressed Reason* as the first immanent critical reflection on European modernity on its own terms, performed in Persian and thus highly translational in its mode of writing.

In virtue of this immanence of thought through translation, Farhadpour's position on the *taqābol* issue sharply distinguishes him from his peers. He knows that occidentosis or 'westoxification' is a poisonous medicine administered to both sides of the *taqābol*: modernity and tradition. For him, 'translation in the broad sense of the word encompasses both our relation to European modernity and our own cultural past. Today we need not only to translate Kant and Hegel but also the writings of Ibn-Sina and Molla-Sadra' (13). Translation is a form of self-reflection that reflects on the other. It generates consciousness of the crisis-ridden modernity into which Iran, like 'all other nations of the word' (15), has been integrated. While the self is fraught with contradictions in the context of modernisation, nation-state building, and capitalist development imposed by the other, the other, too, is entangled with the same conflicts.

Any study of translation in Iran in relation to politics must observe this double relation to the West, one that seeks to intervene not only in the national politics of the target language but in the source language as well. Marxism, in the most diverse shapes that it took since the 1979 revolution, from the works of Lukács to Adorno, was best positioned to show why, on the one hand, translation has always been necessary in modern Iran and how, on the other hand, translation that once backed up a class-conscious politics can offer an immanent, progressive critique of European modernity without falling back into nationalism, traditionalism, or any other reactionary stance vis-à-vis the inevitable historical developments of the modern world.

If we are to grasp the political agency of translation in Iran, we must regard it in relation to the emergence and development of this conceptual trio. Such a perspective will shed a brighter light on the problematic of *taqābol* and further complicate it. Given the role of women as both the object and subject of modern politics in Iran, from Reza Shah's obligatory policy of unveiling to the present-day struggles for their rights, one ought to add a fourth concept to this trio: gender (Sadeghi 2013). But as regards the practice of translation, of these four categories class is best positioned to show why the opposition or the *taqābul* between 'tradition' and 'modernity' ought to be transferred into each opposing term as well.

Dichronism in the 2000s: towards a resolution

During the mid-noughties, in the years immediately preceding the 2009 movement, Far-hadpour and a group of young leftist intellectuals formed the reading and translation circle known as Rokhdad (meaning 'event,' inspired by the political thought of the contemporary French philosopher Alain Badiou). The members of the Rokhdad circle were all based in Tehran and were mainly from a middle- or upper-middle-class background. For some of them, including the present writer as a member, translating meant a means of earning a living. On top of a website devoted to social and political criticism with a sharp theoretical edge and several co-translated works from critical theory and contemporary European radical thought, the circle published four volumes in the series *Ketab-e Rokhdad* (The book of event). These included selected texts by Slavoj Žižek (volume one), Giorgio Agamben, Hannah Arendt, Carl Schmitt, et al. around the topic of violence and law (volume two), Alain Badiou (volume three), and the concept of politics (volume four). The texts would be translated and edited in a collaborative way, accompanied by prefaces, introductions, and footnotes.

The unifying concept running through all the translations was the relationship between critical thinking and an emancipatory politics that, though belonging to the Marxist-socialist tradition, found the language and theoretical means of traditional Marxism in Iran unsatisfying. Recourse to psychoanalysis, theology, aesthetics, and literary theory in their texts and translations signified the desire to find a language to articulate Iran's peculiar, still dichronistic, situation, a path beyond both nativist forms of fundamentalism and liberal-democratic global capitalism. The preface to the first volume of the series sketches the relevance of the project from the standpoint of the politics of translation in contemporary Iran. It draws on Adorno and Horkheimer's insight in their preface to the *Dialectic of Enlightenment*, namely that —I use the Persian translation that Farhadpour and I did—'the particular origin of thinking and its universal perspective have always been inseparable.' It then goes on to state:

> Publishing the *Rokhdad Book* is an attempt to continue thinking in an age in which thinking has turned more than ever into something redundant or perhaps even impossible ... A thinking oriented towards truth is constituted by the tension arising from these two distinct yet inseparable poles.
>
> *(Farhadpour and Mehrgan 2006: 7)*

The preface then goes on to outline the two characters or poles of the Iranian context within which one engages in theoretical-translational practice:

> Insofar as the 'particular origin of thinking' is concerned, that is, the particular social and historical conditions underlying the production of theoretical discourses, there is no doubt that the political turn in our situation calls for a new understanding of theoretical action [*konesh-e nazari*], one which can no longer be subsumed under the general category of 'cultural work' [*kār-e farhangi*], as was done in the previous period. Under the present circumstances, the political act and thinking require a higher degree of forthrightness in theoretical practice, just as theorisation requires a higher degree of reflection and political self-consciousness. Theoretical thinking continues essentially to be nothing but translation in its variegated senses; however,

experience has shown us that realising translation as a creative act owes its success to a great extent to collective work and political insight and commitment.

(Farhadpour and Mehrgan 2006: 7–8)

Written just after the end of the Reformist Era and the beginning of the Ahmadinejad presidency, this statement can be better understood when compared with the one in Farhadpour's *'Aql-e afsordeh* (see Chapter 4), in which there was little talk of politics in relation to translation as an essentially hermeneutic act of cultural self-understanding and maturity. Here, in contrast, politics is an explicit condition for the possibility of translation as a cultural, pedagogical, enlightening activity. The politics in translation and as its condition reveals itself more explicitly when we turn to the second aspect of thinking:

Insofar as the 'universal perspective' of thinking is concerned, our main goal is to grasp what thinking and radical critique in a globalized world means, [...] a critique of the various forms of the realization of the cultural logic of late capitalism or any other ideology that in the form of Buddhism and Kabbalah or 'Maulana [Rumi] according to Madonna' attempts to make life in the commodity chaos of capitalism 'peaceful and fun.' [...] this universal perspective, which unites our voices with those of a Badiou, an Agamben, a Žižek, and a Rancière, is certainly inseparable from its particular origin, that is, from the specific historical circumstances under which we read, translate, and write. It is all too easy to employ a radical critique of postmodern capitalism or to criticize banality in a banal fashion (as performed by the state television cultural programs or the 'cultural' analyses of certain newspapers, and so on). It is our difficult task to stand up against reactionary assaults on thinking and to combine the critique of populist despotism and of false egalitarianism with a resistance to nihilist relativism and neoliberal pluralism.

(Farhadpour and Mehrgan 2006: 9)

The mid-noughties marked a particularly despairing situation both globally—the rise of the US 'war on terror' spearheaded by the Bush administration in Afghanistan and Iraq—and domestically—a harsh neoliberal capitalism disguised as 'justice' (*'adālat*, or in the wrong but more honest-sounding unofficial pronunciation, *'edālat*) in the discourse of Ahmadinejad and his advocates. It is noteworthy that, in colloquial parlance, the Persian word for justice is pronounced *'edālat*, whereas the more official *'adālat* already betrays, at least to my ears, a certain falseness or at least unattainability. The meagre yet promising political opening of the Reformist Era had waned, giving rise to a right-wing populism that pretended to speak for the people who had been overwhelmed by the capitalist liberalism of the previous two presidencies since the end of the Iran–Iraq war. The cultural work that enjoyed the backing of a Reformist state as a vanguard—relaxing censorship for books, short-lived freedom of the press—lost that backing and was forced to rethink its own conditions of possibility.

The moment for experiencing a concrete relationship to politics for the translators and intellectuals of the Rokhdad circle and many others arrived with the remarkable political movement of 2009 (see Postel and Hashemi 2010). The failure of that movement, for all the deep impact it left on the political scene in Iran, put an end to the Rokhdad. Developments since have contributed little to revising the politics of translation in Iran. For one thing, the wave of mostly inadequate and hasty translations of theoretical and literary works, not least under the influence of the works introduced by the Rokhdad circle, has failed to clear the way for a political self-reflection with regard to the dichronistic situation since 1979. For another, the global turn to the populist right with strong nationalist and racist underpinnings coupled with worsened economic lives of the masses domestically has created far more perplexing problems for theoretical thinking, and for translation no less. The simultaneous rise of socialism in recent years, with the revival of the workers' movement in Iran, however, may provide fresh conditions for rethinking and a more creative translational practice. In such a practice, then, navigating between words, sentences, and paragraphs, choosing from them as units of decision making, will not amount to an arbitrary act of private deliberation but involve a necessary expression of how nation, class, and rights are configured in the present situation. Here, perhaps, the political mode of translation as internal to our study of translation, observed in this chapter, necessarily gives way, or ought to give way, to politics as the external mode determining the entire practice of translating and the lives of the translators, no less.

Related topics

Thought/Translation; Translators as Organic Intellectuals; Translating Marx in Japan.

Note

1 Unless otherwise indicated, all translations are mine.

Further reading

Berman, Antoine (1999) *La Traduction-poésie*. Ed. Martine Broda. Strasbourg: Presses Universitaires de Strasbourg. For an English translation of an essay by Berman recapping his argument, see 'Translation and the Trials of the Foreign' in Lawrence Venuti (ed.) (2000) *The Translation Studies Reader*. London: Routledge: 284–297.

Berman's book offers both a historical and systematic account of the key category in the social and political practice of translation: the foreign. This book shows the different modalities by which the foreign affects the familiar through translation.

Berman, Antoine (2018) *The Age of Translation: A Commentary on Walter Benjamin's 'The Task of the Translator'*. Trans. Chantal Write. London: Routledge.

Recently translated into English, this volume contains an in-depth examination of Benjamin's classic essay on translation (originally published as a preface to his translation of poems by Baudelaire) by a key figure in the continental tradition of translation studies.

Barnstone, Willis (1993) *The Poetics of Translation: History, Theory, Practice*. New Haven: Yale University Press.

In a fragmented style of exposition, Barnstone's book explores various aspects of translation from a poetic, not merely linguistic, perspective by placing them within the traditions of letters and reading in Europe.

References

Abazari, Yousef (2009) 'Kalameh be kalameh, shey' bi shey' [Word by Word, Thing by Thing],' [online]. Avaiable at: www.yousefabazari.persianblog.com [accessed 21 February 2019].
Abrahamian, Ervand (1993) *Khomeinism: Essays on the Islamic Republic*. Berkley: University of California Press.

Adib-Soltani, Mirshams-al-Din (tr.) (1983) *Sanjesh-e kherad-e nāb (Critique of Pure Reason) by Immanuel Kant* (1st ed.). Tehran: Amir Kabir.

Adorno, Theodor W. (1991) *Notes to Literature. Vol. 1.* Trans. Sherry Weber Nicholsen. New York: Columbia University Press.

Afari, Janet, and Kevin B. Anderson (2005) *Foucault and the Iranian Revolution. Gender and the Seductions of Islamism.* Chicago: The University of Chicago Press.

Ahmadi, Babak (1998) *Mo'ammā-ye moderniteh (The Enigma of Modernity).* Tehran: Nashr-e markaz.

Al-e Ahmad, Jalal (1984) *Occidentosis: A Plague from the West.* Trans. R. Campbell. Berkley: Mizan.

Apter, Emily (2013) *Against World Literature: On the Politics of Untranslatability.* London: Verso.

Ashouri, Dariush (1997) *Mā va moderniyat (We and Modernity).* Tehran: Mo'assese farhangi-e serat.

Bakhtin, Mikhail (1984) *Problems of Dostoevsky's Poetics.* Trans. Caryl Emerson. Minneapolis: University of Minnesota Press.

Barnstone, Willis (1993) *The Poetics of Translation: History, Theory, Practice.* New Haven: Yale University Press.

Barthes, Roland (1982) *A Barthes Reader.* Ed. Susan Sontag. New York: Hill and Wang.

Bateni, Mohammad-Reza (1988) 'ejāza bedahid ghalat benevisim [Please Let Us Write Incorrect],' *Adine* 24: 26–29.

Benjamin, Walter (1968) *Illuminations.* Trans. Harry Zone. New York: Schocken.

Boase-Beier, Jean (2006) *Stylistic Approaches to Translation.* Manchester: St. Jerome Publishing.

Chilton, Paul, and Christina Schäffner (1997) 'Discourse and Politics,' in *Discourse as Social Interaction* (pp. 303–330). Ed. Teun van Dijk. London: Sage.

Emami, Karim (1994) *Az past va boland-e tarjomeh (On the Ups and Downs of Translation).* Tehran: Niloofar.

Evans, Jonathan, and Fruela Fernandez (2018) 'Introduction: Emancipation, Secret Histories and the Language of Hegemony,' in *Routledge Handbook of Translation and Politics* (pp. 1–15). Eds. Jonathan Evans, and Fruela Fernandez. London: Routledge.

Farhadpour, Morad (1999) *'Aql-e afsordeh: ta'ammolāti dar bāb-e tafakkor-e modern (The Depressed Reason: Reflections on Modern Thought).* Tehran: Negah-e No.

Farhadpour, Morad, and Omid Mehrgan (2006) 'Preface,' in *Slāvoy jijek: nazariyeh, siyāsat, din (Slavoj Zizek: Theory, Politics, Religion)* (pp. 7–13). Eds. M. Farhadpour, O. Mehrgan, and M. Eslami. Ketab-e rokhdaad. Tehran: Gam-e no.

Finch, Geoff (2000) *Linguistic Terms and Concepts.* New York: St Martin's Press.

Ganji, Akbar (2011) 'What Is Our Problem?' in *Civil Society and Democracy in Iran* (pp. 127–159). Ed. Ramin Jahanbegloo. Lanham: Lexington.

Gheissari, Ali, and Vali Nasr (2006) *History and the Quest for Liberty.* Oxford: Oxford University Press.

Gould, Rebecca (2018) 'Hard Translation: Persian Poetry and Post-National Literary Form,' *Forum for Modern Language Studies* 54 (2): 191–206.

Jacquemond, Richard (1992) 'Translation and Cultural Hegemony: The Case of French-Arabic Translation,' in *Rethinking Translation.* Ed. Lawrence Venuti. London: Routledge. 139–158.

Jahanbegloo, Ramin (1994) *Moderniteh, demokrāsi, va rowshanfekrān (Modernity, Democracy, and the Intellelctuals).* Tehran: Nashr-e markaz.

Jakobson, Roman (1987) *Language in Literature.* Ed. Krystyna Pomorska, and Stephen Rudy. Cambridge, MA: Belknap.

Kamshaad, Hasan (2007) *Motarjemān, khā'enān: matteh be khashkhāsh-e chand tarjomeh (Translators, Traitors: Hairsplitting Concerning Some Translations).* Tehran: Ney.

Karoubi, Behrouz (2017) 'A Concise History of Translation in Iran from Antiquity to the Present Time,' *Perspectives* 25 (4): 594–608.

Katouzian, Homa (1981) *The Political Economy of Modern Iran: Despotism and Pseudo-Modernism, 1926–1979.* London: MacMillan.

Katouzian, Homa (2003) *Iranian History and Politics: The Dialectic of State and Society.* London: RoutledgeCurzon.

Khalili, Yasamin, and Ali Khazaeefar (2015) 'Ta'sir-e ide'oloji-ye chāp dar 'arseh-ye entekhāb-e āsār-e adabi jehat-e tarjomeh [The Impacts of Left Ideology on Choosing Literary Works for Translation],' *Faslnāmeh-ye motāli'āt-e zabān va tarjomeh* 3 (Fall 2015): 1–28.

Kianoush, Hasan (2002) *Vājeh-hā-ye barābar-e farhangistān (The Equivalent Words of Farhangestan).* Tehran: Soroush.

Lanham, Richard A. (1991) *A Handlist of Rhetorical Terms* (2nd ed.). Berkley: The University of California Press.

Marashi, Afshin (2008) *Nationalizing Iran: Culture, Power, and the State, 1870–1940*. Seattle: University of Washington Press.

Mason, Ian, and Miranda Stewart (2001) 'Interactional Pragmatics, Face and the Dialogue Interpreter,' in *Triadic Exchanges: Studies in Dialogue Interpreting*. Ed. Ian Mason. Manchester: St. Jerome Publishing. 51–70.

Matin-Asgari, Afshin (2018) *Both Eastern and Western: An Intellectual History of Iranian Modernity*. Cambridge: Cambridge University Press.

Mehrez, Samia (1992) 'Translation and the Postcolonial Experience: The Francophone North African Text,' in *Rethinking Translation*.Ed. Lawrence Venuti. London: Routledge. 120–138.

Mehrgan, Omid (2003) 'Translator's Note to *Nākhoshāyandi-hā-ye farhang* (Das Unbehagen in der Kultur), by Sigmund Freud,' Tehran: Gam-e no.

Mobasheri, Mohammad (tr.) (2013) *Tamaddon va malālāt-hā-ye ān (Das Unbehagen in der Kultur) by Sigmund Freud*. Tehran: Mahi.

Moeen, Mohammad (1998) 'Loghat-e fārsi-ye ebn-e-sinā va [...] [Ibn-Sina's Persian Words and Their Impact on Persian Literature],' in *Moqadameh-ye loghatnāmeh-ye dehkhodā (Preface to the Dehkhoda Dictionary)*. Ed. Mohammad Moeen, and Seyyed Jafar Shahidi. Tehran: The Dehkhoda Dictionary Institute. 67–88.

Moghaddam, Hasan (1922) *Ja'far-Khān az farang bargashteh (Ja'far Khan Has Returned from Europe)*. Tehran: Faruus.

Munday, Jeremy (2007) 'Translating Ideology, a Textual Approach,' *The Translator* 13 (2): 195–217.

Najafi, Abolhasan (1988) *Ghalat nanevisim: farhang-e doshvāri-ha-ye zabān-e fārsi (Let's Not Write Incorrect: The Dictionary of the Difficulties of the Persian Language)*. Tehran: Markaz-e nashr-e daneshgahi.

Najafi, Saleh (2015) 'Ketāb-hā-yi ke nabāyad khānd [Books We Should Not Read],' *Shargh Daily* 1989 (13 April).

Nord, Christiane (1997) *Translating as a Purposeful Activity: Functionalist Approaches Explained*. London: Routledge.

Parks, Tim (2007) *Translating Style*. Manchester: St. Jerome Publishing.

Pooyandeh, Mohamma-Jafar (1998) 'Translator's Note to *Tārikh va āgāhi-ye tabaqāti* (History and Class Consciousness) by Georg Lukács,' Tehran: Tajrobeh. 9–10.

Postel, Daniel, and Nader Hashemi (eds.) (2010) *The People Reloaded: The Green Movement and the Struggle for Iran's Future*. New York: Melville House.

Reiss, Katharina (1971) 'Type, Kind and Individuality of Text: Decision Making in Translation,' in *The Translation Studies Reader*. Ed. Lawrence Venuti. London: Routledge. 161–171.

Sadeghi, Fatemeh (2013) *Kashf-e hejāb: bāzkhāni-ye yek modākheleh-ye modern (Unveiling: Revisiting a Modern Intervention)*. Tehran: Negah-e mo'aser.

Schäffner, Christina (2004) 'Political Discourse Analysis from the Point of View of Translation Studies,' *Journal of Language and Politics* 3 (1): 117–150.

Sciolino, Elaine (2011) *Persian Mirrors: The Elusive Face of Iran*. New York: Fire Press.

Shakeri, Khosro (1974) *Asnād-e tārikhi-ye jonbesh-e kārgari, sosiyāl-demokrāsi va komunisti-ye irān, jeld-e avval (Historical Documents of the Workers', Social Democratic, and Communist Movement in Iran)*. Florence: Mazdak.

Sharifi, Majid (2013) *Imagining Iran: The Tragedy of Subaltern Nationalism*. Lanham: Lexington.

Spivak, Gayatri Chakravorty (1992) 'The Politics of Translation,' in *The Translation Studies Reader*. Ed. Lawrence Venuti. London: Routledge. 397–416.

Tabari, Ehsan (1981) 'Bahsi darbāra-ye semat-hā va vazāyef-e honar [A Discussion about the Status and the Tasks of Art: On the Occasion of the Third Anniversary of the Islamic Republic],' *Shurā-ye nevisandegān va honarmandān-e irān* 5 (Winter): 8–15.

Tavakoli-Targhi, Mohamad (2003) *Tajadod-e bumi (Vernacular Modernity)*. Tehran: Nashr-e tarikh.

Yazdani, Sohrab (2013) *ejtemā'iyun-e 'āmiyun (The Social Democrats)*. Tehran: Ney.

Zibakalam, Sadegh (2001) *Sonnat va moderniteh: risheh-yābi-ye 'elal-e nākāmi-ye eslāhāt va nowsāzi-ye siyāsi dar irān-e 'asr-e qājār (Tradition and Modernity: Finding the Causes of the Failure of Reforms and Political Renewal in the Iran of the Qajar Period)*. Tehran: Rozaneh.

30

Civil resistance through online activist translation in Taiwan's Sunflower Student Movement[1]

Pin-ling Chang

Introduction

The Sunflower Student Movement in early 2014, one of the largest acts of civil disobedience in Taiwan (Wang 2014), sparked many relevant studies of Taiwan–China relations, civil journalism, civil resistance, and use of information technologies in civic engagement (e.g. Fell 2017; Lepesant 2018; Liu and Su 2017), yet few researchers have investigated activist translation activity in this movement, which involved all the aforesaid elements and played a significant role in rallying global support for the movement. In this chapter, I will first give a brief overview of this movement, introduce the internet and communication technologies that facilitated activist translation in the movement, and compare the activist translators and translation in this movement with other international politicised translation communities and activist translation in other place-based protest movements. To explore further the activist translation in this movement, I examine the postings under the 'Protesters occupy Taiwan legislature' assignment on *CNN iReport*, with the reasons for selecting *CNN iReport* data and the five features of its activist translation presented in detail. The last section of this chapter draws on French ethnographer and sociologist Pierre Bourdieu's theory about media and cultural production and his concepts of 'field,' 'habitus,' and 'capital' (Bourdieu 1990, 1993; Bourdieu and Wacquant 1992) to provide an explanation as to what caused the surge of activist translation during the movement and why the activist translators achieved success in the end.

The Sunflower Student Movement: overview

On the evening of 19 March 2014, hundreds of students stormed Taiwan's parliament, also known as the Legislative Yuan in Taiwan, and continued their occupation of the parliament until 10 April 2014. The occupation, later dubbed the Sunflower Student Movement, was initiated mainly by Taiwanese university students over the controversy that the Cross-Strait Service Trade Agreement (CSSTA) between Taiwan and China was passed without thorough bipartisan deliberation and over concerns that the agreement might be 'a cloaked attack on Taiwan's independence from an ever-growing China'

(Roubini and Tashea 2014; Yu and Chen 2014). The Taiwanese government's 'black box negotiations' with China aroused a sense of self-preservation among the public (Brown and Li 2014). In addition to those inside parliament during the occupation, over 100,000 people, connected or mobilised through the internet, supported the movement outside parliament in various ways (Hung 2015).

A few prominent groups or organisations, such as g0v, the Black Island Nation Youth Front, Democratic Front against Cross-Strait Trade in Services Agreement, and Citizen Action Coalition 1985, led or pushed forward the movement by using internet technologies and social media websites. For instance, g0v, which took shape at the end of 2012 and has now become one of Asia's largest open-source communities for presenting the vision of digital natives and helping citizens better understand and monitor how their government works (g0v 2019; Roubini and Tashea 2014), created online public spaces for the movement participants to post, edit, and revise information on the movement both individually and collectively in a real-time manner, with the help of collaboration tools, such as Google Drive, Hackpad, EtherCalc, and GitHub (Roubini and Tashea 2014). Meanwhile, all of the above activist groups created their own websites or Facebook fan pages where members and visitors could share their ideas and opinions. Specifically, during the movement, g0v's Facebook fan page got 350,000 members within a week and a total of more than four million views of its postings (Wu 2014). Aiming to produce as many first-hand and unscreened news reports as possible in a 'professional' manner for the public, dozens of journalism majors at undergraduate and postgraduate levels formed a news team, creating a 'NewseForum' Facebook fan page[2] that later became the official source of information about the movement (Hsu 2014). Social networking media and technologies, such as Facebook, Line, and WhatsApp, were extensively used to mobilise the public for either well-organised or impromptu activities during the movement (Hsu 2014) and particularly effective in rallying support from those who tended to act alone without any organisational or group affiliation. In the event of slow broadband or network congestion, freeware apps that feature text-based instant communication such as Line or WhatsApp could still function properly to maintain public dynamics and coherence. Meanwhile, despite their comparatively inadequate quality of sound and image, the live feeds of the parliament occupation around the clock through UStream were neither vetted nor edited; the 'real-time and all-time' broadcasting of 'original flavour and style' attracted two million viewers (Hsu 2014). The use of internet technologies and social media kept gathering and maintaining the momentum of the movement. To show resistance to the defiant government, more than 500,000 people attended a rally near parliament on 30 March 2014, which was one of the largest acts of Taiwan's civil disobedience (Wang 2014). The government finally bowed to public pressure, with the passing of the CSSTA delayed until now. Arguably, the success of the Sunflower Student Movement could be largely attributed to the proper exertion of the power of information technologies.

Collectives and individuals in Taiwan activist translation

The success of the Sunflower Student Movement in forcing Taiwan's government to withdraw its service trade agreement with China might be partly attributed to the activist translation that made the movement visible and understandable to the world, yet what made this activist translation possible and powerful was information and communication technologies introduced and widespread in recent decades. On the first night of the occupation, two postgraduate journalism students inside parliament produced news reports in Mandarin Chinese and in English by using their smartphones and posted them on

Facebook, YouTube, *CNN iReport*, and other communication apps and websites (Wu 2014: 35). Soon afterwards, inside parliament, many foreign-language majors or people with foreign-language skills were called upon to help with the rapid production of the translation of what concerned the movement into as many as 35 languages to facilitate the circulation of the information about the movement and win global support (Chen 2015). Both inside and outside parliament, some activist translations were collectively produced in relays through use of open-source community websites, such as Hackpad and bulletin board systems (BBS) (Roubini and Tashea 2014; Yu and Chen 2014). The website of Hackpad was swarming with so many users who were concerned with the movement that the huge website traffic paralysed the website five times within three days (Hsu 2014).

Meanwhile, to save time, Google Translate was also used in the preliminary stage of producing translations. As shown in an event log on a GitHub Gist webpage that recorded the process of producing the English translation of a text entitled 'Sunflower Movement Declaration Extract,' the Mandarin Chinese source text was imported to Google Translate library with the source code '# Translate back and forth between Traditional Chinese and English 100 times' (Marsimaria 2015). The benefits of using web-based collaborative real-time text editors were obvious: collective brainstorming, fast delivery, and energy efficiency. However, the quality of translation could not be guaranteed by such methods.

As 'the structure of the movement is simultaneously bottom-up and horizontal' (Roubini and Tashea 2014), the activist translators were not necessarily teamed up with one another. Many people followed along and had their translated texts done on a solitary basis and posted on their personal blogs, Facebook pages, or news media interactive websites, contributing to a surge of amateur translations during a short period of time. This proved the positive effect of social media on the progress in building civil society, which had occurred in other movements, such as the Tunisian revolution in 2011, widely recognised to have been driven by Facebook and Twitter (Kahlaoui 2013). On the plus side, these methods created a wide range of translated reports and stories to help outsiders get a clearer picture of the Sunflower Student Movement. Translators, whether directly involved in on-site protests or following the movement from afar, could voice their concerns or vent their resentment through translation.

The translation activity during the Sunflower Student Movement may be associated with terms such as community translation, translation crowdsourcing, user-generated translation, collaborative translation, or volunteer translation, all of which more or less concern openness and sharing advocated by internet technologies, yet none of these can adequately cover the nature of the translation activity in question. While user-generated translation is done by those who need the translation (Pym 2011: 108), the commonly shared characteristics of the remaining terms 'highlight that it is translation performed voluntarily by [i]nternet users and is usually produced in some form of collaboration often on specific platforms by a group of people forming an online community' (O'Hagan 2011: 14). By contrast, the translation activity during the Sunflower Student Movement aimed to appeal to a global audience and was not necessarily conducted collectively or on specific platforms; to those mostly unprofessional translators, achieving specific political aims was top priority. In general, the translation activity during the movement, which combined technologies, networking, and translation, was a social practice that confirmed Folaron's prediction about the trend in network studies research:

Representation on the Web of th[e] linguistic, cultural diversity, and increased multi-lingual data exchange and communication, will become important factors in future network analysis research, rendered even more complex by diversifying practices of translation assisted by multiple technologies, including a more prominent role for machine translation.

(Folaron 2010: 232)

Activist translation with volunteer translation communities in Europe

Associations or communities of volunteer translators and interpreters are now burgeoning in Europe, such as ECOS, Traduttori per la Pace, and Babels.[3] As the oldest of its kind, ECOS, Traductores e Intérpretes por la solidaridad (ECOS, Translators and Interpreters for Solidarity) was founded around the Faculty of Translation and Interpreting at the University of Granada, Spain, in 1998. The association declares its aim to be providing services of translation and interpreting to disadvantaged groups to promote and achieve equality. More specifically, it trains translators and interpreters, and its members undertake volunteer translation and interpreting tasks for social forums, non-governmental organisations, and other non-profit organisations that share a similar philosophy with ECOS (Gambier 2007: 663–664; García et al. 2011). Similarly, Traduttori per la Pace (Translators for Peace), founded in 1999 and based in Italy, consists of some 300 members. Italian is used as the main language within the association (Baker 2010: 32; Gambier 2007: 664). The association aims to settle international disputes through voluntary translation service 'in every language and by whatever channel' against 'the use of war' and those who wish to join shall abide by 'the inspirational principles and objectives of the Association' (Traduttori per la Pace 1999). Another much larger and organised international network of volunteer interpreters and translators, Babels, was founded mainly to serve the interpreting needs of social forums. In late 2004, the number of its volunteers was said to be more than 7,000, with 63 languages involved (Boéri 2005). Babels involves itself in social movements on a global scale and sees itself as an activist group committed to making the world better in the realms of politics, economy, and the environment (Gambier 2007: 662–663). As indicated above, volunteer translators and interpreters in Europe tend to work within the framework of the voluntary associations, which may receive external funding, provide professional training, and establish online platforms for volunteer translators and interpreters to exchange ideas and collaborate on projects.

By contrast, the ad hoc translators who voluntarily provided their services during Taiwan's Sunflower Student Movement were not affiliated with any translators' or interpreters' association. Some of them worked in groups, but the group members comprised a horizontal, non-hierarchical structure. Each of them still enjoyed much freedom, just like another amorphous crowd of unaffiliated individuals who did their translations alone outside parliament. The common goal of these translators, who belonged to the generation of 'digital natives' (g0v 2019), was not for the greater good of the world but clear and simple—making the Sunflower Student Movement known to and supported by the world and showing their resistance against their government that had ignored the voice of its people, which was actually an outburst of anxiety over Taiwan's increasing economic dependency upon China (Lepesant 2018: 77–78).

This surge of ideologically motivated translation activity ebbed away around the end of the movement.

Activist translation in other place-based protest movements

Baker (2016a) explores how individual volunteer subtitlers helped Egyptian protesters challenge the dominant narratives by making their narratives of the Egyptian revolution of 2011 heard and understood by audiences around the world. The volunteer subtitlers in Baker's study worked within two collectives connected with the Egyptian revolution, Mosireen and Words of Women from the Egyptian revolution, by subtitling the videos made by film makers who might not have taken subtitling into consideration at the time of filmmaking, and therefore, how these subtitlers were positioned in place-based collectives and how they negotiated with the collectives to boost the effect of the political project concerned became the main foci of Baker's study. By contrast, activist translators in Taiwan's Sunflower Student Movement were not necessarily working for collectives; some, if not many, tended to engage in activist translation on a solitary basis. They translated mainly in order to tell stories about the movement and rally global support, unlike the volunteer subtitlers in the Egyptian Revolution of 2011, who resorted to translation as a means of solving the crisis where their current forms of language could not effect change, to foster networks of solidarity among the Egyptians, and to introduce and subtitle documentaries of foreign protest movements for a local Arabic audience (Baker 2016b: 231–233, 2016c: 9).

Translation has played a significant role in the process of democratisation and the progress of democracy. Most studies of activist translators focus on those who received professional training and who work as professional translators and interpreters (Carcelen-Estrada 2018; Doerr 2018). By contrast, although a few of the volunteer translators and interpreters working collectively inside Taiwan's parliament were MA students in translating and interpreting (Chen 2015), most activist translators during the Sunflower Student Movement had not received professional training. They were unfamiliar with professional codes of conduct; hence they did not engage in self-censorship (Merkle 2018: 245–247). Consequently, they could not be expected to maintain neutrality or impartiality in their translations. In some cases, even professional political translators 'openly intervene[d] to challenge cultural and linguistic power asymmetries' (Doerr 2018: 4).

Activist translations during the Sunflower Student Movement—a case of postings on pre-2015 *CNN iReport*

Since the activist translations of the Sunflower Student Movement were scattered on the internet, it is impossible to exhaust all the relevant translations, nor can we reliably generalise concerning the features of the activist translation of the movement by examining the translated texts announced by any certain leading group. Of all the sources of translation output during the movement, *CNN iReport* was one of the few to gather translated materials produced on an individual or collective basis. Tsai (2014) reported that some of the movement participants inside parliament were contacted and encouraged at the very beginning of the movement by *CNN iReport* to provide first-hand videos, photos, and information. This international, open website, aimed at communicating what's happening around the world, was unaffiliated with any group or organisation of Taiwan. Therefore, not only Taiwan-based social movement groups but also individuals who paid close attention to the movement had activist translations, in the form of articles, video clips, or photos, posted on this website.

CNN iReport was first launched in 2006, with a view to tapping into citizen journalism that might provide the news outlet with more first-hand and multifaceted news and stories, particularly around significant world issues. Before its revival in late 2015 amid social media prevalence, *CNN iReport* was affiliated with the mainstream CNN network yet operated on a separate platform (Ingram 2015). In other words, for its first decade, *CNN iReport* might have been largely regarded as a trustworthy global news platform, while its postings were free of prior censorship or interventions. Despite some unfortunate cases of fake news (e.g. Kramer 2008), this practice greatly facilitated news gathering and sharing among world citizens and allowed some significant but initially ignored issues to gain global attention (e.g. Silverman 2012).

Although CNN is a media organisation that 'mediates between society and state, in which the public organi[s]es itself as bearer of public opinion [and] accords with the principle of the public sphere' (Habermas 2010: 115), the pre-2015 *CNN iReport* went beyond Habermas's definition of the public sphere. More precisely, *CNN iReport* at the time of the Sunflower Student Movement was used as a platform for connection and communication between the movement participants and global audience. This platform was not subject to the Taiwanese government (the state) but became a third space where, thanks to internet and communication technologies, unaffiliated individuals and collectives could convey whatever messages about the movement they wanted, without worrying about possible government suppression. The activist translations posted on *CNN iReport* could be seen as citizen journalism, a practice that 'giv[es] voice to those whose voices are ignored or suppressed' and is 'capable of producing counter-publics and counter-discourses' (Rone 2016: 210). Activist translations during the movement were not limited to the lived experiences of the translators themselves and/or the movement participants. In some cases, photos, videos, or reports produced by Taiwan's mainstream media that might echo what the translators wished to say were also reposted to *CNN iReport*, with partial or full translation provided.

During the Sunflower Student Movement (18 March to 10 April 2014), the *CNN iReport* website saw a total of 554 postings under the assignment entitled 'Protesters occupy Taiwan legislature.' One hundred and eight of them included or involved activist Chinese–English translation output concerning the movement. In some cases, external links to translated materials were provided (these are examined in this chapter). A careful review of the translation output shows that, in general, the translations are varied in quality. At the same time, translated texts of high quality were not necessarily a guarantee of their faithfulness to the original. Moreover, partial or summarised translations were commonplace, with the original often mitigated or intensified, which was perhaps due to the translator's incompetence, or emotional involvement, and the nature of the activist translation as news translation on the *CNN iReport* news medium (van Doorslaer 2010: 181–182). Although the nature of a medium limits the ways in which users employ that medium, this in turn has an impact on how content providers devise or present the content. In the case of the activist translation in the Sunflower Student Movement, communication technologies and social media allowed the movement participants to spread online what they saw, heard, or felt in a real-time manner. The urgency and eagerness to share such information contributed to the fact that most of the activist translations were short, brief, improvised, or studded with errors. The activist translations were largely free from prior censorship, thus presenting the 'original flavour and style' of what the translators wished to convey, like the around-the-clock live feeds from the occupied parliament (Hsu 2014). In general, there were five prominent features of such activist translations, which were largely attributed to the use of internet and communication technologies. The following shows the relevant translation examples and possible explanations.

Feature 1: mixture of different genres of source texts and use of translation to support one's opinion

Some of the postings involved translations of a mixture of different genres of source texts, such as video clips and written reports, as shown in Example 1, below.[4] This posting included a video clip and a written text. The video clip started with the subtitle of the translator's own account, with only the last two very short sentences translated, while in the long written message, only the last quotation from a university professor's report involved translation. To avoid confusion, the video subtitle and the written report in Example 1 are separately displayed and italicised, except for the glosses provided by me, and the translation output is underlined and in bold for easy reference.

Example 1—the subtitles of the video clip

As the police tried to pulled (sic) out hundred students and activists in the Taiwan parliament, men and women who were protesting outside climbed into the wall and pushed over the gate to support people in the legislative body.
爬進去, 坐下! (Climb in, sit down!)
Climb in! Sit down!
往前推! (Push forward!)
Push forward!

Example 1——the complete written text

Hundreds of men and women climbed over the wall and pushed over the gate of Taiwan parliament, as the police tried to pulled (sic) out students and activists in the legislative body.

Around 600 students and civic groups stormed the parliament on Tuesday, after the ruling party KMT [Kuomintang] refused to review the Agreement on Trade in Services between Taiwan and China clause-by-clause in the parliament committee. The Cross-Strait trade pact is pending approval by Legislative Yuan, Taiwan's legislative body.

The police blocked all ways into the parliament hall after parliament were stormed, with around 1000 of people protesting outside the parliament peacefully.

At around 03:00AM on Wednesday, people in the hall reported on Facebook (https://www.facebook.com/lslandnationyouth) that police were trying to pull them out. The upset protestors outside then climbed over the wall and pushed over the gate to deter the police from taking over the parliament.

There were no major clashes between people and the police. As the police retreated from their lines, people outside can now provide food supply and enter the parliament hall through windows on the second floor.

*I '**strongly suggest the government suspend the trade pact and restart the negotiation with China,**' Professor Show-ling Jang concluded in a research report on the trade pact. '**The trade pact would not bring positive effect to our country. On the contrary, it could bring huge harm**' to the economy, said the report.*
* Report wrote (sic) by Professor Show-ling Jang:
http://www.slideshare.net/hungchengtu/ss-24730814#btnLast

The underlined quotation in the written text was translated from Professor Show-ling Jang's PowerPoint report on the service trade deal (Jang 2013), but the poster only provided a link to the source material at the end of the posting instead of specifying the exact source sentences of the translation. Comparison of the translation with the source material shows that the translation was produced from the following source text:

整體而言, 服貿協議對我國經濟不但沒有正面影響, 反而有極大傷害, 強烈建議政府應立即中止此協議, 循美韓談判經驗, 重新與中國展開談判。

(Jang 2013: 38)

(As a whole, the Cross-Strait Service Trade Agreement (CSSTA) has no positive influence on but does great harm to our country's economy. It is strongly suggested that the government immediately suspend this agreement and re-open negotiations with China by following the case of the negotiation between the U.S. and South Korea.)

An examination of the source text and the translation indicates that the translation was not faithful to the source text but transedited to support the translator's own opinion. The 'combination of a (hardly re-constructable) multi-source situation with a highly pragmatic use of translation' is 'rather typical of translation in journalism' (van Doorslaer 2010: 182–183). Meanwhile, as Professor Jang teaches at National Taiwan University, a prestigious university in Taiwan, it may be argued that her report was partly translated in order to increase the credibility of the poster's opinion. This view is supported by Duraner's study (2018), in which some pro-LGBTI translators in Turkey are found to first identify a source text that corresponds to their stance and then translate it as a way to 'resist and challenge the dominant narrative' (Duraner 2018).

Feature 2: more than one translation of the same source text

In some cases, the same source texts about the movement were rendered by different translators, thus causing several versions to appear within a very short period of time. For instance, one famous slogan used by the protesters, 當獨裁成事實 革命就是義務 (When the dictatorship is a fact, the revolution is a duty), was translated in three ways on *CNN iReport*:

Example 2: When dictatorship becomes true, revolution is our duty.[5]

Example 3: When dictatorship becomes reality, revolution is our duty![6]

Example 4: When a dictator become a reality, revolution is the obligation.[7]

The slogan, derived from Swiss writer Pascal Mercier's novel *Nachtzug nach Lissabon* (*Night Train to Lisbon*), published in German in 2004 and containing the account of the Carnation Revolution occurring in Lisbon in 1974, was first spray painted on an outer wall of Taiwan's parliament by one protester and soon became one of the main slogans during the Sunflower Student Movement (*Liberty* Times 2014), which is why more than one person provided its Chinese–English translation. The repeated translations also indicate that these activist translators may have acted alone.

Examples 5 and 6 are two different translated subtitles of one video clip embedded in two separate edited video postings. The following extracts are shown in a line-by-line comparison of the source text and its two translations.

Source text line 1: 我們用最高紀律來審議服貿
(We use the highest discipline to examine the service trade deal.)

Example 5: *We're examining CSATS [Cross-Strait Agreement on Trade in Services] with the highest discipline.*[8]
Example 6: *We ask for concerning the trade agreement seriously*[9]
Source text line 2: 記者朋友們 你們不要寫我們是暴民
(Reporter friends, do not write we are mobs.)
Example 5: *Dear reporters, please don't describe us as mobs.*
Example 6: *We are rational and calm.*
Source text line 3: 我們進來沒有破壞任何的束西
(We entered, we did not destroy anything.)
Example 5: *We did not destroy anything in here.*
Example 6: *We did not crash anything in the plenary hall.*

As shown above, Example 5 was generally faithful to the original, while Example 6, although its deviation from the original in both sentence structure and wording resulted in a stronger tone, maintained the general sense of the original. Both subtitled versions were uploaded to *CNN iReport* on the same day, but clearly they were produced separately. This might indicate that the activist translators were eager to convey what they themselves considered important whether or not the same or similar messages had been circulated.

Feature 3: different modes of translation of the same source text

Another unusual situation found in this chapter is that a video clip in which an official was interrogated by pro-movement legislator Kuan Bi-ling about the government's improper action against the protesters was rendered into two modes of translation. One English subtitle translation was first posted on *CNN iReport* (see Example 7),[10] while the next day one English-dubbed version appeared without subtitling (see Example 8).[11] The following shows an extract of the source text and its two translations.

Source text
學生說,『我只能強忍著不安, 想辦法安慰, 因為很多女同學都掉眼淚了
我知道, 我們將被殘暴的對待。』下一秒鐘, 他們說,『我們不準備反抗, 有需要動員
到這麼多鎮暴警察嗎? 如果這是正當執法, 為什麼要把記者驅離呢?』
(A student said, 'I could only suppress my trepidation, trying to comfort, because many female students were crying. 1 knew we were going to be trcatcd brutally. The next second, they [students] said, 'We are not prepared to resist. Is it necessary to mobilise so many riot police? If it is legitimate law enforcement, why were reporters driven away?')
Subtitle translation in Example 7:
The student said 'i could only endure my [t]repidation, and tried to calm other crying students.' 'A lot of female students started to cry.' We knew, we were going to be treated brutally. In the next second, the students said 'We don't want terolt [revolt] against them at all, is the revolt necessary?' 'Is the squelch appropriate? if so, why did they ask the reporters to leave?'
English dubbing in Example 8:
A student said, 'I could only suppress my trepidation and tried to calm others. A lot of female students tried to cry. We knew we were going to be handled with violence. And the next second, the police said, 'We will not permit any resistance.' Is it really necessary to use these many anti-riot police? If this was the legal law enforcement, was it necessary to evict the reporters?

According to the translator in Example 8, who, as was stated at the end of the clip she uploaded, was a student studying abroad at the time, she dubbed the video clip by revising others' translation that had been previously posted online with a view to providing a more appropriate translation and making it more convenient and energy-saving for a foreign audience to watch the clip. This shows that most of the activist translators aimed to increase the international visibility and understanding of the movement by doing whatever they deemed suitable, and that internet and communication technologies allowed people to contribute to the movement without being constrained by time and space.

Feature 4: one translation reviewed and revised online by different internet users

In addition to using web-based collaborative real-time text editors, such as Hackpad, to produce translations during the movement, BBS or discussion forums were also where people might translate collaboratively. For instance, in Example 7, one of the links provided by the translator showed how he sought advice from other internet users on revising and refining his translation posted on the PTT, the largest BBS station in Taiwan, as shown in Figure 30.1.

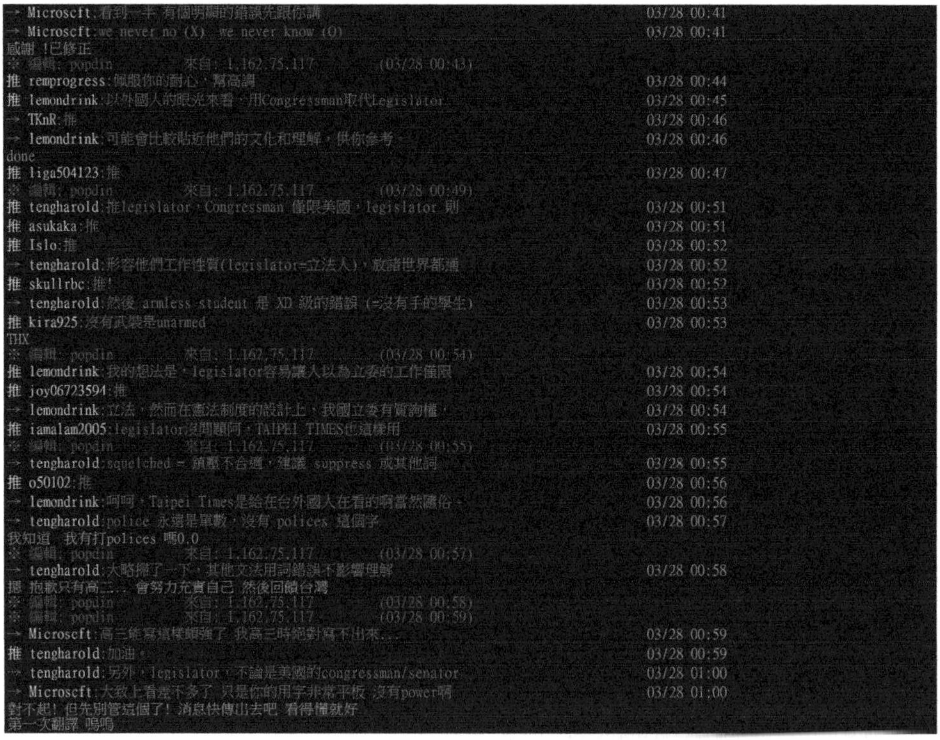

Figure 30.1 A screengrab of the discussions and collaborative translation on the PTT related to Example 7 (Popdin 2014).

One PTT user, 'tengharold,' said that the translation, despite some errors in grammar and wording, was generally understandable, while another user, 'Microscft,' commented that the translation was all right but the wording was very 'flat,' to which the translator responded by saying, 'Sorry! But leave it alone! Spread the messages quickly. It is ok if [the translation] is understandable. First time translating, boo-hoo' (Popdin 2014, my translation). Clearly, since the activist translation for the movement was meant to rally global support, timeliness is an important factor. However, as indicated in the internet users' discussion, the ability of the activist translation to arouse emotion or passion in the audience might be an even weightier concern for some activist translators.

Feature 5: waiving authorship or copyright

Most of the activist translators during the movement did not claim their authorship or copyright; instead, they made it clear that people were welcome to circulate or use the translations without obtaining the translator's consent or quoting the source, which gives even more freedom of reproduction of translations than the concept of 'copyleft' adopted by some foreign networks of volunteer translators such as TLAXCALA (TLAXCALA 2006). For instance, the title of Example 9—'We are Taiwanese! We need the world's attention. Please share the news to everyone you know, and translate it to other languages'—is self-explanatory.[12] Unlike the poster of Example 9, who revealed his identity by providing a link to his Facebook page, the one of Example 10, which was a rebuke against, as said in its title, 'the Fallacy the Premier of Executive Yuan and the Director-General Claimed,' explicitly stated, 'Owing to my identity and individual safety, plus I have no intention to be famous, I will not tell my name. You can treat me as anonymous and share this article.'[13] These two examples indicate that, whether the translators revealed their identities or not, they wished to pass on their translations to a wider audience. Because the activist translators provided their services voluntarily, it was at their discretion how to deal with the original and whether to be visible or invisible to their audience.

The sociology of activist translation in the Sunflower Student Movement

The previous section shows that most of the activist translators in the Sunflower Student Movement were ad hoc translators who received little professional training and had their translations posted on a news medium (*CNN iReport* in question); hence it may be more adequate to analyse their translation activity from perspectives of sociology than of translation theories. This is in part because translation theories tend to focus on professional translators. Also, in the past two decades, French ethnographer and sociologist Pierre Bourdieu's theory about media and cultural production has been widely employed in the field of translation studies to investigate 'the social nature of translation' (Munday 2016: 236). For instance, Hernández-Hernández (Chapter 12) uses Bourdieu's concept of habitus to investigate the activist trajectories and practices of the journalistic translators working for the left-wing French periodical *Le Monde diplomatique*. In this section, Bourdieu's concepts of 'field,' 'habitus,' and 'capital' are drawn on to analyse the activist translation activity during Taiwan's Sunflower Student Movement on pre-2015 *CNN iReport*.

According to Bourdieu, cultural production occurs within a given field that may be subject to 'the field of power,' or a 'meta-field' (Bourdieu and Wacquant 1992: 111). The field possesses varying degrees of autonomy depending on the degree of political and economic dominance the meta-field assumes over the given field (Bourdieu 1993: 37–38). In this chapter, following Bourdieu's theory, the online space for the 'Protesters occupy Taiwan legislature' assignment on *CNN iReport* may be seen as the field where any interested individual or group is eligible to act as a social agent. This field is comparable to a 'game' in which agents as players compete against one another by following implicit but organised rules or regularities to fulfil their belief that winning the game and the stakes, which are 'the product of the competition' (Bourdieu and Wacquant 1992: 98), will earn them credit and success. When the activist translators want their translated postings to become part of CNN news coverage, they play the 'game' seriously in the field by paying attention to translation quality, which explains why activist translations produced by the international group inside Taiwan's parliament were of much higher quality. Of course, all activist translators as social agents in the field are free to post whatever they wish, as at the time of the Sunflower Student Movement, *CNN iReport* did not censor the postings (Ingram 2015). Also, the then Taiwanese government, which dispersed on-site protesters by resorting to violence and law enforcement, had no authority over the field. Consequently, the field, the online space for the assignment in question, was subject to little dominance and enjoyed a high degree of autonomy.

Activist translators in the Sunflower Student Movement belonged to the generation of 'digital natives' (g0v 2019), who navigate through cyberspace with ease and who use communication technologies (heavily) in their everyday life. Some of the student leaders in the movement also had experience in previous smaller-scale student protests, such as the Wild Strawberries Movement in 2008 against the Taiwanese government's violation of people's rights to freedom of assembly and expression when China was involved (Fell 2017). As the habitus of social agents in a field is 'embodied history, internali[s]ed as a second nature and so forgotten as history' and 'the active presence of the whole past of which it is the product' (Bourdieu 1990: 56), it is unsurprising that digital natives in the Sunflower Student Movement could muster public support within a very short period of time by learning from their past movement experience, by using their internet and technological skills, and by appealing to the growing public resentment against China and the pro-China Taiwanese government.

As for the forms of capital possessed by the social agents in the field, the volunteer student translators had educational, linguistic, and technological qualifications as their cultural capital. Meanwhile, there was no lack of social capital on their part. Specifically, as the generation that was most likely to suffer the long-term consequences of Taiwan's trade deal with China, the students as activist translators evoked much identification in their peers and sympathy from their older generations. The informational and communicative use of the internet enabled activist translators to access wider and heterogeneous social networks, thus producing and accumulating social capital (Quan-Haase and Wellman 2004). Furthermore, activist translators in the Sunflower Student Movement provided their service on a voluntary basis, with some movement participants even launching successful fundraising campaigns for the cause (Hsu 2014). This mobilisation greatly reduced the financial advantage of the Taiwanese government, who could not even occupy a dominant position in the field (*CNN iReport*) over these activist translators.

Activist translators during the Sunflower Student Movement were mostly working in the digital world where internet technologies empowered them and set free their translations. By exerting their digital power in cyberspace, the activist translators of the movement helped to claim more public space, gain international attention, and rally global support for the movement. From a sociological perspective, the quality of translation during the movement was not an issue to any party in the field; it was with the high degree of autonomy that the field could enjoy and with as many forms of capital as possible that the supposedly dominated social agents could win this game in civil society and in the age of information technology.

Related topics

Translating Mourning Walls; Translating for *Le Monde diplomatique en español*

Notes

1 This research is supported by Taiwan's Ministry of Science and Technology under grant no. MOST 108-2410-H-033-019–.
2 Available at: www.facebook.com/NewseForum/[accessed 5 July 2019].
3 See Gambier (2007) for an introduction and comparison of more similar networks of volunteer translators/interpreters in Europe.
4 Taiwan4Demo (2014) '[Exclusive] Taiwanese Pushed Over Parliament Gate,' *CNN iReport* [online] 19 March. Available at: http://ireport.cnn.com/docs/DOC-1109099 [accessed 10 April 2014].
5 Badkc (2014) 'Peaceful protest in Nan-jung Square/Protesta pacífica en la plaza Nan-jung,' *CNN iReport* [online] 20 March. Available at: http://ireport.cnn.com/docs/DOC-1109768 [accessed 10 April 2014].
6 jpcy (2014) 'Peaceful Taiwanese Protesters,' *CNN iReport* [online] 20 March. Available at: http://ireport.cnn.com/docs/DOC-1109907 [accessed 10 April 2014].
7 jeffreyfrodo (2014) 'Q&A: Occupying Taiwan Legislature,' *CNN iReport* [online] 23 March. Available at: http://ireport.cnn.com/docs/DOC-1110830 [accessed 10 April 2014].
8 sky40053 (2014) 'The Truth,' *CNN iReport* [online] 21 March. Available at: http://ireport.cnn.com/docs/DOC-1109969 [accessed 10 April 2014].
9 pied225 (2014) 'Real Voices of the Students,' *CNN iReport* [online] 21 March. Available at: http://ireport.cnn.com/docs/DOC-1110266 [accessed 10 April 2014].
10 AlanWang (2014) 'Taiwan Democracy in Peril! Peaceful Protest Ended in Police Brutality,' *CNN iReport* [online] 28 March. Available at: http://ireport.cnn.com/docs/DOC-1113356 [accessed 10 April 2014].
11 Domlim (2014) 'Taiwan Sunflower Student Revolution,' *CNN iReport* [online] 29 March. Available at: http://ireport.cnn.com/docs/DOC-1114178 [accessed 10 April 2014].
12 joyHsu (2014) 'We are Taiwanese! We need the world's attention. Please share the news to everyone you know, and translate it to other languages,' *CNN iReport* [online] 19 March. Available at: http://ireport.cnn.com/docs/DOC-1109046 [accessed 10 April 2014].
13 TCH318 (2014) 'About the Fallacy the Premier of Executive Yuan and the Director-General Claimed,' *CNN iReport* [online] 27 March. Available at: http://ireport.cnn.com/docs/DOC-1113107 [accessed 10 April 2014].

Further reading

Baker, Mona (2016) 'The Prefigurative Politics of Translation in Place-Based Movements of Protest: Subtitling in the Egyptian Revolution,' *The Translator* 22(1): 1–21.

This paper explores how individual volunteer subtitlers helped Egyptian protesters challenge the dominant narrative by making their narratives of the Egyptian Revolution of 2011 heard and understood by audiences across the world while negotiating their position within the collectives they worked for.

Doerr, Nicole (2018) *Political Translation: How Social Movement Democracies Survive*. Cambridge: Cambridge University Press.

This book, based on three case studies set in American and European contexts, looks at translators' critical capacity from interdisciplinary perspectives and how political translators and interpreters have exerted their language power in grassroots democratic practices and helped push forward the progress of democracy.

Fell, Dafydd (ed.) (2017) *Taiwan's Social Movements under Ma Ying-jeou*. London:Routledge.

This edited book contains several chapters that look at Taiwan's Sunflower Student Movement in terms of its origins, structures, strategies, and the China factor and how civic activism and protest in Taiwan might achieve success.

Hung, Chenling (ed.) (2015) *Sunflower Movement, New Citizenry, and New Media*. Taipei: Net and Books.

This edited book was produced as documentary evidence of the Sunflower Student Movement by students and teachers in journalism at National Taiwan University, many of whom were the movement participants inside Taiwan's parliament at the time. The book includes in-depth interviews with most prominent individuals and groups during the movement.

References

Baker, Mona (2010) 'Translation and Activism: Emerging Patterns of Narrative Community,' in *Translation, Resistance, Activism*. Ed. Maria Tymoczko. Amherst: University of Massachusetts Press. 23–41.

Baker, Mona (2016a) 'The Prefigurative Politics of Translation in Place-Based Movements of Protest: Subtitling in the Egyptian Revolution,' *The Translator* 22(1): 1–21.

Baker, Mona (2016b) 'Interview with Philip Rizk,' in *Translating Dissent: Voices from and with the Egyptian Revolution*. Ed. Mona Baker. London: Routledge. 225–238.

Baker, Mona (2016c) 'Beyond the Spectacle: Translation and Solidarity in Protest Movements,' in *Translating Dissent: Voices from and with the Egyptian Revolution*. Ed. Mona Baker. London: Routledge. 1–18.

Boéri, Julie (2005) 'Babels and the Politics of Language at the Heart of the Social Forum,' in *Academia.edu* [online]. Available at: www.academia.edu/512895/Babels_and_the_Politics_of_Language_at_the_Heart_of_the_Social_Forum [accessed 5 July 2019].

Bourdieu, Pierre (1990) *The Logic of Practice*. Trans. Richard Nice. Cambridge: Polity Press.

Bourdieu, Pierre (1993) *The Field of Cultural Production: Essays on Art and Literature*. Cambridge: Polity Press.

Bourdieu, Pierre, and Loïc J. D. Wacquant (1992) *An Invitation to Reflexive Sociology*. Chicago: The University of Chicago Press.

Brown, Sophie, and Zoe Li (2014) 'Taiwan Police Clash with Students in Protests over Trade Deal,' in *CNN* [online] 25 March. Available at: https://edition.cnn.com/2014/03/24/world/asia/taiwan-trade-student-protest/index.html [accessed 4 July 2019].

Carcelen-Estrada, Antonia (2018) 'Translation and Activism,' in *The Routledge Handbook of Translation and Politics*. Eds. Fruela Fernández and Evans Jonathan London: Routledge. 254–269.

Chen, Pinchie (2015) '125人14國語言: 太陽花國際部向世界發聲 [125 People 14 Languages: The Sunflower Movement International Division Speaks to the World],' in *Sunflower Movement, New Citizenry, and New Media*. Ed. Chenling Hung. Taipei: Net and Books. 250–266.

Doerr, Nicole (2018) *Political Translation: How Social Movement Democracies Survive*. Cambridge: Cambridge University Press.

Duraner, Jasmin Esin (2018) 'News Translation as a Way of Activism: The Case of LGBTI News Turkey,' paper presented at the IATIS 6th International Conference, Hong Kong, 3-6 July.

Fell, Dafydd (ed.) (2017) *Taiwan's Social Movements under Ma Ying-jeou*. London: Routledge.

Folaron, Deborah (2010) 'Networking and Volunteer Translators,' in *Handbook of Translation Studies* Vol. 1. Eds. Yves Gambier and Luc van Doorslaer. Amsterdam: John Benjamins. 231–234.

Gambier, Yves (2007) 'Réseaux de Traducteurs/Interprètes Bénévoles,' *Meta* 52(4): 658–672.

García, Eloísa Monteoliva, Esther Romero Gutiérrez, Leticia Sánchez Balsalobre, and Jesús de Manuel Jerez (2011) 'ECOS: 10 años rompiendo las barreras del silencio y de las lenguas [ECOS: 10 Years Breaking the Barriers of Silence and Languages],' in *ECOS* [online]14 April. Available at: https://ecosteis.wordpress.com/2011/04/14/ecos-10-anos-rompiendo-las-barreras-del-silencio-y-de-las-lenguas/ [accessed 4 July 2019].

g0v (2019) 'Introduction to g0v,' in *g0v.tw* [online]. Available at: https://g0v.tw/en-US/about.html [accessed 5 July 2019].

Habermas, Jurgen (2010) 'The Public Sphere: An Encyclopedia Article (1964),' in *The Idea of the Public Sphere: A Reader*. Eds. Jostein Gripsrud, Hallvard Moe, Anders Molander and Murdock Graham. Lanham: Lexington Books. 114–120.

Hsu, Renchuan (2014) '太陽花學運科技大搜祕! [the Technologies Used in the Sunflower Student Movement!],' in *Global Views Monthly* [online] 29 April. Available at: www.gvm.com.tw/article. html?id=52313 [accessed 5 July 2019].

Hung, Chenling (ed.) (2015) *Sunflower Movement, New Citizenry, and New Media*. Taipei: Net and Books.

Ingram, Mathew (2015) 'CNN Is Rebooting Its iReport Site Thanks to Social Media,' in *Fortune* [online] 12 November. Available at: http://fortune.com/2015/11/12/cnn-ireport/ [accessed 5 July 2019].

Jang, Showling (2013) '兩岸服貿協議對我國的衝擊分析 [The Analysis of the Impact of the Cross-strait Service Trade Agreement on Our Country],' in *LinkedIn SlideShare* [online]. Available at: www.slideshare.net/hungchengtu/ss-24730814#btnLast [accessed 4 July 2019].

Kahlaoui, Tarek (2013) 'The Powers of Social Media,' in *Making of the Tunisian Revolution: Contexts, Architects, Prospects*. Ed. Nouri Gana. Edinburgh: Edinburgh University Press. 147–158.

Kramer, Staci D. (2008) 'CNN's iReport under Fire for Fake Jobs Health Report,' in *CBS News* [online] 4 October. Available at: www.cbsnews.com/news/cnns-ireport-under-fire-for-fake-jobs-health-report/ [accessed 3 July 2019].

Lepesant, Tanguy (2018) 'Taiwanese Youth and National Identity under Ma Ying-jeou,' in *Changing Taiwanese Identities*. Eds. J. Bruce and Kang Peter. London: Routledge. 64–85.

Liberty Times (2014) '佔領國會》「當獨裁成為事實, 革命就是義務」 [Occupy Parliament: When Dictatorship Becomes a Fact, Revolution Is a Duty],' in *Liberty Times* [online] 21 March. Available at: https://news.ltn.com.tw/news/politics/breakingnews/972799 [accessed 4 July 2019].

Liu, Shihchun, and Herng Su (2017) 'Mediating the Sunflower Movement: Hybrid Media Networks in a Digital Age,' *Information Society* 33: 147–188.

Marsimaria (2015) 'Sunflower Movement Declaration Extract,' in *GitHub Gist* [online] 28 March. Available at: https://gist.github.com/marsimaria/c5b1cb22024263de5b8e [accessed 4 July 2019].

Merkle, Denise (2018) 'Translation and Censorship,' in *The Routledge Handbook of Translation and Politics*. Eds. Fruela Fernández and Jonathan Evans. London: Routledge. 238–253.

Munday, Jeremy (2016) *Introducing Translation Studies: Theories and Applications* (4th ed). London: Routledge.

O'Hagan, Minako (2011) 'Community Translation: Translation as a Social Activity and Its Possible Consequences in the Advent of Web 2.0 And Beyond,' *Linguistica Antverpiensia, New Series—Themes in Translation Studies* 10: 11–23.

Popdin (2014) '[分享] 翻譯 管碧玲質詢影片 ([share] Translation Video of Kuan Bi-Ling's Interrogation),' in *the FuMouDiscuss Board of PTT* [online] 28 March. Available at: www.ptt.cc/bbs/FuMou Discuss/M.1395937640.A.B73.html [accessed 4 July 2019].

Pym, Anthony (2011) 'Translation Research Terms: A Tentative Glossary for Moments of Perplexity and Dispute,' in *Translation Research Project* 3. Ed. Anthony Pym. Tarragona: Intercultural Studies Group. 75–110.

Quan-Haase, Anabel, and Barry Wellman (2004) 'How Does the Internet Affect Social Capital?' in *Social Capital and Information Technology*. Eds. Marleen Huysman and Wulk Volker. Cambridge, MA: MIT Press. 113–131.

Rone, Julia (2016) 'The People Formerly Known as the Oligarchy: The Co-optation of Citizen Journalism,' in *Citizen Media and Public Spaces: Diverse Expressions of Citizenship and Dissent*. Eds. Mona Baker and Bolette B. Blaagaard. London: Routledge. 208–224.

Roubini, Sonia, and Jason R. Tashea (2014) 'After Sunflower Movement, Taiwan's G0v Uses Open Source to Open the Government,' in *Personal Democracy Media* [online] 5 November. Available online: http://techpresident.com/news/wegov/25339/sunflower-movement-g0v-taiwan-open-govern ment [accessed 4 July 2019].

Silverman, Craig (2012) 'How CNN's iReport Verifies Its Citizen Content,' in *The Poynter Institute* [online] 26 January. Available at: www.poynter.org/reporting-editing/2012/how-cnns-ireport-veri fies-its-citizen-content/ [accessed 3 July 2019].

TLAXCALA (2006) 'Tlaxcala's Manifesto,' in *TLAXCALA: The Translators' Network for Linguistic Diversity* [online] 21 February. Available at: www.tlaxcala.es/manifiesto.asp?section=2&lg=en [accessed 4 July 2019].

Traduttori per la Pace (1999) 'The Charter of Translators for Peace,' in *Traduttori per la Pace* [online] 24 May. Available at: http://web.tiscali.it/traduttoriperlapace/ [accessed 4 July 2019].

Tsai, Chiren (2014) '學生攻占立院 CNN開專區報導 [Students Occupy the Parliament; CNN Sets up Special Zone for Reports],' in *United Daily News* [online] 19 March. Available at: www.udn.com/2014/3/19/NEWS/NATIONAL/NATS6/8557746.shtml [accessed 15 October 2019].

van Doorslaer, Luc (2010) 'Journalism and Translation,' in *Handbook of Translation Studies* Vol. 1. Eds. Yves Gambier and Luc van Doorslaer. Amsterdam: John Benjamins. 180–184.

Wang, Yuchung (2014) '50萬黑潮上凱道 林飛帆要馬出面回應 [Five Hundred Thousand People in Black Took to Ketagalan Boulevard; Lin Feifan Demanded President Ma's Response],' in *Liberty Times* [online] 30 March. Available at: http://news.ltn.com.tw/news/politics/breakingnews/978491 [accessed 4 July 2019].

Wu, Chungchieh (2014) '史上最大學運推手: 免費網路工具 (The Greatest Driving Force behind the Student Movement: Free Internet Tools),' *Business Weekly* 1377: 34–36.

Yu, Aili, and Chiling Chen (2014) '野百合時代過去: 科技, 引爆不一樣的組織動員力 [The Age of the Wild Lily Student Movement Has Passed! Technology Ignites Different Mobilisation Power],' in *MANAGER Today* [online] 31 March. Available at: www.managertoday.com.tw/articles/view/39715 [accessed 4 July 2019].

31

Afterword

Postcolonialism, activism, and translation

Paul F. Bandia

The subject of activism is currently front and centre in many academic disciplines in the humanities and the social sciences. The growing influence of Cultural Studies and Post-colonial Studies has been instrumental in fostering interest in activism, and the latter's definition and application are multiple and varied depending on whether activism is viewed as a physical manifestation or intervention in support of a cause or as a scientific construct enabling research into various forms of actions or resistance by oppressed or marginalised groups in situations characterised by unequal power relations. There is no resistance, hence no activism, without oppression, deprivation, or abuse. Such resistance can take many forms, ranging from passive expressions of rejection to physical acts of resistance, including aggression. The contributions to this volume testify to the broad understanding of activism in contemporary scholarship, as they deal with the subject from a variety of perspectives. They are united by the concept of translational activism, which is the main focus of the volume.

There is a growing interest in translation and activism as a subfield in translation studies, often discussed in tandem with the related topic of translation and conflict. Although there is an obvious overlap between the two topics, they should not be con-flated. While the latter addresses the role of translation or translators in zones of conflict, clashes, or war, the former deals with deliberate attempts by translators, interpreters, or language providers to intervene on behalf of the marginalised or subordinate groups in order to facilitate communication or redress what they consider unfairness based on asymmetrical power relations. As mentioned earlier, though some manifestations of activism are passive, activism always implies some form of deliberate intent or action, a form of opposition or resistance to power, as it were. In other words, 'translation and conflict' may simply concern itself with the role of the language provider as mediator or go-between of the parties involved in the conflict, including those responsible for conflict resolution, such as peace-keepers, international courts, and war tribunals. 'Translation and activism,' on the other hand, highlights the agency of the translator or interpreter (or language provider) as the initiator, or proactive catalyst, with the expressed desire to sway or determine the outcome of a situation arising between parties circumscribed by conditions determined by power differentials.

The postcolonial condition is highly conducive to situations of activism. It is therefore not surprising that the majority of contributions in this volume derive from postcolonial contexts, or situations dealing with subaltern or marginalised peoples, or those communities living on the periphery of our globalised world. Translational activism could be internal to the postcolony or could be external to it, that is, it can be found in situations where postcolonial subjects find themselves on the receiving end of the imposition of power, such as in the case of migrants, refugees, and asylum seekers. When such activism is internal to the postcolony it is often a reaction or resistance based on the dynamics of class and power governing the relations between the masses and the elite. The activist translation of the Moroccan testimonial literature from the 'Years of Lead' (1956–1999) in this volume is a good example of such activism internal to the postcolony. It has to do with co-writing with political prisoners as translational activism to bear witness to oppression under an autocratic political regime. An example, in this volume, of translational activism outside the postcolony, yet systematically involving postcolonial subjects, is the case of refugees or asylum seekers in California who are given support as language minorities in a context where such support is crucial for the adequate institutional representation of facts to ensure a fair trial. The language facilitators in this instance go beyond merely providing translation services; they also intervene to make sure their clients are not limited in their case by ingrained cultural inhibitions, and that their dossiers are presented in conformity with institutional requirements in order to maximise their chances of success.

It can be argued that translation, by its very nature, is activist within the postcolonial context, as it is often ideologically charged with the need or desire for linguistic or cultural representation of minority or marginalised societies. As aptly stated in the introduction to this volume, 'translation-as-activism lies at the heart of their anticolonial agenda' (1). Postcoloniality evokes translation, not only in the sense of what some theorists have inferred to be a translated state of being (Casanova 2004), marked by its hybridity and polyphony (Bhabha 2004), but also as a strategy of cultural assertion and resistance to western imperialism. Postcoloniality, translation, and activism go hand in hand in the historical struggle for the liberation of colonised or dominated societies. The anticolonialist discourse of the years immediately preceding decolonisation was indeed activist in that it sought to resist colonial imposition, and translational in that it mobilised the aesthetic and cultural resources of colonised peoples in the language of the coloniser to counter colonialist misrepresentations. By the same token, postcolonialist discourse following the independence of formerly colonised nations is at once activist and translational in that there is a desire for cultural assertion or affirmation on the world stage in the global colonial language.

Anticolonialism and activism

The link between anticolonialist movements and activism is enabled by what can be construed literally and metaphorically as activism through translational acts of resistance. In the African context, anticolonial movements were guided by the philosophical writings and aesthetic productions of thinkers such as the Martinican Frantz Fanon, the Senegalese poet and statesman Léopold Sédar Senghor, the Martinican poet Aimé Césaire, Amilcar Cabral of Guinea Bissau, and the African-American scholar W.E.B. Du Bois. Today it is generally acknowledged that the writings of Frantz Fanon constituted the basic philosophical and ideological point of reference for anticolonial movements.

Having fought against the French colonisation of Algeria, Fanon used his expertise as a psychiatrist to analyse the effects of colonialism on the psyche of the colonised. He diagnosed and raised awareness of what is generally referred to as colonial mentality. Simply put, colonial mentality is the condition whereby the colonised engages subconsciously in the mimicry of the coloniser, having been brainwashed into rejecting his or her own culture as primitive and believing in the innate superiority of the coloniser's culture. This is a critique levelled at the colonised bourgeoisie whom Fanon depicts as clones of the colonial power and the weak link in the anticolonial struggle (Fanon 1952, 1961). Fanon further denounces what he refers to as 'colonial essentialism,' that is, the abnegation of responsibility by the colonised through the facile attribution to colonisation of all that is wrong with postcolonial society. In his view the initial phase of mimicry of colonial culture is eventually negated by the rise of cultural nationalism whereby the colonised begins to reject colonial culture as a consequence of growing resistance to colonial rule. The colonised now draw from their past to assert their indigenous identity. As stated in Young (2015: 99), 'native languages are reappraised, revalued, and chosen over the colonial idiom, local literature is rediscovered and championed, new works are written, and western clothes are discarded in favor of indigenous dress.' Not only is Fanon's anticolonial activism evident in his decision to join the Algerian resistance to French colonialism; his writings are exhortations to combat and to resist all forms of domination of oppressed peoples. Through psychiatry Fanon aptly captures or translates the angst of the postcolonial subject and the psychological realities of the postcolonial condition. It is therefore not surprising that Fanon's works have been translated in so many languages and have constituted the rallying point for many revolutionary movements. In the introduction to this volume, reference is made to the translation of Fanon's *The Wretched of the Earth* into Persian to illustrate the timeliness of activist translation. Apparently, this translation, done in 1963, helped the spread of anticolonial ideas in Iran and contributed to 'toppling a colonialist-dependent political regime, leading to the 1979 Islamic revolution' (4). The importance of Fanon's work for activist and revolutionary movements can be seen in *Translating Frantz Fanon Across Continents and Languages*, a volume edited by Kathryn Batchelor and Sue-Ann Harding and published by Routledge in 2017, which offers a comprehensive exploration of the translations and reception of *The Wretched of the Earth* and other texts.

The *Négritude* movement, the brainchild of Senghor, was mainly inspired by Fanon's philosophical musings, and recast African culture in terms that extolled its beauty and value in order to counter colonialist claims of primitivism. The concept of *négritude* was defined to propagate a universal valuation of Africa and its peoples across the globe. Senghor's famous poem, *Femme noire*, an ode to the Black woman, was above all a poem about love of country, of the African woman as custodian of culture, of African civilisation. His contemporary, the Martinican poet Aimé Césaire, also founder of the *négritude* movement, takes up a similar theme in his well-known book of poems, *Cahier d'un retour au pays natal* (1939) (*Notebook of a Return to my Native Land*) (1995). These works are activist in that they propagated a kind of cultural nationalism that encouraged pride in once-denigrated cultures resulting in confidence in the use of the colonial language in ways that reflected local idioms in Africa and the Caribbean. The works of these *négritude* poets have been translated into several languages and have been a reference point for many contemporary revolutionary movements.

While the *négritude* movement was mainly Francophone, in Anglophone Africa there was allegiance to a similar movement, known as the Pan-Africanist movement, whose

517

leader was the African-American scholar W.E.B. Du Bois. This was a worldwide move-ment that sought to strengthen bonds among African peoples on the continent and in the diaspora. The aim was to counter the effects of slavery and colonisation and to mend the ensuing divisions by highlighting the communality of all peoples of African descent. Amilcar Cabral, the anticolonial leader and theorist from Guinea Bissau, summed up nicely the importance of cultural nationalism when he declared that culture was indeed a weapon of resistance (Cabral 1973: 59–60; also cited in Young 2015: 100). The con-ceptualisation of the translation of revolutionary classics as translational activism is taken up in this volume in Yang's study of the translation of Karl Marx's theory for the Japanese New Left movement of the twentieth century (Chapter 5), Kuan-yen Liu's dis-cussion of the politicisation of the theory of evolution in the late-Qing Chinese transla-tion of social Darwinism (Chapter 27), and Wróblewska's chapter that examines how the translation of Gramsci's prison notebooks into Italian, English, and Polish challenges or reinforces asymmetrical relations of power (Chapter 2).

Postcolonialism and activism

Postcolonialism has become a theoretical construct that seeks to account for the chal-lenges to (as well as the analysis of) oppressive forms of western power and hegem-ony. It gives voice to the marginalised to denounce or counter the historic exploitation and oppression of peoples and societies of the global South. To the extent that postcolonialism is fundamentally engaged with denouncing all forms of oppression, including race, gender, class, and the environment, it is the locus of activ-ism directed at the residual effects of colonialism. Postcolonialism enables the subal-tern to take charge of their own history as active and speaking subjects rather than objects of the narratives of dominant or imperial powers. This switching of roles is tantamount to translating oneself from the perspective of the dominant to that of the subordinated (Young 2015: 150). Postcolonial activism therefore seeks to redress or challenge hegemonic representations of postcolonial subjects. This kind of activism is more readily expressed in literature which has generally followed two routes, namely, in literature confronting the postcolony and the colonial metropole and in literary and cultural productions dealing specifically with the postcolony, elucidating issues of class and power, as well as the effects of neocolonialism. In both cases language plays an important role as global monolingualism is resisted and rejected in favor of heterogeneity and multilingualism, which have become a firewall against the con-tinued imposition of the will or power of the metropole and the means for asserting subaltern identities. In this volume Kilolo alludes to this preference for multilingual-ism, as a conversation that takes place across and among multiple African languages, rather than adopting a single unifying language (Chapter 21).

The voices of indigenous people must be heard and their modes of knowledge pro-duction appreciated, and not become submerged in the generalised practice of a single unifying language, the colonial language. Also in this volume, Mourad argues for giving voice to indigenous people by employing the metaphor of the activist translator as *marron* and of translation as *marronage*, a concept drawn from Caribbean history, which signifies the determination of indigenous people of the Carib Territory to escape slavery at all costs (Chapter 10). This metaphor is a pithy encapsulation of the confrontation between the postcolony and the colonial metropole, whereby the postcolonial subject seeks to circumvent dominant colonial impositions. Shwaikh's chapter also argues against totalising colonialist representations by highlighting indigenous perspectives (Chapter 8).

The activism involved in issues related to the dynamic of class and power in the post-colony is expressed through class struggles between the elite and the masses, as well as through other forms of opposition involving dictatorships, wars and child soldiering, gender inequality, mineral exploitation, and environmental concerns. This kind of activism is translational mainly in terms of its modes of expression in literature, cinema, and other audiovisual and artistic media. Such translational activism can take the form of resistance, dissidence, protest, reform, and overthrow, and is driven by translators who give voice to the oppressed or the underrepresented.

Often the challenge to authority is conveyed through the privileging of cultural and linguistic multiplicity over the homogenising representation of the postcolony. Linguistic vernacularisation is mobilised as a translational act of resistance to power and assertion of identity for the marginalised or oppressed populations. Activist translators, who in this context are often creative writers, are often eager to deconstruct the language of officialdom, highly dependent on metropolitan norms, by emphasising the hybridity, heterogeneity, and multilingualism of postcolonial societies. There is a conscious effort to resist the effects of neocolonialism, which, together with globalisation, continue to maintain the postcolony in a state of dependency. The corrupt exploitation of natural resources and the ensuing damage to the environment, as well as the cruel use of child soldiers to fight internecine wars for personal benefit, have figured prominently in literary and audiovisual productions that have translated the predominant attitude of the masses vis-à-vis the excesses of the ruling class. Migration, both outward and inward, to the postcolony has contributed to complexifying translational activism, inasmuch as the relocation of cultures and languages is bound to enhance the need for translation and intercultural communication. Globalisation—economic, cultural, and linguistic—has raised awareness worldwide of the need to preserve minority cultures and languages whose very survival may be threatened. Translational activism through multilingual and multicultural practices has been instrumental in slowing the rush toward global monolingualism. English has been forced to take on a variety of local inflections in communities where English is used as a global language.

There is also the situation in settler colonies where translational activism has been front and centre in efforts of reconciliation between the settlers and the indigenous peoples. In settler colonies, indigenous populations have lived for centuries with separate identities from the main population. Power is in the hands of the descendants of settlers who inherited the privilege of the dominant population and tacitly continued the colonial domination of indigenous peoples. The sense of guilt towards indigenous people and the desire for restitution have led to several truth and reconciliation commissions, such as in South Africa and Canada, which required the intervention of translators as language facilitators during public hearings which were often highly emotionally charged. Besides providing interlingual translation, the translators were often expected to accompany witnesses and assist them through emotionally draining testimonies.

The subject of translational activism is extremely rich and quite timely, and this volume provides the most comprehensive, varied, and exhaustive treatment yet. The broad definition of the subject allows for an inclusive and interdisciplinary approach that opens up exciting and new dimensions on the study of translation and activism. The numerous contributions as well as the spatial and temporal reach of the volume will constitute the basis of research in this area of translation studies for a long time to come.

References

Batchelor, Kathryn, and Sue-Ann Harding (eds.) (2017) *Translating Frantz Fanon across Continents and Languages*. New York and London: Routledge.

Bhabha, Homi (2004) *The Location of Culture*. New York and London: Routledge.

Cabral, Amilcar (1973) *Return to the Source: Selected Speeches by Amilcar Cabral*. New York: Monthly Review Press with Africa Information Service.

Casanova, Pascale (2004) *The World Republic of Letters*. Tr. M. B. DeBevoise. Cambridge, MA: Harvard University Press.

Césaire, Aimé (1995 [1939]) *Cahier d'un retour au pays natal* (*Notebook of a Return to My Native Land*) Tr. Mireille Rosello and Annie Pritchard. Newcastle upon Tyne: Bloodaxe Books.

Fanon, Frantz (1952) *Black Skin, White Masks*. Tr. Charles Lam Markmann. London: Pluto Press.

Fanon, Frantz (1961) *The Wretched of the Earth*. Tr. Constance Farrington. New York: Grove Press.

Young, Robert J. C. (2015) *Empire, Colony, Postcolony*. Sussex: Wiley Blackwell.

Index

Page locators in **bold** and *italics* refer to tables and images, respectively.

Index